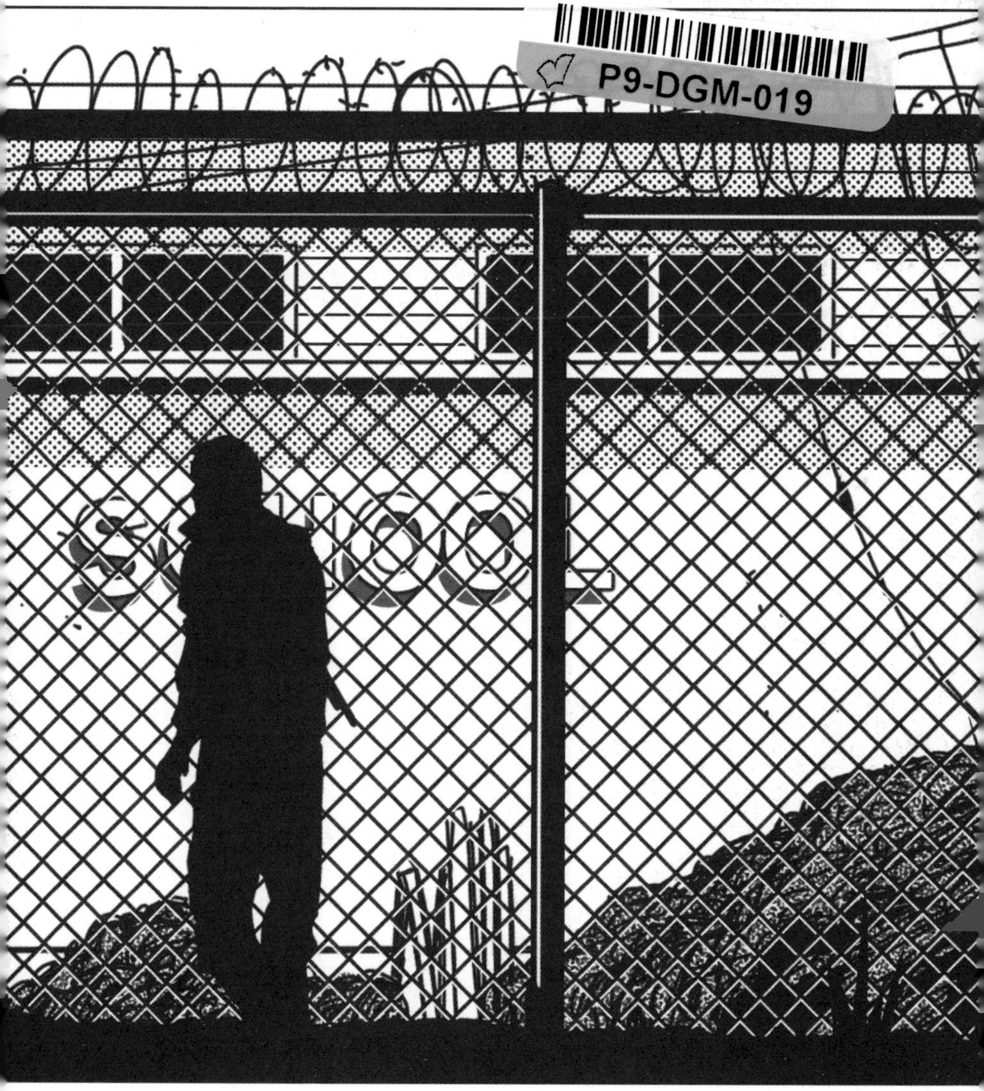

WRITTEN BY
AMANDA HOCKING AND TONY LEE

ART BY
STEVE UY

LETTERS BY
BILL TORTOLINI

INTRODUCTION

I always knew I wanted *The Hollows* series to be a graphic novel. There's something so visual about fighting off zombies and I couldn't be more thrilled about the way this series has turned out.

Growing up reading comics – everything from Batman to Calvin & Hobbes in the Sunday paper – it had always been a dream of mine to see my stories in the comics. But since I completely lacked any ability to draw, I slowly let the idea die and assumed it wasn't to be. Now, with the completion of *The Hollows*, I can happily say that it's a dream come true.

Seeing Remy, Lazlo, and especially Ripley, come to life on the pages is amazing. Steve Uy's artwork in creating the hollowed out world that they inhabit is perfect. The earlier introductions of the characters and the story by Tony Lee is exactly what I'd envisioned for them.

If you're already familiar with the series, I hope you enjoy seeing the story in a new light as much I have. And if you're new to it, welcome to the Hollowland.

Amanda Hocking

CHAPTER ONE

THE BEGINNING
OF THE END

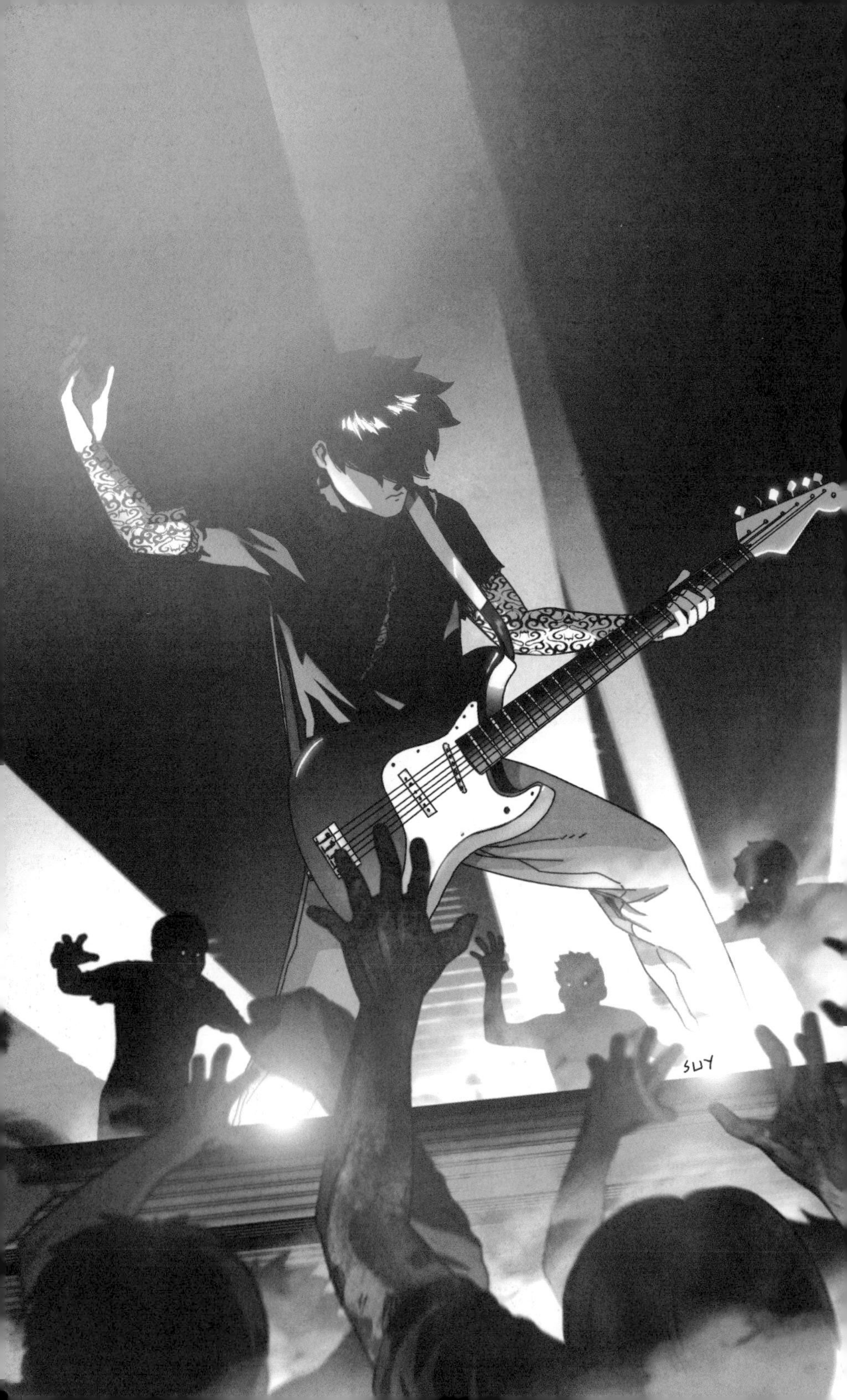
SUY

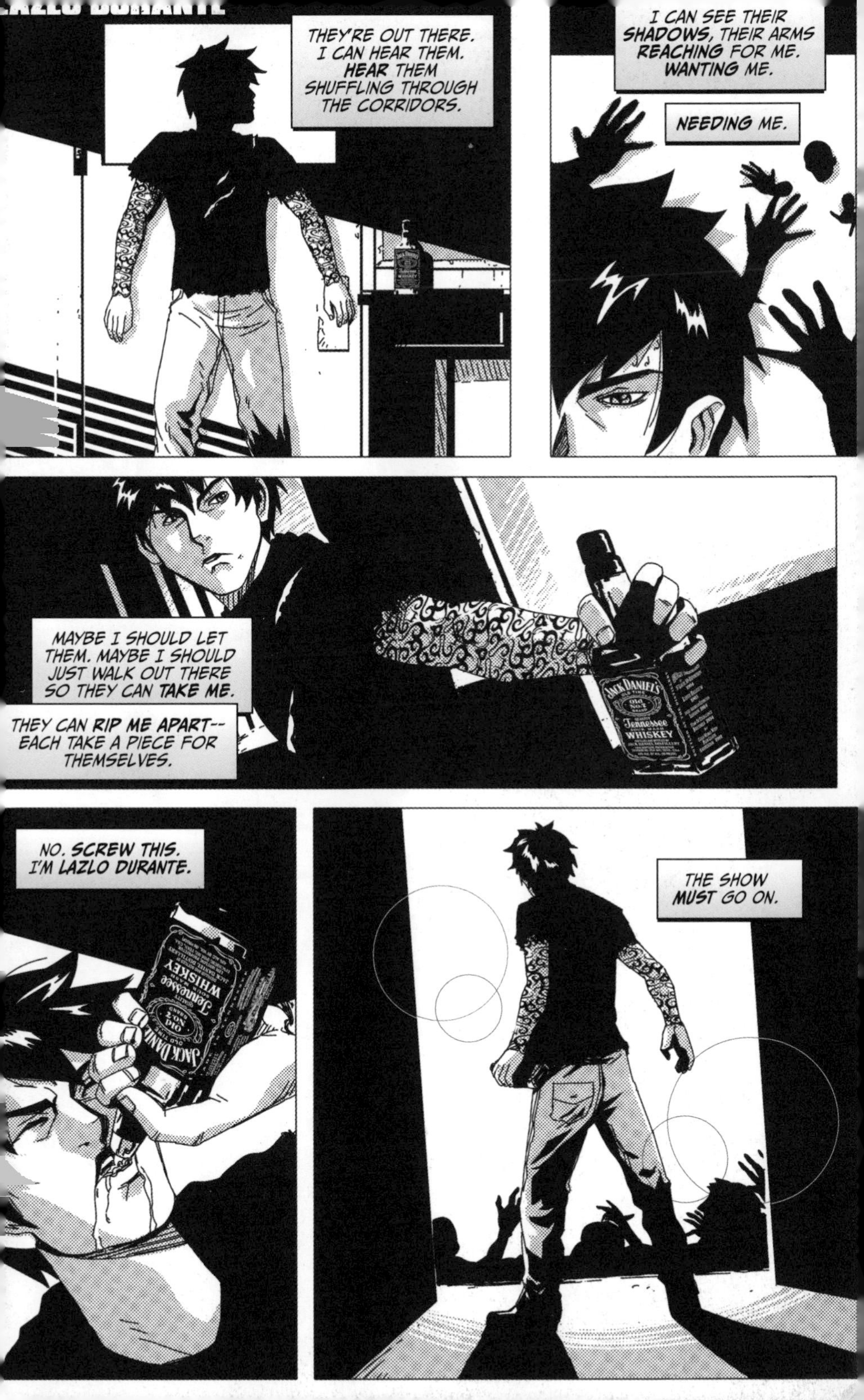
THEY'RE OUT THERE. I CAN HEAR THEM. HEAR THEM SHUFFLING THROUGH THE CORRIDORS.
I CAN SEE THEIR SHADOWS, THEIR ARMS REACHING FOR ME. WANTING ME.
NEEDING ME.
MAYBE I SHOULD LET THEM. MAYBE I SHOULD JUST WALK OUT THERE SO THEY CAN TAKE ME.
THEY CAN RIP ME APART-- EACH TAKE A PIECE FOR THEMSELVES.
JACK DANIEL'S
Tennessee
WHISKEY
NO. SCREW THIS. I'M LAZLO DURANTE.
THE SHOW MUST GO ON.

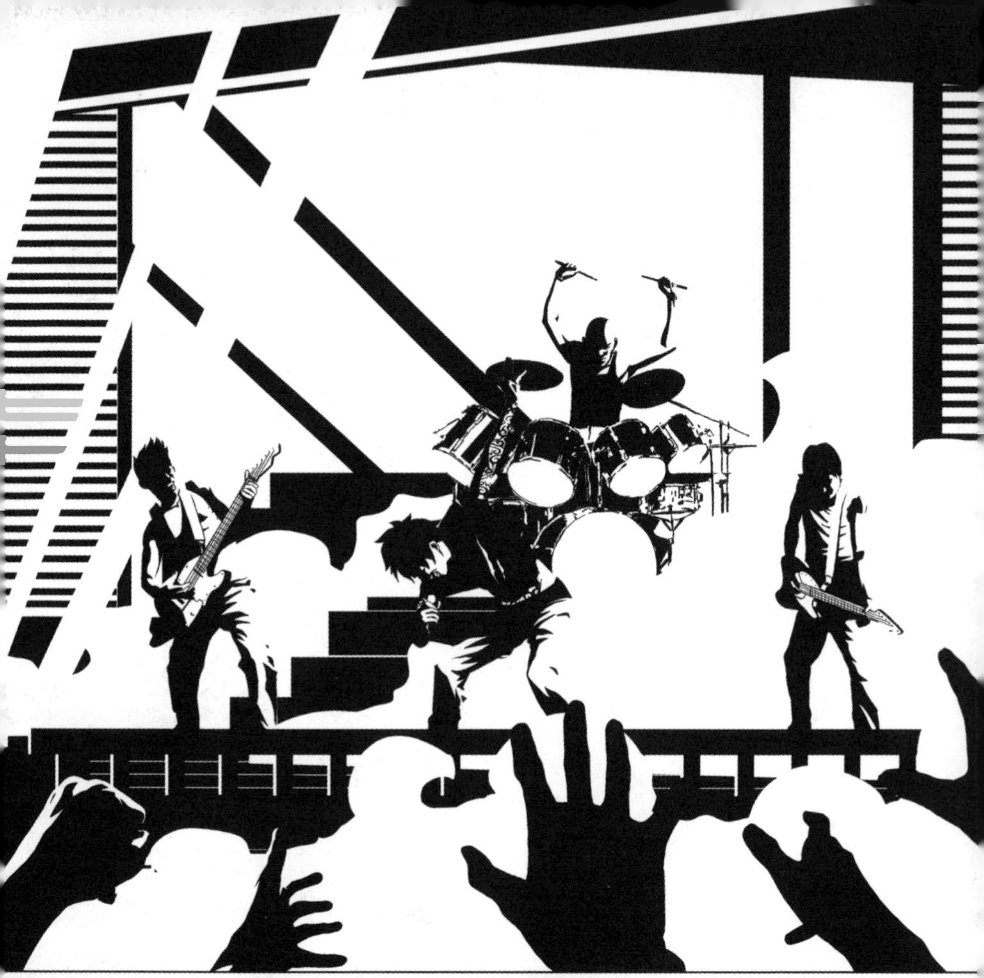

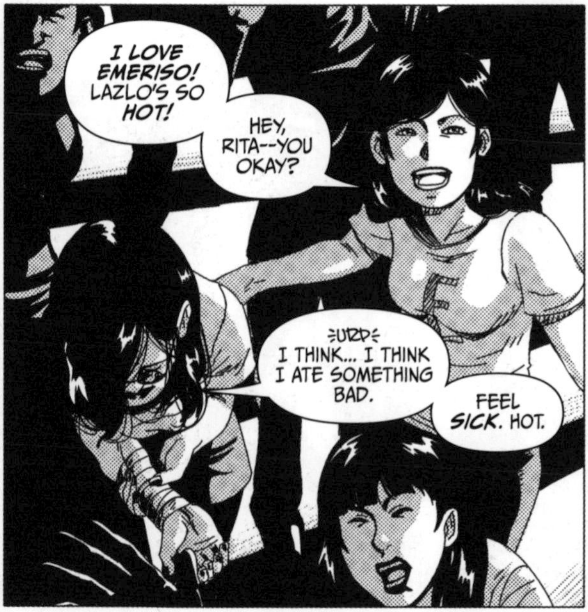

I LOVE EMERISO! LAZLO'S SO HOT!
HEY, RITA--YOU OKAY?
URP
I THINK... I THINK I ATE SOMETHING BAD.
FEEL SICK. HOT.

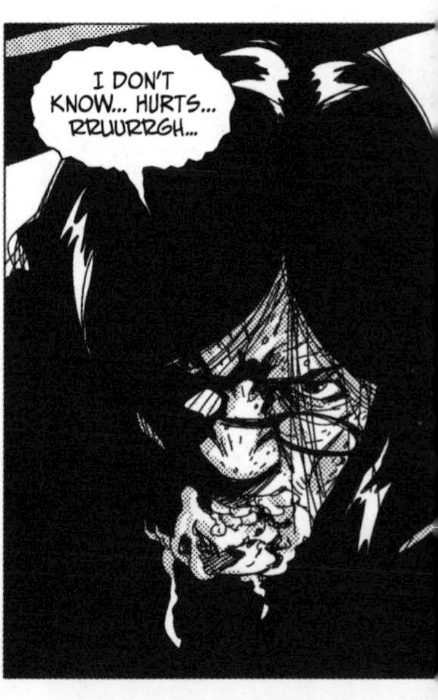

I DON'T KNOW... HURTS... RRUURRGH...

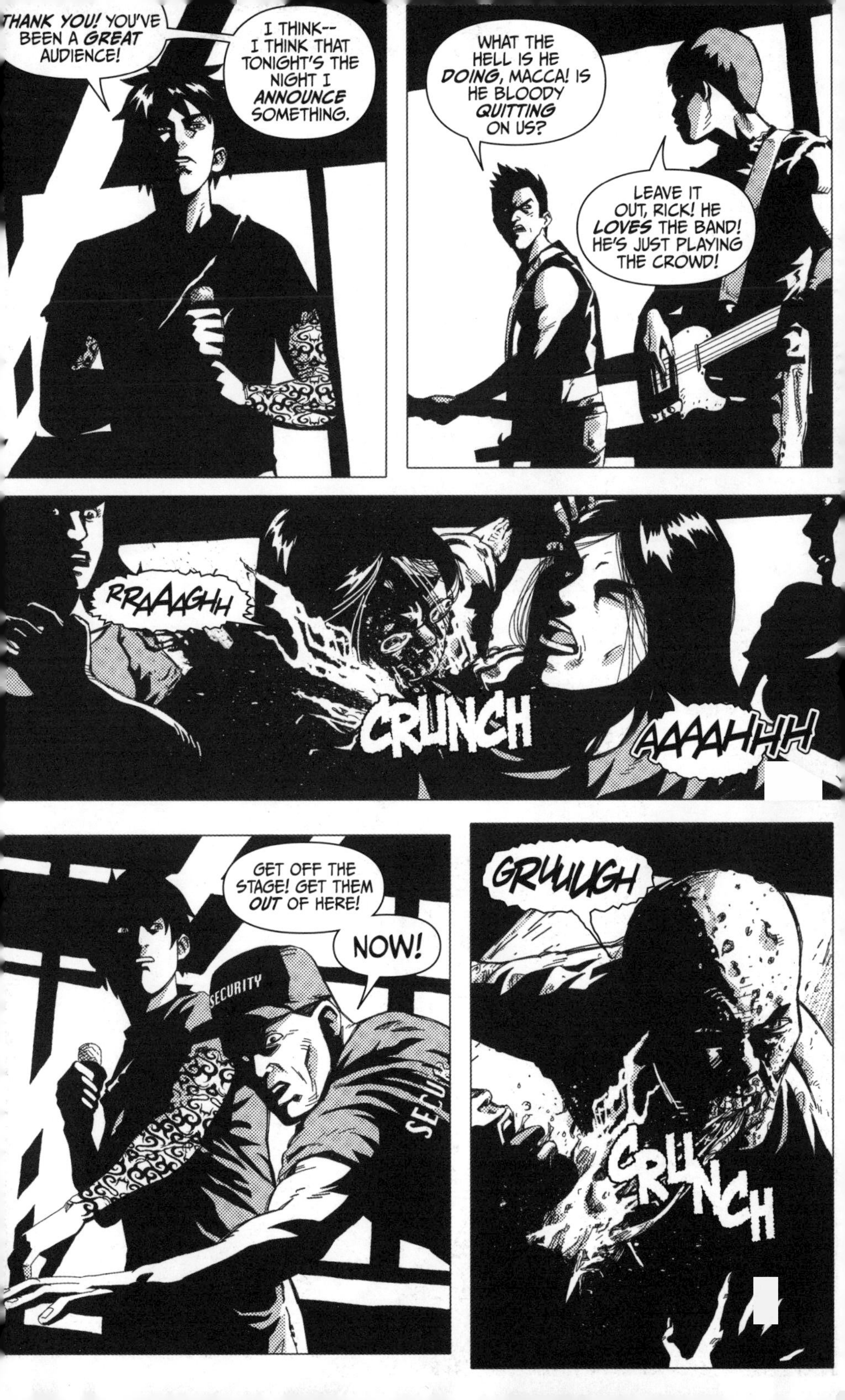
THANK YOU! YOU'VE BEEN A GREAT AUDIENCE!
I THINK-- I THINK THAT TONIGHT'S THE NIGHT I ANNOUNCE SOMETHING.
WHAT THE HELL IS HE DOING, MACCA! IS HE BLOODY QUITTING ON US?
LEAVE IT OUT, RICK! HE LOVES THE BAND! HE'S JUST PLAYING THE CROWD!
RRAAAGHH
CRUNCH
AAAAHHH
GET OFF THE STAGE! GET THEM OUT OF HERE!
NOW!
SECURITY
SECU
GRUUUGH
CRUNCH

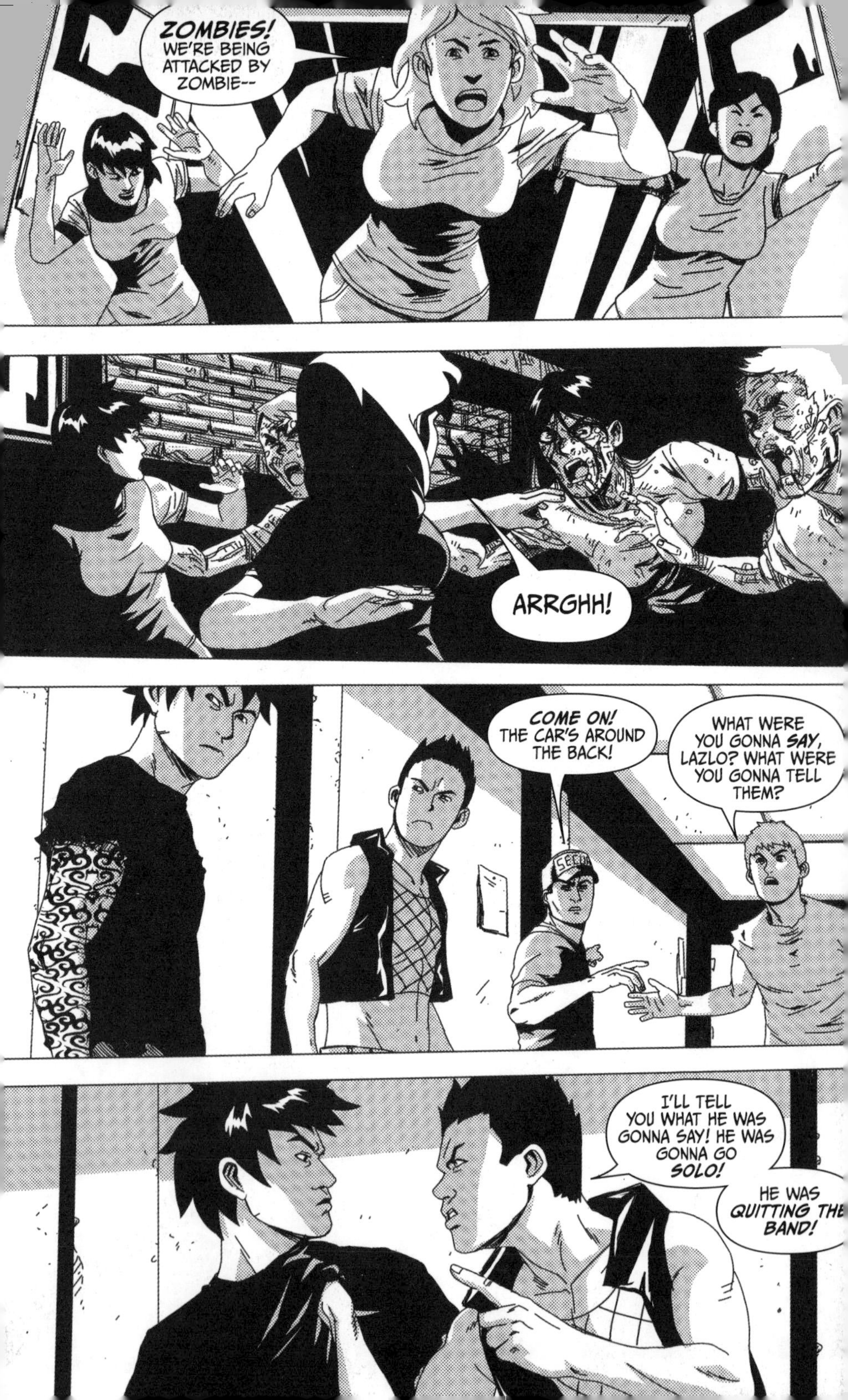
ZOMBIES! WE'RE BEING ATTACKED BY ZOMBIE--
ARRGHH!
COME ON! THE CAR'S AROUND THE BACK!
WHAT WERE YOU GONNA SAY, LAZLO? WHAT WERE YOU GONNA TELL THEM?
I'LL TELL YOU WHAT HE WAS GONNA SAY! HE WAS GONNA GO SOLO!
HE WAS QUITTING THE BAND!

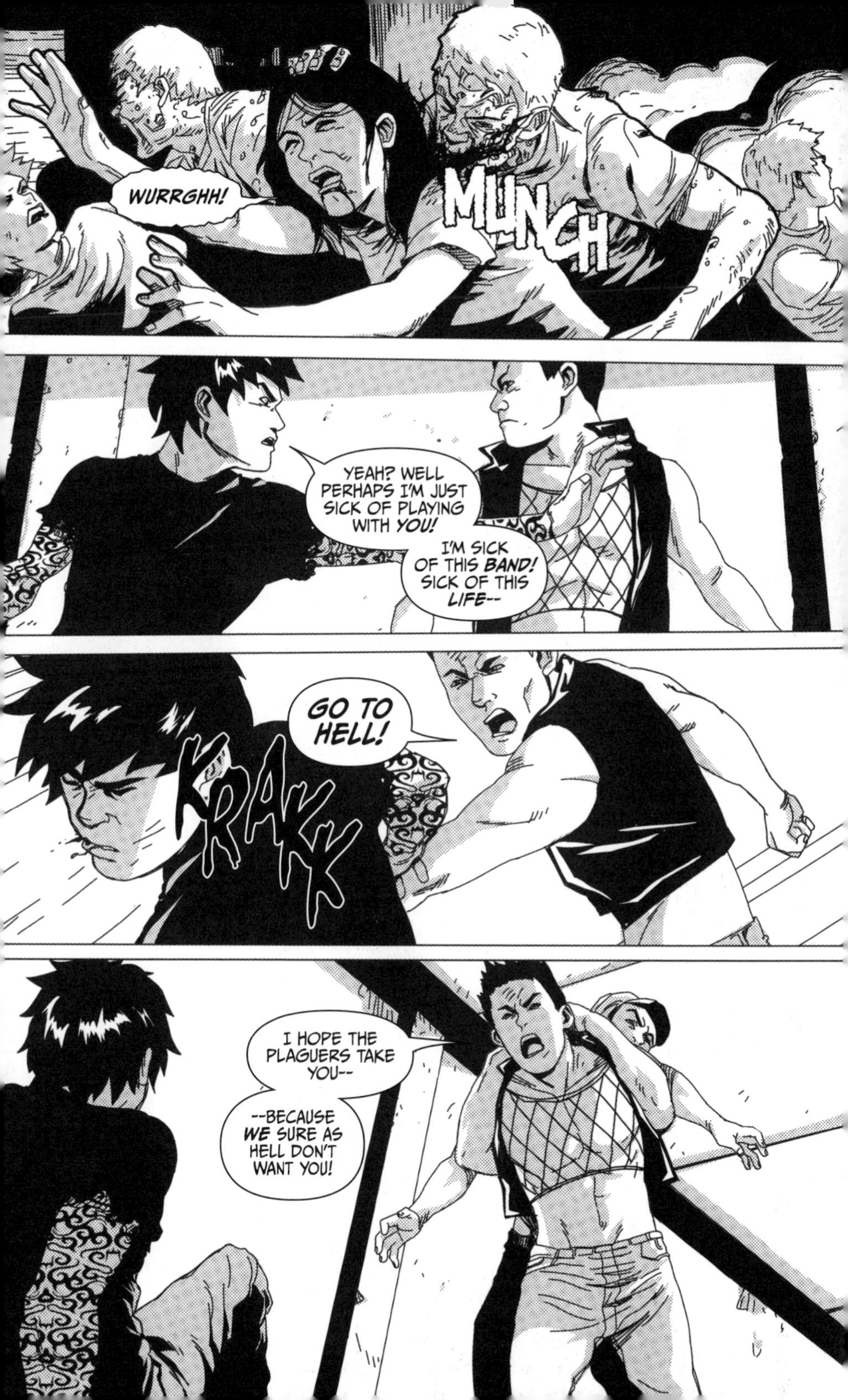
WURRGHH!
MUNCH
YEAH? WELL PERHAPS I'M JUST SICK OF PLAYING WITH *YOU!*
I'M SICK OF THIS *BAND!* SICK OF THIS *LIFE--*
GO TO HELL!
KRAKK
I HOPE THE PLAGUERS TAKE YOU--
--BECAUSE *WE* SURE AS HELL DON'T WANT YOU!

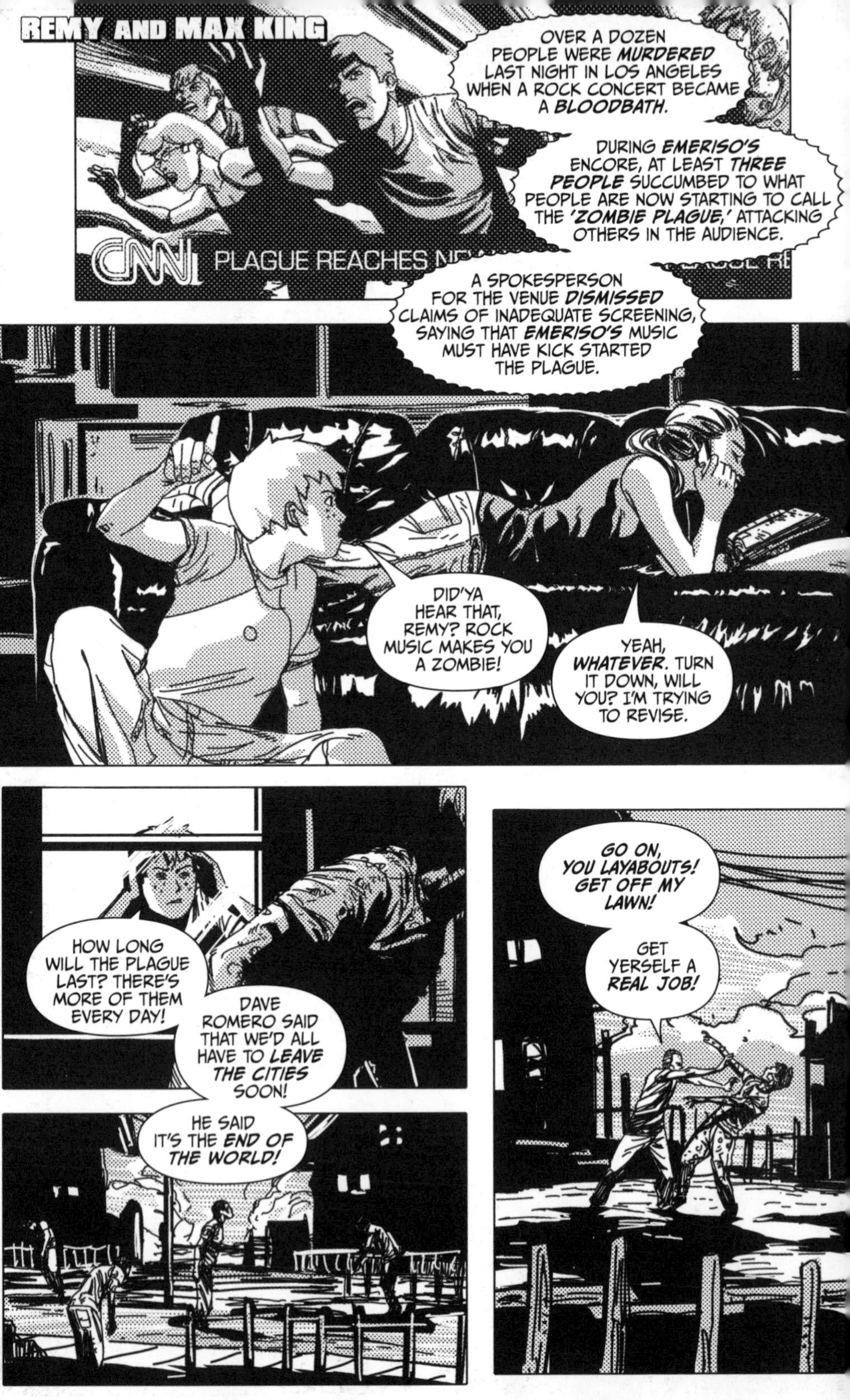
REMY AND MAX KING
OVER A DOZEN PEOPLE WERE *MURDERED* LAST NIGHT IN LOS ANGELES WHEN A ROCK CONCERT BECAME A *BLOODBATH*.
DURING *EMERISO'S* ENCORE, AT LEAST *THREE PEOPLE* SUCCUMBED TO WHAT PEOPLE ARE NOW STARTING TO CALL THE *'ZOMBIE PLAGUE,'* ATTACKING OTHERS IN THE AUDIENCE.
CNN PLAGUE REACHES
A SPOKESPERSON FOR THE VENUE *DISMISSED* CLAIMS OF INADEQUATE SCREENING, SAYING THAT *EMERISO'S* MUSIC MUST HAVE KICK STARTED THE PLAGUE.
DID'YA HEAR THAT, REMY? ROCK MUSIC MAKES YOU A ZOMBIE!
YEAH, *WHATEVER*. TURN IT DOWN, WILL YOU? I'M TRYING TO REVISE.
HOW LONG WILL THE PLAGUE LAST? THERE'S MORE OF THEM EVERY DAY!
DAVE ROMERO SAID THAT WE'D ALL HAVE TO *LEAVE THE CITIES* SOON!
HE SAID IT'S THE *END OF THE WORLD!*
GO ON, YOU LAYABOUTS! GET OFF MY LAWN!
GET YERSELF A *REAL JOB!*

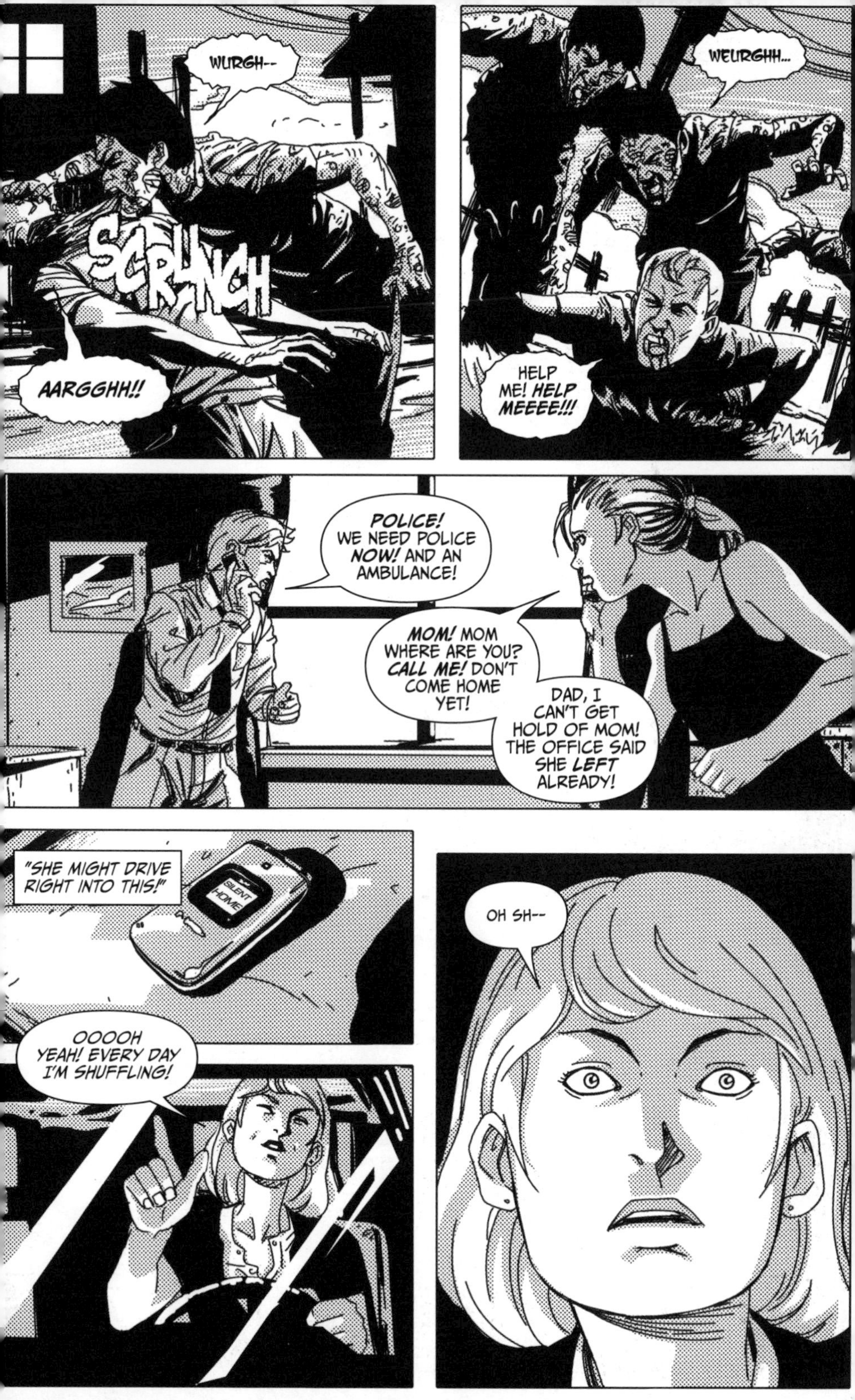
WURGH--
SCRUNCH
AARGGHH!!
WEURGHH...
HELP ME! HELP MEEEE!!!
POLICE! WE NEED POLICE NOW! AND AN AMBULANCE!
MOM! MOM WHERE ARE YOU? CALL ME! DON'T COME HOME YET!
DAD, I CAN'T GET HOLD OF MOM! THE OFFICE SAID SHE LEFT ALREADY!
"SHE MIGHT DRIVE RIGHT INTO THIS!"
SILENT
HOME
OOOOH YEAH! EVERY DAY I'M SHUFFLING!
OH SH--

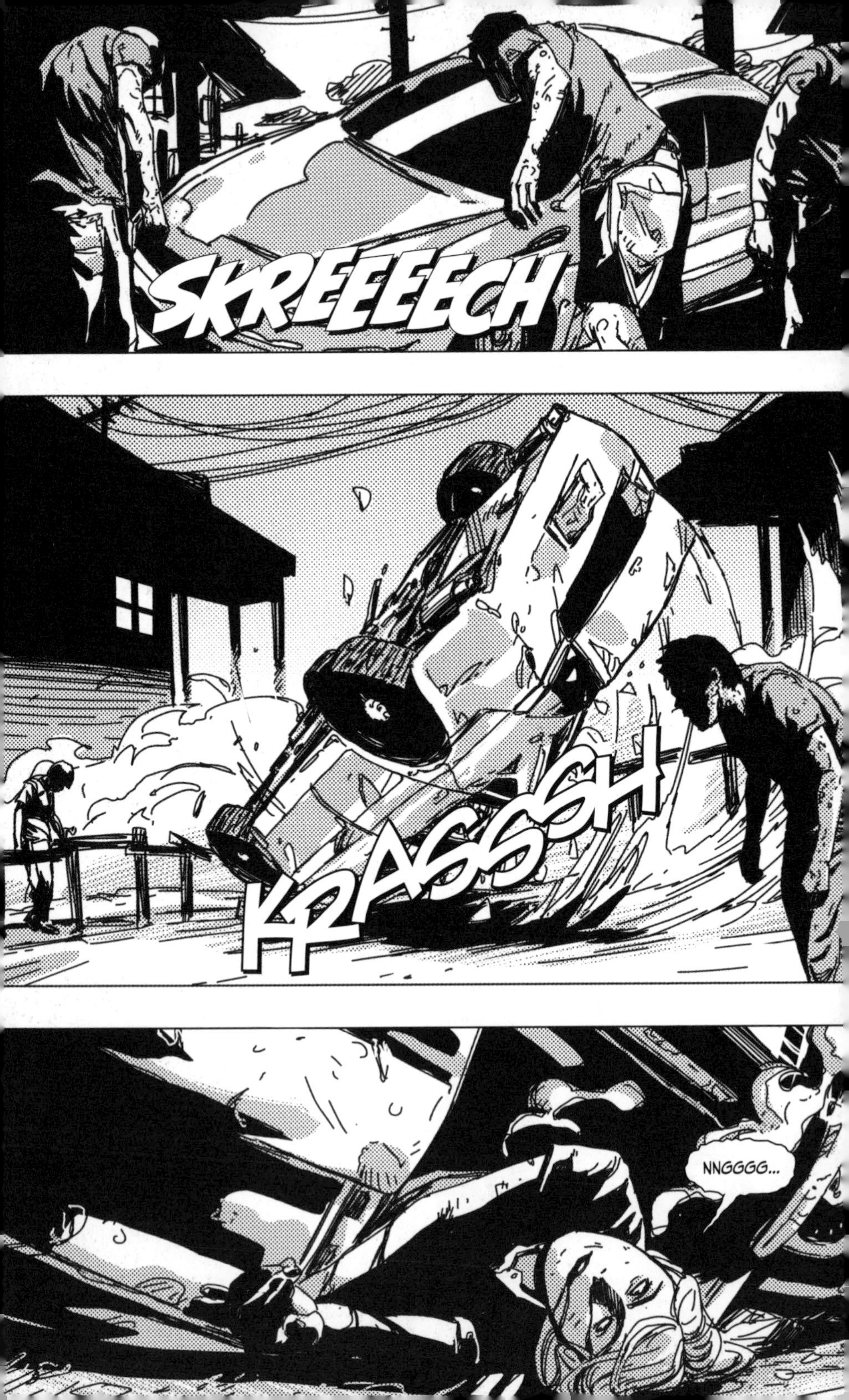
SKREEEECH
KRASSSH
NNGGGG...

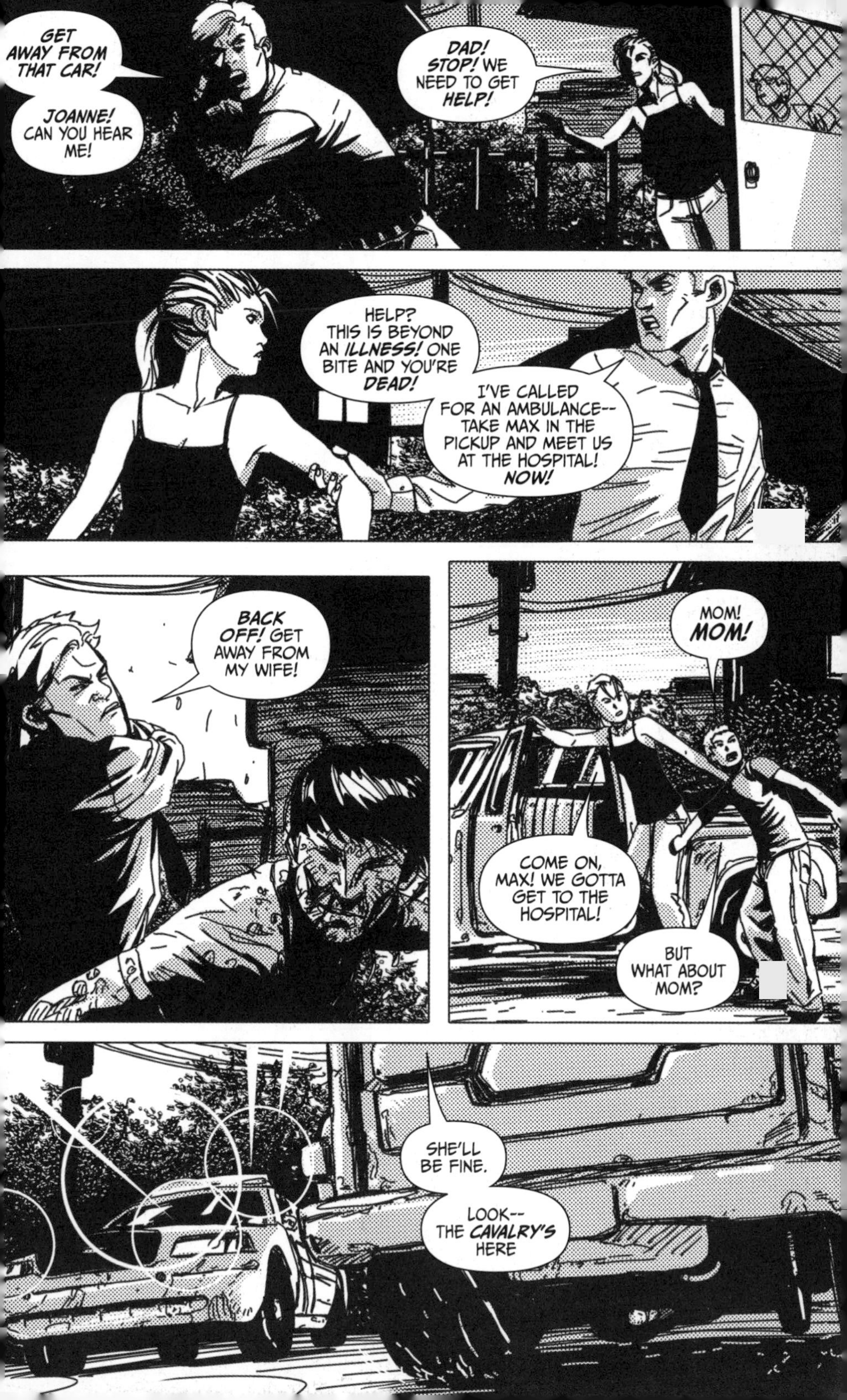
GET AWAY FROM THAT CAR!
JOANNE! CAN YOU HEAR ME!
DAD! STOP! WE NEED TO GET HELP!
HELP? THIS IS BEYOND AN ILLNESS! ONE BITE AND YOU'RE DEAD!
I'VE CALLED FOR AN AMBULANCE-- TAKE MAX IN THE PICKUP AND MEET US AT THE HOSPITAL! NOW!
BACK OFF! GET AWAY FROM MY WIFE!
MOM! MOM!
COME ON, MAX! WE GOTTA GET TO THE HOSPITAL!
BUT WHAT ABOUT MOM?
SHE'LL BE FINE.
LOOK-- THE CAVALRY'S HERE

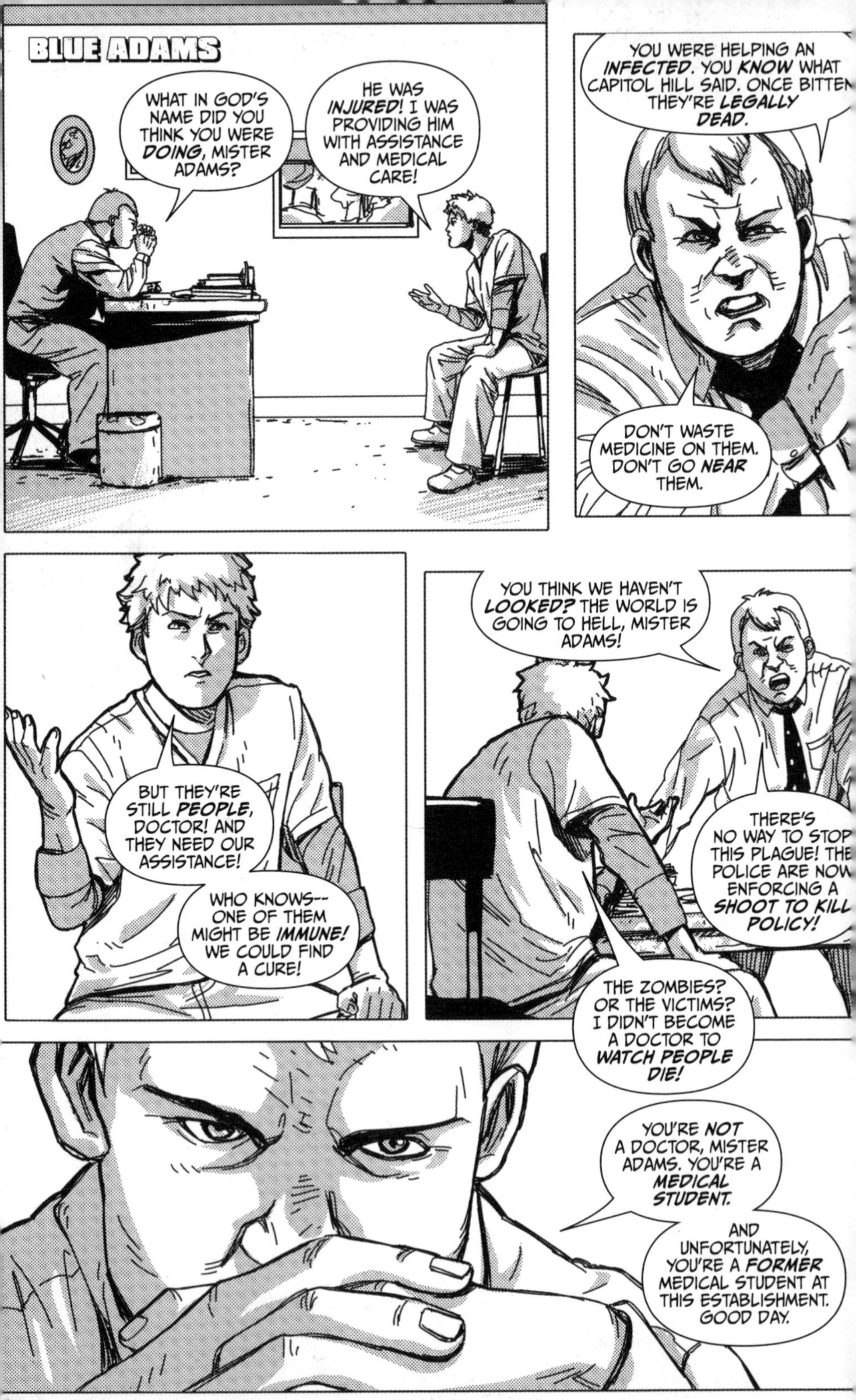
BLUE ADAMS
WHAT IN GOD'S NAME DID YOU THINK YOU WERE DOING, MISTER ADAMS?
HE WAS INJURED! I WAS PROVIDING HIM WITH ASSISTANCE AND MEDICAL CARE!
YOU WERE HELPING AN INFECTED. YOU KNOW WHAT CAPITOL HILL SAID. ONCE BITTEN THEY'RE LEGALLY DEAD.
DON'T WASTE MEDICINE ON THEM. DON'T GO NEAR THEM.
BUT THEY'RE STILL PEOPLE, DOCTOR! AND THEY NEED OUR ASSISTANCE!
WHO KNOWS-- ONE OF THEM MIGHT BE IMMUNE! WE COULD FIND A CURE!
YOU THINK WE HAVEN'T LOOKED? THE WORLD IS GOING TO HELL, MISTER ADAMS!
THERE'S NO WAY TO STOP THIS PLAGUE! THE POLICE ARE NOW ENFORCING A SHOOT TO KILL POLICY!
THE ZOMBIES? OR THE VICTIMS? I DIDN'T BECOME A DOCTOR TO WATCH PEOPLE DIE!
YOU'RE NOT A DOCTOR, MISTER ADAMS. YOU'RE A MEDICAL STUDENT.
AND UNFORTUNATELY, YOU'RE A FORMER MEDICAL STUDENT AT THIS ESTABLISHMENT. GOOD DAY.

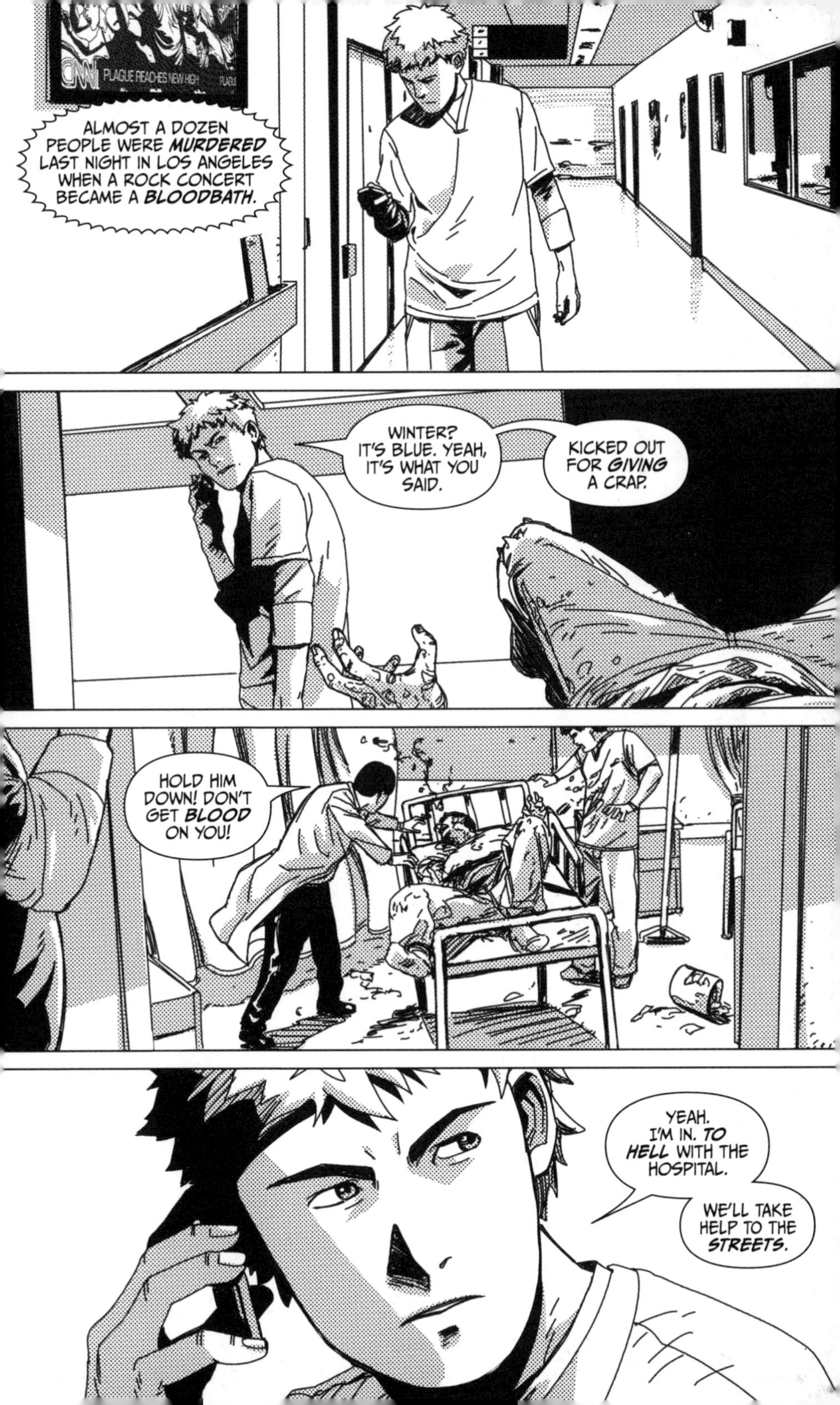
CNN PLAGUE REACHES NEW HIGH
ALMOST A DOZEN PEOPLE WERE MURDERED LAST NIGHT IN LOS ANGELES WHEN A ROCK CONCERT BECAME A BLOODBATH.
WINTER? IT'S BLUE. YEAH, IT'S WHAT YOU SAID.
KICKED OUT FOR GIVING A CRAP.
HOLD HIM DOWN! DON'T GET BLOOD ON YOU!
YEAH. I'M IN. TO HELL WITH THE HOSPITAL.
WE'LL TAKE HELP TO THE STREETS.

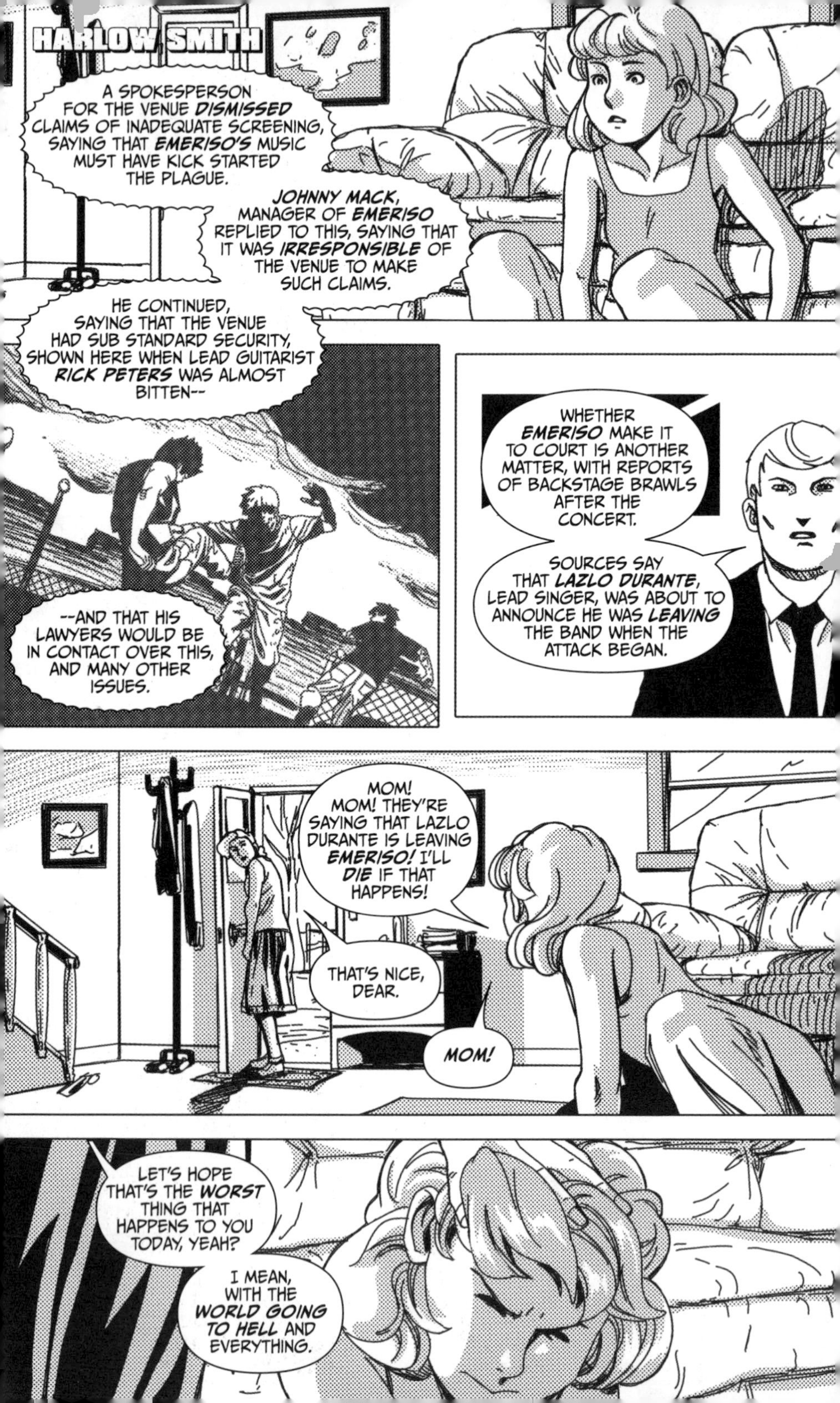
HARLOW SMITH
A SPOKESPERSON FOR THE VENUE *DISMISSED* CLAIMS OF INADEQUATE SCREENING, SAYING THAT *EMERISO'S* MUSIC MUST HAVE KICK STARTED THE PLAGUE.
JOHNNY MACK, MANAGER OF *EMERISO* REPLIED TO THIS, SAYING THAT IT WAS *IRRESPONSIBLE* OF THE VENUE TO MAKE SUCH CLAIMS.
HE CONTINUED, SAYING THAT THE VENUE HAD SUB STANDARD SECURITY, SHOWN HERE WHEN LEAD GUITARIST *RICK PETERS* WAS ALMOST BITTEN--
--AND THAT HIS LAWYERS WOULD BE IN CONTACT OVER THIS, AND MANY OTHER ISSUES.
WHETHER *EMERISO* MAKE IT TO COURT IS ANOTHER MATTER, WITH REPORTS OF BACKSTAGE BRAWLS AFTER THE CONCERT.
SOURCES SAY THAT *LAZLO DURANTE*, LEAD SINGER, WAS ABOUT TO ANNOUNCE HE WAS *LEAVING* THE BAND WHEN THE ATTACK BEGAN.
MOM! MOM! THEY'RE SAYING THAT LAZLO DURANTE IS LEAVING *EMERISO!* I'LL *DIE* IF THAT HAPPENS!
THAT'S NICE, DEAR.
MOM!
LET'S HOPE THAT'S THE *WORST* THING THAT HAPPENS TO YOU TODAY, YEAH?
I MEAN, WITH THE *WORLD GOING TO HELL* AND EVERYTHING.

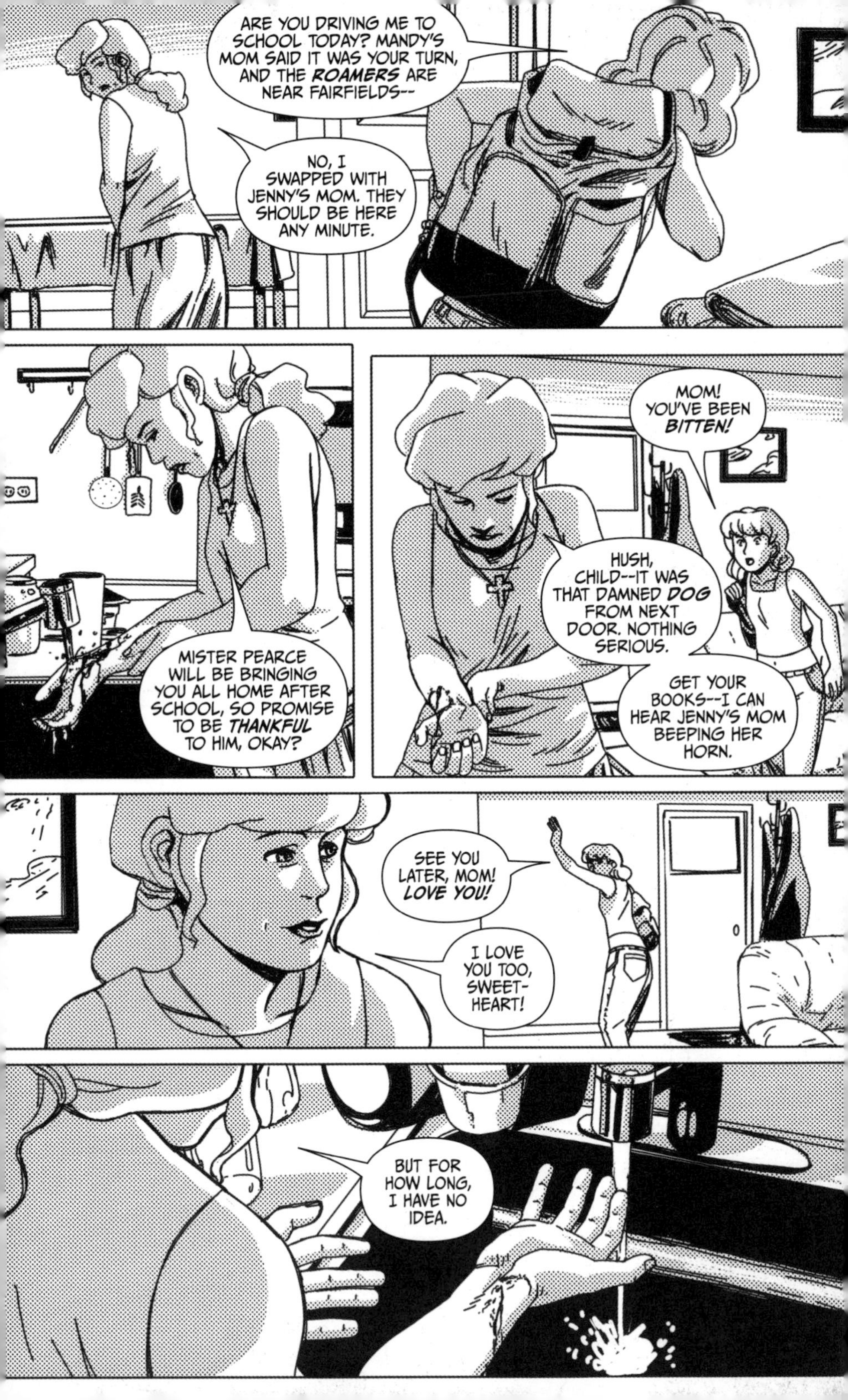
ARE YOU DRIVING ME TO SCHOOL TODAY? MANDY'S MOM SAID IT WAS YOUR TURN, AND THE ***ROAMERS*** ARE NEAR FAIRFIELDS--
NO, I SWAPPED WITH JENNY'S MOM. THEY SHOULD BE HERE ANY MINUTE.
MISTER PEARCE WILL BE BRINGING YOU ALL HOME AFTER SCHOOL, SO PROMISE TO BE ***THANKFUL*** TO HIM, OKAY?
MOM! YOU'VE BEEN ***BITTEN!***
HUSH, CHILD--IT WAS THAT DAMNED ***DOG*** FROM NEXT DOOR. NOTHING SERIOUS.
GET YOUR BOOKS--I CAN HEAR JENNY'S MOM BEEPING HER HORN.
SEE YOU LATER, MOM! ***LOVE YOU!***
I LOVE YOU TOO, SWEET-HEART!
BUT FOR HOW LONG, I HAVE NO IDEA.

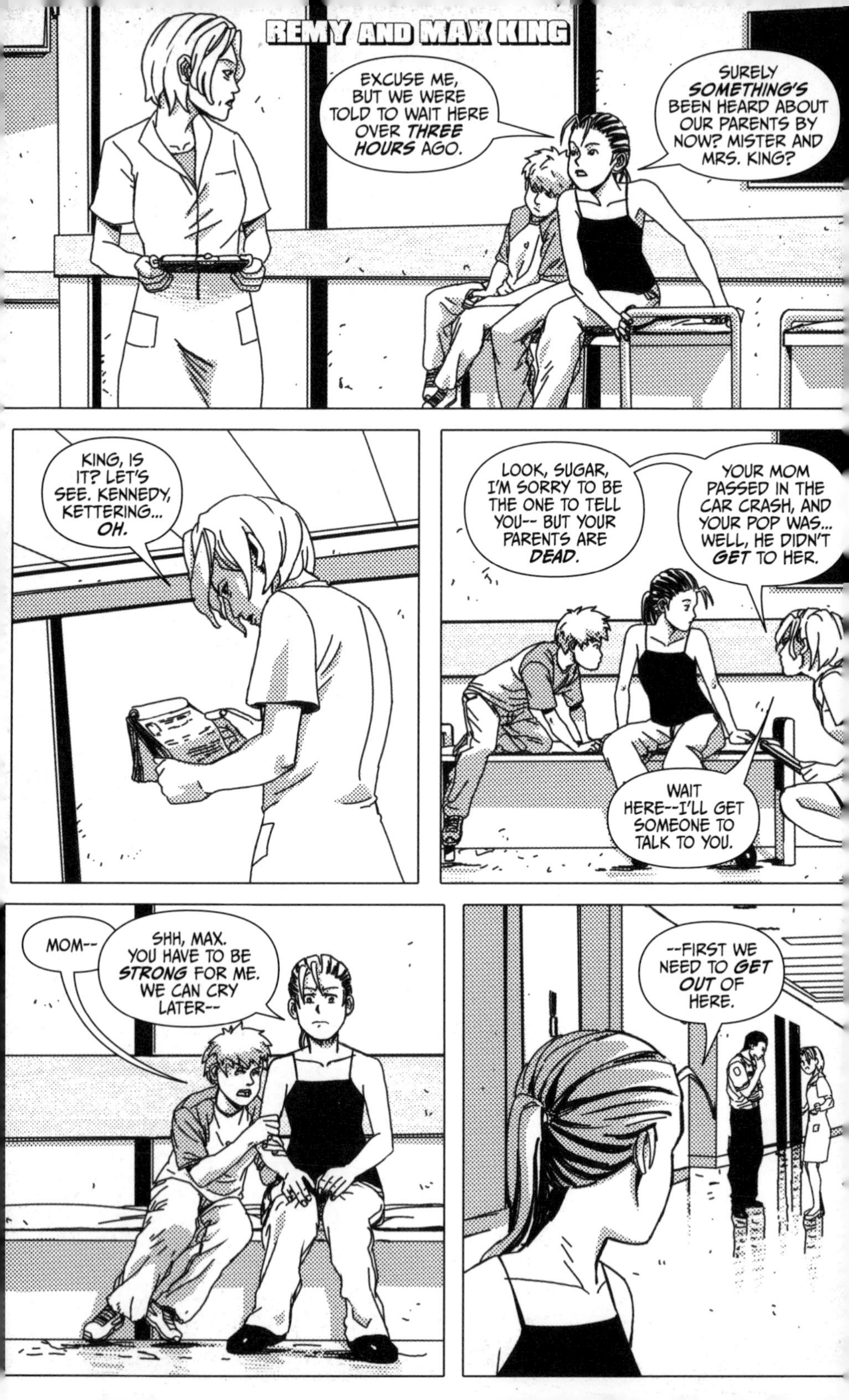
REMY AND MAX KING
EXCUSE ME, BUT WE WERE TOLD TO WAIT HERE OVER *THREE HOURS* AGO.
SURELY *SOMETHING'S* BEEN HEARD ABOUT OUR PARENTS BY NOW? MISTER AND MRS. KING?
KING, IS IT? LET'S SEE. KENNEDY, KETTERING... *OH.*
LOOK, SUGAR, I'M SORRY TO BE THE ONE TO TELL YOU-- BUT YOUR PARENTS ARE *DEAD.*
YOUR MOM PASSED IN THE CAR CRASH, AND YOUR POP WAS... WELL, HE DIDN'T *GET* TO HER.
WAIT HERE--I'LL GET SOMEONE TO TALK TO YOU.
MOM--
SHH, MAX. YOU HAVE TO BE *STRONG* FOR ME. WE CAN CRY LATER--
--FIRST WE NEED TO *GET OUT* OF HERE.

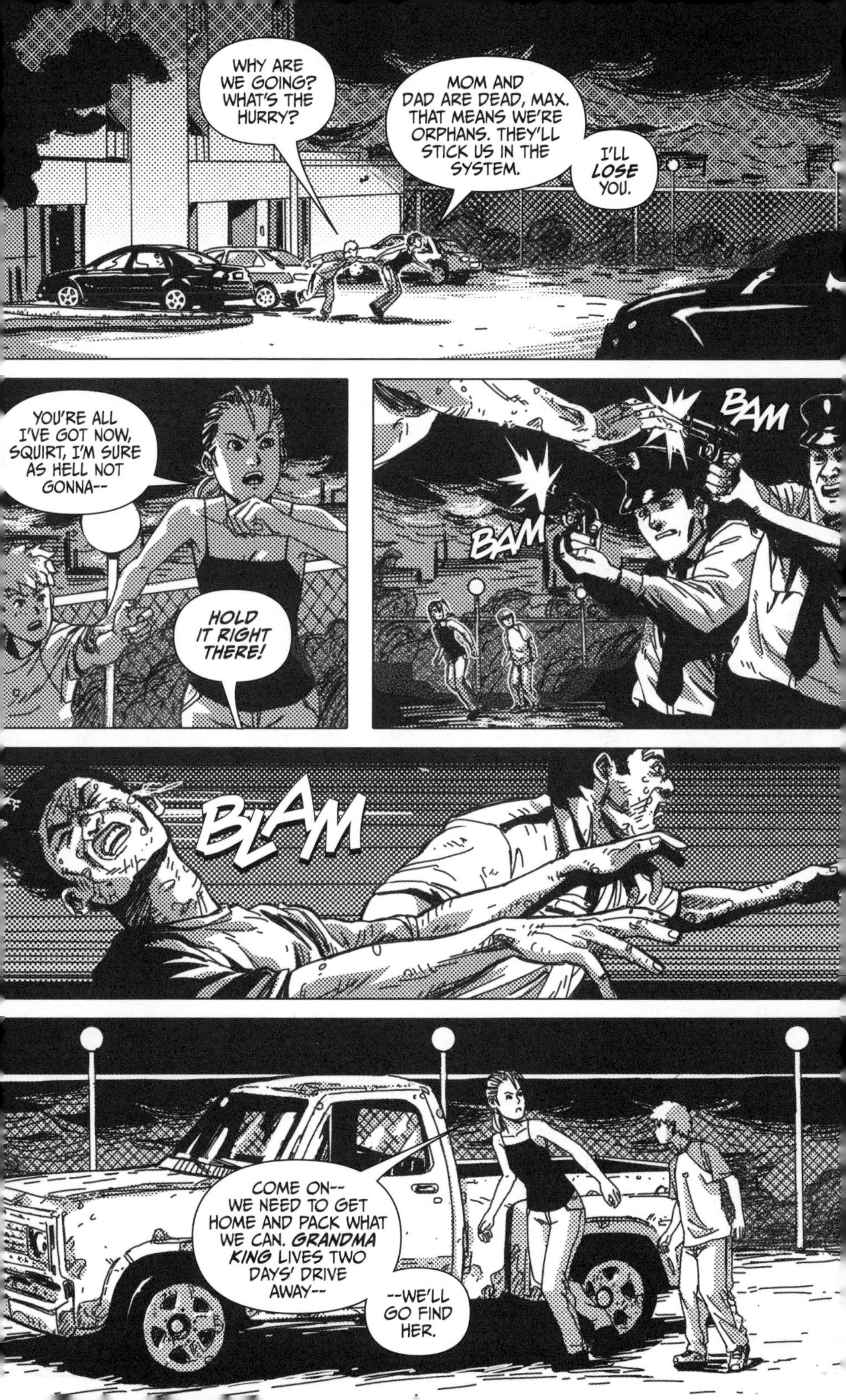
WHY ARE WE GOING? WHAT'S THE HURRY?
MOM AND DAD ARE DEAD, MAX. THAT MEANS WE'RE ORPHANS. THEY'LL STICK US IN THE SYSTEM.
I'LL LOSE YOU.
YOU'RE ALL I'VE GOT NOW, SQUIRT, I'M SURE AS HELL NOT GONNA--
HOLD IT RIGHT THERE!
BAM
BAM
BLAM
COME ON-- WE NEED TO GET HOME AND PACK WHAT WE CAN. GRANDMA KING LIVES TWO DAYS' DRIVE AWAY--
--WE'LL GO FIND HER.

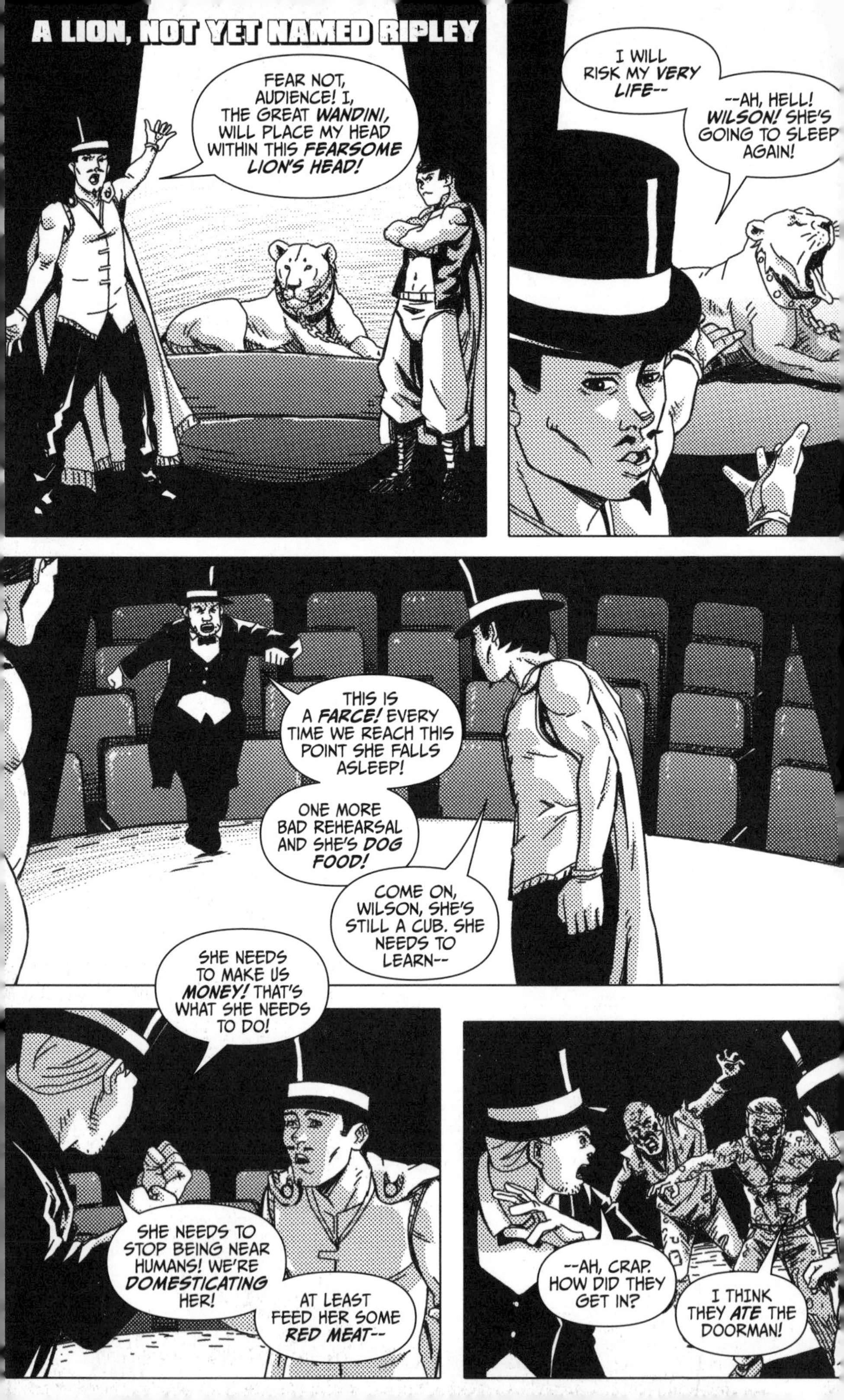
A LION, NOT YET NAMED RIPLEY
FEAR NOT, AUDIENCE! I, THE GREAT WANDINI, WILL PLACE MY HEAD WITHIN THIS FEARSOME LION'S HEAD!
I WILL RISK MY VERY LIFE--
--AH, HELL! WILSON! SHE'S GOING TO SLEEP AGAIN!
THIS IS A FARCE! EVERY TIME WE REACH THIS POINT SHE FALLS ASLEEP!
ONE MORE BAD REHEARSAL AND SHE'S DOG FOOD!
COME ON, WILSON, SHE'S STILL A CUB. SHE NEEDS TO LEARN--
SHE NEEDS TO MAKE US MONEY! THAT'S WHAT SHE NEEDS TO DO!
SHE NEEDS TO STOP BEING NEAR HUMANS! WE'RE DOMESTICATING HER!
AT LEAST FEED HER SOME RED MEAT--
--AH, CRAP. HOW DID THEY GET IN?
I THINK THEY ATE THE DOORMAN!

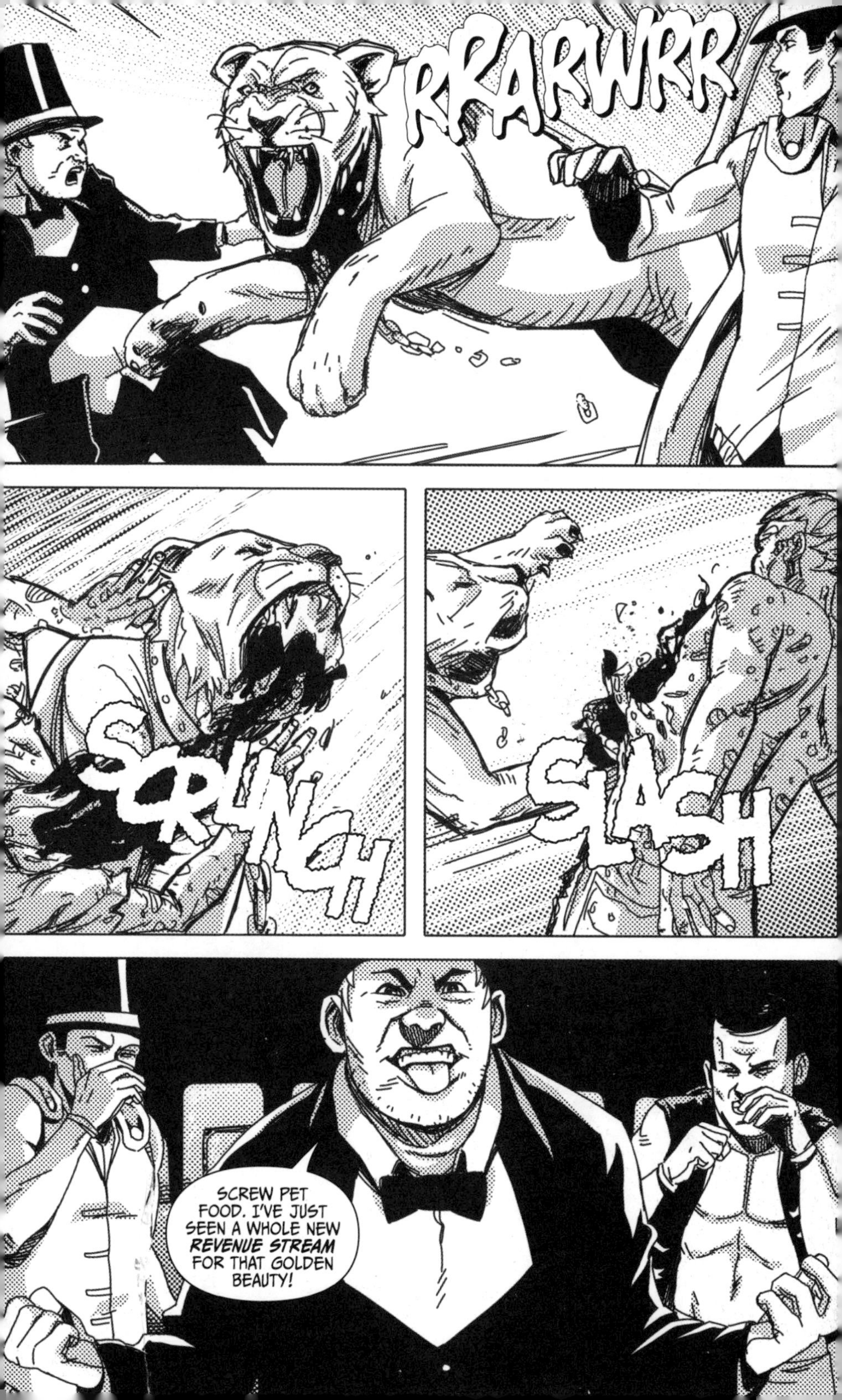
RRARWRR
SCRUNCH
SLASH
SCREW PET FOOD. I'VE JUST SEEN A WHOLE NEW ***REVENUE STREAM*** FOR THAT GOLDEN BEAUTY!

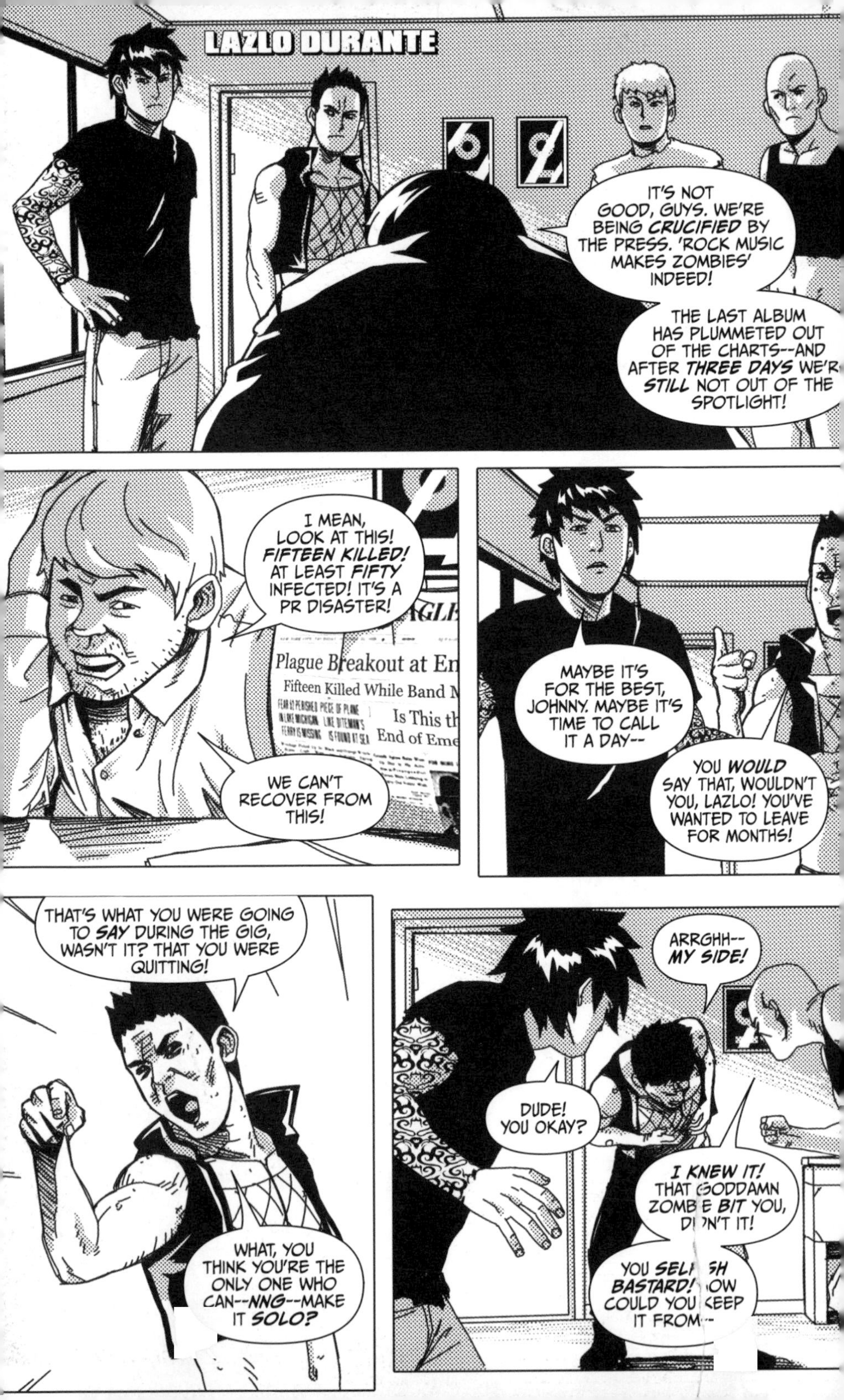
LAZLO DURANTE
IT'S NOT GOOD, GUYS. WE'RE BEING *CRUCIFIED* BY THE PRESS. 'ROCK MUSIC MAKES ZOMBIES' INDEED!
THE LAST ALBUM HAS PLUMMETED OUT OF THE CHARTS--AND AFTER *THREE DAYS* WE'R *STILL* NOT OUT OF THE SPOTLIGHT!
I MEAN, LOOK AT THIS! *FIFTEEN KILLED!* AT LEAST *FIFTY* INFECTED! IT'S A PR DISASTER!
Plague Breakout at Em
Fifteen Killed While Band M
Is This th
End of Eme
WE CAN'T RECOVER FROM THIS!
MAYBE IT'S FOR THE BEST, JOHNNY. MAYBE IT'S TIME TO CALL IT A DAY--
YOU *WOULD* SAY THAT, WOULDN'T YOU, LAZLO! YOU'VE WANTED TO LEAVE FOR MONTHS!
THAT'S WHAT YOU WERE GOING TO *SAY* DURING THE GIG, WASN'T IT? THAT YOU WERE QUITTING!
WHAT, YOU THINK YOU'RE THE ONLY ONE WHO CAN--*NNG*--MAKE IT *SOLO?*
ARRGHH-- *MY SIDE!*
DUDE! YOU OKAY?
I KNEW IT! THAT GODDAMN ZOMB E *BIT* YOU, D N'T IT!
YOU *SEL SH BASTARD!* OW COULD YOU KEEP IT FROM--

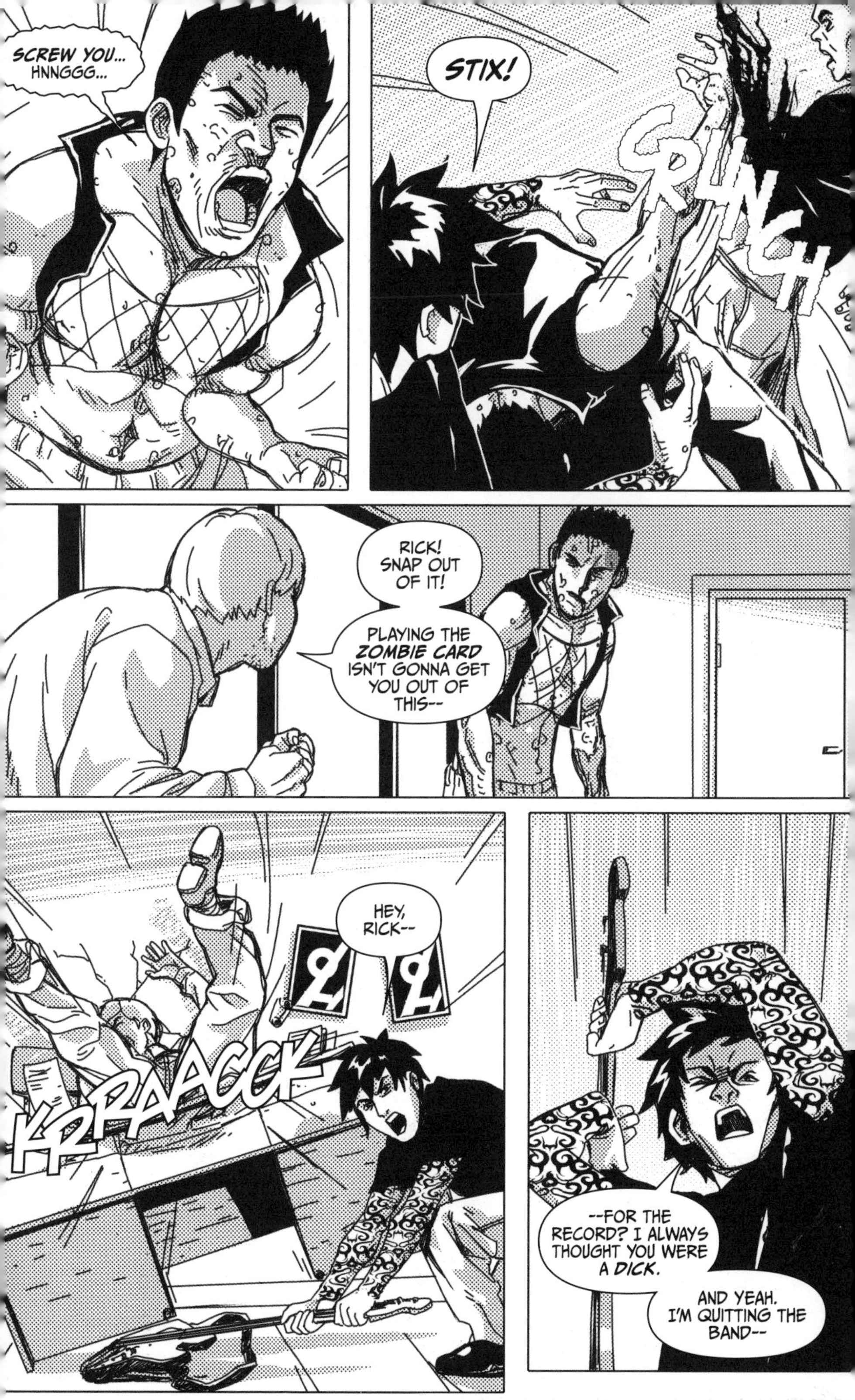
SCREW YOU... HNNGGG...
STIX!
CRUNCH
RICK! SNAP OUT OF IT!
PLAYING THE ZOMBIE CARD ISN'T GONNA GET YOU OUT OF THIS--
HEY, RICK--
KRRAACCK
--FOR THE RECORD? I ALWAYS THOUGHT YOU WERE A DICK.
AND YEAH. I'M QUITTING THE BAND--

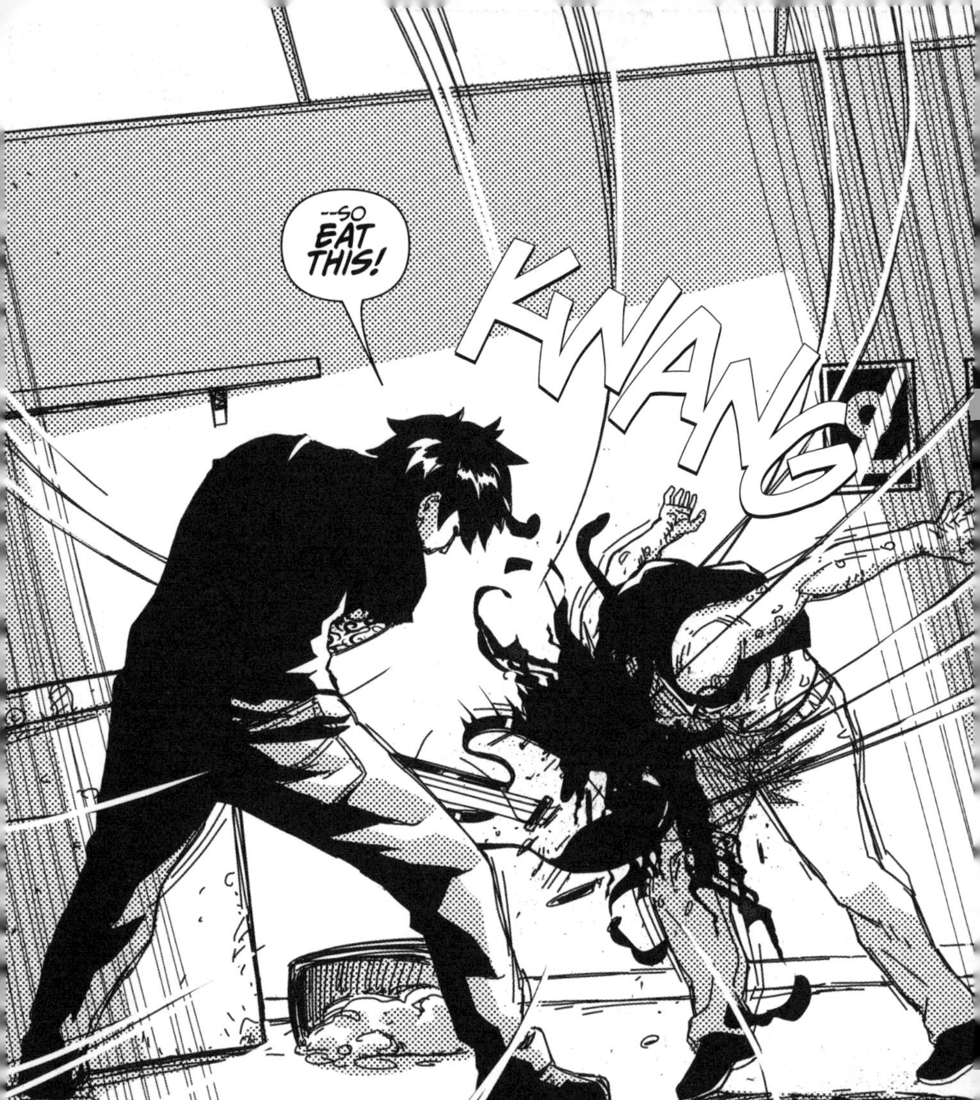
--SO EAT THIS!
KWANG!!
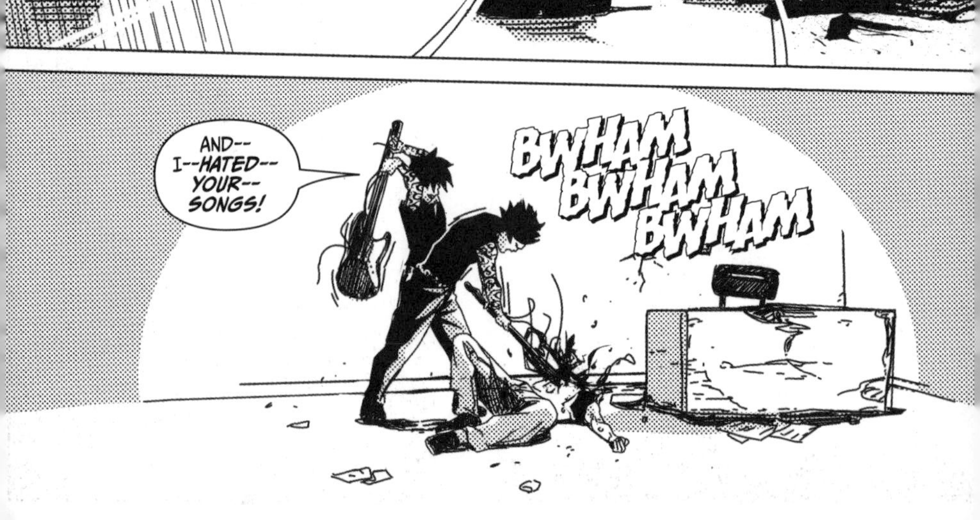
AND-- I--HATED-- YOUR-- SONGS!
BWHAM BWHAM BWHAM

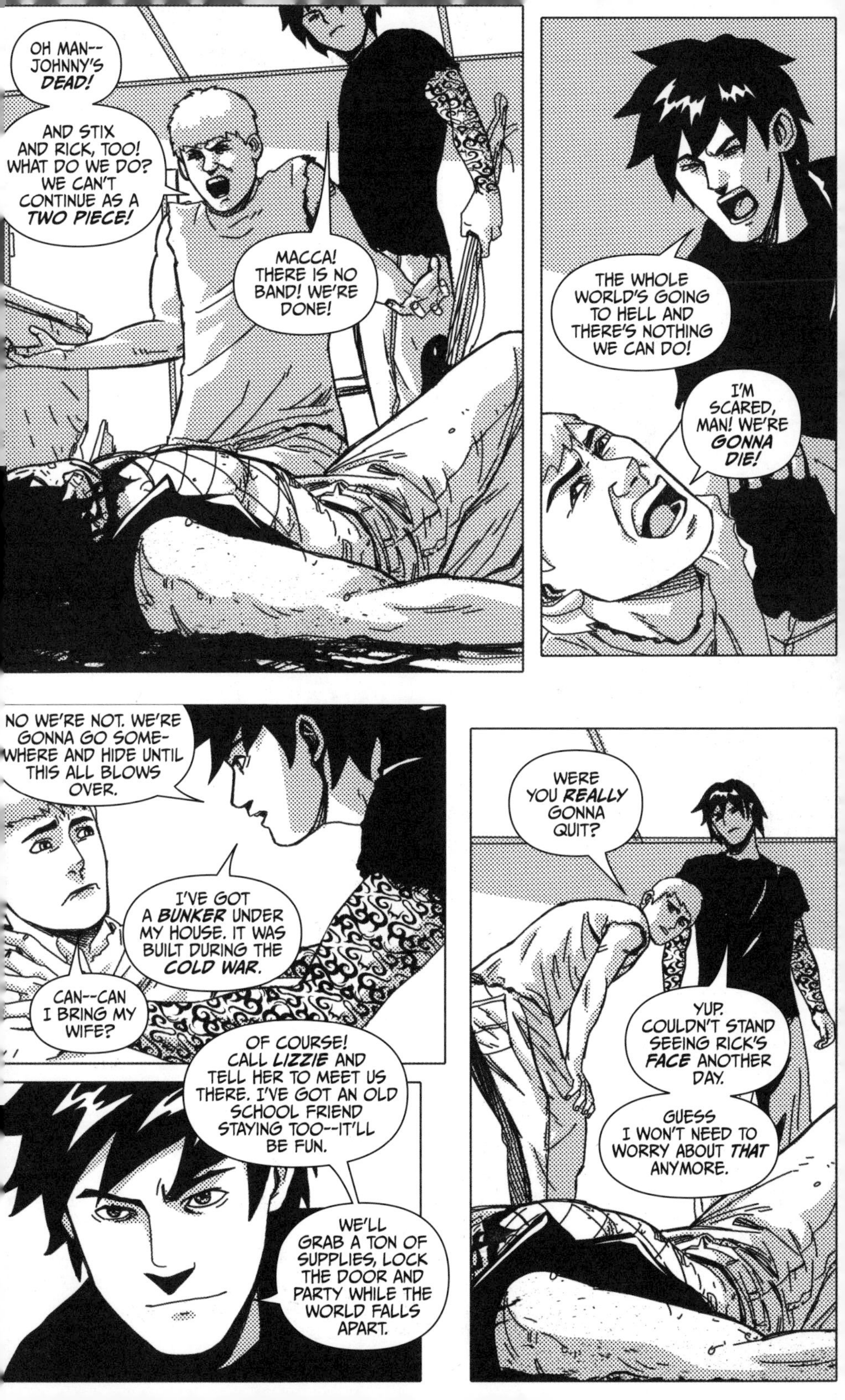
OH MAN--JOHNNY'S DEAD!
AND STIX AND RICK, TOO! WHAT DO WE DO? WE CAN'T CONTINUE AS A TWO PIECE!
MACCA! THERE IS NO BAND! WE'RE DONE!
THE WHOLE WORLD'S GOING TO HELL AND THERE'S NOTHING WE CAN DO!
I'M SCARED, MAN! WE'RE GONNA DIE!
NO WE'RE NOT. WE'RE GONNA GO SOME-WHERE AND HIDE UNTIL THIS ALL BLOWS OVER.
I'VE GOT A BUNKER UNDER MY HOUSE. IT WAS BUILT DURING THE COLD WAR.
CAN--CAN I BRING MY WIFE?
OF COURSE! CALL LIZZIE AND TELL HER TO MEET US THERE. I'VE GOT AN OLD SCHOOL FRIEND STAYING TOO--IT'LL BE FUN.
WE'LL GRAB A TON OF SUPPLIES, LOCK THE DOOR AND PARTY WHILE THE WORLD FALLS APART.
WERE YOU REALLY GONNA QUIT?
YUP. COULDN'T STAND SEEING RICK'S FACE ANOTHER DAY.
GUESS I WON'T NEED TO WORRY ABOUT THAT ANYMORE.

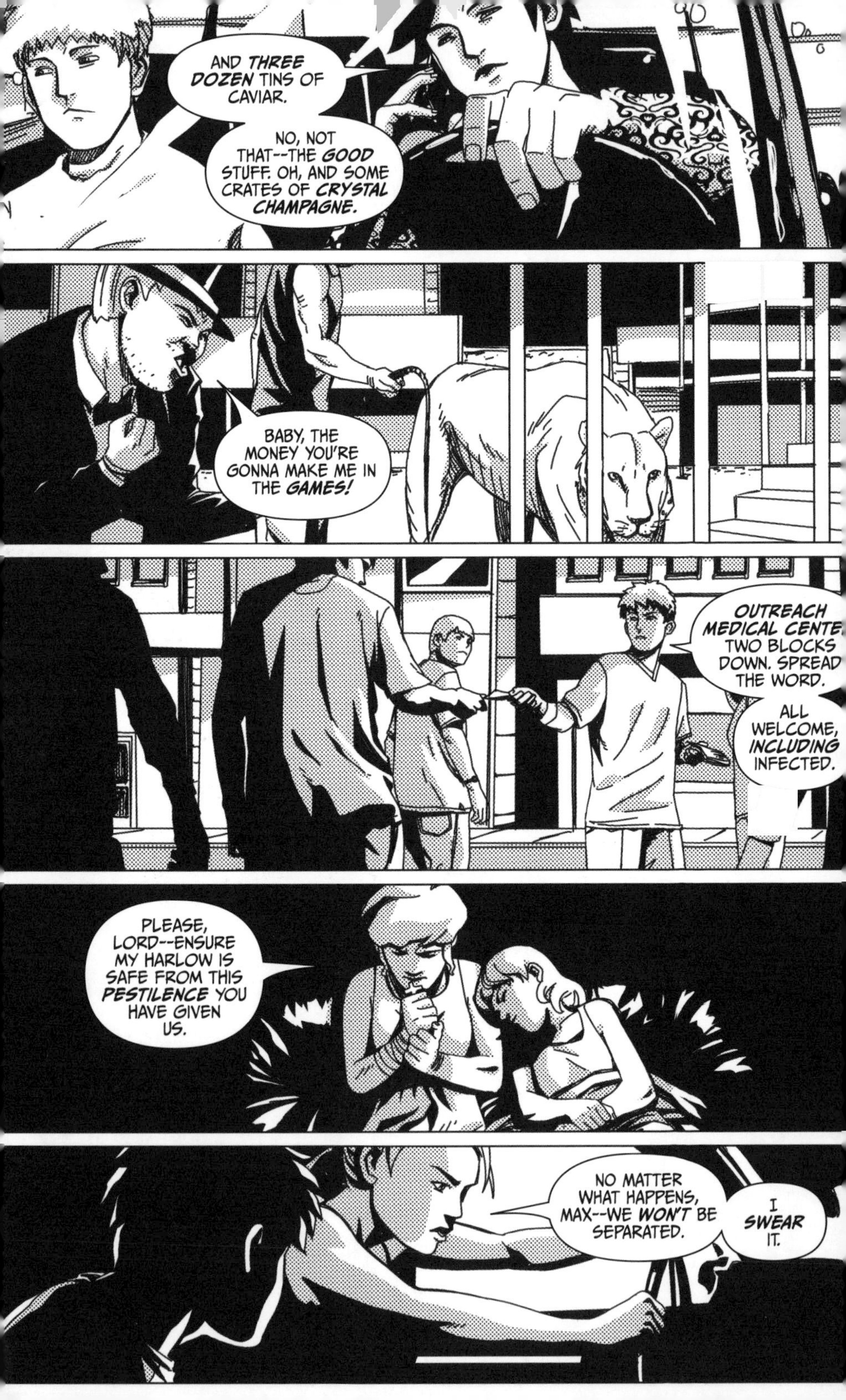
AND THREE DOZEN TINS OF CAVIAR.
NO, NOT THAT--THE GOOD STUFF. OH, AND SOME CRATES OF CRYSTAL CHAMPAGNE.
BABY, THE MONEY YOU'RE GONNA MAKE ME IN THE GAMES!
OUTREACH MEDICAL CENTE TWO BLOCKS DOWN. SPREAD THE WORD.
ALL WELCOME, INCLUDING INFECTED.
PLEASE, LORD--ENSURE MY HARLOW IS SAFE FROM THIS PESTILENCE YOU HAVE GIVEN US.
NO MATTER WHAT HAPPENS, MAX--WE WON'T BE SEPARATED.
I SWEAR IT.

CHAPTER TWO

RADIO SILENCE

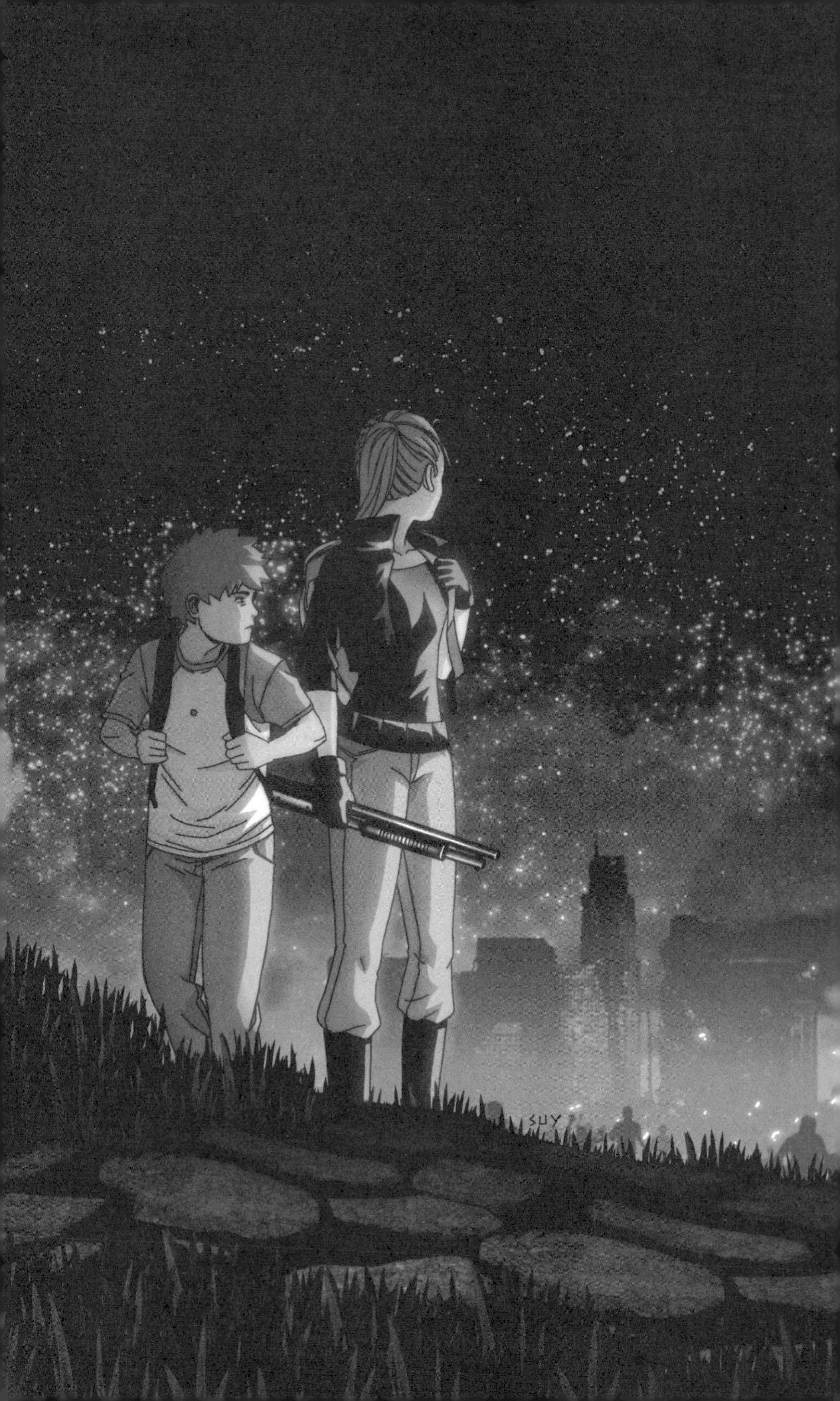
SUY

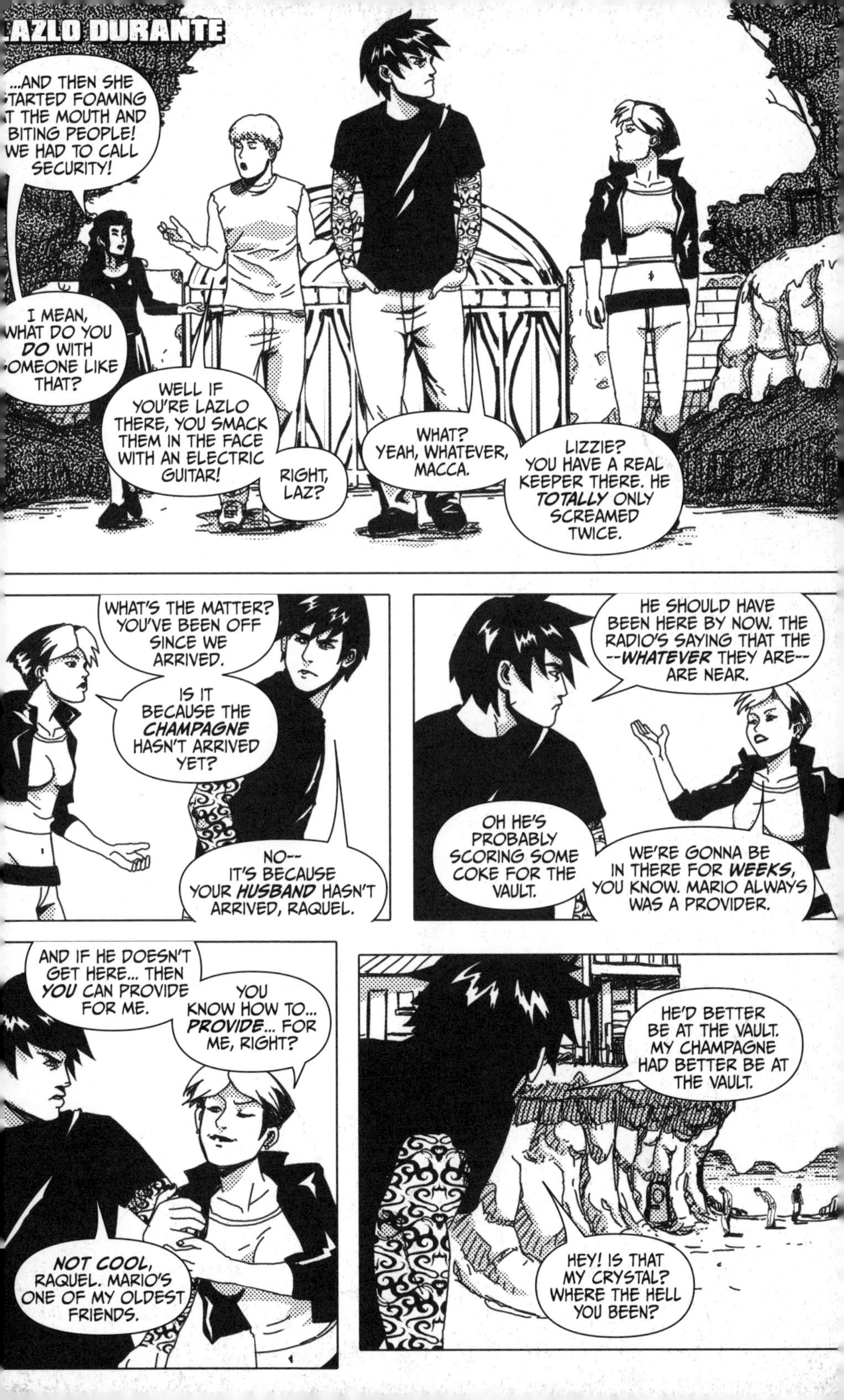
LAZLO DURANTE
...AND THEN SHE STARTED FOAMING AT THE MOUTH AND BITING PEOPLE! WE HAD TO CALL SECURITY!
I MEAN, WHAT DO YOU *DO* WITH SOMEONE LIKE THAT?
WELL IF YOU'RE LAZLO THERE, YOU SMACK THEM IN THE FACE WITH AN ELECTRIC GUITAR!
RIGHT, LAZ?
WHAT? YEAH, WHATEVER, MACCA.
LIZZIE? YOU HAVE A REAL KEEPER THERE. HE *TOTALLY* ONLY SCREAMED TWICE.
WHAT'S THE MATTER? YOU'VE BEEN OFF SINCE WE ARRIVED.
IS IT BECAUSE THE *CHAMPAGNE* HASN'T ARRIVED YET?
NO-- IT'S BECAUSE YOUR *HUSBAND* HASN'T ARRIVED, RAQUEL.
HE SHOULD HAVE BEEN HERE BY NOW. THE RADIO'S SAYING THAT THE --*WHATEVER* THEY ARE-- ARE NEAR.
OH HE'S PROBABLY SCORING SOME COKE FOR THE VAULT.
WE'RE GONNA BE IN THERE FOR *WEEKS*, YOU KNOW. MARIO ALWAYS WAS A PROVIDER.
AND IF HE DOESN'T GET HERE... THEN *YOU* CAN PROVIDE FOR ME.
YOU KNOW HOW TO... *PROVIDE*... FOR ME, RIGHT?
NOT COOL, RAQUEL. MARIO'S ONE OF MY OLDEST FRIENDS.
HE'D BETTER BE AT THE VAULT. MY CHAMPAGNE HAD BETTER BE AT THE VAULT.
HEY! IS THAT MY CRYSTAL? WHERE THE HELL YOU BEEN?

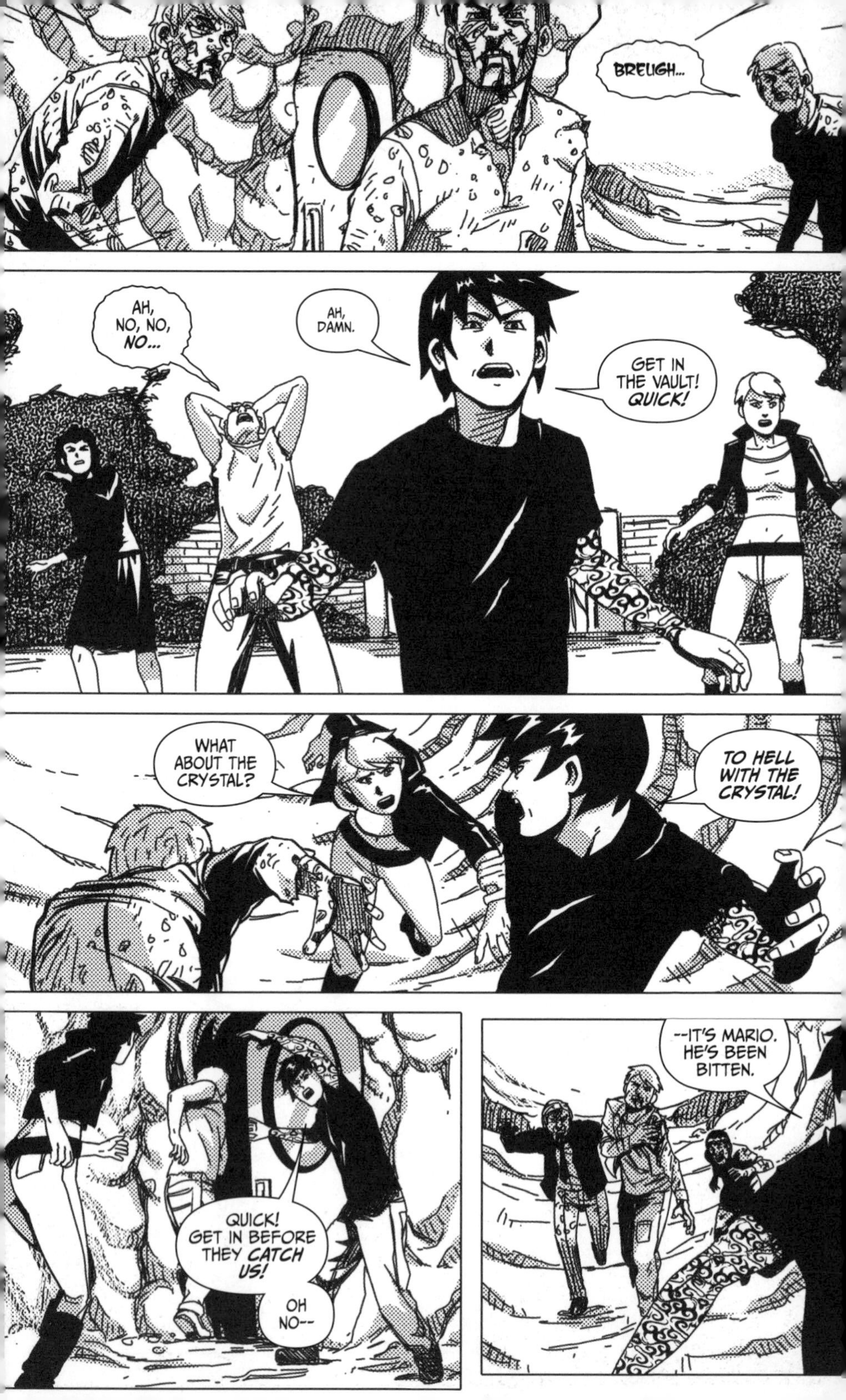
BREUGH...
AH, NO, NO, *NO...*
AH, DAMN.
GET IN THE VAULT! *QUICK!*
WHAT ABOUT THE CRYSTAL?
TO HELL WITH THE CRYSTAL!
QUICK! GET IN BEFORE THEY *CATCH US!*
OH NO--
--IT'S MARIO. HE'S BEEN BITTEN.

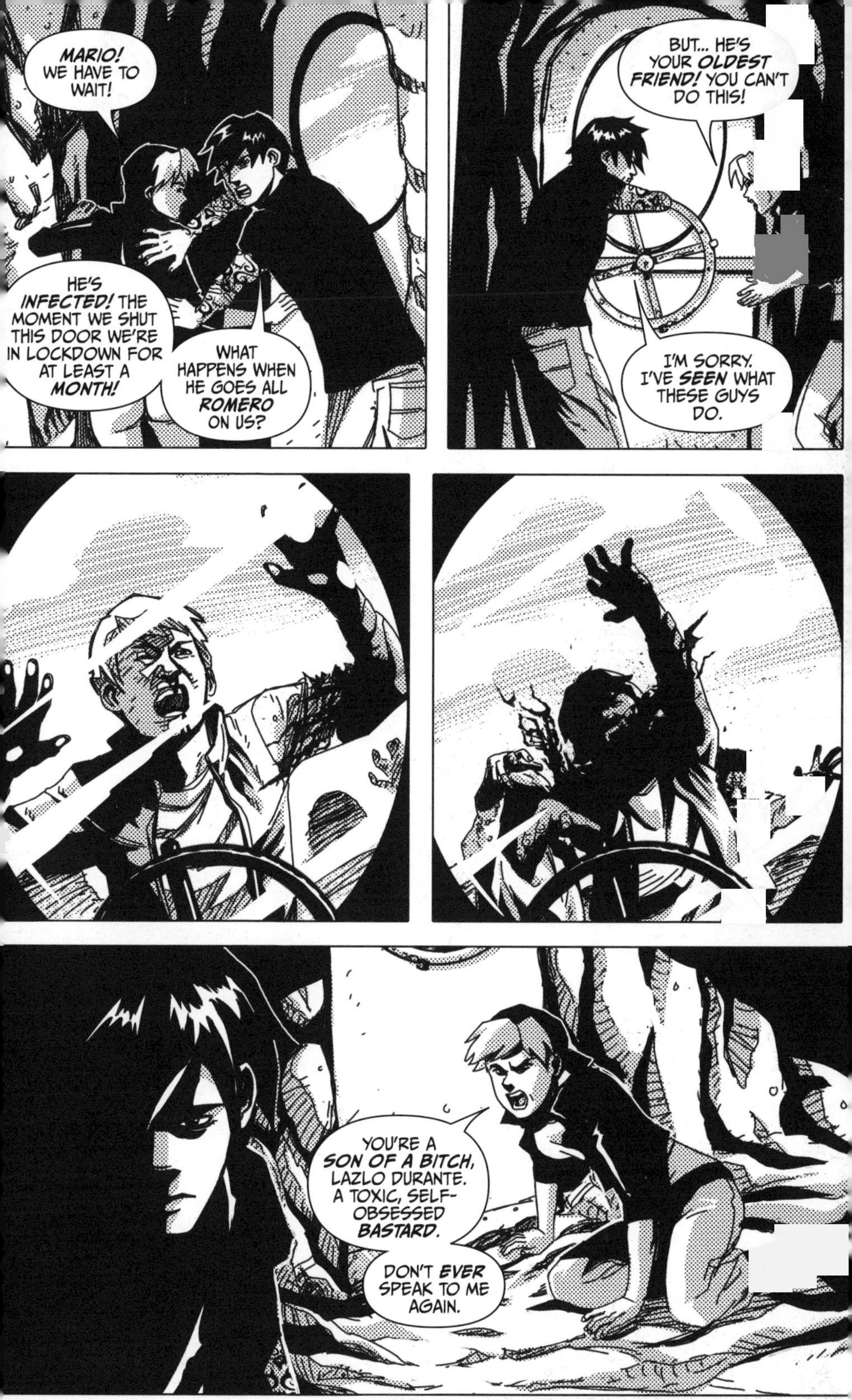
MARIO! WE HAVE TO WAIT!
HE'S INFECTED! THE MOMENT WE SHUT THIS DOOR WE'RE IN LOCKDOWN FOR AT LEAST A MONTH!
WHAT HAPPENS WHEN HE GOES ALL ROMERO ON US?
BUT... HE'S YOUR OLDEST FRIEND! YOU CAN'T DO THIS!
I'M SORRY. I'VE SEEN WHAT THESE GUYS DO.
YOU'RE A SON OF A BITCH, LAZLO DURANTE. A TOXIC, SELF-OBSESSED BASTARD.
DON'T EVER SPEAK TO ME AGAIN.

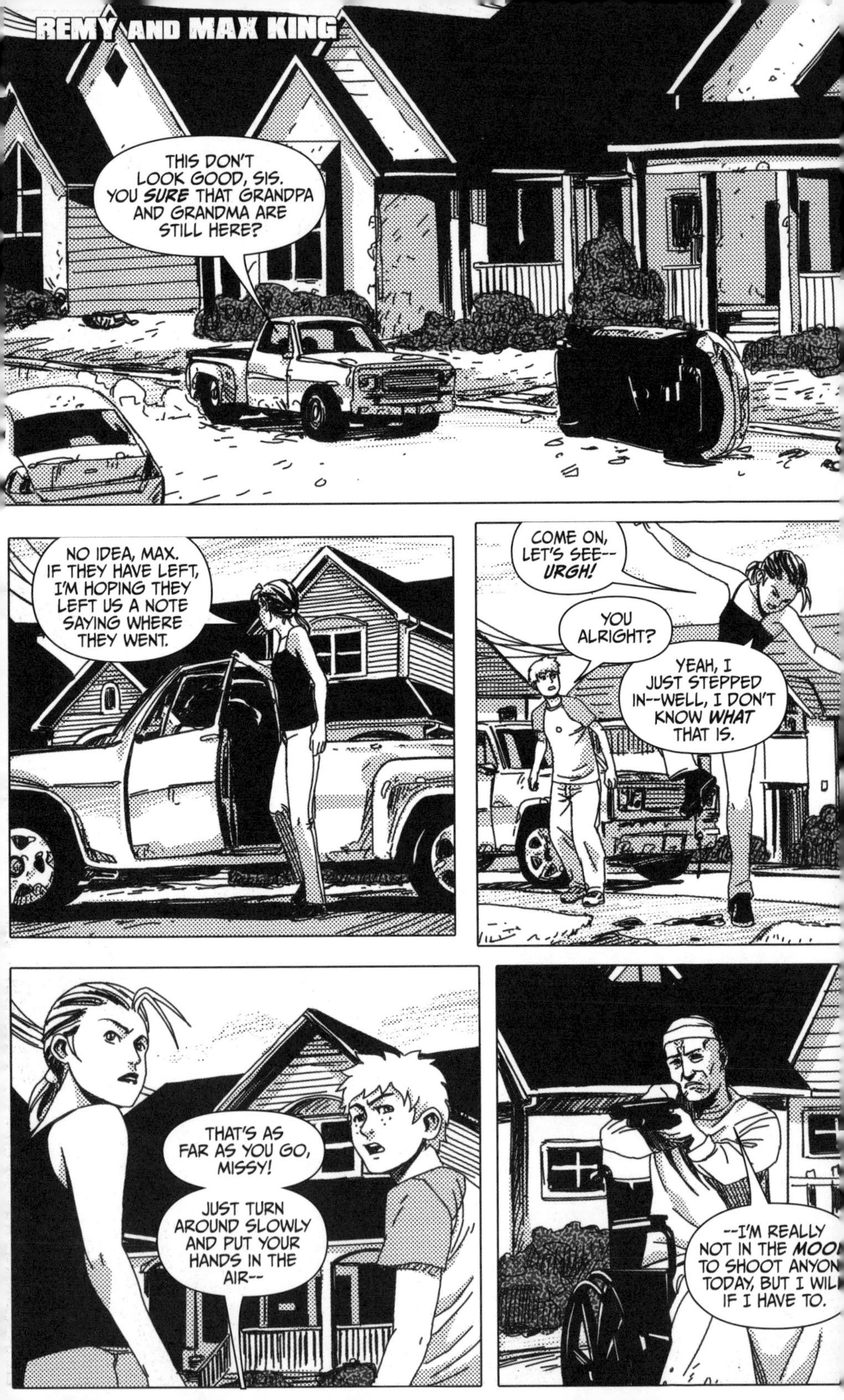
REMY AND MAX KING
THIS DON'T LOOK GOOD, SIS. YOU SURE THAT GRANDPA AND GRANDMA ARE STILL HERE?
NO IDEA, MAX. IF THEY HAVE LEFT, I'M HOPING THEY LEFT US A NOTE SAYING WHERE THEY WENT.
COME ON, LET'S SEE-- URGH!
YOU ALRIGHT?
YEAH, I JUST STEPPED IN--WELL, I DON'T KNOW WHAT THAT IS.
THAT'S AS FAR AS YOU GO, MISSY!
JUST TURN AROUND SLOWLY AND PUT YOUR HANDS IN THE AIR--
--I'M REALLY NOT IN THE MOO
TO SHOOT ANYON
TODAY, BUT I WIL
IF I HAVE TO.

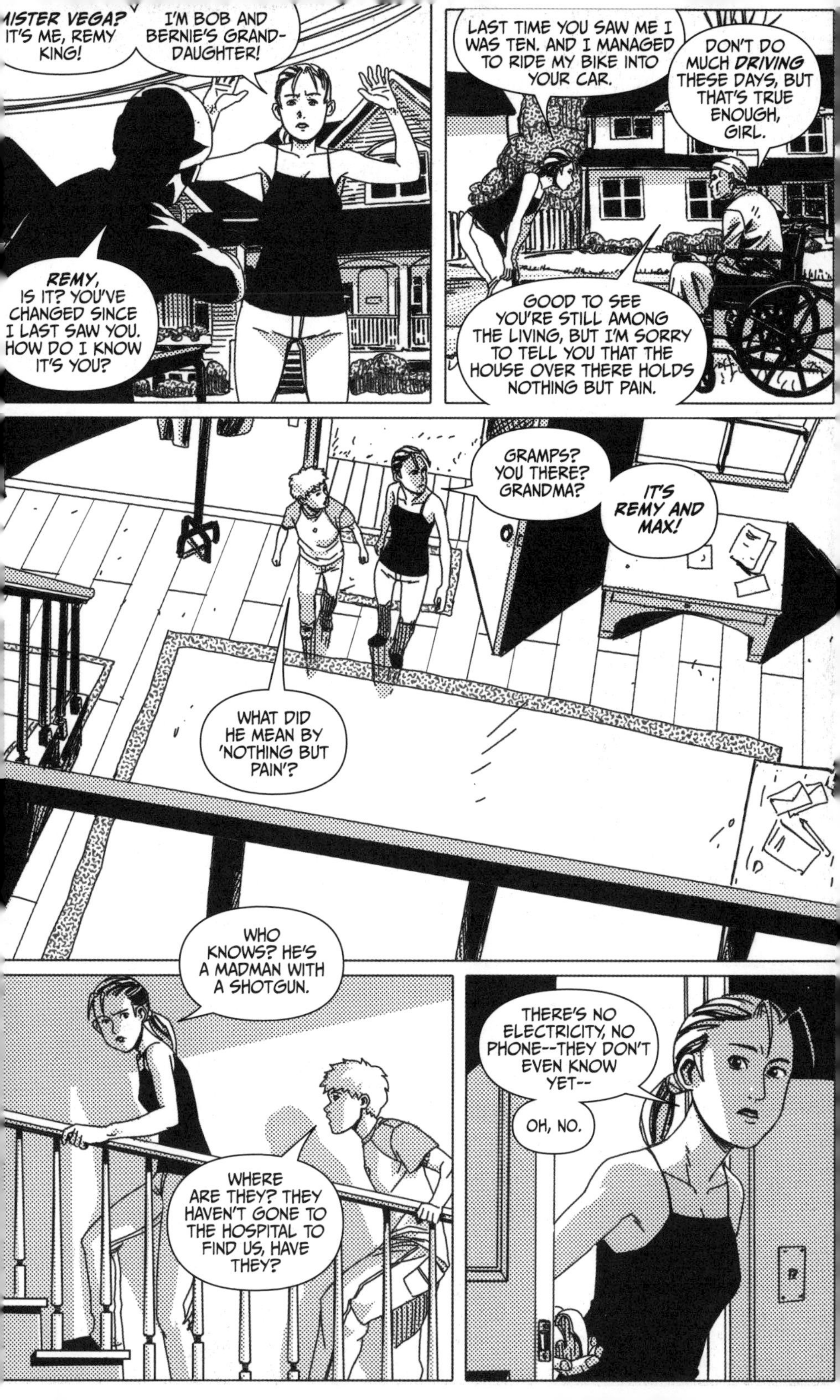
MISTER VEGA? IT'S ME, REMY KING!
I'M BOB AND BERNIE'S GRAND-DAUGHTER!
REMY, IS IT? YOU'VE CHANGED SINCE I LAST SAW YOU. HOW DO I KNOW IT'S YOU?
LAST TIME YOU SAW ME I WAS TEN. AND I MANAGED TO RIDE MY BIKE INTO YOUR CAR.
DON'T DO MUCH DRIVING THESE DAYS, BUT THAT'S TRUE ENOUGH, GIRL.
GOOD TO SEE YOU'RE STILL AMONG THE LIVING, BUT I'M SORRY TO TELL YOU THAT THE HOUSE OVER THERE HOLDS NOTHING BUT PAIN.
GRAMPS? YOU THERE? GRANDMA?
IT'S REMY AND MAX!
WHAT DID HE MEAN BY 'NOTHING BUT PAIN'?
WHO KNOWS? HE'S A MADMAN WITH A SHOTGUN.
WHERE ARE THEY? THEY HAVEN'T GONE TO THE HOSPITAL TO FIND US, HAVE THEY?
THERE'S NO ELECTRICITY, NO PHONE--THEY DON'T EVEN KNOW YET--
OH, NO.

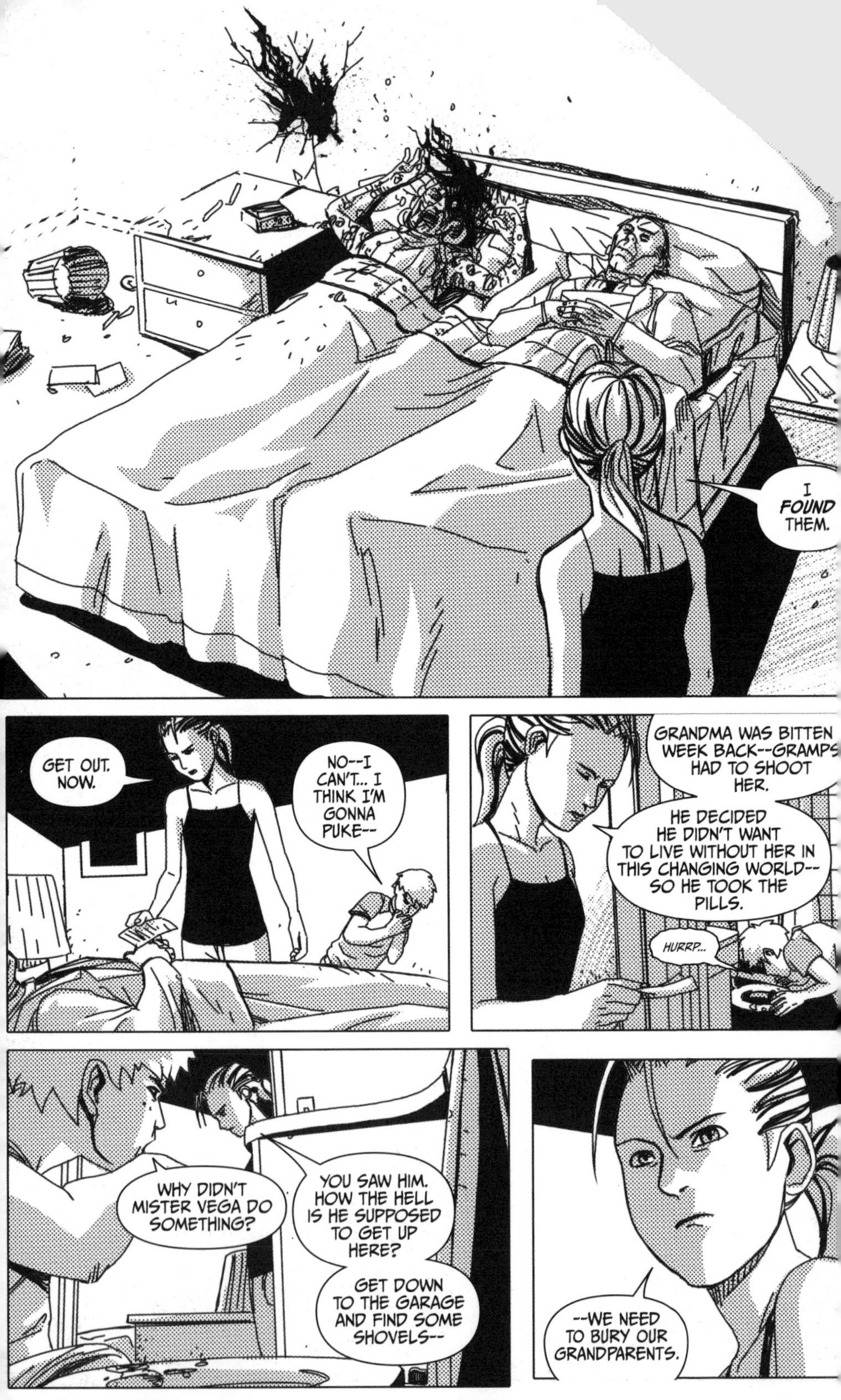
I FOUND THEM.
GET OUT. NOW.
NO--I CAN'T... I THINK I'M GONNA PUKE--
GRANDMA WAS BITTEN WEEK BACK--GRAMPS HAD TO SHOOT HER.
HE DECIDED HE DIDN'T WANT TO LIVE WITHOUT HER IN THIS CHANGING WORLD-- SO HE TOOK THE PILLS.
HURRP...
WHY DIDN'T MISTER VEGA DO SOMETHING?
YOU SAW HIM. HOW THE HELL IS HE SUPPOSED TO GET UP HERE?
GET DOWN TO THE GARAGE AND FIND SOME SHOVELS--
--WE NEED TO BURY OUR GRANDPARENTS.

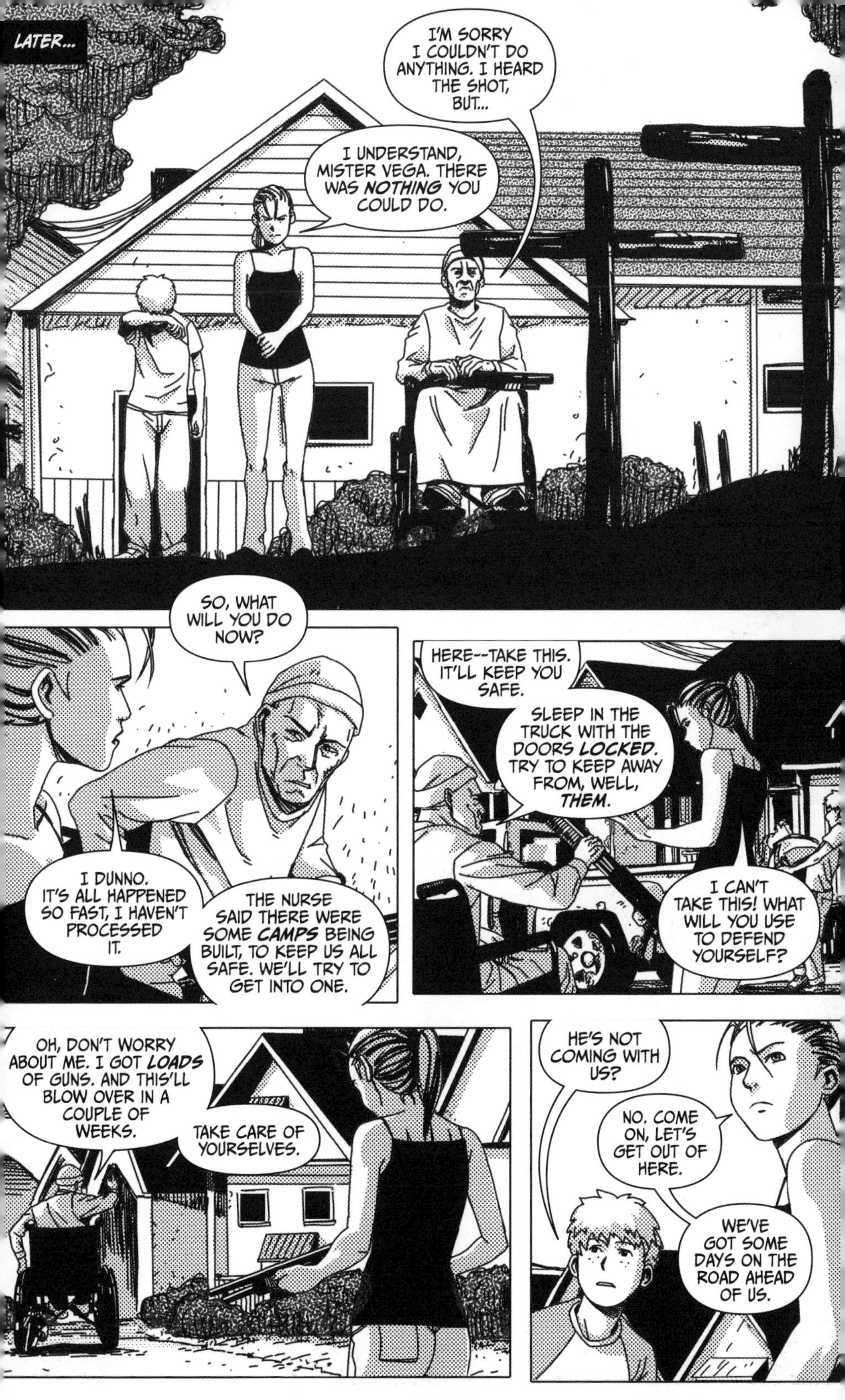
LATER...
I'M SORRY I COULDN'T DO ANYTHING. I HEARD THE SHOT, BUT...
I UNDERSTAND, MISTER VEGA. THERE WAS *NOTHING* YOU COULD DO.
SO, WHAT WILL YOU DO NOW?
I DUNNO. IT'S ALL HAPPENED SO FAST, I HAVEN'T PROCESSED IT.
THE NURSE SAID THERE WERE SOME *CAMPS* BEING BUILT, TO KEEP US ALL SAFE. WE'LL TRY TO GET INTO ONE.
HERE--TAKE THIS. IT'LL KEEP YOU SAFE.
SLEEP IN THE TRUCK WITH THE DOORS *LOCKED*. TRY TO KEEP AWAY FROM, WELL, *THEM*.
I CAN'T TAKE THIS! WHAT WILL YOU USE TO DEFEND YOURSELF?
OH, DON'T WORRY ABOUT ME. I GOT *LOADS* OF GUNS. AND THIS'LL BLOW OVER IN A COUPLE OF WEEKS.
TAKE CARE OF YOURSELVES.
HE'S NOT COMING WITH US?
NO. COME ON, LET'S GET OUT OF HERE.
WE'VE GOT SOME DAYS ON THE ROAD AHEAD OF US.

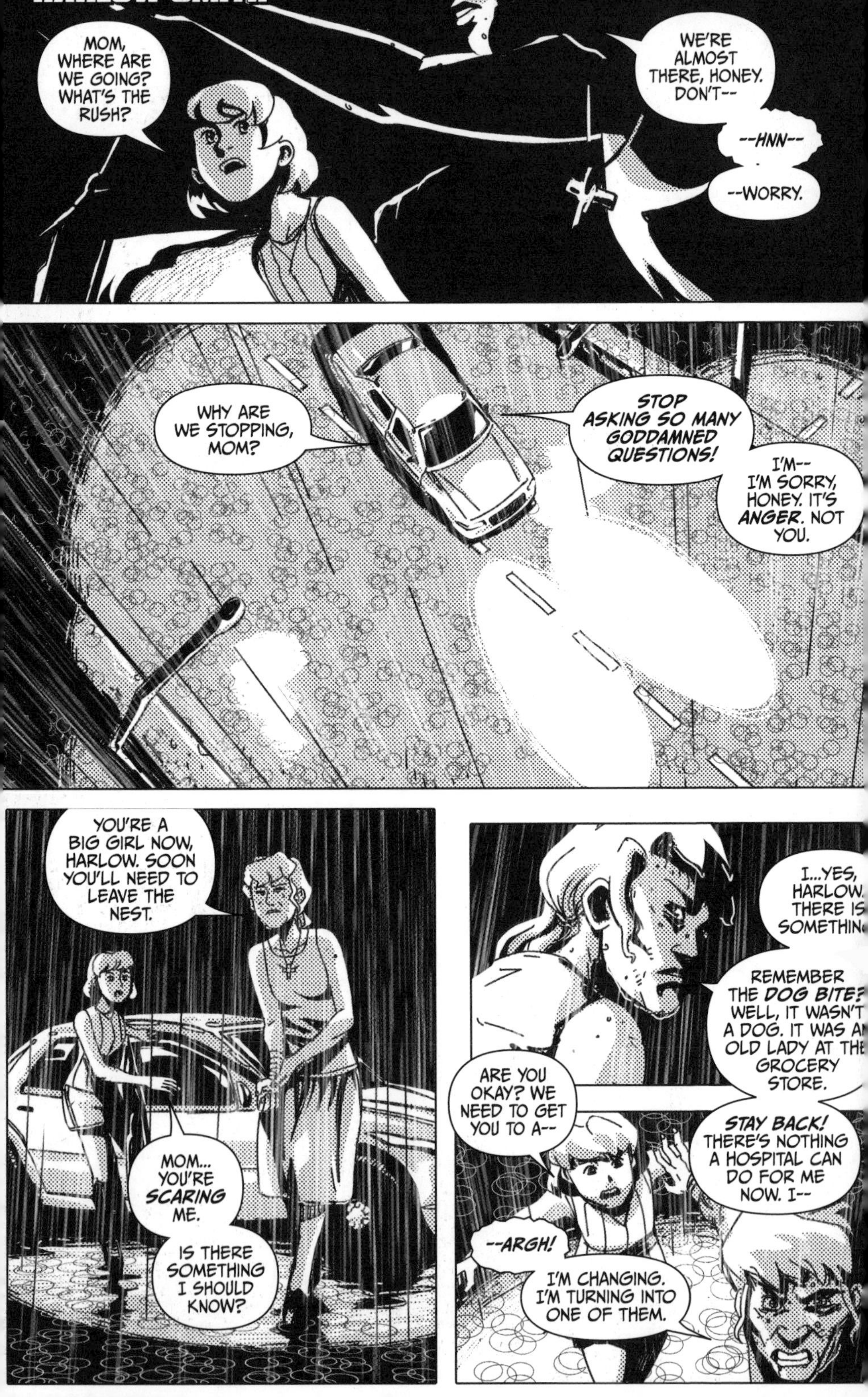
MOM, WHERE ARE WE GOING? WHAT'S THE RUSH?
WE'RE ALMOST THERE, HONEY. DON'T--
--HNN--
--WORRY.
WHY ARE WE STOPPING, MOM?
STOP ASKING SO MANY GODDAMNED QUESTIONS!
I'M-- I'M SORRY, HONEY. IT'S ANGER. NOT YOU.
YOU'RE A BIG GIRL NOW, HARLOW. SOON YOU'LL NEED TO LEAVE THE NEST.
MOM... YOU'RE SCARING ME.
IS THERE SOMETHING I SHOULD KNOW?
I...YES, HARLOW. THERE IS SOMETHIN
REMEMBER THE DOG BITE? WELL, IT WASN'T A DOG. IT WAS A OLD LADY AT THE GROCERY STORE.
ARE YOU OKAY? WE NEED TO GET YOU TO A--
STAY BACK! THERE'S NOTHING A HOSPITAL CAN DO FOR ME NOW. I--
--ARGH!
I'M CHANGING. I'M TURNING INTO ONE OF THEM.

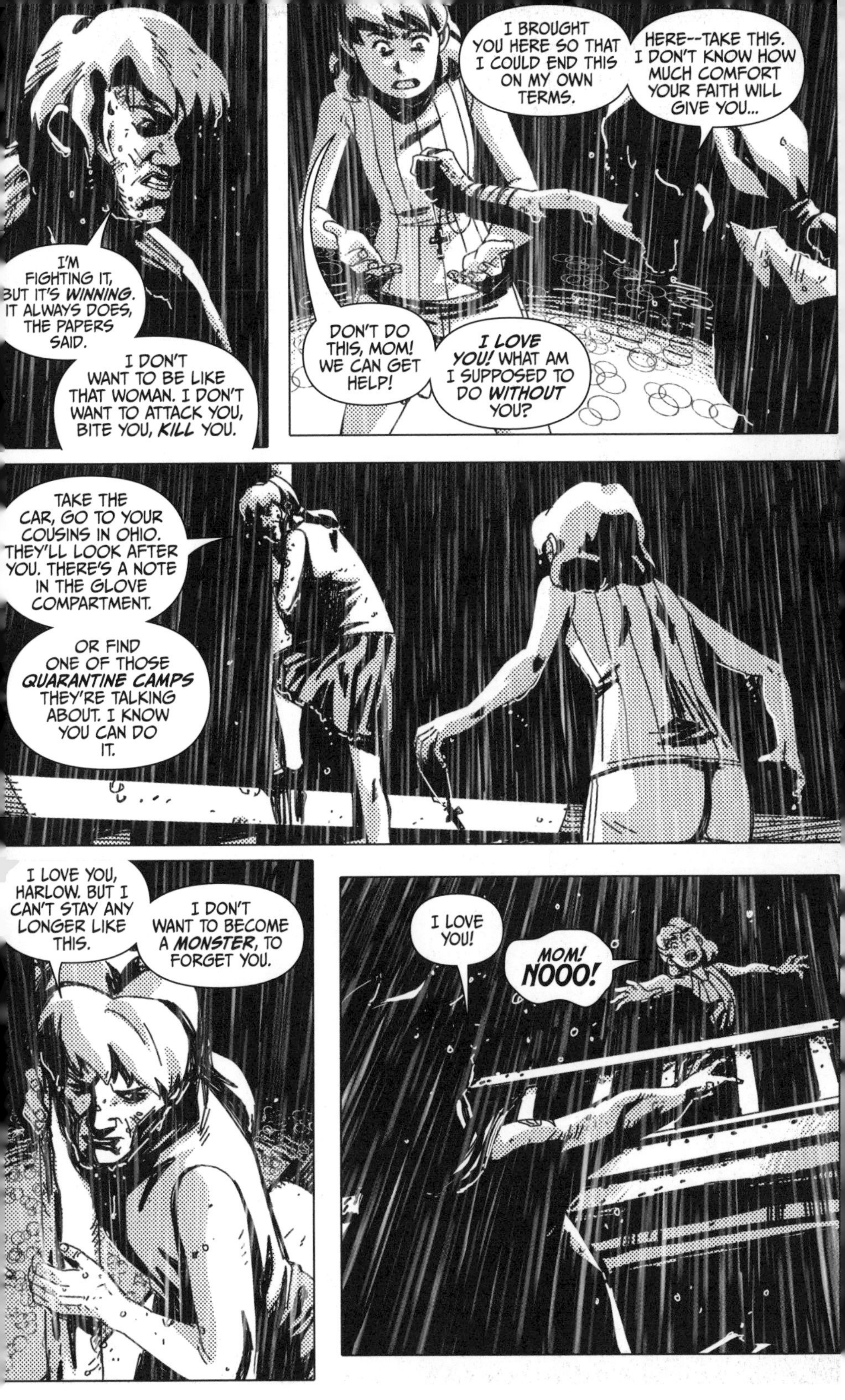
I'M FIGHTING IT, BUT IT'S **WINNING**. IT ALWAYS DOES, THE PAPERS SAID.
I DON'T WANT TO BE LIKE THAT WOMAN. I DON'T WANT TO ATTACK YOU, BITE YOU, **KILL** YOU.
I BROUGHT YOU HERE SO THAT I COULD END THIS ON MY OWN TERMS.
HERE--TAKE THIS. I DON'T KNOW HOW MUCH COMFORT YOUR FAITH WILL GIVE YOU...
DON'T DO THIS, MOM! WE CAN GET HELP!
I LOVE YOU! WHAT AM I SUPPOSED TO DO ***WITHOUT*** YOU?
TAKE THE CAR, GO TO YOUR COUSINS IN OHIO. THEY'LL LOOK AFTER YOU. THERE'S A NOTE IN THE GLOVE COMPARTMENT.
OR FIND ONE OF THOSE ***QUARANTINE CAMPS*** THEY'RE TALKING ABOUT. I KNOW YOU CAN DO IT.
I LOVE YOU, HARLOW. BUT I CAN'T STAY ANY LONGER LIKE THIS.
I DON'T WANT TO BECOME A ***MONSTER***, TO FORGET YOU.
I LOVE YOU!
MOM! NOOO!

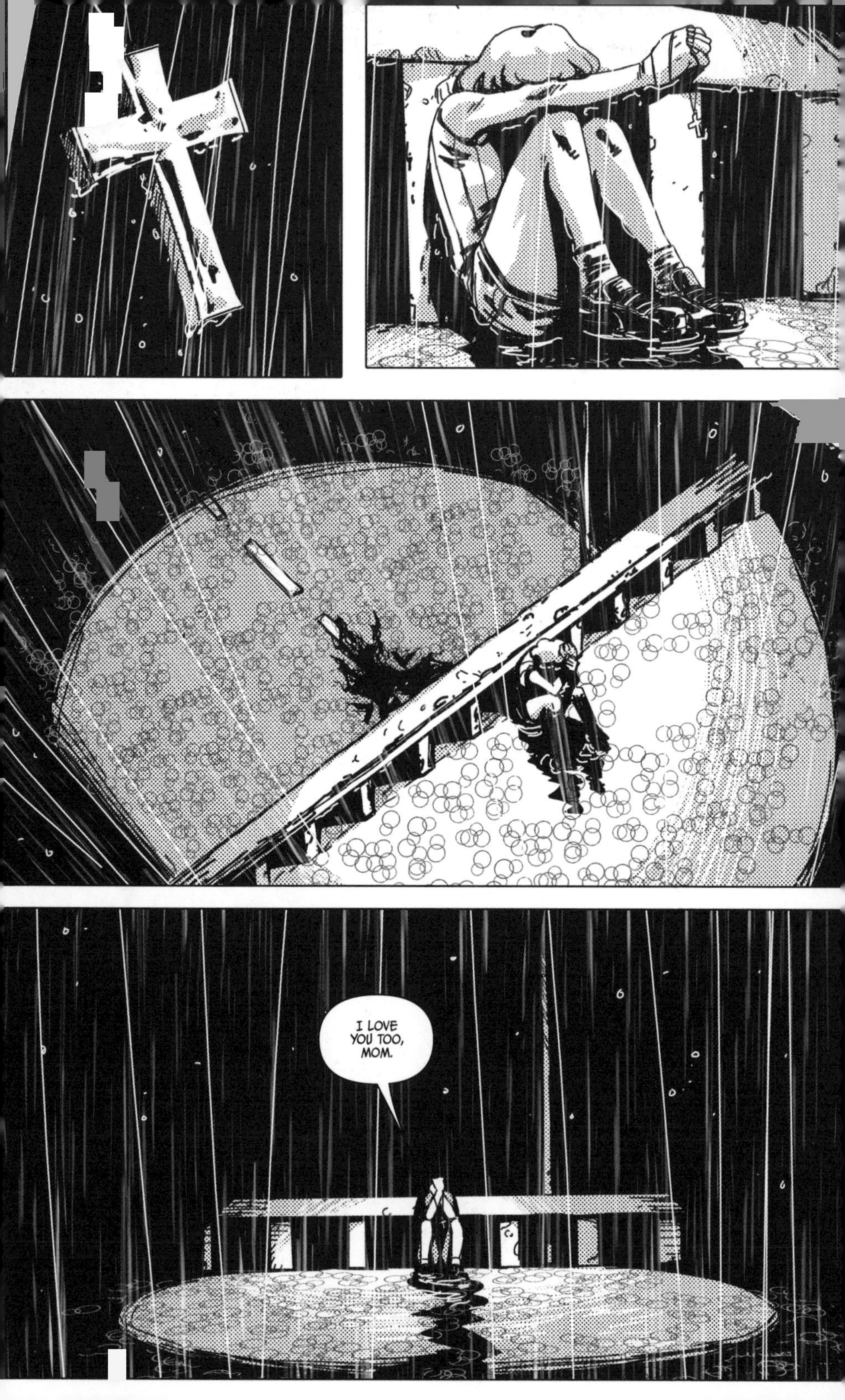
I LOVE YOU TOO, MOM.

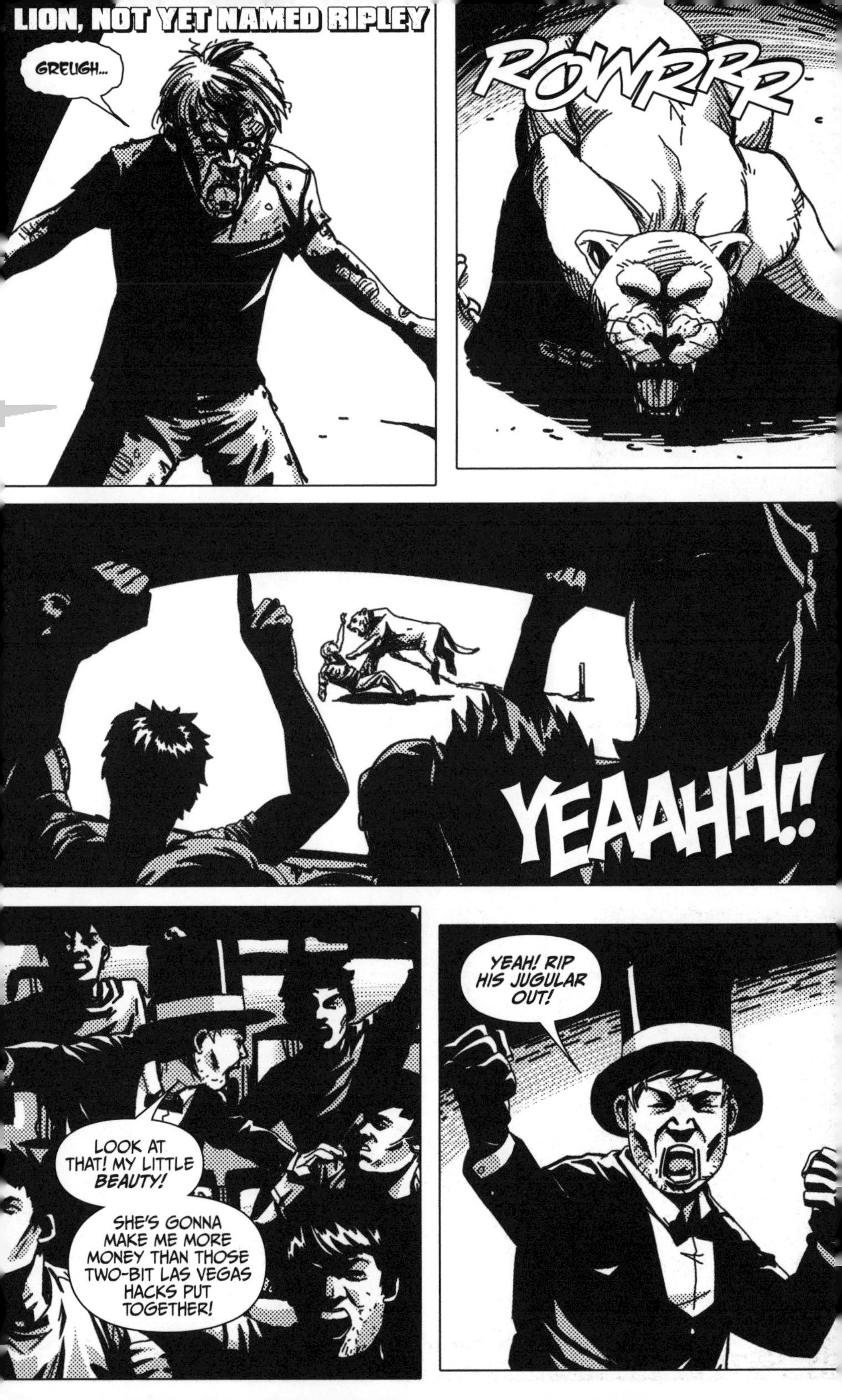
LION, NOT YET NAMED RIPLEY
GREUGH...
ROWRRR
YEAAHH!!
LOOK AT THAT! MY LITTLE *BEAUTY!*
SHE'S GONNA MAKE ME MORE MONEY THAN THOSE TWO-BIT LAS VEGAS HACKS PUT TOGETHER!
YEAH! RIP HIS JUGULAR OUT!

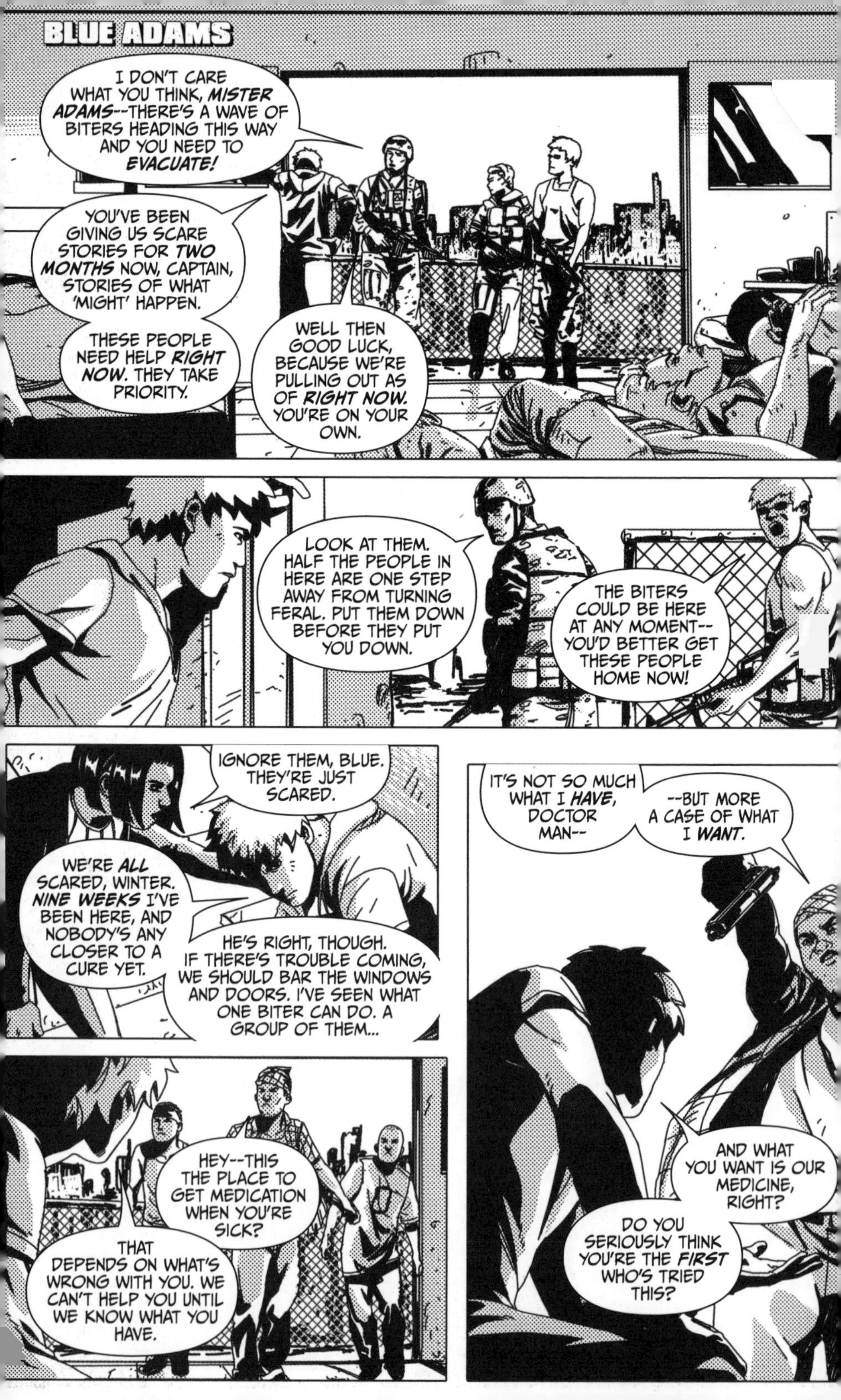
I DON'T CARE WHAT YOU THINK, *MISTER ADAMS*--THERE'S A WAVE OF BITERS HEADING THIS WAY AND YOU NEED TO *EVACUATE!*
YOU'VE BEEN GIVING US SCARE STORIES FOR *TWO MONTHS* NOW, CAPTAIN, STORIES OF WHAT 'MIGHT' HAPPEN.
THESE PEOPLE NEED HELP *RIGHT NOW*. THEY TAKE PRIORITY.
WELL THEN GOOD LUCK, BECAUSE WE'RE PULLING OUT AS OF *RIGHT NOW.* YOU'RE ON YOUR OWN.
LOOK AT THEM. HALF THE PEOPLE IN HERE ARE ONE STEP AWAY FROM TURNING FERAL. PUT THEM DOWN BEFORE THEY PUT YOU DOWN.
THE BITERS COULD BE HERE AT ANY MOMENT--YOU'D BETTER GET THESE PEOPLE HOME NOW!
IGNORE THEM, BLUE. THEY'RE JUST SCARED.
WE'RE *ALL* SCARED, WINTER. *NINE WEEKS* I'VE BEEN HERE, AND NOBODY'S ANY CLOSER TO A CURE YET.
HE'S RIGHT, THOUGH. IF THERE'S TROUBLE COMING, WE SHOULD BAR THE WINDOWS AND DOORS. I'VE SEEN WHAT ONE BITER CAN DO. A GROUP OF THEM...
HEY--THIS THE PLACE TO GET MEDICATION WHEN YOU'RE SICK?
THAT DEPENDS ON WHAT'S WRONG WITH YOU. WE CAN'T HELP YOU UNTIL WE KNOW WHAT YOU HAVE.
IT'S NOT SO MUCH WHAT I *HAVE*, DOCTOR MAN--
--BUT MORE A CASE OF WHAT I *WANT*.
AND WHAT YOU WANT IS OUR MEDICINE, RIGHT?
DO YOU SERIOUSLY THINK YOU'RE THE *FIRST* WHO'S TRIED THIS?

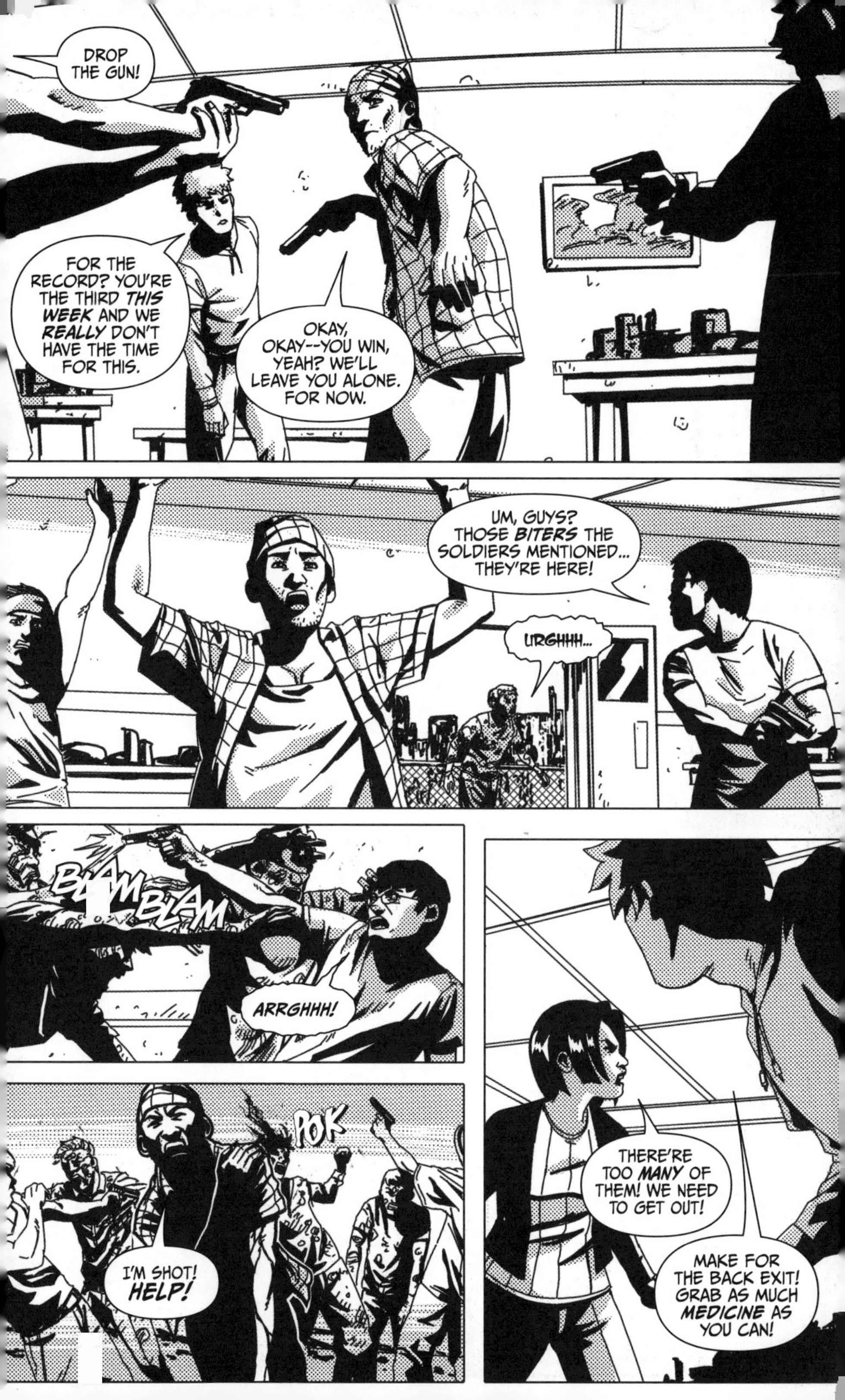
DROP THE GUN!
FOR THE RECORD? YOU'RE THE THIRD THIS WEEK AND WE REALLY DON'T HAVE THE TIME FOR THIS.
OKAY, OKAY--YOU WIN, YEAH? WE'LL LEAVE YOU ALONE. FOR NOW.
UM, GUYS? THOSE BITERS THE SOLDIERS MENTIONED... THEY'RE HERE!
URGHHH...
BLAM BLAM BLAM
ARRGHHH!
POK
I'M SHOT! HELP!
THERE'RE TOO MANY OF THEM! WE NEED TO GET OUT!
MAKE FOR THE BACK EXIT! GRAB AS MUCH MEDICINE AS YOU CAN!

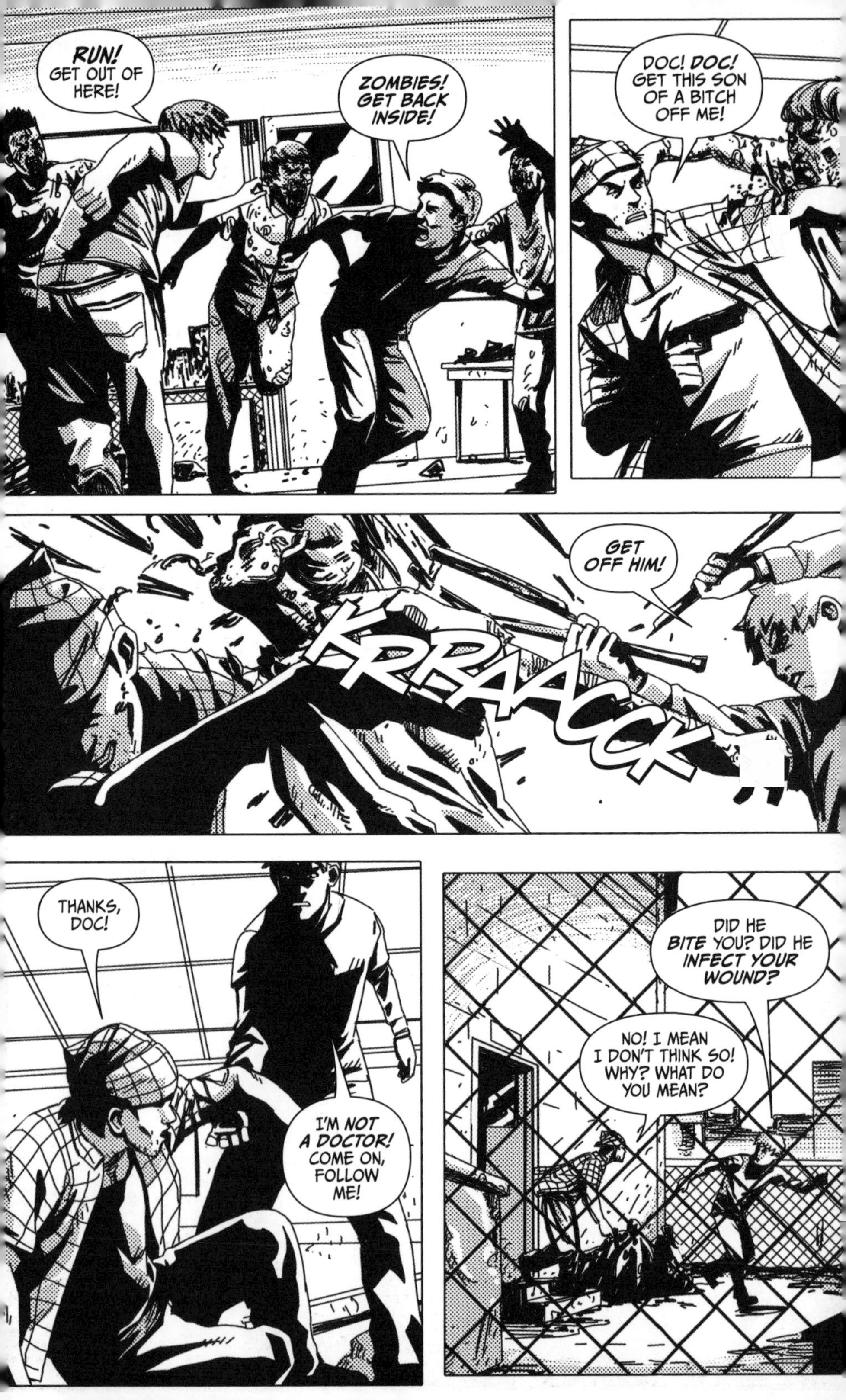
RUN! GET OUT OF HERE!
ZOMBIES! GET BACK INSIDE!
DOC! DOC! GET THIS SON OF A BITCH OFF ME!
GET OFF HIM!
KRRAACCK
THANKS, DOC!
I'M NOT A DOCTOR! COME ON, FOLLOW ME!
DID HE BITE YOU? DID HE INFECT YOUR WOUND?
NO! I MEAN I DON'T THINK SO! WHY? WHAT DO YOU MEAN?

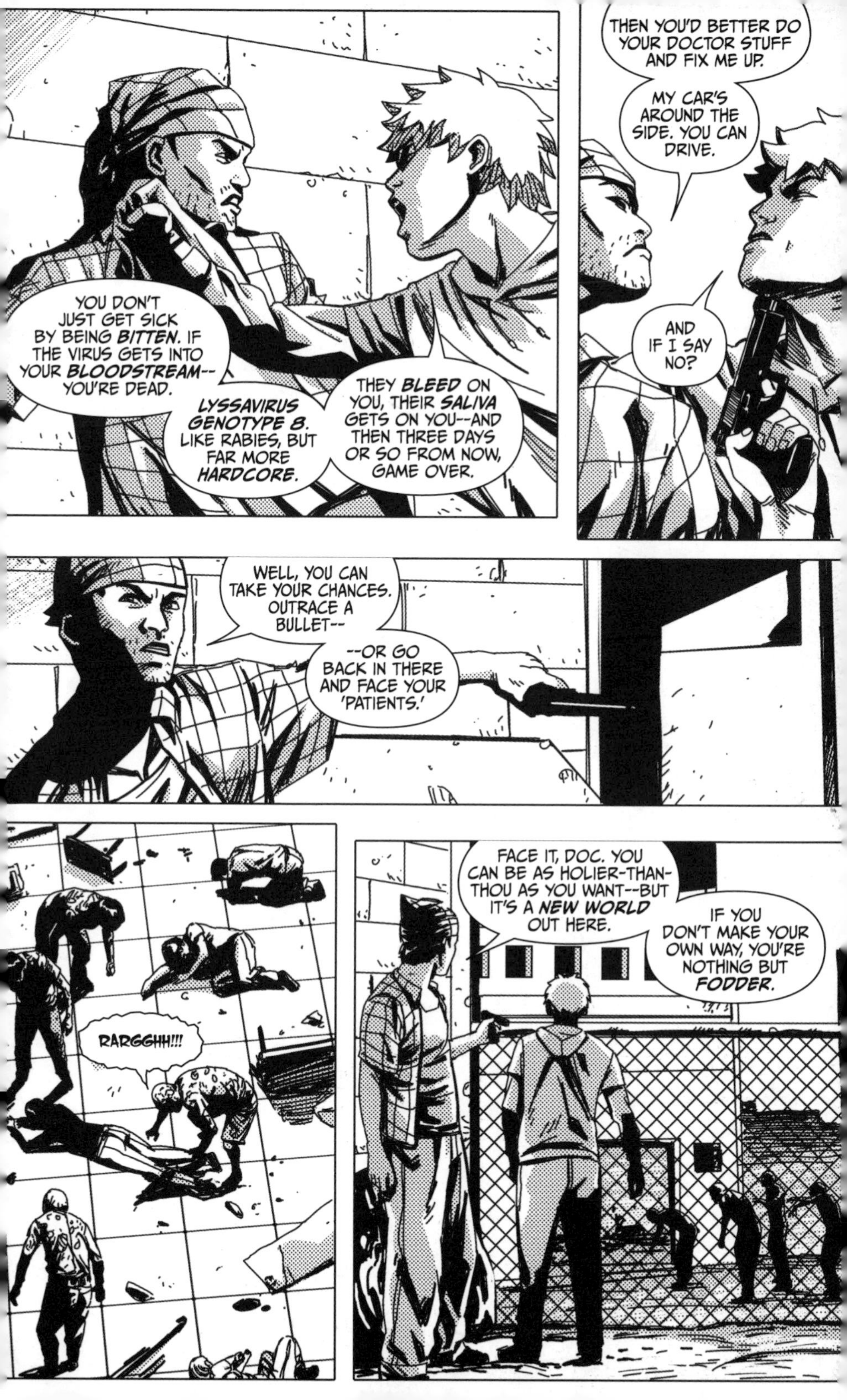
YOU DON'T JUST GET SICK BY BEING BITTEN. IF THE VIRUS GETS INTO YOUR BLOODSTREAM--YOU'RE DEAD.
LYSSAVIRUS GENOTYPE 8. LIKE RABIES, BUT FAR MORE HARDCORE.
THEY BLEED ON YOU, THEIR SALIVA GETS ON YOU--AND THEN THREE DAYS OR SO FROM NOW, GAME OVER.
THEN YOU'D BETTER DO YOUR DOCTOR STUFF AND FIX ME UP.
MY CAR'S AROUND THE SIDE. YOU CAN DRIVE.
AND IF I SAY NO?
WELL, YOU CAN TAKE YOUR CHANCES. OUTRACE A BULLET--
--OR GO BACK IN THERE AND FACE YOUR 'PATIENTS.'
RARGGHH!!!
FACE IT, DOC. YOU CAN BE AS HOLIER-THAN-THOU AS YOU WANT--BUT IT'S A NEW WORLD OUT HERE.
IF YOU DON'T MAKE YOUR OWN WAY, YOU'RE NOTHING BUT FODDER.

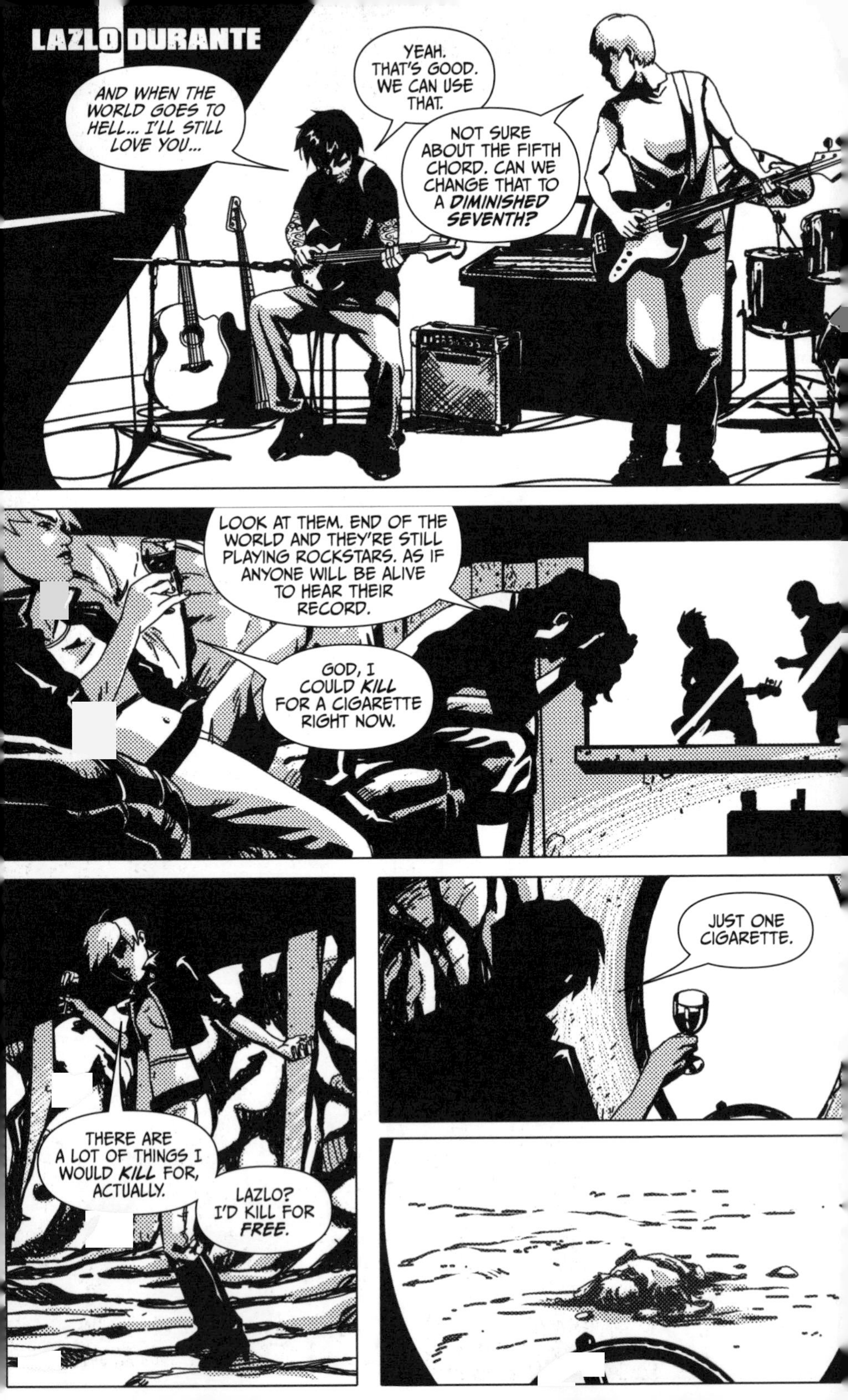
LAZLO DURANTE
AND WHEN THE WORLD GOES TO HELL... I'LL STILL LOVE YOU...
YEAH. THAT'S GOOD. WE CAN USE THAT.
NOT SURE ABOUT THE FIFTH CHORD. CAN WE CHANGE THAT TO A *DIMINISHED SEVENTH?*
LOOK AT THEM. END OF THE WORLD AND THEY'RE STILL PLAYING ROCKSTARS. AS IF ANYONE WILL BE ALIVE TO HEAR THEIR RECORD.
GOD, I COULD *KILL* FOR A CIGARETTE RIGHT NOW.
THERE ARE A LOT OF THINGS I WOULD *KILL* FOR, ACTUALLY.
LAZLO? I'D KILL FOR *FREE.*
JUST ONE CIGARETTE.

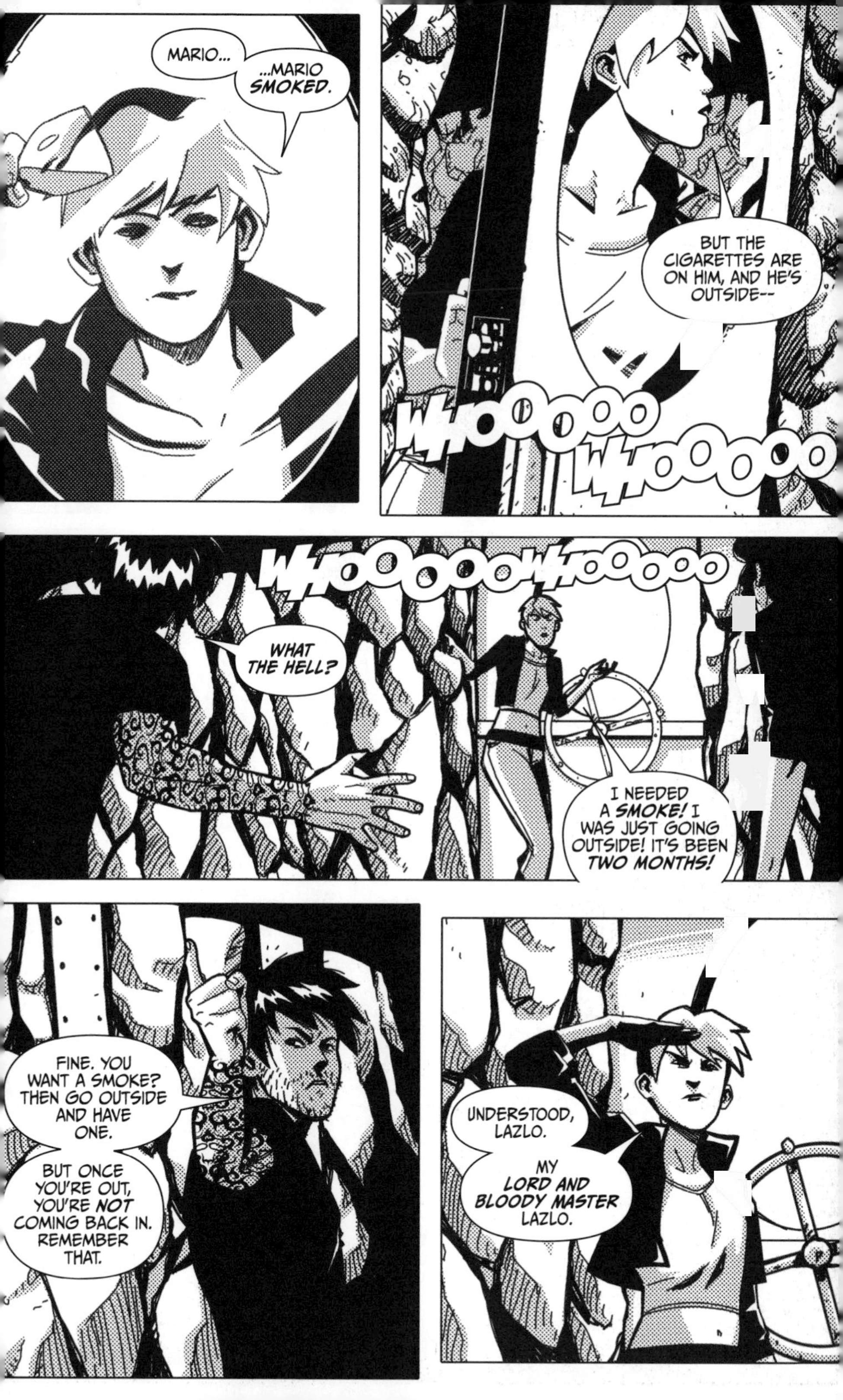
MARIO...
...MARIO SMOKED.
BUT THE CIGARETTES ARE ON HIM, AND HE'S OUTSIDE--
WHOOOOO WHOOOOOO
WHOOOOOOWHOOOOOO
WHAT THE HELL?
I NEEDED A SMOKE! I WAS JUST GOING OUTSIDE! IT'S BEEN TWO MONTHS!
FINE. YOU WANT A SMOKE? THEN GO OUTSIDE AND HAVE ONE.
BUT ONCE YOU'RE OUT, YOU'RE NOT COMING BACK IN. REMEMBER THAT.
UNDERSTOOD, LAZLO.
MY LORD AND BLOODY MASTER LAZLO.

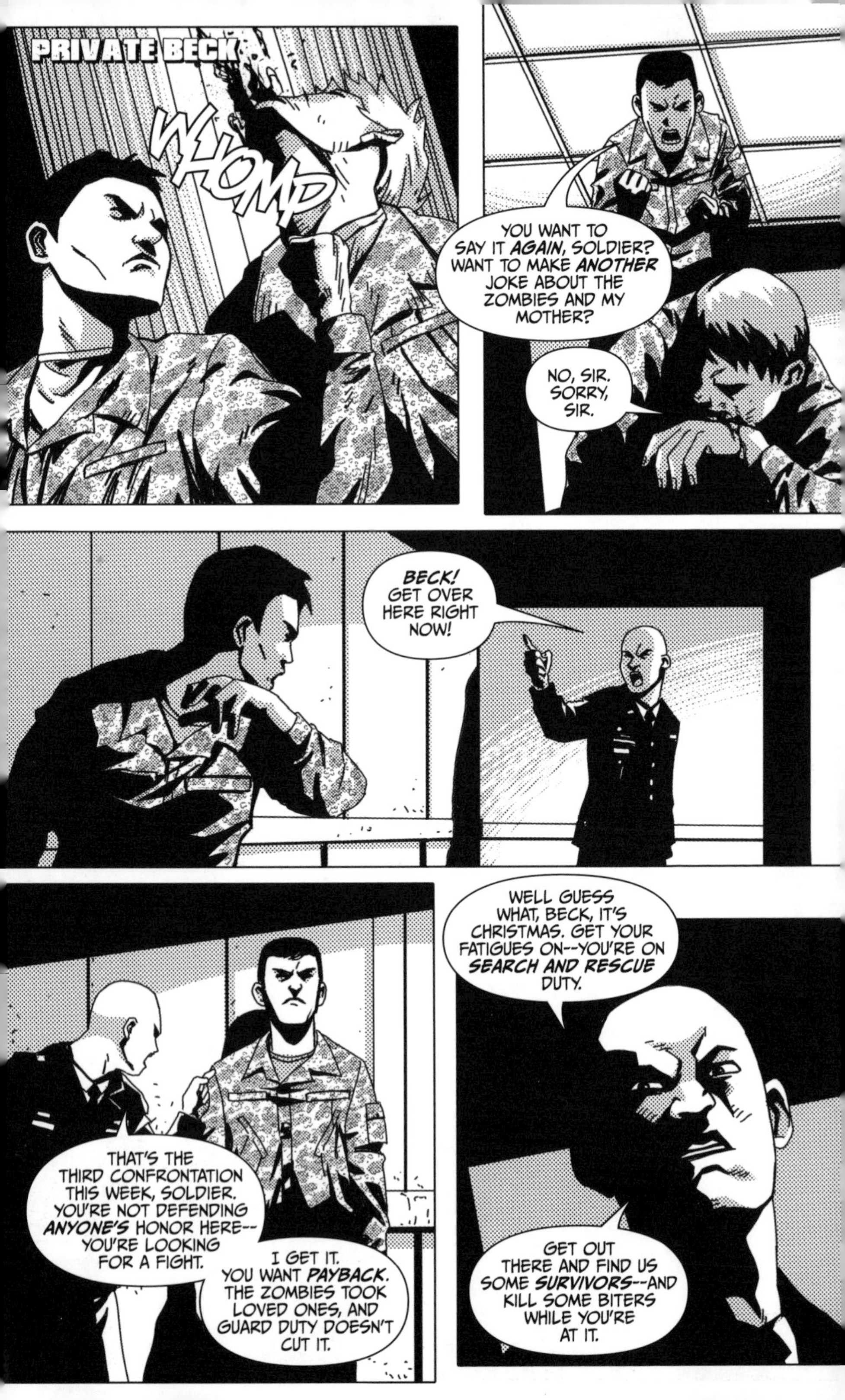
PRIVATE BECK
WHOMP
YOU WANT TO SAY IT *AGAIN*, SOLDIER? WANT TO MAKE *ANOTHER* JOKE ABOUT THE ZOMBIES AND MY MOTHER?
NO, SIR. SORRY, SIR.
BECK! GET OVER HERE RIGHT NOW!
THAT'S THE THIRD CONFRONTATION THIS WEEK, SOLDIER. YOU'RE NOT DEFENDING *ANYONE'S* HONOR HERE--YOU'RE LOOKING FOR A FIGHT.
I GET IT. YOU WANT *PAYBACK*. THE ZOMBIES TOOK LOVED ONES, AND GUARD DUTY DOESN'T CUT IT.
WELL GUESS WHAT, BECK, IT'S CHRISTMAS. GET YOUR FATIGUES ON--YOU'RE ON *SEARCH AND RESCUE* DUTY.
GET OUT THERE AND FIND US SOME *SURVIVORS*--AND KILL SOME BITERS WHILE YOU'RE AT IT.

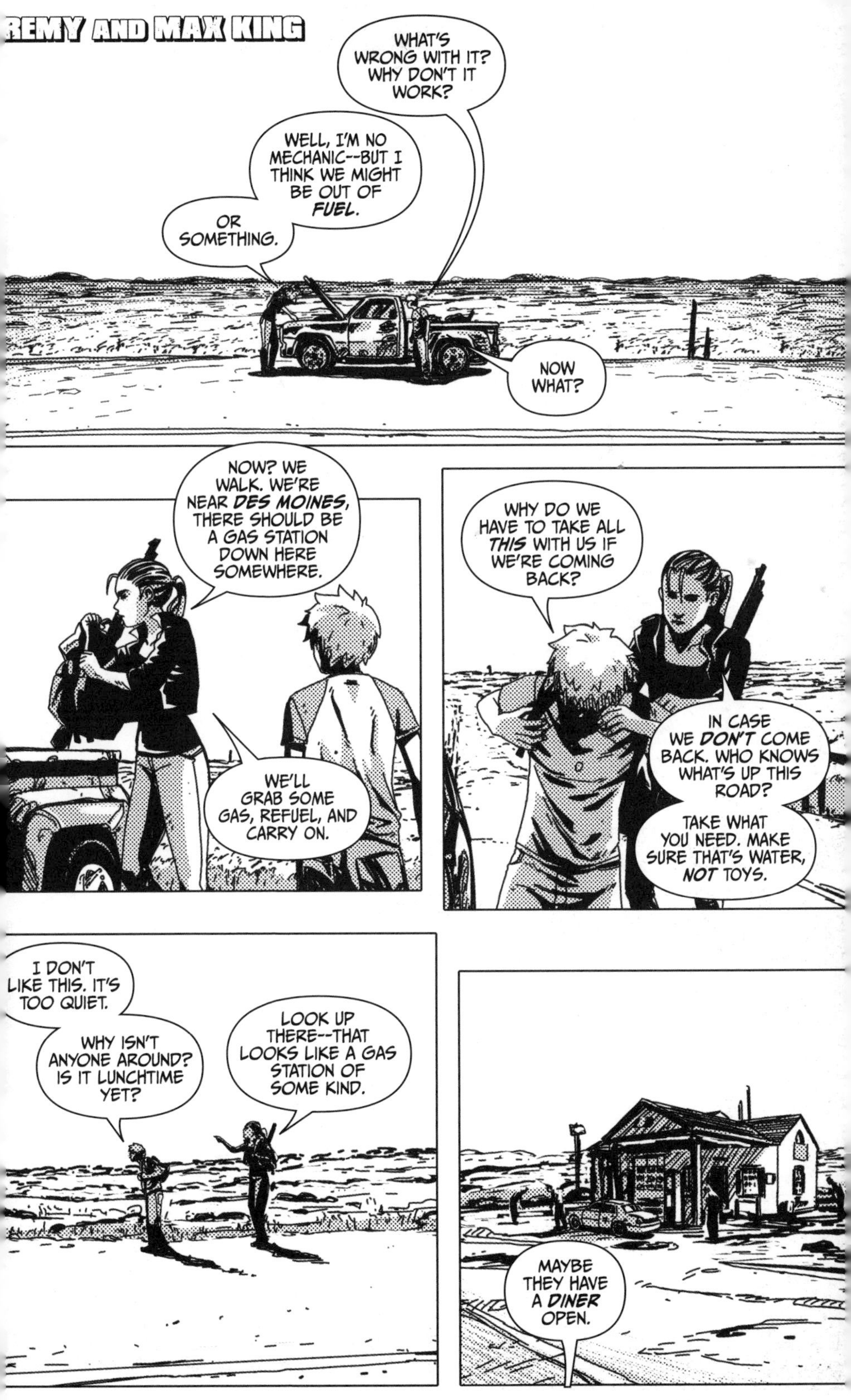
WHAT'S WRONG WITH IT? WHY DON'T IT WORK?
WELL, I'M NO MECHANIC--BUT I THINK WE MIGHT BE OUT OF *FUEL*.
OR SOMETHING.
NOW WHAT?
NOW? WE WALK. WE'RE NEAR *DES MOINES*, THERE SHOULD BE A GAS STATION DOWN HERE SOMEWHERE.
WE'LL GRAB SOME GAS, REFUEL, AND CARRY ON.
WHY DO WE HAVE TO TAKE ALL *THIS* WITH US IF WE'RE COMING BACK?
IN CASE WE *DON'T* COME BACK. WHO KNOWS WHAT'S UP THIS ROAD?
TAKE WHAT YOU NEED. MAKE SURE THAT'S WATER, *NOT* TOYS.
I DON'T LIKE THIS. IT'S TOO QUIET.
WHY ISN'T ANYONE AROUND? IS IT LUNCHTIME YET?
LOOK UP THERE--THAT LOOKS LIKE A GAS STATION OF SOME KIND.
MAYBE THEY HAVE A *DINER* OPEN.

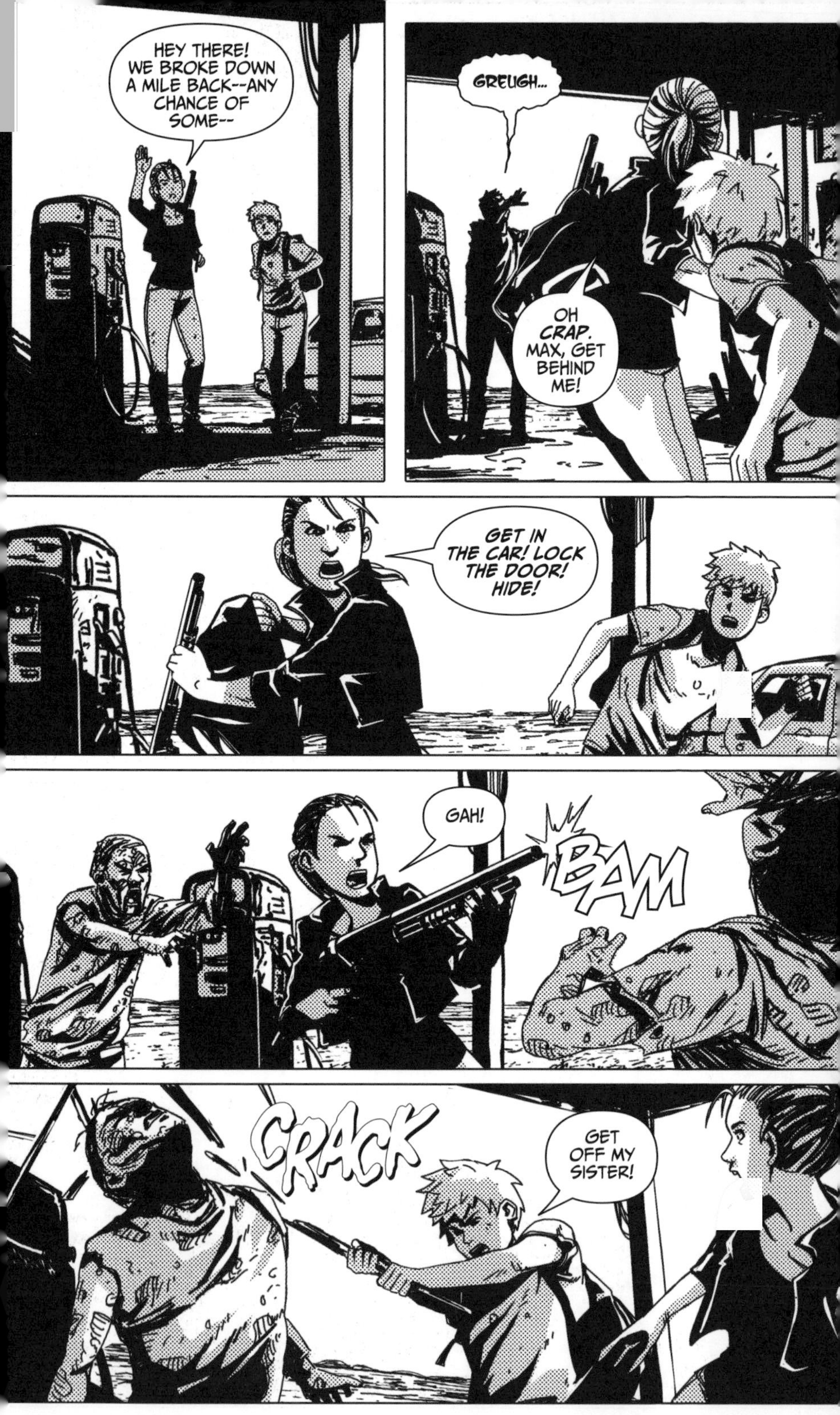
HEY THERE! WE BROKE DOWN A MILE BACK--ANY CHANCE OF SOME--
GREUGH...
OH *CRAP.* MAX, GET BEHIND ME!
GET IN THE CAR! LOCK THE DOOR! HIDE!
GAH!
BAM
CRACK
GET OFF MY SISTER!

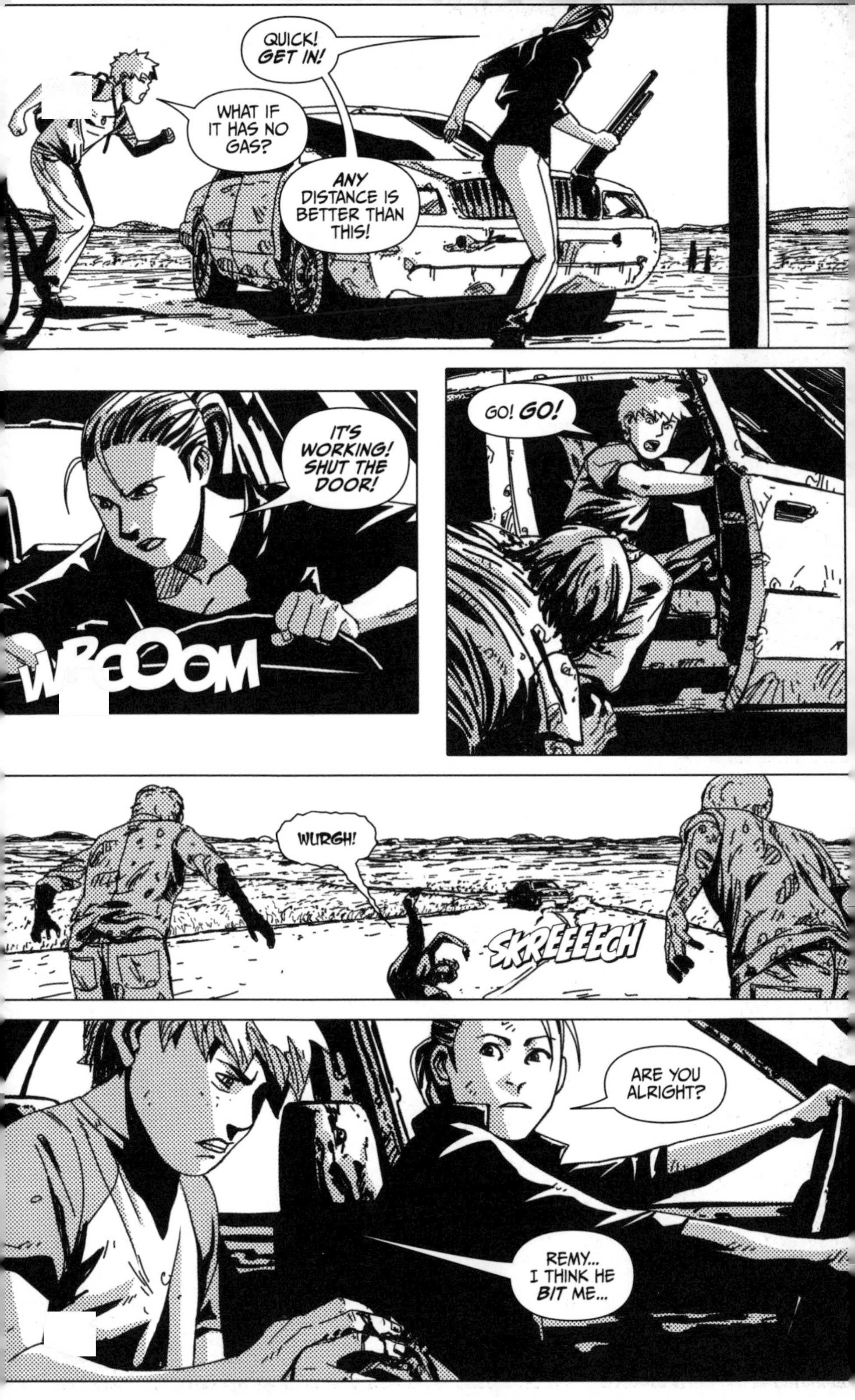
QUICK! GET IN!
WHAT IF IT HAS NO GAS?
ANY DISTANCE IS BETTER THAN THIS!
IT'S WORKING! SHUT THE DOOR!
WROOOM
GO! GO!
WURGH!
SKREEEECH
ARE YOU ALRIGHT?
REMY... I THINK HE BIT ME...

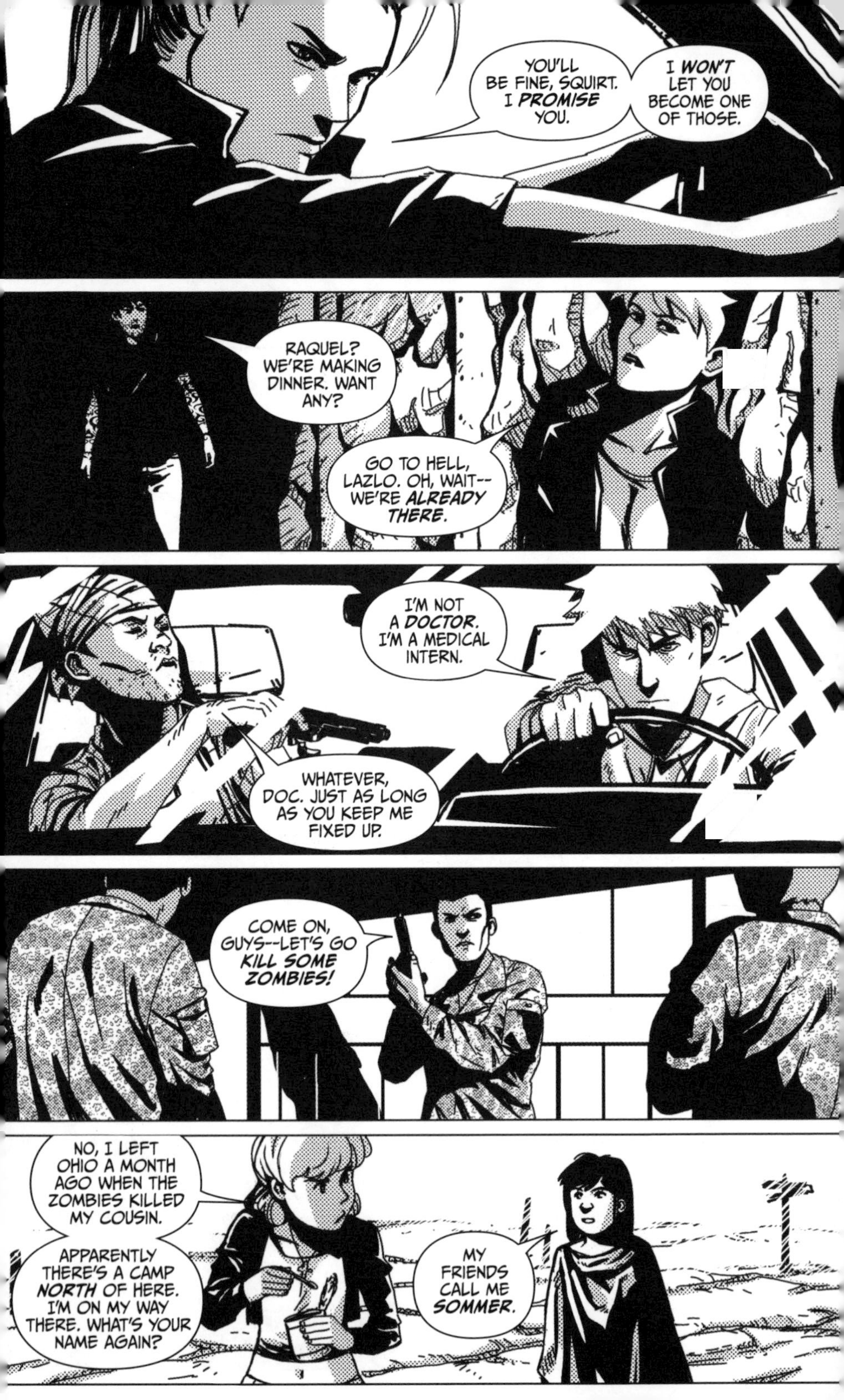

YOU'LL BE FINE, SQUIRT. I *PROMISE* YOU.
I *WON'T* LET YOU BECOME ONE OF THOSE.
RAQUEL? WE'RE MAKING DINNER. WANT ANY?
GO TO HELL, LAZLO. OH, WAIT-- WE'RE *ALREADY THERE.*
I'M NOT A *DOCTOR.* I'M A MEDICAL INTERN.
WHATEVER, DOC. JUST AS LONG AS YOU KEEP ME FIXED UP.
COME ON, GUYS--LET'S GO *KILL SOME ZOMBIES!*
NO, I LEFT OHIO A MONTH AGO WHEN THE ZOMBIES KILLED MY COUSIN.
APPARENTLY THERE'S A CAMP *NORTH* OF HERE. I'M ON MY WAY THERE. WHAT'S YOUR NAME AGAIN?
MY FRIENDS CALL ME *SOMMER.*

CHAPTER THREE

MOVIN' ON

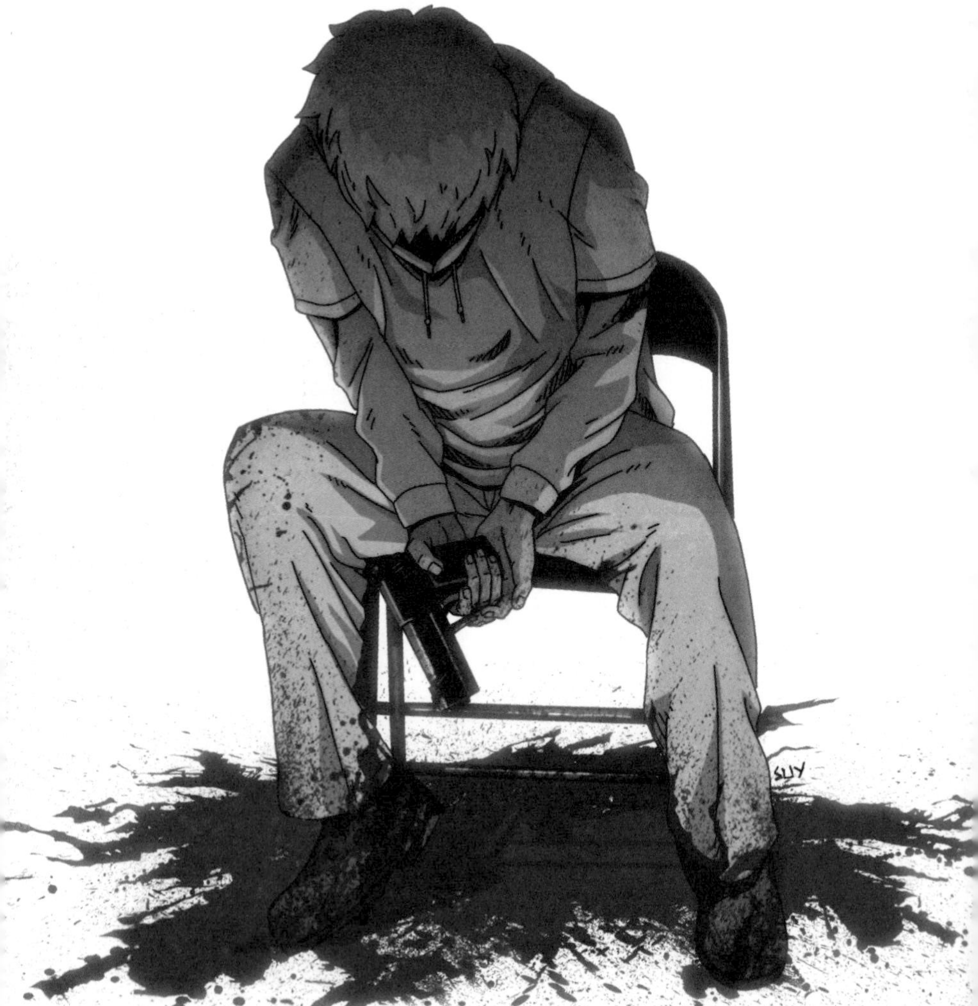
SUY

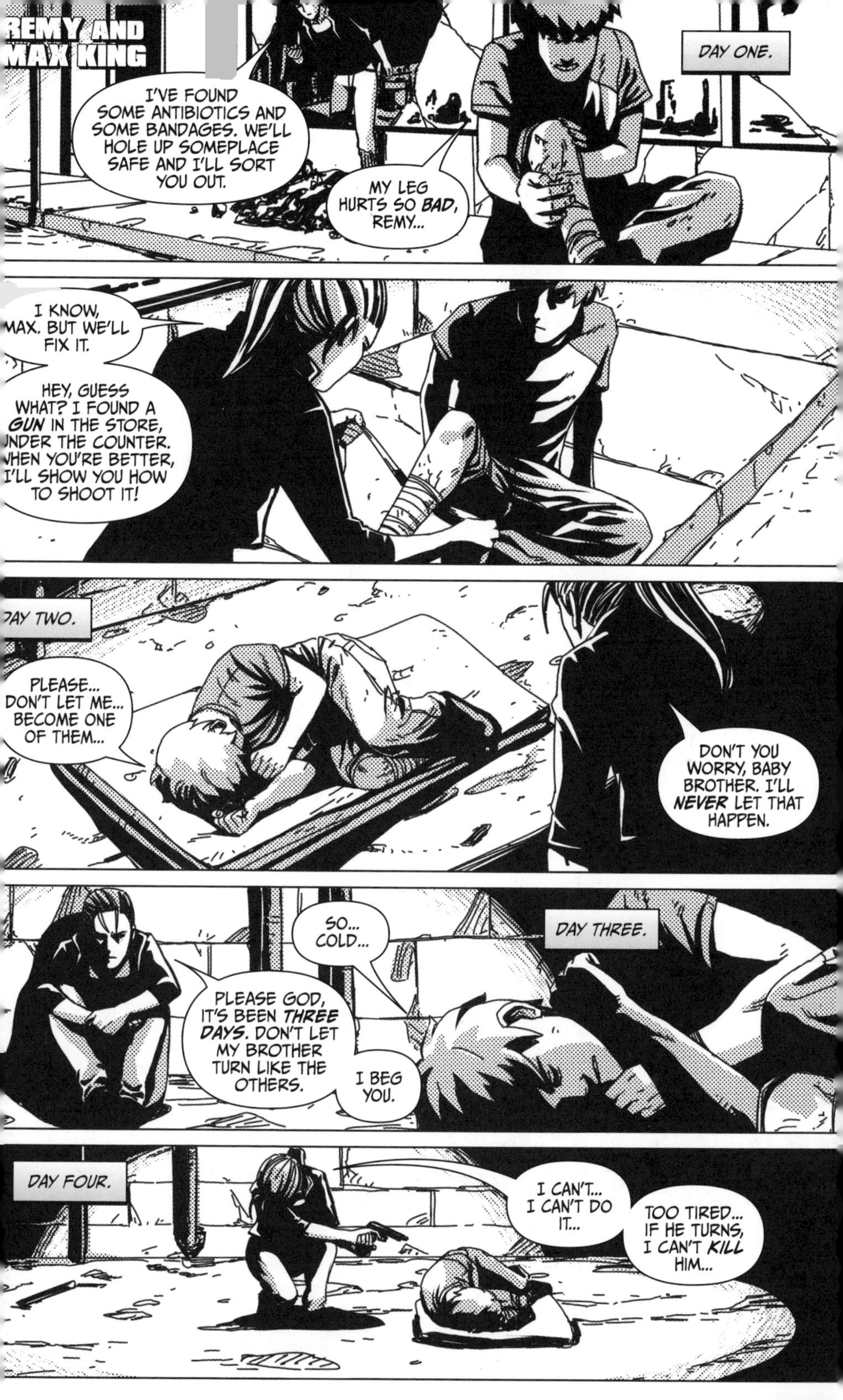
REMY AND MAX KING
DAY ONE.
I'VE FOUND SOME ANTIBIOTICS AND SOME BANDAGES. WE'LL HOLE UP SOMEPLACE SAFE AND I'LL SORT YOU OUT.
MY LEG HURTS SO BAD, REMY...
I KNOW, MAX. BUT WE'LL FIX IT.
HEY, GUESS WHAT? I FOUND A GUN IN THE STORE, UNDER THE COUNTER. WHEN YOU'RE BETTER, I'LL SHOW YOU HOW TO SHOOT IT!
DAY TWO.
PLEASE... DON'T LET ME... BECOME ONE OF THEM...
DON'T YOU WORRY, BABY BROTHER. I'LL NEVER LET THAT HAPPEN.
SO... COLD...
DAY THREE.
PLEASE GOD, IT'S BEEN THREE DAYS. DON'T LET MY BROTHER TURN LIKE THE OTHERS.
I BEG YOU.
DAY FOUR.
I CAN'T... I CAN'T DO IT...
TOO TIRED... IF HE TURNS, I CAN'T KILL HIM...

LOOK AT YOU! THE ANGER, THE RAISED BLOOD PRESSURE--YOU HAVE *LYSSAVIRUS GENOTYPE 8!*

IT'S JUST A MATTER OF TIME! I'M *SORRY!*

COME ON, MAN! IT'S BEEN *THREE DAYS!* I'VE DONE *EVERYTHING* THAT I CAN!

LET ME GO!

SORRY? YOU WERE SUPPOSED TO *CURE* ME, DOC! NOW WHAT DO I.. DO I...

RRUUR--GGGHHH...

OH DAMN. DAMN, DAMN, DAMN.

COME ON! BREAK!

BRUUR--RGHH!!!!

NOT LIKE THIS! *NOT LIKE THIS!*

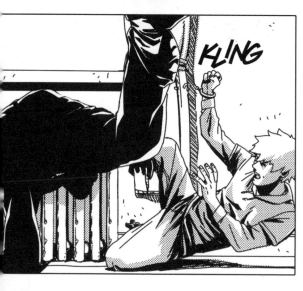

KLING

THREE DAYS YOU'VE KEPT ME HERE, YOU SON OF A BITCH--

THREE DAYS!

BLAM

THUDD

I REALLY HAVE TO GET OUT OF LOS ANGELES.

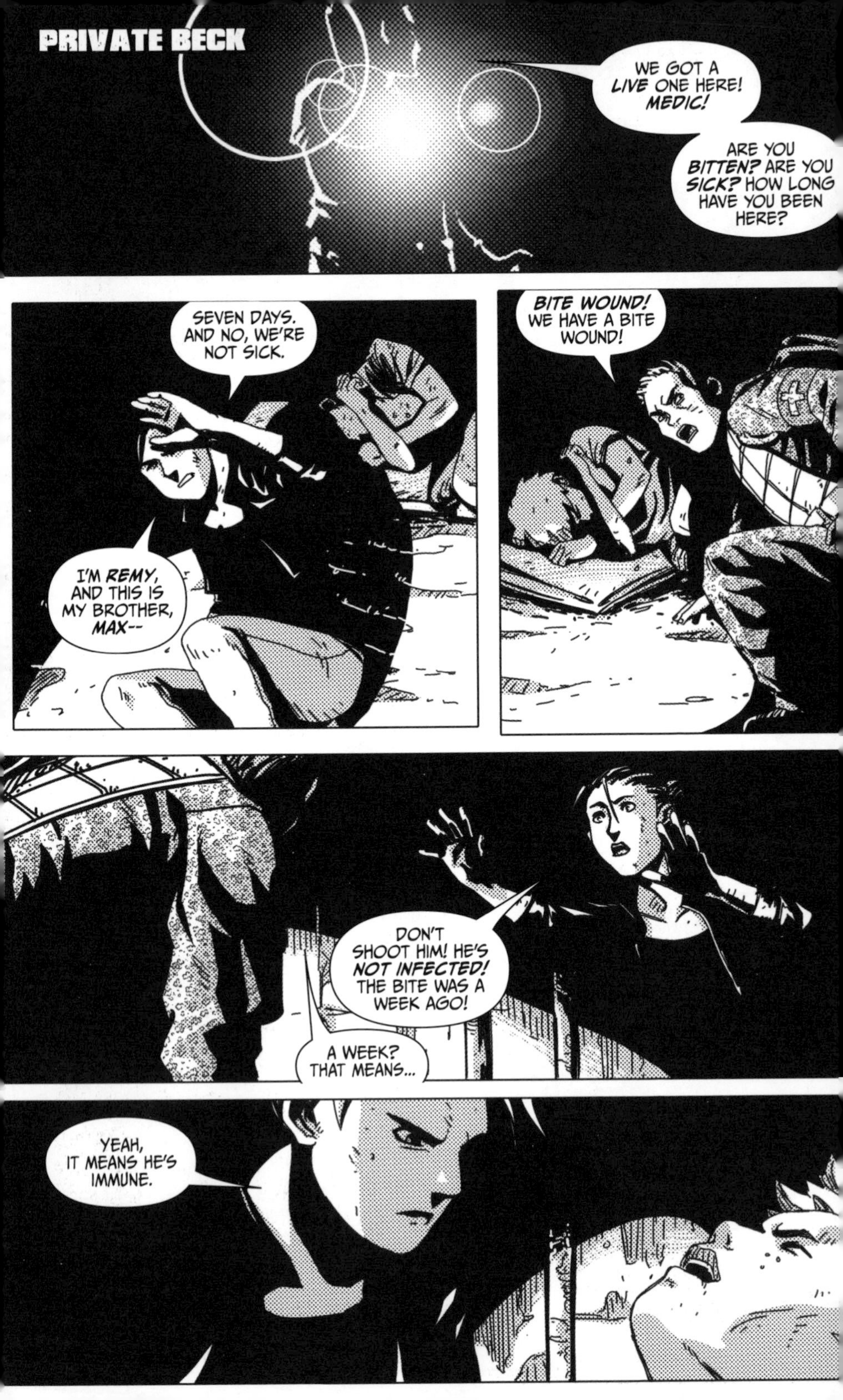
PRIVATE BECK
WE GOT A *LIVE* ONE HERE! ***MEDIC!***
ARE YOU ***BITTEN?*** ARE YOU ***SICK?*** HOW LONG HAVE YOU BEEN HERE?
SEVEN DAYS. AND NO, WE'RE NOT SICK.
I'M ***REMY***, AND THIS IS MY BROTHER, ***MAX***--
BITE WOUND! WE HAVE A BITE WOUND!
DON'T SHOOT HIM! HE'S ***NOT INFECTED!*** THE BITE WAS A WEEK AGO!
A WEEK? THAT MEANS...
YEAH, IT MEANS HE'S IMMUNE.

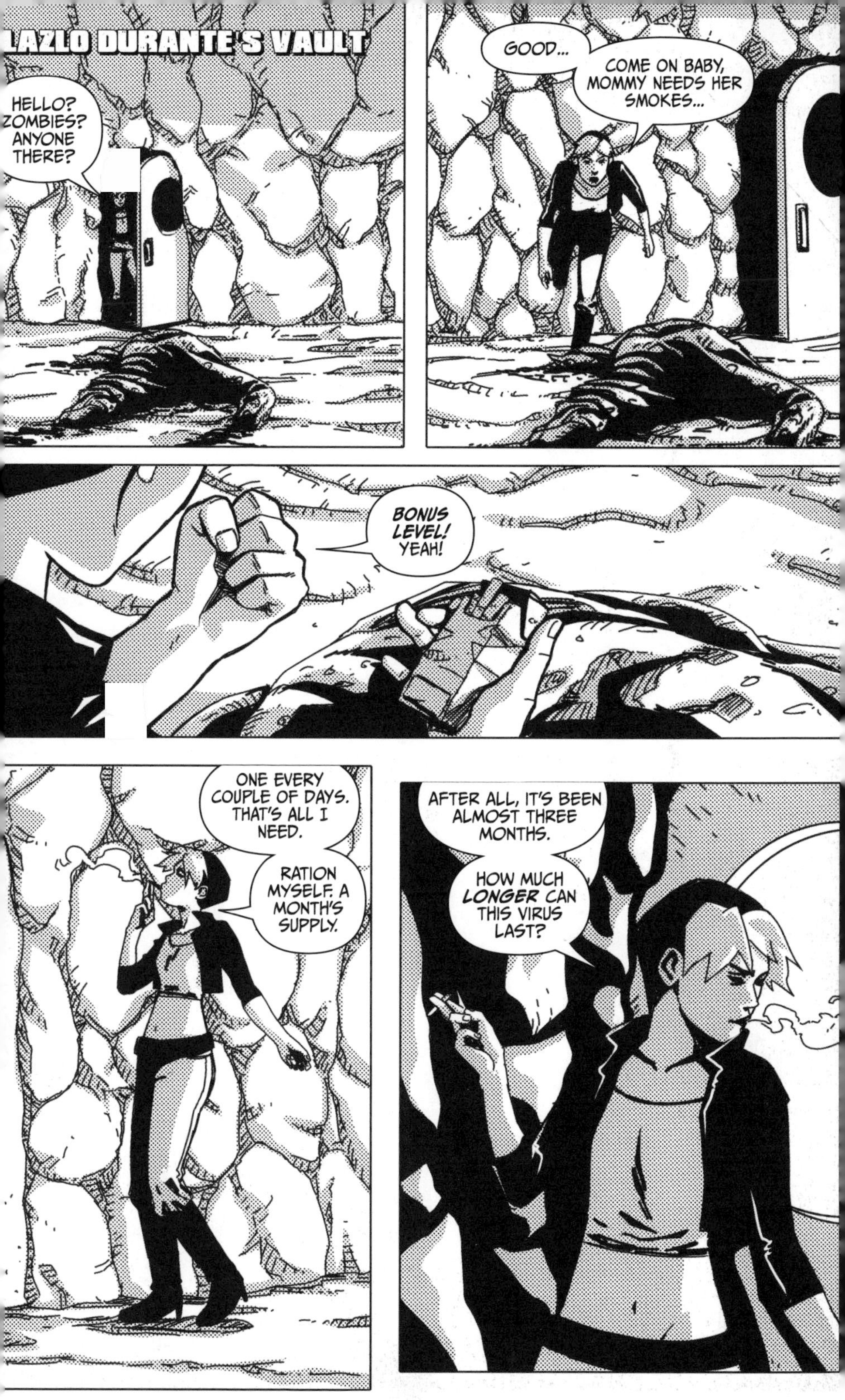
LAZLO DURANTE'S VAULT
HELLO? ZOMBIES? ANYONE THERE?
GOOD...
COME ON BABY, MOMMY NEEDS HER SMOKES...
BONUS LEVEL! YEAH!
ONE EVERY COUPLE OF DAYS. THAT'S ALL I NEED.
RATION MYSELF. A MONTH'S SUPPLY.
AFTER ALL, IT'S BEEN ALMOST THREE MONTHS.
HOW MUCH LONGER CAN THIS VIRUS LAST?

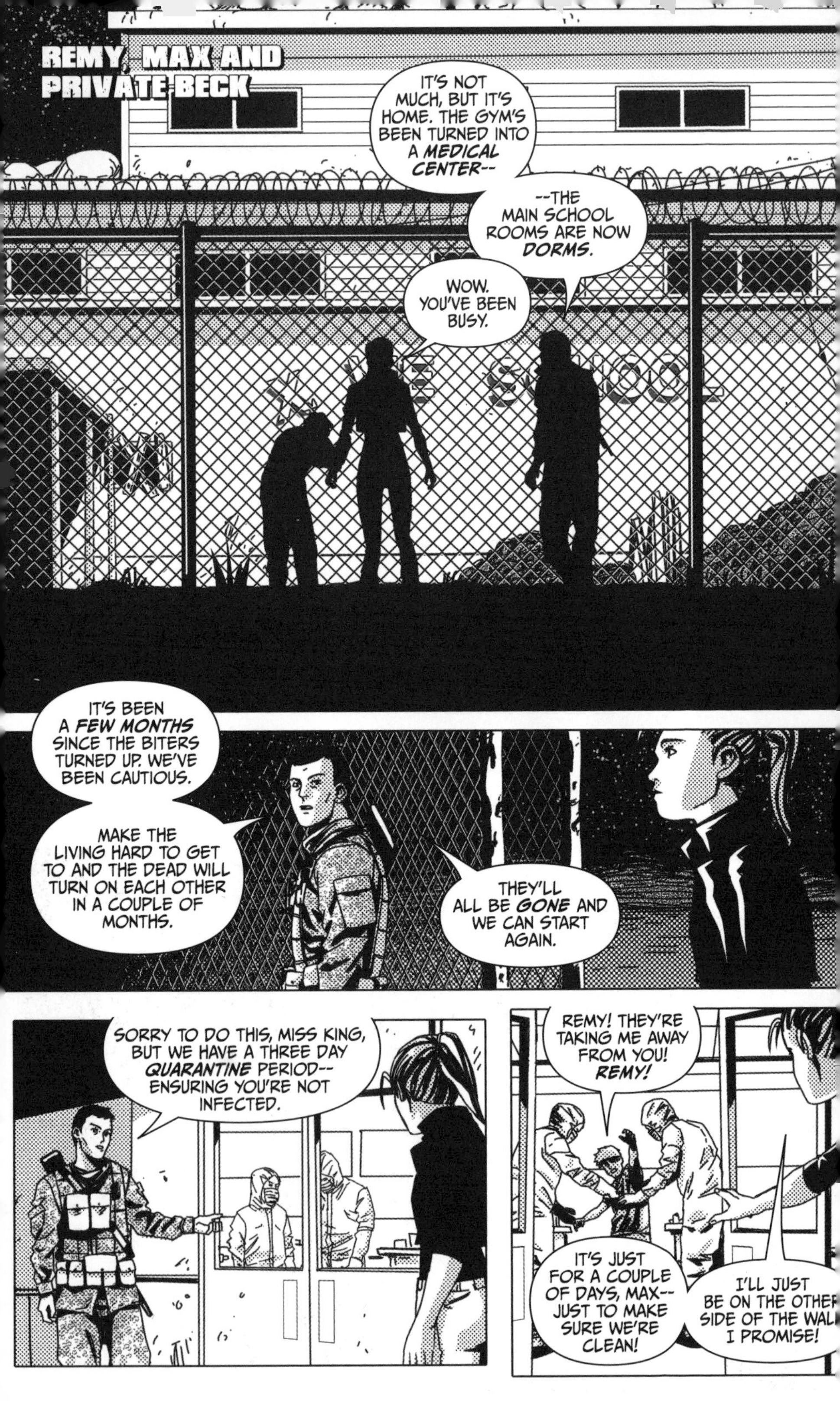
REMY, MAX AND PRIVATE BECK
IT'S NOT MUCH, BUT IT'S HOME. THE GYM'S BEEN TURNED INTO A MEDICAL CENTER--
--THE MAIN SCHOOL ROOMS ARE NOW DORMS.
WOW. YOU'VE BEEN BUSY.
IT'S BEEN A FEW MONTHS SINCE THE BITERS TURNED UP. WE'VE BEEN CAUTIOUS.
MAKE THE LIVING HARD TO GET TO AND THE DEAD WILL TURN ON EACH OTHER IN A COUPLE OF MONTHS.
THEY'LL ALL BE GONE AND WE CAN START AGAIN.
SORRY TO DO THIS, MISS KING, BUT WE HAVE A THREE DAY QUARANTINE PERIOD-- ENSURING YOU'RE NOT INFECTED.
REMY! THEY'RE TAKING ME AWAY FROM YOU! REMY!
IT'S JUST FOR A COUPLE OF DAYS, MAX-- JUST TO MAKE SURE WE'RE CLEAN!
I'LL JUST BE ON THE OTHER SIDE OF THE WALL I PROMISE!

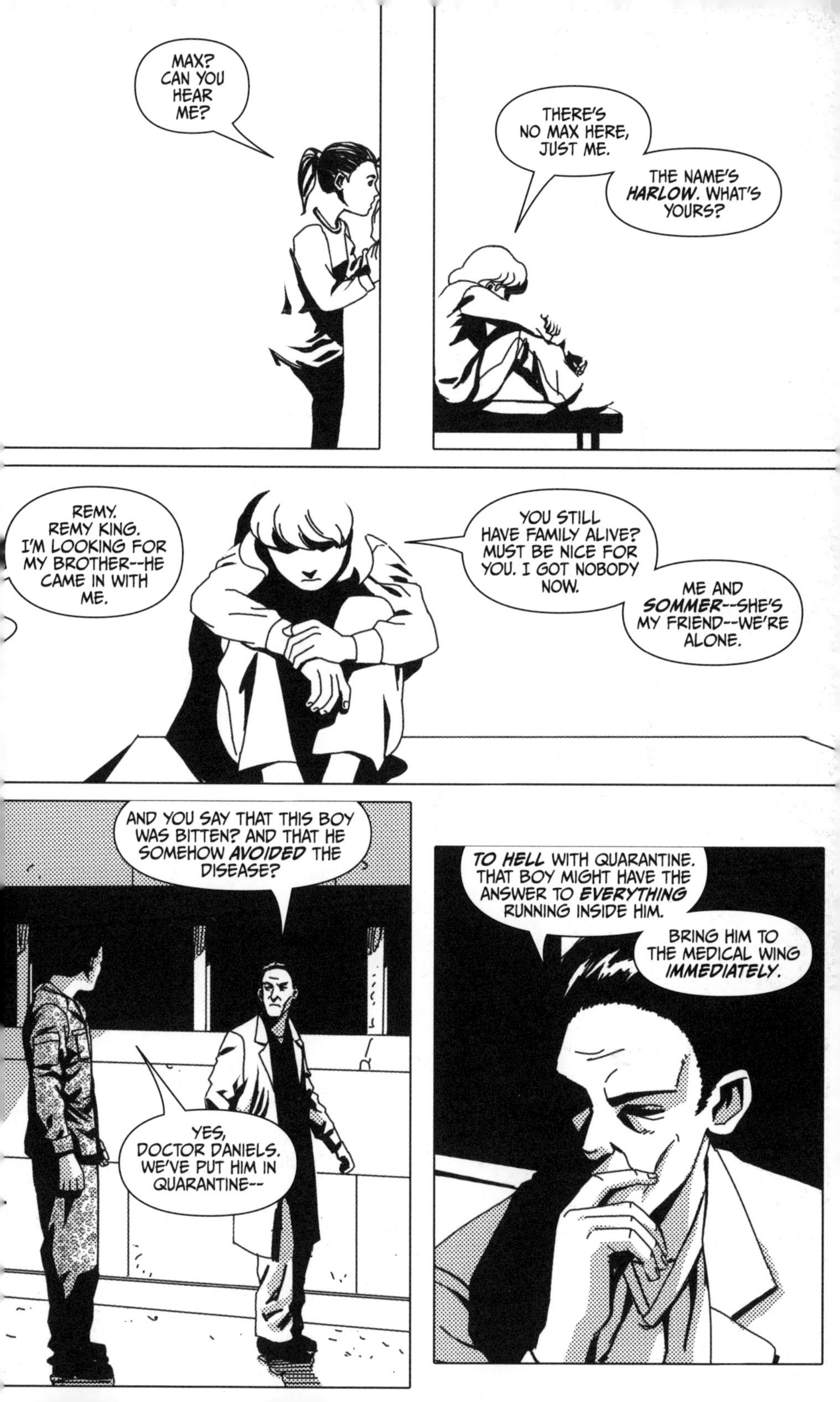
MAX? CAN YOU HEAR ME?
THERE'S NO MAX HERE, JUST ME.
THE NAME'S HARLOW. WHAT'S YOURS?
REMY. REMY KING. I'M LOOKING FOR MY BROTHER--HE CAME IN WITH ME.
YOU STILL HAVE FAMILY ALIVE? MUST BE NICE FOR YOU. I GOT NOBODY NOW.
ME AND SOMMER--SHE'S MY FRIEND--WE'RE ALONE.
AND YOU SAY THAT THIS BOY WAS BITTEN? AND THAT HE SOMEHOW AVOIDED THE DISEASE?
YES, DOCTOR DANIELS. WE'VE PUT HIM IN QUARANTINE--
TO HELL WITH QUARANTINE. THAT BOY MIGHT HAVE THE ANSWER TO EVERYTHING RUNNING INSIDE HIM.
BRING HIM TO THE MEDICAL WING IMMEDIATELY.

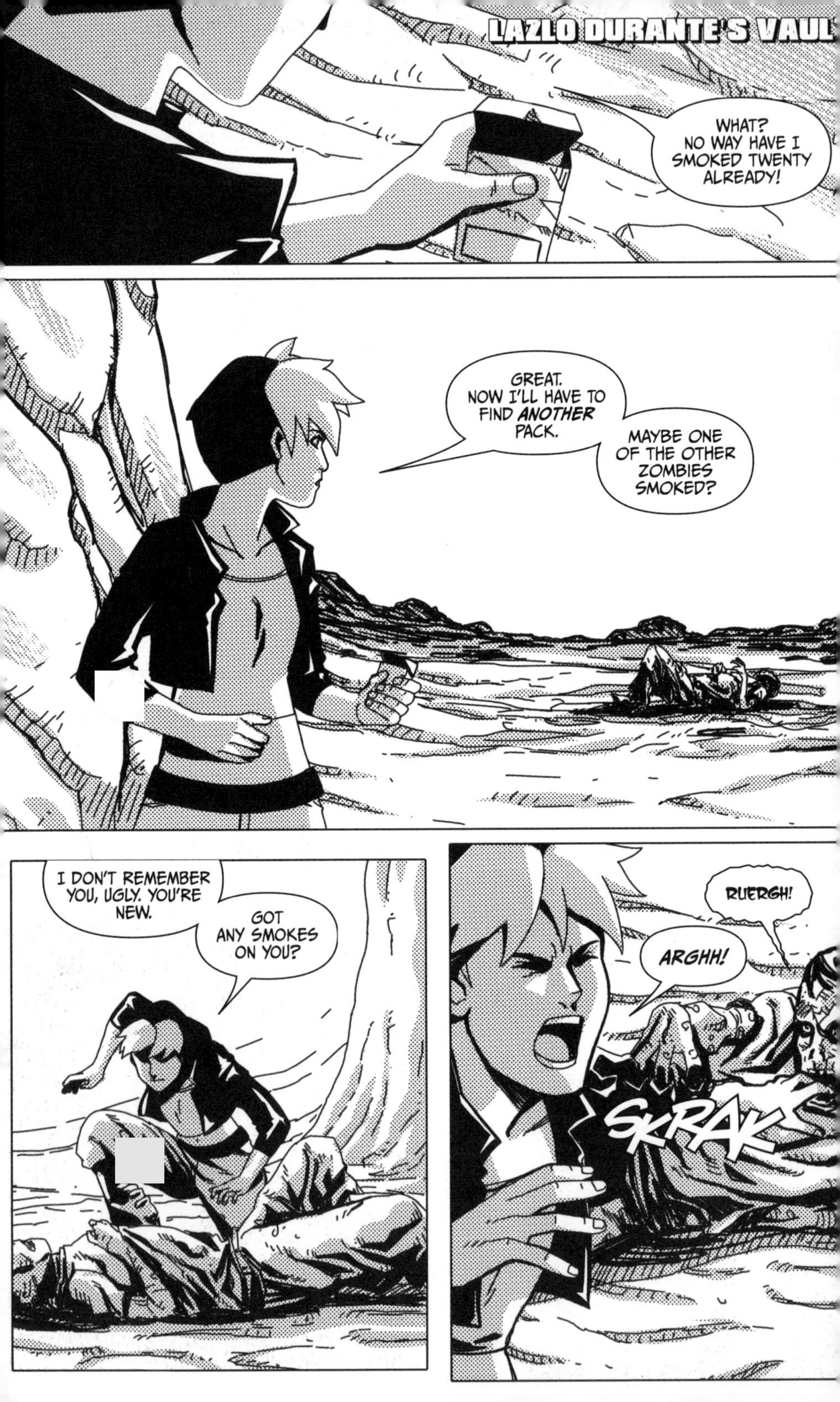
WHAT? NO WAY HAVE I SMOKED TWENTY ALREADY!
GREAT. NOW I'LL HAVE TO FIND ANOTHER PACK.
MAYBE ONE OF THE OTHER ZOMBIES SMOKED?
I DON'T REMEMBER YOU, UGLY. YOU'RE NEW.
GOT ANY SMOKES ON YOU?
RUERGH!
ARGHH!
SKRAK

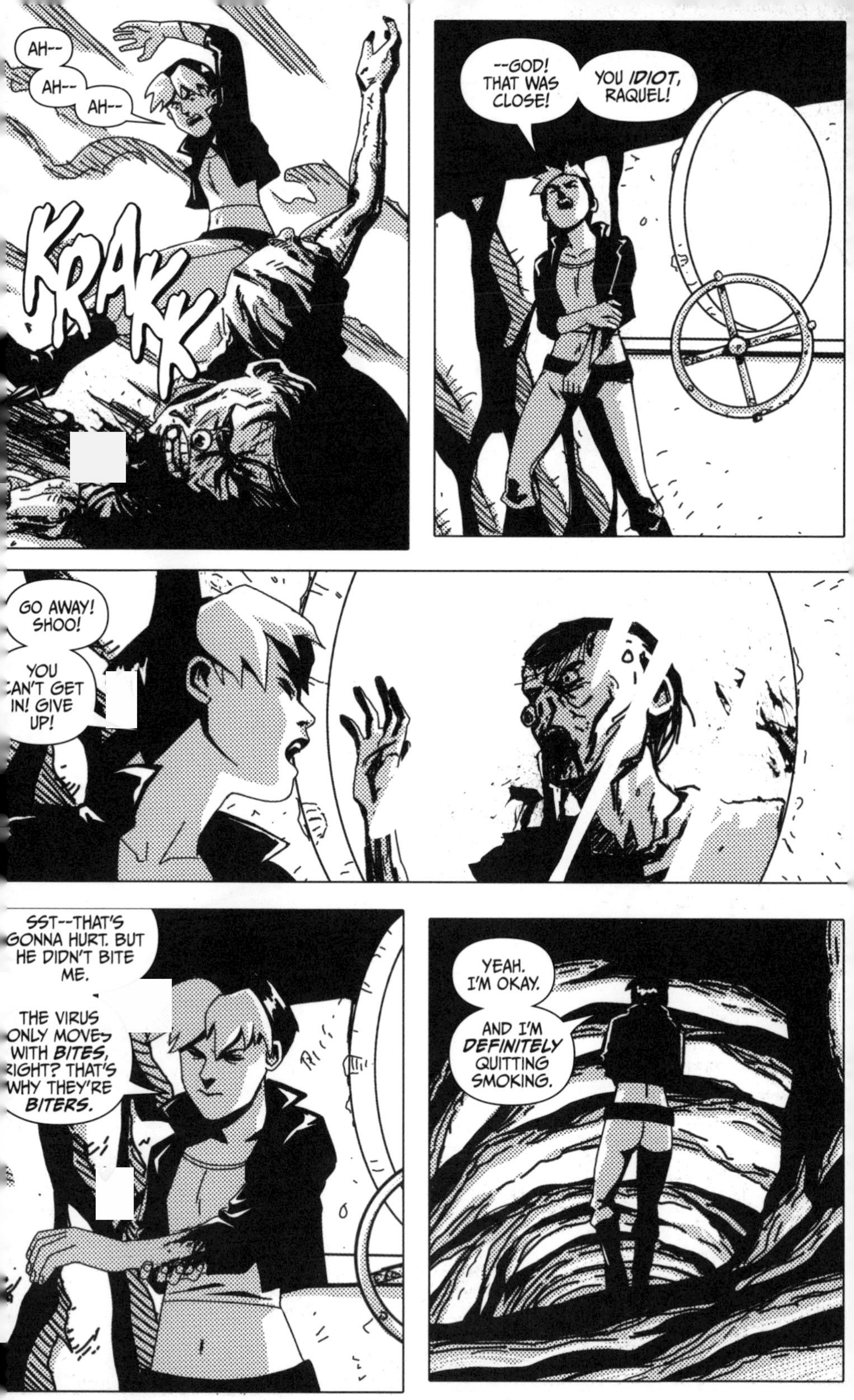
AH--
AH--
AH--
KRAKK
--GOD! THAT WAS CLOSE!
YOU *IDIOT*, RAQUEL!
GO AWAY! SHOO!
YOU CAN'T GET IN! GIVE UP!
SST--THAT'S GONNA HURT. BUT HE DIDN'T BITE ME.
THE VIRUS ONLY MOVES WITH *BITES*, RIGHT? THAT'S WHY THEY'RE *BITERS*.
YEAH. I'M OKAY.
AND I'M *DEFINITELY* QUITTING SMOKING.

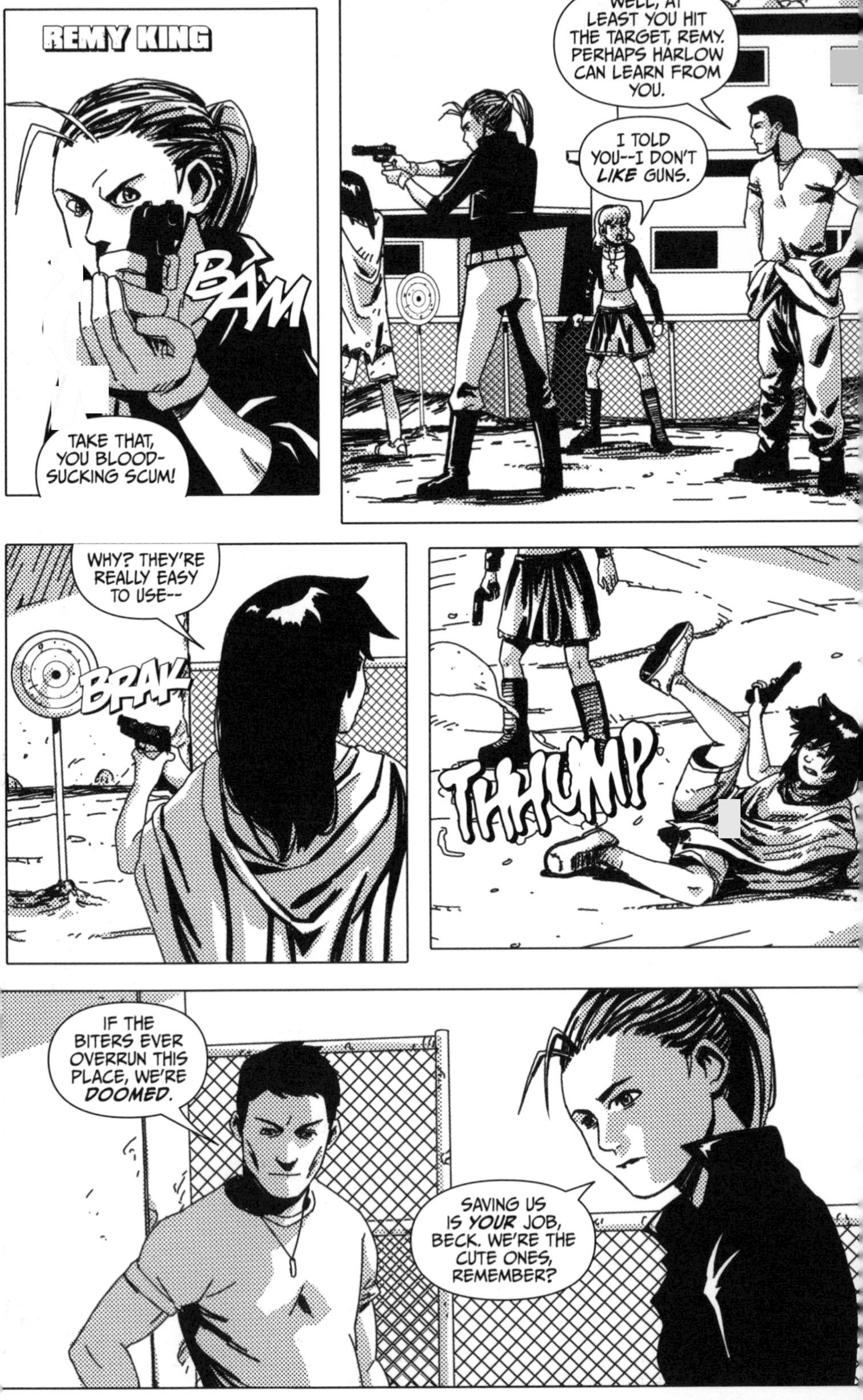
REMY KING
BAM
TAKE THAT, YOU BLOOD-SUCKING SCUM!
WELL, AT LEAST YOU HIT THE TARGET, REMY. PERHAPS HARLOW CAN LEARN FROM YOU.
I TOLD YOU--I DON'T LIKE GUNS.
WHY? THEY'RE REALLY EASY TO USE--
BRAK
THHUMP
IF THE BITERS EVER OVERRUN THIS PLACE, WE'RE DOOMED.
SAVING US IS YOUR JOB, BECK. WE'RE THE CUTE ONES, REMEMBER?

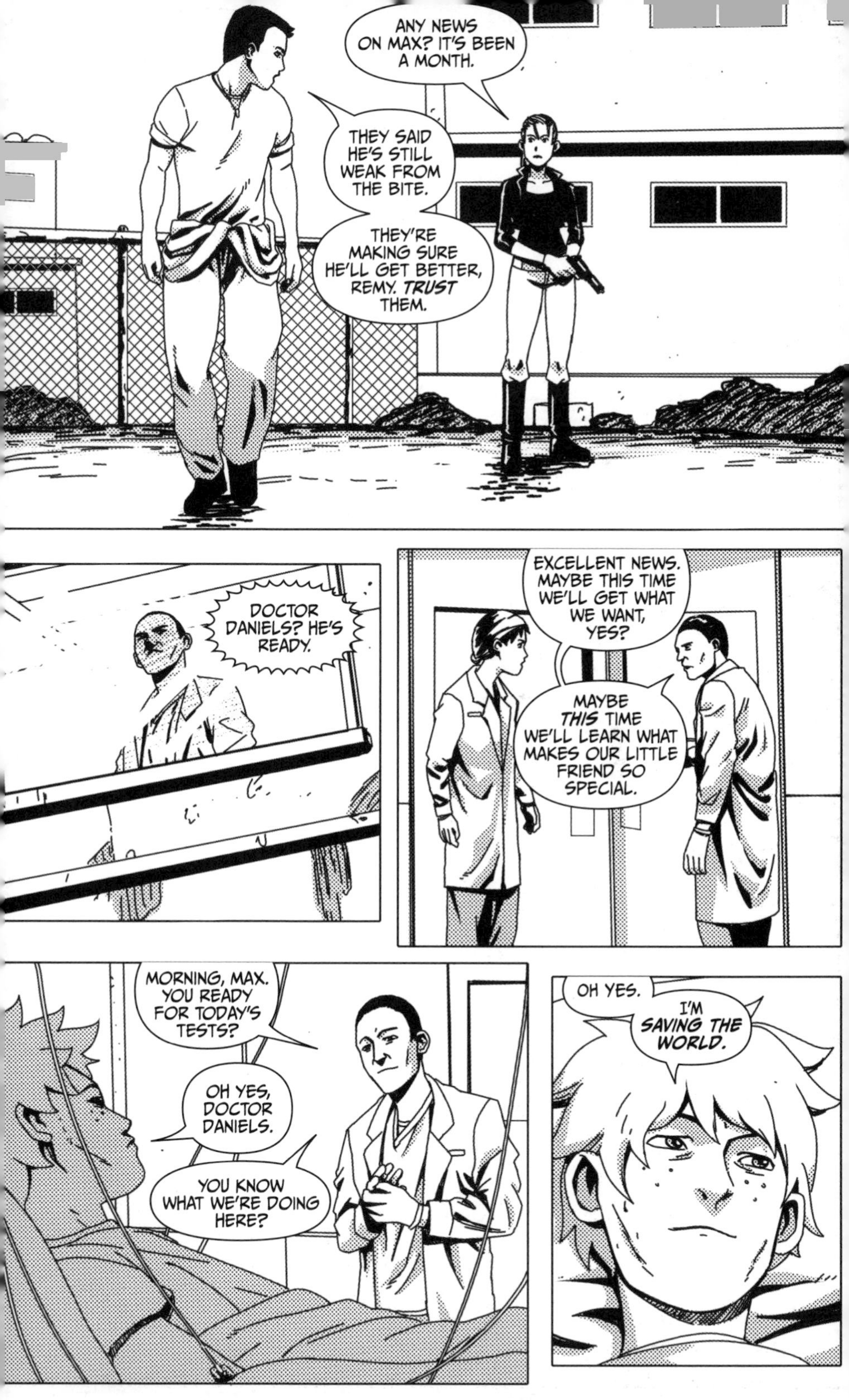
ANY NEWS ON MAX? IT'S BEEN A MONTH.
THEY SAID HE'S STILL WEAK FROM THE BITE.
THEY'RE MAKING SURE HE'LL GET BETTER, REMY. *TRUST* THEM.
DOCTOR DANIELS? HE'S READY.
EXCELLENT NEWS. MAYBE THIS TIME WE'LL GET WHAT WE WANT, YES?
MAYBE *THIS* TIME WE'LL LEARN WHAT MAKES OUR LITTLE FRIEND SO SPECIAL.
MORNING, MAX. YOU READY FOR TODAY'S TESTS?
OH YES, DOCTOR DANIELS.
YOU KNOW WHAT WE'RE DOING HERE?
OH YES.
I'M *SAVING THE WORLD.*

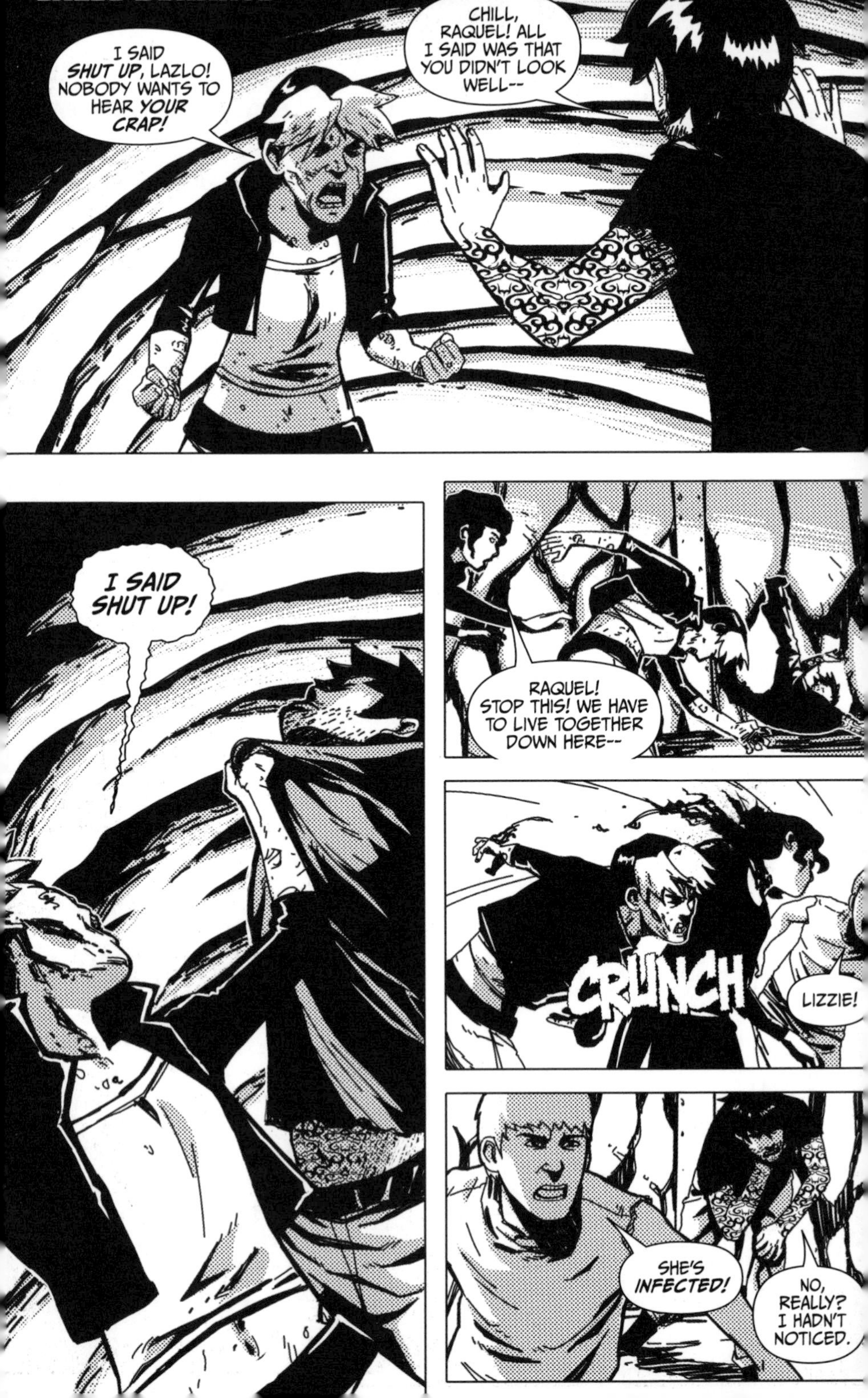
I SAID *SHUT UP*, LAZLO! NOBODY WANTS TO HEAR *YOUR CRAP!*
CHILL, RAQUEL! ALL I SAID WAS THAT YOU DIDN'T LOOK WELL--
I SAID SHUT UP!
RAQUEL! STOP THIS! WE HAVE TO LIVE TOGETHER DOWN HERE--
CRUNCH
LIZZIE!
SHE'S *INFECTED!*
NO, REALLY? I HADN'T NOTICED.

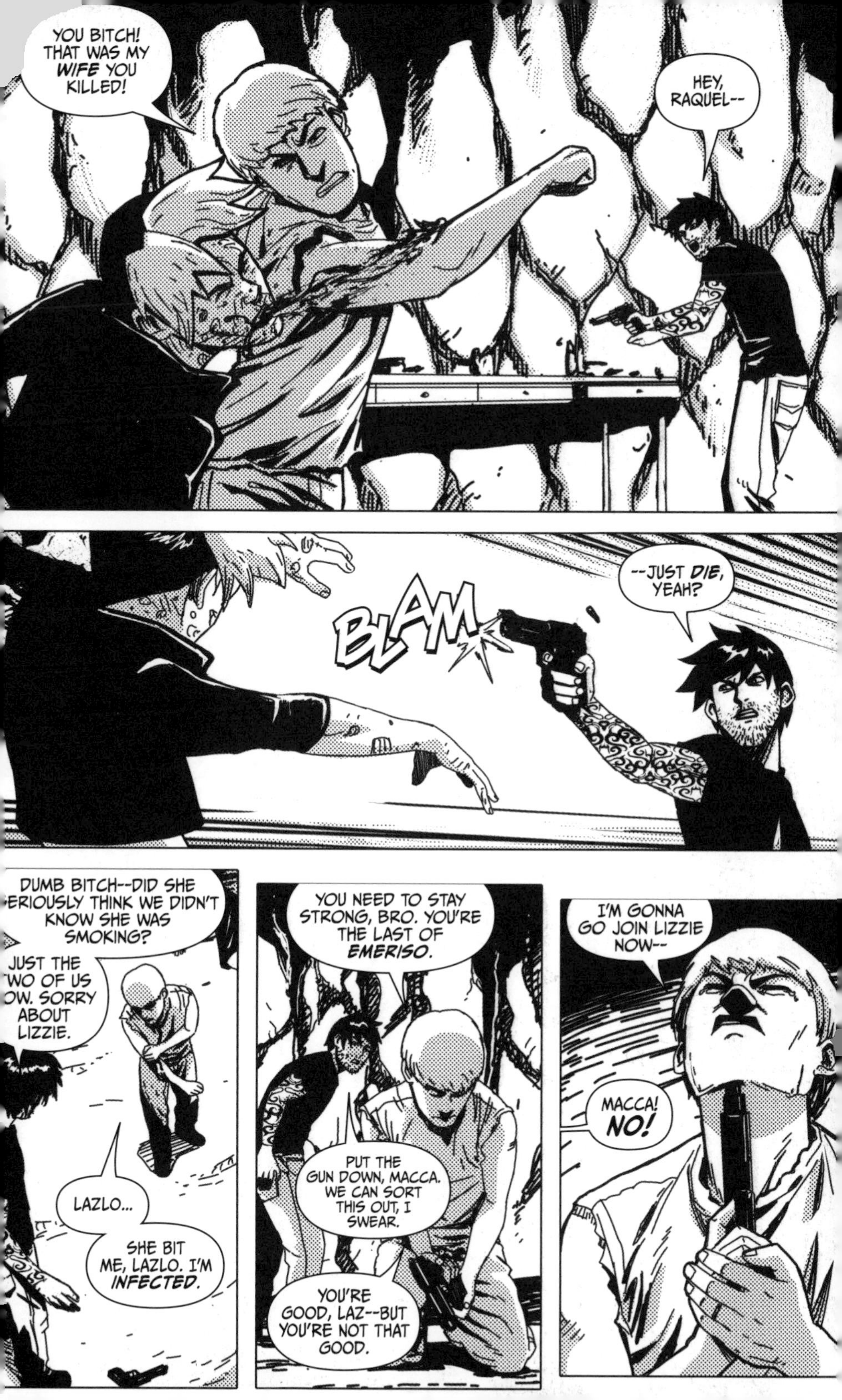
YOU BITCH! THAT WAS MY WIFE YOU KILLED!
HEY, RAQUEL--
BLAM
--JUST DIE, YEAH?
DUMB BITCH--DID SHE SERIOUSLY THINK WE DIDN'T KNOW SHE WAS SMOKING?
JUST THE TWO OF US NOW. SORRY ABOUT LIZZIE.
LAZLO...
SHE BIT ME, LAZLO. I'M INFECTED.
YOU NEED TO STAY STRONG, BRO. YOU'RE THE LAST OF EMERISO.
PUT THE GUN DOWN, MACCA. WE CAN SORT THIS OUT, I SWEAR.
YOU'RE GOOD, LAZ--BUT YOU'RE NOT THAT GOOD.
I'M GONNA GO JOIN LIZZIE NOW--
MACCA! NO!

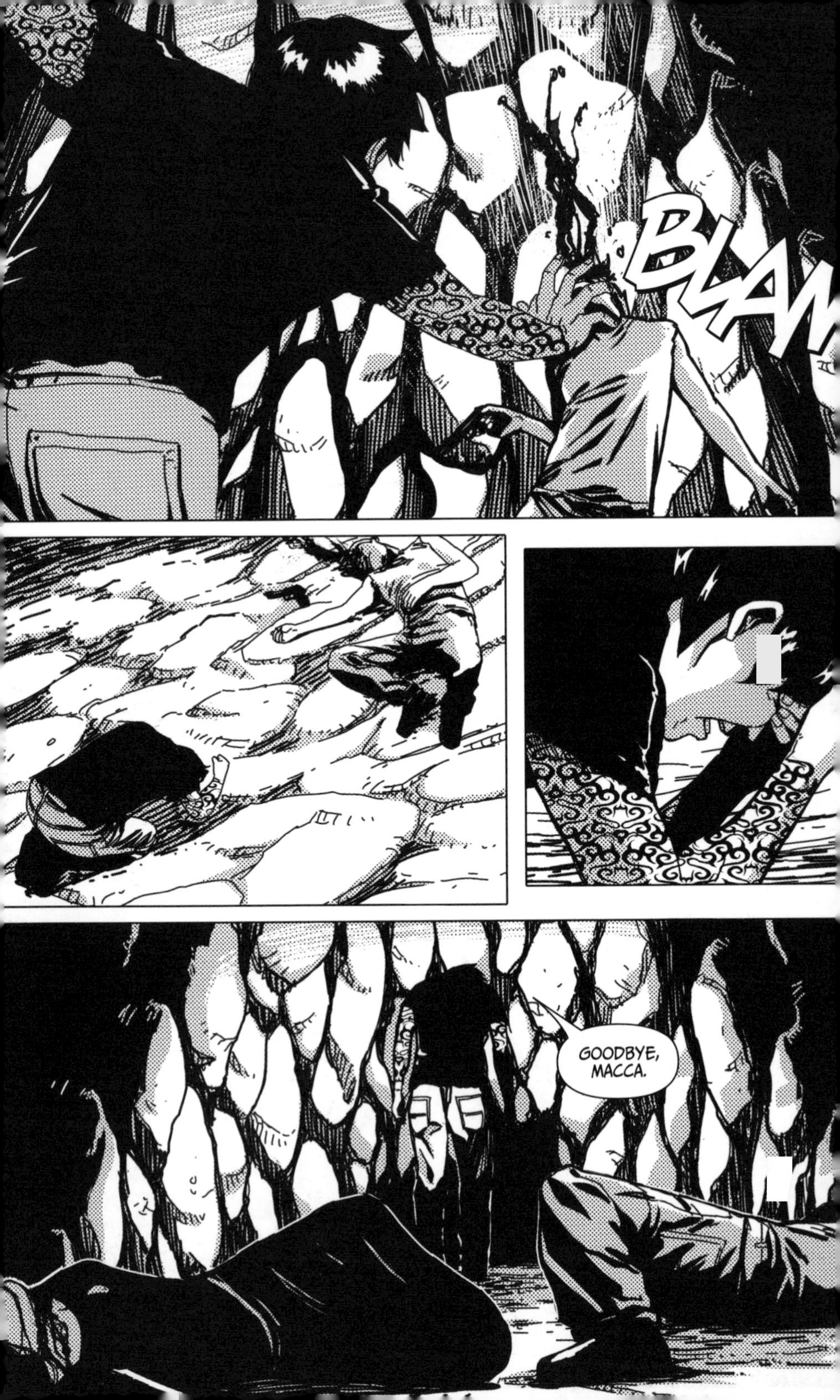
BLAM
GOODBYE, MACCA.

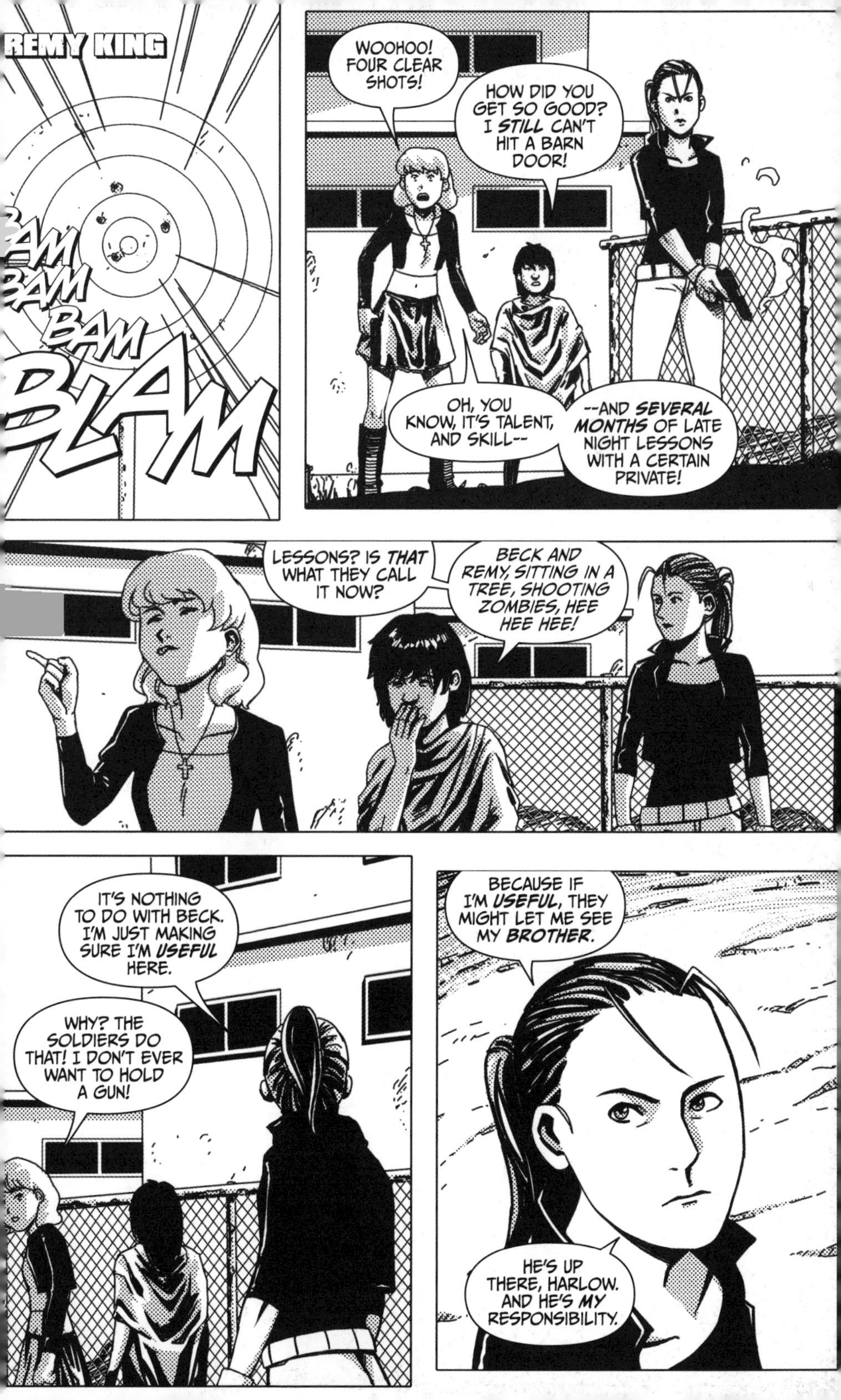
BAM
BAM
BAM
BLAM
WOOHOO! FOUR CLEAR SHOTS!
HOW DID YOU GET SO GOOD? I STILL CAN'T HIT A BARN DOOR!
OH, YOU KNOW, IT'S TALENT, AND SKILL--
--AND SEVERAL MONTHS OF LATE NIGHT LESSONS WITH A CERTAIN PRIVATE!
LESSONS? IS THAT WHAT THEY CALL IT NOW?
BECK AND REMY, SITTING IN A TREE, SHOOTING ZOMBIES, HEE HEE HEE!
IT'S NOTHING TO DO WITH BECK. I'M JUST MAKING SURE I'M USEFUL HERE.
WHY? THE SOLDIERS DO THAT! I DON'T EVER WANT TO HOLD A GUN!
BECAUSE IF I'M USEFUL, THEY MIGHT LET ME SEE MY BROTHER.
HE'S UP THERE, HARLOW. AND HE'S MY RESPONSIBILITY.

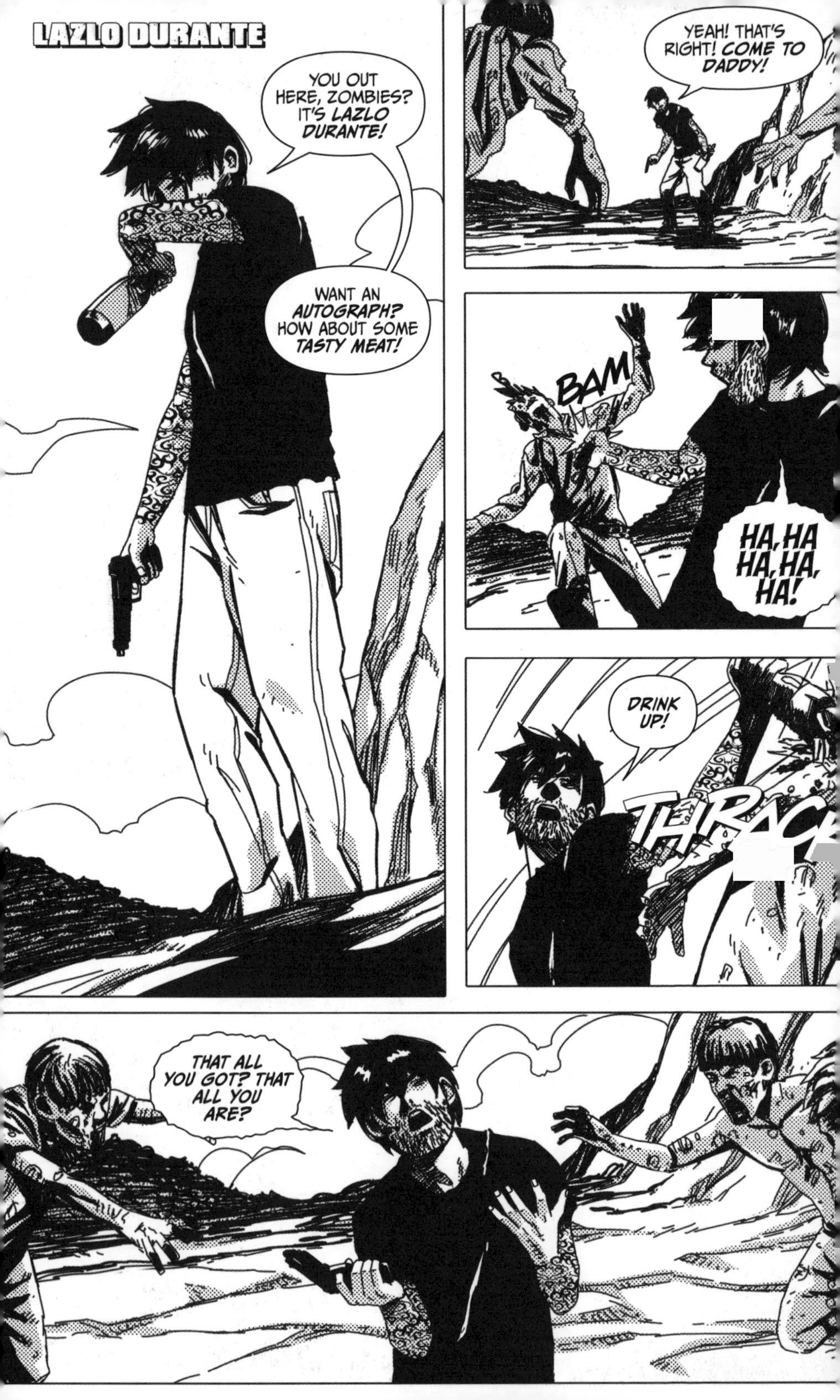
LAZLO DURANTE
YOU OUT HERE, ZOMBIES? IT'S LAZLO DURANTE!
WANT AN AUTOGRAPH? HOW ABOUT SOME TASTY MEAT!
YEAH! THAT'S RIGHT! COME TO DADDY!
BAM
HA, HA HA, HA, HA!
DRINK UP!
THRACK
THAT ALL YOU GOT? THAT ALL YOU ARE?

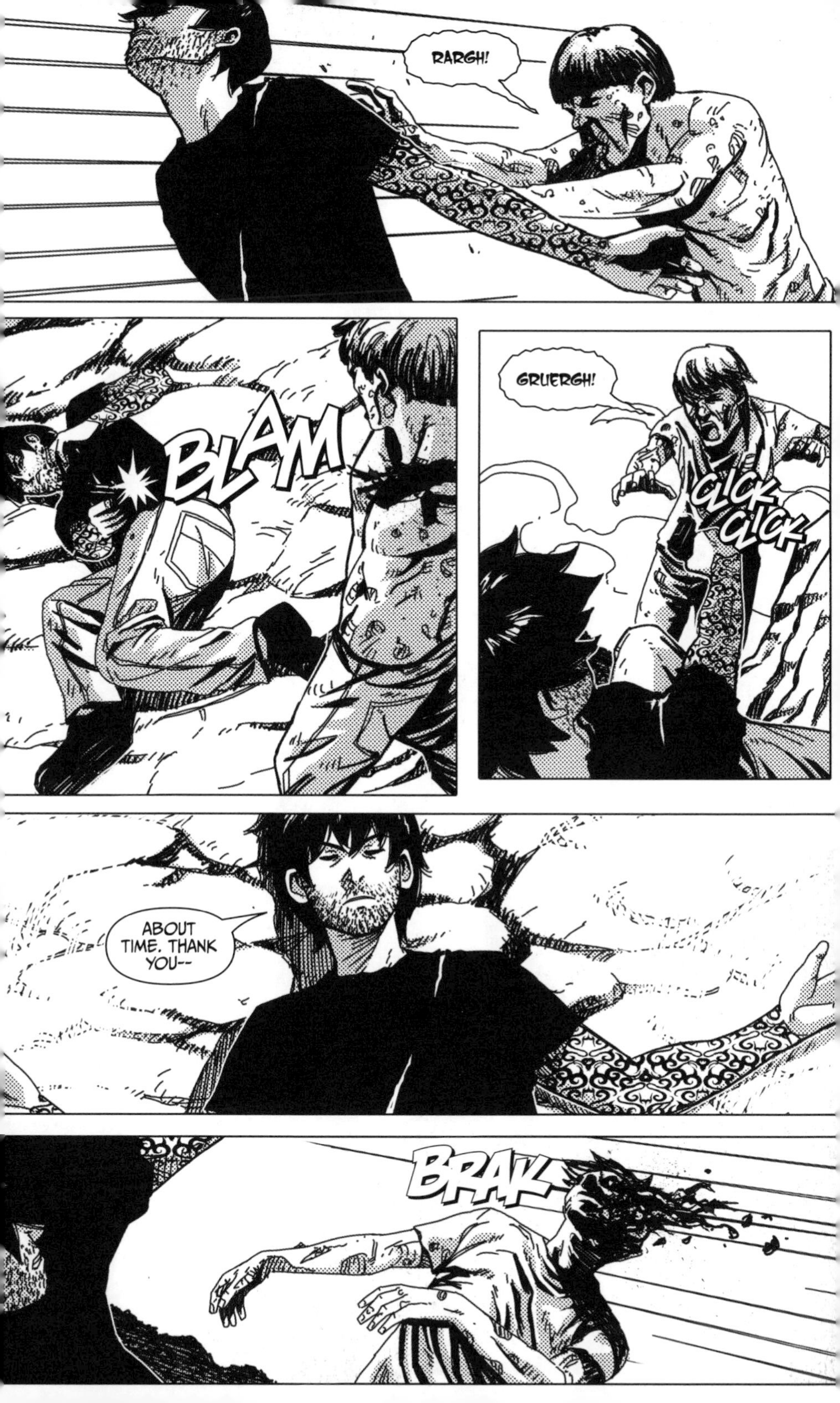
RARGH!
BLAM
GRUERGH!
CLICK CLICK
ABOUT TIME. THANK YOU--
BRAK

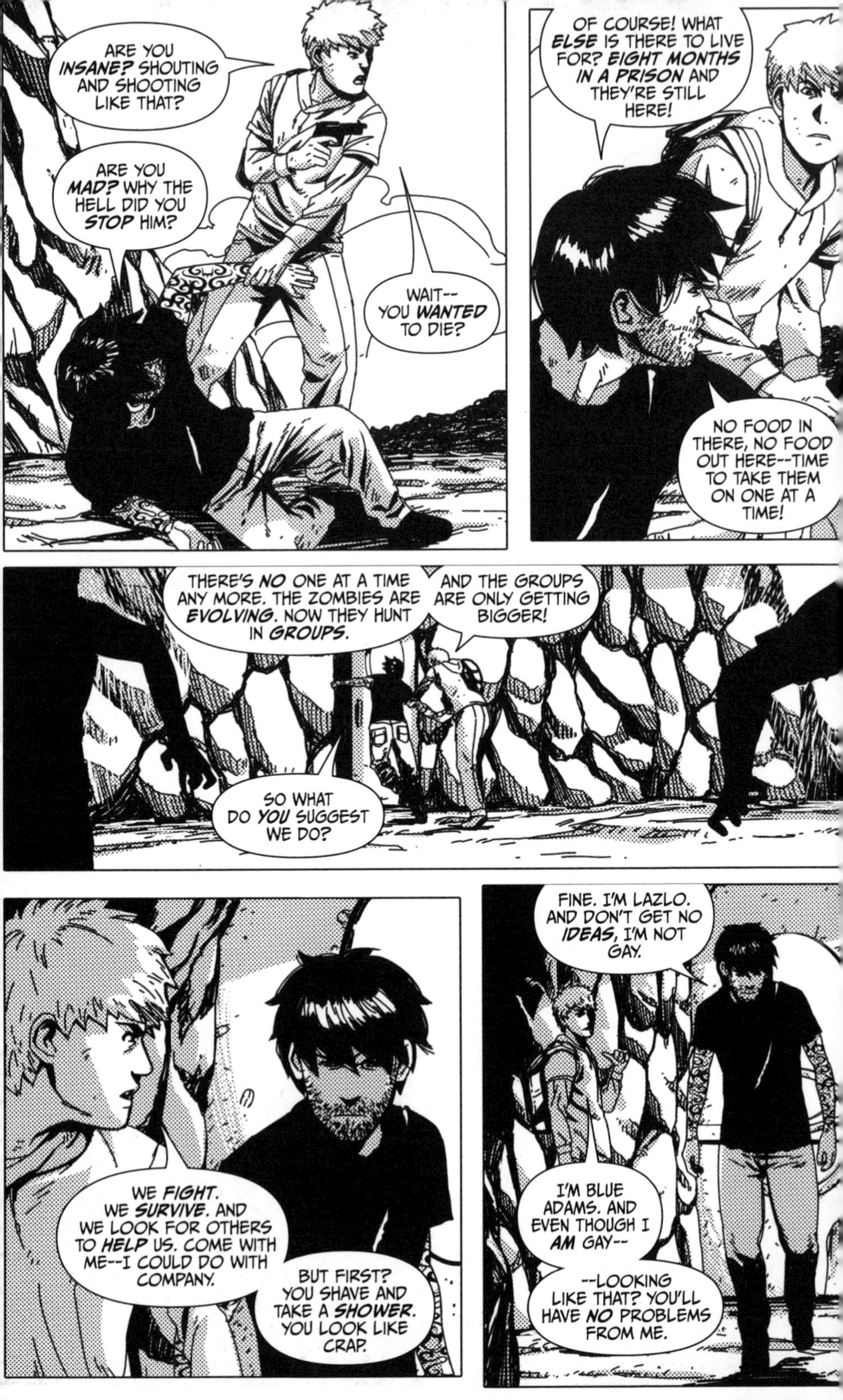
ARE YOU INSANE? SHOUTING AND SHOOTING LIKE THAT?
ARE YOU MAD? WHY THE HELL DID YOU STOP HIM?
WAIT-- YOU WANTED TO DIE?
OF COURSE! WHAT ELSE IS THERE TO LIVE FOR? EIGHT MONTHS IN A PRISON AND THEY'RE STILL HERE!
NO FOOD IN THERE, NO FOOD OUT HERE--TIME TO TAKE THEM ON ONE AT A TIME!
THERE'S NO ONE AT A TIME ANY MORE. THE ZOMBIES ARE EVOLVING. NOW THEY HUNT IN GROUPS.
AND THE GROUPS ARE ONLY GETTING BIGGER!
SO WHAT DO YOU SUGGEST WE DO?
WE FIGHT. WE SURVIVE. AND WE LOOK FOR OTHERS TO HELP US. COME WITH ME--I COULD DO WITH COMPANY.
BUT FIRST? YOU SHAVE AND TAKE A SHOWER. YOU LOOK LIKE CRAP.
FINE. I'M LAZLO. AND DON'T GET NO IDEAS, I'M NOT GAY.
I'M BLUE ADAMS. AND EVEN THOUGH I AM GAY--
--LOOKING LIKE THAT? YOU'LL HAVE NO PROBLEMS FROM ME.

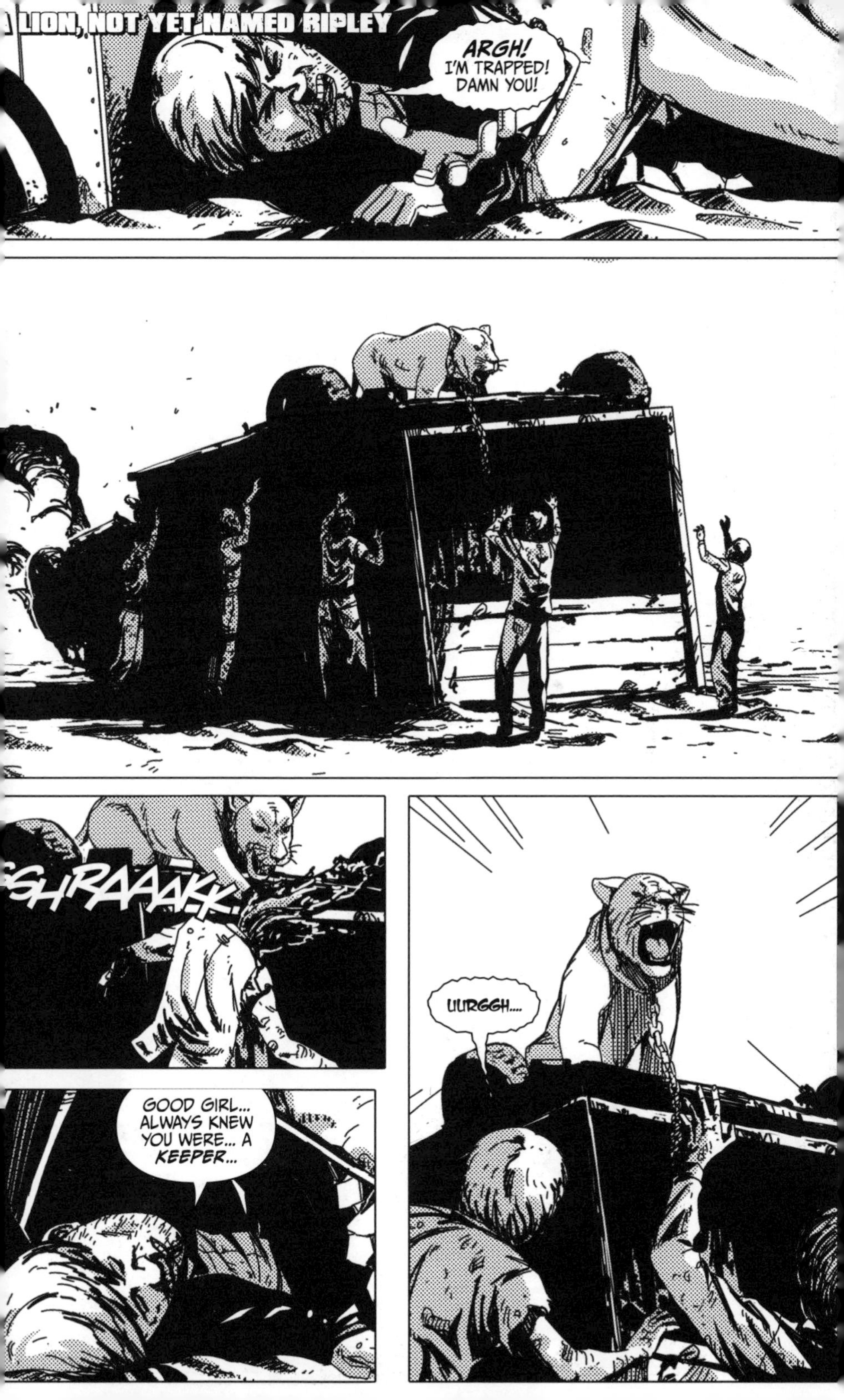

LION, NOT YET NAMED RIPLEY
ARGH! I'M TRAPPED! DAMN YOU!
SHRAAAKK
UURGGH....
GOOD GIRL... ALWAYS KNEW YOU WERE... A KEEPER...

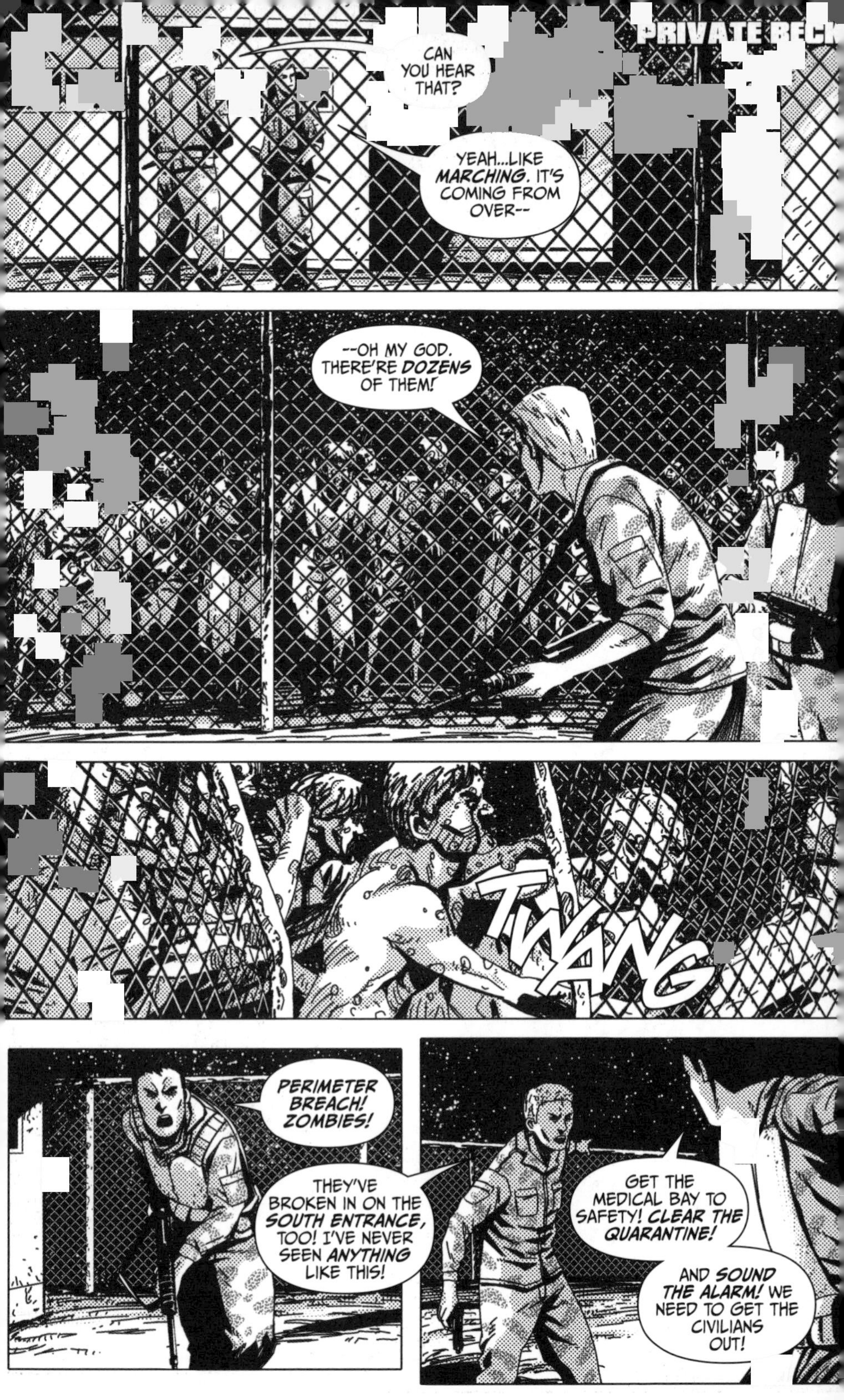
PRIVATE BECK
CAN YOU HEAR THAT?
YEAH...LIKE MARCHING. IT'S COMING FROM OVER--
--OH MY GOD. THERE'RE DOZENS OF THEM!
TWANG
PERIMETER BREACH! ZOMBIES!
THEY'VE BROKEN IN ON THE SOUTH ENTRANCE, TOO! I'VE NEVER SEEN ANYTHING LIKE THIS!
GET THE MEDICAL BAY TO SAFETY! CLEAR THE QUARANTINE!
AND SOUND THE ALARM! WE NEED TO GET THE CIVILIANS OUT!

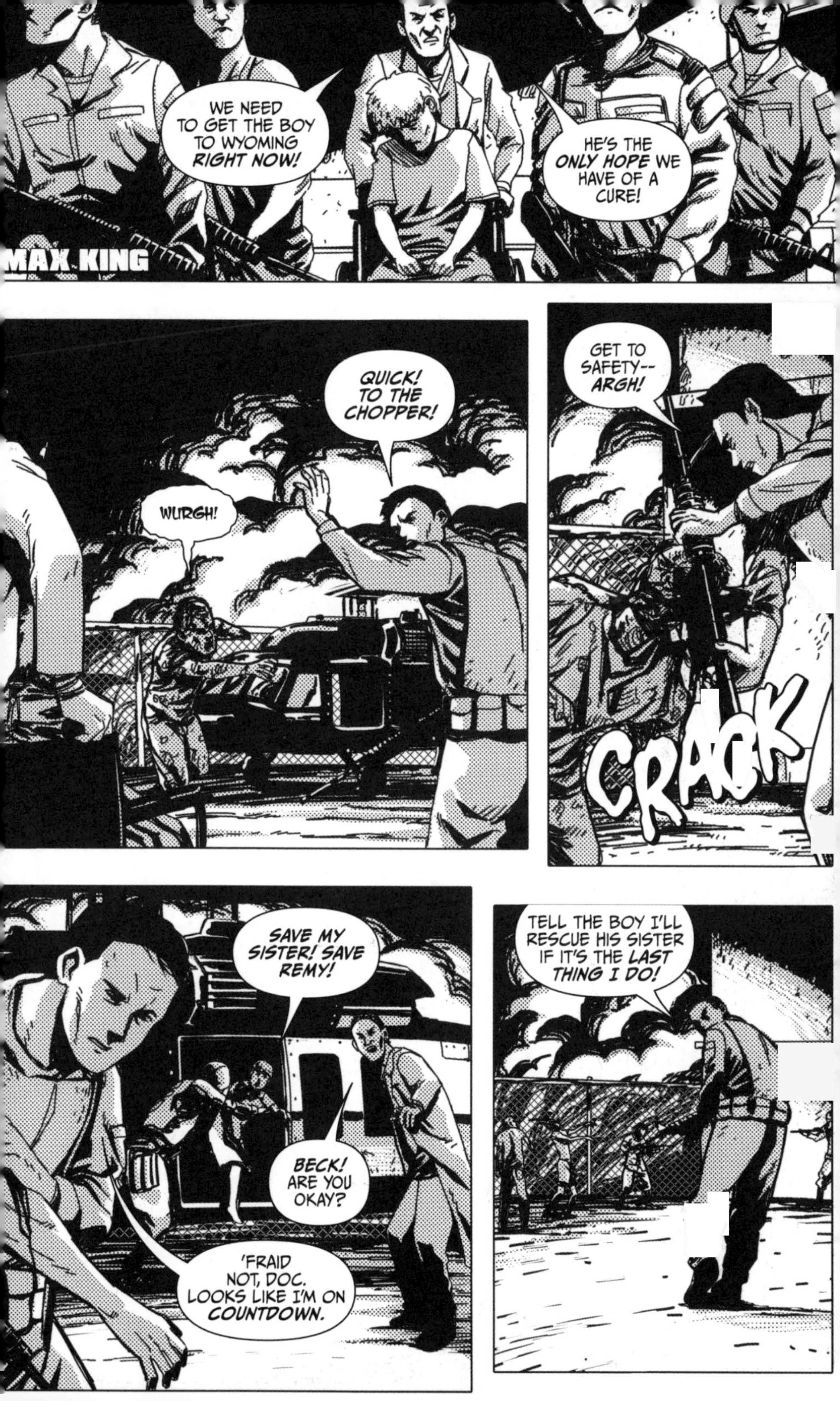
MAX KING
WE NEED TO GET THE BOY TO WYOMING RIGHT NOW!
HE'S THE ONLY HOPE WE HAVE OF A CURE!
QUICK! TO THE CHOPPER!
WURGH!
GET TO SAFETY-- ARGH!
CRACK
SAVE MY SISTER! SAVE REMY!
BECK! ARE YOU OKAY?
'FRAID NOT, DOC. LOOKS LIKE I'M ON COUNTDOWN.
TELL THE BOY I'LL RESCUE HIS SISTER IF IT'S THE LAST THING I DO!

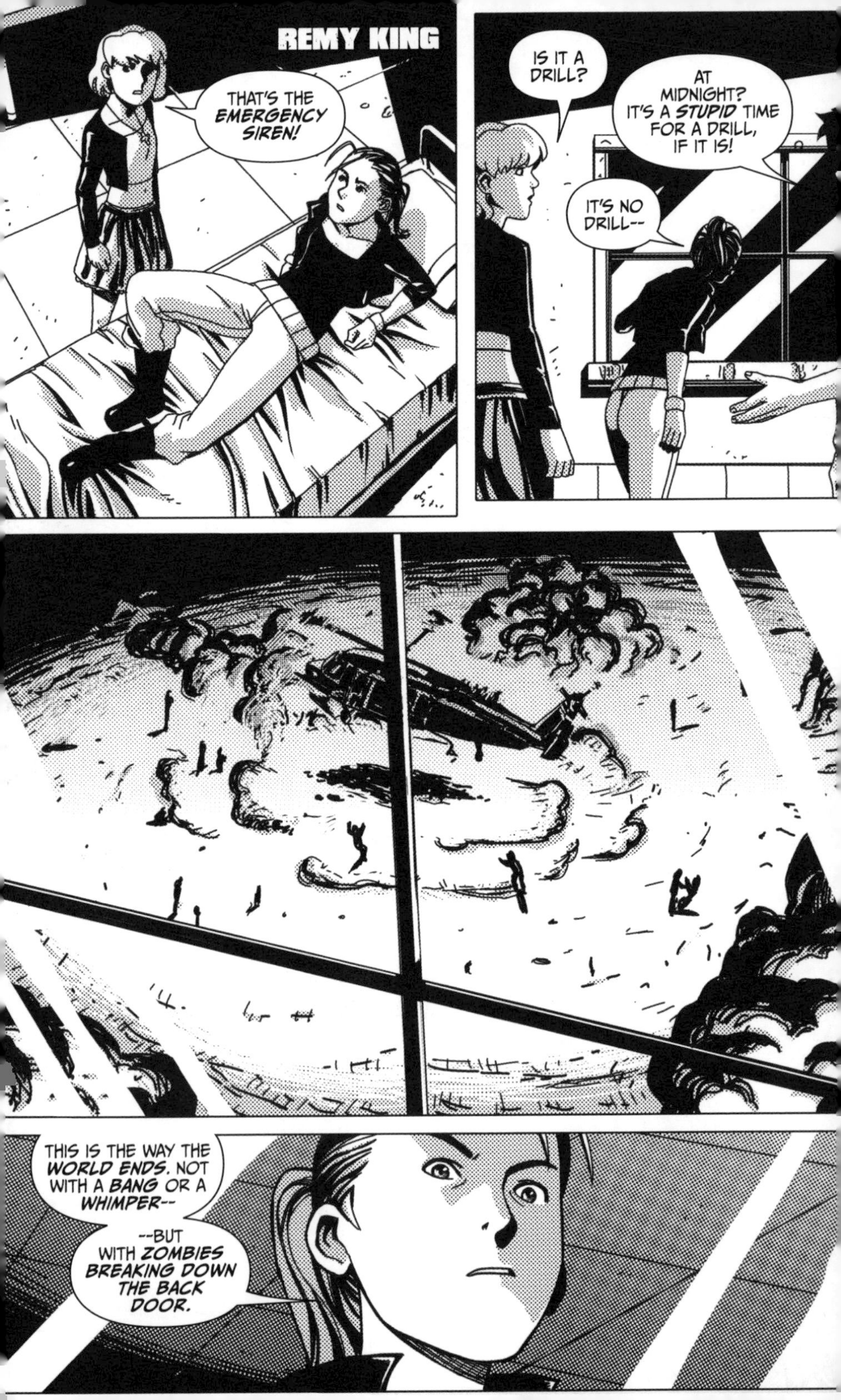
REMY KING
THAT'S THE EMERGENCY SIREN!
IS IT A DRILL?
AT MIDNIGHT? IT'S A STUPID TIME FOR A DRILL, IF IT IS!
IT'S NO DRILL--
THIS IS THE WAY THE WORLD ENDS. NOT WITH A BANG OR A WHIMPER--
--BUT WITH ZOMBIES BREAKING DOWN THE BACK DOOR.

CHAPTER FOUR

FORCED EVICTION

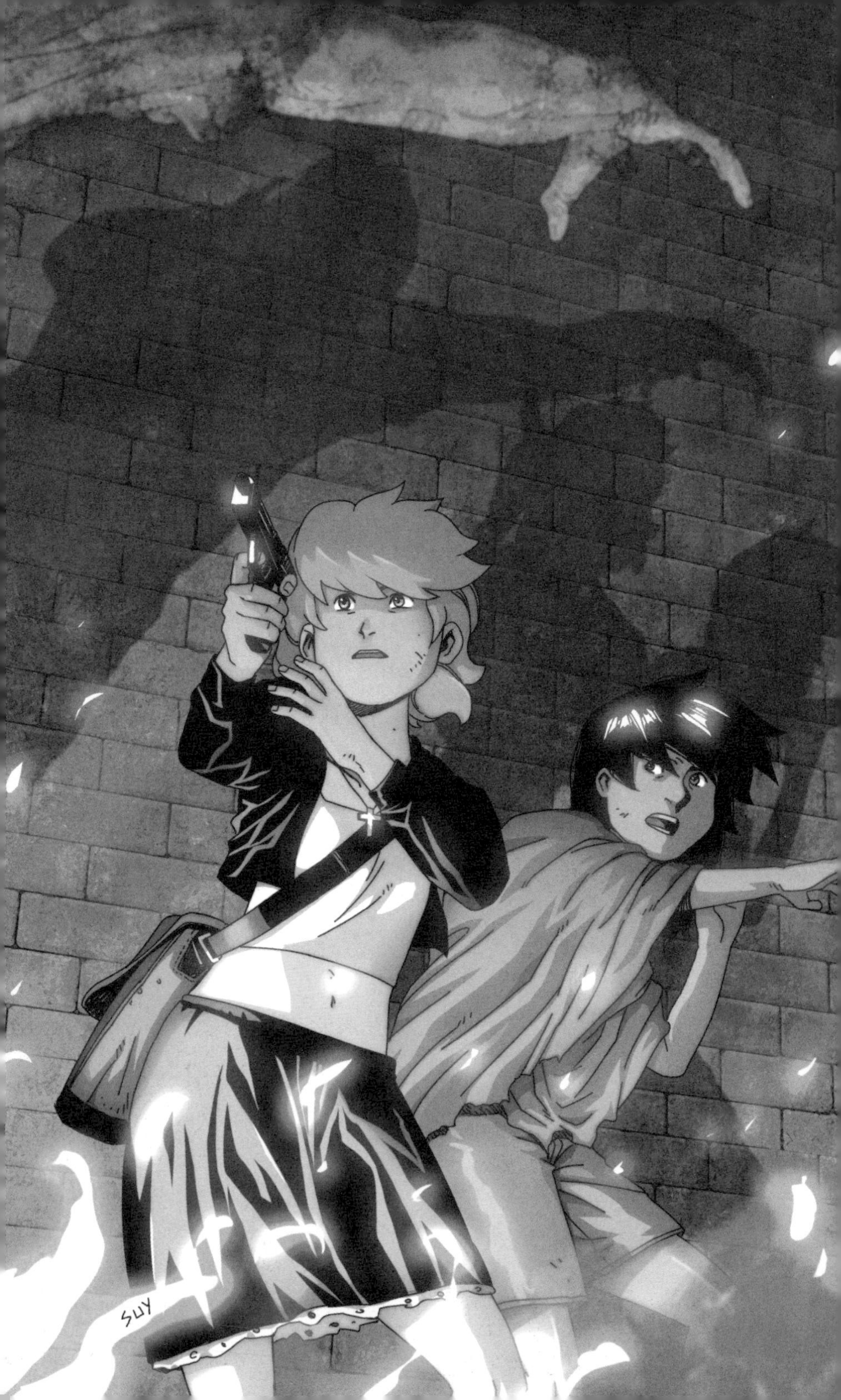
SUY

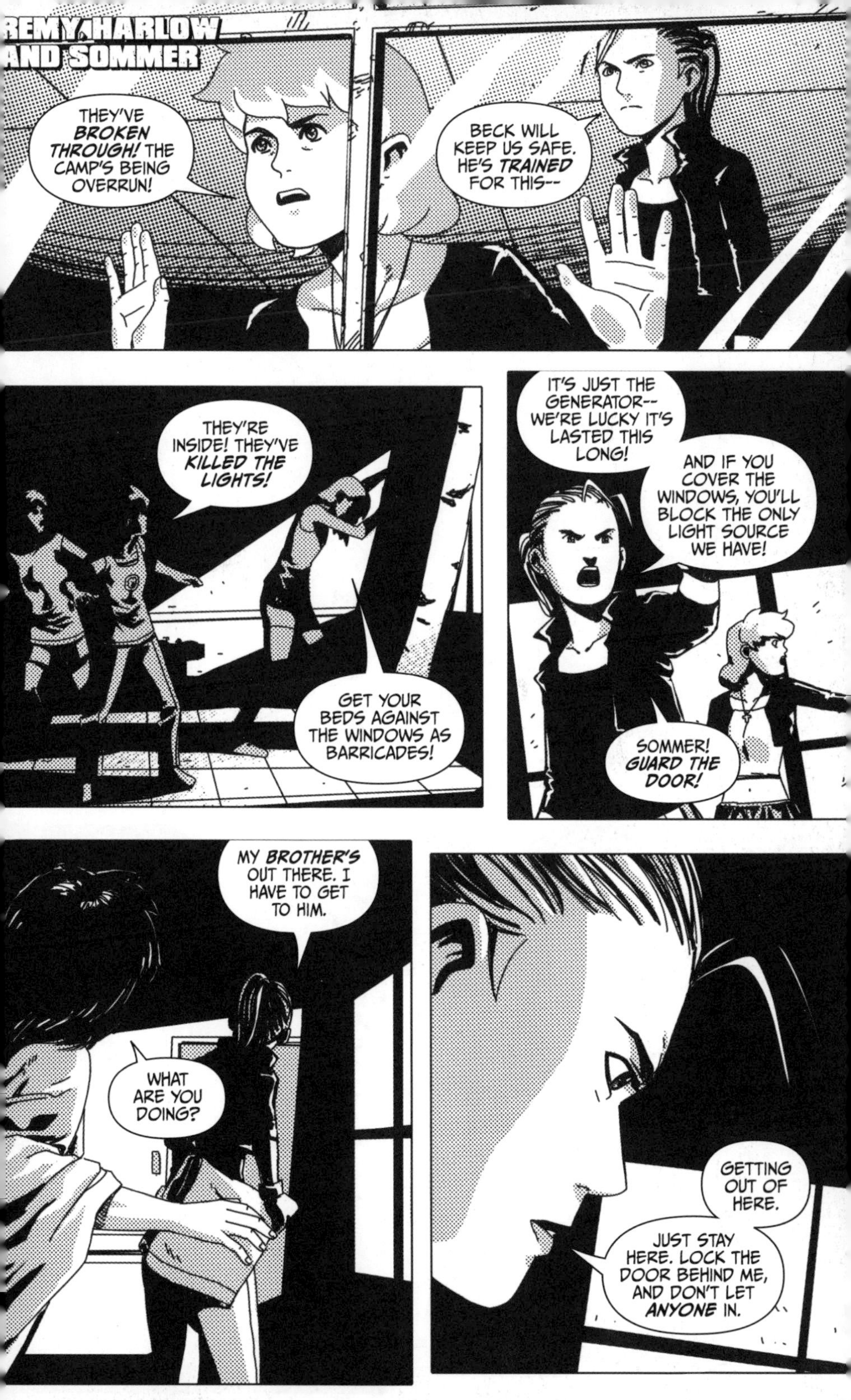
REMY, HARLOW AND SOMMER
THEY'VE BROKEN THROUGH! THE CAMP'S BEING OVERRUN!
BECK WILL KEEP US SAFE. HE'S TRAINED FOR THIS--
THEY'RE INSIDE! THEY'VE KILLED THE LIGHTS!
GET YOUR BEDS AGAINST THE WINDOWS AS BARRICADES!
IT'S JUST THE GENERATOR-- WE'RE LUCKY IT'S LASTED THIS LONG!
AND IF YOU COVER THE WINDOWS, YOU'LL BLOCK THE ONLY LIGHT SOURCE WE HAVE!
SOMMER! GUARD THE DOOR!
MY BROTHER'S OUT THERE. I HAVE TO GET TO HIM.
WHAT ARE YOU DOING?
GETTING OUT OF HERE.
JUST STAY HERE. LOCK THE DOOR BEHIND ME, AND DON'T LET ANYONE IN.

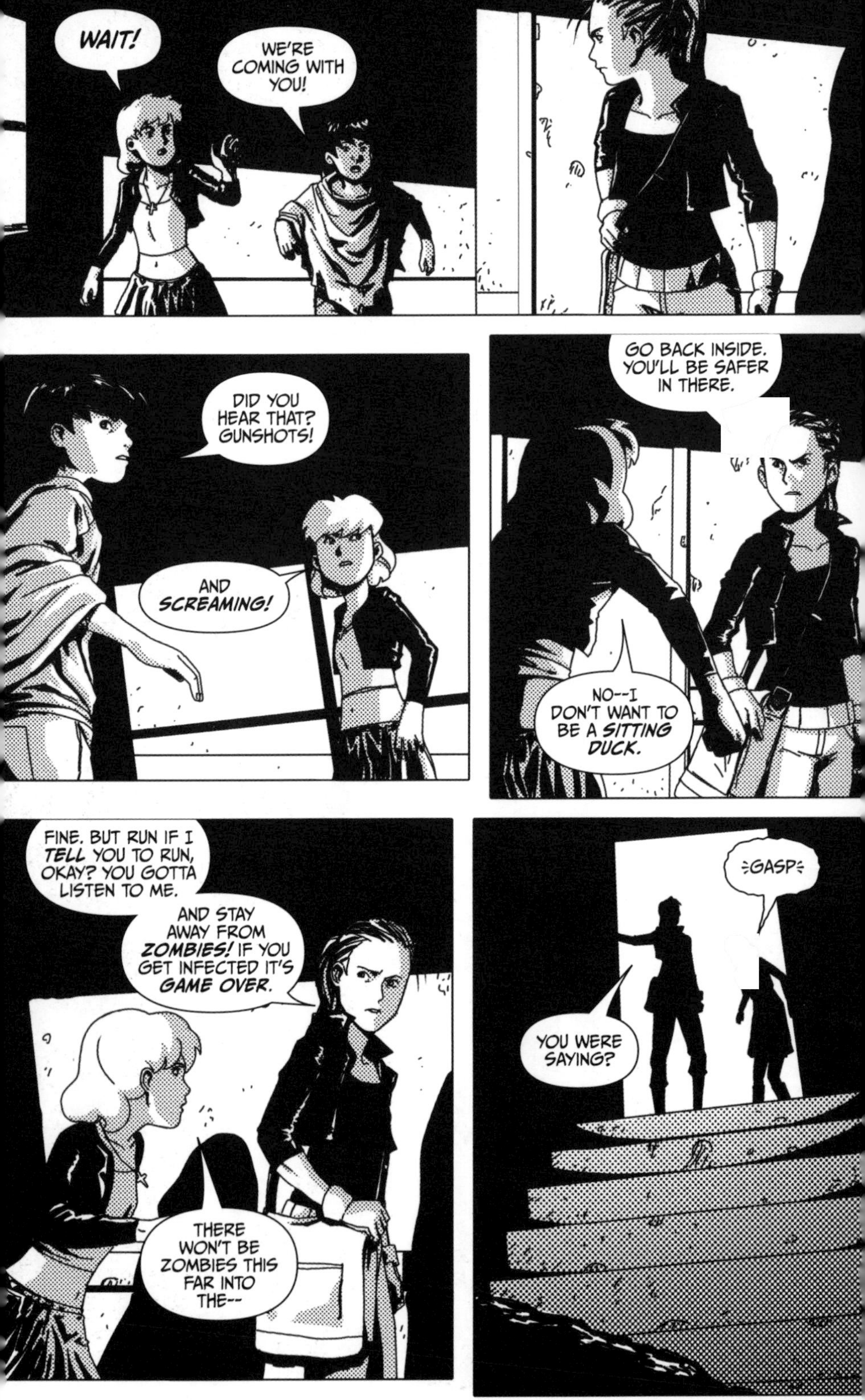
WAIT!
WE'RE COMING WITH YOU!
DID YOU HEAR THAT? GUNSHOTS!
AND SCREAMING!
GO BACK INSIDE. YOU'LL BE SAFER IN THERE.
NO--I DON'T WANT TO BE A SITTING DUCK.
FINE. BUT RUN IF I TELL YOU TO RUN, OKAY? YOU GOTTA LISTEN TO ME.
AND STAY AWAY FROM ZOMBIES! IF YOU GET INFECTED IT'S GAME OVER.
THERE WON'T BE ZOMBIES THIS FAR INTO THE--
GASP
YOU WERE SAYING?

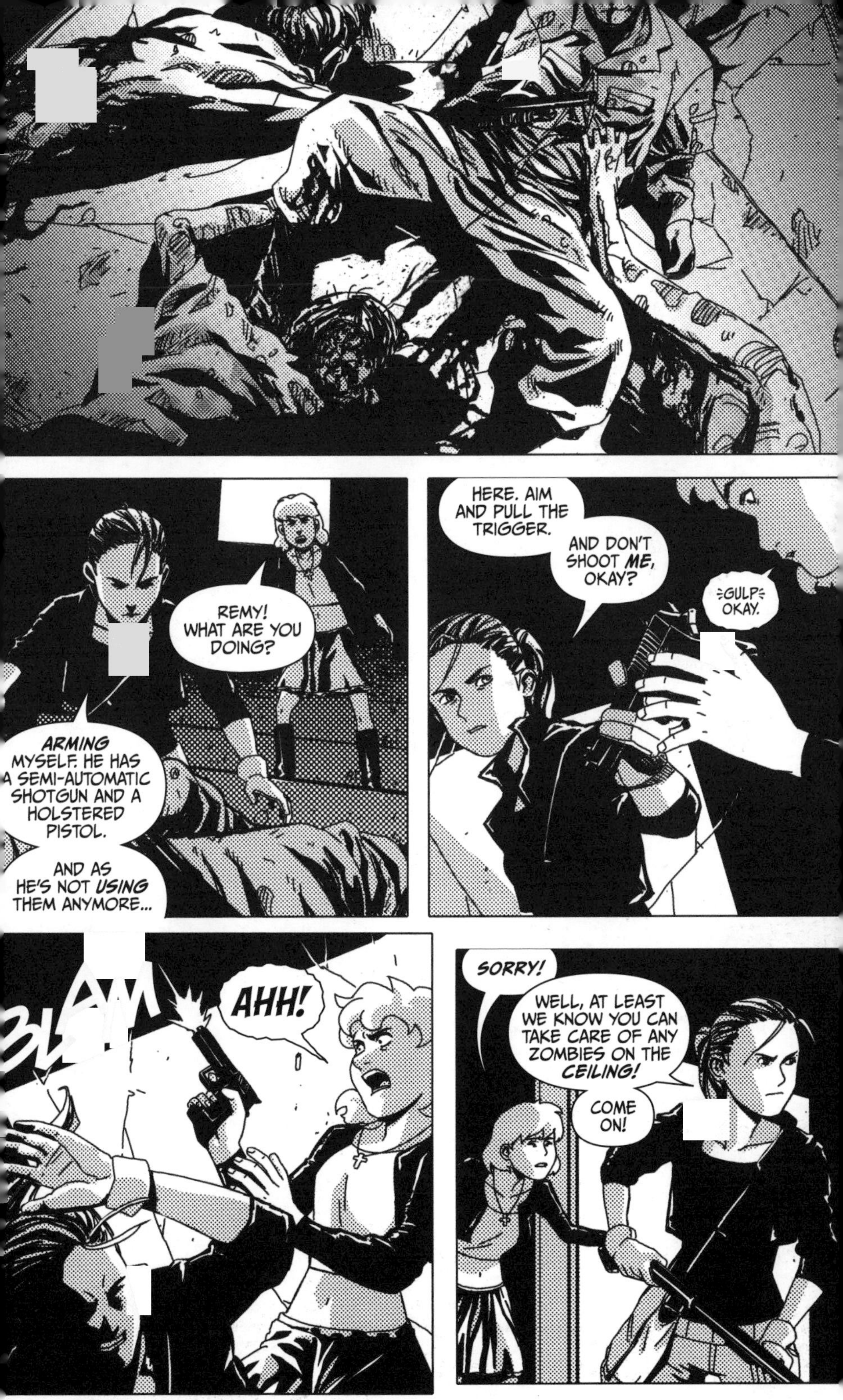

REMY! WHAT ARE YOU DOING?
ARMING MYSELF. HE HAS A SEMI-AUTOMATIC SHOTGUN AND A HOLSTERED PISTOL.
AND AS HE'S NOT *USING* THEM ANYMORE...
HERE. AIM AND PULL THE TRIGGER.
AND DON'T SHOOT *ME*, OKAY?
GULP OKAY.
AHH!
SORRY!
WELL, AT LEAST WE KNOW YOU CAN TAKE CARE OF ANY ZOMBIES ON THE *CEILING*!
COME ON!

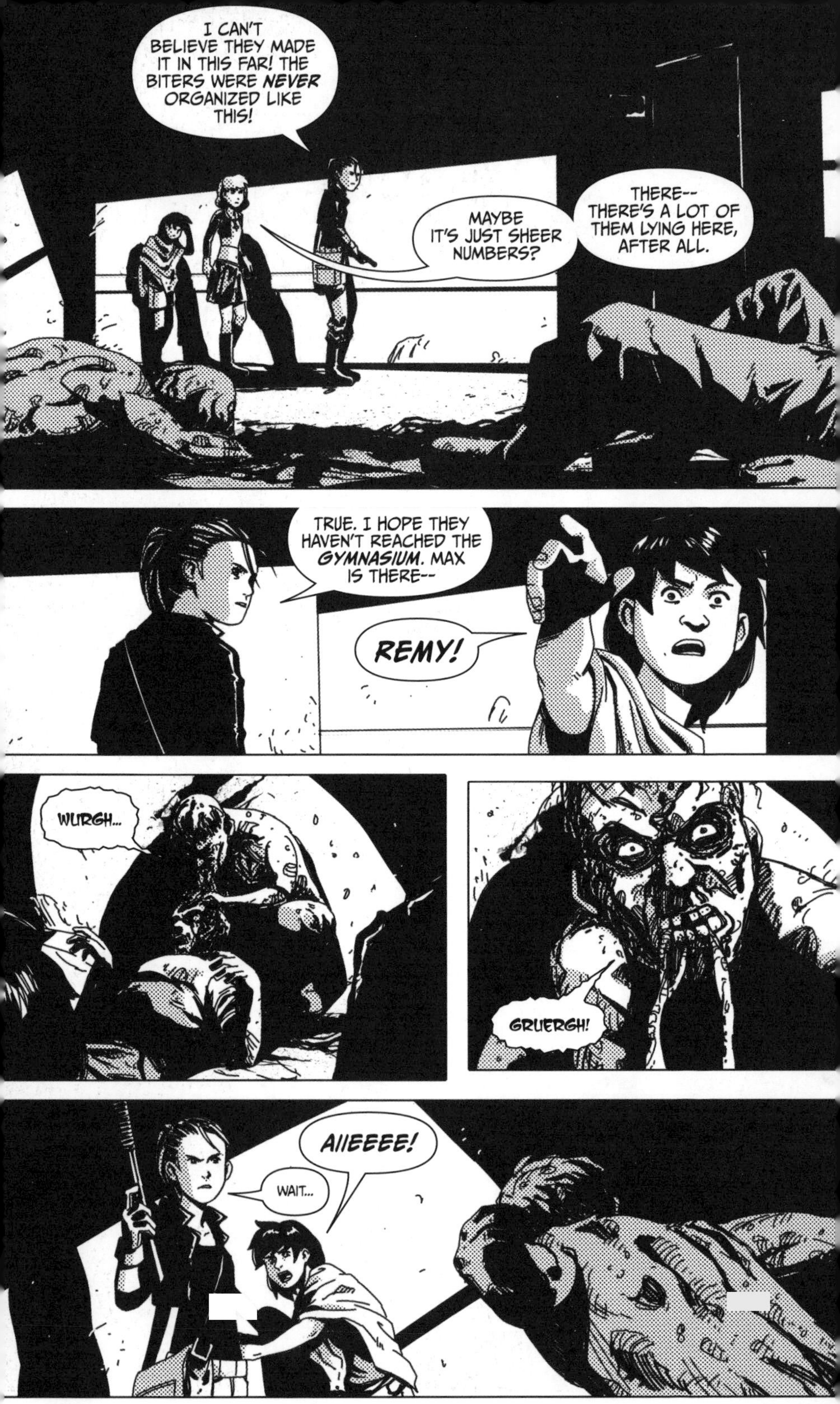
I CAN'T BELIEVE THEY MADE IT IN THIS FAR! THE BITERS WERE *NEVER* ORGANIZED LIKE THIS!
MAYBE IT'S JUST SHEER NUMBERS?
THERE-- THERE'S A LOT OF THEM LYING HERE, AFTER ALL.
TRUE. I HOPE THEY HAVEN'T REACHED THE *GYMNASIUM*. MAX IS THERE--
REMY!
WURGH...
GRUERGH!
WAIT...
AIIEEEE!

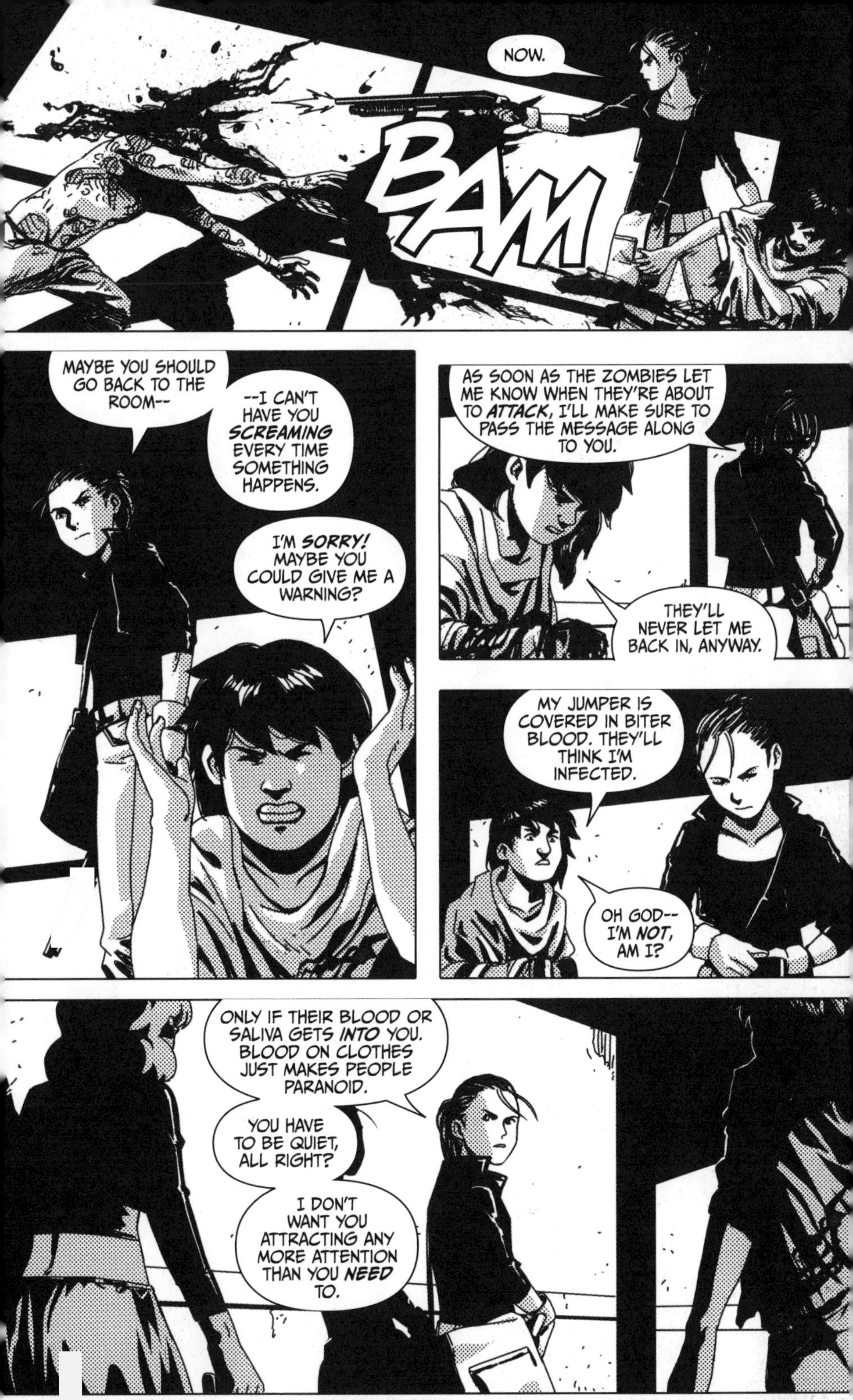
NOW.
BAM
MAYBE YOU SHOULD GO BACK TO THE ROOM--
--I CAN'T HAVE YOU *SCREAMING* EVERY TIME SOMETHING HAPPENS.
I'M *SORRY!* MAYBE YOU COULD GIVE ME A WARNING?
AS SOON AS THE ZOMBIES LET ME KNOW WHEN THEY'RE ABOUT TO *ATTACK*, I'LL MAKE SURE TO PASS THE MESSAGE ALONG TO YOU.
THEY'LL NEVER LET ME BACK IN, ANYWAY.
MY JUMPER IS COVERED IN BITER BLOOD. THEY'LL THINK I'M INFECTED.
OH GOD-- I'M *NOT*, AM I?
ONLY IF THEIR BLOOD OR SALIVA GETS *INTO* YOU. BLOOD ON CLOTHES JUST MAKES PEOPLE PARANOID.
YOU HAVE TO BE QUIET, ALL RIGHT?
I DON'T WANT YOU ATTRACTING ANY MORE ATTENTION THAN YOU *NEED* TO.

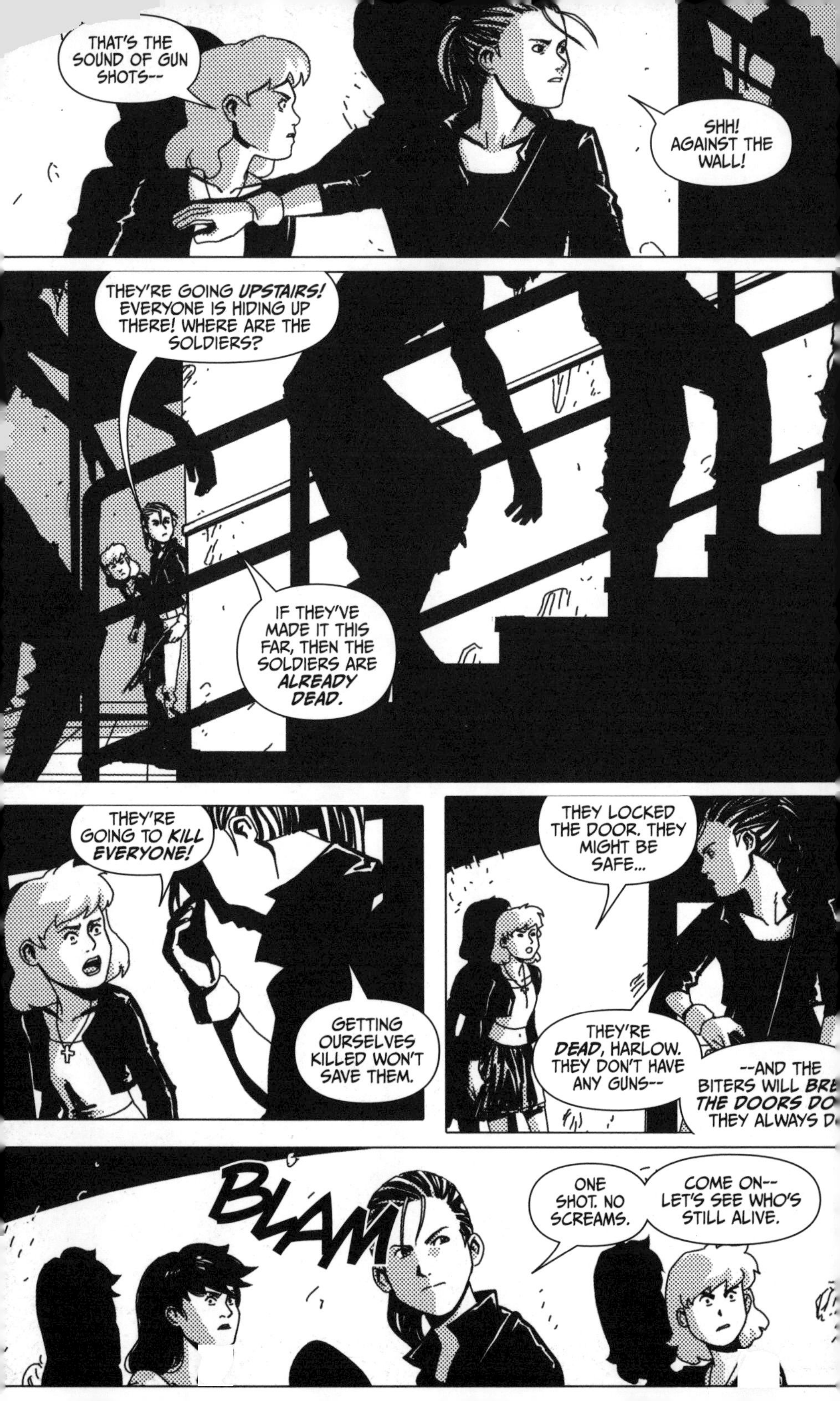
THAT'S THE SOUND OF GUN SHOTS--
SHH! AGAINST THE WALL!
THEY'RE GOING *UPSTAIRS!* EVERYONE IS HIDING UP THERE! WHERE ARE THE SOLDIERS?
IF THEY'VE MADE IT THIS FAR, THEN THE SOLDIERS ARE ***ALREADY DEAD.***
THEY'RE GOING TO ***KILL EVERYONE!***
GETTING OURSELVES KILLED WON'T SAVE THEM.
THEY LOCKED THE DOOR. THEY MIGHT BE SAFE...
THEY'RE ***DEAD,*** HARLOW. THEY DON'T HAVE ANY GUNS--
BLAM
ONE SHOT. NO SCREAMS.
COME ON-- LET'S SEE WHO'S STILL ALIVE.

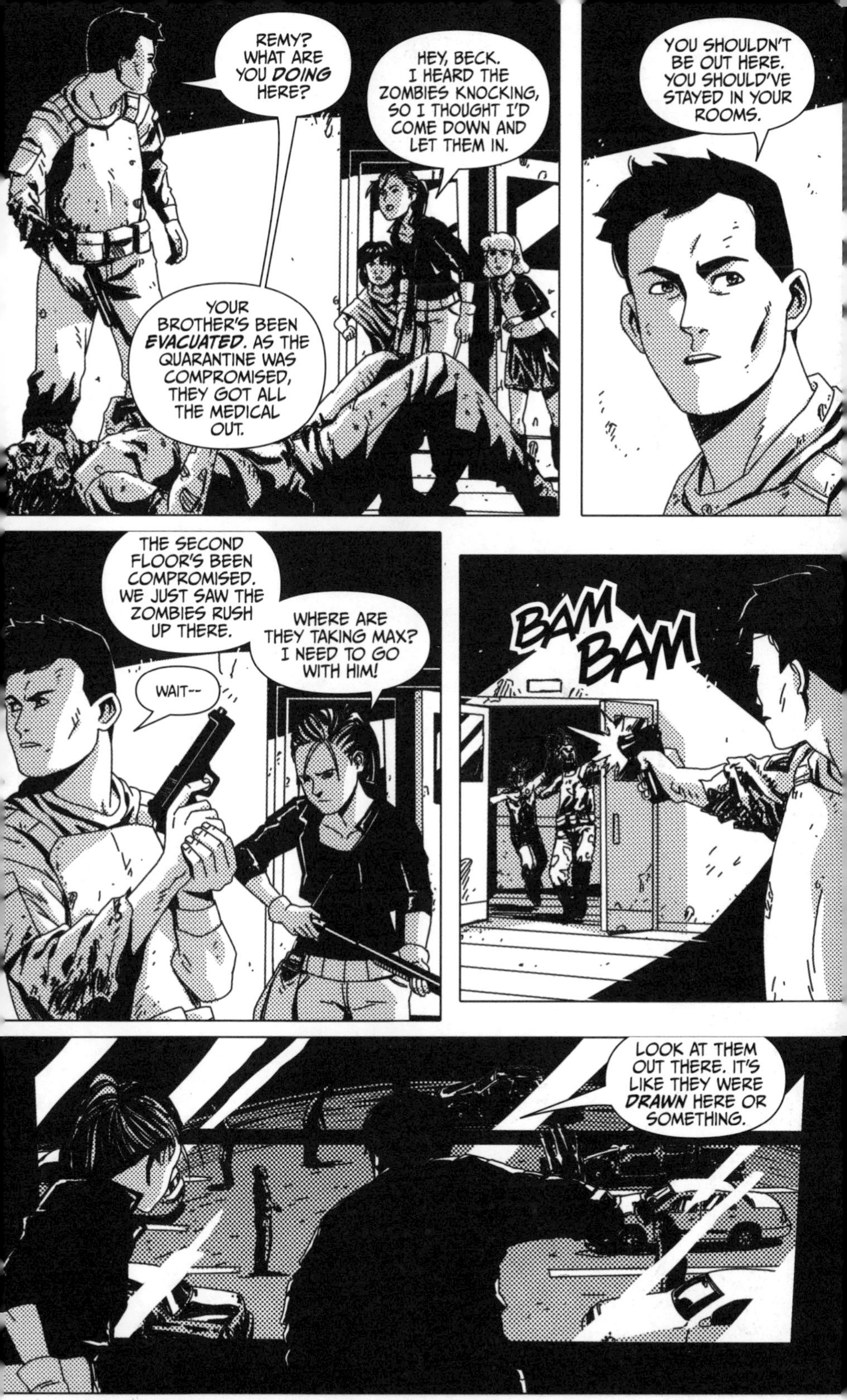
REMY? WHAT ARE YOU *DOING* HERE?
HEY, BECK. I HEARD THE ZOMBIES KNOCKING, SO I THOUGHT I'D COME DOWN AND LET THEM IN.
YOUR BROTHER'S BEEN *EVACUATED*. AS THE QUARANTINE WAS COMPROMISED, THEY GOT ALL THE MEDICAL OUT.
YOU SHOULDN'T BE OUT HERE. YOU SHOULD'VE STAYED IN YOUR ROOMS.
THE SECOND FLOOR'S BEEN COMPROMISED. WE JUST SAW THE ZOMBIES RUSH UP THERE.
WAIT--
WHERE ARE THEY TAKING MAX? I NEED TO GO WITH HIM!
BAM
BAM
LOOK AT THEM OUT THERE. IT'S LIKE THEY WERE *DRAWN* HERE OR SOMETHING.

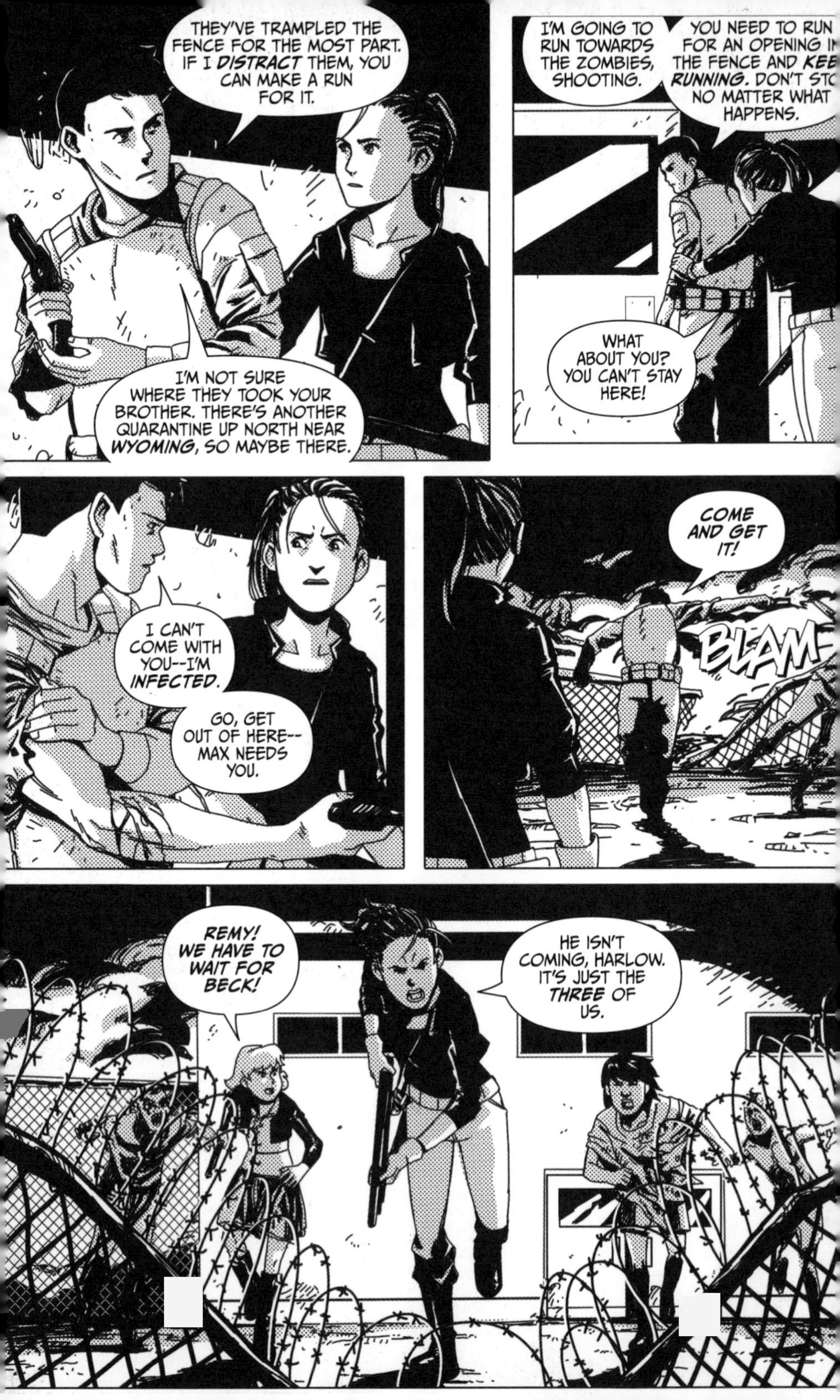
THEY'VE TRAMPLED THE FENCE FOR THE MOST PART. IF I *DISTRACT* THEM, YOU CAN MAKE A RUN FOR IT.
I'M NOT SURE WHERE THEY TOOK YOUR BROTHER. THERE'S ANOTHER QUARANTINE UP NORTH NEAR *WYOMING*, SO MAYBE THERE.
I'M GOING TO RUN TOWARDS THE ZOMBIES, SHOOTING.
YOU NEED TO RUN FOR AN OPENING IN THE FENCE AND *KEEP RUNNING.* DON'T STOP NO MATTER WHAT HAPPENS.
WHAT ABOUT YOU? YOU CAN'T STAY HERE!
I CAN'T COME WITH YOU--I'M *INFECTED.*
GO, GET OUT OF HERE-- MAX NEEDS YOU.
COME AND GET IT!
BLAM
REMY! WE HAVE TO WAIT FOR BECK!
HE ISN'T COMING, HARLOW. IT'S JUST THE *THREE* OF US.

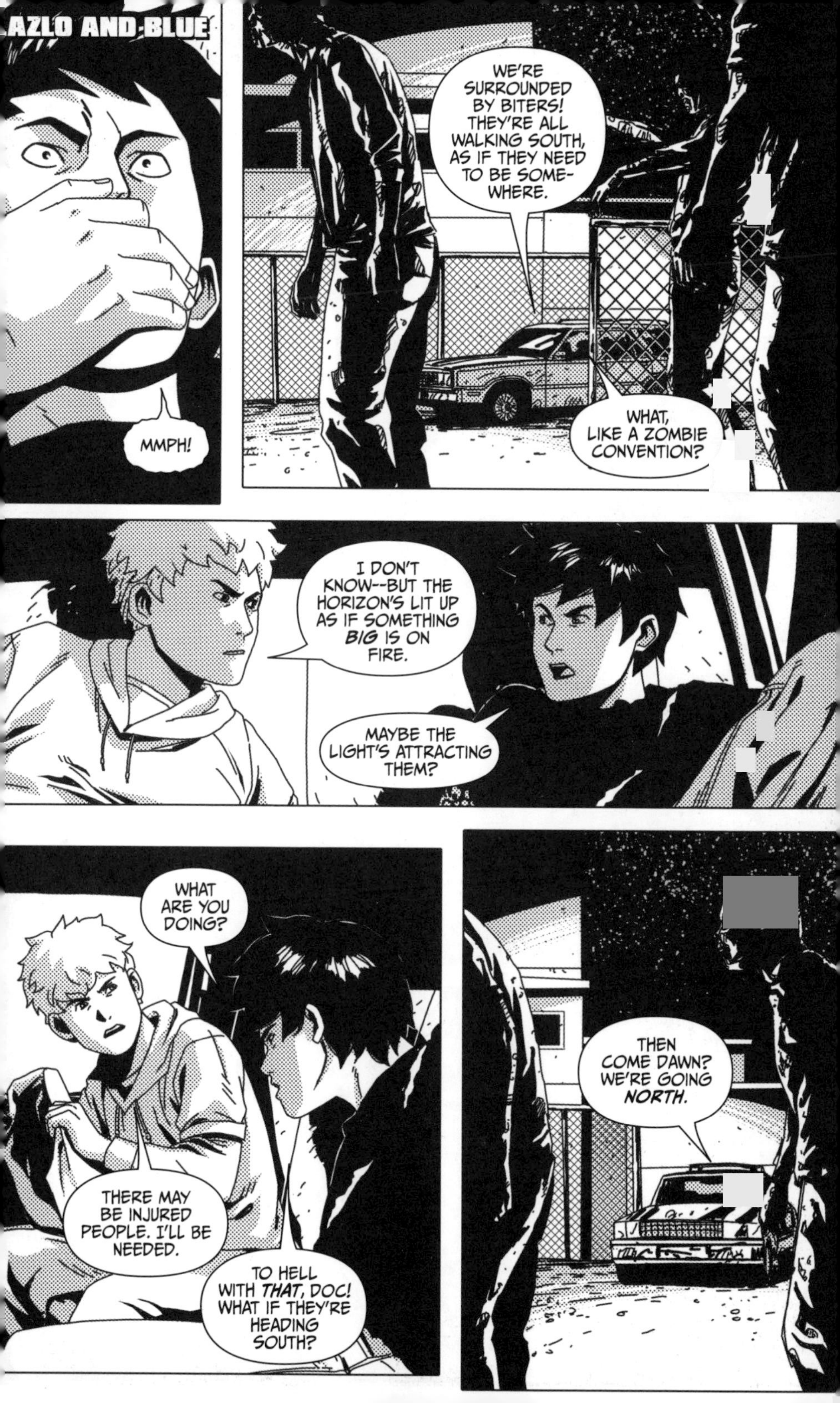
MMPH!
WE'RE SURROUNDED BY BITERS! THEY'RE ALL WALKING SOUTH, AS IF THEY NEED TO BE SOME-WHERE.
WHAT, LIKE A ZOMBIE CONVENTION?
I DON'T KNOW--BUT THE HORIZON'S LIT UP AS IF SOMETHING *BIG* IS ON FIRE.
MAYBE THE LIGHT'S ATTRACTING THEM?
WHAT ARE YOU DOING?
THERE MAY BE INJURED PEOPLE. I'LL BE NEEDED.
TO HELL WITH *THAT*, DOC! WHAT IF THEY'RE HEADING SOUTH?
THEN COME DAWN? WE'RE GOING *NORTH*.

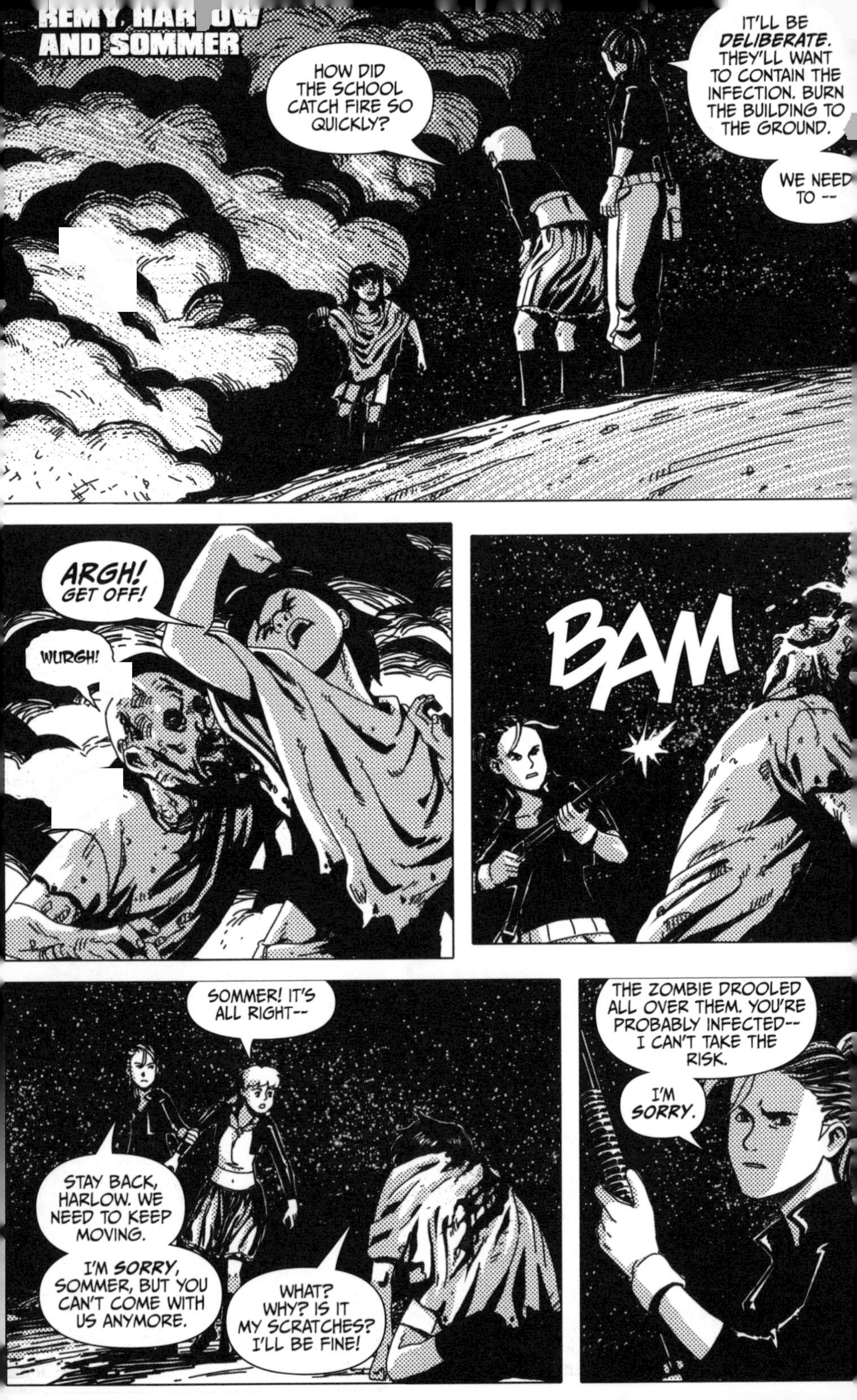

AND SOMMER
HOW DID THE SCHOOL CATCH FIRE SO QUICKLY?
IT'LL BE *DELIBERATE*. THEY'LL WANT TO CONTAIN THE INFECTION. BURN THE BUILDING TO THE GROUND.
WE NEED TO --
ARGH! GET OFF!
WURGH!
BAM
SOMMER! IT'S ALL RIGHT--
STAY BACK, HARLOW. WE NEED TO KEEP MOVING.
I'M *SORRY*, SOMMER, BUT YOU CAN'T COME WITH US ANYMORE.
WHAT? WHY? IS IT MY SCRATCHES? I'LL BE FINE!
THE ZOMBIE DROOLED ALL OVER THEM. YOU'RE PROBABLY INFECTED-- I CAN'T TAKE THE RISK.
I'M *SORRY*.

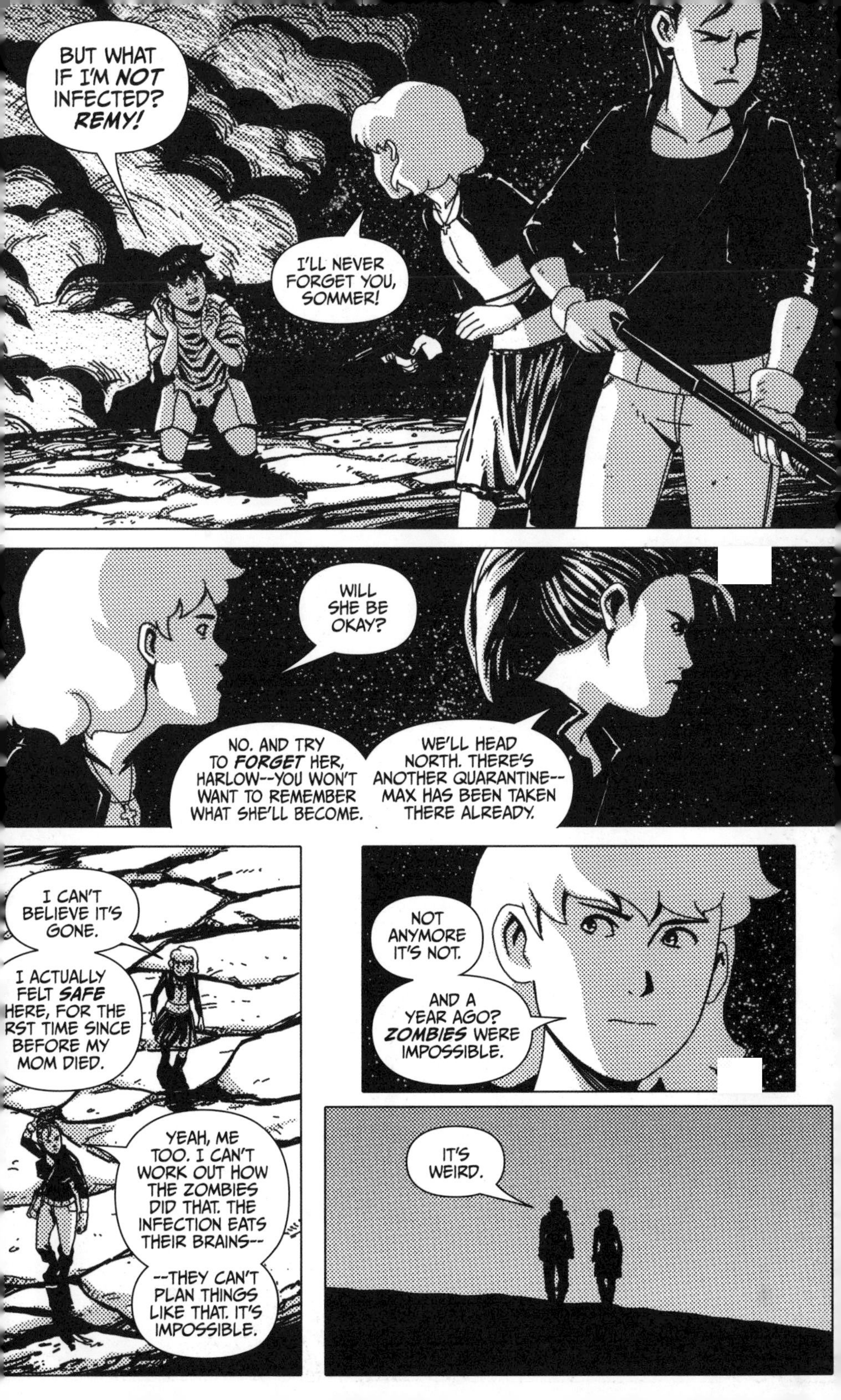
BUT WHAT IF I'M NOT INFECTED? REMY!
I'LL NEVER FORGET YOU, SOMMER!
WILL SHE BE OKAY?
NO. AND TRY TO FORGET HER, HARLOW--YOU WON'T WANT TO REMEMBER WHAT SHE'LL BECOME.
WE'LL HEAD NORTH. THERE'S ANOTHER QUARANTINE--MAX HAS BEEN TAKEN THERE ALREADY.
I CAN'T BELIEVE IT'S GONE.
I ACTUALLY FELT SAFE HERE, FOR THE RST TIME SINCE BEFORE MY MOM DIED.
YEAH, ME TOO. I CAN'T WORK OUT HOW THE ZOMBIES DID THAT. THE INFECTION EATS THEIR BRAINS--
--THEY CAN'T PLAN THINGS LIKE THAT. IT'S IMPOSSIBLE.
NOT ANYMORE IT'S NOT.
AND A YEAR AGO? ZOMBIES WERE IMPOSSIBLE.
IT'S WEIRD.

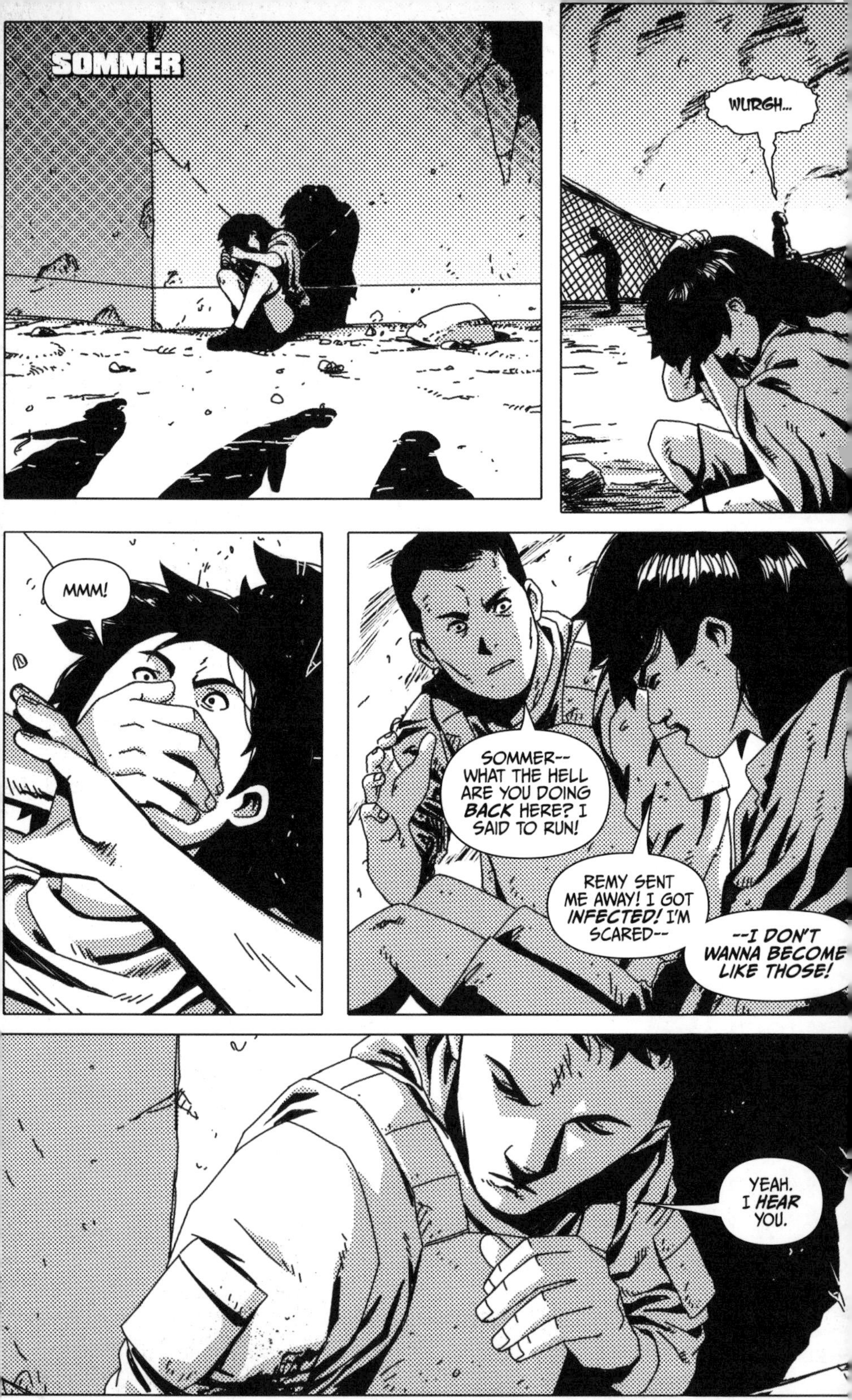
SOMMER
WURGH...
MMM!
SOMMER-- WHAT THE HELL ARE YOU DOING BACK HERE? I SAID TO RUN!
REMY SENT ME AWAY! I GOT INFECTED! I'M SCARED--
--I DON'T WANNA BECOME LIKE THOSE!
YEAH. I HEAR YOU.

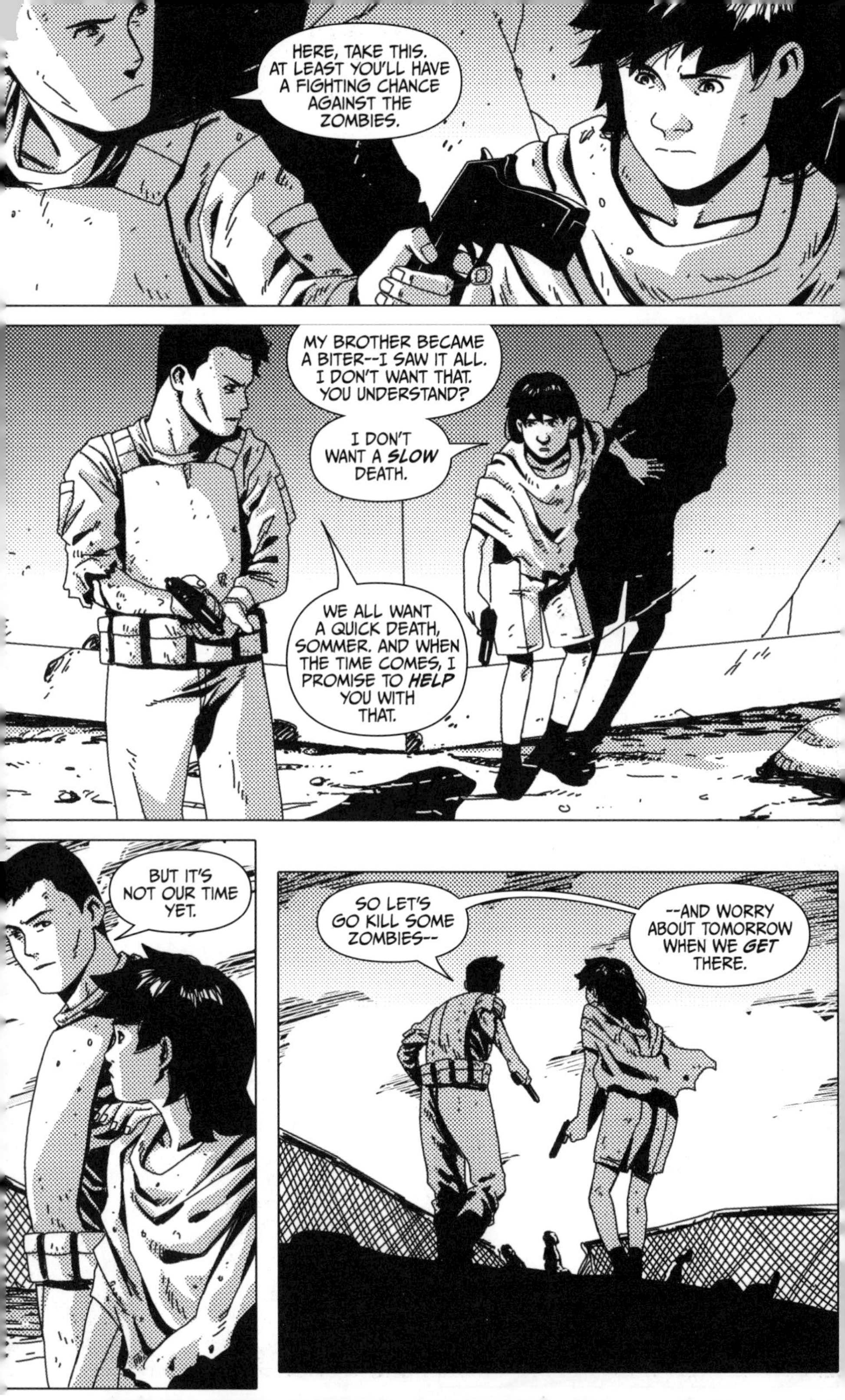
HERE, TAKE THIS. AT LEAST YOU'LL HAVE A FIGHTING CHANCE AGAINST THE ZOMBIES.
MY BROTHER BECAME A BITER--I SAW IT ALL. I DON'T WANT THAT. YOU UNDERSTAND?
I DON'T WANT A *SLOW* DEATH.
WE ALL WANT A QUICK DEATH, SOMMER. AND WHEN THE TIME COMES, I PROMISE TO *HELP* YOU WITH THAT.
BUT IT'S NOT OUR TIME YET.
SO LET'S GO KILL SOME ZOMBIES--
--AND WORRY ABOUT TOMORROW WHEN WE *GET* THERE.

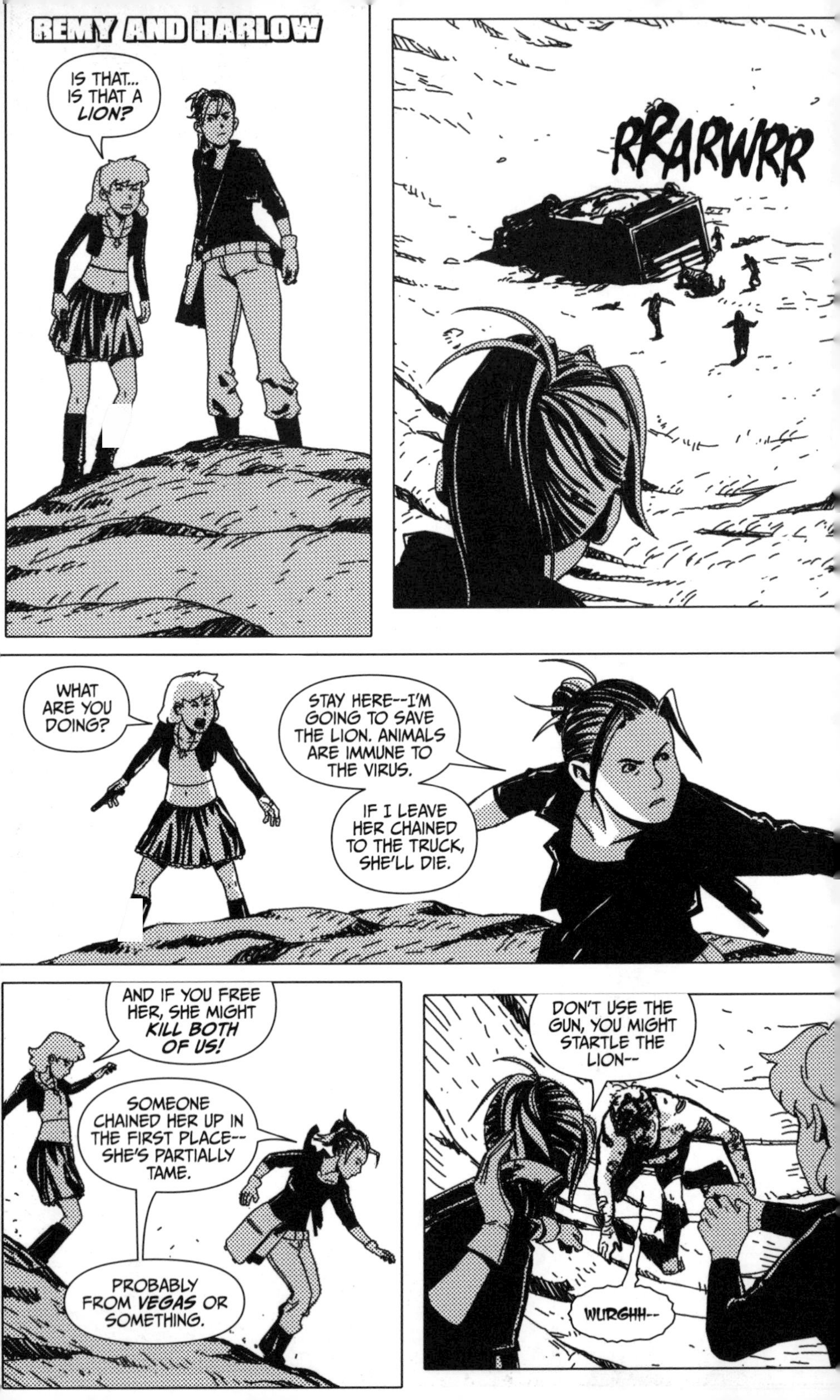
REMY AND HARLOW
IS THAT... IS THAT A LION?
RRARWRR
WHAT ARE YOU DOING?
STAY HERE--I'M GOING TO SAVE THE LION. ANIMALS ARE IMMUNE TO THE VIRUS.
IF I LEAVE HER CHAINED TO THE TRUCK, SHE'LL DIE.
AND IF YOU FREE HER, SHE MIGHT KILL BOTH OF US!
SOMEONE CHAINED HER UP IN THE FIRST PLACE--SHE'S PARTIALLY TAME.
PROBABLY FROM VEGAS OR SOMETHING.
DON'T USE THE GUN, YOU MIGHT STARTLE THE LION--
WURGHH--

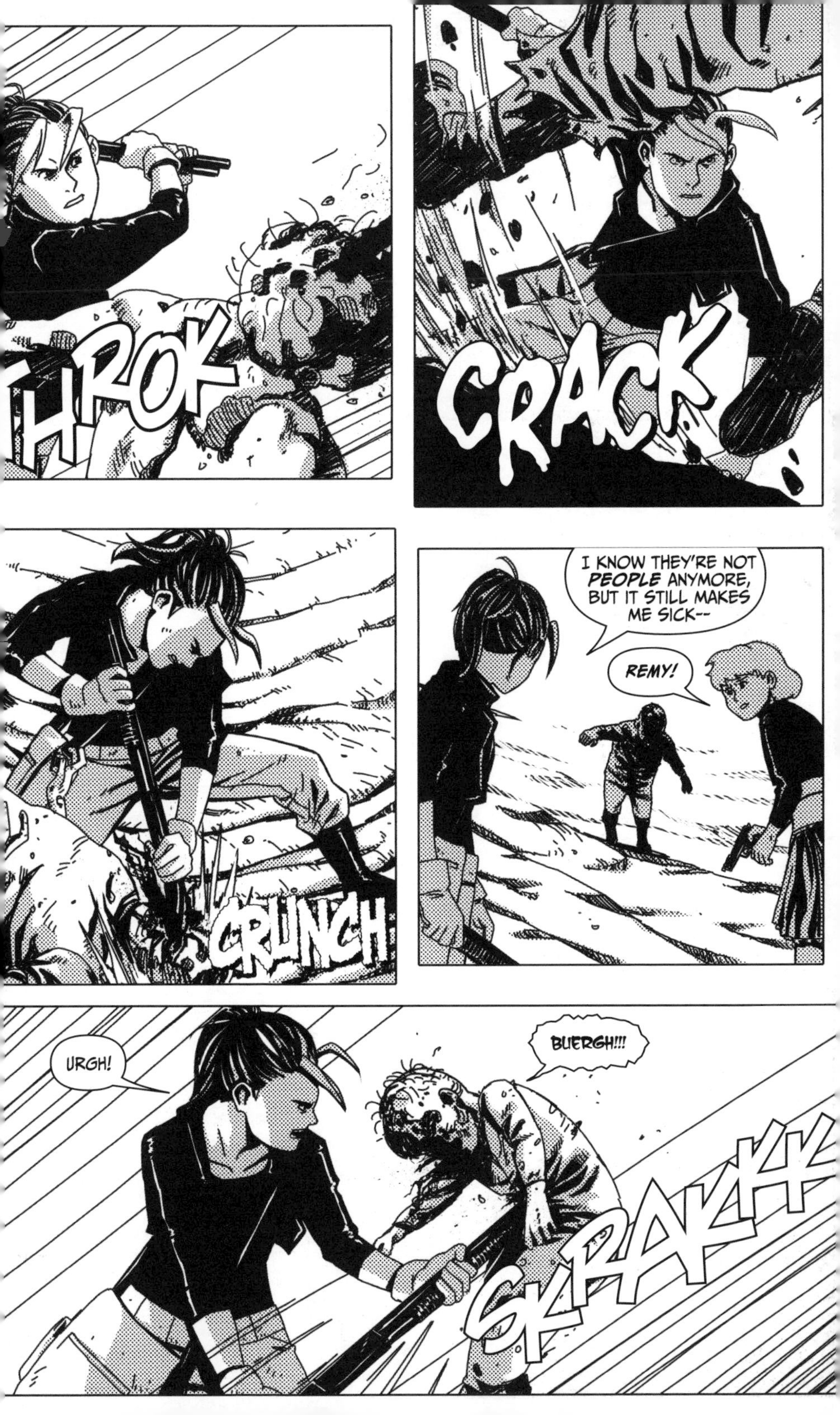

THROK
CRACK
CRUNCH
I KNOW THEY'RE NOT *PEOPLE* ANYMORE, BUT IT STILL MAKES ME SICK--
REMY!
URGH!
BUERGH!!!
SKRAKK

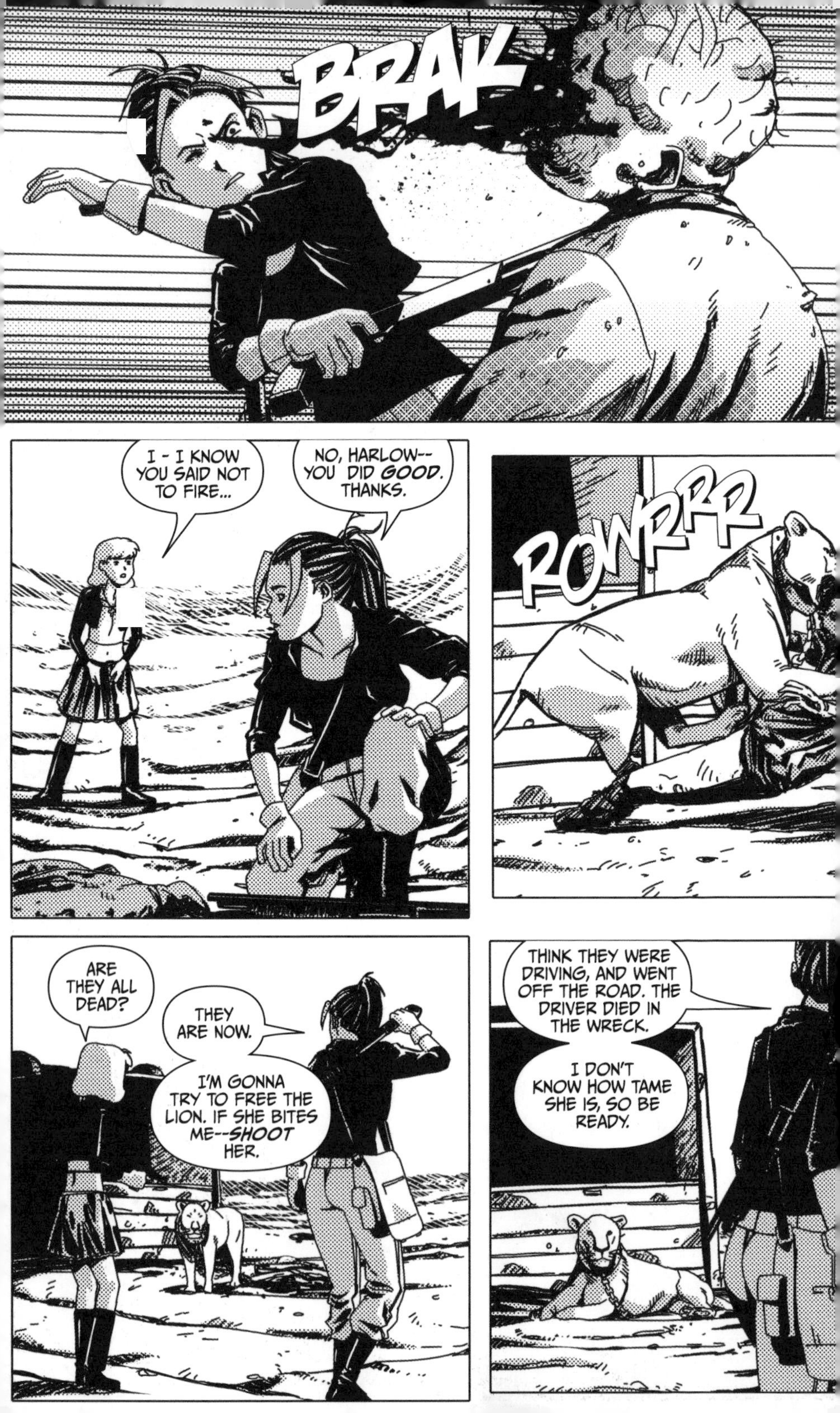
BRAK
I - I KNOW YOU SAID NOT TO FIRE...
NO, HARLOW-- YOU DID *GOOD*. THANKS.
ROWRRR
ARE THEY ALL DEAD?
THEY ARE NOW.
I'M GONNA TRY TO FREE THE LION. IF SHE BITES ME--*SHOOT* HER.
THINK THEY WERE DRIVING, AND WENT OFF THE ROAD. THE DRIVER DIED IN THE WRECK.
I DON'T KNOW HOW TAME SHE IS, SO BE READY.

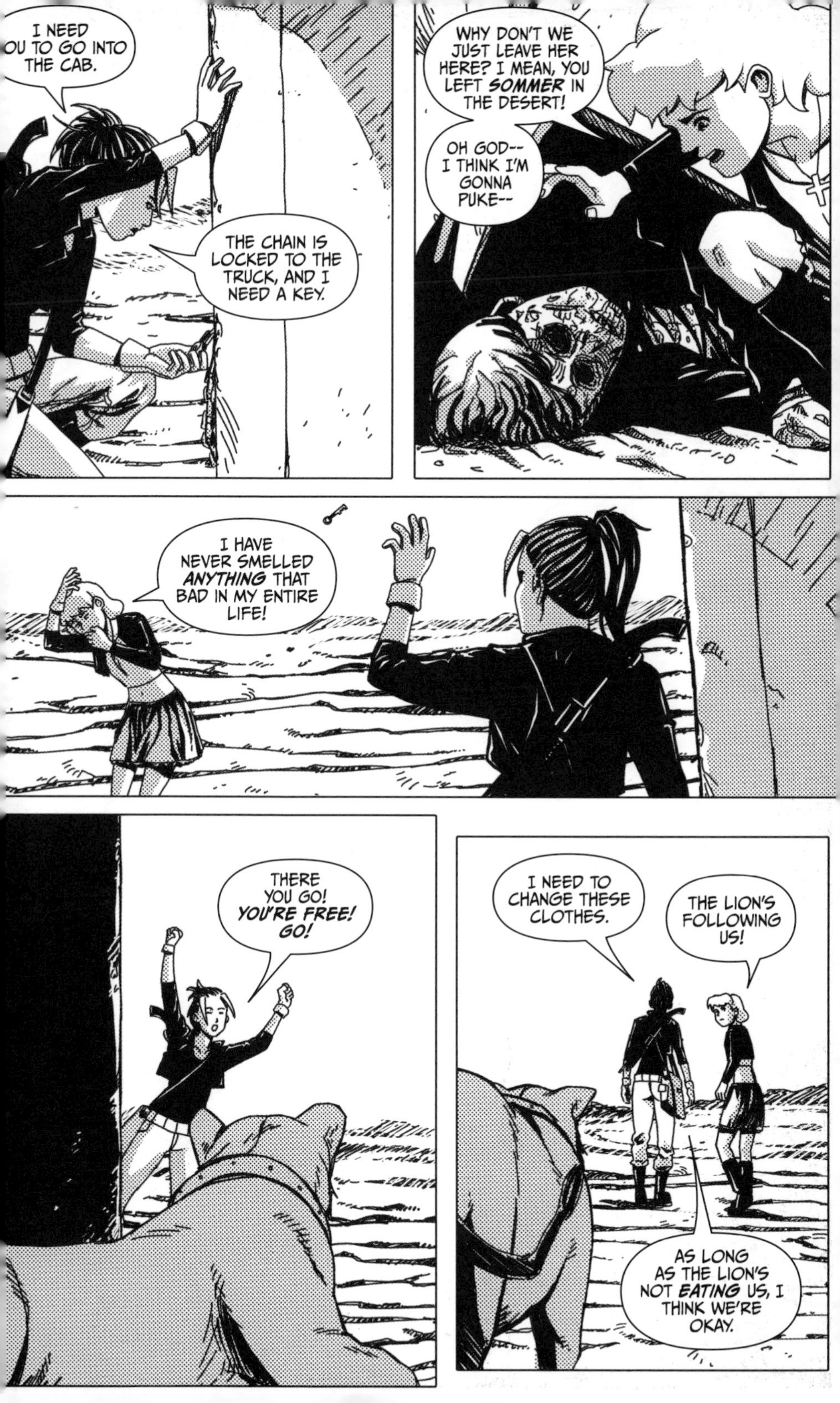

I NEED OU TO GO INTO THE CAB.
THE CHAIN IS LOCKED TO THE TRUCK, AND I NEED A KEY.
WHY DON'T WE JUST LEAVE HER HERE? I MEAN, YOU LEFT **SOMMER** IN THE DESERT!
OH GOD-- I THINK I'M GONNA PUKE--
I HAVE NEVER SMELLED **ANYTHING** THAT BAD IN MY ENTIRE LIFE!
THERE YOU GO! **YOU'RE FREE! GO!**
I NEED TO CHANGE THESE CLOTHES.
THE LION'S FOLLOWING US!
AS LONG AS THE LION'S NOT **EATING** US, I THINK WE'RE OKAY.

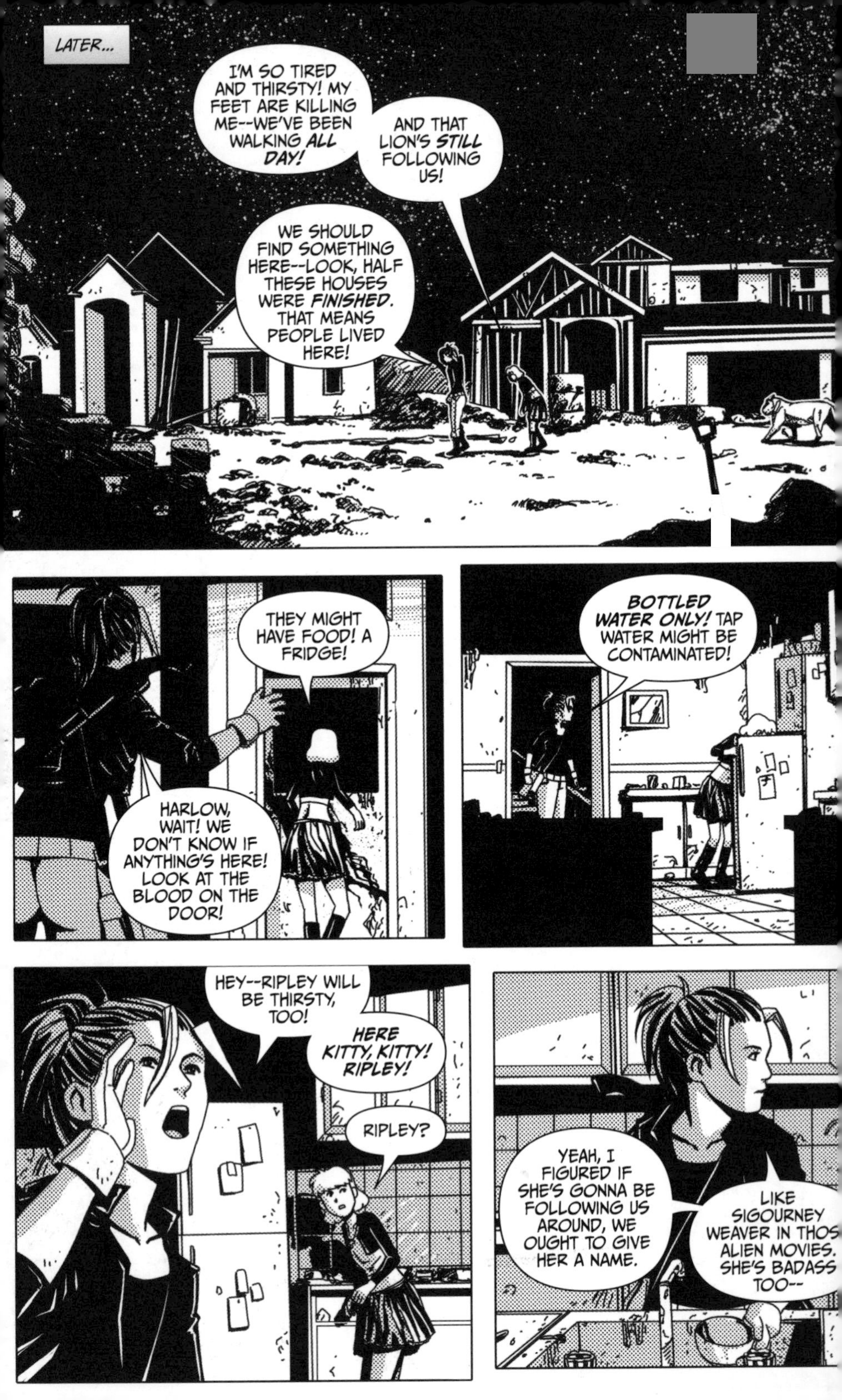
LATER...
I'M SO TIRED AND THIRSTY! MY FEET ARE KILLING ME--WE'VE BEEN WALKING ALL DAY!
AND THAT LION'S STILL FOLLOWING US!
WE SHOULD FIND SOMETHING HERE--LOOK, HALF THESE HOUSES WERE FINISHED. THAT MEANS PEOPLE LIVED HERE!
THEY MIGHT HAVE FOOD! A FRIDGE!
HARLOW, WAIT! WE DON'T KNOW IF ANYTHING'S HERE! LOOK AT THE BLOOD ON THE DOOR!
BOTTLED WATER ONLY! TAP WATER MIGHT BE CONTAMINATED!
HEY--RIPLEY WILL BE THIRSTY, TOO!
HERE KITTY, KITTY! RIPLEY!
RIPLEY?
YEAH, I FIGURED IF SHE'S GONNA BE FOLLOWING US AROUND, WE OUGHT TO GIVE HER A NAME.
LIKE SIGOURNEY WEAVER IN THOS ALIEN MOVIES. SHE'S BADASS TOO--

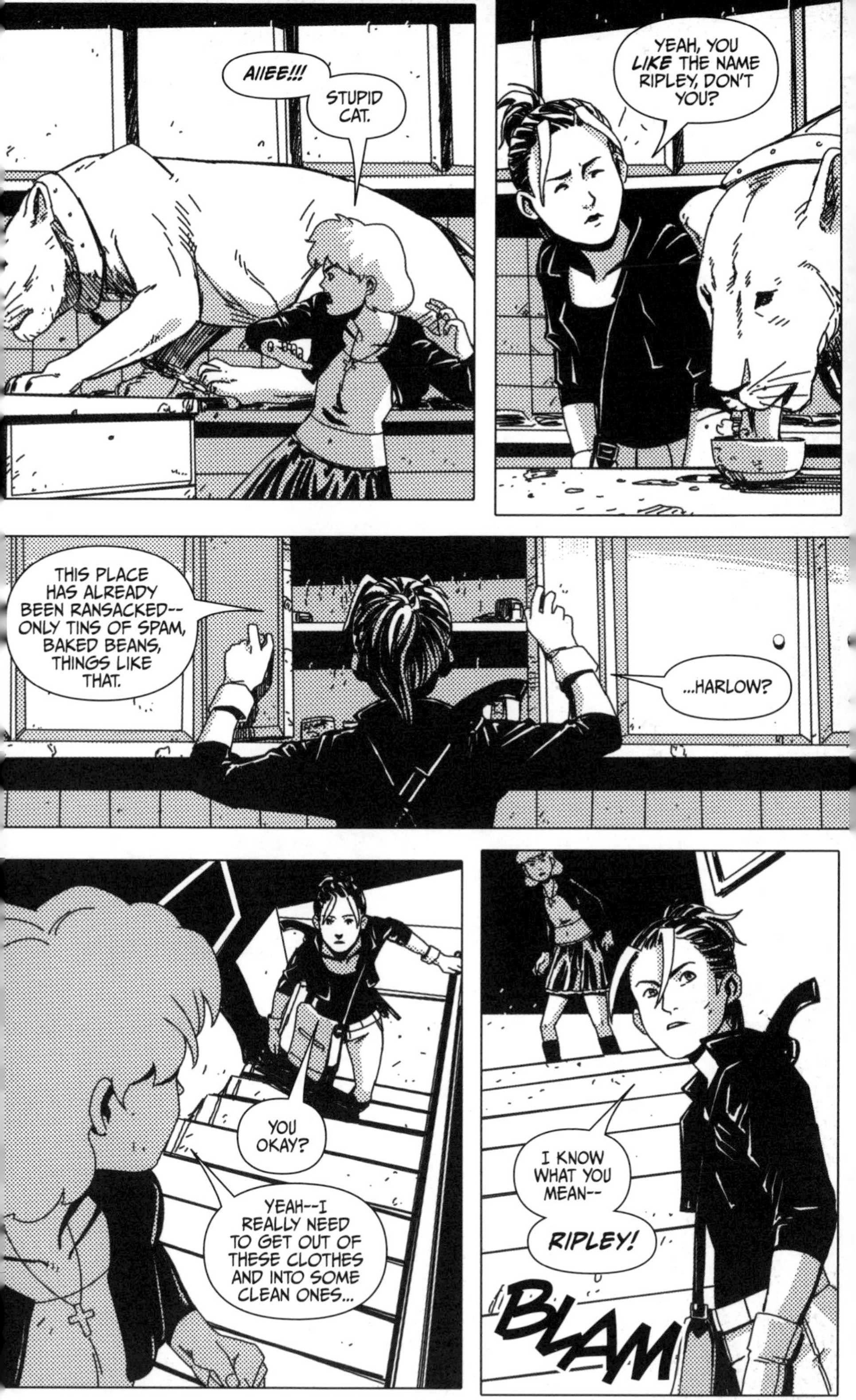
AIIEE!!!
STUPID CAT.
YEAH, YOU LIKE THE NAME RIPLEY, DON'T YOU?
THIS PLACE HAS ALREADY BEEN RANSACKED-- ONLY TINS OF SPAM, BAKED BEANS, THINGS LIKE THAT.
...HARLOW?
YOU OKAY?
YEAH--I REALLY NEED TO GET OUT OF THESE CLOTHES AND INTO SOME CLEAN ONES...
I KNOW WHAT YOU MEAN--
RIPLEY!
BLAM

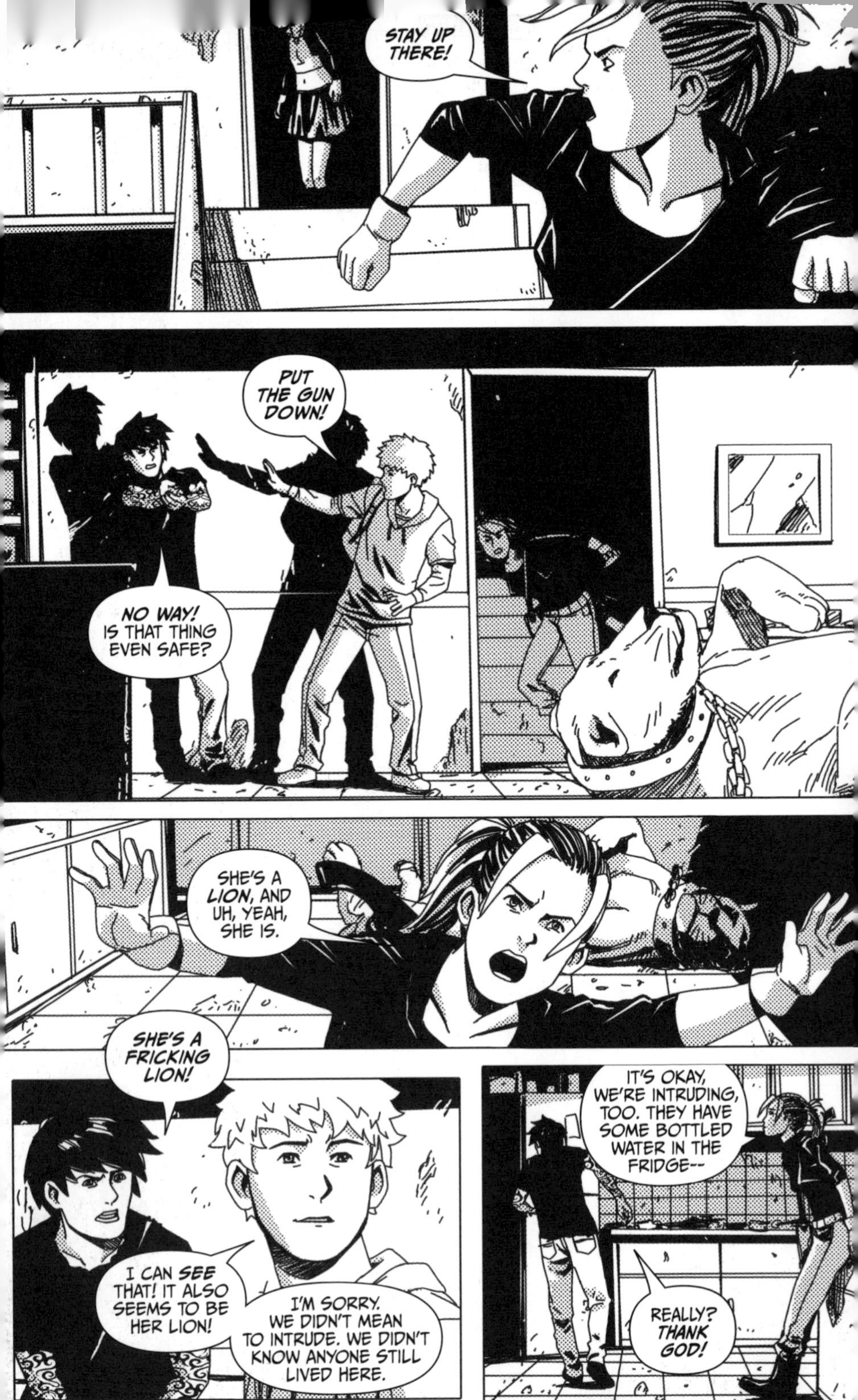
STAY UP THERE!
PUT THE GUN DOWN!
NO WAY! IS THAT THING EVEN SAFE?
SHE'S A LION, AND UH, YEAH, SHE IS.
SHE'S A FRICKING LION!
I CAN SEE THAT! IT ALSO SEEMS TO BE HER LION!
I'M SORRY. WE DIDN'T MEAN TO INTRUDE. WE DIDN'T KNOW ANYONE STILL LIVED HERE.
IT'S OKAY, WE'RE INTRUDING, TOO. THEY HAVE SOME BOTTLED WATER IN THE FRIDGE--
REALLY? THANK GOD!

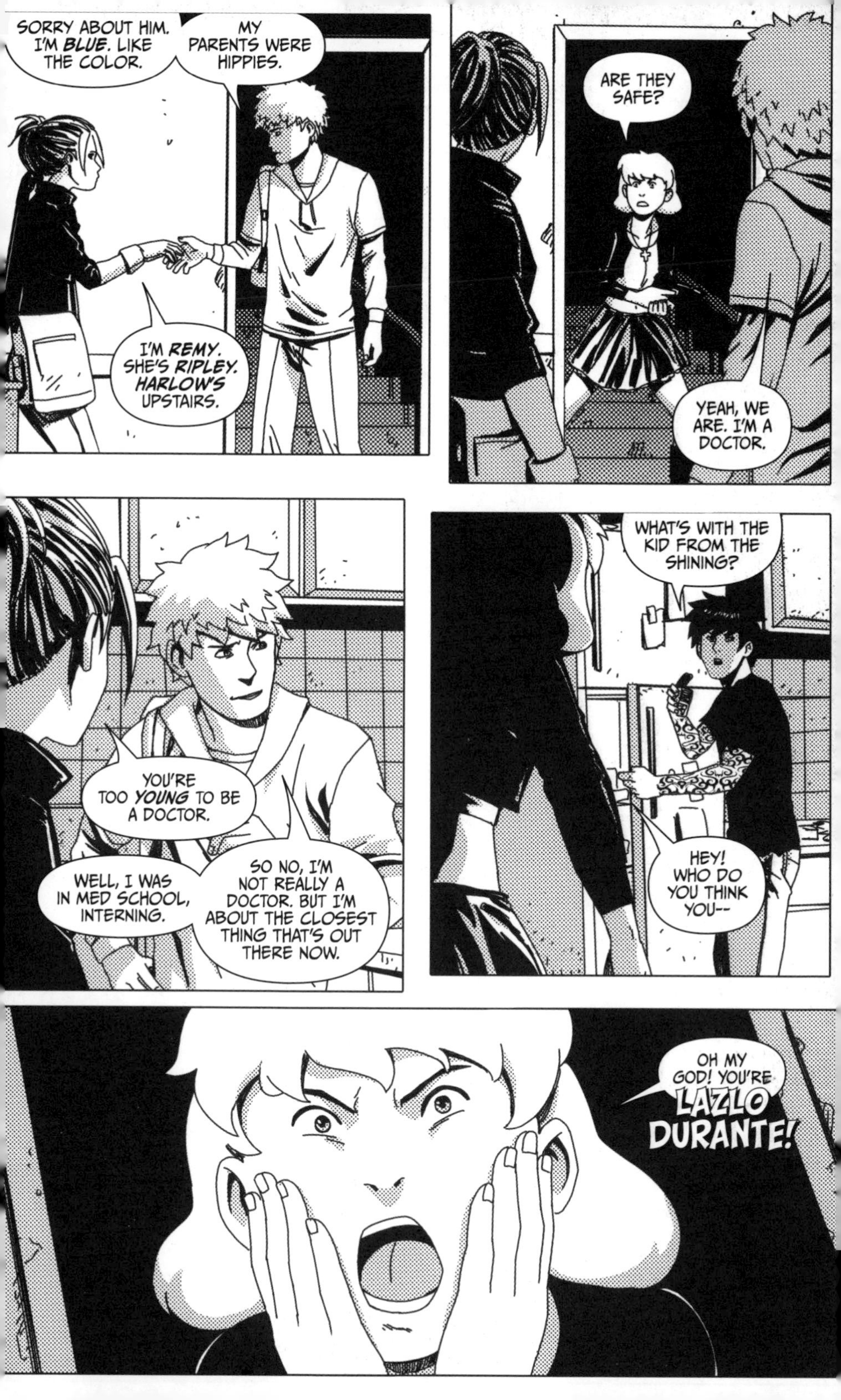
SORRY ABOUT HIM. I'M BLUE. LIKE THE COLOR.
MY PARENTS WERE HIPPIES.
I'M REMY. SHE'S RIPLEY. HARLOW'S UPSTAIRS.
ARE THEY SAFE?
YEAH, WE ARE. I'M A DOCTOR.
YOU'RE TOO YOUNG TO BE A DOCTOR.
WELL, I WAS IN MED SCHOOL, INTERNING.
SO NO, I'M NOT REALLY A DOCTOR. BUT I'M ABOUT THE CLOSEST THING THAT'S OUT THERE NOW.
WHAT'S WITH THE KID FROM THE SHINING?
HEY! WHO DO YOU THINK YOU--
OH MY GOD! YOU'RE LAZLO DURANTE!

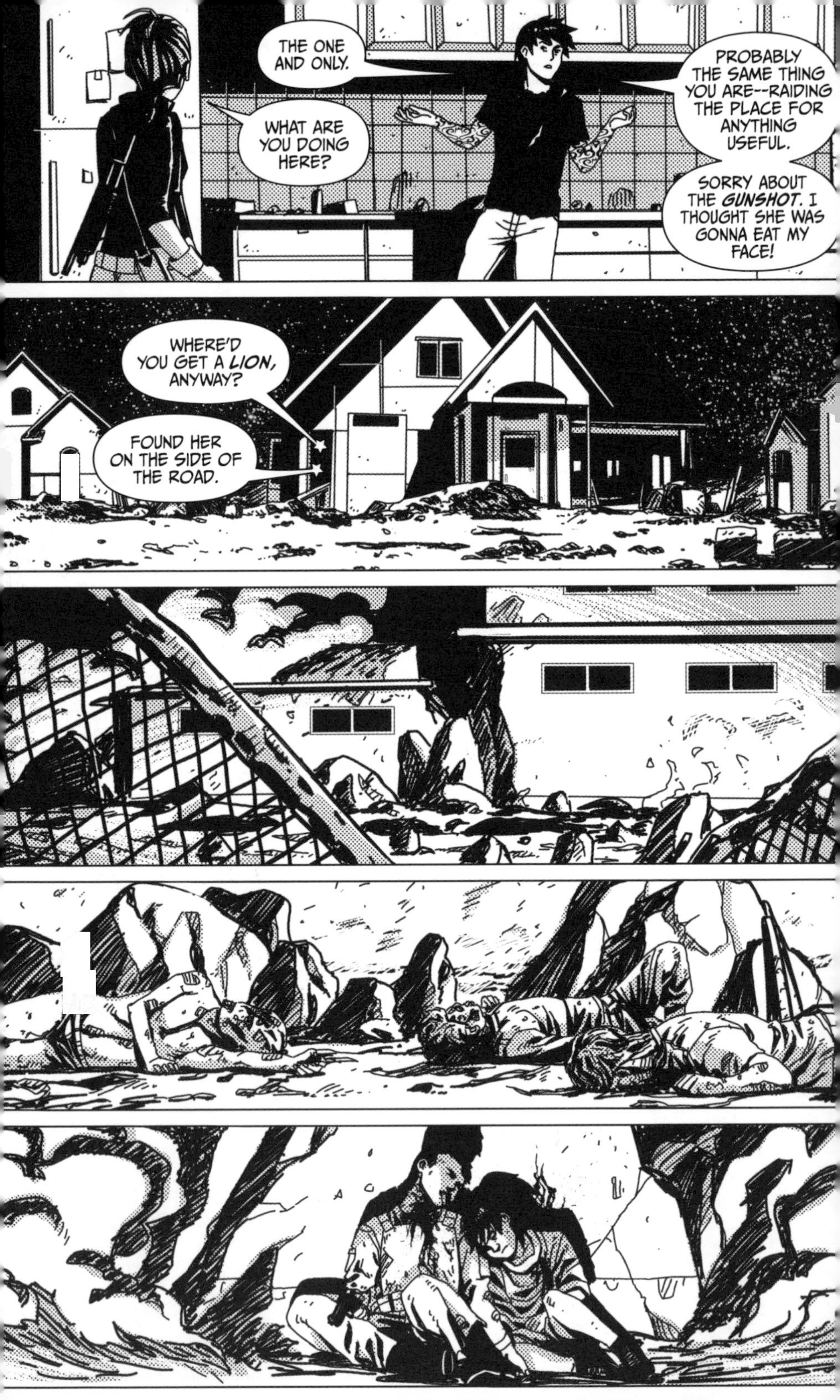

THE ONE AND ONLY.
WHAT ARE YOU DOING HERE?
PROBABLY THE SAME THING YOU ARE--RAIDING THE PLACE FOR ANYTHING USEFUL.
SORRY ABOUT THE **GUNSHOT**. I THOUGHT SHE WAS GONNA EAT MY FACE!
WHERE'D YOU GET A *LION*, ANYWAY?
FOUND HER ON THE SIDE OF THE ROAD.

CHAPTER FIVE

AND THEN THERE
WERE FIVE

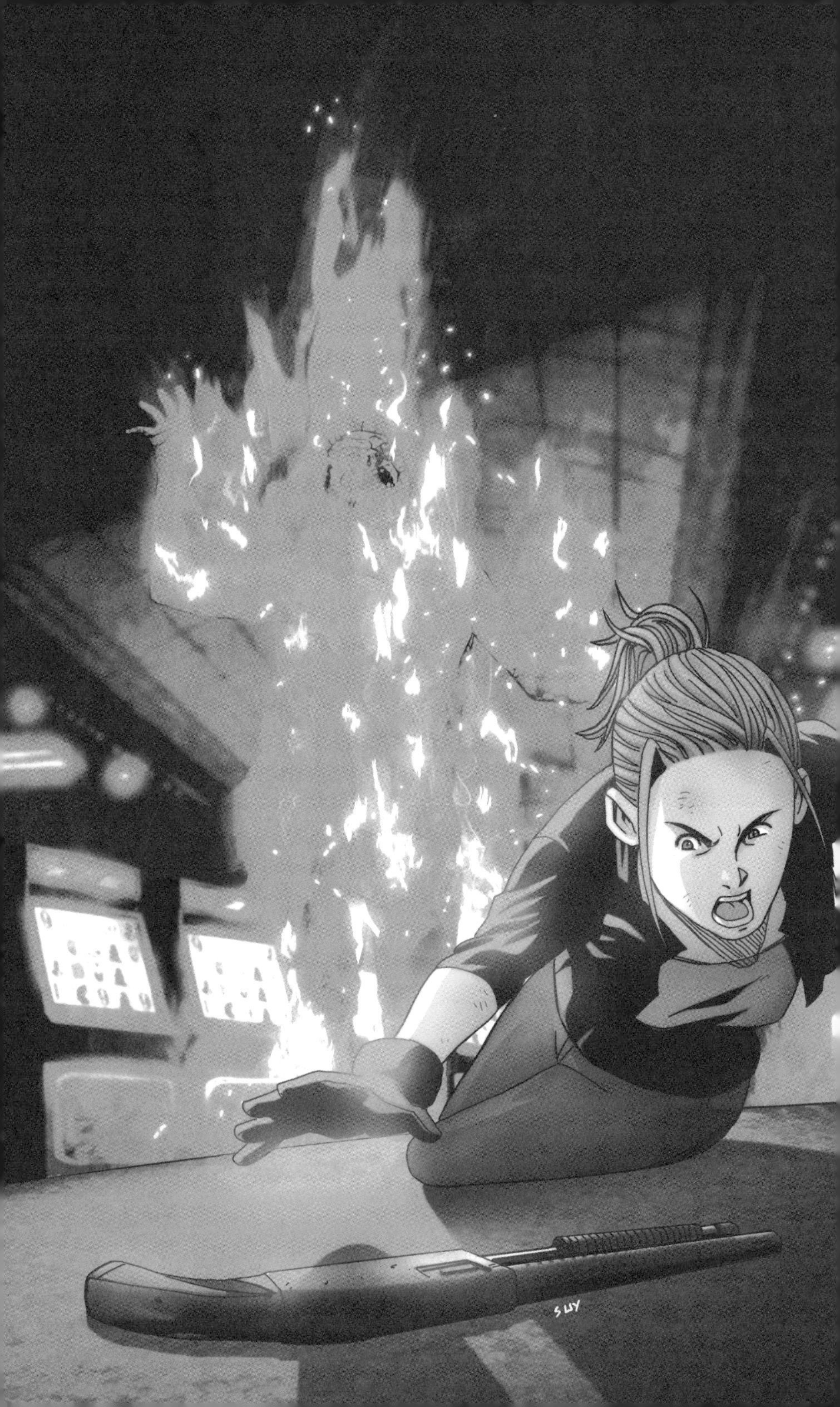
SUY

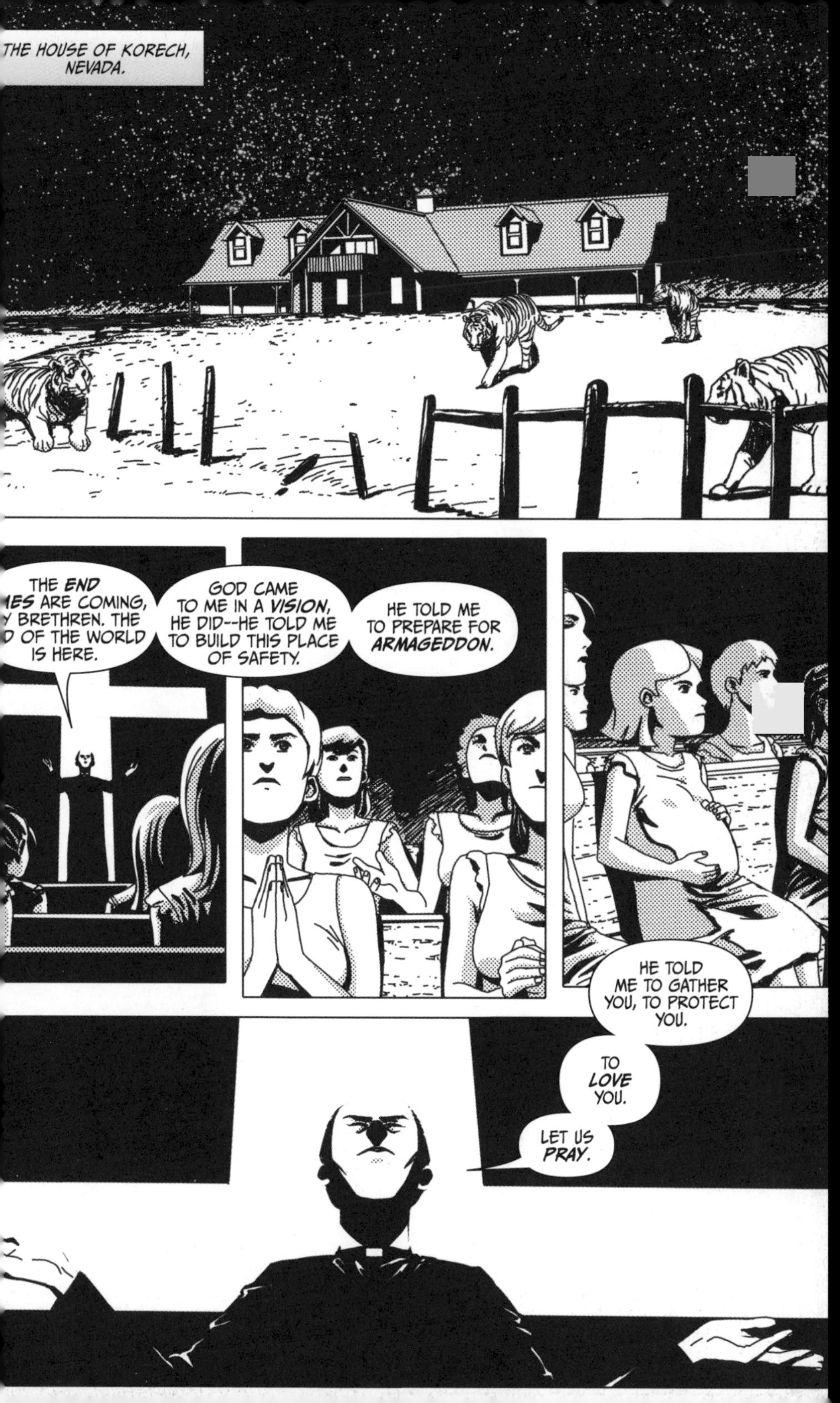
THE HOUSE OF KORECH, NEVADA.
THE END IES ARE COMING, Y BRETHREN. THE D OF THE WORLD IS HERE.
GOD CAME TO ME IN A VISION, HE DID--HE TOLD ME TO BUILD THIS PLACE OF SAFETY.
HE TOLD ME TO PREPARE FOR ARMAGEDDON.
HE TOLD ME TO GATHER YOU, TO PROTECT YOU.
TO LOVE YOU.
LET US PRAY.

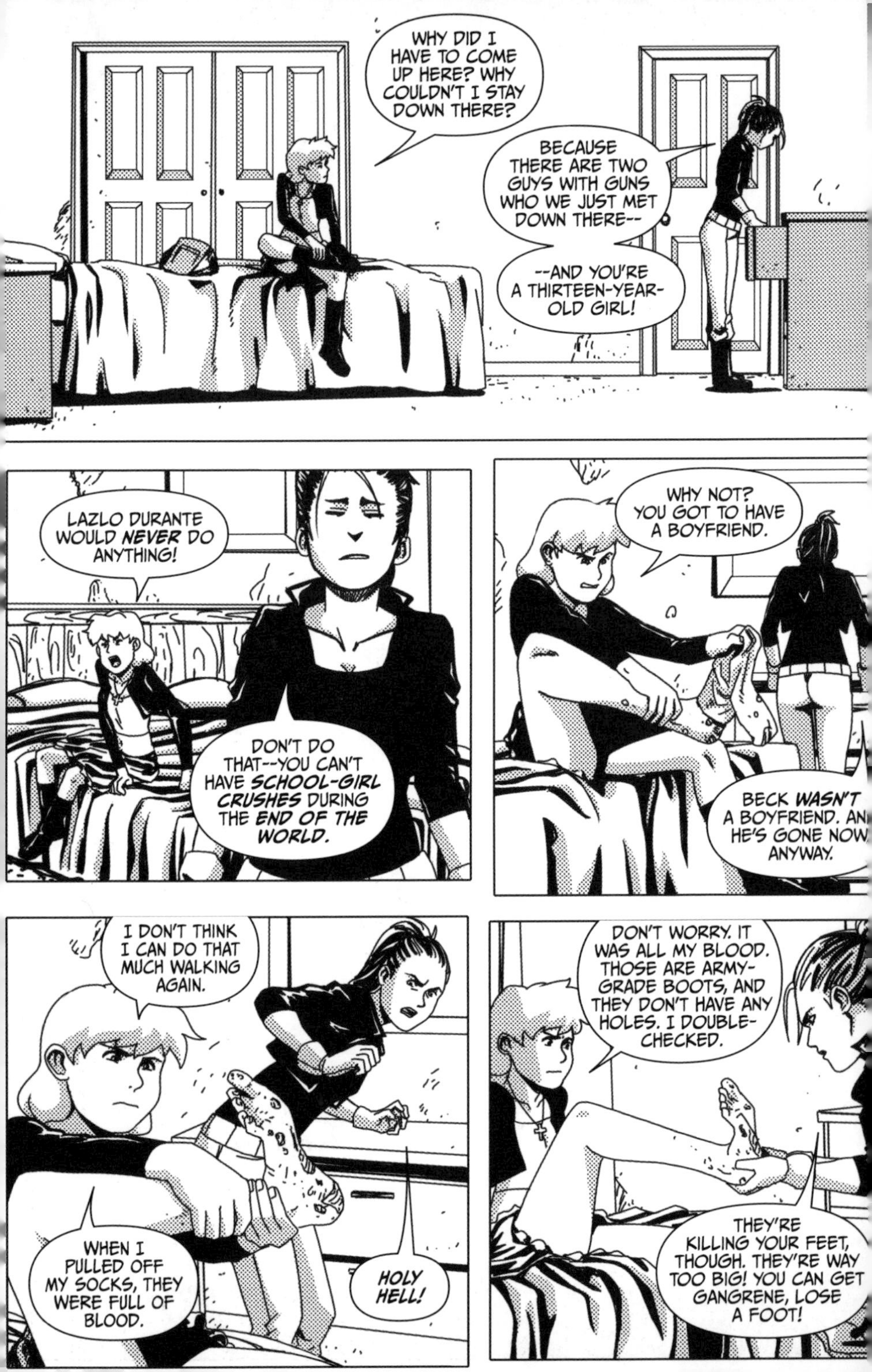

WHY DID I HAVE TO COME UP HERE? WHY COULDN'T I STAY DOWN THERE?
BECAUSE THERE ARE TWO GUYS WITH GUNS WHO WE JUST MET DOWN THERE--
--AND YOU'RE A THIRTEEN-YEAR-OLD GIRL!
LAZLO DURANTE WOULD **NEVER** DO ANYTHING!
DON'T DO THAT--YOU CAN'T HAVE **SCHOOL-GIRL CRUSHES** DURING THE **END OF THE WORLD.**
WHY NOT? YOU GOT TO HAVE A BOYFRIEND.
BECK **WASN'T** A BOYFRIEND. AN HE'S GONE NOW ANYWAY.
I DON'T THINK I CAN DO THAT MUCH WALKING AGAIN.
WHEN I PULLED OFF MY SOCKS, THEY WERE FULL OF BLOOD.
HOLY HELL!
DON'T WORRY. IT WAS ALL MY BLOOD. THOSE ARE ARMY-GRADE BOOTS, AND THEY DON'T HAVE ANY HOLES. I DOUBLE-CHECKED.
THEY'RE KILLING YOUR FEET, THOUGH. THEY'RE WAY TOO BIG! YOU CAN GET GANGRENE, LOSE A FOOT!

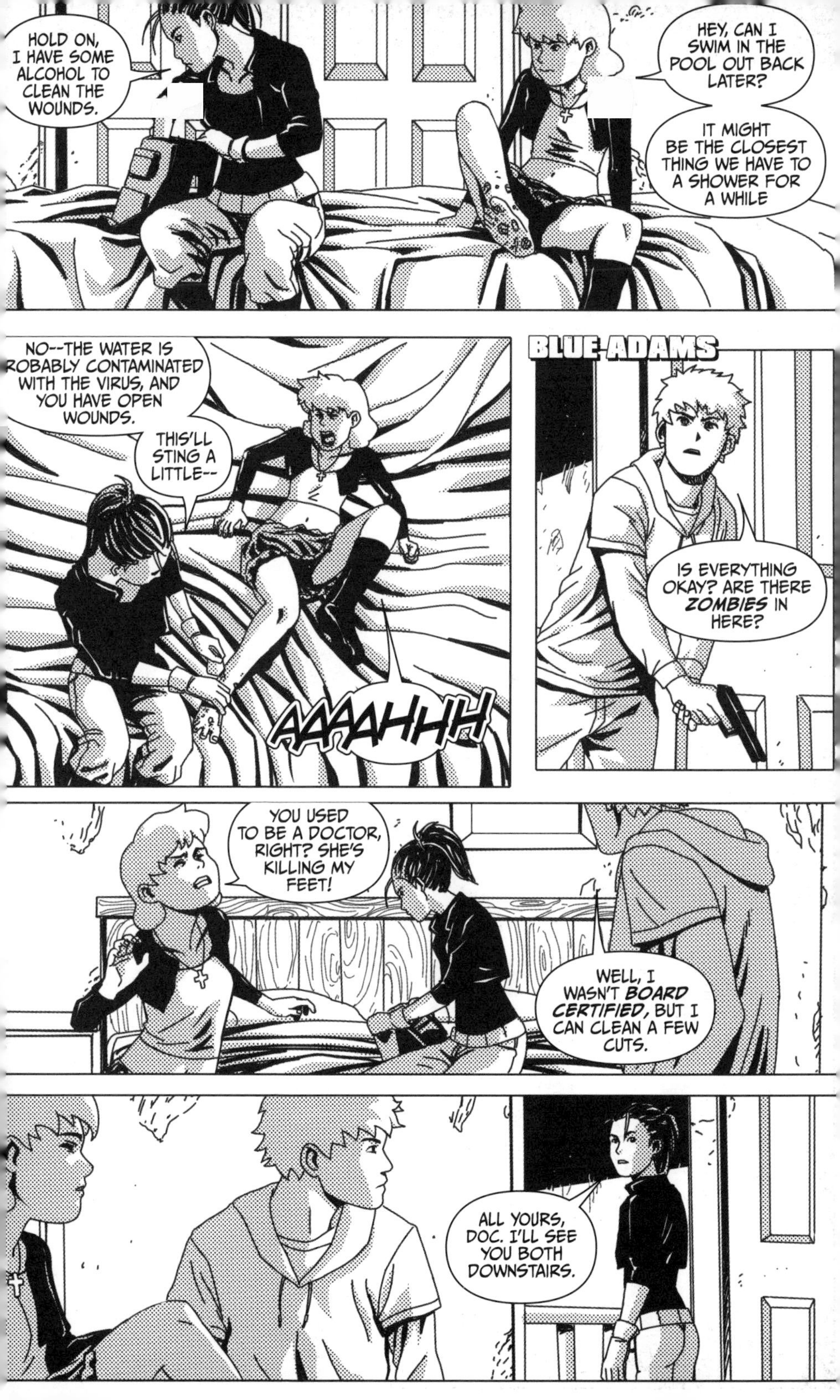
HOLD ON, I HAVE SOME ALCOHOL TO CLEAN THE WOUNDS.
HEY, CAN I SWIM IN THE POOL OUT BACK LATER?
IT MIGHT BE THE CLOSEST THING WE HAVE TO A SHOWER FOR A WHILE
NO--THE WATER IS ROBABLY CONTAMINATED WITH THE VIRUS, AND YOU HAVE OPEN WOUNDS.
THIS'LL STING A LITTLE--
AAAAHHH
BLUE ADAMS
IS EVERYTHING OKAY? ARE THERE *ZOMBIES* IN HERE?
YOU USED TO BE A DOCTOR, RIGHT? SHE'S KILLING MY FEET!
WELL, I WASN'T ***BOARD CERTIFIED,*** BUT I CAN CLEAN A FEW CUTS.
ALL YOURS, DOC. I'LL SEE YOU BOTH DOWNSTAIRS.

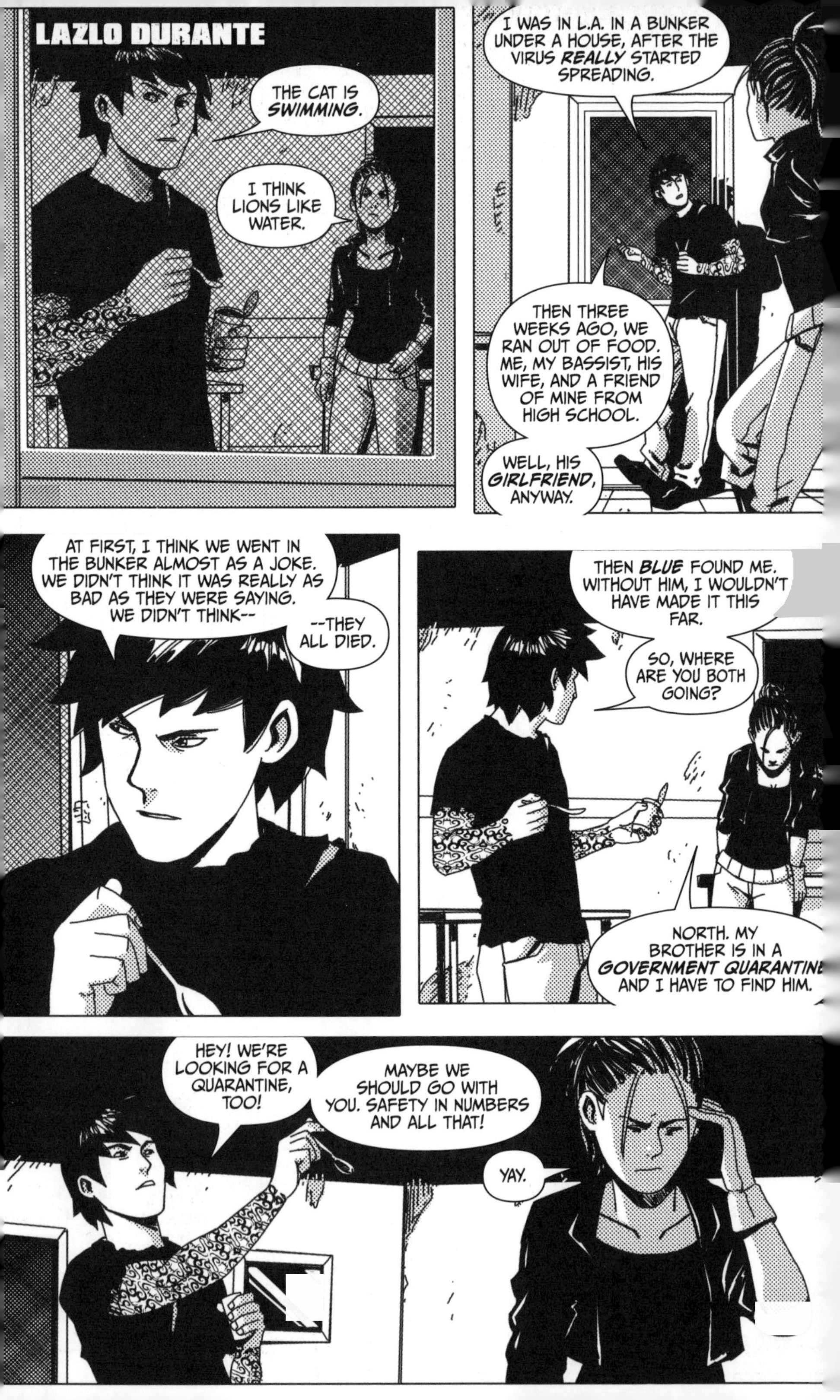
LAZLO DURANTE
THE CAT IS SWIMMING.
I THINK LIONS LIKE WATER.
I WAS IN L.A. IN A BUNKER UNDER A HOUSE, AFTER THE VIRUS REALLY STARTED SPREADING.
THEN THREE WEEKS AGO, WE RAN OUT OF FOOD. ME, MY BASSIST, HIS WIFE, AND A FRIEND OF MINE FROM HIGH SCHOOL.
WELL, HIS GIRLFRIEND, ANYWAY.
AT FIRST, I THINK WE WENT IN THE BUNKER ALMOST AS A JOKE. WE DIDN'T THINK IT WAS REALLY AS BAD AS THEY WERE SAYING. WE DIDN'T THINK--
--THEY ALL DIED.
THEN BLUE FOUND ME. WITHOUT HIM, I WOULDN'T HAVE MADE IT THIS FAR.
SO, WHERE ARE YOU BOTH GOING?
NORTH. MY BROTHER IS IN A GOVERNMENT QUARANTINE AND I HAVE TO FIND HIM.
HEY! WE'RE LOOKING FOR A QUARANTINE, TOO!
MAYBE WE SHOULD GO WITH YOU. SAFETY IN NUMBERS AND ALL THAT!
YAY.

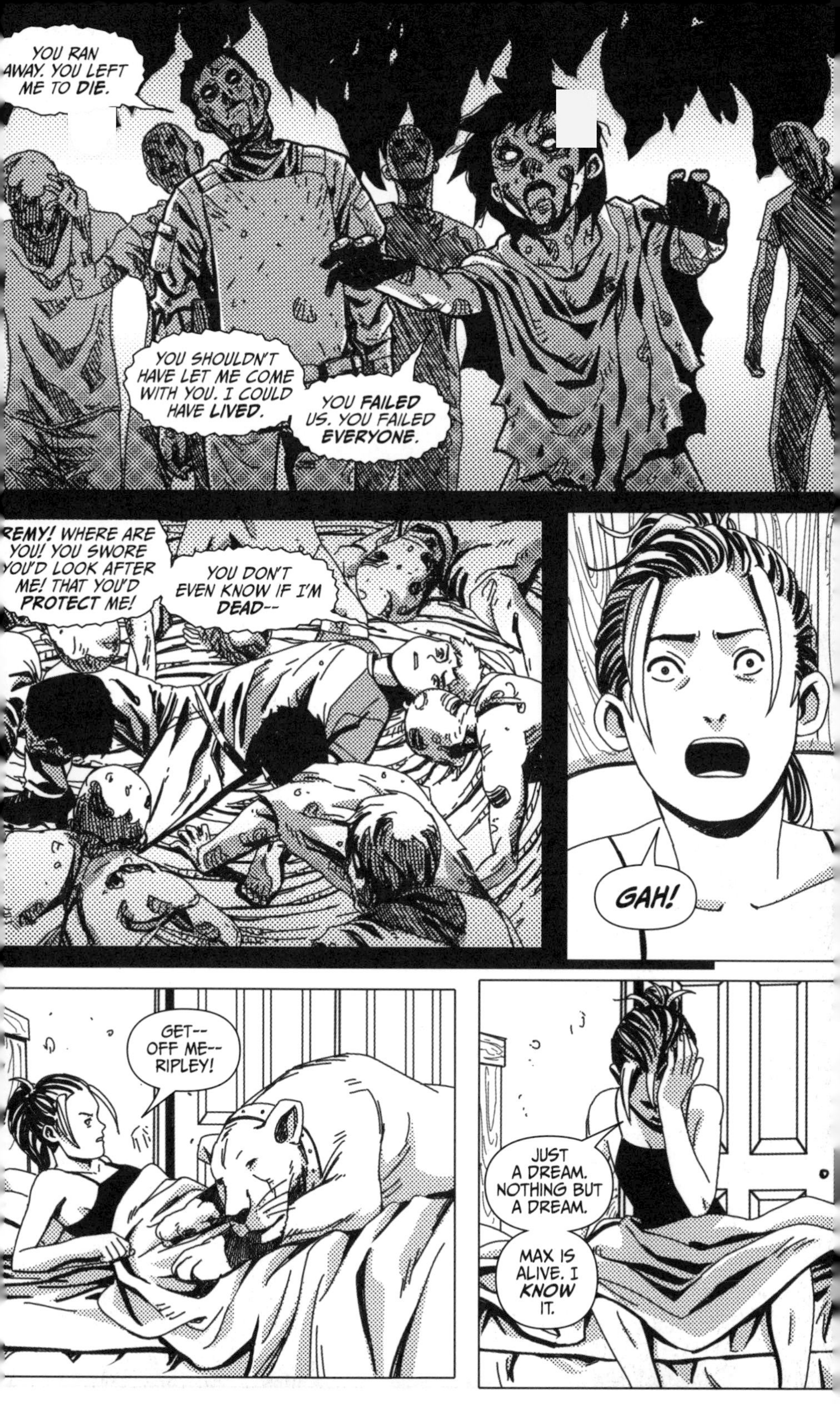
YOU RAN AWAY. YOU LEFT ME TO DIE.
YOU SHOULDN'T HAVE LET ME COME WITH YOU. I COULD HAVE LIVED.
YOU FAILED US. YOU FAILED EVERYONE.
REMY! WHERE ARE YOU! YOU SWORE YOU'D LOOK AFTER ME! THAT YOU'D PROTECT ME!
YOU DON'T EVEN KNOW IF I'M DEAD--
GAH!
GET-- OFF ME-- RIPLEY!
JUST A DREAM. NOTHING BUT A DREAM.
MAX IS ALIVE. I KNOW IT.

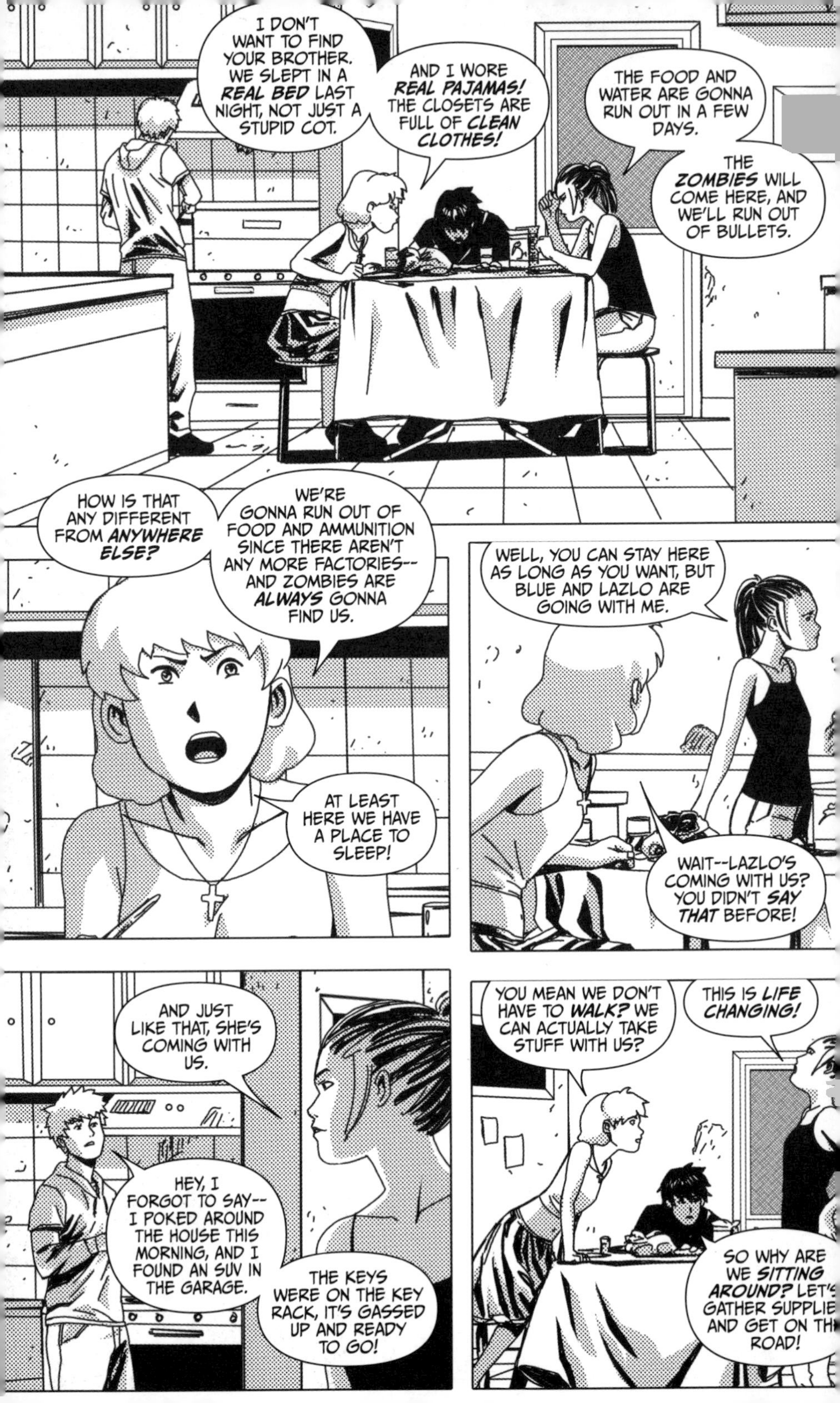
I DON'T WANT TO FIND YOUR BROTHER. WE SLEPT IN A REAL BED LAST NIGHT, NOT JUST A STUPID COT.
AND I WORE REAL PAJAMAS! THE CLOSETS ARE FULL OF CLEAN CLOTHES!
THE FOOD AND WATER ARE GONNA RUN OUT IN A FEW DAYS.
THE ZOMBIES WILL COME HERE, AND WE'LL RUN OUT OF BULLETS.
HOW IS THAT ANY DIFFERENT FROM ANYWHERE ELSE?
WE'RE GONNA RUN OUT OF FOOD AND AMMUNITION SINCE THERE AREN'T ANY MORE FACTORIES-- AND ZOMBIES ARE ALWAYS GONNA FIND US.
AT LEAST HERE WE HAVE A PLACE TO SLEEP!
WELL, YOU CAN STAY HERE AS LONG AS YOU WANT, BUT BLUE AND LAZLO ARE GOING WITH ME.
WAIT--LAZLO'S COMING WITH US? YOU DIDN'T SAY THAT BEFORE!
AND JUST LIKE THAT, SHE'S COMING WITH US.
HEY, I FORGOT TO SAY-- I POKED AROUND THE HOUSE THIS MORNING, AND I FOUND AN SUV IN THE GARAGE.
THE KEYS WERE ON THE KEY RACK, IT'S GASSED UP AND READY TO GO!
YOU MEAN WE DON'T HAVE TO WALK? WE CAN ACTUALLY TAKE STUFF WITH US?
THIS IS LIFE CHANGING!
SO WHY ARE WE SITTING AROUND? LET'S GATHER SUPPLIES AND GET ON THE ROAD!

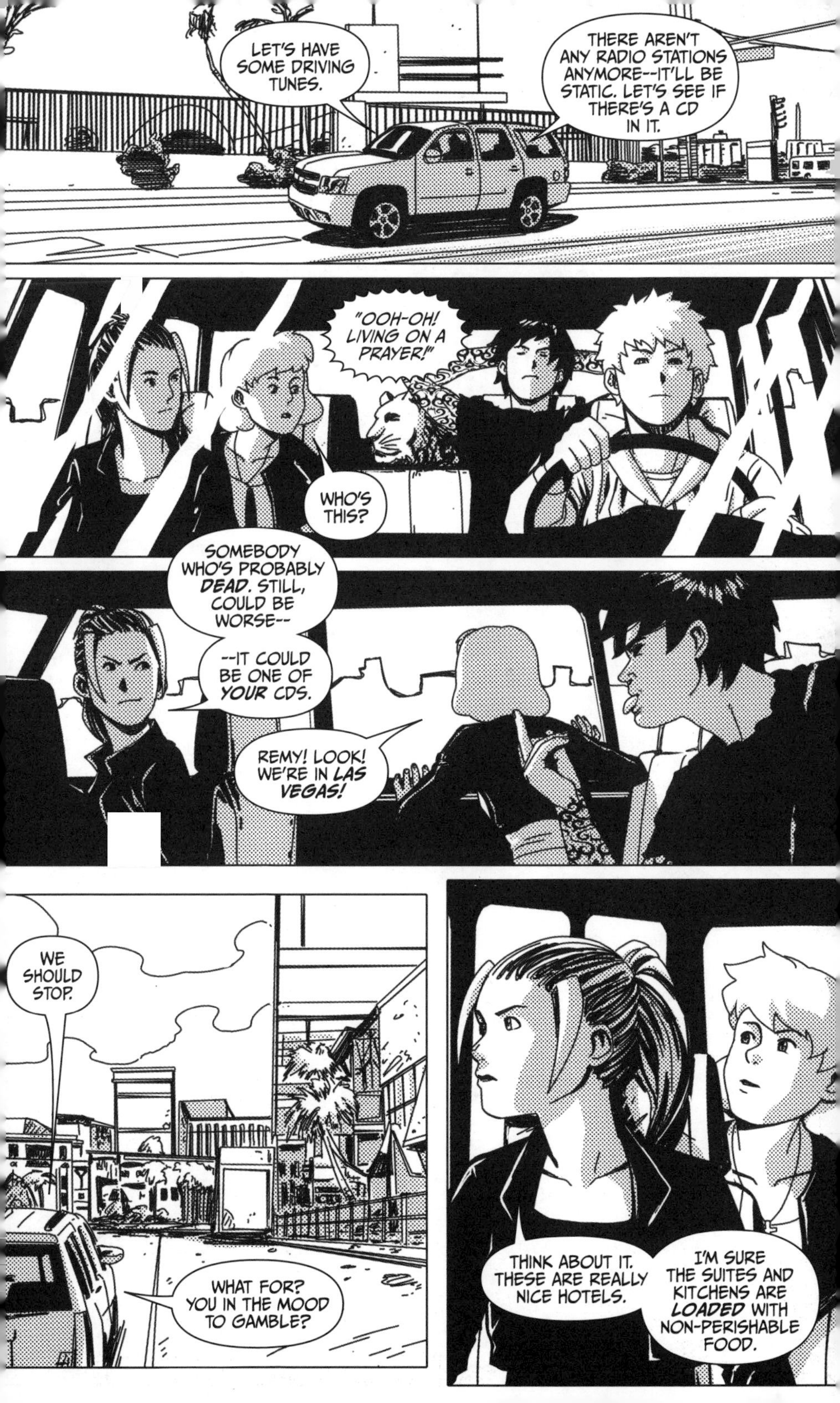
LET'S HAVE SOME DRIVING TUNES.
THERE AREN'T ANY RADIO STATIONS ANYMORE--IT'LL BE STATIC. LET'S SEE IF THERE'S A CD IN IT.
"OOH-OH! LIVING ON A PRAYER!"
WHO'S THIS?
SOMEBODY WHO'S PROBABLY DEAD. STILL, COULD BE WORSE--
--IT COULD BE ONE OF YOUR CDS.
REMY! LOOK! WE'RE IN LAS VEGAS!
WE SHOULD STOP.
WHAT FOR? YOU IN THE MOOD TO GAMBLE?
THINK ABOUT IT. THESE ARE REALLY NICE HOTELS.
I'M SURE THE SUITES AND KITCHENS ARE LOADED WITH NON-PERISHABLE FOOD.

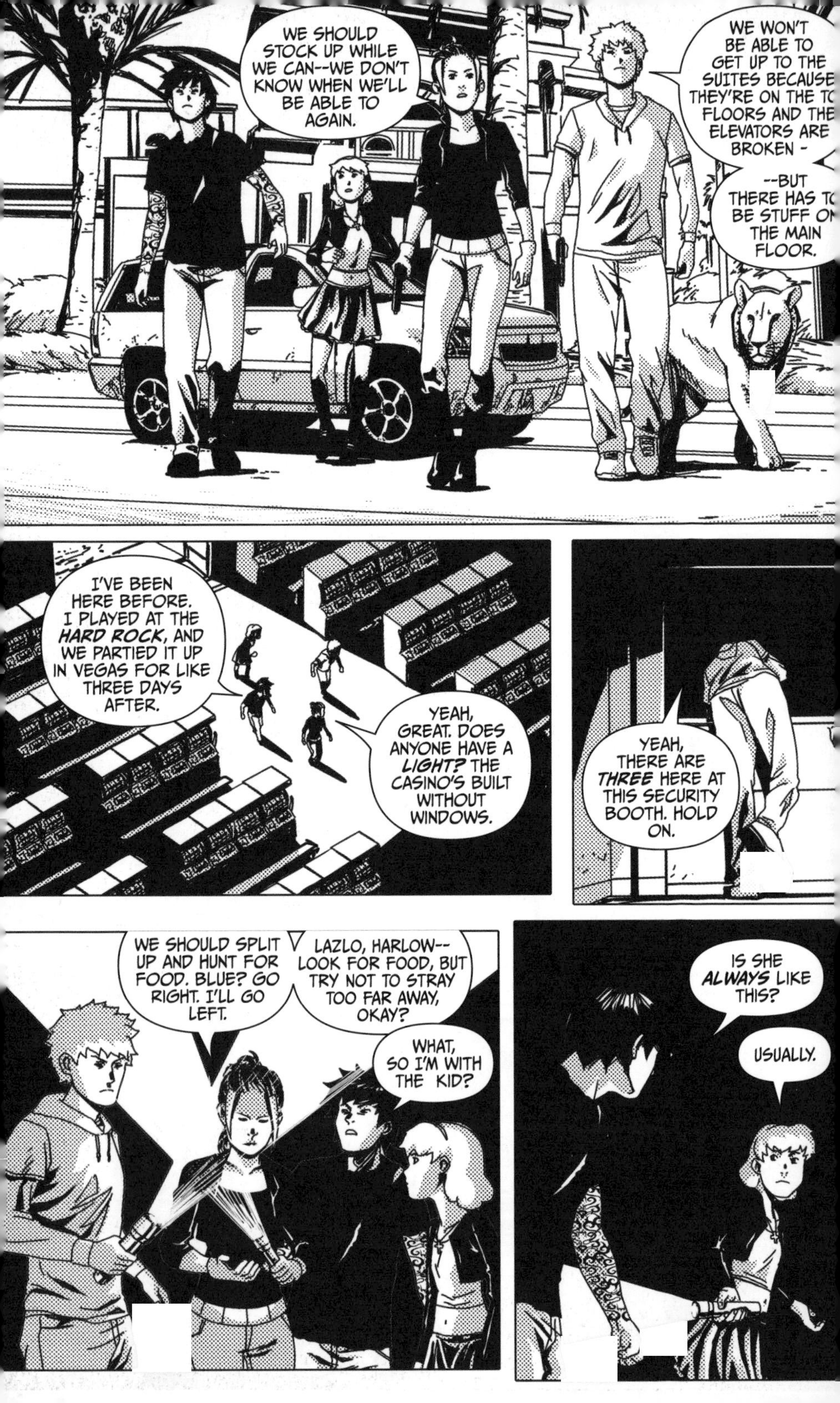
WE SHOULD STOCK UP WHILE WE CAN--WE DON'T KNOW WHEN WE'LL BE ABLE TO AGAIN.
WE WON'T BE ABLE TO GET UP TO THE SUITES BECAUSE THEY'RE ON THE TO FLOORS AND THE ELEVATORS ARE BROKEN -
--BUT THERE HAS TO BE STUFF ON THE MAIN FLOOR.
I'VE BEEN HERE BEFORE. I PLAYED AT THE HARD ROCK, AND WE PARTIED IT UP IN VEGAS FOR LIKE THREE DAYS AFTER.
YEAH, GREAT. DOES ANYONE HAVE A LIGHT? THE CASINO'S BUILT WITHOUT WINDOWS.
YEAH, THERE ARE THREE HERE AT THIS SECURITY BOOTH. HOLD ON.
WE SHOULD SPLIT UP AND HUNT FOR FOOD. BLUE? GO RIGHT. I'LL GO LEFT.
LAZLO, HARLOW-- LOOK FOR FOOD, BUT TRY NOT TO STRAY TOO FAR AWAY, OKAY?
WHAT, SO I'M WITH THE KID?
IS SHE ALWAYS LIKE THIS?
USUALLY.

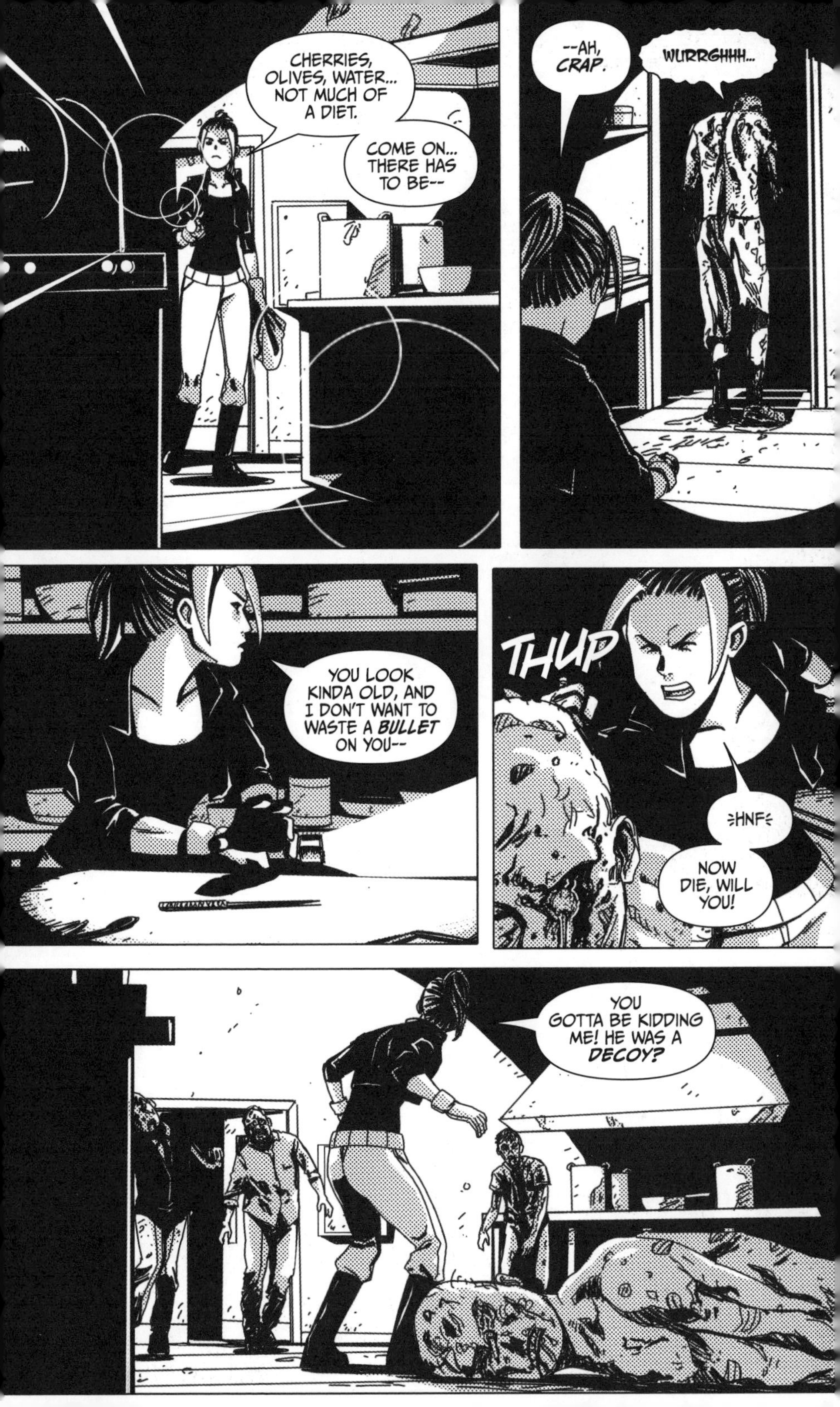
CHERRIES, OLIVES, WATER... NOT MUCH OF A DIET.
COME ON... THERE HAS TO BE--
--AH, CRAP.
WURRGHHH...
YOU LOOK KINDA OLD, AND I DON'T WANT TO WASTE A BULLET ON YOU--
THUP
HNF
NOW DIE, WILL YOU!
YOU GOTTA BE KIDDING ME! HE WAS A DECOY?

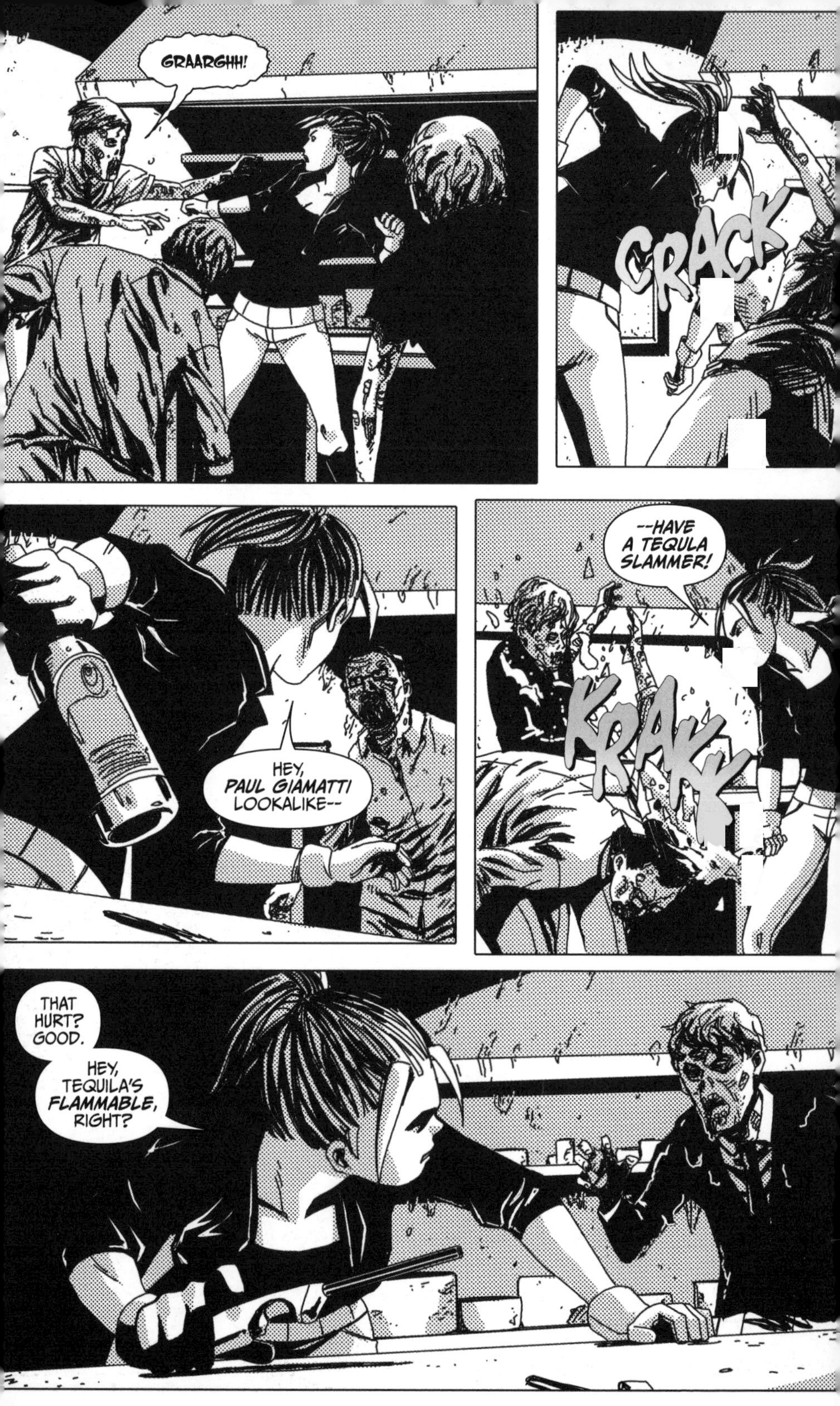
GRAARGHH!
CRACK
HEY, PAUL GIAMATTI LOOKALIKE--
--HAVE A TEQUILA SLAMMER!
KRAKK
THAT HURT? GOOD.
HEY, TEQUILA'S FLAMMABLE, RIGHT?

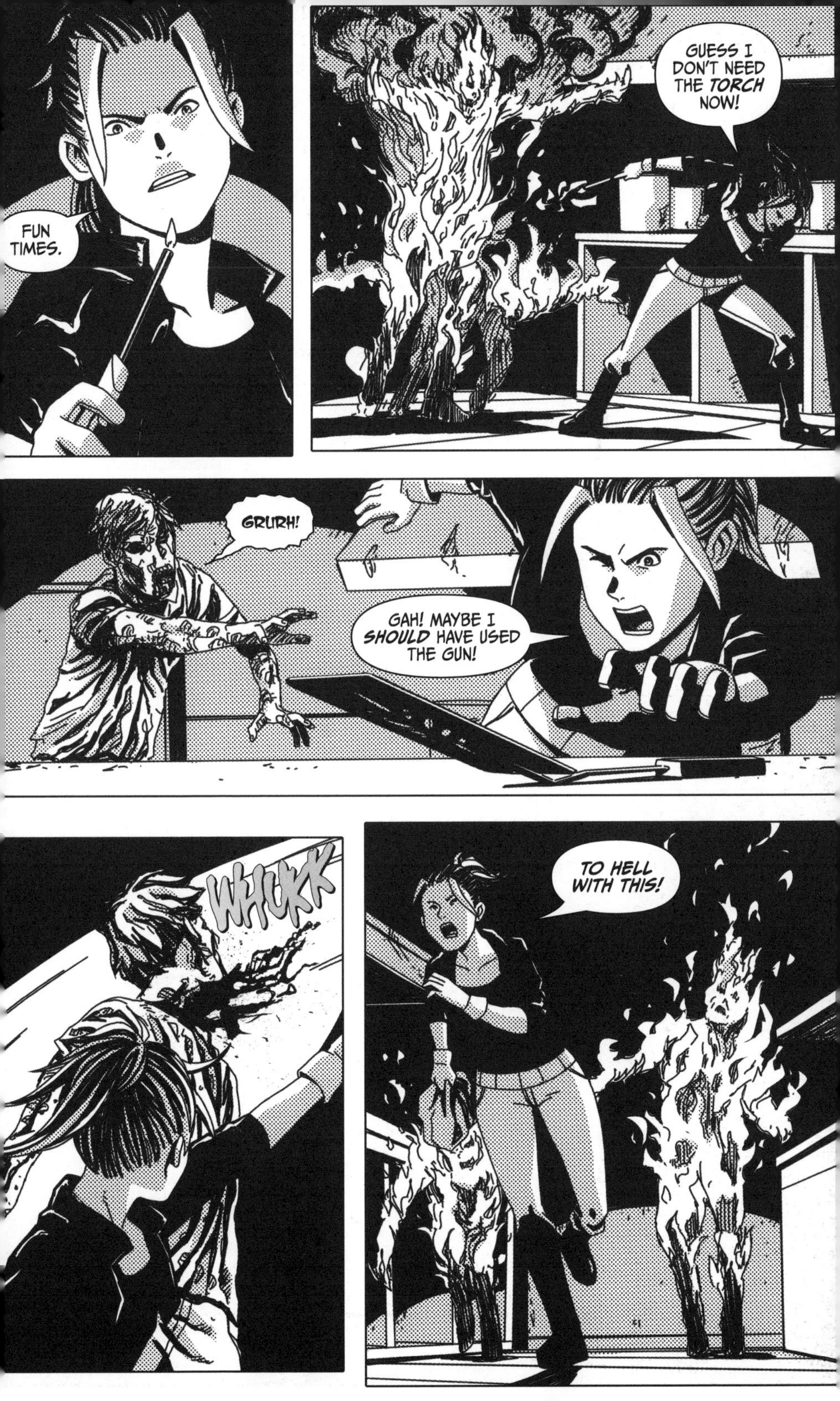
FUN TIMES.
GUESS I DON'T NEED THE *TORCH* NOW!
GRURH!
GAH! MAYBE I *SHOULD* HAVE USED THE GUN!
WHUKK
TO HELL WITH THIS!

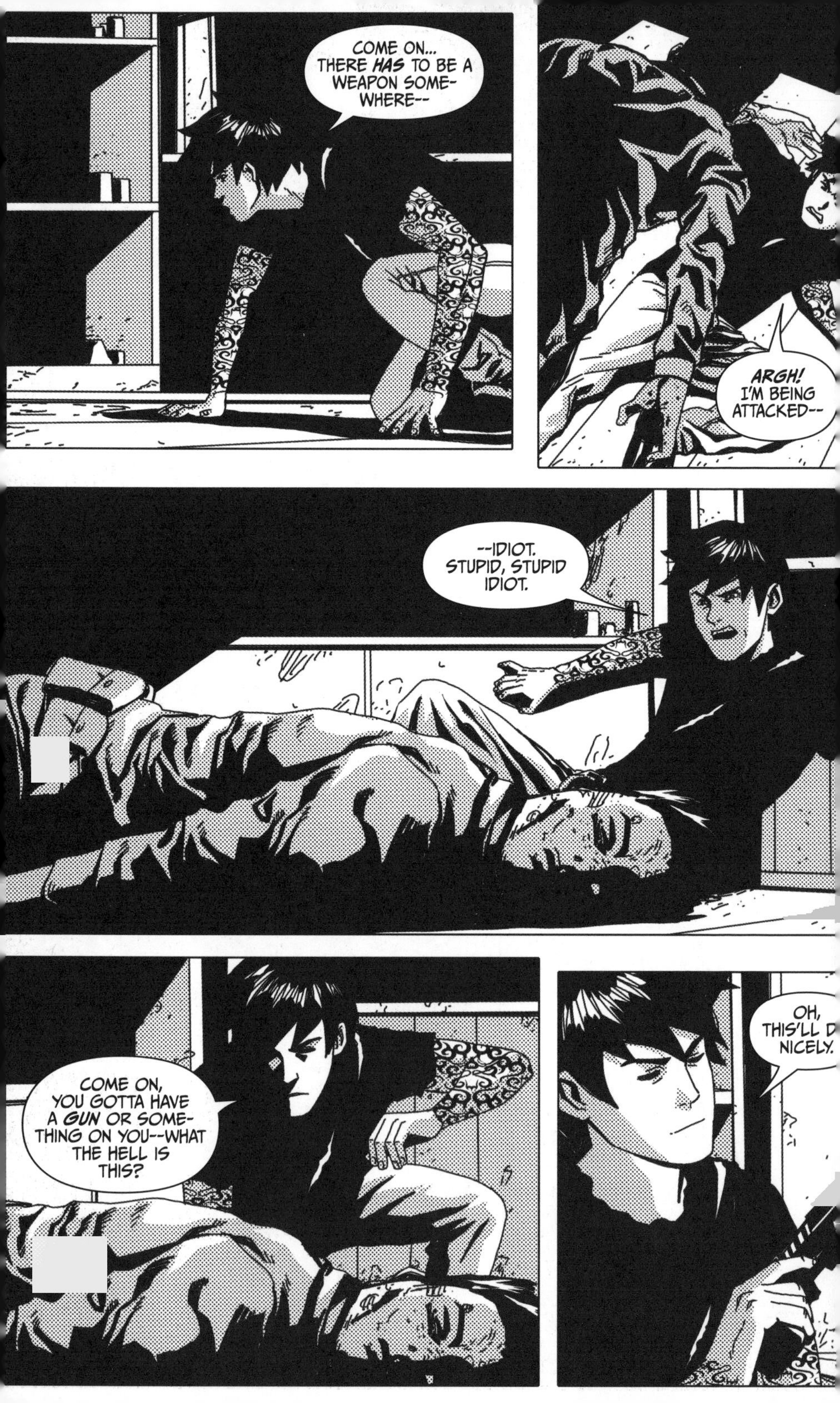
COME ON... THERE *HAS* TO BE A WEAPON SOME-WHERE--
ARGH! I'M BEING ATTACKED--
--IDIOT. STUPID, STUPID IDIOT.
COME ON, YOU GOTTA HAVE A *GUN* OR SOME-THING ON YOU--WHAT THE HELL IS THIS?
OH, THIS'LL D NICELY.

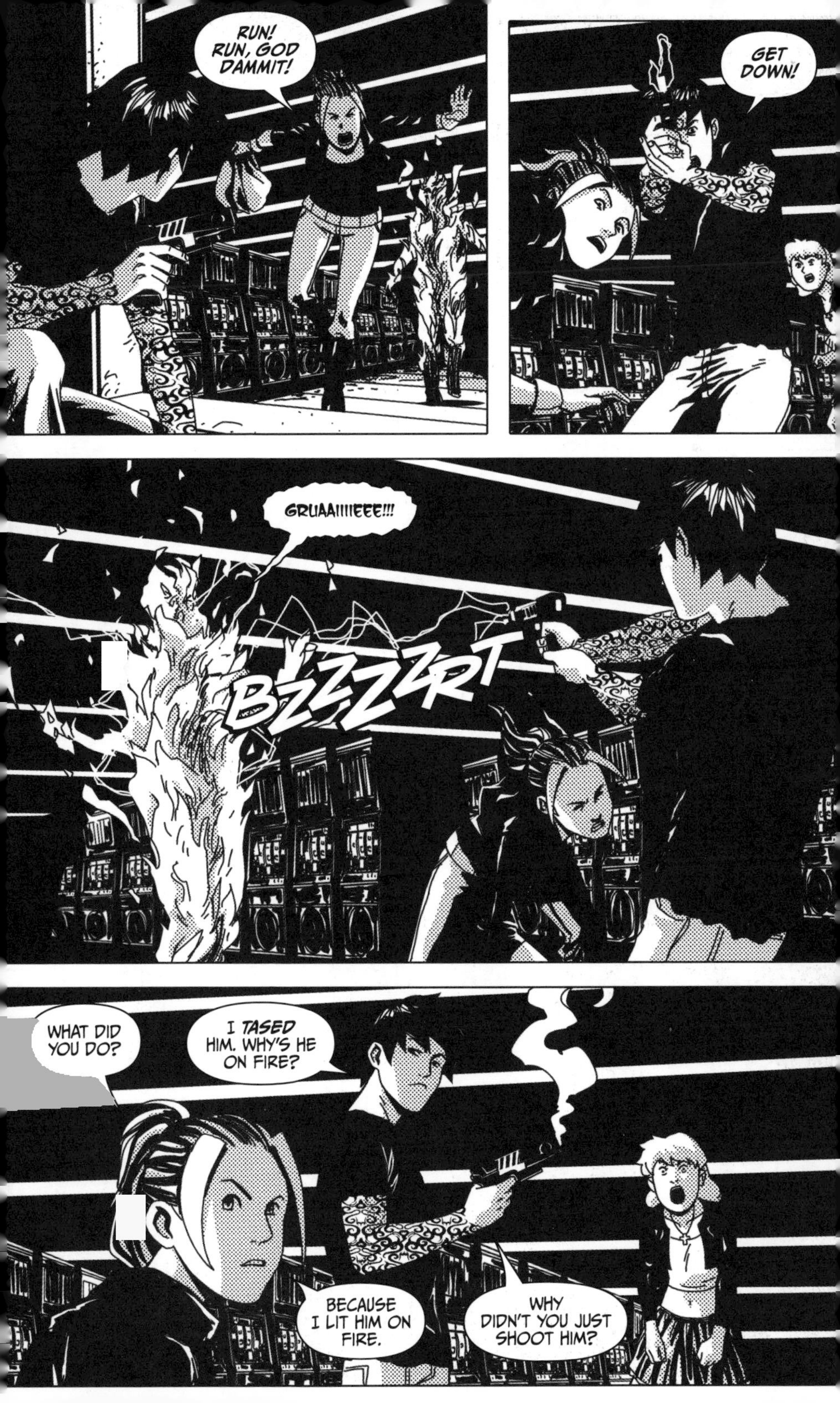
RUN! RUN, GOD DAMMIT!
GET DOWN!
GRUAAIIIIEEE!!!
BZZZZRT
WHAT DID YOU DO?
I TASED HIM. WHY'S HE ON FIRE?
BECAUSE I LIT HIM ON FIRE.
WHY DIDN'T YOU JUST SHOOT HIM?

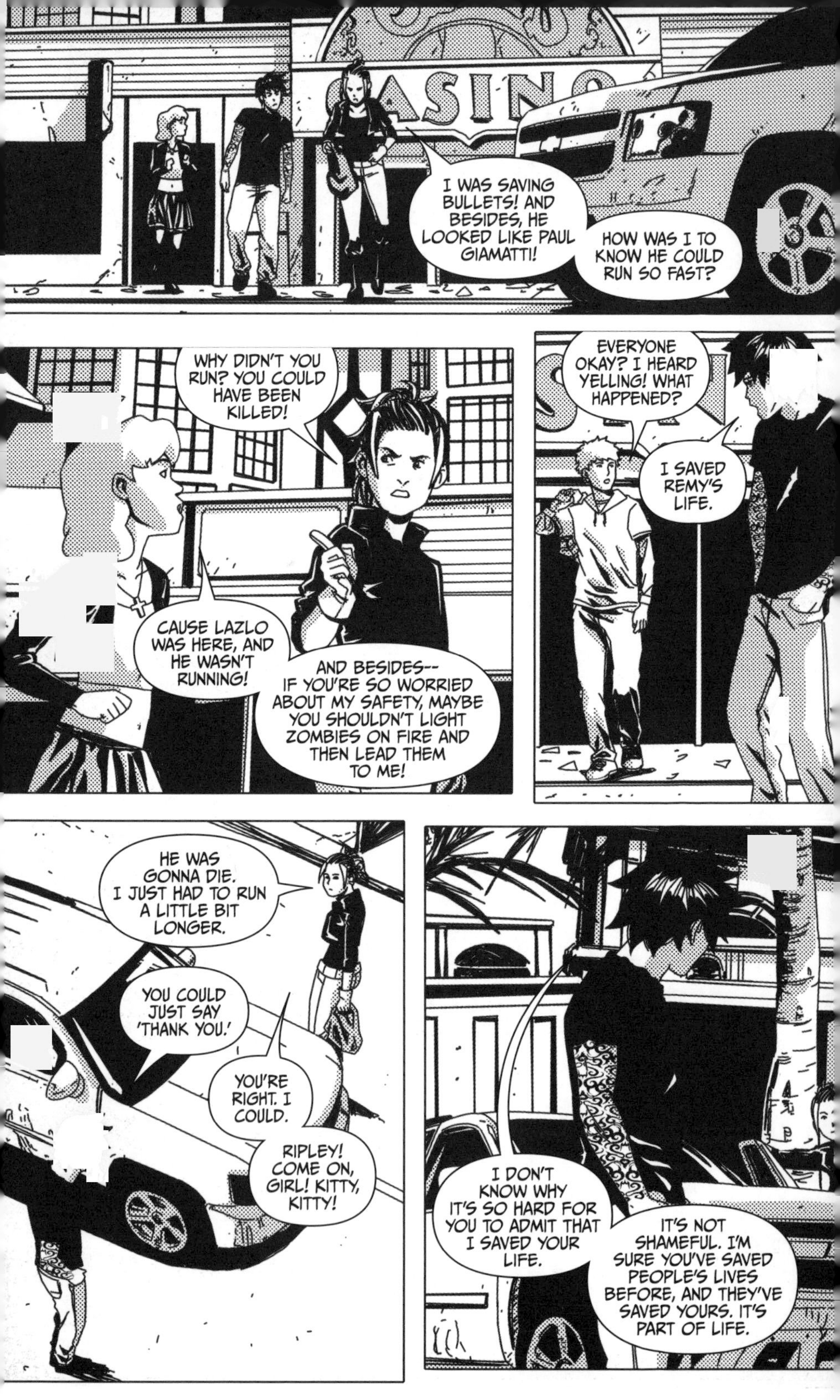
CASINO
I WAS SAVING BULLETS! AND BESIDES, HE LOOKED LIKE PAUL GIAMATTI!
HOW WAS I TO KNOW HE COULD RUN SO FAST?
WHY DIDN'T YOU RUN? YOU COULD HAVE BEEN KILLED!
CAUSE LAZLO WAS HERE, AND HE WASN'T RUNNING!
AND BESIDES-- IF YOU'RE SO WORRIED ABOUT MY SAFETY, MAYBE YOU SHOULDN'T LIGHT ZOMBIES ON FIRE AND THEN LEAD THEM TO ME!
EVERYONE OKAY? I HEARD YELLING! WHAT HAPPENED?
I SAVED REMY'S LIFE.
HE WAS GONNA DIE. I JUST HAD TO RUN A LITTLE BIT LONGER.
YOU COULD JUST SAY 'THANK YOU.'
YOU'RE RIGHT. I COULD.
RIPLEY! COME ON, GIRL! KITTY, KITTY!
I DON'T KNOW WHY IT'S SO HARD FOR YOU TO ADMIT THAT I SAVED YOUR LIFE.
IT'S NOT SHAMEFUL. I'M SURE YOU'VE SAVED PEOPLE'S LIVES BEFORE, AND THEY'VE SAVED YOURS. IT'S PART OF LIFE.

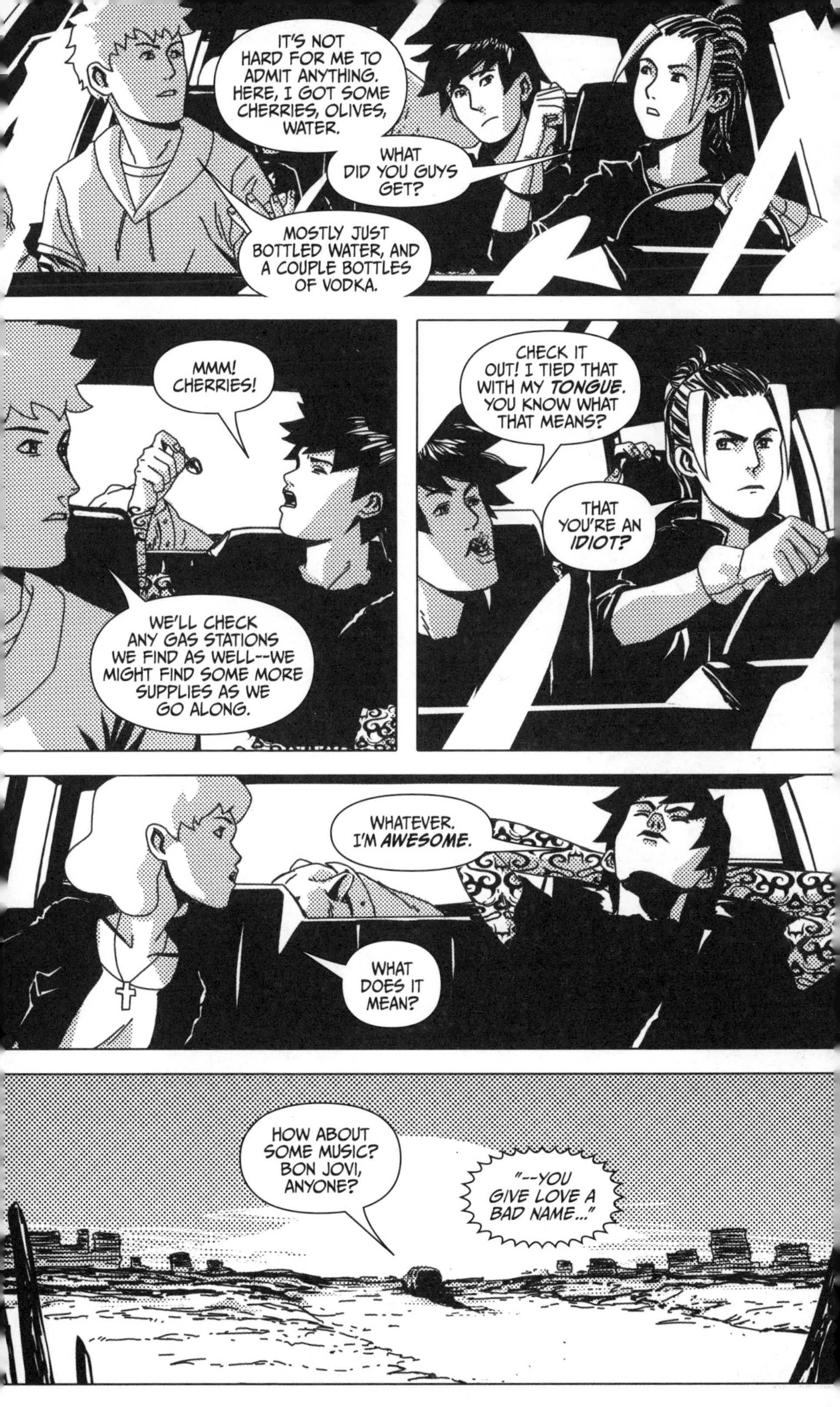
IT'S NOT HARD FOR ME TO ADMIT ANYTHING. HERE, I GOT SOME CHERRIES, OLIVES, WATER.
WHAT DID YOU GUYS GET?
MOSTLY JUST BOTTLED WATER, AND A COUPLE BOTTLES OF VODKA.
MMM! CHERRIES!
WE'LL CHECK ANY GAS STATIONS WE FIND AS WELL--WE MIGHT FIND SOME MORE SUPPLIES AS WE GO ALONG.
CHECK IT OUT! I TIED THAT WITH MY TONGUE. YOU KNOW WHAT THAT MEANS?
THAT YOU'RE AN IDIOT?
WHATEVER. I'M AWESOME.
WHAT DOES IT MEAN?
HOW ABOUT SOME MUSIC? BON JOVI, ANYONE?
"--YOU GIVE LOVE A BAD NAME..."

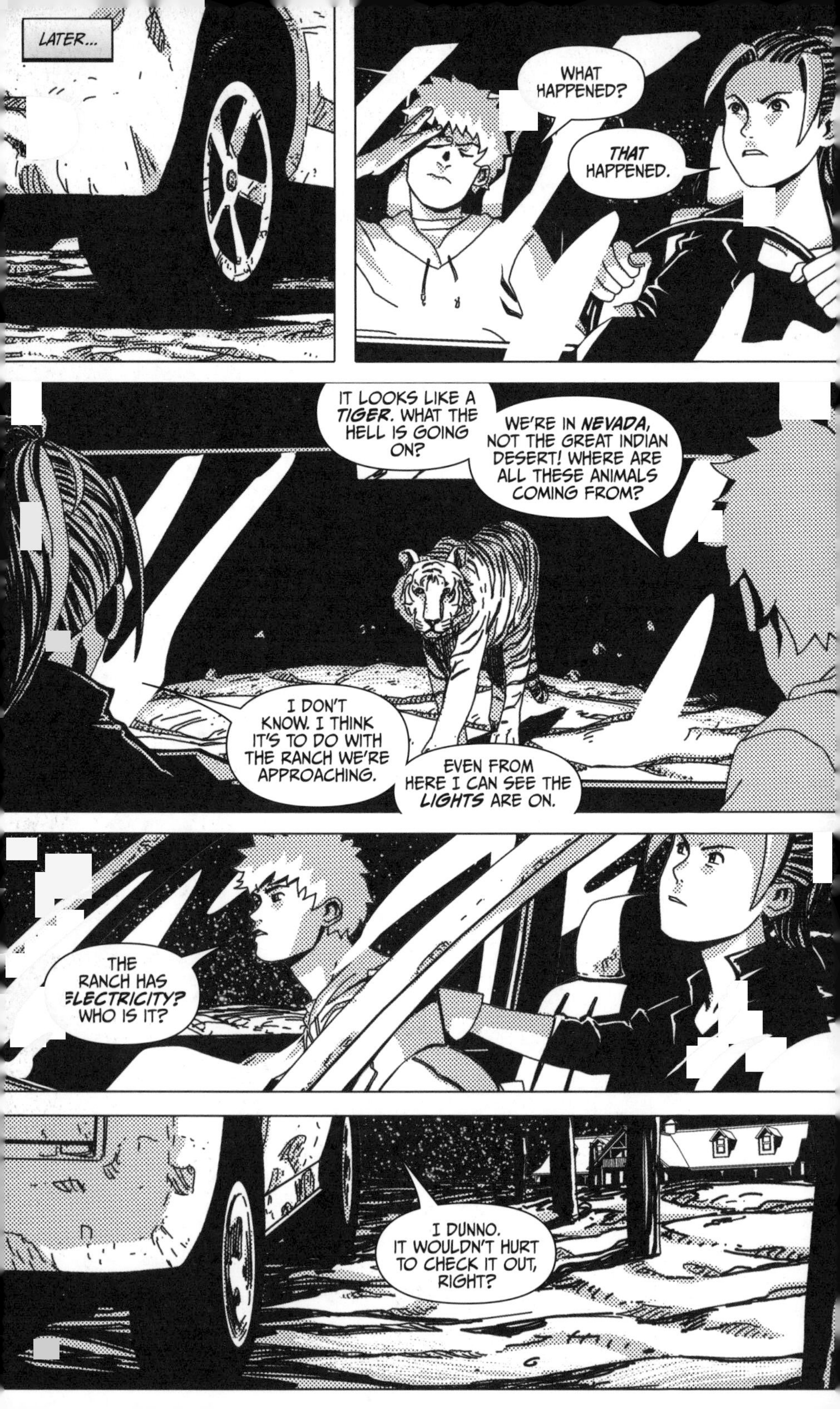
LATER...
WHAT HAPPENED?
THAT HAPPENED.
IT LOOKS LIKE A TIGER. WHAT THE HELL IS GOING ON?
WE'RE IN NEVADA, NOT THE GREAT INDIAN DESERT! WHERE ARE ALL THESE ANIMALS COMING FROM?
I DON'T KNOW. I THINK IT'S TO DO WITH THE RANCH WE'RE APPROACHING.
EVEN FROM HERE I CAN SEE THE LIGHTS ARE ON.
THE RANCH HAS ELECTRICITY? WHO IS IT?
I DUNNO. IT WOULDN'T HURT TO CHECK IT OUT, RIGHT?

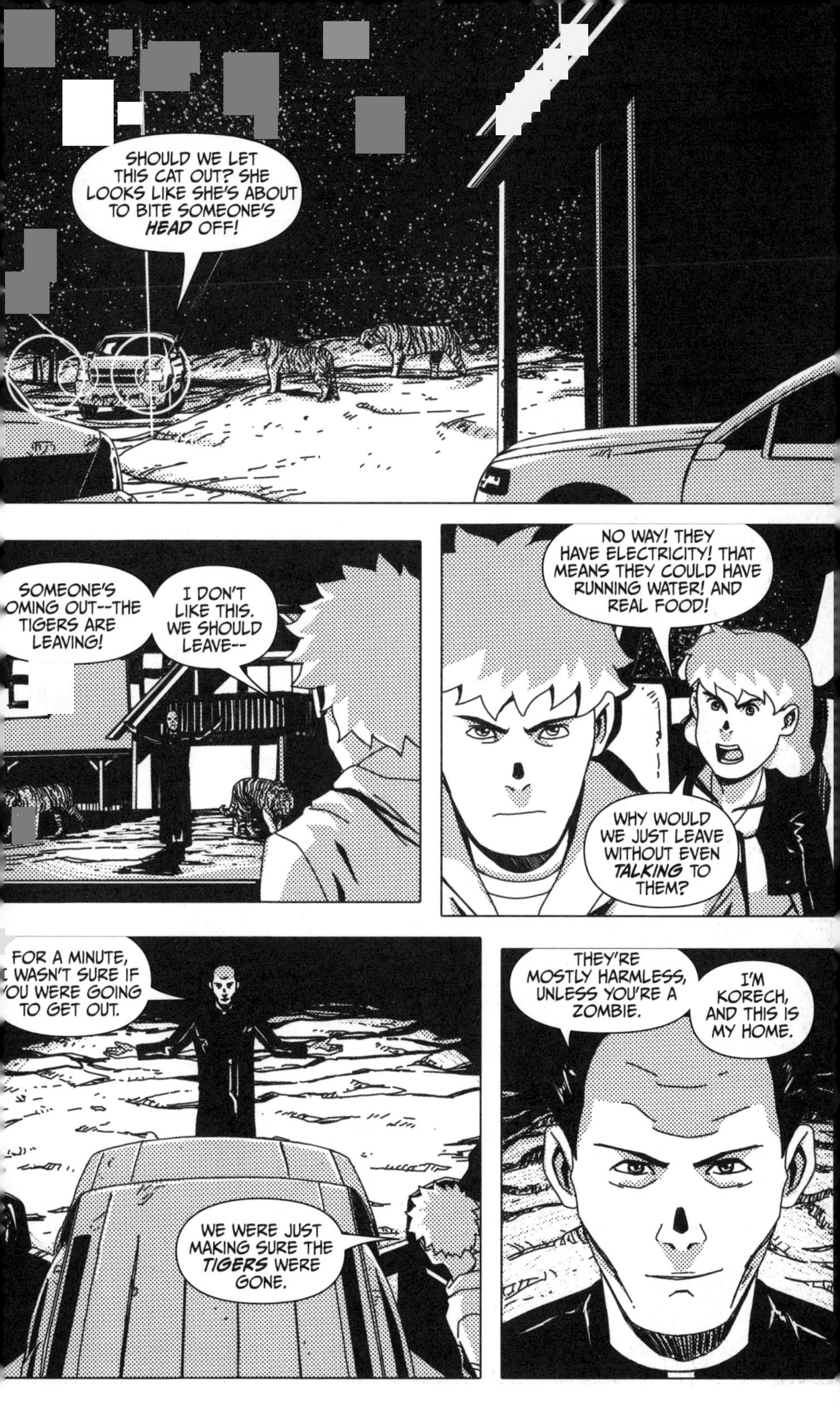

SHOULD WE LET THIS CAT OUT? SHE LOOKS LIKE SHE'S ABOUT TO BITE SOMEONE'S *HEAD* OFF!
SOMEONE'S OMING OUT--THE TIGERS ARE LEAVING!
I DON'T LIKE THIS. WE SHOULD LEAVE--
NO WAY! THEY HAVE ELECTRICITY! THAT MEANS THEY COULD HAVE RUNNING WATER! AND REAL FOOD!
WHY WOULD WE JUST LEAVE WITHOUT EVEN *TALKING* TO THEM?
FOR A MINUTE, WASN'T SURE IF OU WERE GOING TO GET OUT.
WE WERE JUST MAKING SURE THE *TIGERS* WERE GONE.
THEY'RE MOSTLY HARMLESS, UNLESS YOU'RE A ZOMBIE.
I'M KORECH, AND THIS IS MY HOME.

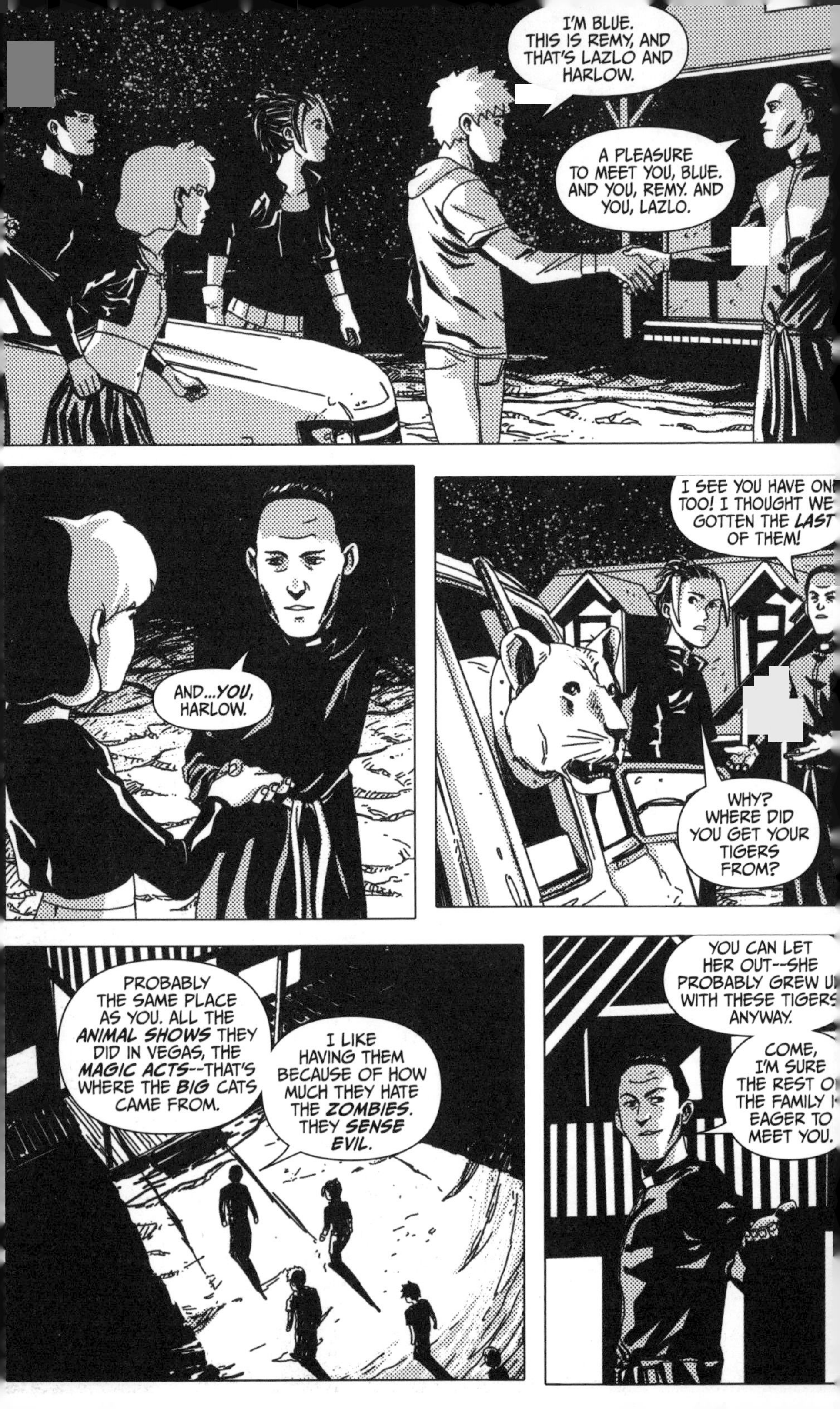
I'M BLUE. THIS IS REMY, AND THAT'S LAZLO AND HARLOW.
A PLEASURE TO MEET YOU, BLUE. AND YOU, REMY. AND YOU, LAZLO.
AND...*YOU,* HARLOW.
I SEE YOU HAVE ON TOO! I THOUGHT WE GOTTEN THE *LAST* OF THEM!
WHY? WHERE DID YOU GET YOUR TIGERS FROM?
PROBABLY THE SAME PLACE AS YOU. ALL THE *ANIMAL SHOWS* THEY DID IN VEGAS, THE *MAGIC ACTS*--THAT'S WHERE THE *BIG* CATS CAME FROM.
I LIKE HAVING THEM BECAUSE OF HOW MUCH THEY HATE THE *ZOMBIES*. THEY *SENSE EVIL*.
YOU CAN LET HER OUT--SHE PROBABLY GREW U WITH THESE TIGERS ANYWAY.
COME, I'M SURE THE REST O THE FAMILY I EAGER TO MEET YOU.

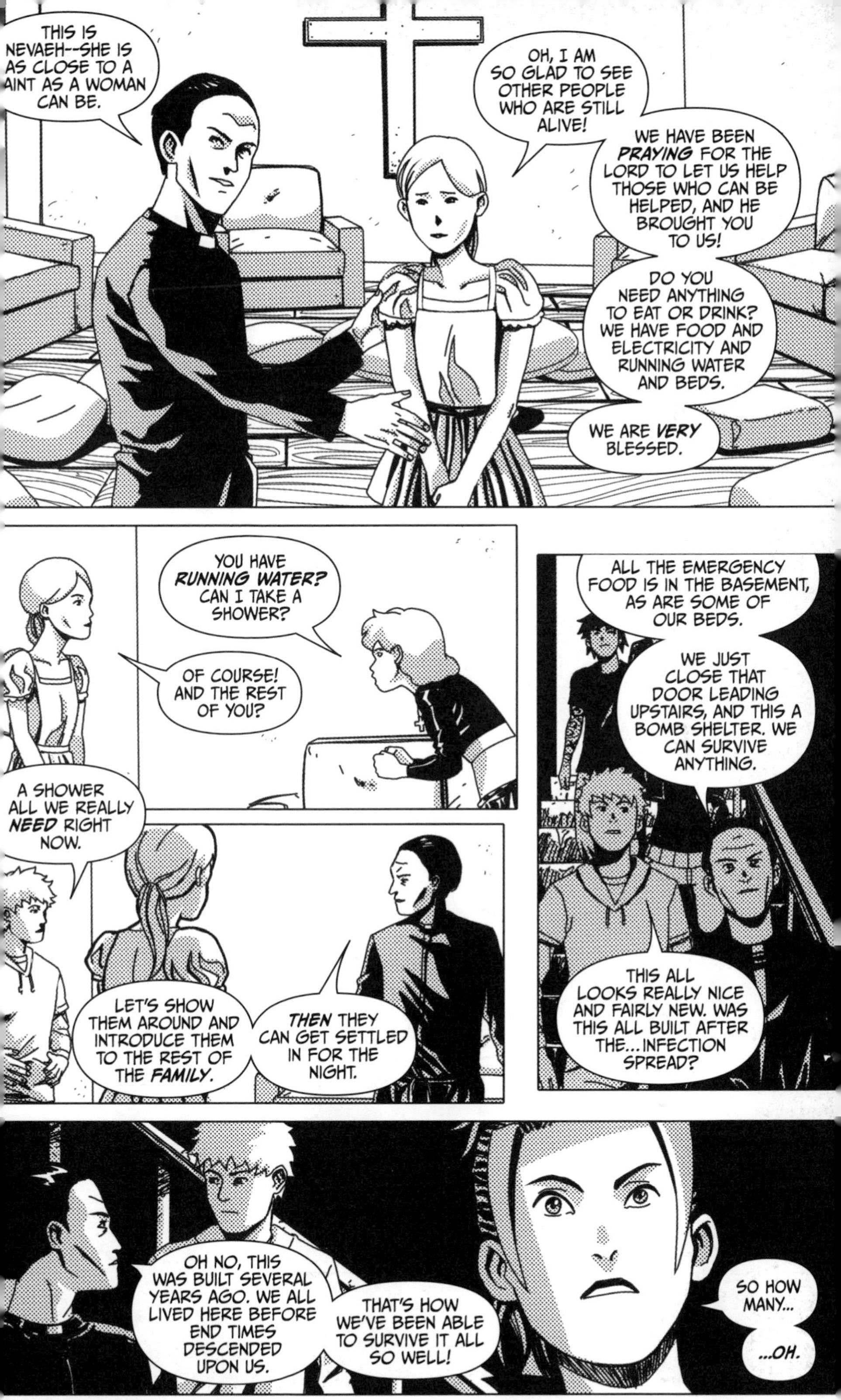
THIS IS NEVAEH--SHE IS AS CLOSE TO A AINT AS A WOMAN CAN BE.
OH, I AM SO GLAD TO SEE OTHER PEOPLE WHO ARE STILL ALIVE!
WE HAVE BEEN *PRAYING* FOR THE LORD TO LET US HELP THOSE WHO CAN BE HELPED, AND HE BROUGHT YOU TO US!
DO YOU NEED ANYTHING TO EAT OR DRINK? WE HAVE FOOD AND ELECTRICITY AND RUNNING WATER AND BEDS.
WE ARE *VERY* BLESSED.
YOU HAVE *RUNNING WATER?* CAN I TAKE A SHOWER?
OF COURSE! AND THE REST OF YOU?
A SHOWER ALL WE REALLY *NEED* RIGHT NOW.
LET'S SHOW THEM AROUND AND INTRODUCE THEM TO THE REST OF THE *FAMILY*.
THEN THEY CAN GET SETTLED IN FOR THE NIGHT.
ALL THE EMERGENCY FOOD IS IN THE BASEMENT, AS ARE SOME OF OUR BEDS.
WE JUST CLOSE THAT DOOR LEADING UPSTAIRS, AND THIS A BOMB SHELTER. WE CAN SURVIVE ANYTHING.
THIS ALL LOOKS REALLY NICE AND FAIRLY NEW. WAS THIS ALL BUILT AFTER THE...INFECTION SPREAD?
OH NO, THIS WAS BUILT SEVERAL YEARS AGO. WE ALL LIVED HERE BEFORE END TIMES DESCENDED UPON US.
THAT'S HOW WE'VE BEEN ABLE TO SURVIVE IT ALL SO WELL!
SO HOW MANY...
...OH.

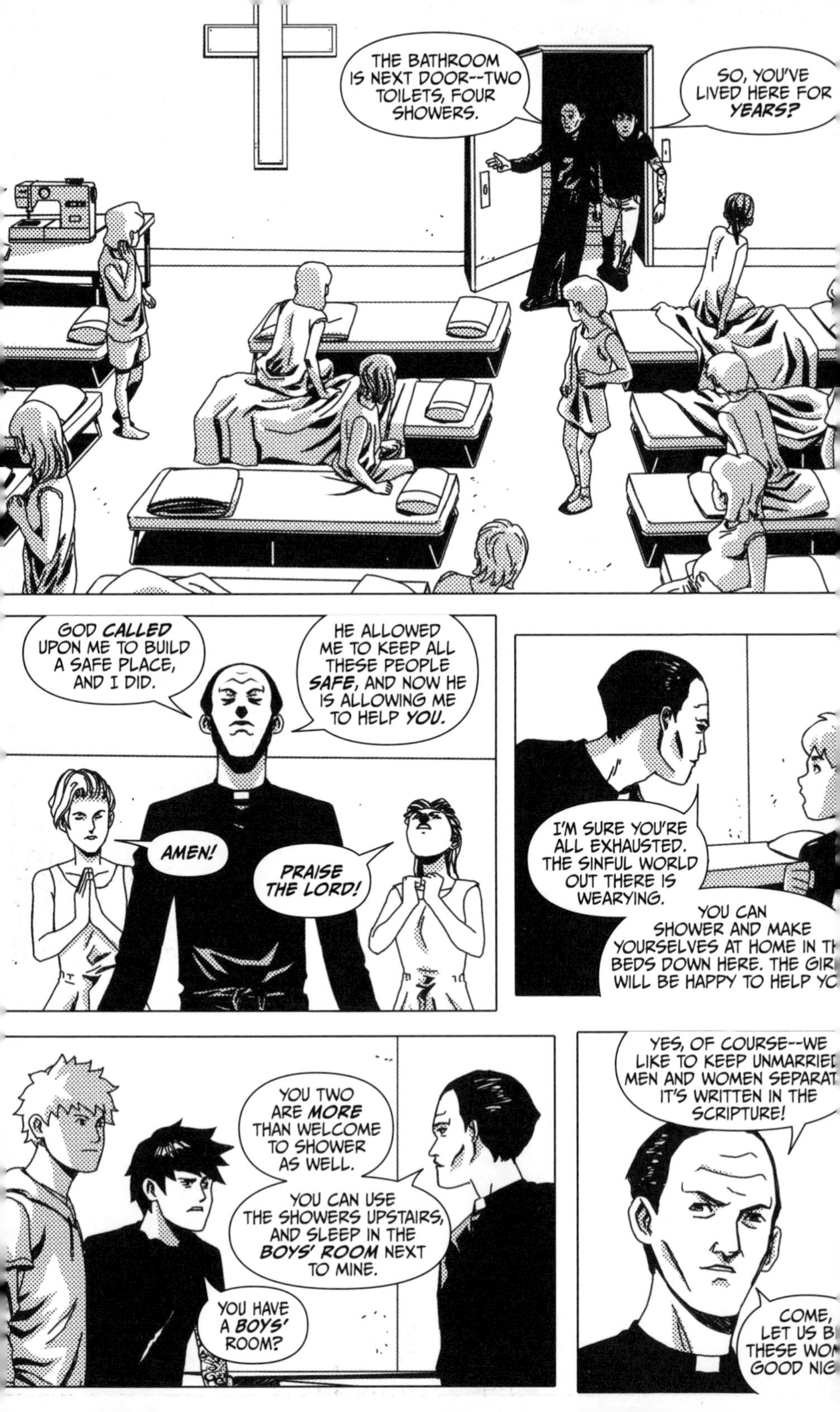
THE BATHROOM IS NEXT DOOR--TWO TOILETS, FOUR SHOWERS.
SO, YOU'VE LIVED HERE FOR *YEARS?*
GOD *CALLED* UPON ME TO BUILD A SAFE PLACE, AND I DID.
HE ALLOWED ME TO KEEP ALL THESE PEOPLE *SAFE*, AND NOW HE IS ALLOWING ME TO HELP *YOU.*
AMEN!
PRAISE THE LORD!
I'M SURE YOU'RE ALL EXHAUSTED. THE SINFUL WORLD OUT THERE IS WEARYING.
YOU CAN SHOWER AND MAKE YOURSELVES AT HOME IN TH BEDS DOWN HERE. THE GIR WILL BE HAPPY TO HELP YO
YOU TWO ARE *MORE* THAN WELCOME TO SHOWER AS WELL.
YOU CAN USE THE SHOWERS UPSTAIRS, AND SLEEP IN THE *BOYS' ROOM* NEXT TO MINE.
YOU HAVE A *BOYS'* ROOM?
YES, OF COURSE--WE LIKE TO KEEP UNMARRIED MEN AND WOMEN SEPARAT IT'S WRITTEN IN THE SCRIPTURE!
COME, LET US B THESE WOM GOOD NIG

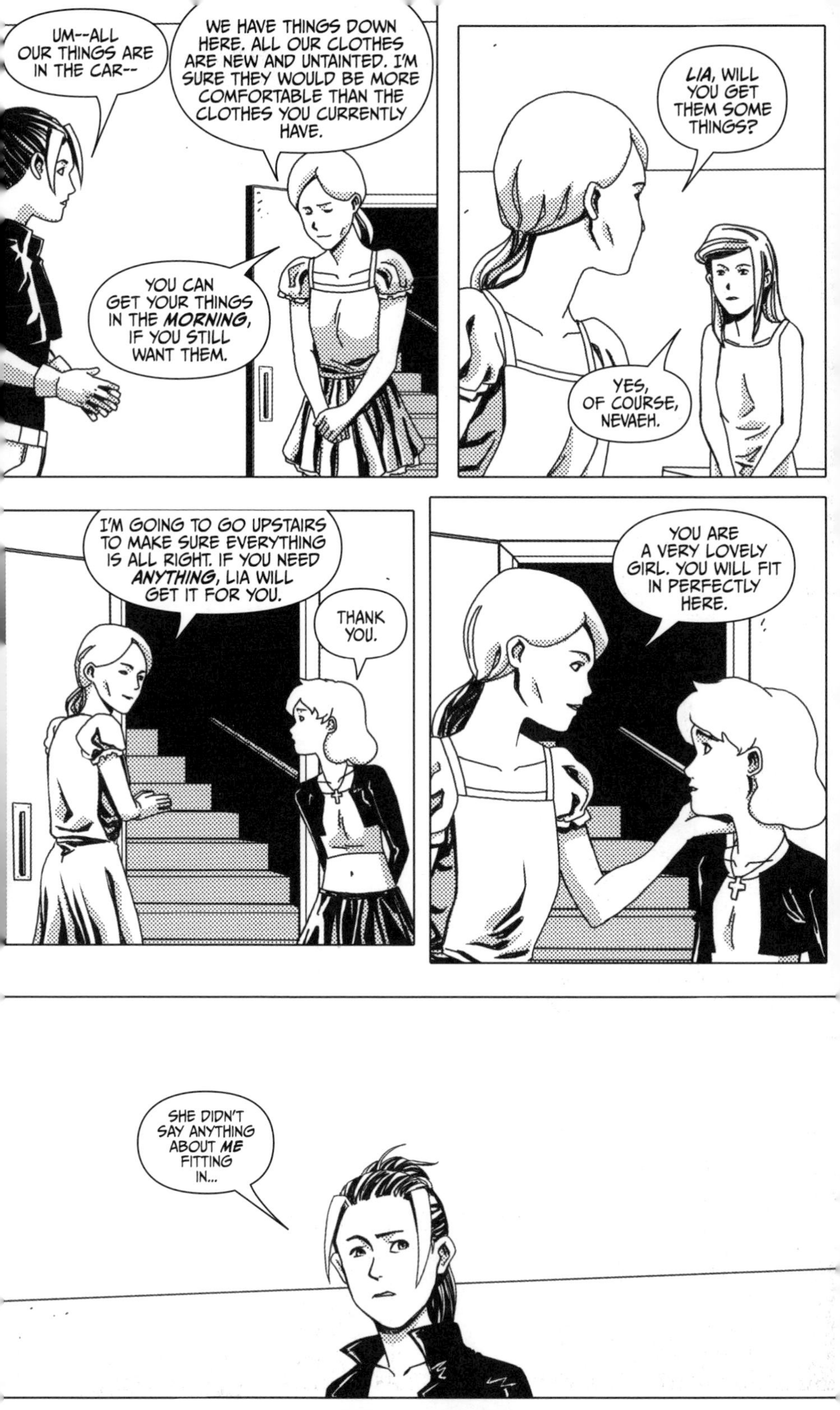
UM--ALL OUR THINGS ARE IN THE CAR--
WE HAVE THINGS DOWN HERE. ALL OUR CLOTHES ARE NEW AND UNTAINTED. I'M SURE THEY WOULD BE MORE COMFORTABLE THAN THE CLOTHES YOU CURRENTLY HAVE.
YOU CAN GET YOUR THINGS IN THE ***MORNING***, IF YOU STILL WANT THEM.
LIA, WILL YOU GET THEM SOME THINGS?
YES, OF COURSE, NEVAEH.
I'M GOING TO GO UPSTAIRS TO MAKE SURE EVERYTHING IS ALL RIGHT. IF YOU NEED ***ANYTHING***, LIA WILL GET IT FOR YOU.
THANK YOU.
YOU ARE A VERY LOVELY GIRL. YOU WILL FIT IN PERFECTLY HERE.
SHE DIDN'T SAY ANYTHING ABOUT ***ME*** FITTING IN...

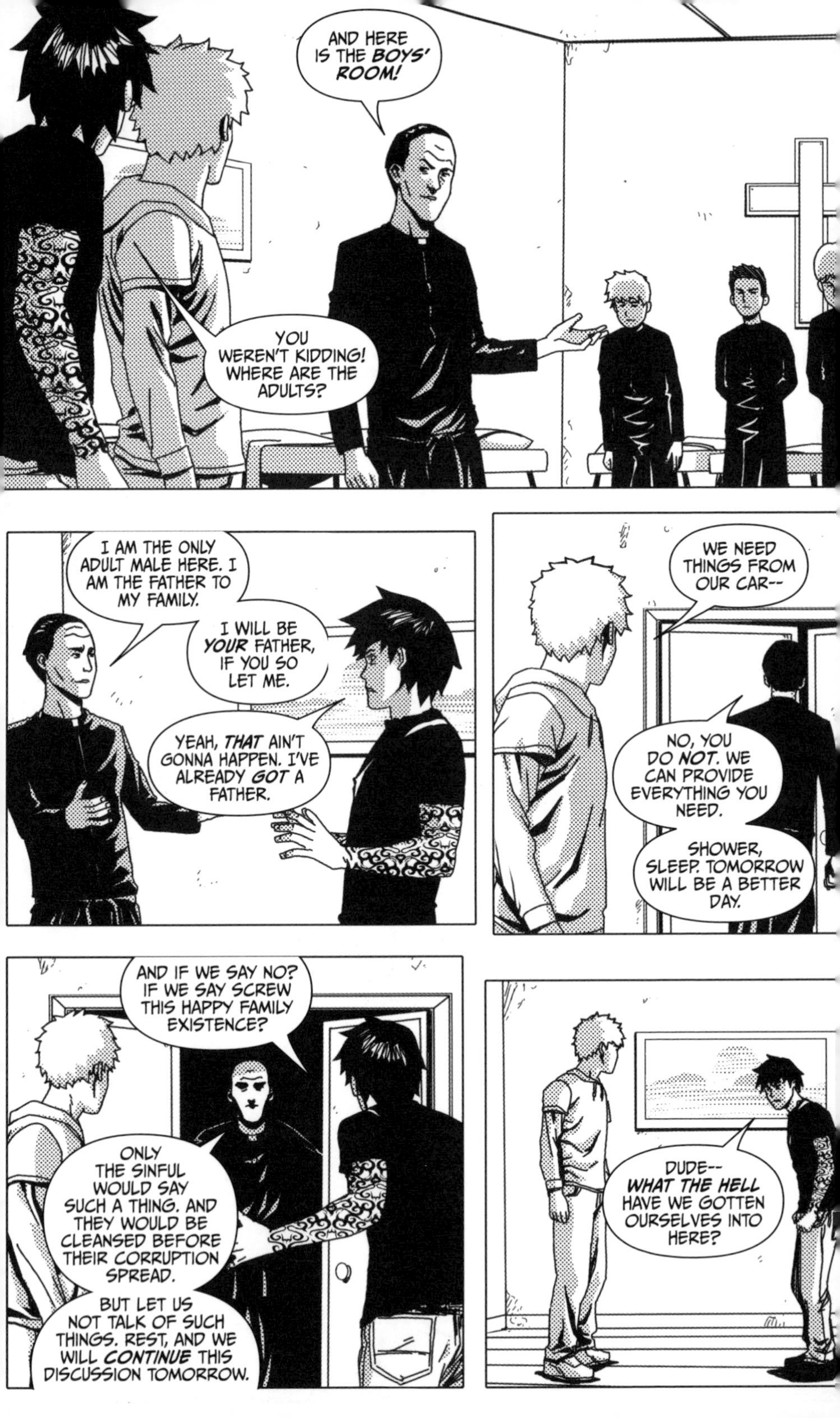
AND HERE IS THE *BOYS'* *ROOM!*
YOU WEREN'T KIDDING! WHERE ARE THE ADULTS?
I AM THE ONLY ADULT MALE HERE. I AM THE FATHER TO MY FAMILY.
I WILL BE *YOUR* FATHER, IF YOU SO LET ME.
YEAH, *THAT* AIN'T GONNA HAPPEN. I'VE ALREADY *GOT* A FATHER.
WE NEED THINGS FROM OUR CAR--
NO, YOU DO *NOT*. WE CAN PROVIDE EVERYTHING YOU NEED.
SHOWER, SLEEP. TOMORROW WILL BE A BETTER DAY.
AND IF WE SAY NO? IF WE SAY SCREW THIS HAPPY FAMILY EXISTENCE?
ONLY THE SINFUL WOULD SAY SUCH A THING. AND THEY WOULD BE CLEANSED BEFORE THEIR CORRUPTION SPREAD.
BUT LET US NOT TALK OF SUCH THINGS. REST, AND WE WILL *CONTINUE* THIS DISCUSSION TOMORROW.
DUDE-- *WHAT THE HELL* HAVE WE GOTTEN OURSELVES INTO HERE?

CHAPTER SIX

THE OLD TIME
RELIGION

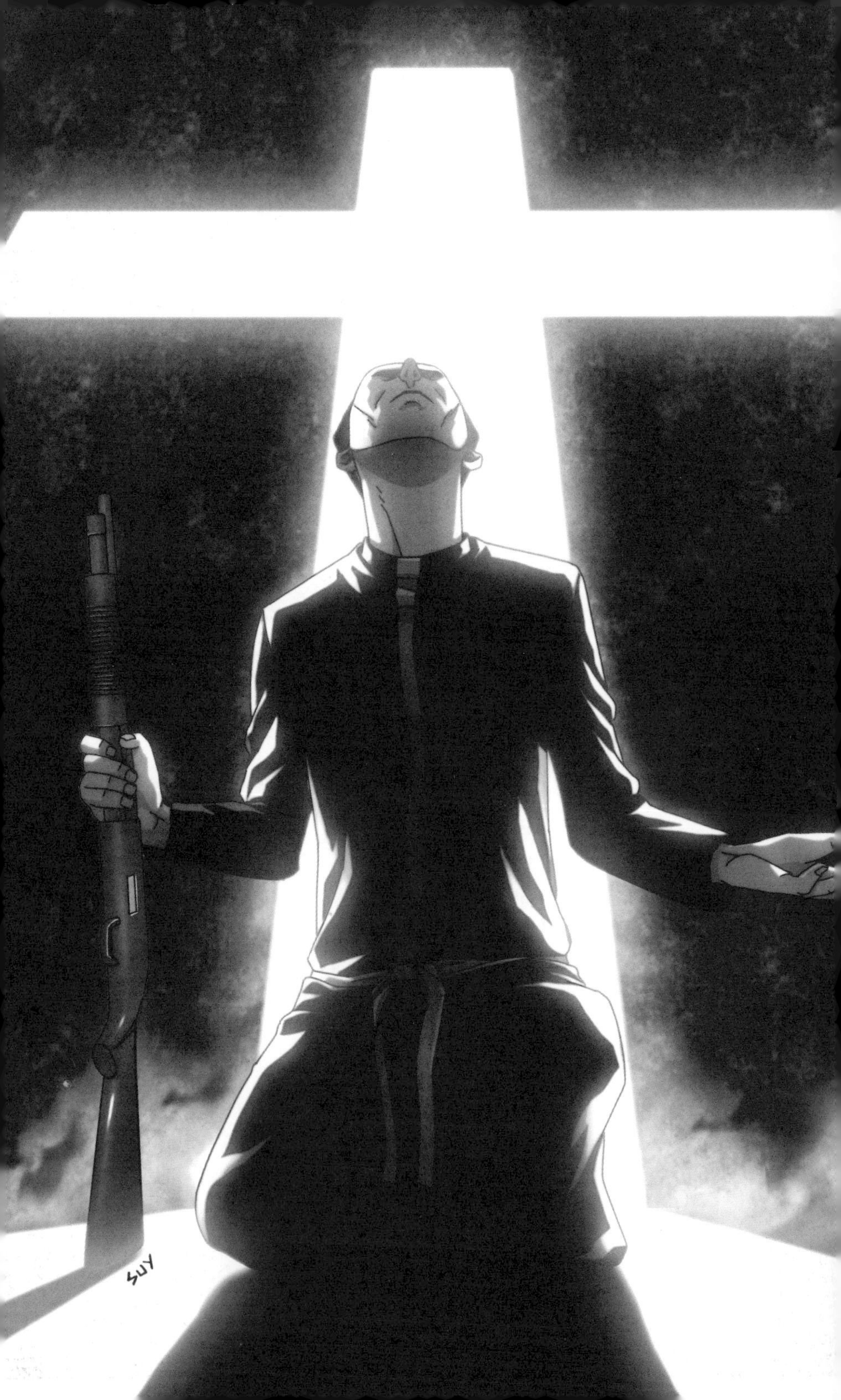
SUY

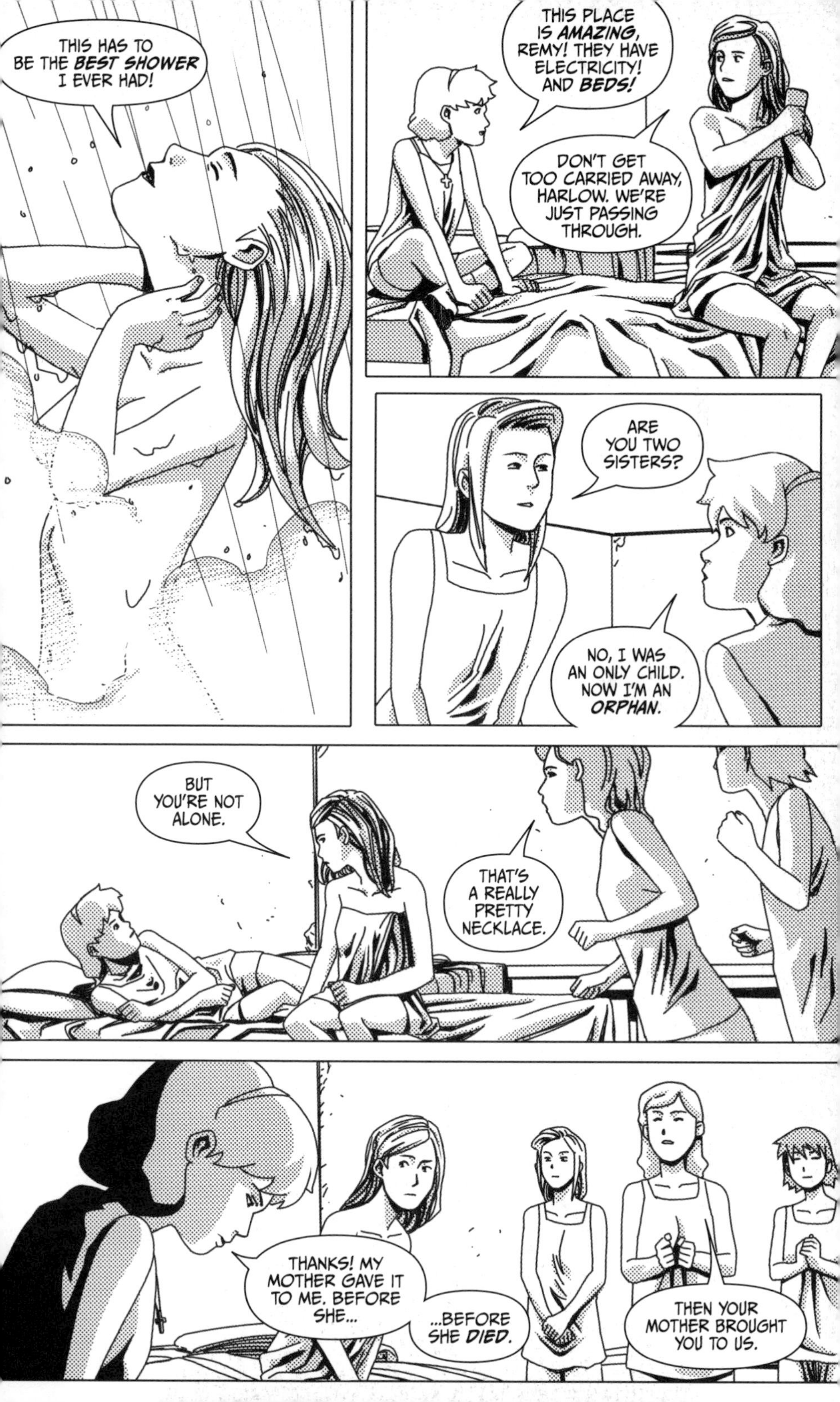
THIS HAS TO BE THE BEST SHOWER I EVER HAD!
THIS PLACE IS AMAZING, REMY! THEY HAVE ELECTRICITY! AND BEDS!
DON'T GET TOO CARRIED AWAY, HARLOW. WE'RE JUST PASSING THROUGH.
ARE YOU TWO SISTERS?
NO, I WAS AN ONLY CHILD. NOW I'M AN ORPHAN.
BUT YOU'RE NOT ALONE.
THAT'S A REALLY PRETTY NECKLACE.
THANKS! MY MOTHER GAVE IT TO ME. BEFORE SHE...
...BEFORE SHE DIED.
THEN YOUR MOTHER BROUGHT YOU TO US.

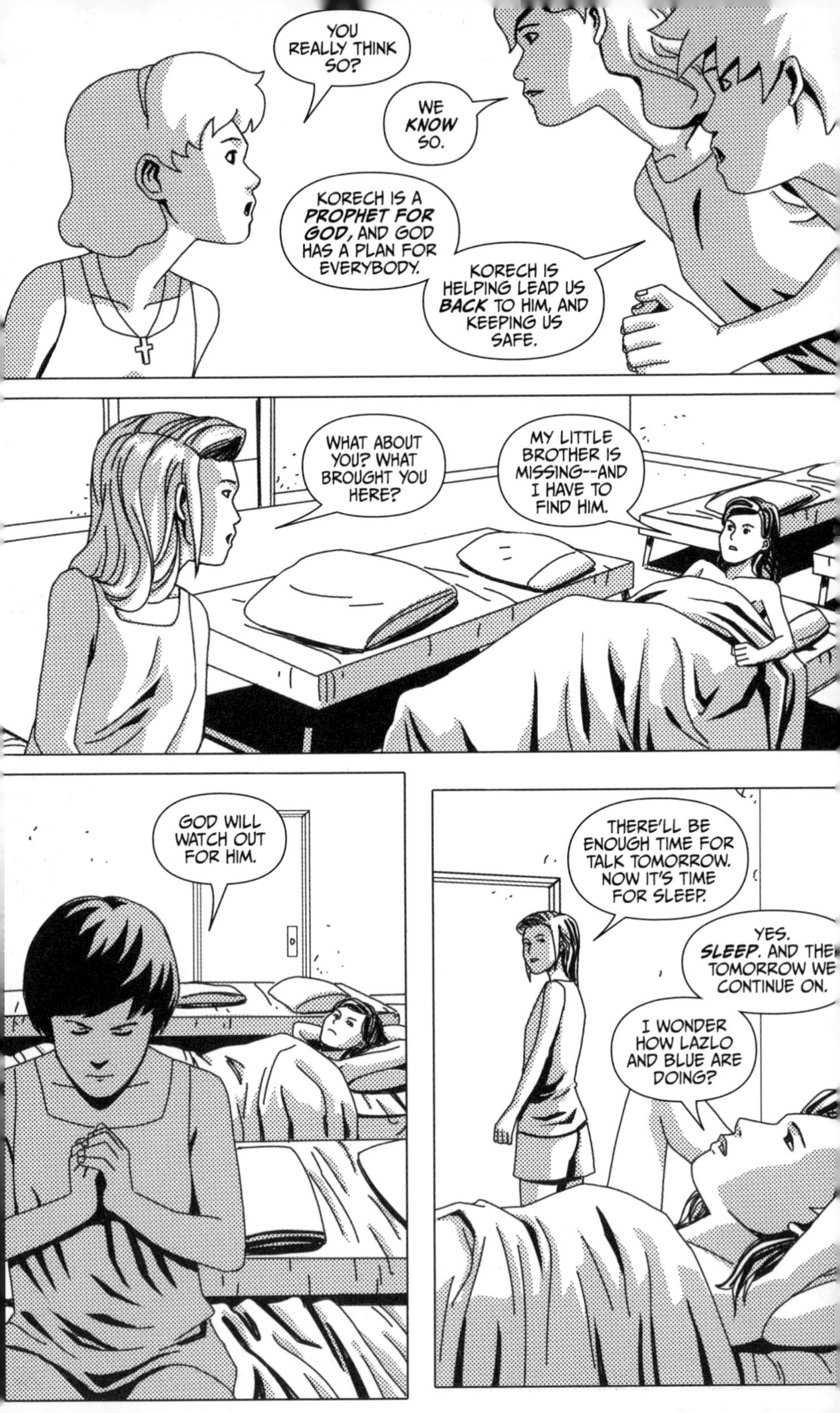
YOU REALLY THINK SO?
WE *KNOW* SO.
KORECH IS A ***PROPHET FOR GOD,*** AND GOD HAS A PLAN FOR EVERYBODY.
KORECH IS HELPING LEAD US ***BACK*** TO HIM, AND KEEPING US SAFE.
WHAT ABOUT YOU? WHAT BROUGHT YOU HERE?
MY LITTLE BROTHER IS MISSING--AND I HAVE TO FIND HIM.
GOD WILL WATCH OUT FOR HIM.
THERE'LL BE ENOUGH TIME FOR TALK TOMORROW. NOW IT'S TIME FOR SLEEP.
YES. ***SLEEP***. AND THE TOMORROW WE CONTINUE ON.
I WONDER HOW LAZLO AND BLUE ARE DOING?

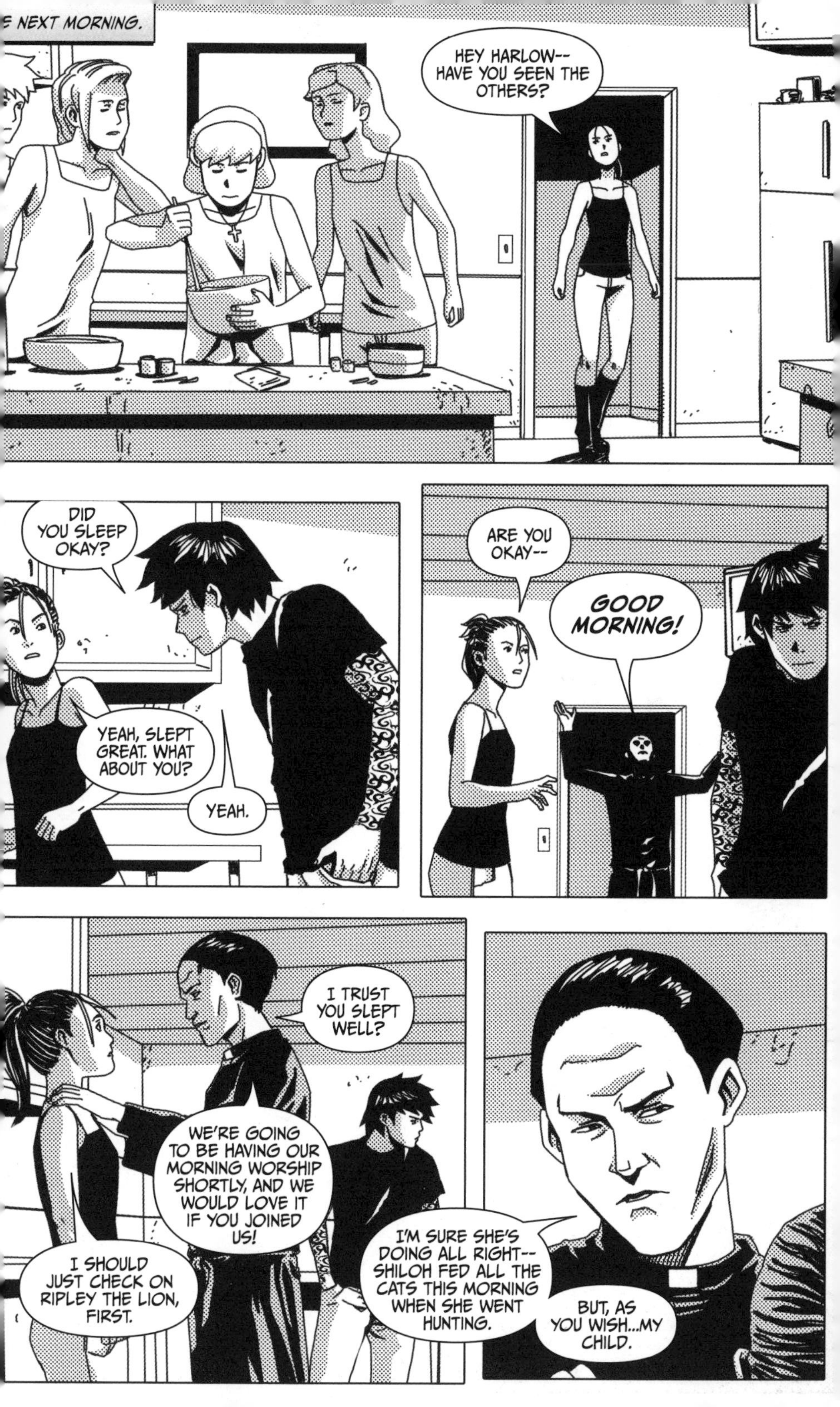
E NEXT MORNING.
HEY HARLOW-- HAVE YOU SEEN THE OTHERS?
DID YOU SLEEP OKAY?
YEAH, SLEPT GREAT. WHAT ABOUT YOU?
YEAH.
ARE YOU OKAY--
GOOD MORNING!
I TRUST YOU SLEPT WELL?
WE'RE GOING TO BE HAVING OUR MORNING WORSHIP SHORTLY, AND WE WOULD LOVE IT IF YOU JOINED US!
I SHOULD JUST CHECK ON RIPLEY THE LION, FIRST.
I'M SURE SHE'S DOING ALL RIGHT-- SHILOH FED ALL THE CATS THIS MORNING WHEN SHE WENT HUNTING.
BUT, AS YOU WISH...MY CHILD.

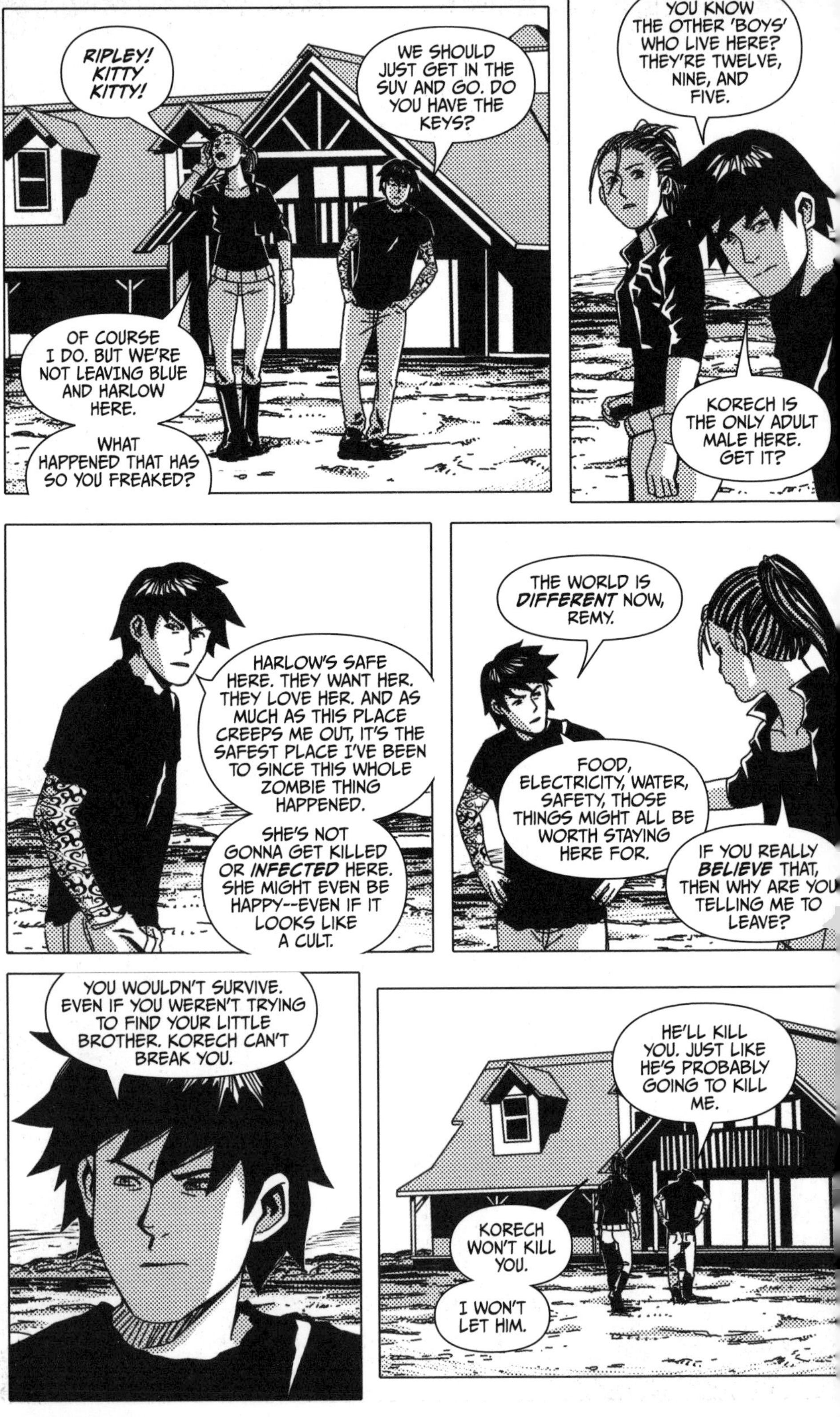
RIPLEY! KITTY KITTY!
WE SHOULD JUST GET IN THE SUV AND GO. DO YOU HAVE THE KEYS?
OF COURSE I DO. BUT WE'RE NOT LEAVING BLUE AND HARLOW HERE.
WHAT HAPPENED THAT HAS SO YOU FREAKED?
YOU KNOW THE OTHER 'BOYS' WHO LIVE HERE? THEY'RE TWELVE, NINE, AND FIVE.
KORECH IS THE ONLY ADULT MALE HERE. GET IT?
HARLOW'S SAFE HERE. THEY WANT HER. THEY LOVE HER. AND AS MUCH AS THIS PLACE CREEPS ME OUT, IT'S THE SAFEST PLACE I'VE BEEN TO SINCE THIS WHOLE ZOMBIE THING HAPPENED.
SHE'S NOT GONNA GET KILLED OR INFECTED HERE. SHE MIGHT EVEN BE HAPPY--EVEN IF IT LOOKS LIKE A CULT.
THE WORLD IS DIFFERENT NOW, REMY.
FOOD, ELECTRICITY, WATER, SAFETY, THOSE THINGS MIGHT ALL BE WORTH STAYING HERE FOR.
IF YOU REALLY BELIEVE THAT, THEN WHY ARE YOU TELLING ME TO LEAVE?
YOU WOULDN'T SURVIVE. EVEN IF YOU WEREN'T TRYING TO FIND YOUR LITTLE BROTHER. KORECH CAN'T BREAK YOU.
HE'LL KILL YOU. JUST LIKE HE'S PROBABLY GOING TO KILL ME.
KORECH WON'T KILL YOU.
I WON'T LET HIM.

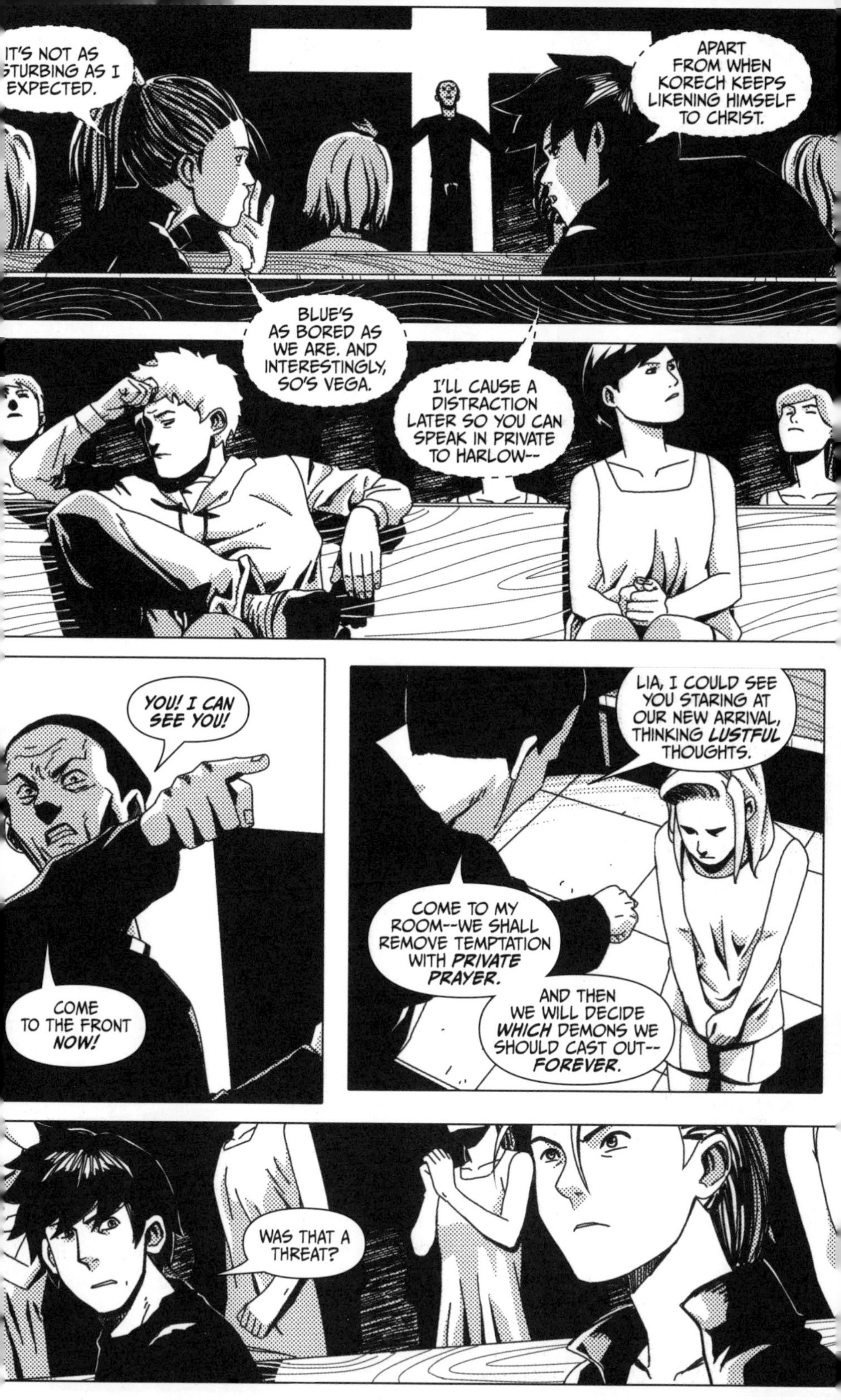
IT'S NOT AS STURBING AS I EXPECTED.
APART FROM WHEN KORECH KEEPS LIKENING HIMSELF TO CHRIST.
BLUE'S AS BORED AS WE ARE. AND INTERESTINGLY, SO'S VEGA.
I'LL CAUSE A DISTRACTION LATER SO YOU CAN SPEAK IN PRIVATE TO HARLOW--
YOU! I CAN SEE YOU!
COME TO THE FRONT ***NOW!***
LIA, I COULD SEE YOU STARING AT OUR NEW ARRIVAL, THINKING ***LUSTFUL*** THOUGHTS.
COME TO MY ROOM--WE SHALL REMOVE TEMPTATION WITH ***PRIVATE PRAYER.***
AND THEN WE WILL DECIDE ***WHICH*** DEMONS WE SHOULD CAST OUT-- ***FOREVER.***
WAS THAT A THREAT?

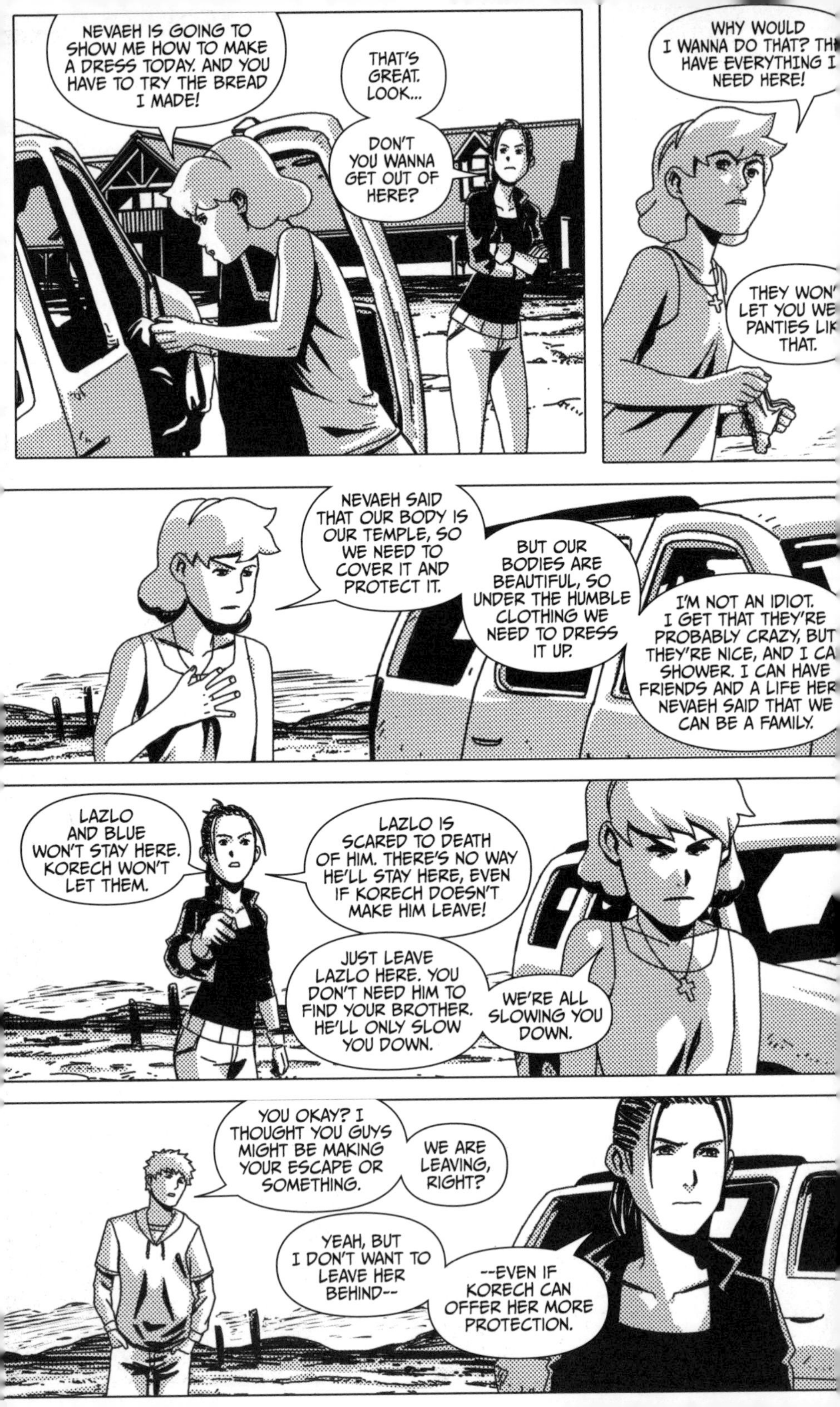
NEVAEH IS GOING TO SHOW ME HOW TO MAKE A DRESS TODAY. AND YOU HAVE TO TRY THE BREAD I MADE!
THAT'S GREAT. LOOK...
DON'T YOU WANNA GET OUT OF HERE?
WHY WOULD I WANNA DO THAT? TH HAVE EVERYTHING I NEED HERE!
THEY WON' LET YOU WE PANTIES LIK THAT.
NEVAEH SAID THAT OUR BODY IS OUR TEMPLE, SO WE NEED TO COVER IT AND PROTECT IT.
BUT OUR BODIES ARE BEAUTIFUL, SO UNDER THE HUMBLE CLOTHING WE NEED TO DRESS IT UP.
I'M NOT AN IDIOT. I GET THAT THEY'RE PROBABLY CRAZY, BUT THEY'RE NICE, AND I CA SHOWER. I CAN HAVE FRIENDS AND A LIFE HER NEVAEH SAID THAT WE CAN BE A FAMILY.
LAZLO AND BLUE WON'T STAY HERE. KORECH WON'T LET THEM.
LAZLO IS SCARED TO DEATH OF HIM. THERE'S NO WAY HE'LL STAY HERE, EVEN IF KORECH DOESN'T MAKE HIM LEAVE!
JUST LEAVE LAZLO HERE. YOU DON'T NEED HIM TO FIND YOUR BROTHER. HE'LL ONLY SLOW YOU DOWN.
WE'RE ALL SLOWING YOU DOWN.
YOU OKAY? I THOUGHT YOU GUYS MIGHT BE MAKING YOUR ESCAPE OR SOMETHING.
WE ARE LEAVING, RIGHT?
YEAH, BUT I DON'T WANT TO LEAVE HER BEHIND--
--EVEN IF KORECH CAN OFFER HER MORE PROTECTION.

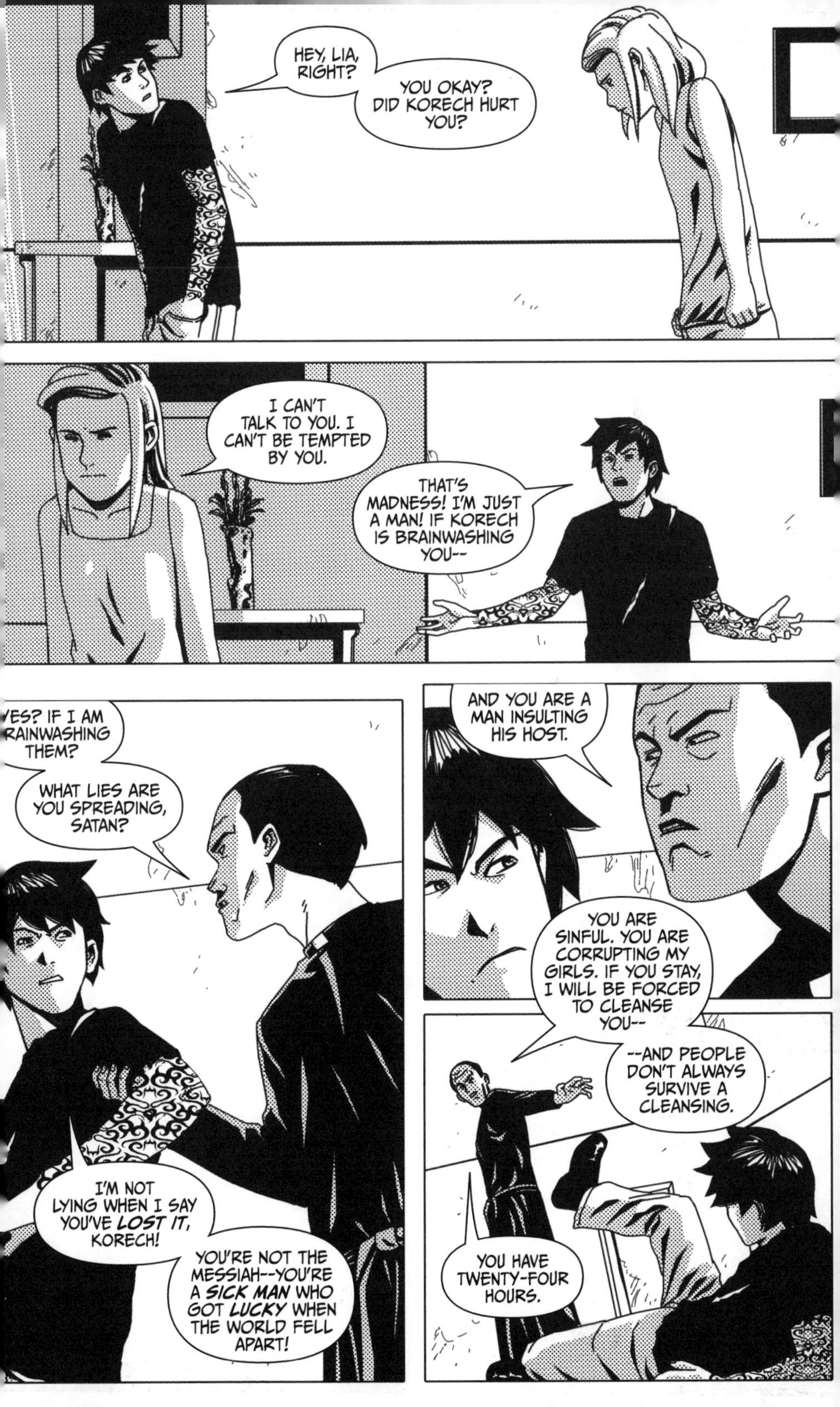
HEY, LIA, RIGHT?
YOU OKAY? DID KORECH HURT YOU?
I CAN'T TALK TO YOU. I CAN'T BE TEMPTED BY YOU.
THAT'S MADNESS! I'M JUST A MAN! IF KORECH IS BRAINWASHING YOU--
YES? IF I AM BRAINWASHING THEM?
WHAT LIES ARE YOU SPREADING, SATAN?
I'M NOT LYING WHEN I SAY YOU'VE LOST IT, KORECH!
YOU'RE NOT THE MESSIAH--YOU'RE A SICK MAN WHO GOT LUCKY WHEN THE WORLD FELL APART!
AND YOU ARE A MAN INSULTING HIS HOST.
YOU ARE SINFUL. YOU ARE CORRUPTING MY GIRLS. IF YOU STAY, I WILL BE FORCED TO CLEANSE YOU--
--AND PEOPLE DON'T ALWAYS SURVIVE A CLEANSING.
YOU HAVE TWENTY-FOUR HOURS.

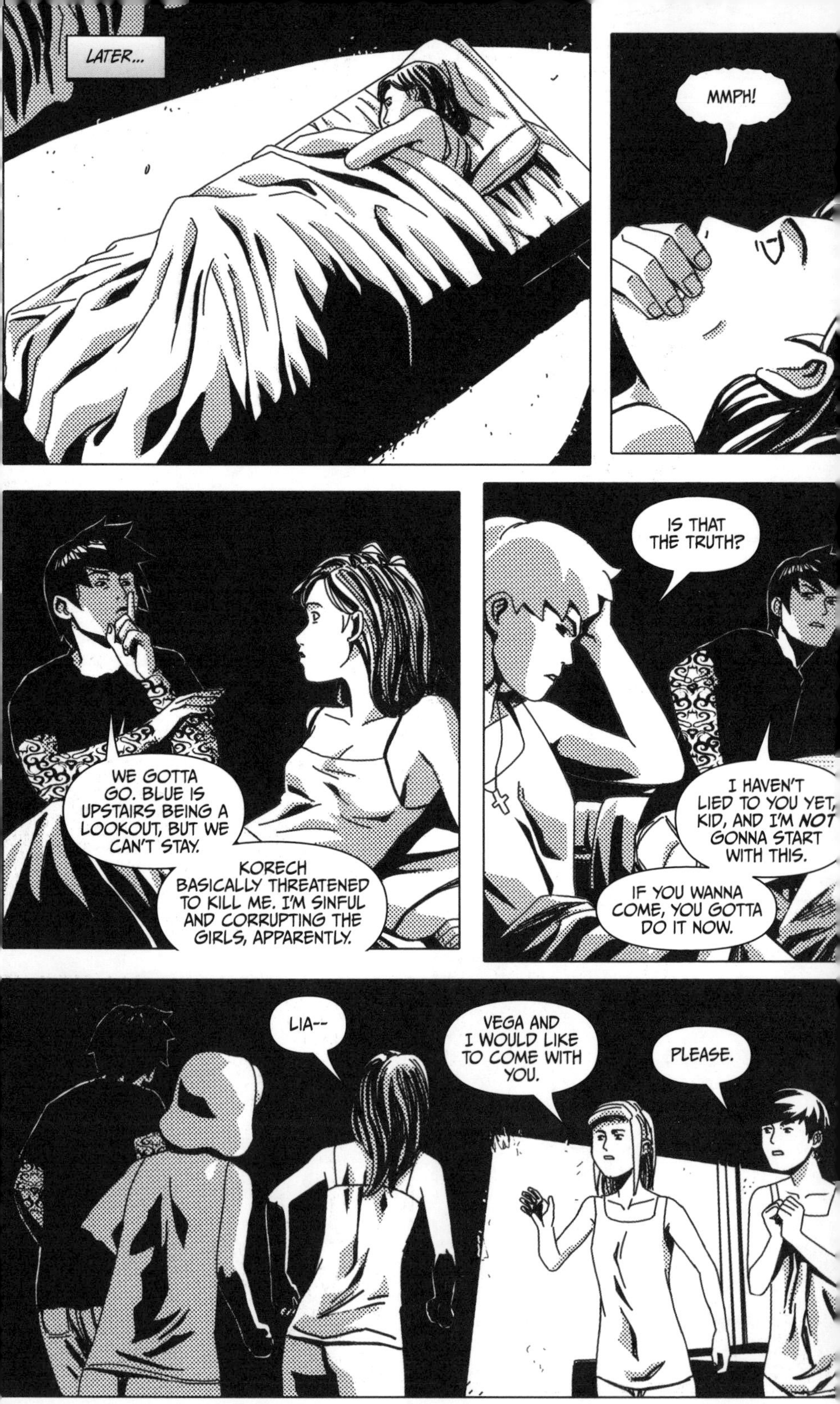
LATER...
MMPH!
WE GOTTA GO. BLUE IS UPSTAIRS BEING A LOOKOUT, BUT WE CAN'T STAY.
KORECH BASICALLY THREATENED TO KILL ME. I'M SINFUL AND CORRUPTING THE GIRLS, APPARENTLY.
IS THAT THE TRUTH?
I HAVEN'T LIED TO YOU YET, KID, AND I'M *NOT* GONNA START WITH THIS.
IF YOU WANNA COME, YOU GOTTA DO IT NOW.
LIA--
VEGA AND I WOULD LIKE TO COME WITH YOU.
PLEASE.

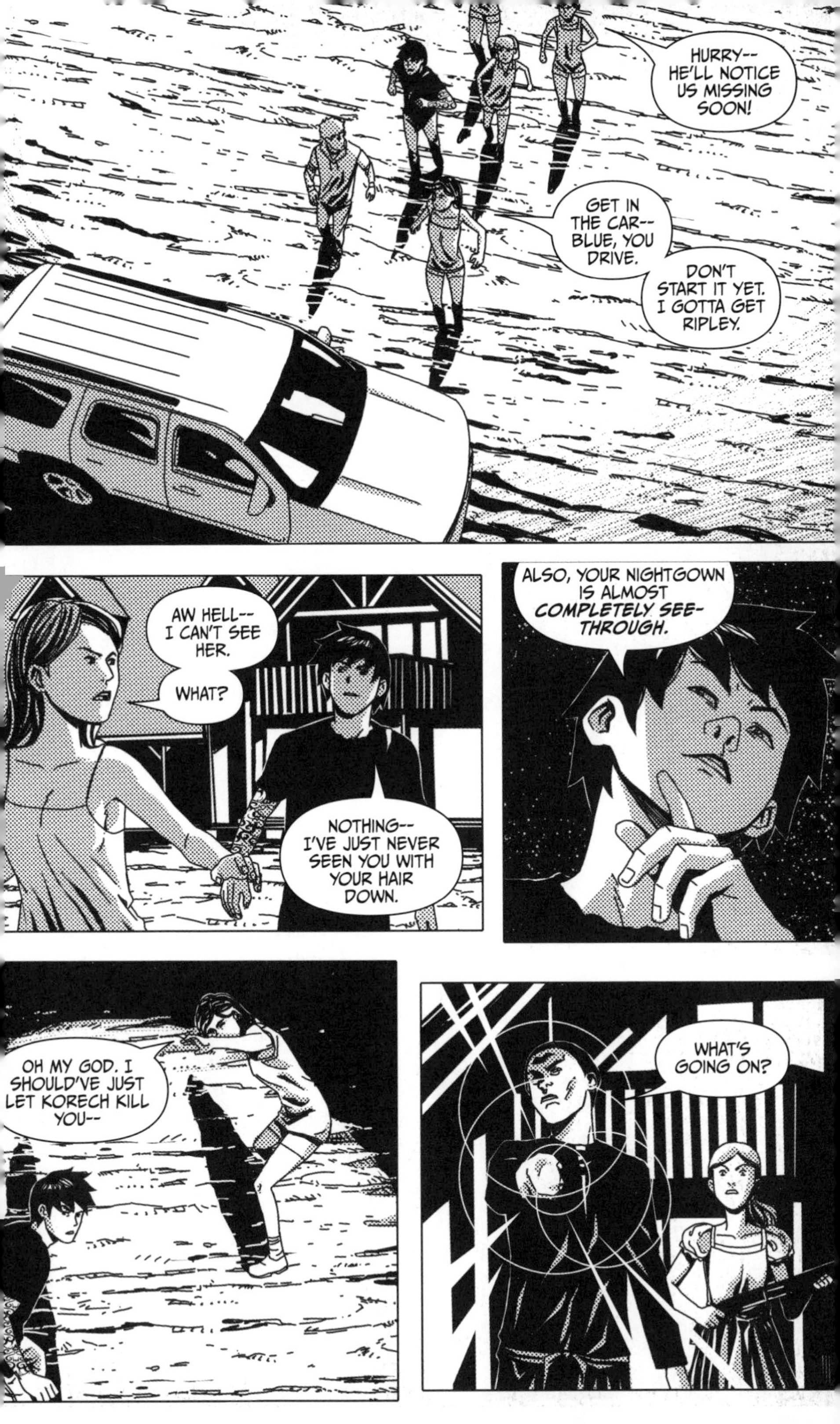
HURRY-- HE'LL NOTICE US MISSING SOON!
GET IN THE CAR-- BLUE, YOU DRIVE.
DON'T START IT YET. I GOTTA GET RIPLEY.
AW HELL-- I CAN'T SEE HER.
WHAT?
NOTHING-- I'VE JUST NEVER SEEN YOU WITH YOUR HAIR DOWN.
ALSO, YOUR NIGHTGOWN IS ALMOST *COMPLETELY SEE-THROUGH.*
OH MY GOD. I SHOULD'VE JUST LET KORECH KILL YOU--
WHAT'S GOING ON?

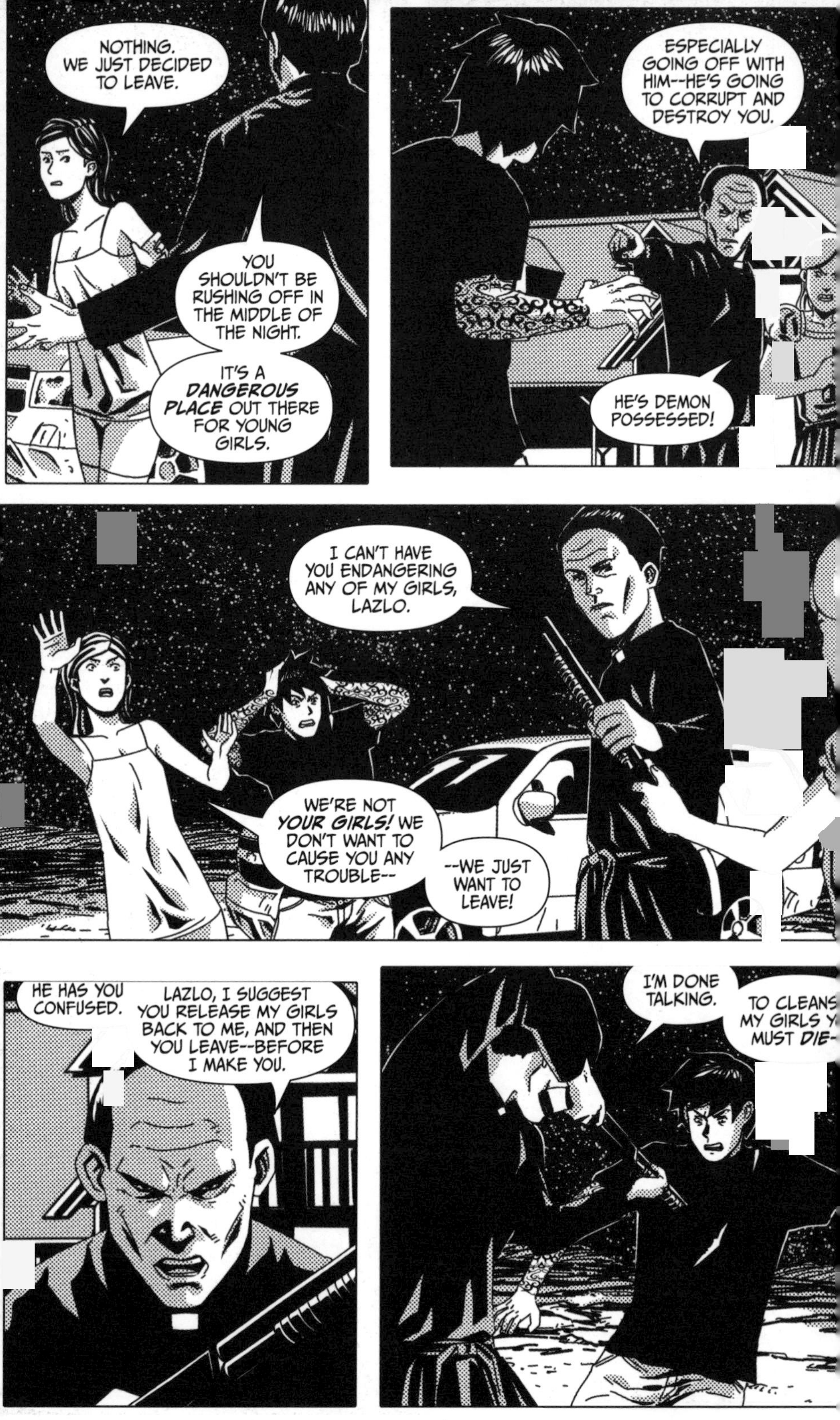
NOTHING. WE JUST DECIDED TO LEAVE.
YOU SHOULDN'T BE RUSHING OFF IN THE MIDDLE OF THE NIGHT.
IT'S A DANGEROUS PLACE OUT THERE FOR YOUNG GIRLS.
ESPECIALLY GOING OFF WITH HIM--HE'S GOING TO CORRUPT AND DESTROY YOU.
HE'S DEMON POSSESSED!
I CAN'T HAVE YOU ENDANGERING ANY OF MY GIRLS, LAZLO.
WE'RE NOT YOUR GIRLS! WE DON'T WANT TO CAUSE YOU ANY TROUBLE--
--WE JUST WANT TO LEAVE!
HE HAS YOU CONFUSED.
LAZLO, I SUGGEST YOU RELEASE MY GIRLS BACK TO ME, AND THEN YOU LEAVE--BEFORE I MAKE YOU.
I'M DONE TALKING.
TO CLEANS MY GIRLS Y MUST DIE-

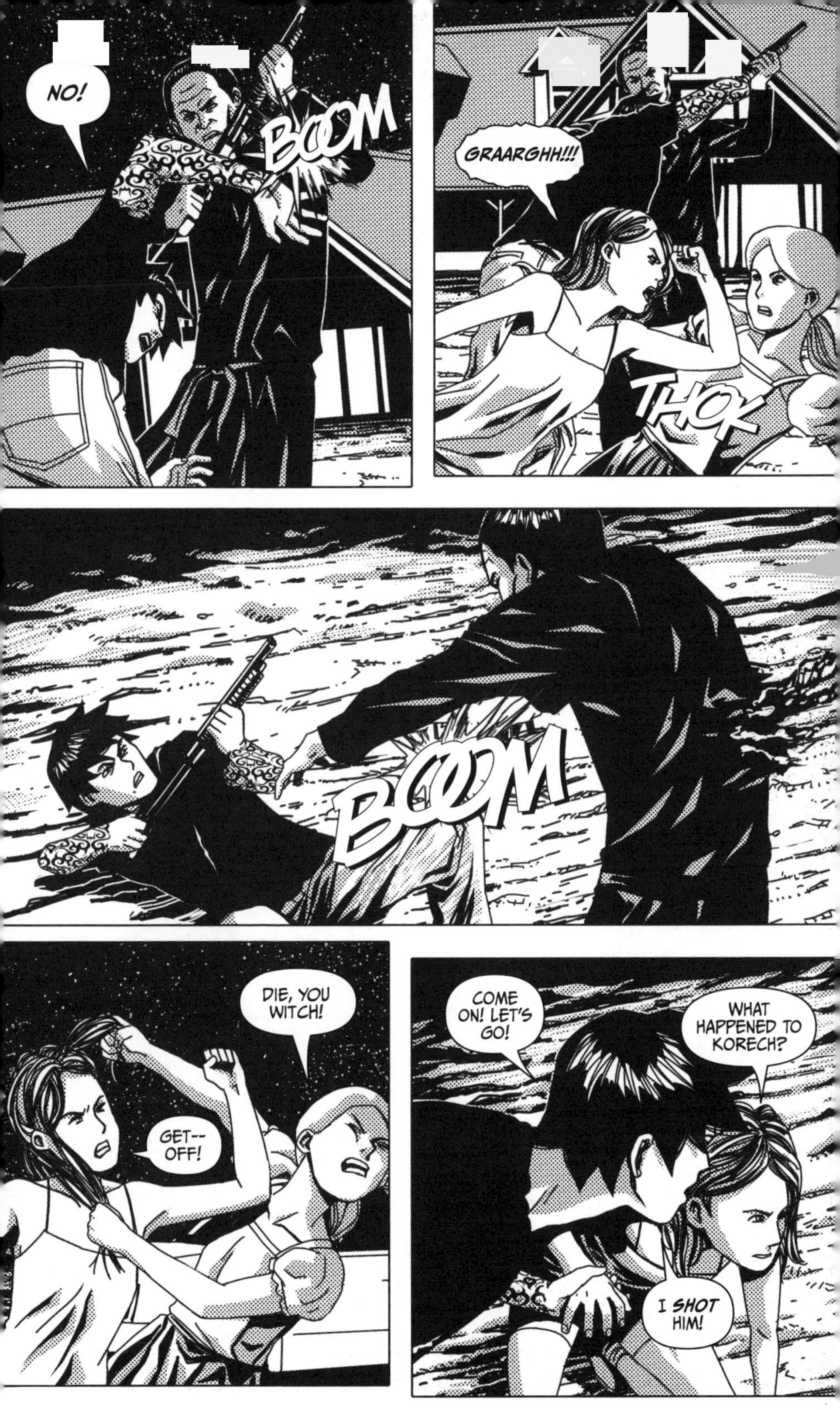
NO!
BOOM
GRAARGHH!!!
THOK
BOOM
DIE, YOU WITCH!
GET-- OFF!
COME ON! LET'S GO!
WHAT HAPPENED TO KORECH?
I SHOT HIM!

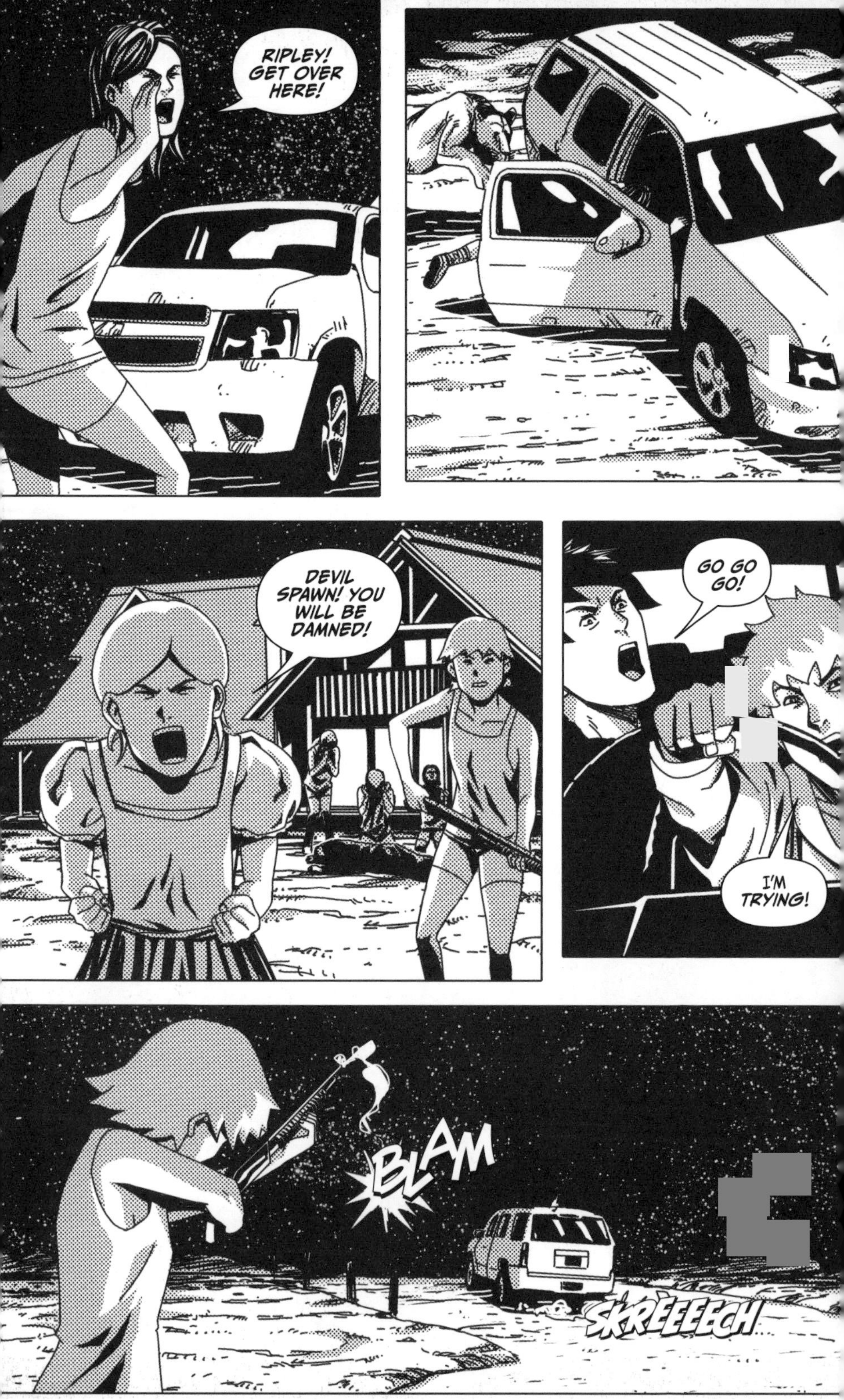
RIPLEY! GET OVER HERE!
DEVIL SPAWN! YOU WILL BE DAMNED!
GO GO GO!
I'M TRYING!
BLAM
SKREEEECH

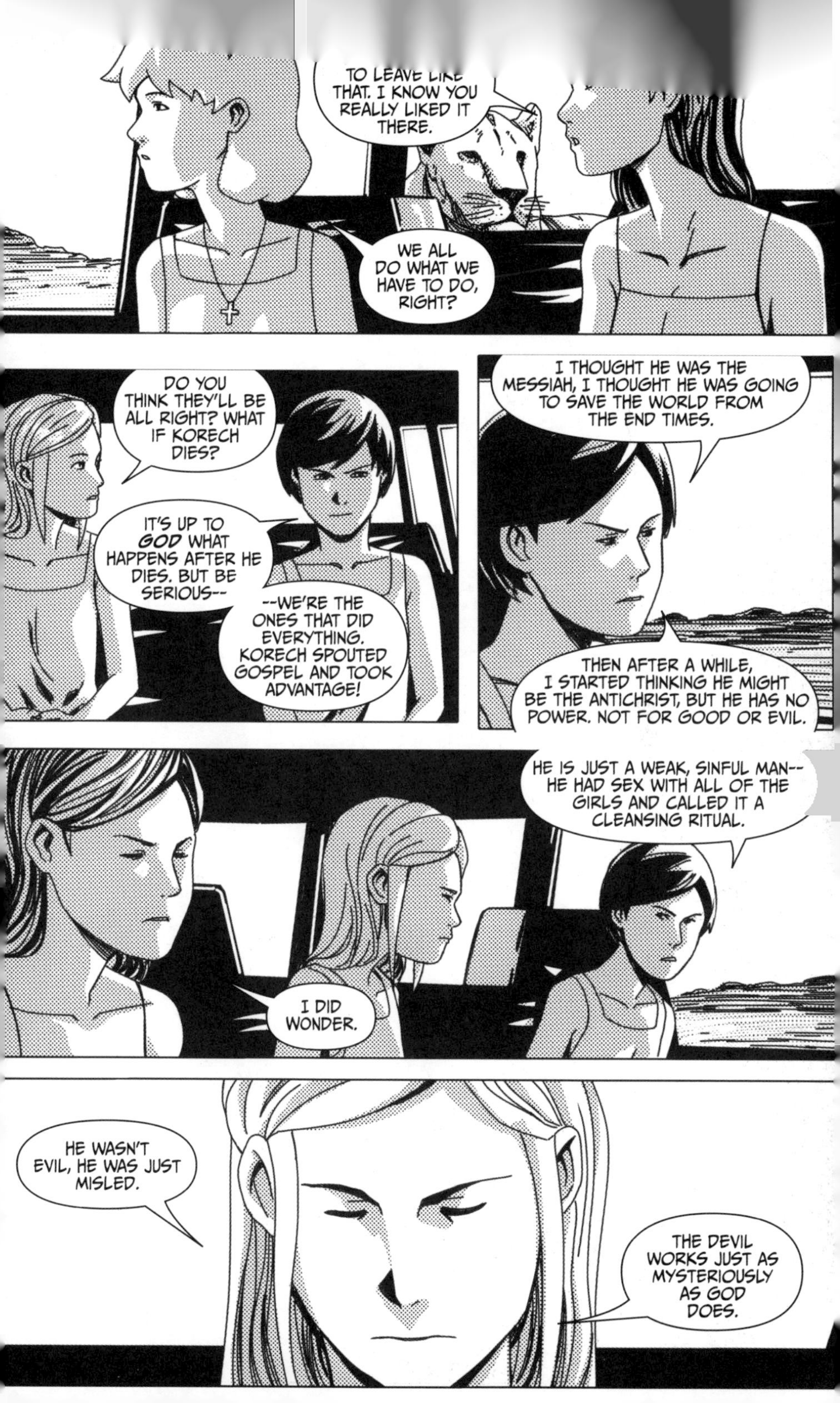
TO LEAVE LIKE THAT. I KNOW YOU REALLY LIKED IT THERE.
WE ALL DO WHAT WE HAVE TO DO, RIGHT?
DO YOU THINK THEY'LL BE ALL RIGHT? WHAT IF KORECH DIES?
IT'S UP TO GOD WHAT HAPPENS AFTER HE DIES. BUT BE SERIOUS--
--WE'RE THE ONES THAT DID EVERYTHING. KORECH SPOUTED GOSPEL AND TOOK ADVANTAGE!
I THOUGHT HE WAS THE MESSIAH, I THOUGHT HE WAS GOING TO SAVE THE WORLD FROM THE END TIMES.
THEN AFTER A WHILE, I STARTED THINKING HE MIGHT BE THE ANTICHRIST, BUT HE HAS NO POWER. NOT FOR GOOD OR EVIL.
HE IS JUST A WEAK, SINFUL MAN-- HE HAD SEX WITH ALL OF THE GIRLS AND CALLED IT A CLEANSING RITUAL.
I DID WONDER.
HE WASN'T EVIL, HE WAS JUST MISLED.
THE DEVIL WORKS JUST AS MYSTERIOUSLY AS GOD DOES.

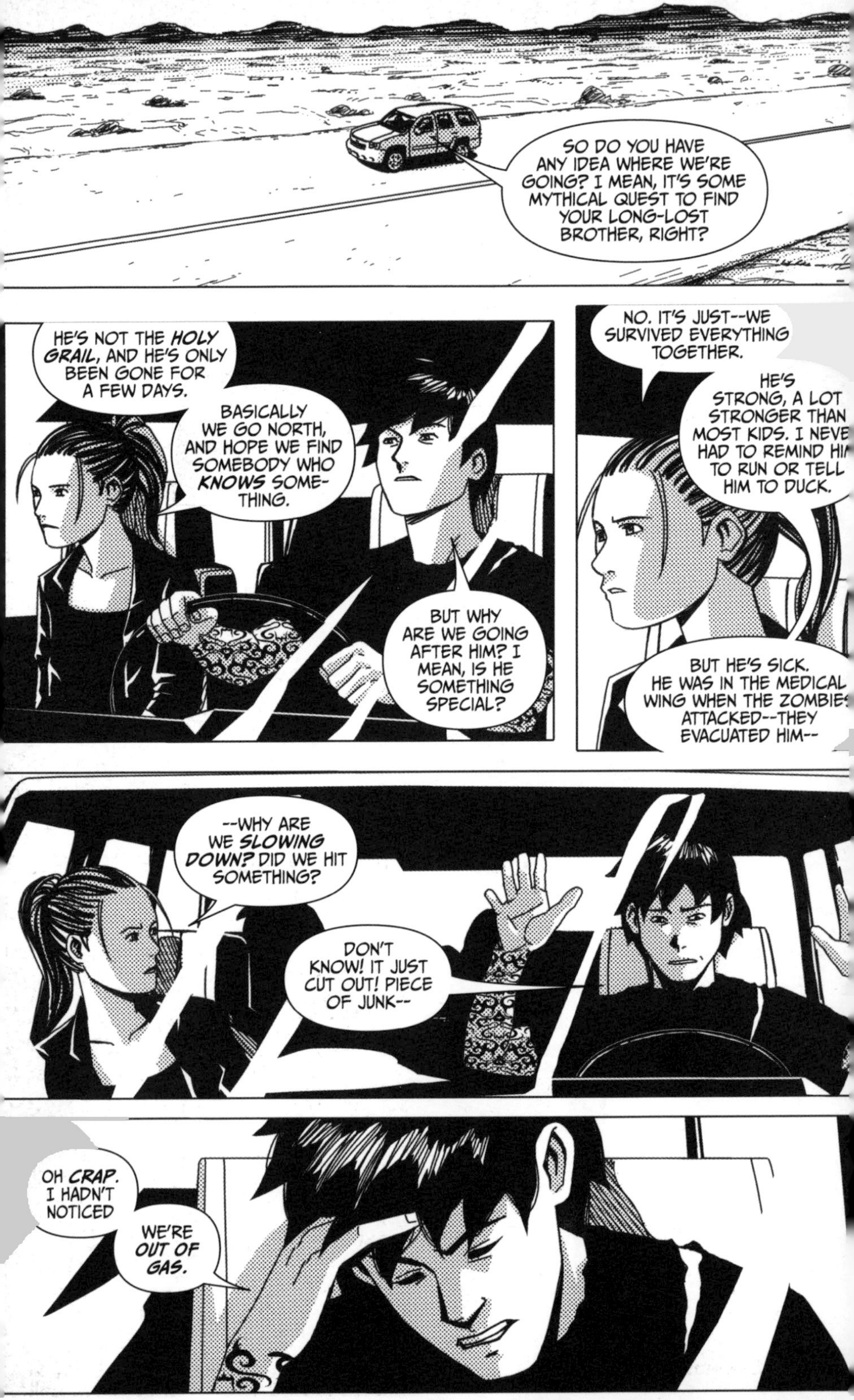
SO DO YOU HAVE ANY IDEA WHERE WE'RE GOING? I MEAN, IT'S SOME MYTHICAL QUEST TO FIND YOUR LONG-LOST BROTHER, RIGHT?
HE'S NOT THE HOLY GRAIL, AND HE'S ONLY BEEN GONE FOR A FEW DAYS.
BASICALLY WE GO NORTH, AND HOPE WE FIND SOMEBODY WHO KNOWS SOME-THING.
BUT WHY ARE WE GOING AFTER HIM? I MEAN, IS HE SOMETHING SPECIAL?
NO. IT'S JUST--WE SURVIVED EVERYTHING TOGETHER.
HE'S STRONG, A LOT STRONGER THAN MOST KIDS. I NEVE HAD TO REMIND HI TO RUN OR TELL HIM TO DUCK.
BUT HE'S SICK. HE WAS IN THE MEDICAL WING WHEN THE ZOMBIE ATTACKED--THEY EVACUATED HIM--
--WHY ARE WE SLOWING DOWN? DID WE HIT SOMETHING?
DON'T KNOW! IT JUST CUT OUT! PIECE OF JUNK--
OH CRAP. I HADN'T NOTICED
WE'RE OUT OF GAS.

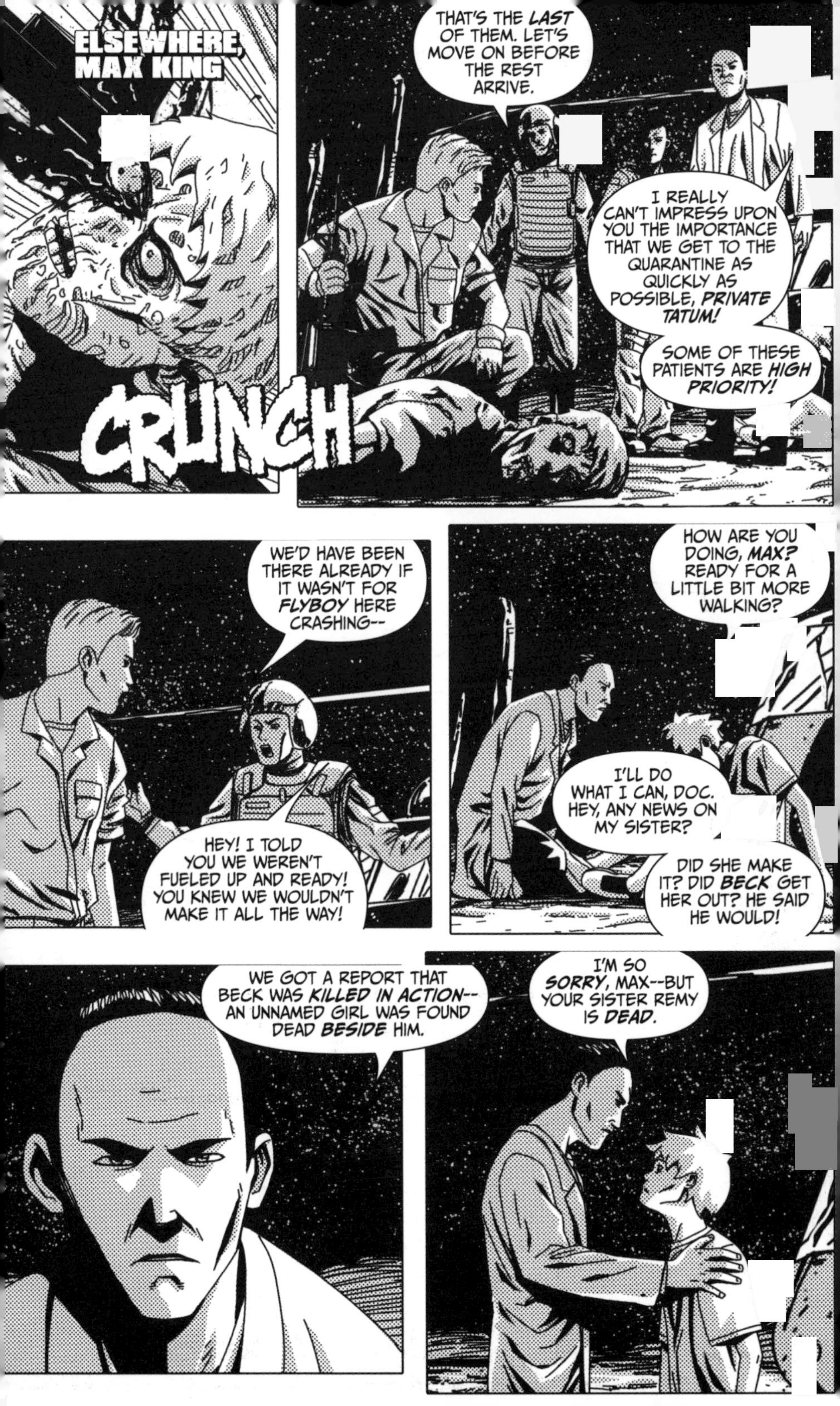
ELSEWHERE, MAX KING
CRUNCH
THAT'S THE LAST OF THEM. LET'S MOVE ON BEFORE THE REST ARRIVE.
I REALLY CAN'T IMPRESS UPON YOU THE IMPORTANCE THAT WE GET TO THE QUARANTINE AS QUICKLY AS POSSIBLE, PRIVATE TATUM!
SOME OF THESE PATIENTS ARE HIGH PRIORITY!
WE'D HAVE BEEN THERE ALREADY IF IT WASN'T FOR FLYBOY HERE CRASHING--
HEY! I TOLD YOU WE WEREN'T FUELED UP AND READY! YOU KNEW WE WOULDN'T MAKE IT ALL THE WAY!
HOW ARE YOU DOING, MAX? READY FOR A LITTLE BIT MORE WALKING?
I'LL DO WHAT I CAN, DOC. HEY, ANY NEWS ON MY SISTER?
DID SHE MAKE IT? DID BECK GET HER OUT? HE SAID HE WOULD!
WE GOT A REPORT THAT BECK WAS KILLED IN ACTION-- AN UNNAMED GIRL WAS FOUND DEAD BESIDE HIM.
I'M SO SORRY, MAX--BUT YOUR SISTER REMY IS DEAD.

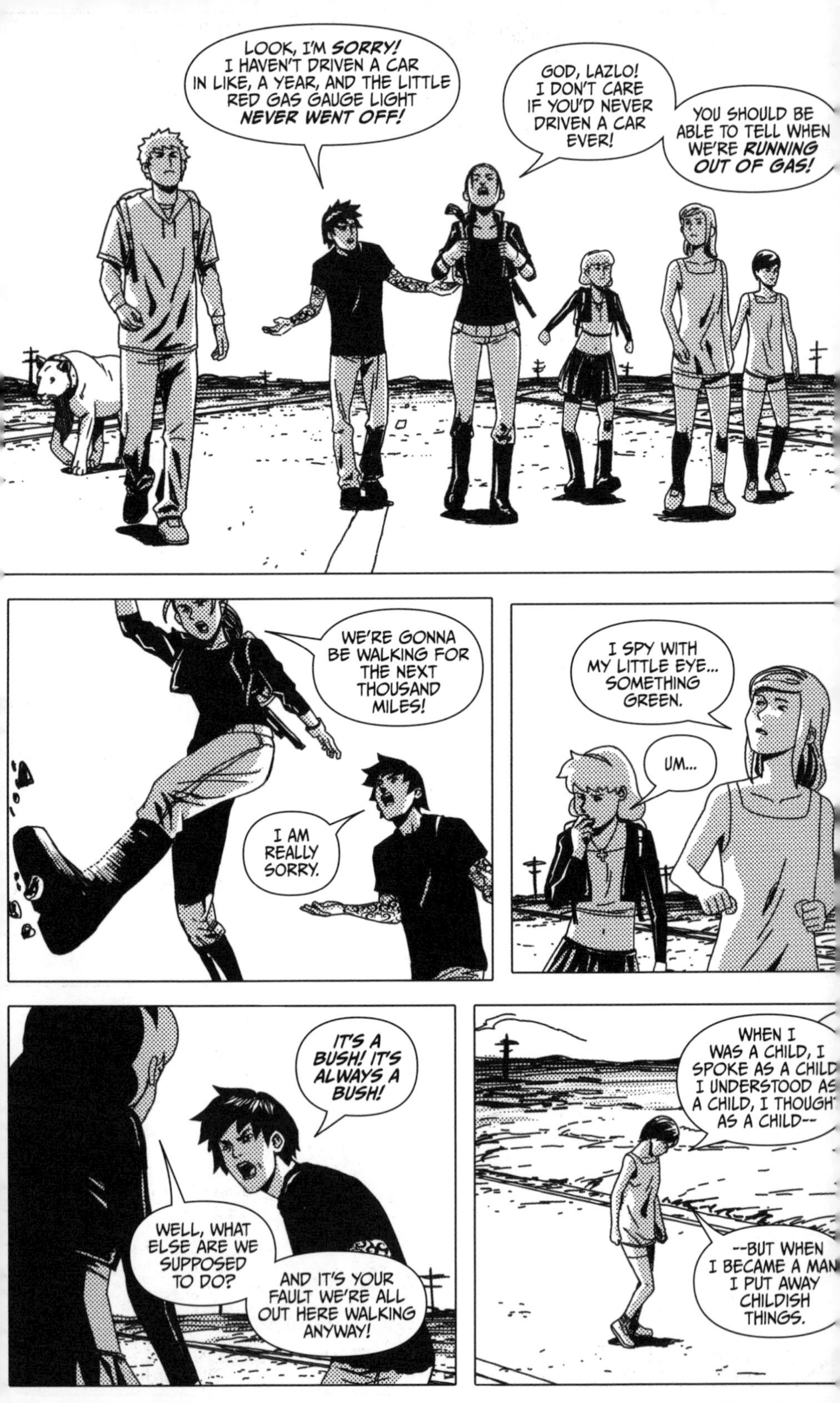

LOOK, I'M SORRY! I HAVEN'T DRIVEN A CAR IN LIKE, A YEAR, AND THE LITTLE RED GAS GAUGE LIGHT NEVER WENT OFF!
GOD, LAZLO! I DON'T CARE IF YOU'D NEVER DRIVEN A CAR EVER!
YOU SHOULD BE ABLE TO TELL WHEN WE'RE RUNNING OUT OF GAS!
WE'RE GONNA BE WALKING FOR THE NEXT THOUSAND MILES!
I AM REALLY SORRY.
I SPY WITH MY LITTLE EYE... SOMETHING GREEN.
UM...
IT'S A BUSH! IT'S ALWAYS A BUSH!
WELL, WHAT ELSE ARE WE SUPPOSED TO DO?
AND IT'S YOUR FAULT WE'RE ALL OUT HERE WALKING ANYWAY!
WHEN I WAS A CHILD, I SPOKE AS A CHILD I UNDERSTOOD AS A CHILD, I THOUGHT AS A CHILD--
--BUT WHEN I BECAME A MAN I PUT AWAY CHILDISH THINGS.

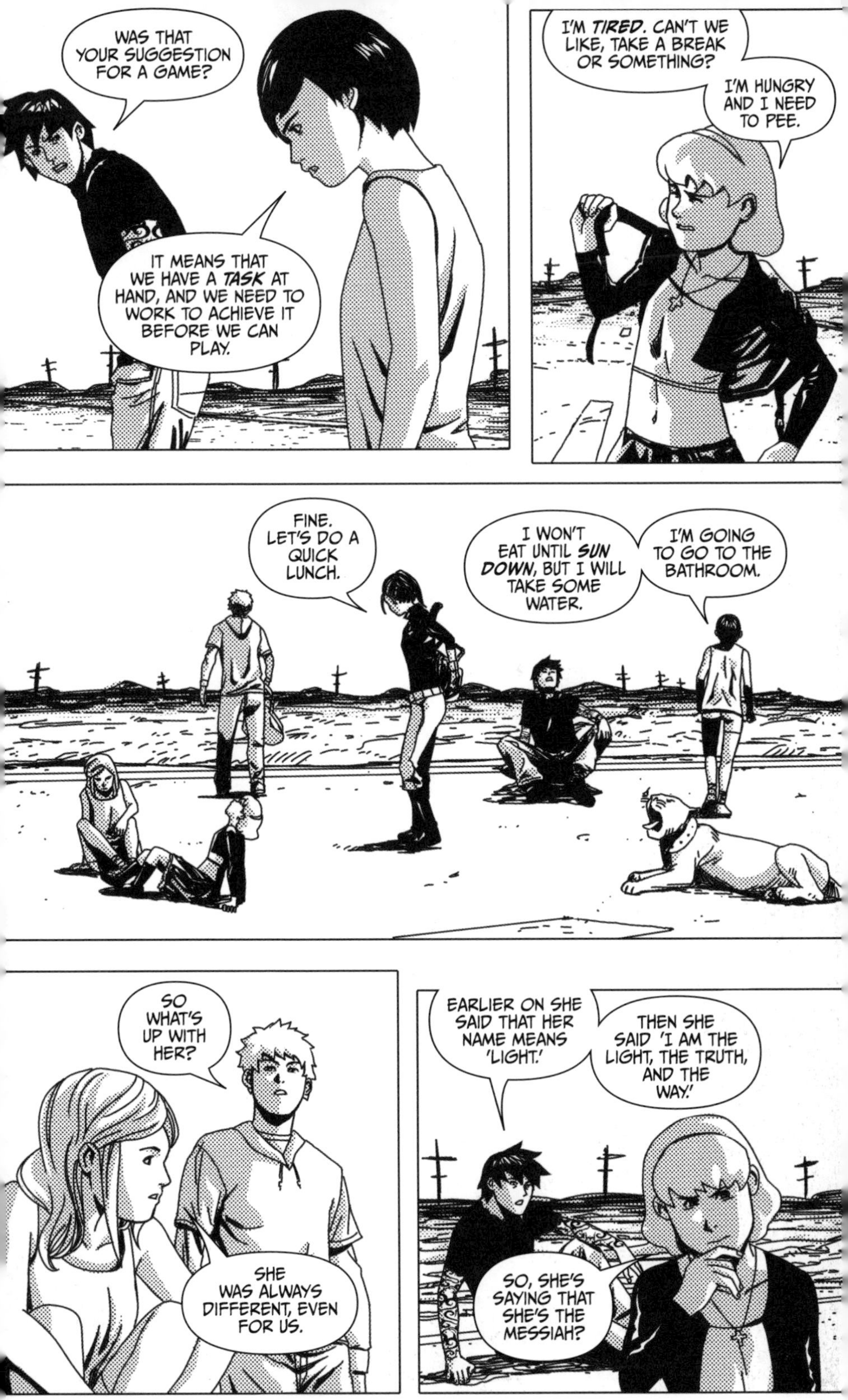
WAS THAT YOUR SUGGESTION FOR A GAME?
IT MEANS THAT WE HAVE A *TASK* AT HAND, AND WE NEED TO WORK TO ACHIEVE IT BEFORE WE CAN PLAY.
I'M *TIRED*. CAN'T WE LIKE, TAKE A BREAK OR SOMETHING?
I'M HUNGRY AND I NEED TO PEE.
FINE. LET'S DO A QUICK LUNCH.
I WON'T EAT UNTIL *SUN DOWN*, BUT I WILL TAKE SOME WATER.
I'M GOING TO GO TO THE BATHROOM.
SO WHAT'S UP WITH HER?
SHE WAS ALWAYS DIFFERENT, EVEN FOR US.
EARLIER ON SHE SAID THAT HER NAME MEANS 'LIGHT.'
THEN SHE SAID 'I AM THE LIGHT, THE TRUTH, AND THE WAY.'
SO, SHE'S SAYING THAT SHE'S THE MESSIAH?

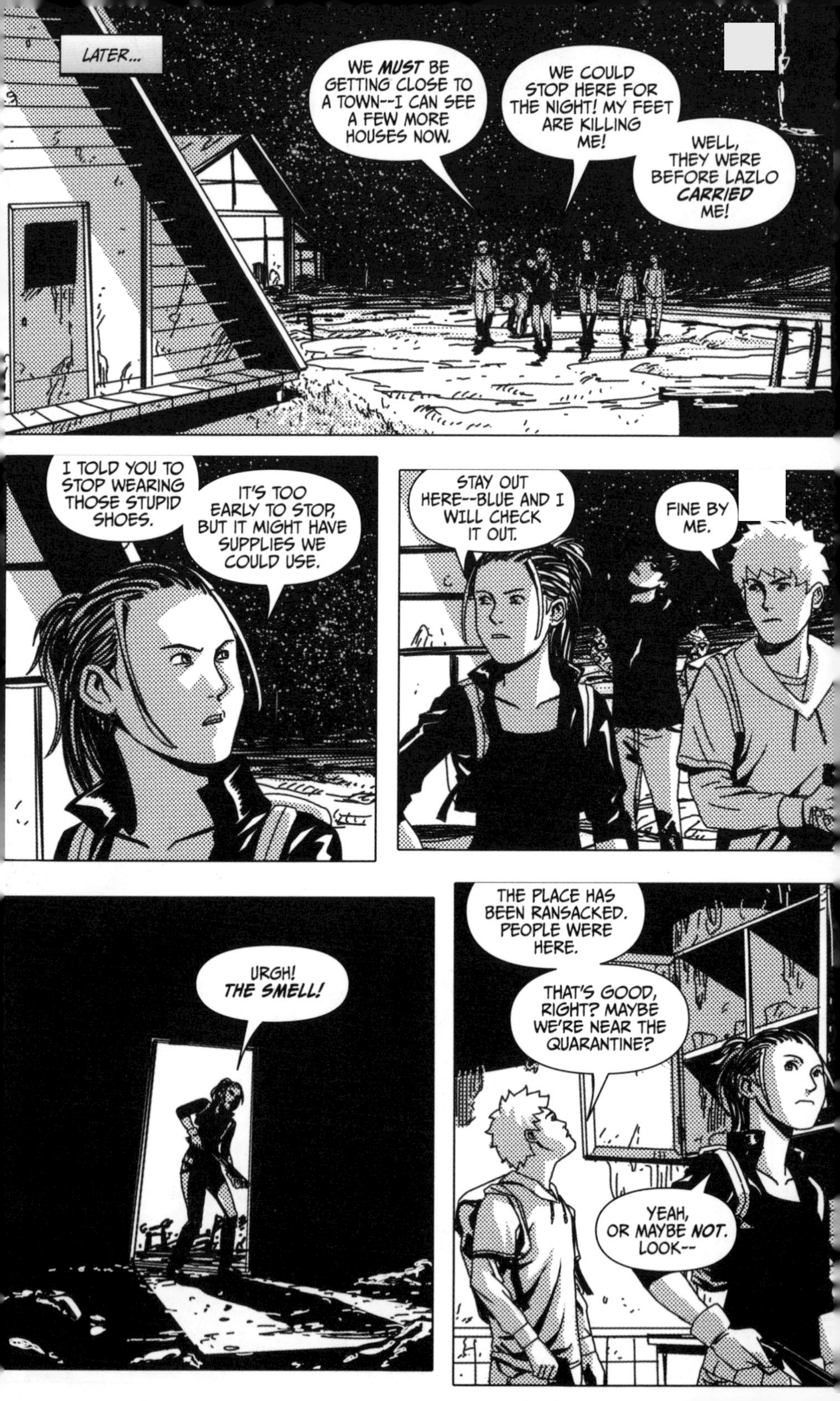
LATER...
WE MUST BE GETTING CLOSE TO A TOWN--I CAN SEE A FEW MORE HOUSES NOW.
WE COULD STOP HERE FOR THE NIGHT! MY FEET ARE KILLING ME!
WELL, THEY WERE BEFORE LAZLO CARRIED ME!
I TOLD YOU TO STOP WEARING THOSE STUPID SHOES.
IT'S TOO EARLY TO STOP, BUT IT MIGHT HAVE SUPPLIES WE COULD USE.
STAY OUT HERE--BLUE AND I WILL CHECK IT OUT.
FINE BY ME.
URGH! THE SMELL!
THE PLACE HAS BEEN RANSACKED. PEOPLE WERE HERE.
THAT'S GOOD, RIGHT? MAYBE WE'RE NEAR THE QUARANTINE?
YEAH, OR MAYBE NOT. LOOK--

HELTER SKELTER

WHAT'S IT MEAN?

IT'S A SONG BY THE *BEATLES*. AND IN THE *CHARLES MANSON MURDERS*, AFTER THEY BRUTALLY MURDERED PEOPLE--

--THEY WROTE 'HELTER SKELTER' ON THE REFRIGERATOR IN BLOOD.

SOMEBODY'S EMULATING CHARLES MANSON?

THEY PROBABLY DID IT AS A JOKE.

REAL FUNNY.

WE'RE NOT STAYING HERE. WE CAN TRY FURTHER INTO THE TOWN.

BUT MY FEET!

WE ARE *NOT* STAYING HERE, HARLOW.

TIME TO MOVE ON.

THIS IS WHAT THE OUTSIDE WORLD IS LIKE?

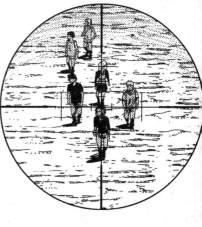

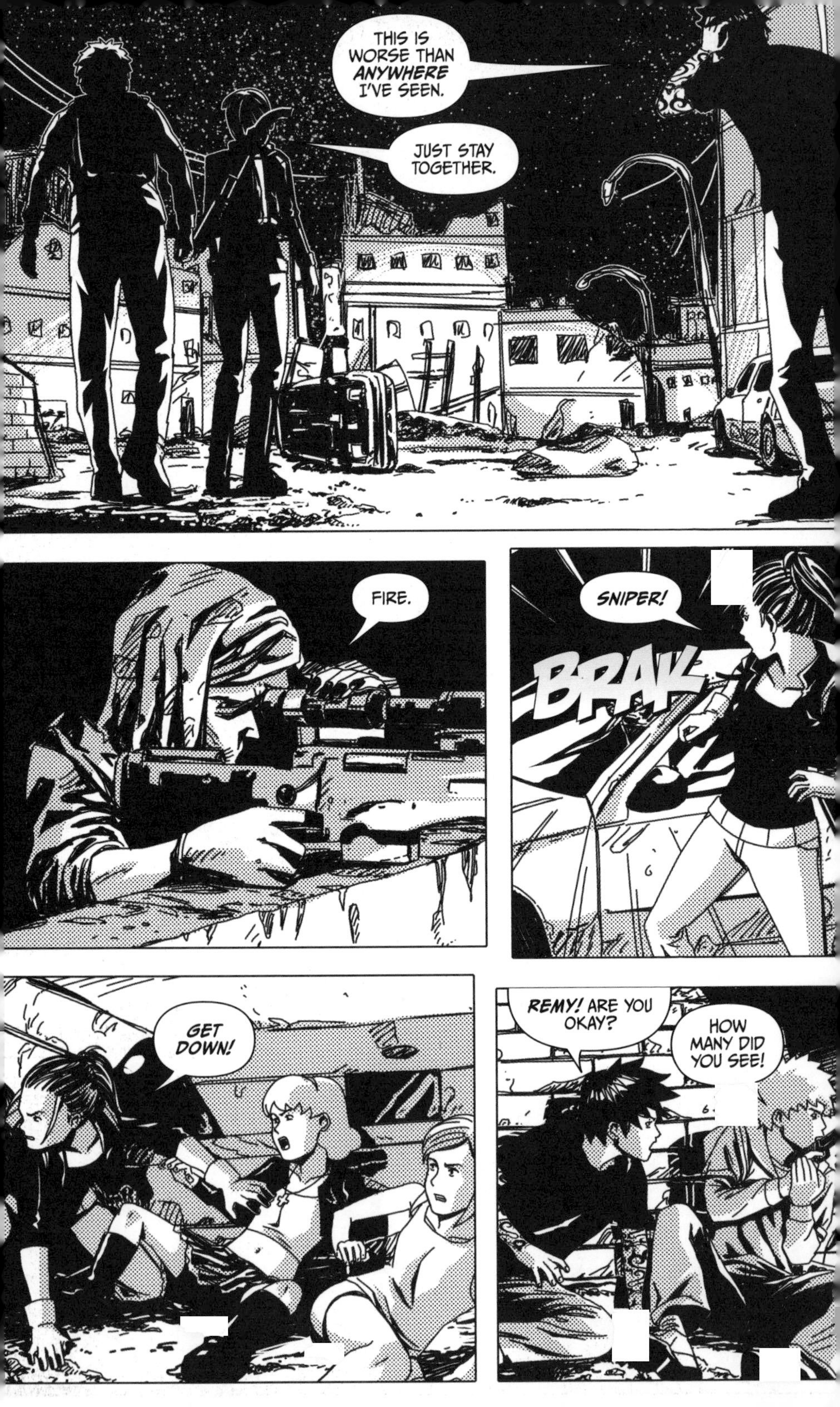
THIS IS WORSE THAN *ANYWHERE* I'VE SEEN.
JUST STAY TOGETHER.
FIRE.
SNIPER!
BRAK
GET DOWN!
REMY! ARE YOU OKAY?
HOW MANY DID YOU SEE!

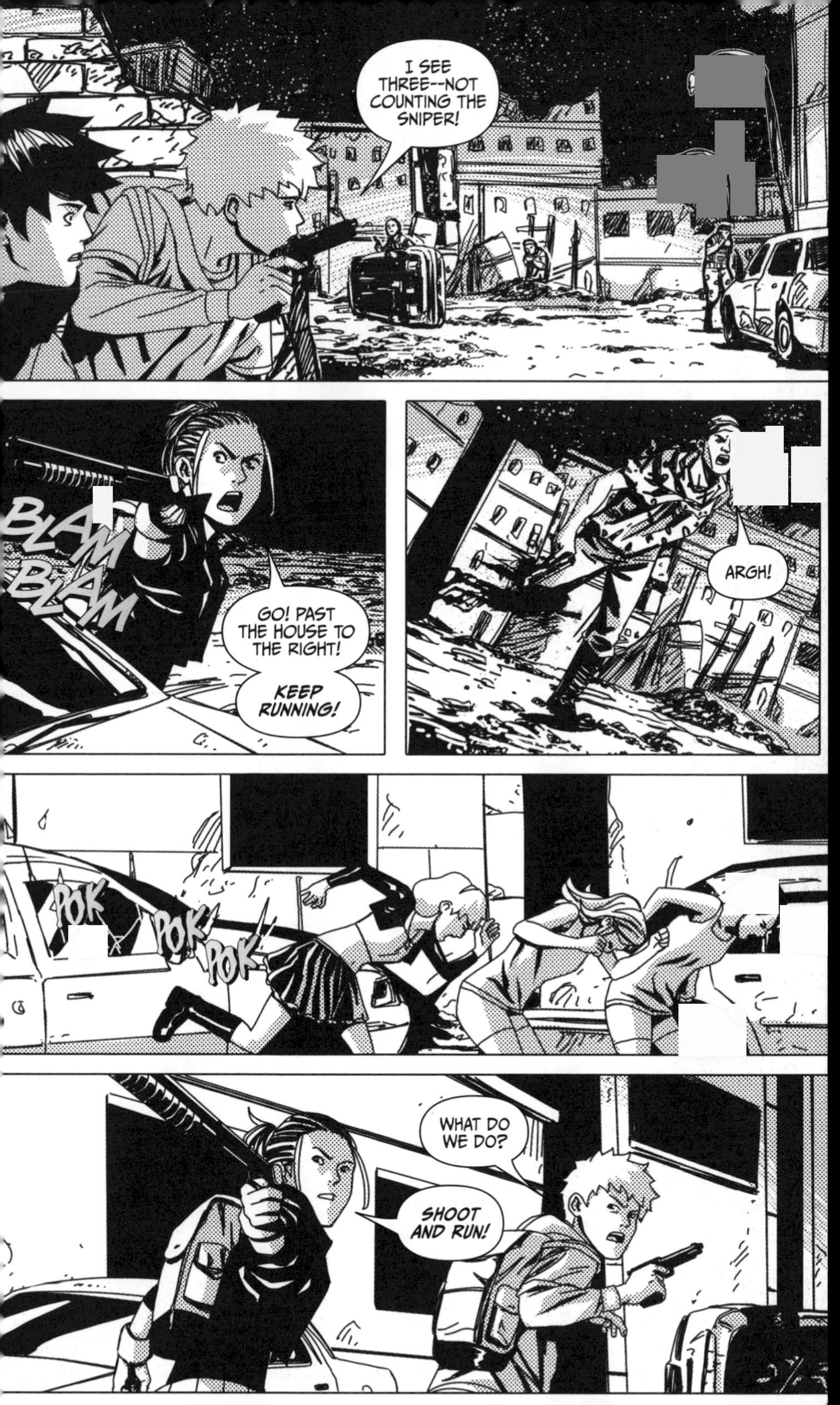

I SEE THREE--NOT COUNTING THE SNIPER!
BLAM BLAM
GO! PAST THE HOUSE TO THE RIGHT!
KEEP RUNNING!
ARGH!
POK
POK
POK
WHAT DO WE DO?
SHOOT AND RUN!

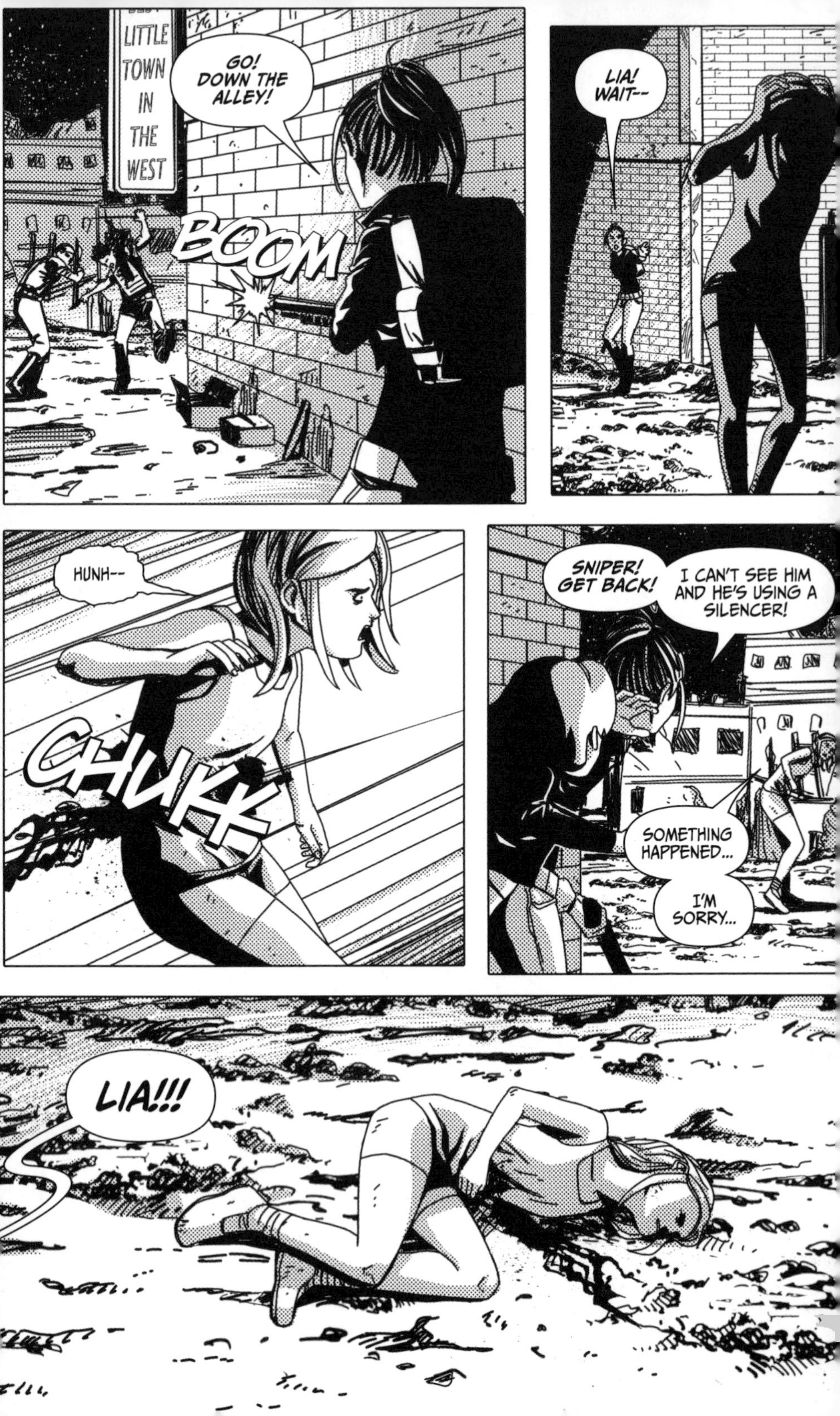
LITTLE TOWN IN THE WEST
GO! DOWN THE ALLEY!
BOOM
LIA! WAIT--
HUNH--
CHUKK
SNIPER! GET BACK!
I CAN'T SEE HIM AND HE'S USING A SILENCER!
SOMETHING HAPPENED...
I'M SORRY...
LIA!!!

CHAPTER SEVEN

SURROUNDED BY MARAUDERS

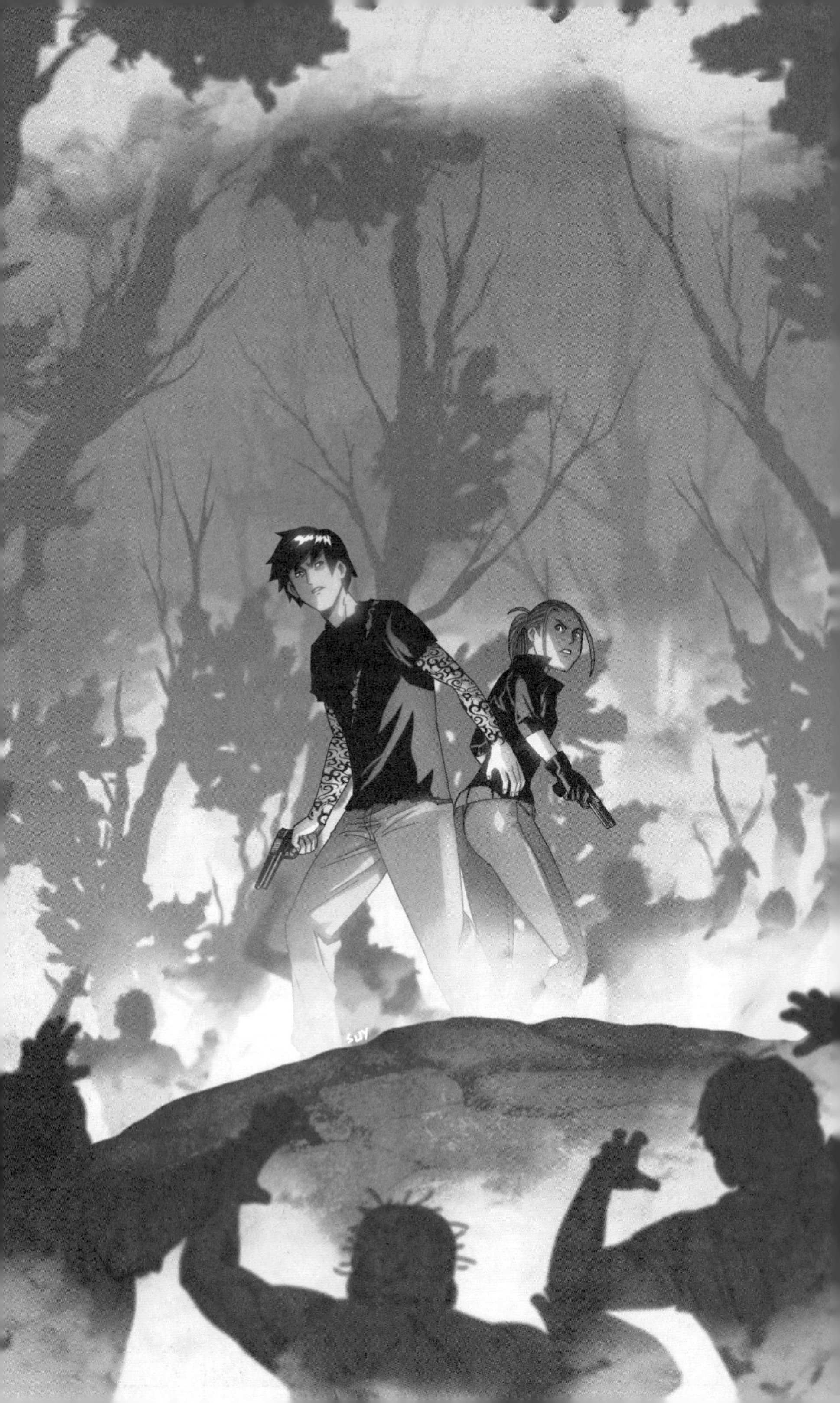

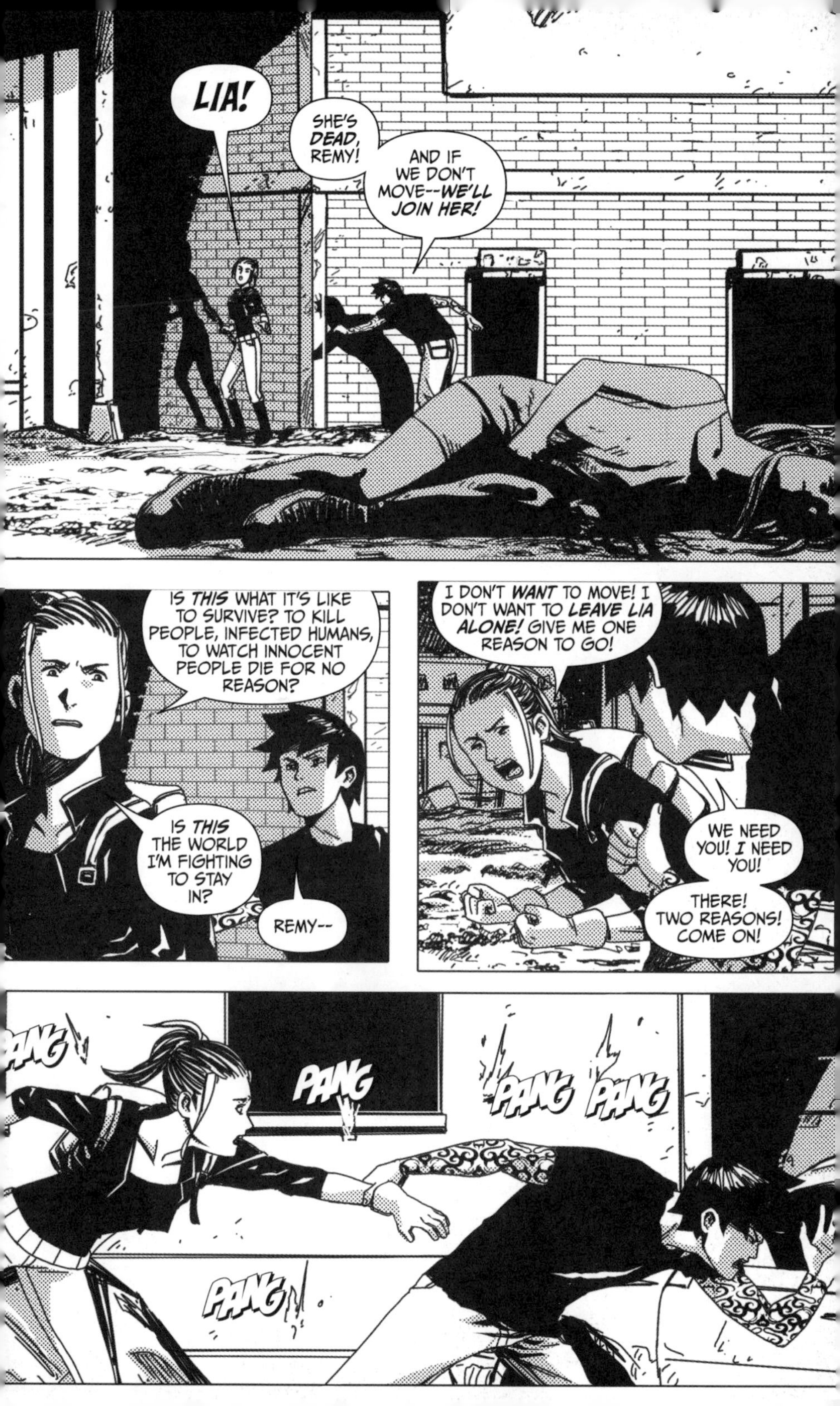
LIA!
SHE'S DEAD, REMY!
AND IF WE DON'T MOVE--WE'LL JOIN HER!
IS THIS WHAT IT'S LIKE TO SURVIVE? TO KILL PEOPLE, INFECTED HUMANS, TO WATCH INNOCENT PEOPLE DIE FOR NO REASON?
IS THIS THE WORLD I'M FIGHTING TO STAY IN?
REMY--
I DON'T WANT TO MOVE! I DON'T WANT TO LEAVE LIA ALONE! GIVE ME ONE REASON TO GO!
WE NEED YOU! I NEED YOU!
THERE! TWO REASONS! COME ON!
PANG
PANG
PANG PANG
PANG

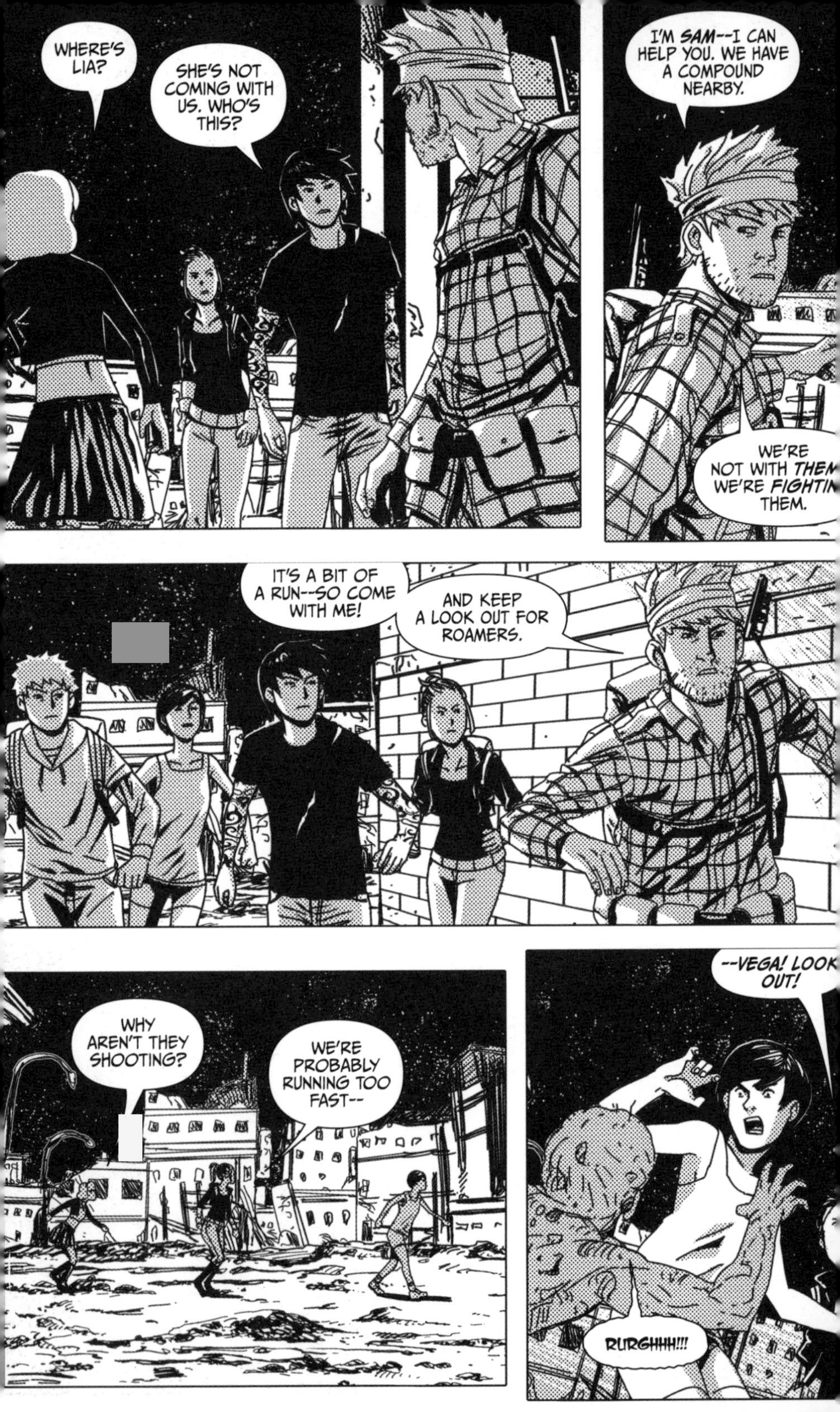
WHERE'S LIA?
SHE'S NOT COMING WITH US. WHO'S THIS?
I'M *SAM*--I CAN HELP YOU. WE HAVE A COMPOUND NEARBY.
WE'RE NOT WITH *THEM* WE'RE *FIGHTIN* THEM.
IT'S A BIT OF A RUN--SO COME WITH ME!
AND KEEP A LOOK OUT FOR ROAMERS.
WHY AREN'T THEY SHOOTING?
WE'RE PROBABLY RUNNING TOO FAST--
--VEGA! LOOK OUT!
RURGHHH!!!

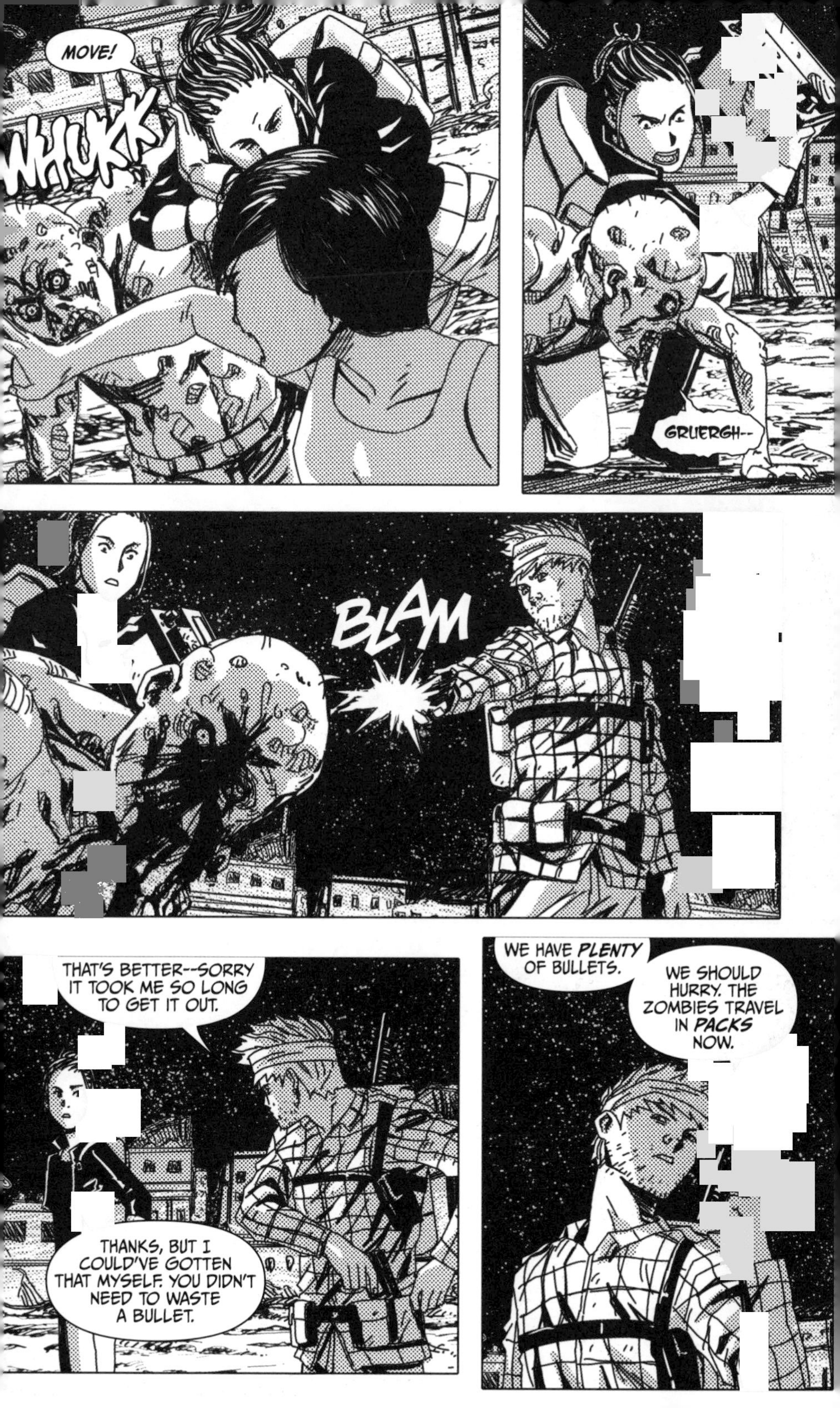
MOVE!
WHUKK
GRUERGH--
BLAM
THAT'S BETTER--SORRY IT TOOK ME SO LONG TO GET IT OUT.
THANKS, BUT I COULD'VE GOTTEN THAT MYSELF. YOU DIDN'T NEED TO WASTE A BULLET.
WE HAVE PLENTY OF BULLETS.
WE SHOULD HURRY. THE ZOMBIES TRAVEL IN PACKS NOW.

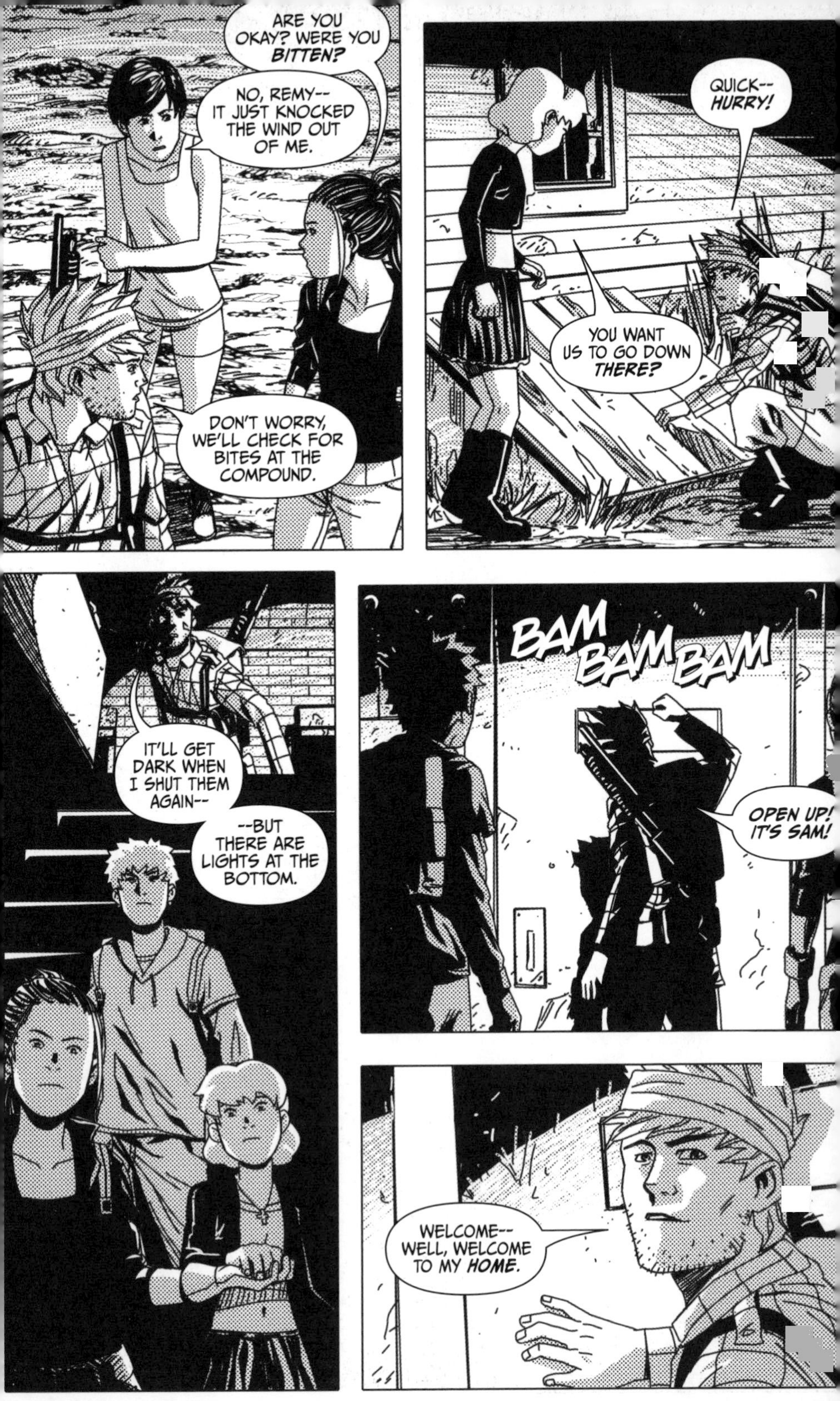
ARE YOU OKAY? WERE YOU *BITTEN?*
NO, REMY-- IT JUST KNOCKED THE WIND OUT OF ME.
DON'T WORRY, WE'LL CHECK FOR BITES AT THE COMPOUND.
QUICK-- *HURRY!*
YOU WANT US TO GO DOWN *THERE?*
IT'LL GET DARK WHEN I SHUT THEM AGAIN--
--BUT THERE ARE LIGHTS AT THE BOTTOM.
BAM BAM BAM
OPEN UP! IT'S SAM!
WELCOME-- WELL, WELCOME TO MY *HOME.*

FOUND THEM OUT IN THE STREETS.

HELLO--
I'M *LONDON*,
AND THIS IS *HOPE*.
THIS IS OUR
COMPOUND.

YOU ALL LOOK VERY WORN. HOW LONG HAVE YOU BEEN TRAVELING?

A WHILE.

THEY HAD A RUN-IN WITH THE *MARAUDERS*.

MARAUDERS?

THE MEN WITH GUNS IN BLACK CAMOUFLAGE. THEY RAIDED AN *ARMY BASE*, AND THEY'VE BEEN TRYING TO RULE THE TOWN WITH NIHILISTIC BRUTALITY.

WE'VE BEEN MAINTAINING A STRONGHOLD AGAINST THEM.

AH--REMY *SHOT* SOME OF THEM.

HOW MANY DID YOU KILL?

NOT THE TIME, LAZLO.

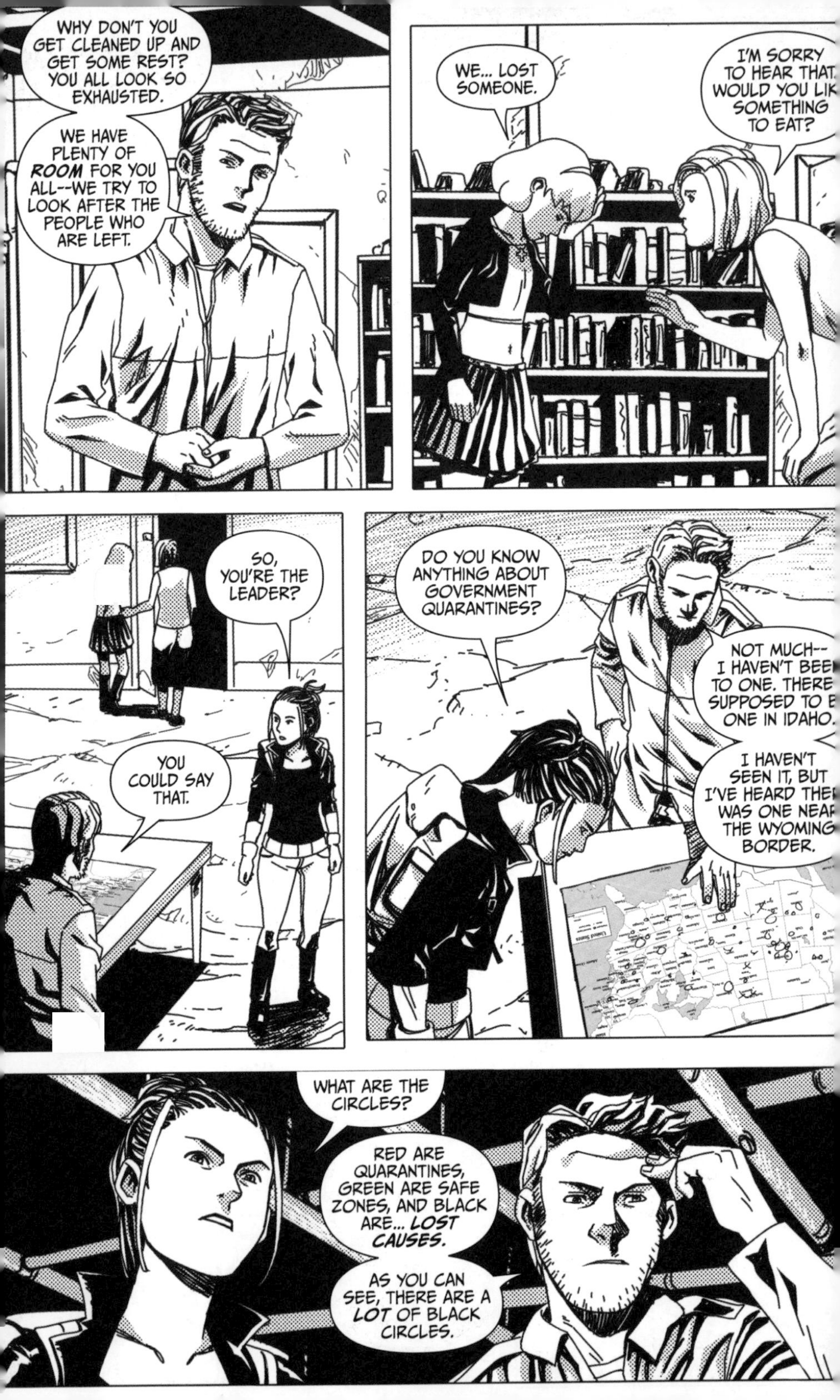
WHY DON'T YOU GET CLEANED UP AND GET SOME REST? YOU ALL LOOK SO EXHAUSTED.
WE HAVE PLENTY OF ROOM FOR YOU ALL--WE TRY TO LOOK AFTER THE PEOPLE WHO ARE LEFT.
WE... LOST SOMEONE.
I'M SORRY TO HEAR THAT. WOULD YOU LIK SOMETHING TO EAT?
SO, YOU'RE THE LEADER?
YOU COULD SAY THAT.
DO YOU KNOW ANYTHING ABOUT GOVERNMENT QUARANTINES?
NOT MUCH-- I HAVEN'T BEE TO ONE. THERE SUPPOSED TO B ONE IN IDAHO.
I HAVEN'T SEEN IT, BUT I'VE HEARD THE WAS ONE NEAR THE WYOMING BORDER.
WHAT ARE THE CIRCLES?
RED ARE QUARANTINES, GREEN ARE SAFE ZONES, AND BLACK ARE... LOST CAUSES.
AS YOU CAN SEE, THERE ARE A LOT OF BLACK CIRCLES.

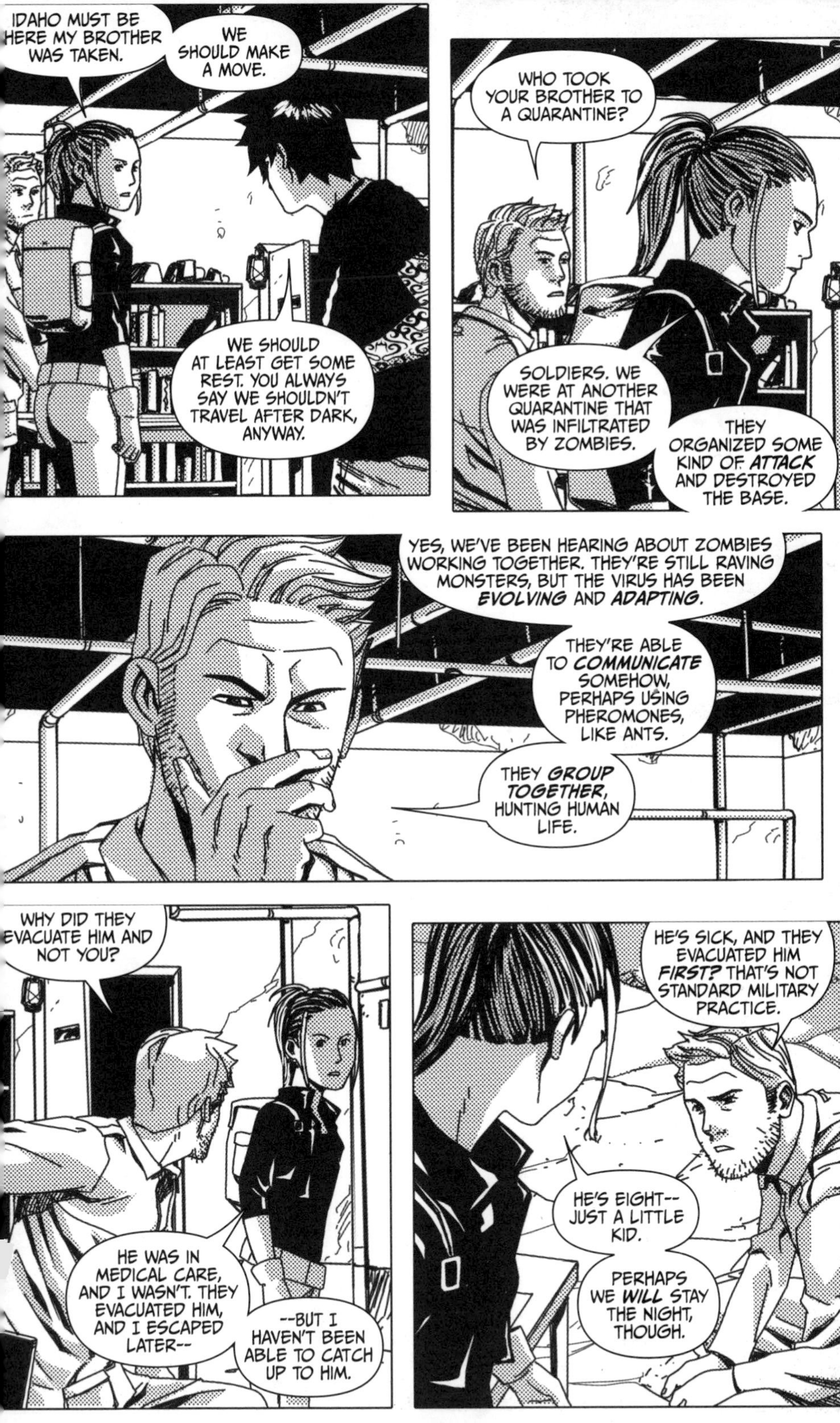
IDAHO MUST BE HERE MY BROTHER WAS TAKEN.
WE SHOULD MAKE A MOVE.
WE SHOULD AT LEAST GET SOME REST. YOU ALWAYS SAY WE SHOULDN'T TRAVEL AFTER DARK, ANYWAY.
WHO TOOK YOUR BROTHER TO A QUARANTINE?
SOLDIERS. WE WERE AT ANOTHER QUARANTINE THAT WAS INFILTRATED BY ZOMBIES.
THEY ORGANIZED SOME KIND OF *ATTACK* AND DESTROYED THE BASE.
YES, WE'VE BEEN HEARING ABOUT ZOMBIES WORKING TOGETHER. THEY'RE STILL RAVING MONSTERS, BUT THE VIRUS HAS BEEN ***EVOLVING*** AND ***ADAPTING***.
THEY'RE ABLE TO ***COMMUNICATE*** SOMEHOW, PERHAPS USING PHEROMONES, LIKE ANTS.
THEY ***GROUP TOGETHER***, HUNTING HUMAN LIFE.
WHY DID THEY EVACUATE HIM AND NOT YOU?
HE WAS IN MEDICAL CARE, AND I WASN'T. THEY EVACUATED HIM, AND I ESCAPED LATER--
--BUT I HAVEN'T BEEN ABLE TO CATCH UP TO HIM.
HE'S SICK, AND THEY EVACUATED HIM ***FIRST?*** THAT'S NOT STANDARD MILITARY PRACTICE.
HE'S EIGHT-- JUST A LITTLE KID.
PERHAPS WE ***WILL*** STAY THE NIGHT, THOUGH.

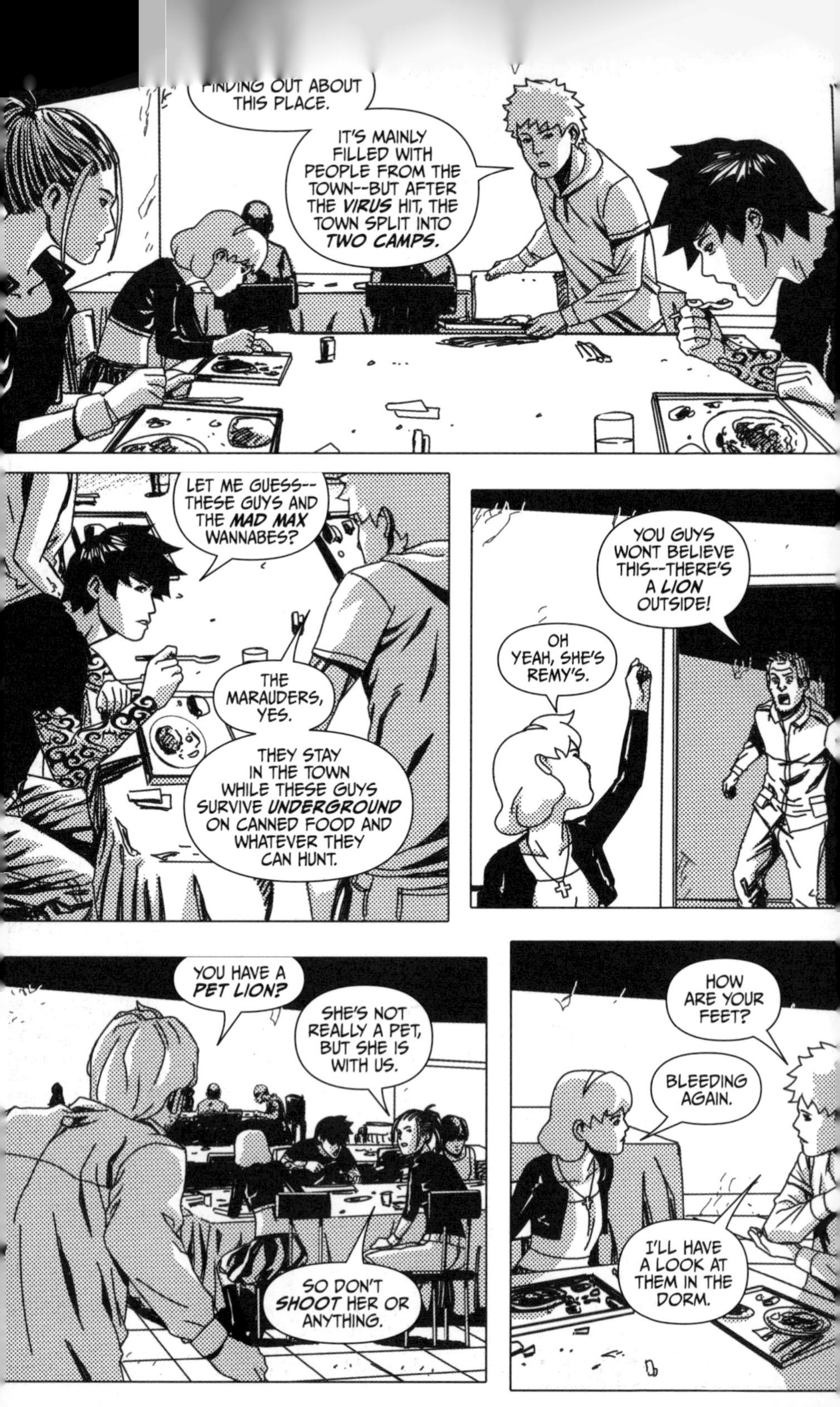
FINDING OUT ABOUT THIS PLACE.
IT'S MAINLY FILLED WITH PEOPLE FROM THE TOWN--BUT AFTER THE VIRUS HIT, THE TOWN SPLIT INTO TWO CAMPS.
LET ME GUESS-- THESE GUYS AND THE MAD MAX WANNABES?
THE MARAUDERS, YES.
THEY STAY IN THE TOWN WHILE THESE GUYS SURVIVE UNDERGROUND ON CANNED FOOD AND WHATEVER THEY CAN HUNT.
YOU GUYS WONT BELIEVE THIS--THERE'S A LION OUTSIDE!
OH YEAH, SHE'S REMY'S.
YOU HAVE A PET LION?
SHE'S NOT REALLY A PET, BUT SHE IS WITH US.
SO DON'T SHOOT HER OR ANYTHING.
HOW ARE YOUR FEET?
BLEEDING AGAIN.
I'LL HAVE A LOOK AT THEM IN THE DORM.

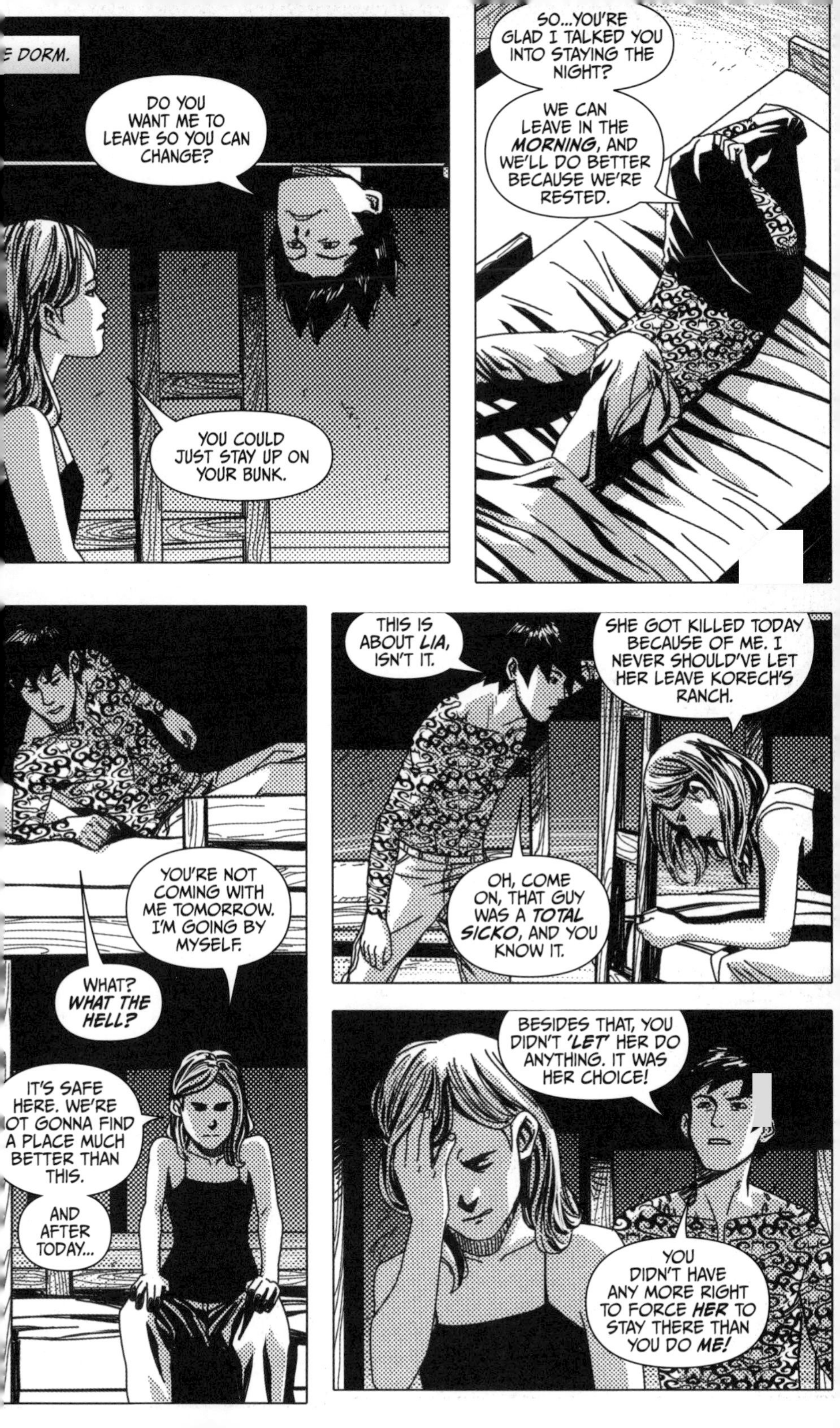
E DORM.
DO YOU WANT ME TO LEAVE SO YOU CAN CHANGE?
YOU COULD JUST STAY UP ON YOUR BUNK.
SO...YOU'RE GLAD I TALKED YOU INTO STAYING THE NIGHT?
WE CAN LEAVE IN THE *MORNING*, AND WE'LL DO BETTER BECAUSE WE'RE RESTED.
YOU'RE NOT COMING WITH ME TOMORROW. I'M GOING BY MYSELF.
WHAT? *WHAT THE HELL?*
IT'S SAFE HERE. WE'RE OT GONNA FIND A PLACE MUCH BETTER THAN THIS.
AND AFTER TODAY...
THIS IS ABOUT *LIA*, ISN'T IT.
SHE GOT KILLED TODAY BECAUSE OF ME. I NEVER SHOULD'VE LET HER LEAVE KORECH'S RANCH.
OH, COME ON, THAT GUY WAS A *TOTAL SICKO*, AND YOU KNOW IT.
BESIDES THAT, YOU DIDN'T *'LET'* HER DO ANYTHING. IT WAS HER CHOICE!
YOU DIDN'T HAVE ANY MORE RIGHT TO FORCE *HER* TO STAY THERE THAN YOU DO *ME!*

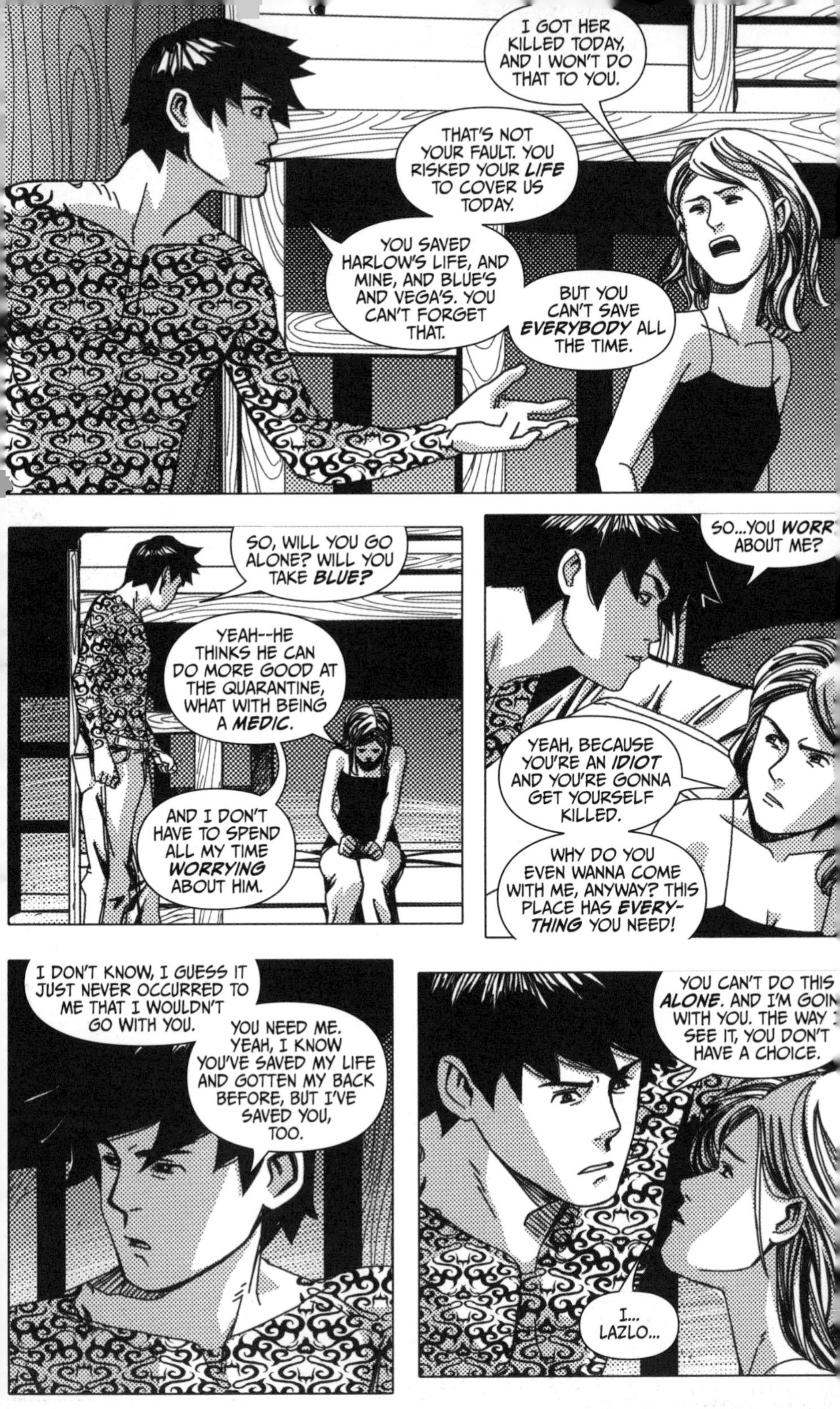

I GOT HER KILLED TODAY, AND I WON'T DO THAT TO YOU.
THAT'S NOT YOUR FAULT. YOU RISKED YOUR LIFE TO COVER US TODAY.
YOU SAVED HARLOW'S LIFE, AND MINE, AND BLUE'S AND VEGA'S. YOU CAN'T FORGET THAT.
BUT YOU CAN'T SAVE EVERYBODY ALL THE TIME.
SO, WILL YOU GO ALONE? WILL YOU TAKE BLUE?
YEAH--HE THINKS HE CAN DO MORE GOOD AT THE QUARANTINE, WHAT WITH BEING A MEDIC.
AND I DON'T HAVE TO SPEND ALL MY TIME WORRYING ABOUT HIM.
SO...YOU WORR ABOUT ME?
YEAH, BECAUSE YOU'RE AN IDIOT AND YOU'RE GONNA GET YOURSELF KILLED.
WHY DO YOU EVEN WANNA COME WITH ME, ANYWAY? THIS PLACE HAS EVERY-THING YOU NEED!
I DON'T KNOW, I GUESS IT JUST NEVER OCCURRED TO ME THAT I WOULDN'T GO WITH YOU.
YOU NEED ME. YEAH, I KNOW YOU'VE SAVED MY LIFE AND GOTTEN MY BACK BEFORE, BUT I'VE SAVED YOU, TOO.
YOU CAN'T DO THIS ALONE. AND I'M GOIN WITH YOU. THE WAY I SEE IT, YOU DON'T HAVE A CHOICE.
I... LAZLO...

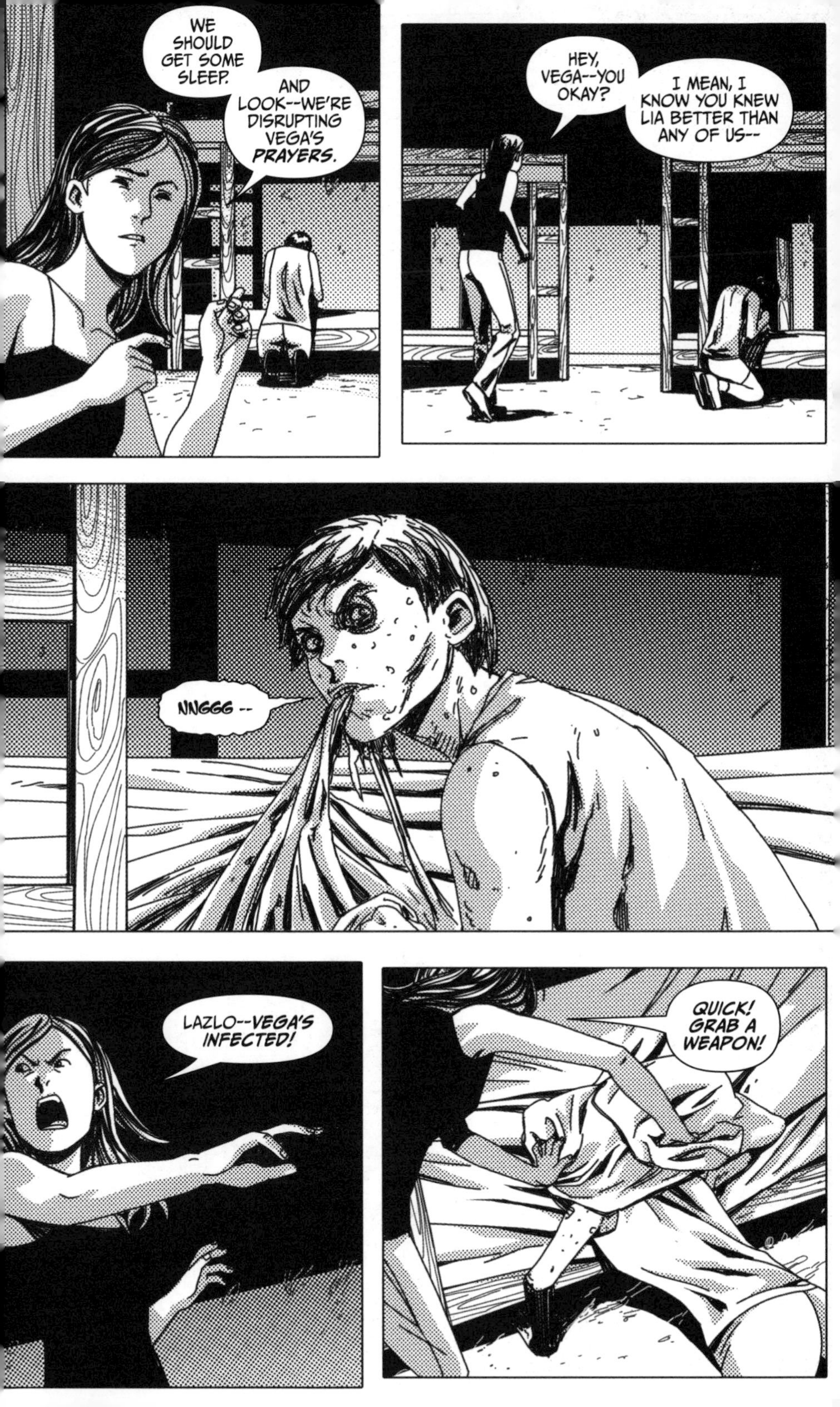
WE SHOULD GET SOME SLEEP.
AND LOOK--WE'RE DISRUPTING VEGA'S *PRAYERS.*
HEY, VEGA--YOU OKAY?
I MEAN, I KNOW YOU KNEW LIA BETTER THAN ANY OF US--
NNGGG --
LAZLO--*VEGA'S INFECTED!*
QUICK! GRAB A WEAPON!

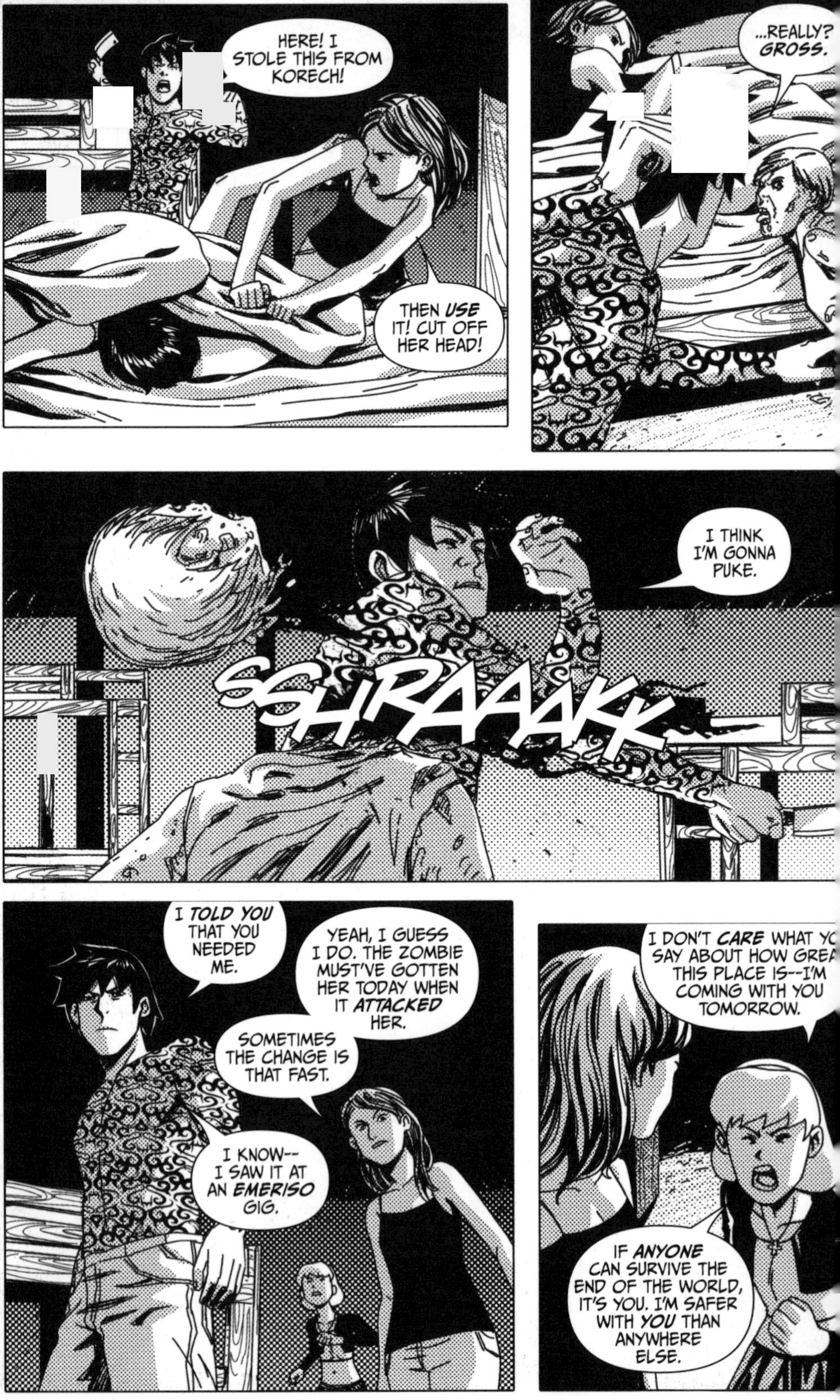

HERE! I STOLE THIS FROM KORECH!
THEN USE IT! CUT OFF HER HEAD!
...REALLY? GROSS.
I THINK I'M GONNA PUKE.
SSHRAAAKK
I TOLD YOU THAT YOU NEEDED ME.
YEAH, I GUESS I DO. THE ZOMBIE MUST'VE GOTTEN HER TODAY WHEN IT ATTACKED HER.
SOMETIMES THE CHANGE IS THAT FAST.
I KNOW-- I SAW IT AT AN EMERISO GIG.
I DON'T CARE WHAT YO SAY ABOUT HOW GREA THIS PLACE IS--I'M COMING WITH YOU TOMORROW.
IF ANYONE CAN SURVIVE THE END OF THE WORLD, IT'S YOU. I'M SAFER WITH YOU THAN ANYWHERE ELSE.

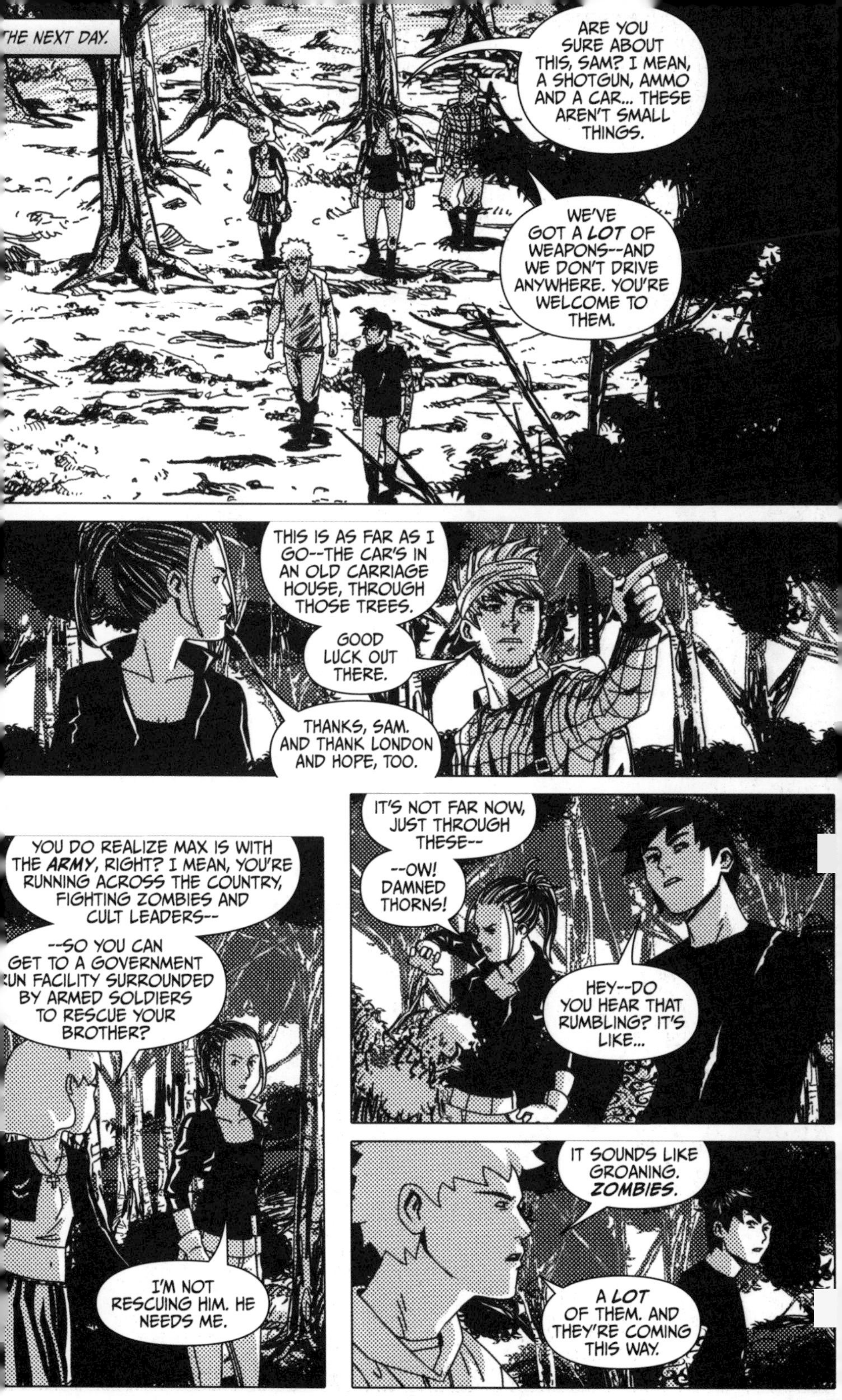

THE NEXT DAY.
ARE YOU SURE ABOUT THIS, SAM? I MEAN, A SHOTGUN, AMMO AND A CAR... THESE AREN'T SMALL THINGS.
WE'VE GOT A *LOT* OF WEAPONS--AND WE DON'T DRIVE ANYWHERE. YOU'RE WELCOME TO THEM.
THIS IS AS FAR AS I GO--THE CAR'S IN AN OLD CARRIAGE HOUSE, THROUGH THOSE TREES.
GOOD LUCK OUT THERE.
THANKS, SAM. AND THANK LONDON AND HOPE, TOO.
YOU DO REALIZE MAX IS WITH THE *ARMY*, RIGHT? I MEAN, YOU'RE RUNNING ACROSS THE COUNTRY, FIGHTING ZOMBIES AND CULT LEADERS--
--SO YOU CAN GET TO A GOVERNMENT RUN FACILITY SURROUNDED BY ARMED SOLDIERS TO RESCUE YOUR BROTHER?
I'M NOT RESCUING HIM. HE NEEDS ME.
IT'S NOT FAR NOW, JUST THROUGH THESE--
--OW! DAMNED THORNS!
HEY--DO YOU HEAR THAT RUMBLING? IT'S LIKE...
IT SOUNDS LIKE GROANING. *ZOMBIES*.
A *LOT* OF THEM. AND THEY'RE COMING THIS WAY.

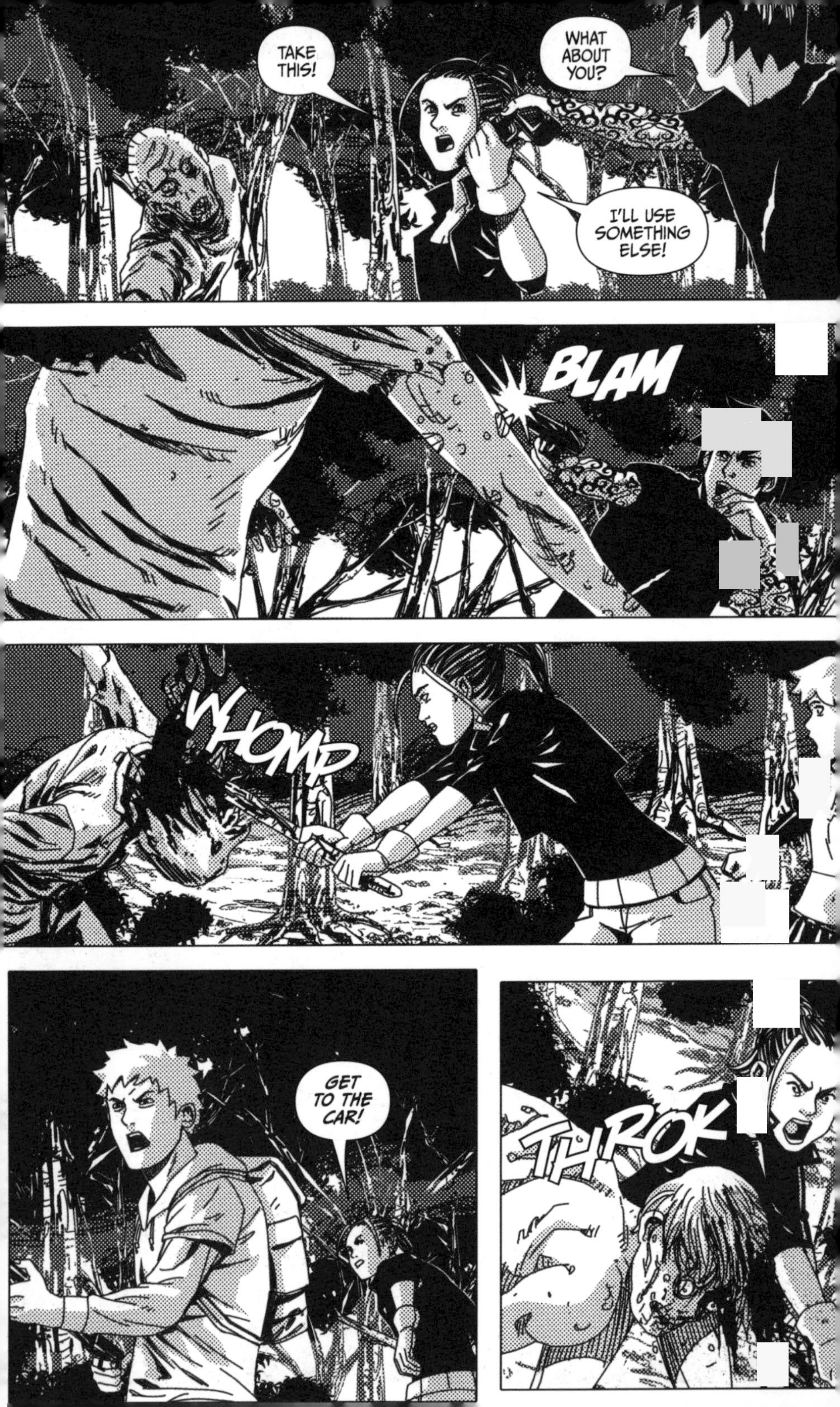
TAKE THIS!
WHAT ABOUT YOU?
I'LL USE SOMETHING ELSE!
BLAM
WHOMP
GET TO THE CAR!
THROK

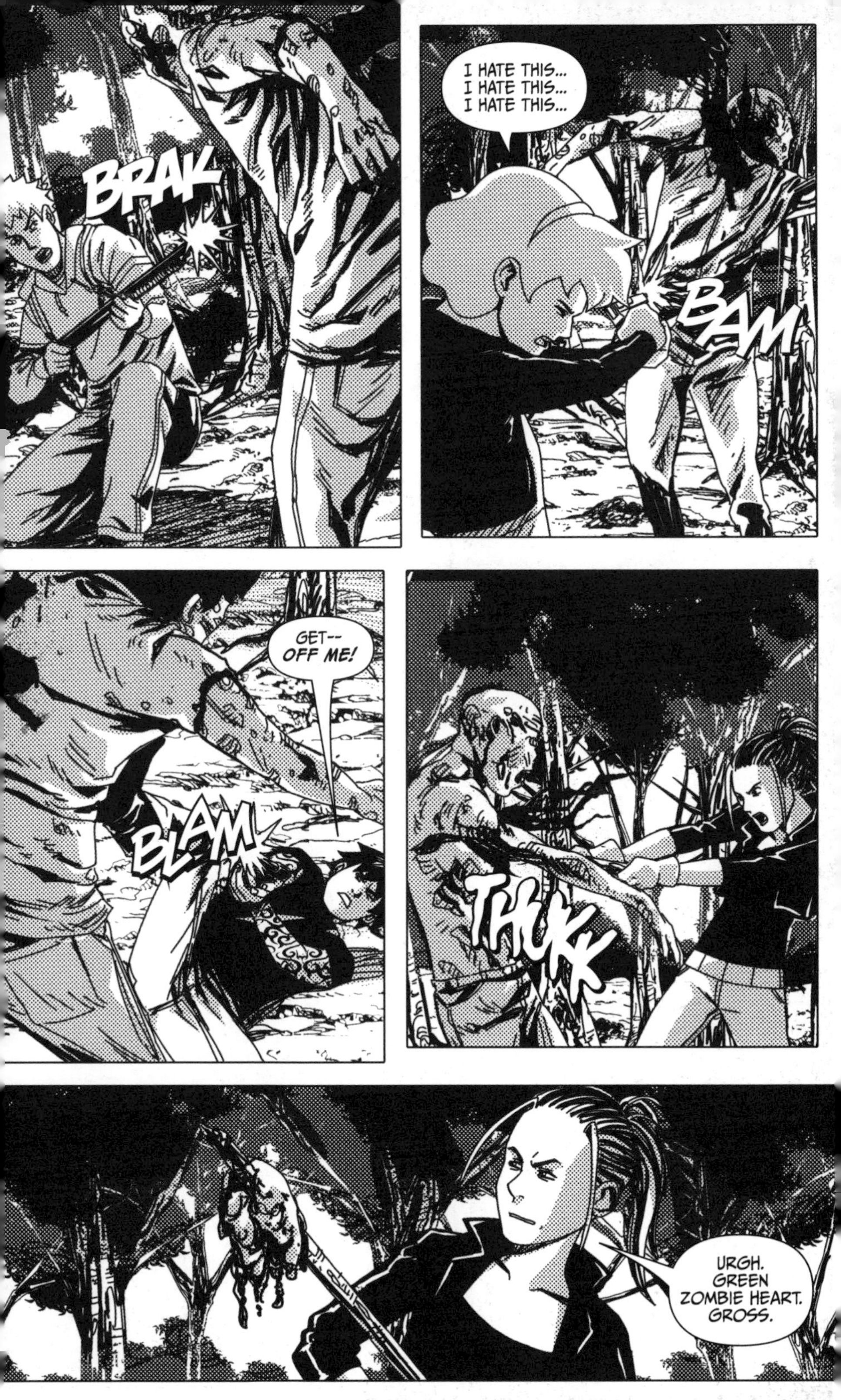
BRAK
I HATE THIS... I HATE THIS... I HATE THIS...
BAM
GET-- OFF ME!
BLAM
THUKK
URGH. GREEN ZOMBIE HEART. GROSS.

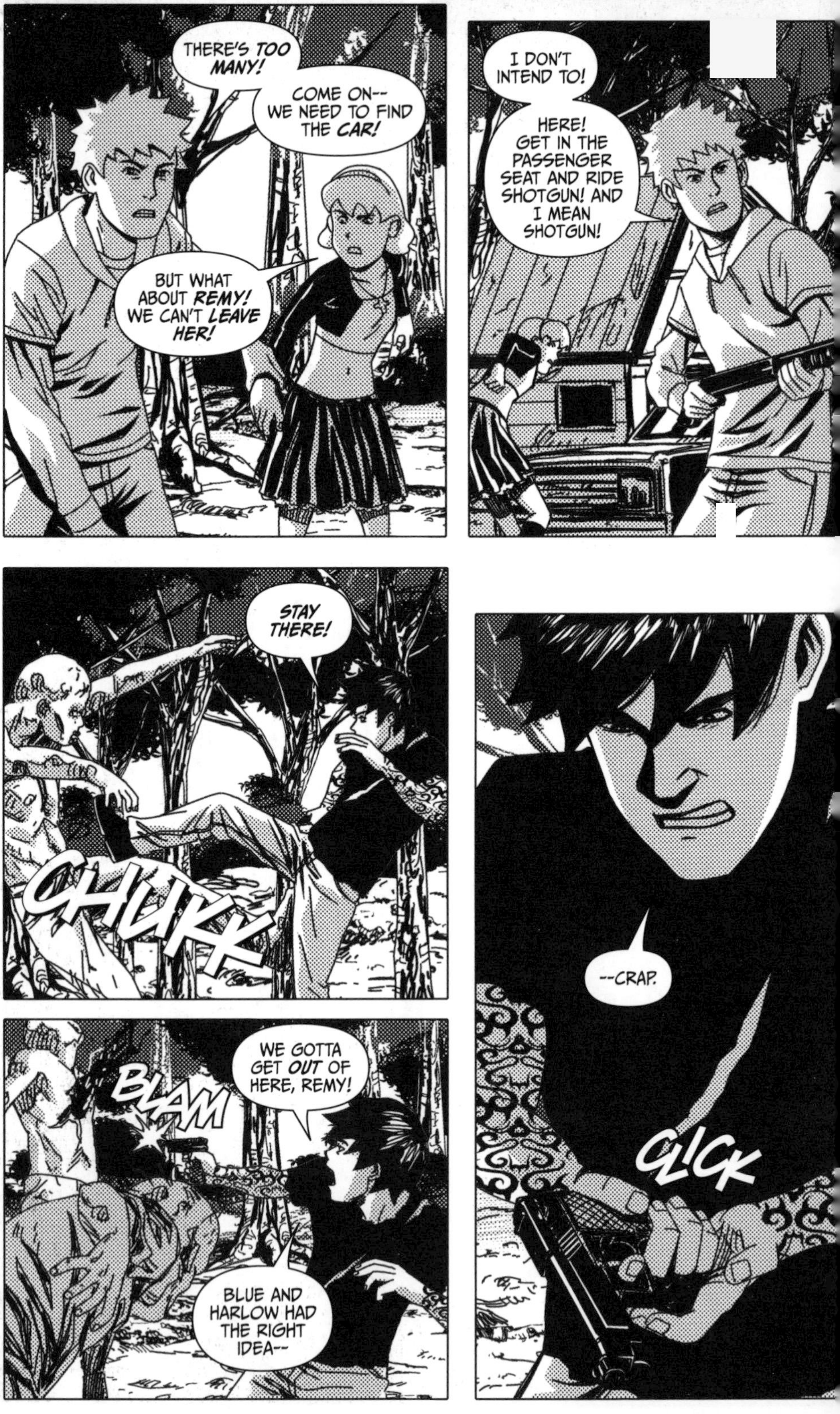
THERE'S *TOO MANY!*
COME ON-- WE NEED TO FIND THE *CAR!*
BUT WHAT ABOUT ***REMY!*** WE CAN'T *LEAVE HER!*
I DON'T INTEND TO!
HERE! GET IN THE PASSENGER SEAT AND RIDE SHOTGUN! AND I MEAN SHOTGUN!
STAY THERE!
CHUKK
BLAM
WE GOTTA GET *OUT* OF HERE, REMY!
BLUE AND HARLOW HAD THE RIGHT IDEA--
--CRAP.
CLICK

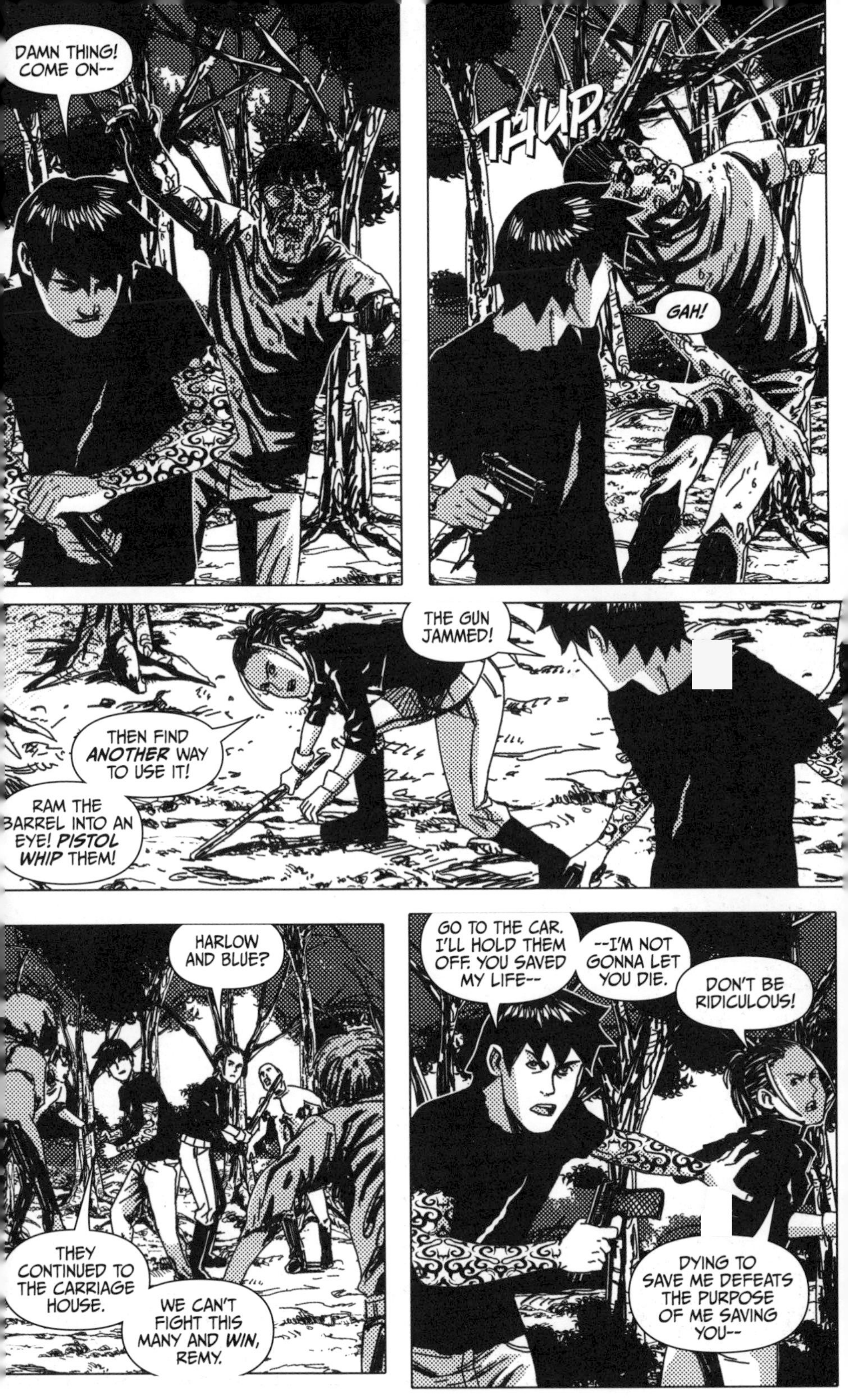
DAMN THING! COME ON--
THUP
GAH!
THE GUN JAMMED!
THEN FIND *ANOTHER* WAY TO USE IT!
RAM THE BARREL INTO AN EYE! *PISTOL WHIP* THEM!
HARLOW AND BLUE?
THEY CONTINUED TO THE CARRIAGE HOUSE.
WE CAN'T FIGHT THIS MANY AND *WIN*, REMY.
GO TO THE CAR. I'LL HOLD THEM OFF. YOU SAVED MY LIFE--
--I'M NOT GONNA LET YOU DIE.
DON'T BE RIDICULOUS!
DYING TO SAVE ME DEFEATS THE PURPOSE OF ME SAVING YOU--

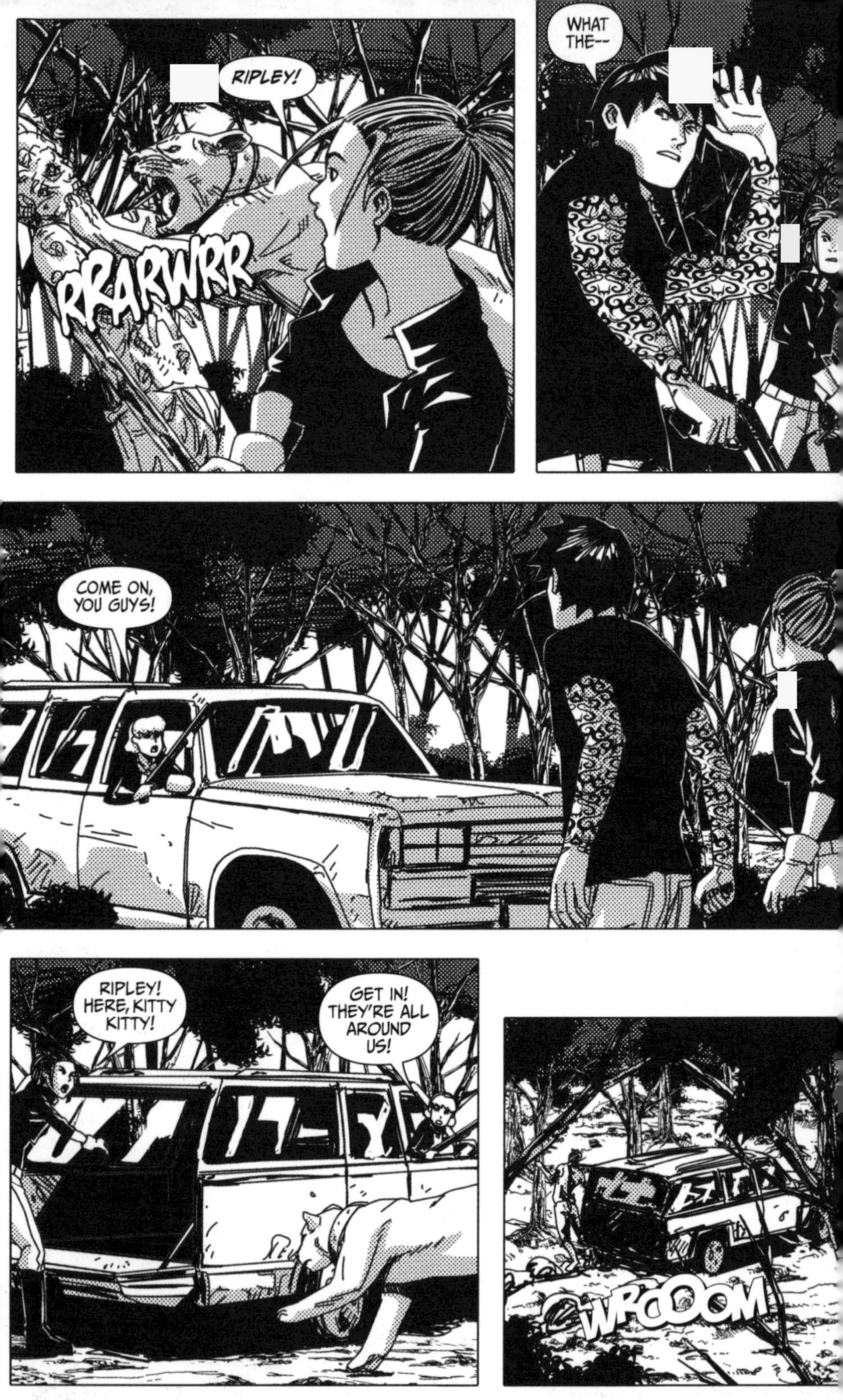
RIPLEY!
RRARWRR
WHAT THE--
COME ON, YOU GUYS!
RIPLEY! HERE, KITTY KITTY!
GET IN! THEY'RE ALL AROUND US!
WRCOOOM

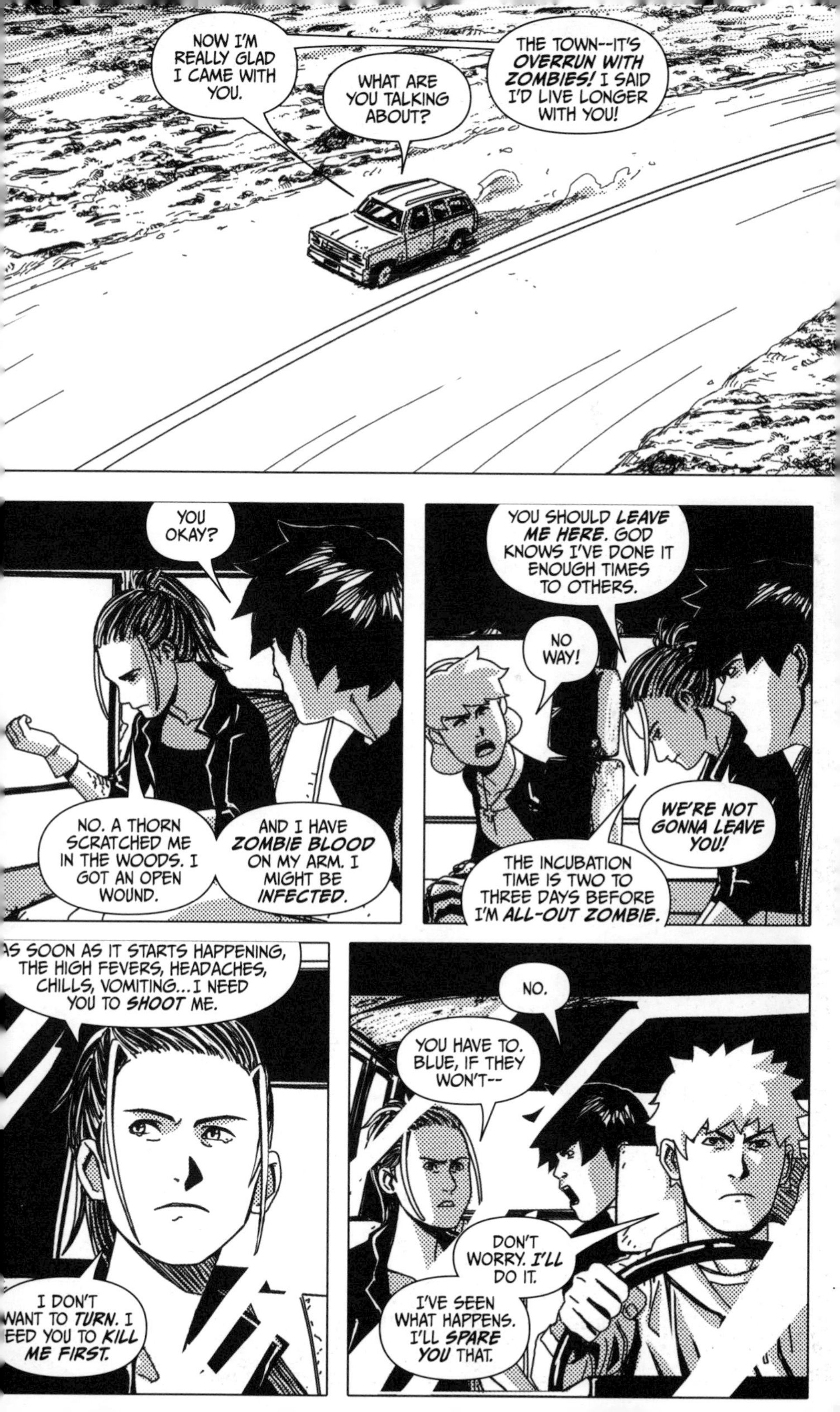
NOW I'M REALLY GLAD I CAME WITH YOU.
WHAT ARE YOU TALKING ABOUT?
THE TOWN--IT'S OVERRUN WITH ZOMBIES! I SAID I'D LIVE LONGER WITH YOU!
YOU OKAY?
NO. A THORN SCRATCHED ME IN THE WOODS. I GOT AN OPEN WOUND.
AND I HAVE ZOMBIE BLOOD ON MY ARM. I MIGHT BE INFECTED.
YOU SHOULD LEAVE ME HERE. GOD KNOWS I'VE DONE IT ENOUGH TIMES TO OTHERS.
NO WAY!
WE'RE NOT GONNA LEAVE YOU!
THE INCUBATION TIME IS TWO TO THREE DAYS BEFORE I'M ALL-OUT ZOMBIE.
AS SOON AS IT STARTS HAPPENING, THE HIGH FEVERS, HEADACHES, CHILLS, VOMITING...I NEED YOU TO SHOOT ME.
I DON'T WANT TO TURN. I NEED YOU TO KILL ME FIRST.
NO.
YOU HAVE TO. BLUE, IF THEY WON'T--
DON'T WORRY. I'LL DO IT.
I'VE SEEN WHAT HAPPENS. I'LL SPARE YOU THAT.

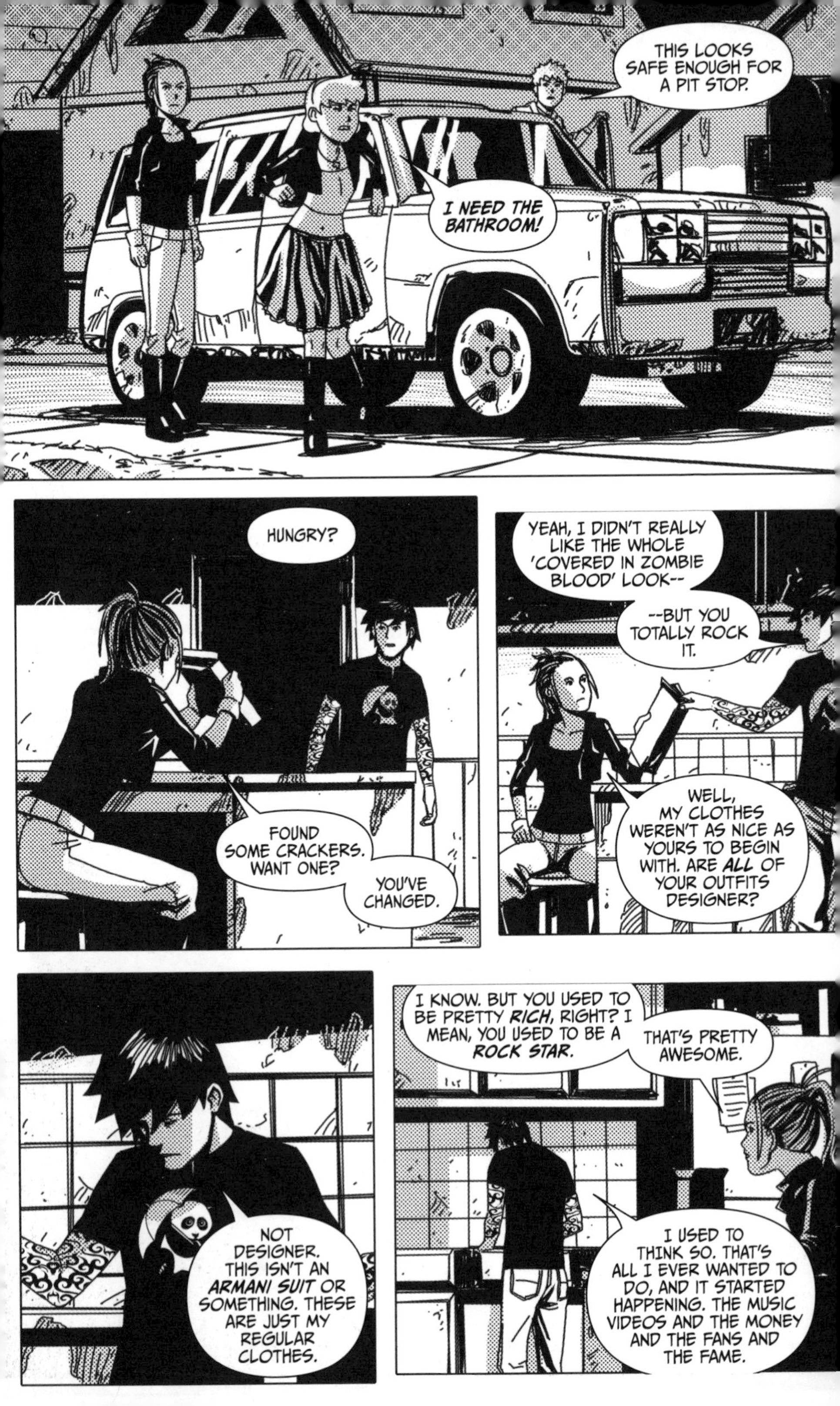
THIS LOOKS SAFE ENOUGH FOR A PIT STOP.
I NEED THE BATHROOM!
HUNGRY?
FOUND SOME CRACKERS. WANT ONE?
YOU'VE CHANGED.
YEAH, I DIDN'T REALLY LIKE THE WHOLE 'COVERED IN ZOMBIE BLOOD' LOOK--
--BUT YOU TOTALLY ROCK IT.
WELL, MY CLOTHES WEREN'T AS NICE AS YOURS TO BEGIN WITH. ARE ALL OF YOUR OUTFITS DESIGNER?
NOT DESIGNER. THIS ISN'T AN ARMANI SUIT OR SOMETHING. THESE ARE JUST MY REGULAR CLOTHES.
I KNOW. BUT YOU USED TO BE PRETTY RICH, RIGHT? I MEAN, YOU USED TO BE A ROCK STAR.
THAT'S PRETTY AWESOME.
I USED TO THINK SO. THAT'S ALL I EVER WANTED TO DO, AND IT STARTED HAPPENING. THE MUSIC VIDEOS AND THE MONEY AND THE FANS AND THE FAME.

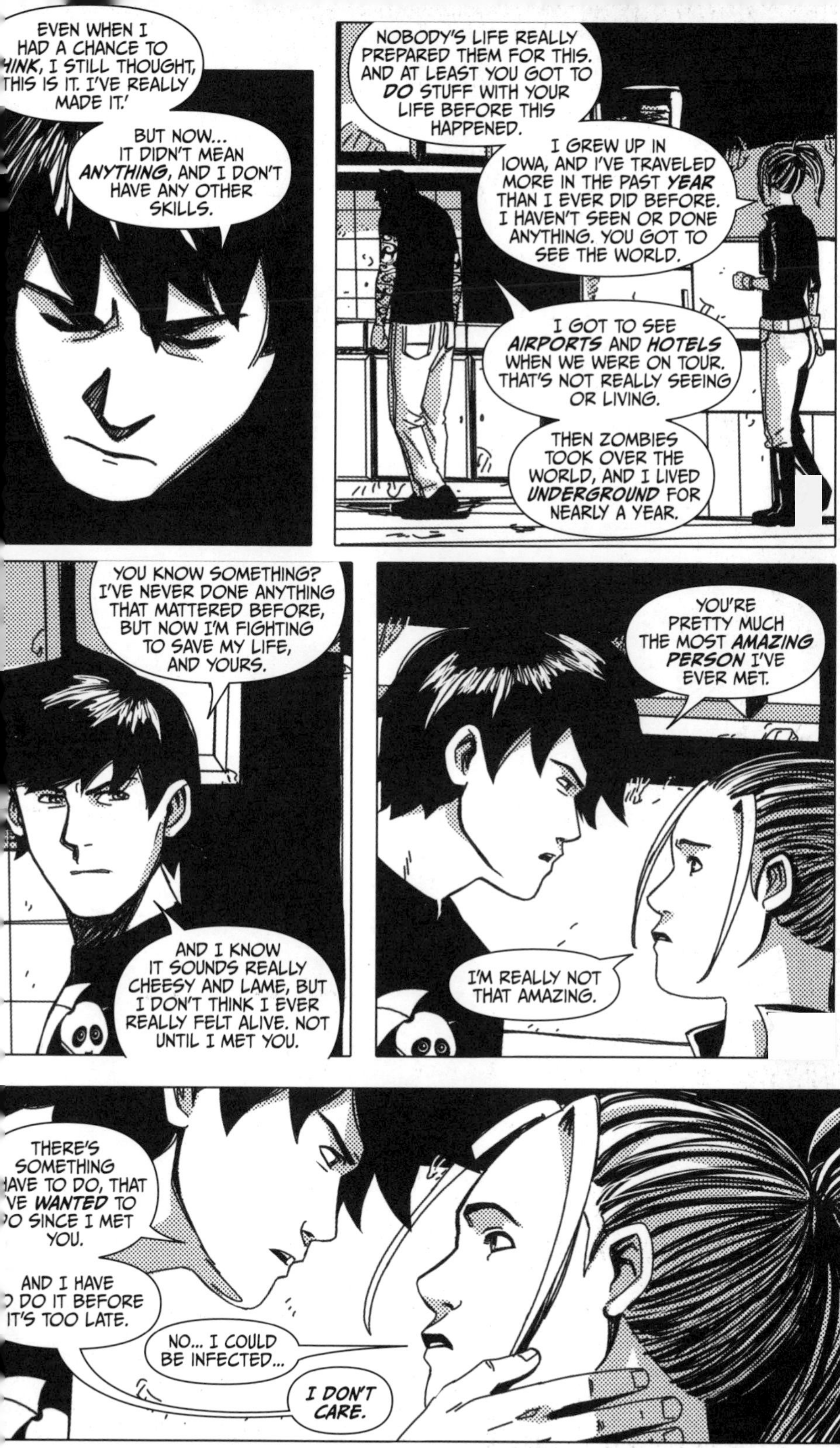

EVEN WHEN I HAD A CHANCE TO HINK, I STILL THOUGHT, THIS IS IT. I'VE REALLY MADE IT.'
BUT NOW... IT DIDN'T MEAN ANYTHING, AND I DON'T HAVE ANY OTHER SKILLS.
NOBODY'S LIFE REALLY PREPARED THEM FOR THIS. AND AT LEAST YOU GOT TO DO STUFF WITH YOUR LIFE BEFORE THIS HAPPENED.
I GREW UP IN IOWA, AND I'VE TRAVELED MORE IN THE PAST YEAR THAN I EVER DID BEFORE. I HAVEN'T SEEN OR DONE ANYTHING. YOU GOT TO SEE THE WORLD.
I GOT TO SEE AIRPORTS AND HOTELS WHEN WE WERE ON TOUR. THAT'S NOT REALLY SEEING OR LIVING.
THEN ZOMBIES TOOK OVER THE WORLD, AND I LIVED UNDERGROUND FOR NEARLY A YEAR.
YOU KNOW SOMETHING? I'VE NEVER DONE ANYTHING THAT MATTERED BEFORE, BUT NOW I'M FIGHTING TO SAVE MY LIFE, AND YOURS.
AND I KNOW IT SOUNDS REALLY CHEESY AND LAME, BUT I DON'T THINK I EVER REALLY FELT ALIVE. NOT UNTIL I MET YOU.
YOU'RE PRETTY MUCH THE MOST AMAZING PERSON I'VE EVER MET.
I'M REALLY NOT THAT AMAZING.
THERE'S SOMETHING HAVE TO DO, THAT VE WANTED TO O SINCE I MET YOU.
AND I HAVE O DO IT BEFORE IT'S TOO LATE.
NO... I COULD BE INFECTED...
I DON'T CARE.

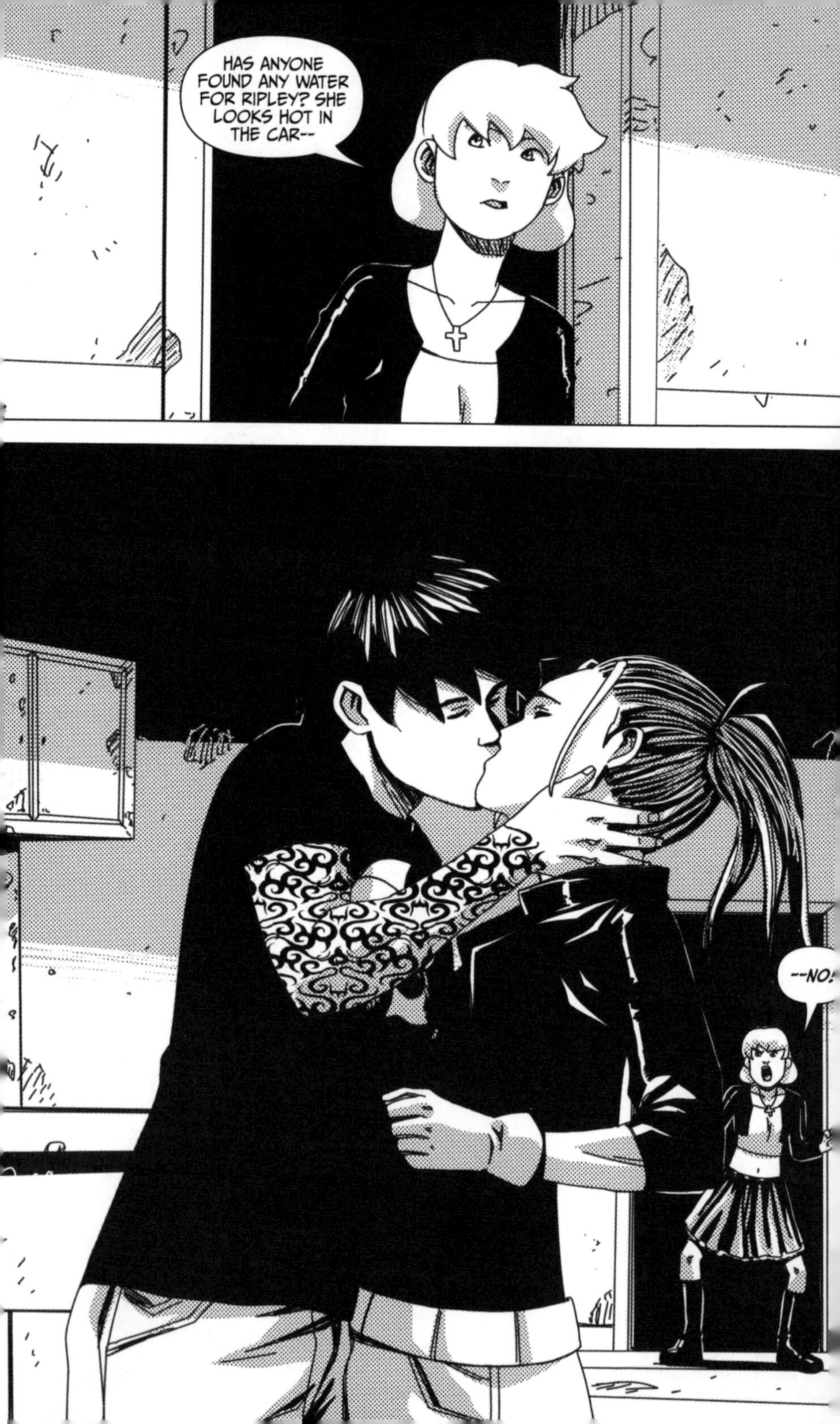
HAS ANYONE FOUND ANY WATER FOR RIPLEY? SHE LOOKS HOT IN THE CAR--
--NO!

CHAPTER EIGHT

UNITED BUT DIVIDED

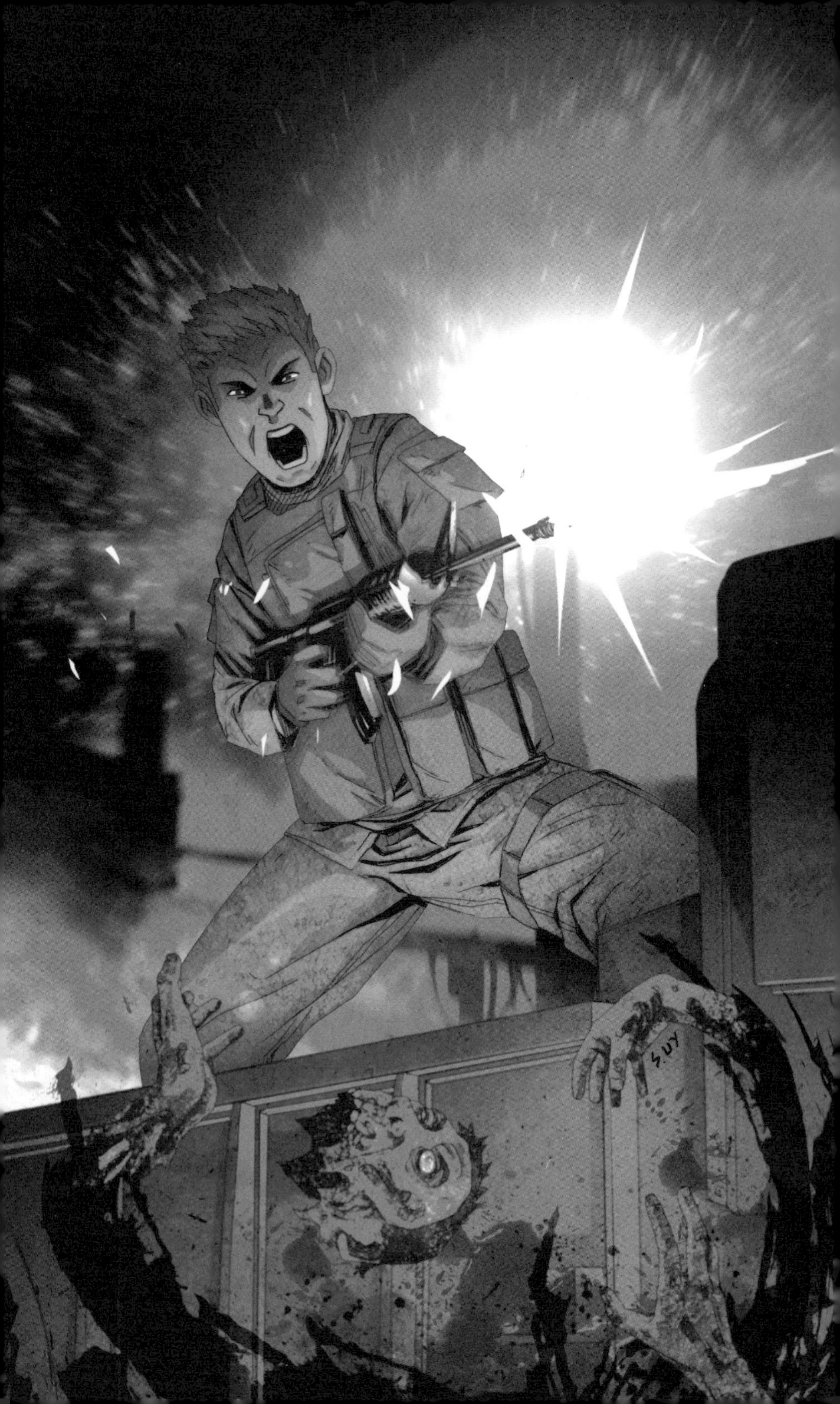
S.UY

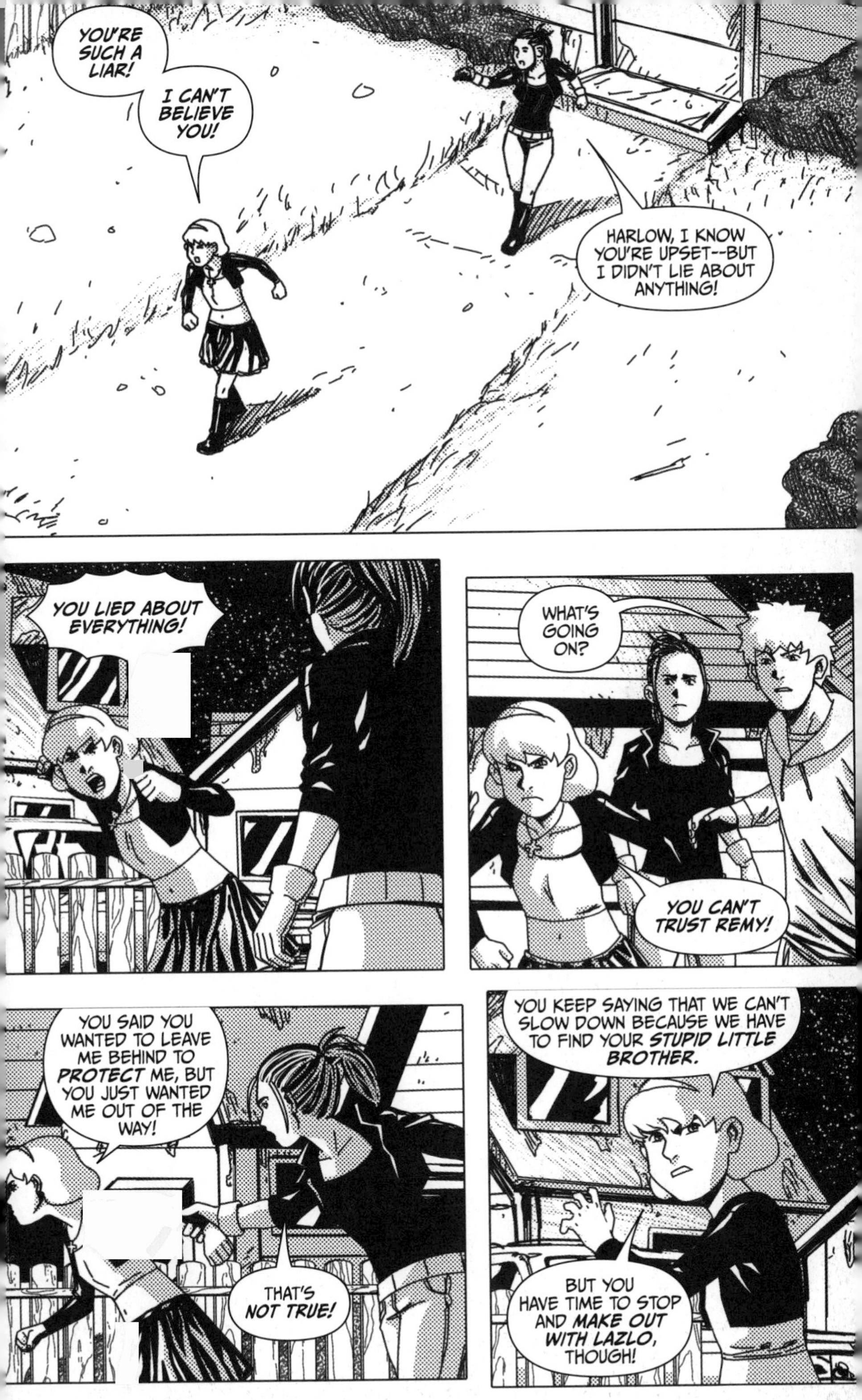
YOU'RE SUCH A LIAR!
I CAN'T BELIEVE YOU!
HARLOW, I KNOW YOU'RE UPSET--BUT I DIDN'T LIE ABOUT ANYTHING!
YOU LIED ABOUT EVERYTHING!
WHAT'S GOING ON?
YOU CAN'T TRUST REMY!
YOU SAID YOU WANTED TO LEAVE ME BEHIND TO PROTECT ME, BUT YOU JUST WANTED ME OUT OF THE WAY!
THAT'S NOT TRUE!
YOU KEEP SAYING THAT WE CAN'T SLOW DOWN BECAUSE WE HAVE TO FIND YOUR STUPID LITTLE BROTHER.
BUT YOU HAVE TIME TO STOP AND MAKE OUT WITH LAZLO, THOUGH!

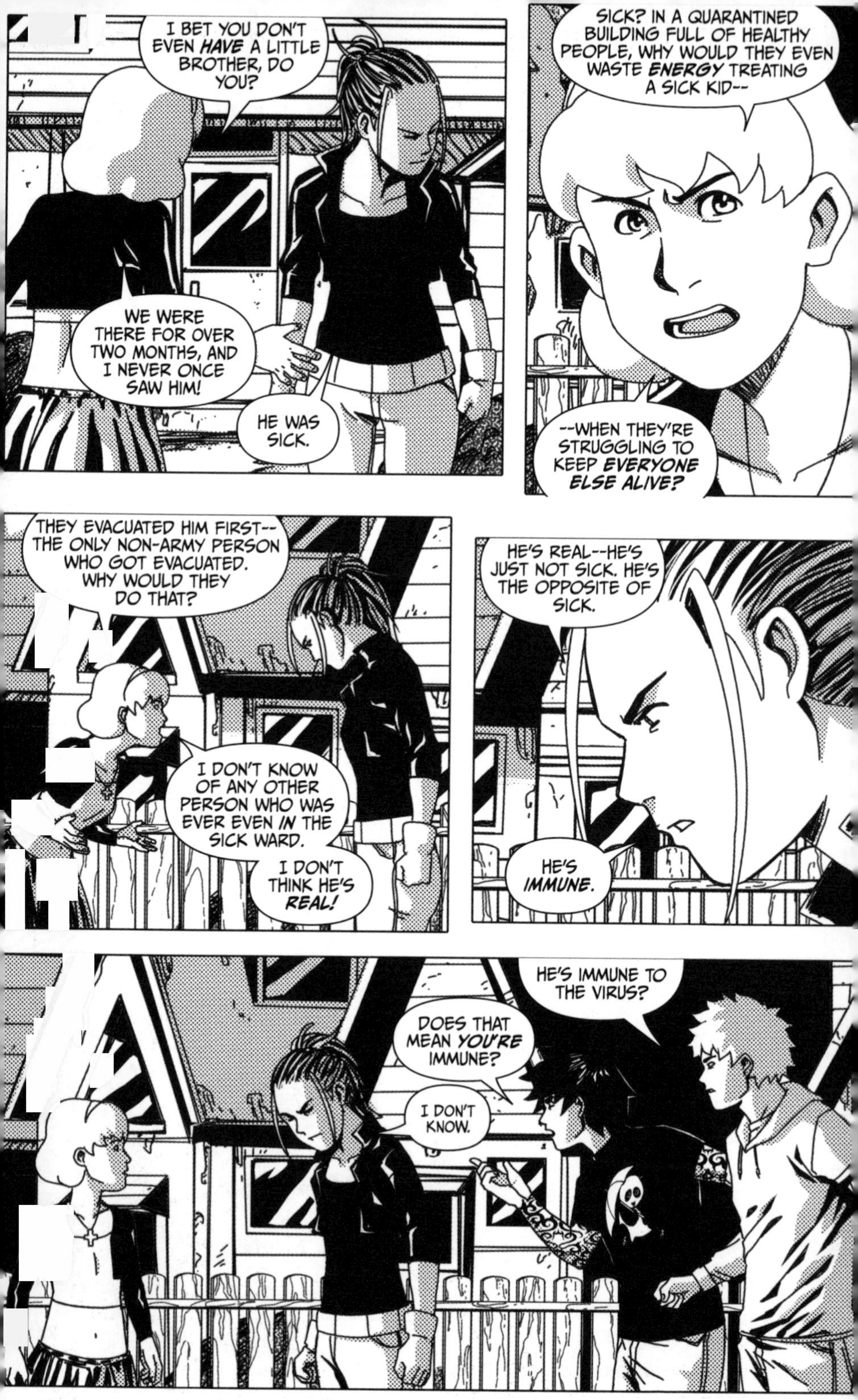
I BET YOU DON'T EVEN *HAVE* A LITTLE BROTHER, DO YOU?
WE WERE THERE FOR OVER TWO MONTHS, AND I NEVER ONCE SAW HIM!
HE WAS SICK.
SICK? IN A QUARANTINED BUILDING FULL OF HEALTHY PEOPLE, WHY WOULD THEY EVEN WASTE *ENERGY* TREATING A SICK KID--
--WHEN THEY'RE STRUGGLING TO KEEP *EVERYONE ELSE ALIVE?*
THEY EVACUATED HIM FIRST-- THE ONLY NON-ARMY PERSON WHO GOT EVACUATED. WHY WOULD THEY DO THAT?
I DON'T KNOW OF ANY OTHER PERSON WHO WAS EVER EVEN *IN* THE SICK WARD.
I DON'T THINK HE'S *REAL!*
HE'S REAL--HE'S JUST NOT SICK. HE'S THE OPPOSITE OF SICK.
HE'S *IMMUNE.*
HE'S IMMUNE TO THE VIRUS?
DOES THAT MEAN *YOU'RE* IMMUNE?
I DON'T KNOW.

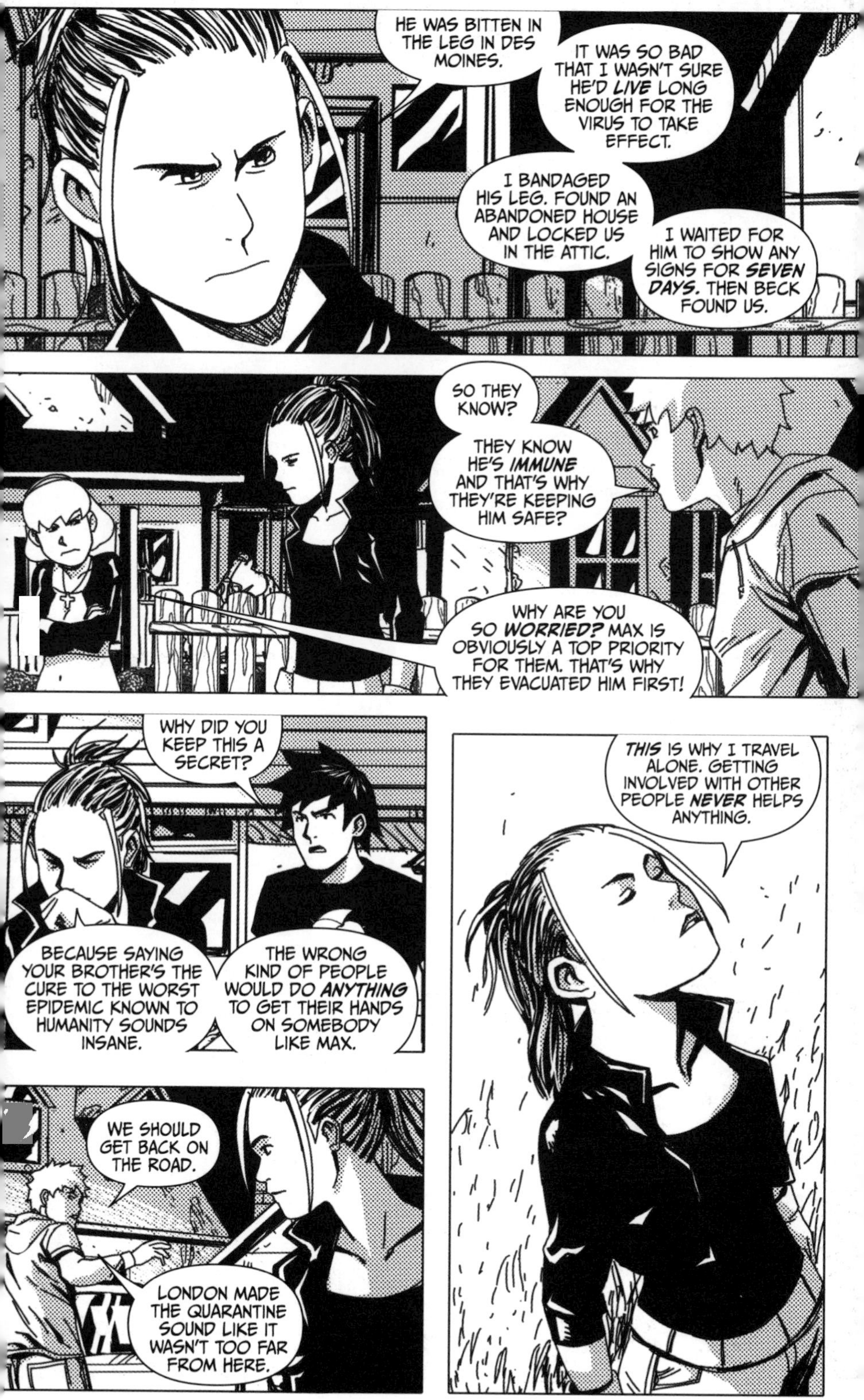
HE WAS BITTEN IN THE LEG IN DES MOINES.
IT WAS SO BAD THAT I WASN'T SURE HE'D LIVE LONG ENOUGH FOR THE VIRUS TO TAKE EFFECT.
I BANDAGED HIS LEG. FOUND AN ABANDONED HOUSE AND LOCKED US IN THE ATTIC.
I WAITED FOR HIM TO SHOW ANY SIGNS FOR SEVEN DAYS. THEN BECK FOUND US.
SO THEY KNOW?
THEY KNOW HE'S IMMUNE AND THAT'S WHY THEY'RE KEEPING HIM SAFE?
WHY ARE YOU SO WORRIED? MAX IS OBVIOUSLY A TOP PRIORITY FOR THEM. THAT'S WHY THEY EVACUATED HIM FIRST!
WHY DID YOU KEEP THIS A SECRET?
BECAUSE SAYING YOUR BROTHER'S THE CURE TO THE WORST EPIDEMIC KNOWN TO HUMANITY SOUNDS INSANE.
THE WRONG KIND OF PEOPLE WOULD DO ANYTHING TO GET THEIR HANDS ON SOMEBODY LIKE MAX.
WE SHOULD GET BACK ON THE ROAD.
LONDON MADE THE QUARANTINE SOUND LIKE IT WASN'T TOO FAR FROM HERE.
THIS IS WHY I TRAVEL ALONE. GETTING INVOLVED WITH OTHER PEOPLE NEVER HELPS ANYTHING.

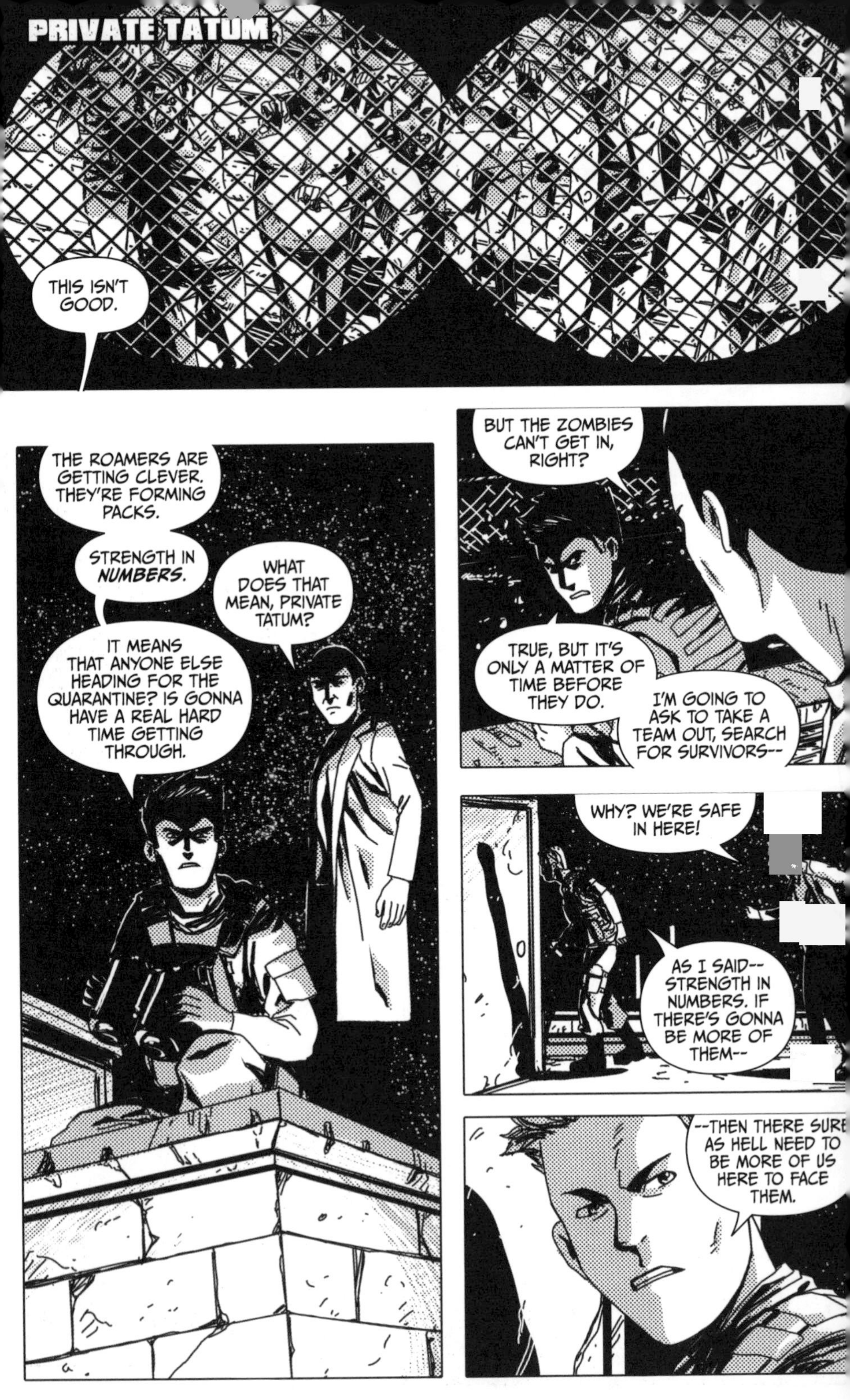
PRIVATE TATUM
THIS ISN'T GOOD.
THE ROAMERS ARE GETTING CLEVER. THEY'RE FORMING PACKS.
STRENGTH IN *NUMBERS*.
WHAT DOES THAT MEAN, PRIVATE TATUM?
IT MEANS THAT ANYONE ELSE HEADING FOR THE QUARANTINE? IS GONNA HAVE A REAL HARD TIME GETTING THROUGH.
BUT THE ZOMBIES CAN'T GET IN, RIGHT?
TRUE, BUT IT'S ONLY A MATTER OF TIME BEFORE THEY DO.
I'M GOING TO ASK TO TAKE A TEAM OUT, SEARCH FOR SURVIVORS--
WHY? WE'RE SAFE IN HERE!
AS I SAID-- STRENGTH IN NUMBERS. IF THERE'S GONNA BE MORE OF THEM--
--THEN THERE SURE AS HELL NEED TO BE MORE OF US HERE TO FACE THEM.

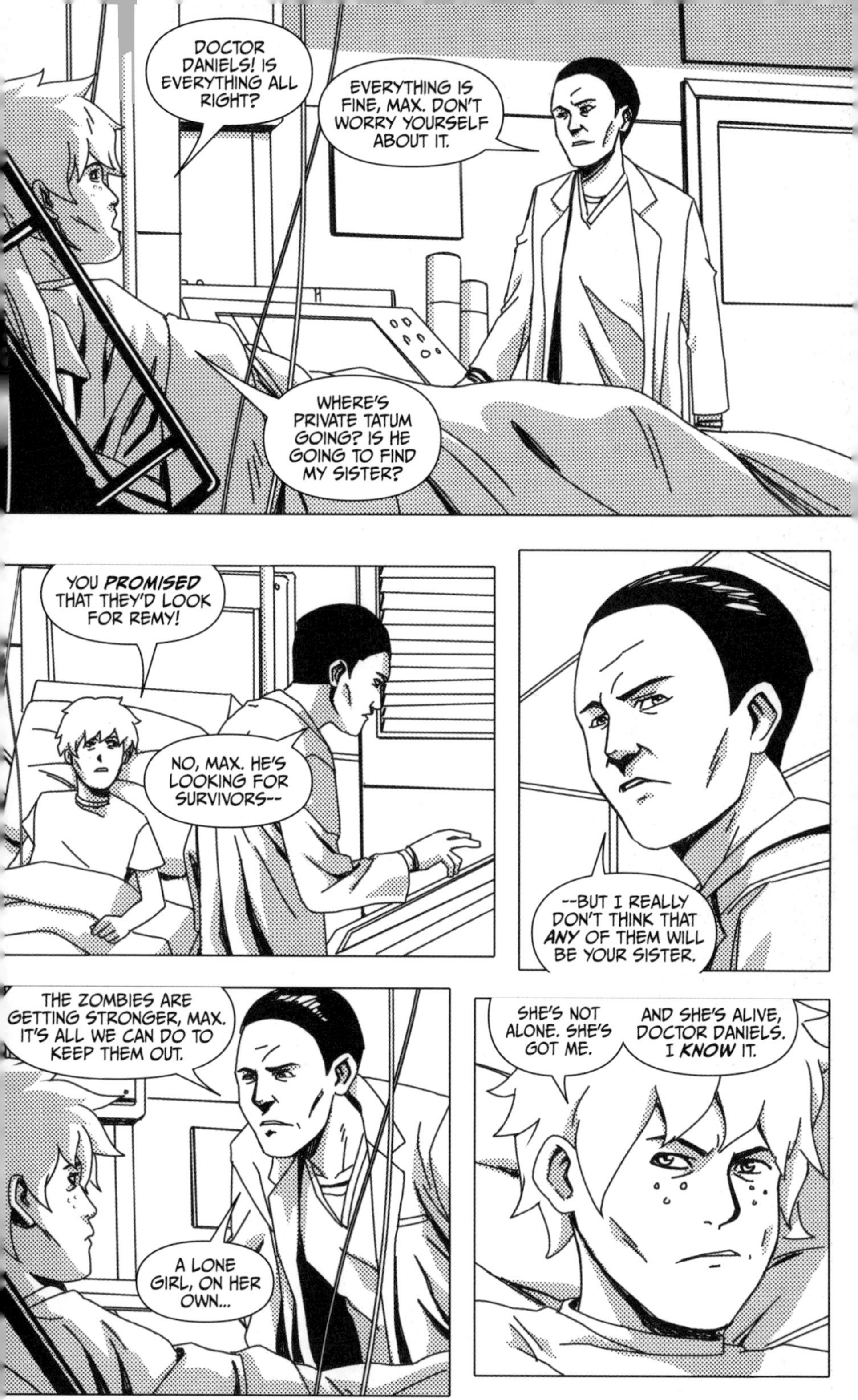
DOCTOR DANIELS! IS EVERYTHING ALL RIGHT?
EVERYTHING IS FINE, MAX. DON'T WORRY YOURSELF ABOUT IT.
WHERE'S PRIVATE TATUM GOING? IS HE GOING TO FIND MY SISTER?
YOU *PROMISED* THAT THEY'D LOOK FOR REMY!
NO, MAX. HE'S LOOKING FOR SURVIVORS--
--BUT I REALLY DON'T THINK THAT *ANY* OF THEM WILL BE YOUR SISTER.
THE ZOMBIES ARE GETTING STRONGER, MAX. IT'S ALL WE CAN DO TO KEEP THEM OUT.
A LONE GIRL, ON HER OWN...
SHE'S NOT ALONE. SHE'S GOT ME.
AND SHE'S ALIVE, DOCTOR DANIELS. I *KNOW* IT.

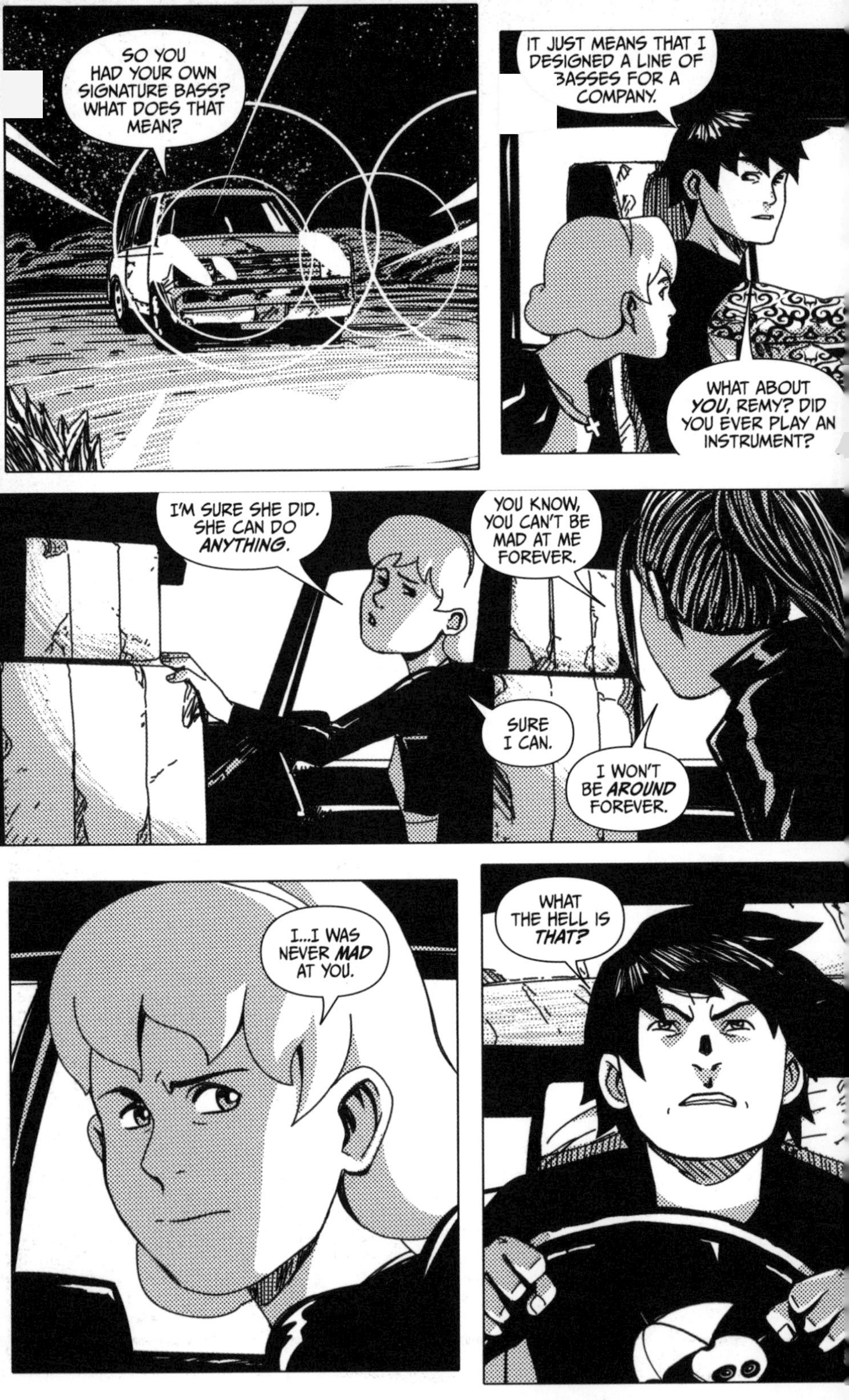
SO YOU HAD YOUR OWN SIGNATURE BASS? WHAT DOES THAT MEAN?
IT JUST MEANS THAT I DESIGNED A LINE OF BASSES FOR A COMPANY.
WHAT ABOUT *YOU*, REMY? DID YOU EVER PLAY AN INSTRUMENT?
I'M SURE SHE DID. SHE CAN DO *ANYTHING*.
YOU KNOW, YOU CAN'T BE MAD AT ME FOREVER.
SURE I CAN.
I WON'T BE *AROUND* FOREVER.
I...I WAS NEVER *MAD* AT YOU.
WHAT THE HELL IS *THAT?*

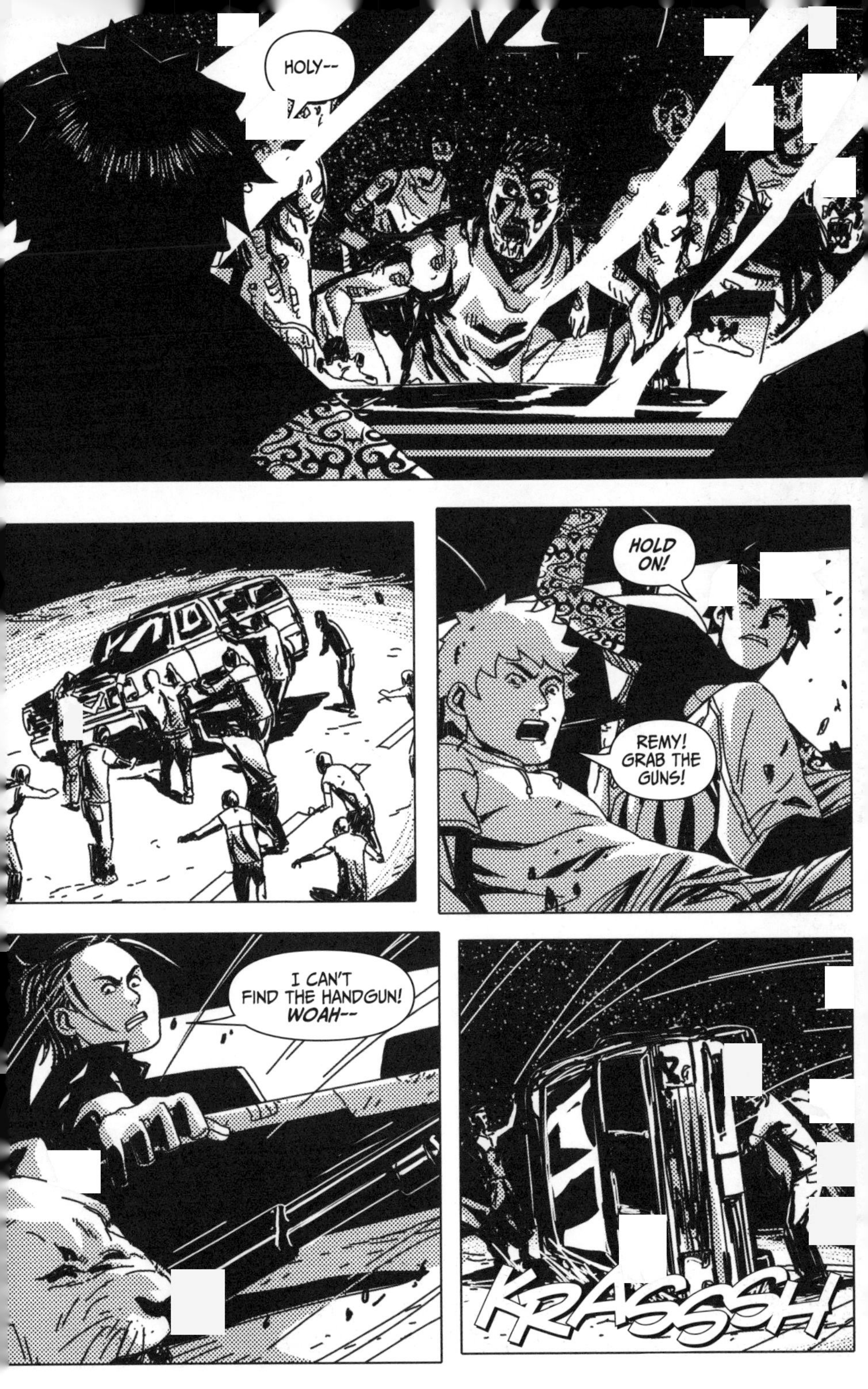
HOLY--
HOLD ON!
REMY! GRAB THE GUNS!
I CAN'T FIND THE HANDGUN! WOAH--
KRASSSH

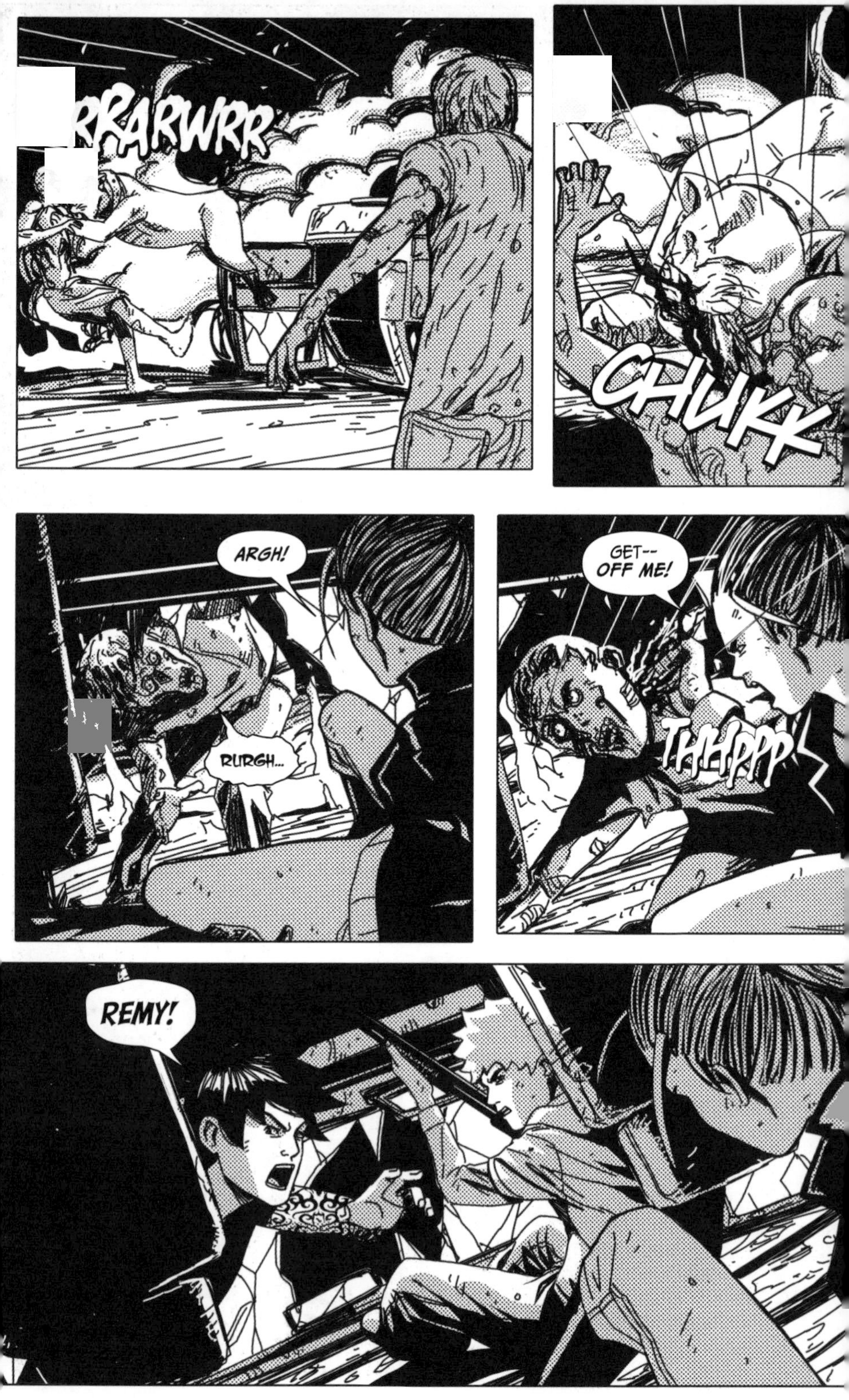
RRARWRR
CHUKK
ARGH!
RURGH...
GET-- OFF ME!
THHPPP
REMY!

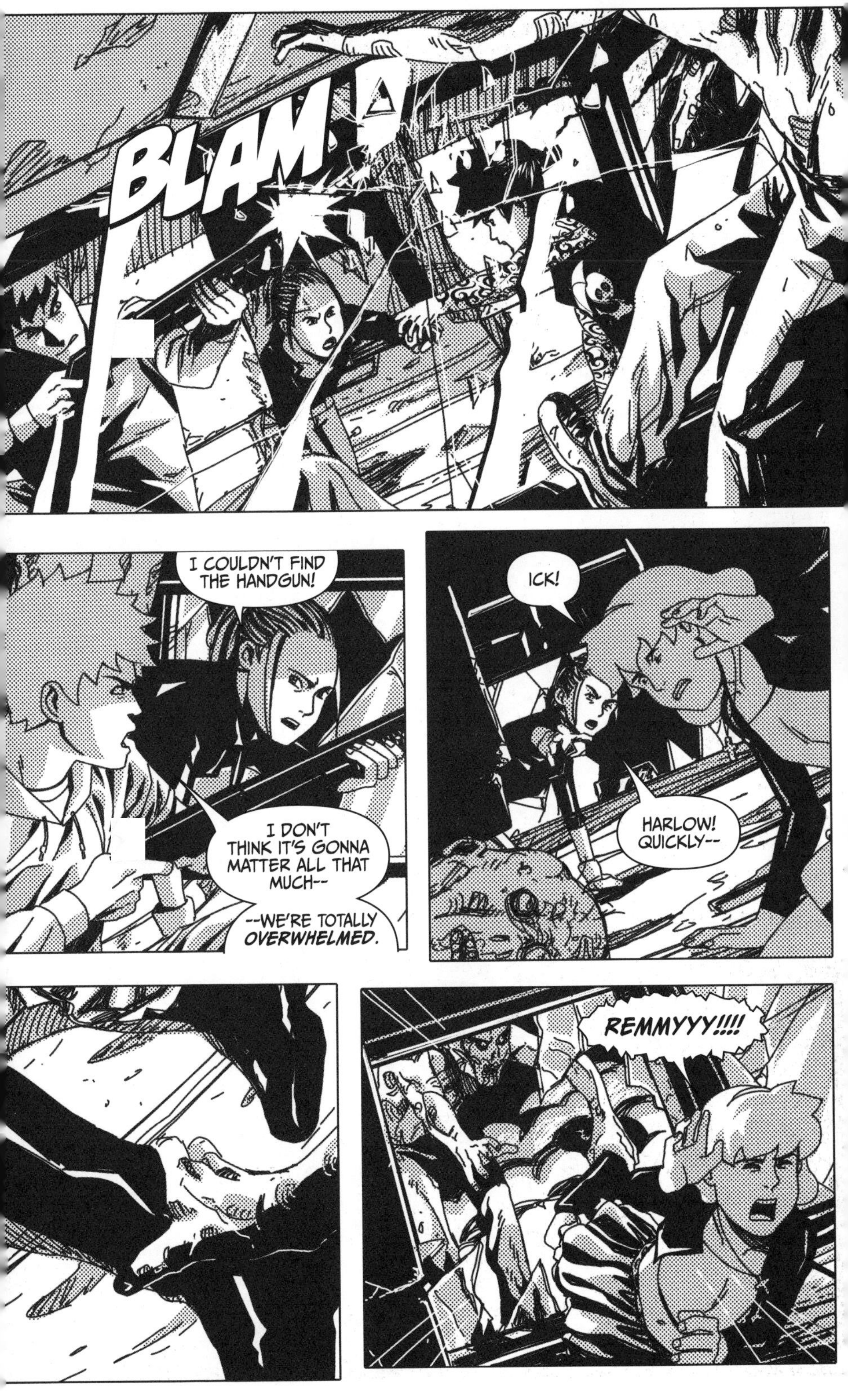
BLAM
I COULDN'T FIND THE HANDGUN!
I DON'T THINK IT'S GONNA MATTER ALL THAT MUCH--
--WE'RE TOTALLY *OVERWHELMED*.
ICK!
HARLOW! QUICKLY--
REMMYYY!!!!

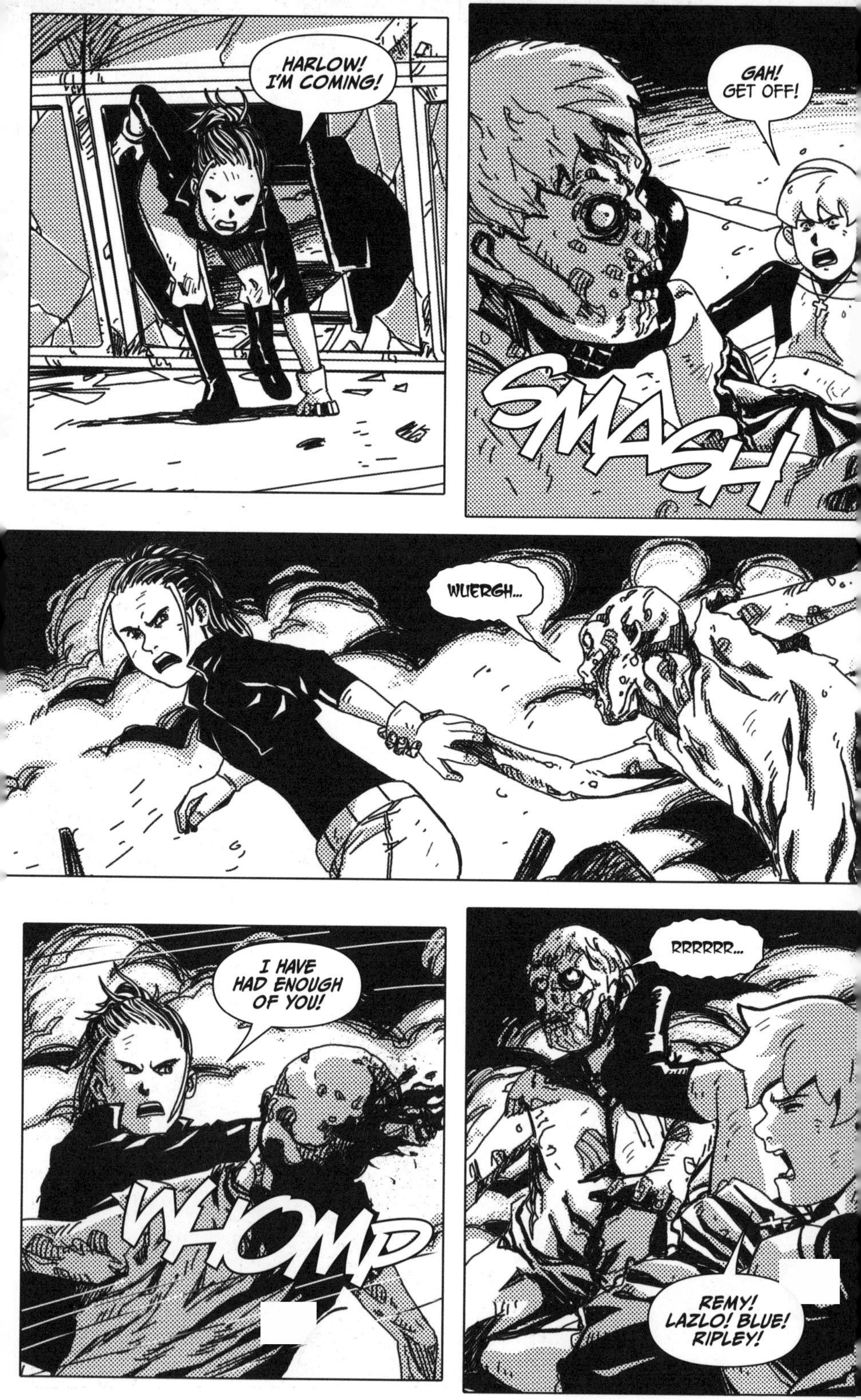
HARLOW! I'M COMING!
GAH! GET OFF!
SMASH
WUERGH...
I HAVE HAD ENOUGH OF YOU!
WHOMP
RRRRRR...
REMY! LAZLO! BLUE! RIPLEY!

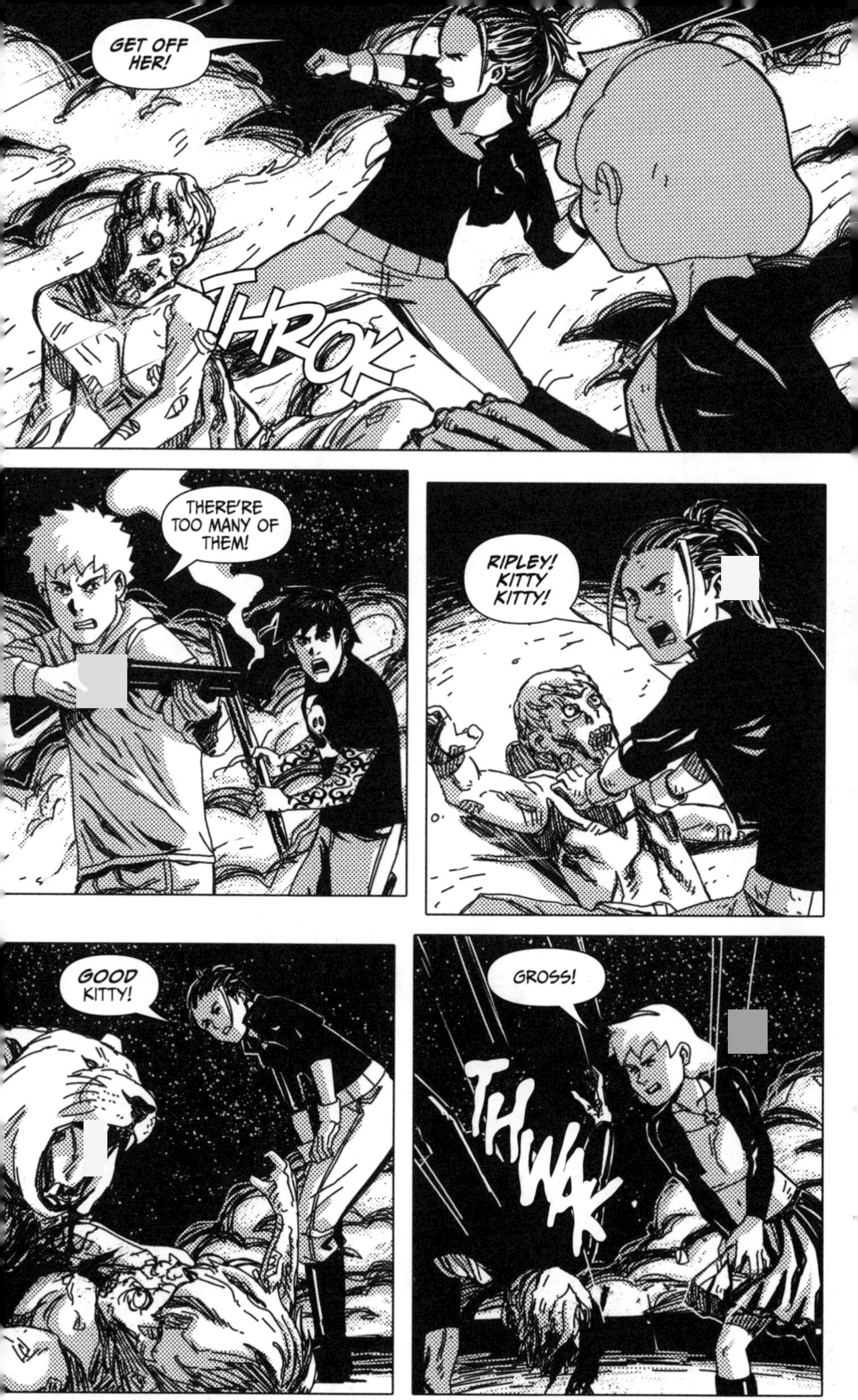
GET OFF HER!
THROK
THERE'RE TOO MANY OF THEM!
RIPLEY! KITTY KITTY!
GOOD KITTY!
GROSS!
THWAK

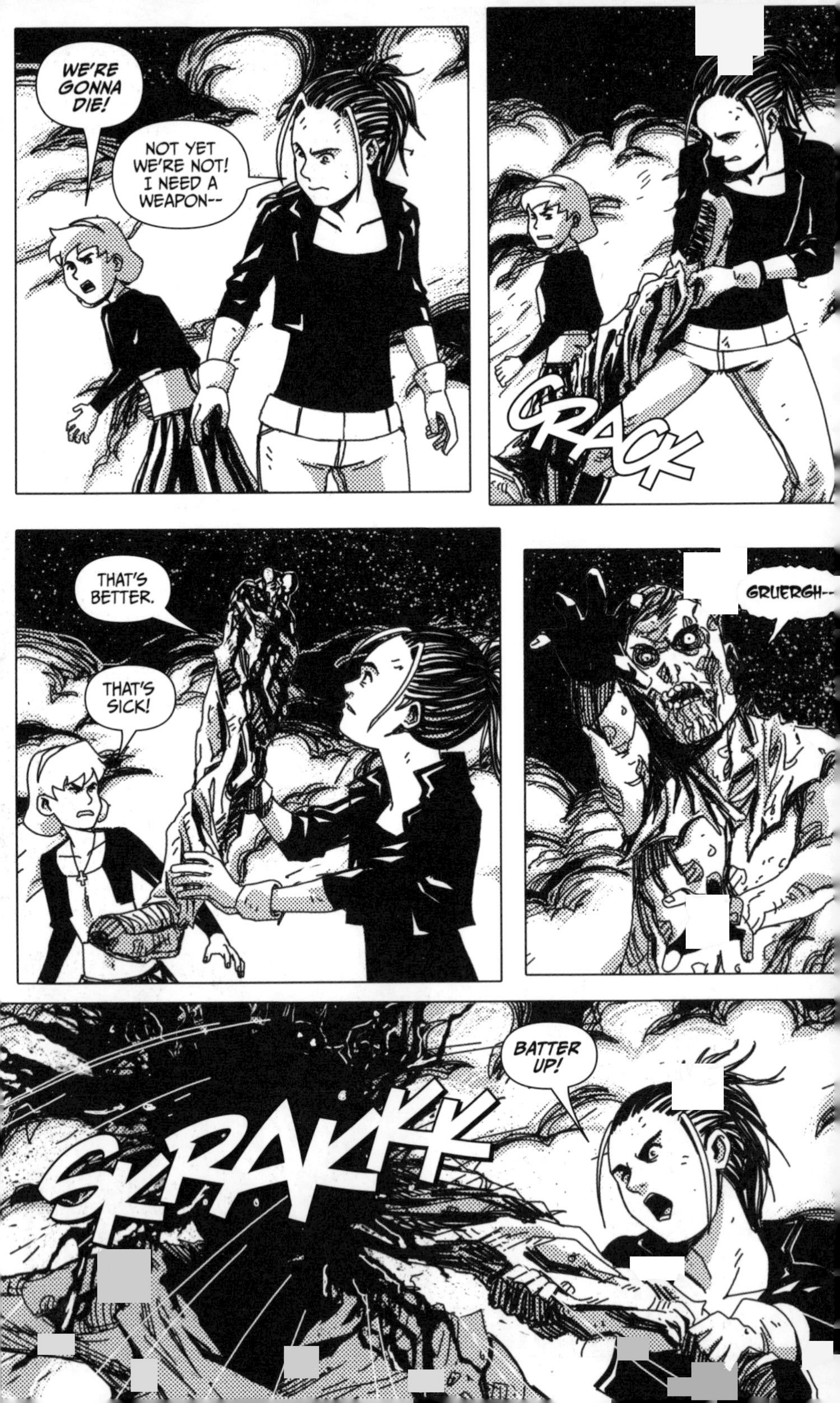
WE'RE GONNA DIE!
NOT YET WE'RE NOT! I NEED A WEAPON--
CRACK
THAT'S BETTER.
THAT'S SICK!
GRUERGH--
BATTER UP!
SKRAKK

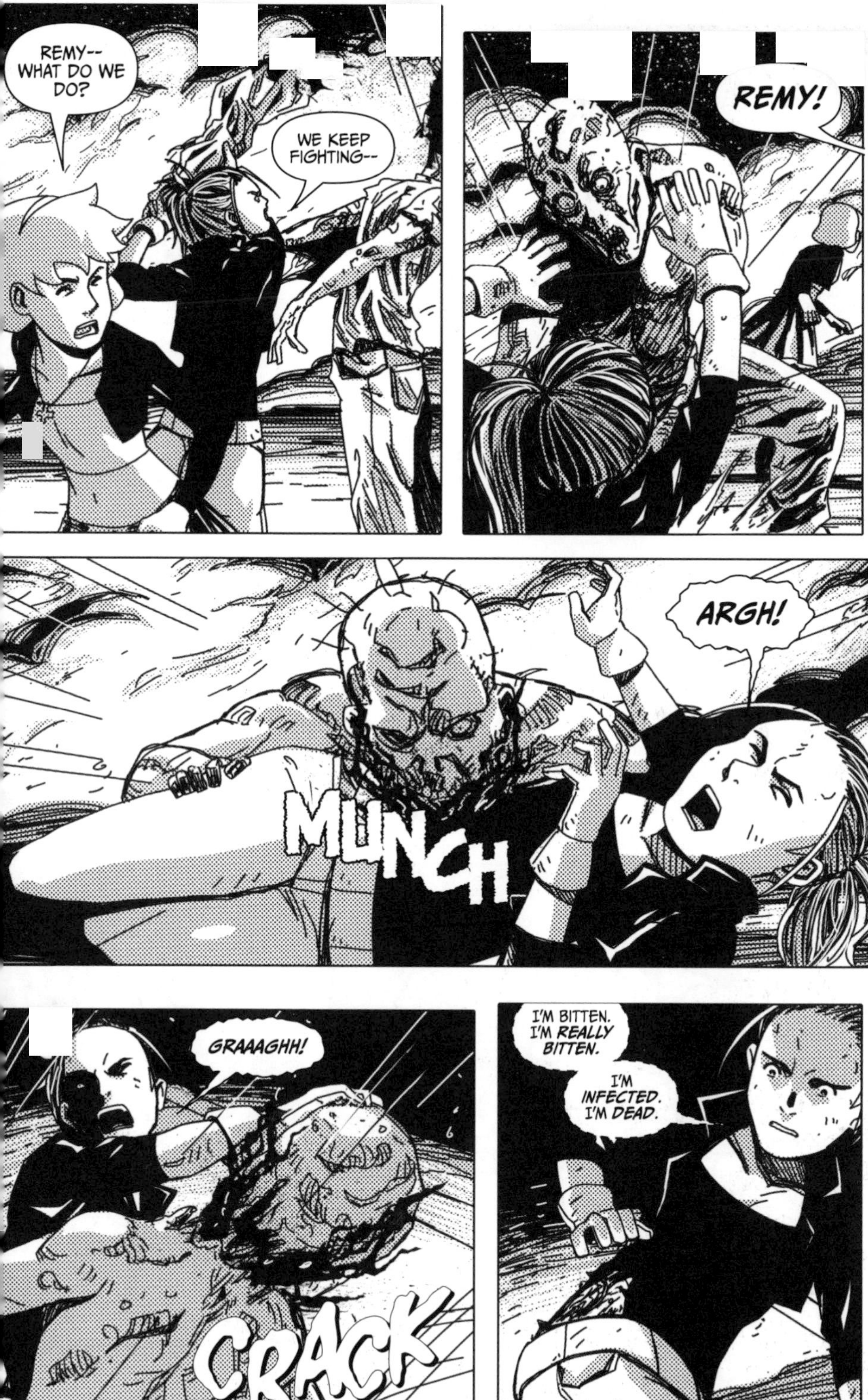
REMY-- WHAT DO WE DO?
WE KEEP FIGHTING--
REMY!
ARGH!
MUNCH
GRAAAGHH!
CRACK
I'M BITTEN. I'M *REALLY* BITTEN.
I'M *INFECTED.* I'M *DEAD.*

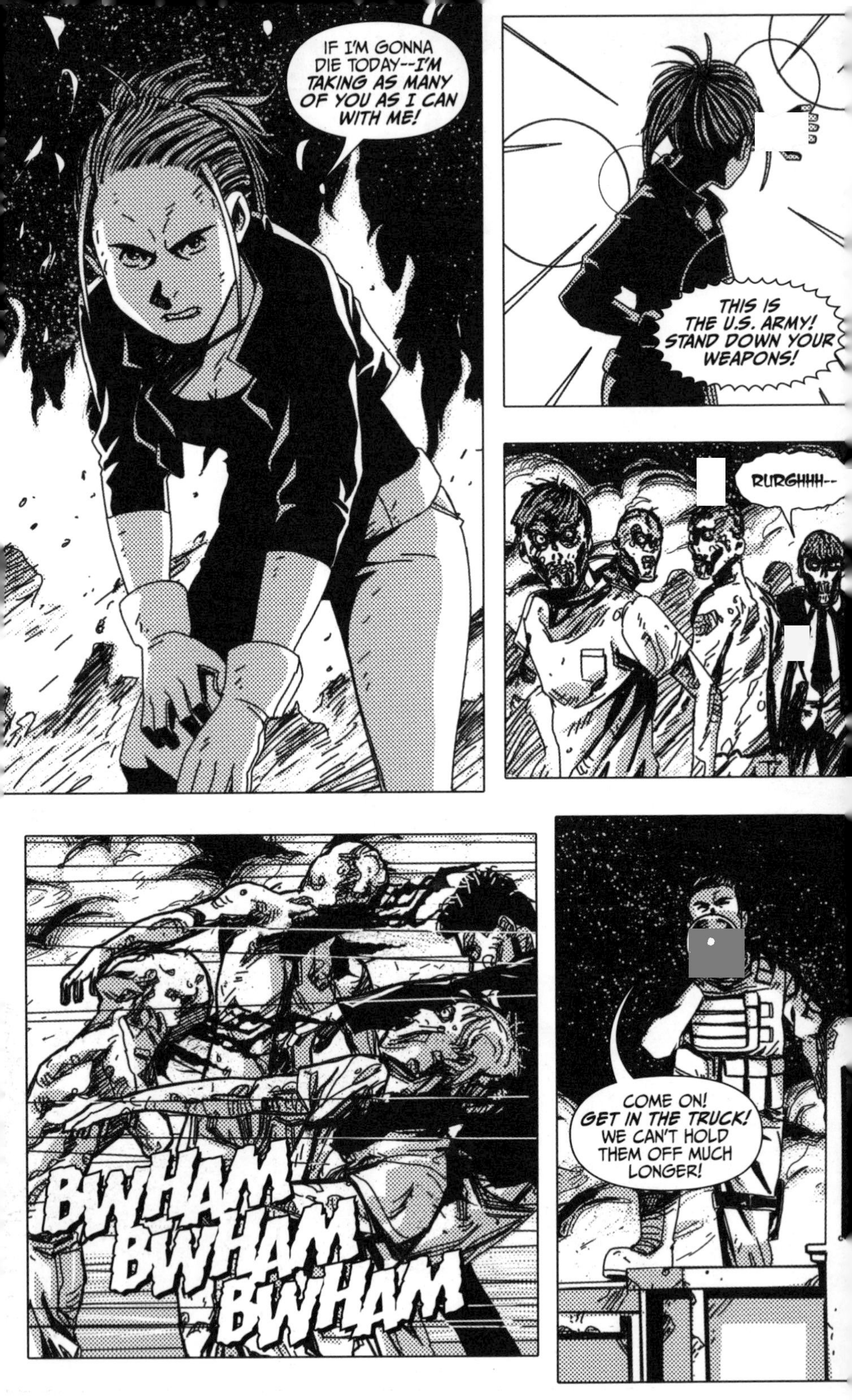
IF I'M GONNA DIE TODAY--I'M TAKING AS MANY OF YOU AS I CAN WITH ME!
THIS IS THE U.S. ARMY! STAND DOWN YOUR WEAPONS!
RURGHHH--
BWHAM BWHAM BWHAM
COME ON! GET IN THE TRUCK! WE CAN'T HOLD THEM OFF MUCH LONGER!

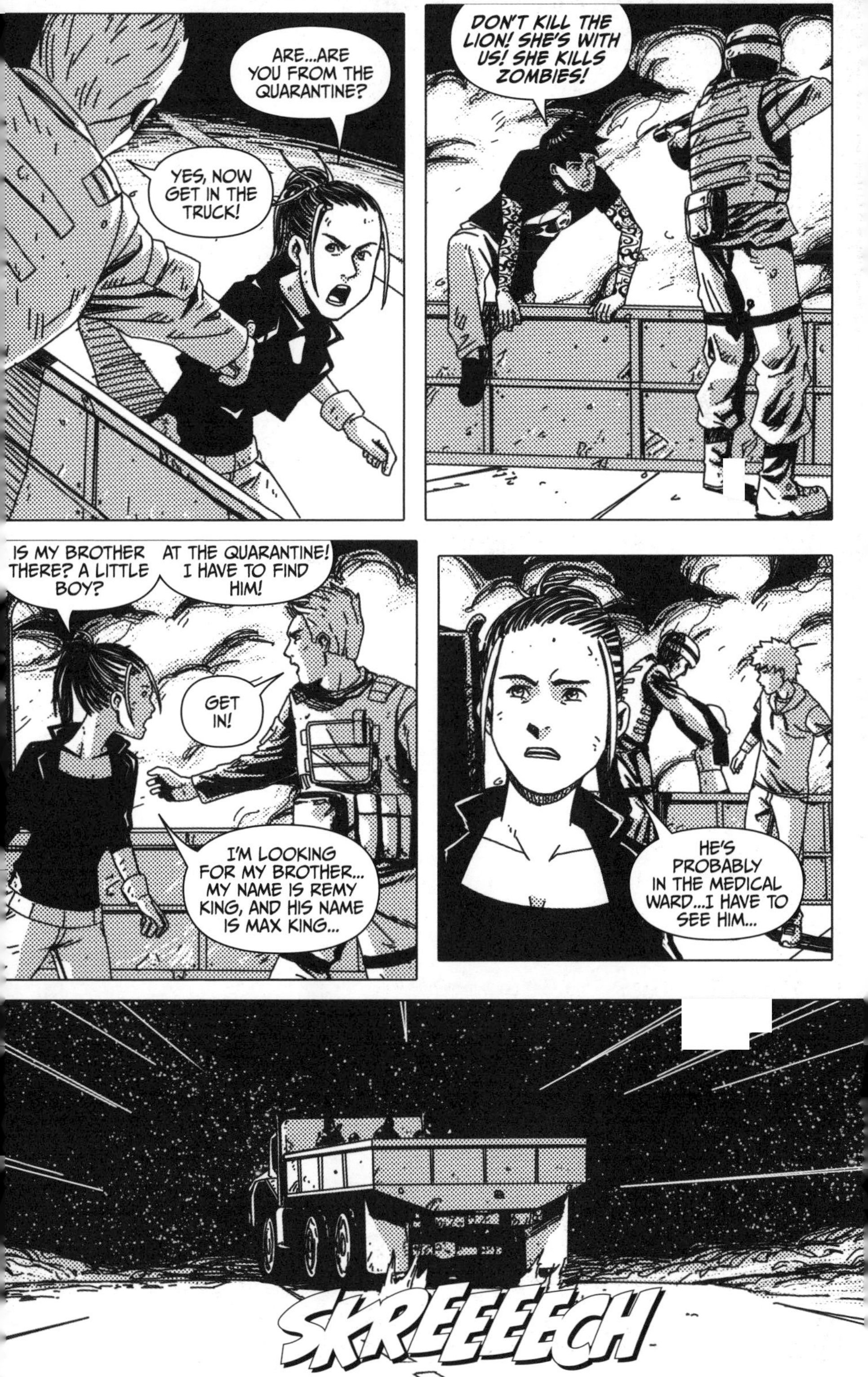
ARE...ARE YOU FROM THE QUARANTINE?
YES, NOW GET IN THE TRUCK!
DON'T KILL THE LION! SHE'S WITH US! SHE KILLS ZOMBIES!
IS MY BROTHER THERE? A LITTLE BOY?
AT THE QUARANTINE! I HAVE TO FIND HIM!
GET IN!
I'M LOOKING FOR MY BROTHER... MY NAME IS REMY KING, AND HIS NAME IS MAX KING...
HE'S PROBABLY IN THE MEDICAL WARD...I HAVE TO SEE HIM...
SKREEEECH

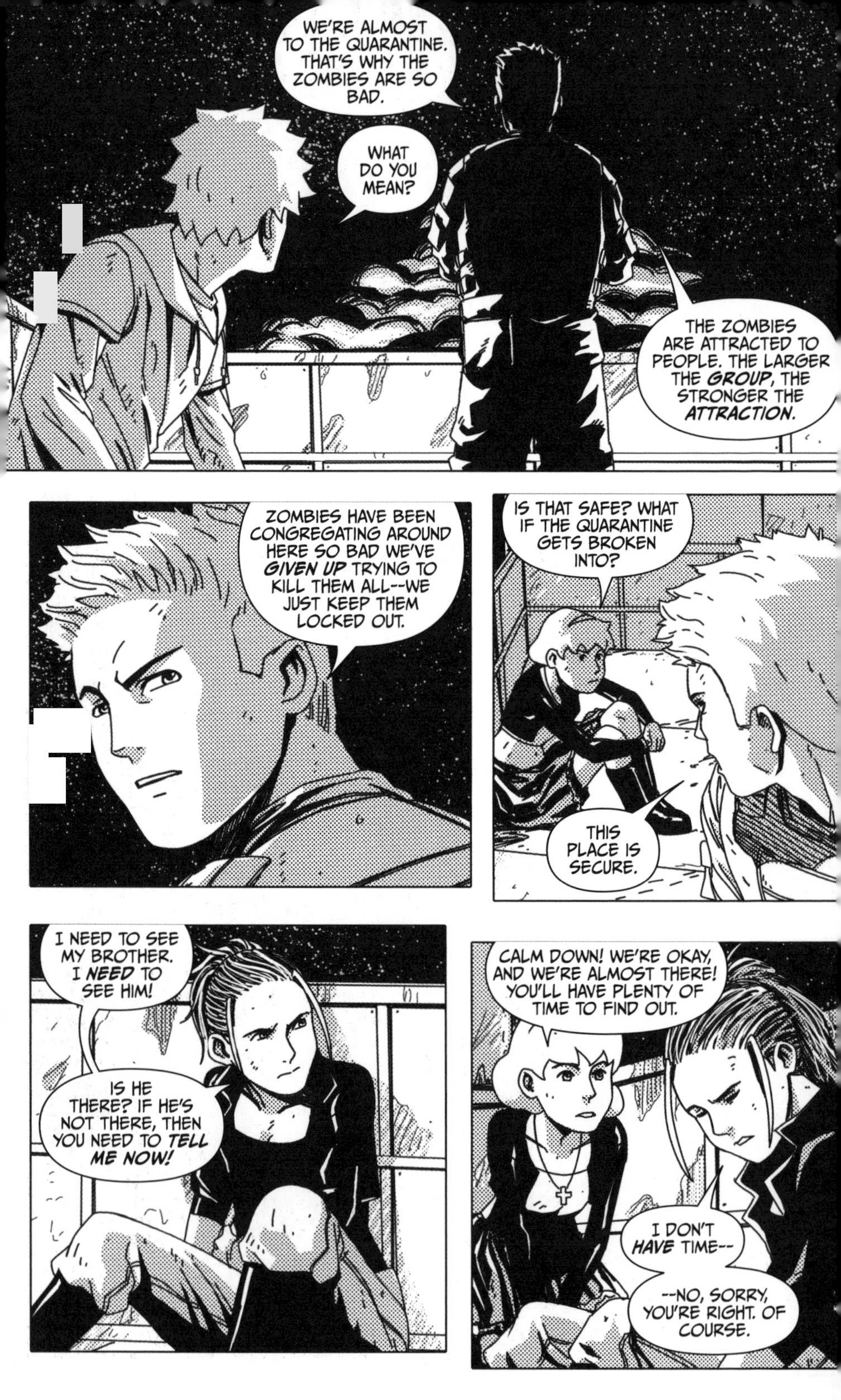

WE'RE ALMOST TO THE QUARANTINE. THAT'S WHY THE ZOMBIES ARE SO BAD.
WHAT DO YOU MEAN?
THE ZOMBIES ARE ATTRACTED TO PEOPLE. THE LARGER THE GROUP, THE STRONGER THE ATTRACTION.
ZOMBIES HAVE BEEN CONGREGATING AROUND HERE SO BAD WE'VE GIVEN UP TRYING TO KILL THEM ALL--WE JUST KEEP THEM LOCKED OUT.
IS THAT SAFE? WHAT IF THE QUARANTINE GETS BROKEN INTO?
THIS PLACE IS SECURE.
I NEED TO SEE MY BROTHER. I NEED TO SEE HIM!
IS HE THERE? IF HE'S NOT THERE, THEN YOU NEED TO TELL ME NOW!
CALM DOWN! WE'RE OKAY, AND WE'RE ALMOST THERE! YOU'LL HAVE PLENTY OF TIME TO FIND OUT.
I DON'T HAVE TIME--
--NO, SORRY, YOU'RE RIGHT. OF COURSE.

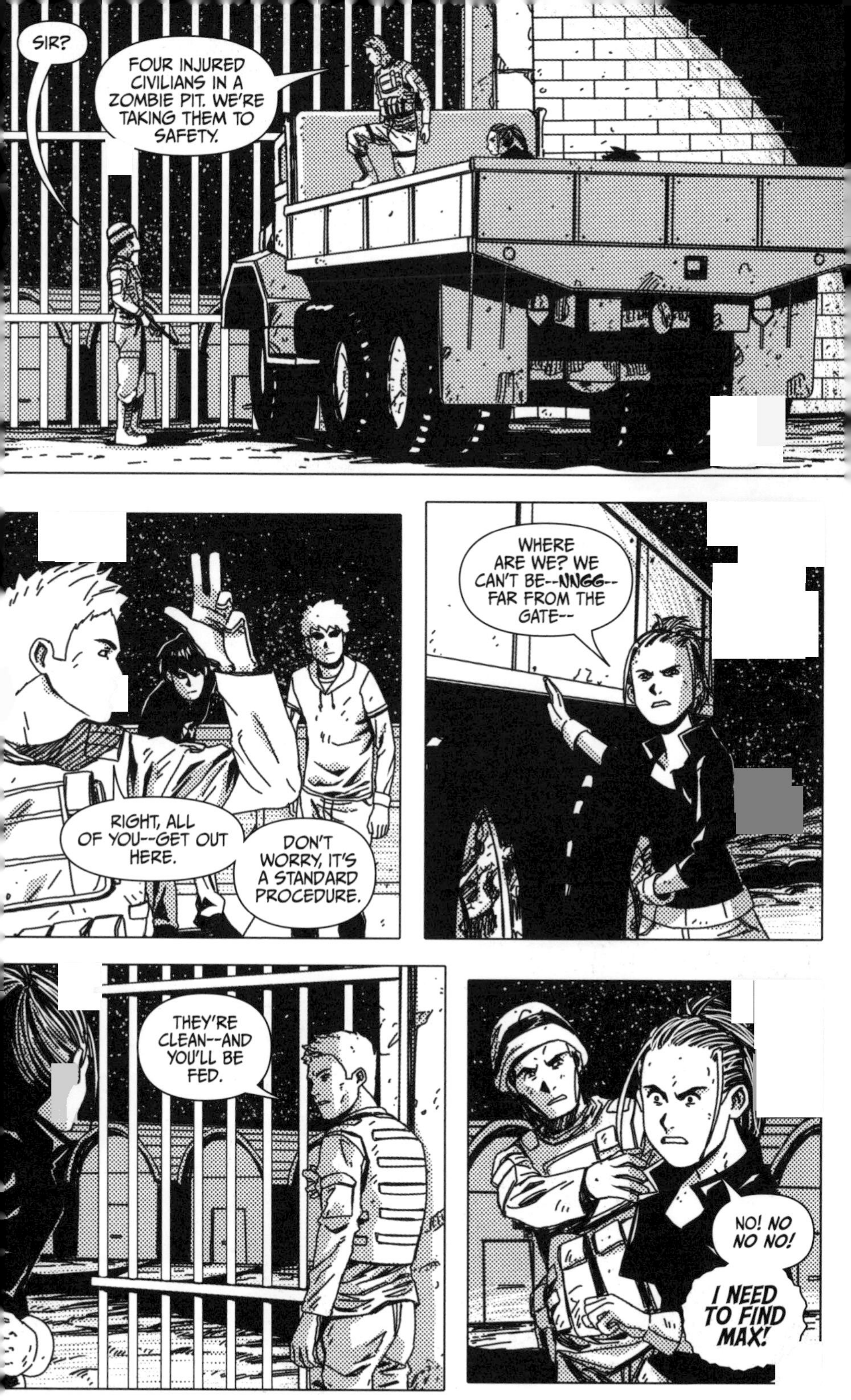
SIR?
FOUR INJURED CIVILIANS IN A ZOMBIE PIT. WE'RE TAKING THEM TO SAFETY.
RIGHT, ALL OF YOU--GET OUT HERE.
DON'T WORRY, IT'S A STANDARD PROCEDURE.
WHERE ARE WE? WE CAN'T BE--NNGG--FAR FROM THE GATE--
THEY'RE CLEAN--AND YOU'LL BE FED.
NO! NO NO NO!
I NEED TO FIND MAX!

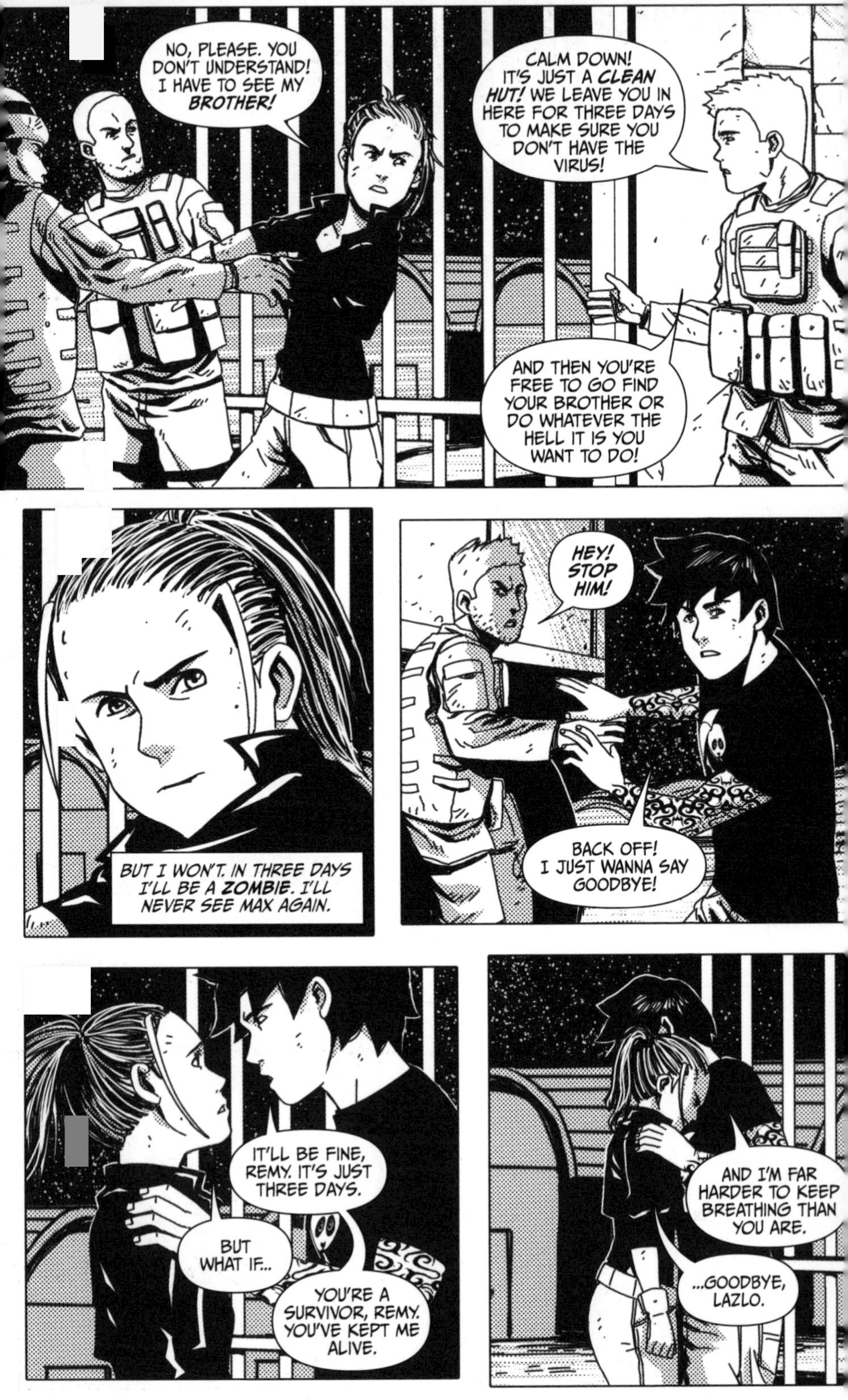
NO, PLEASE. YOU DON'T UNDERSTAND! I HAVE TO SEE MY **BROTHER!**
CALM DOWN! IT'S JUST A ***CLEAN HUT!*** WE LEAVE YOU IN HERE FOR THREE DAYS TO MAKE SURE YOU DON'T HAVE THE VIRUS!
AND THEN YOU'RE FREE TO GO FIND YOUR BROTHER OR DO WHATEVER THE HELL IT IS YOU WANT TO DO!
*BUT I WON'T. IN THREE DAYS I'LL BE A **ZOMBIE**. I'LL NEVER SEE MAX AGAIN.*
HEY! STOP HIM!
BACK OFF! I JUST WANNA SAY GOODBYE!
IT'LL BE FINE, REMY. IT'S JUST THREE DAYS.
BUT WHAT IF...
YOU'RE A SURVIVOR, REMY. YOU'VE KEPT ME ALIVE.
AND I'M FAR HARDER TO KEEP BREATHING THAN YOU ARE.
...GOODBYE, LAZLO.

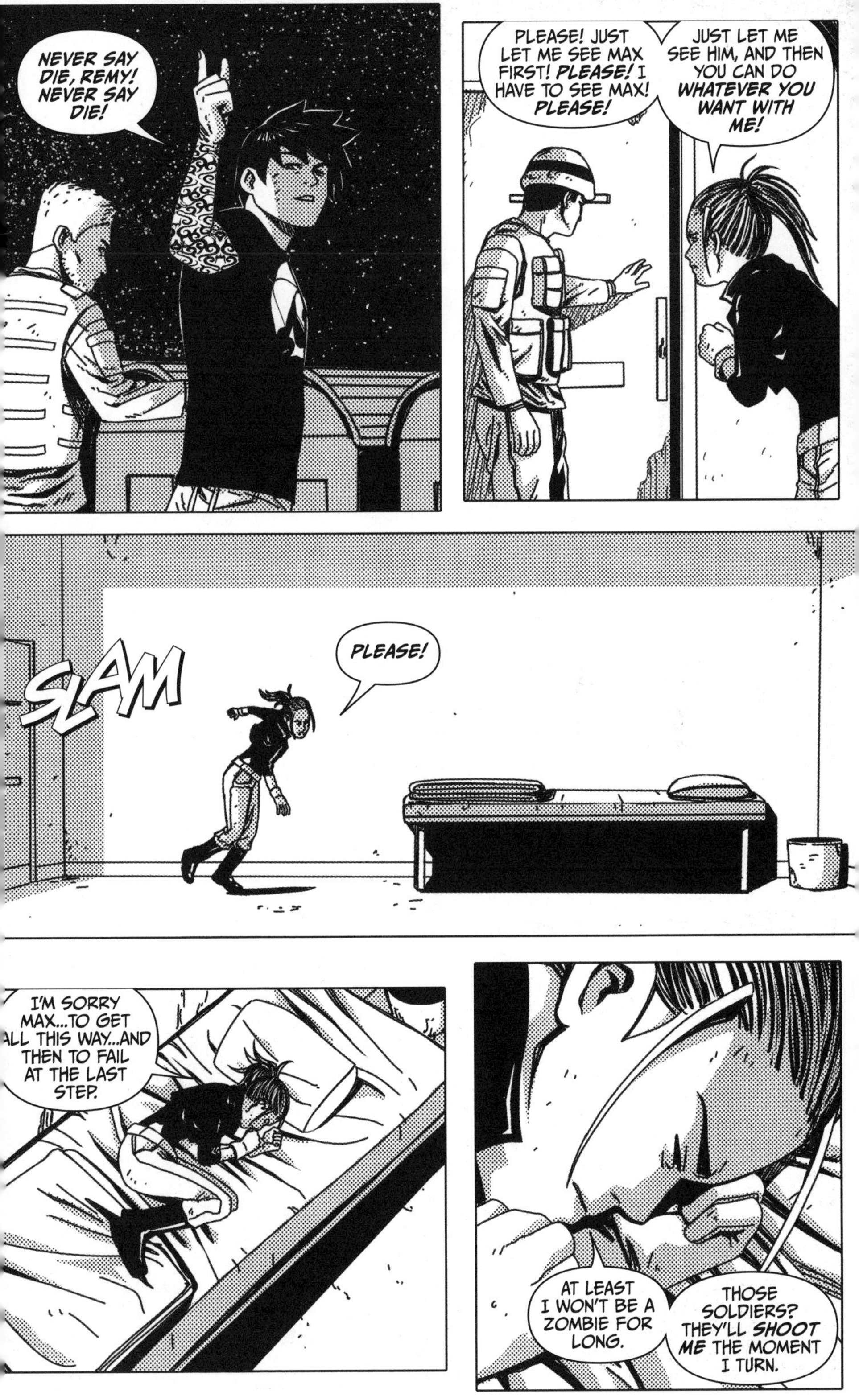

NEVER SAY DIE, REMY! NEVER SAY DIE!
PLEASE! JUST LET ME SEE MAX FIRST! PLEASE! I HAVE TO SEE MAX! PLEASE!
JUST LET ME SEE HIM, AND THEN YOU CAN DO WHATEVER YOU WANT WITH ME!
SLAM
PLEASE!
I'M SORRY MAX...TO GET ALL THIS WAY...AND THEN TO FAIL AT THE LAST STEP.
AT LEAST I WON'T BE A ZOMBIE FOR LONG.
THOSE SOLDIERS? THEY'LL SHOOT ME THE MOMENT I TURN.

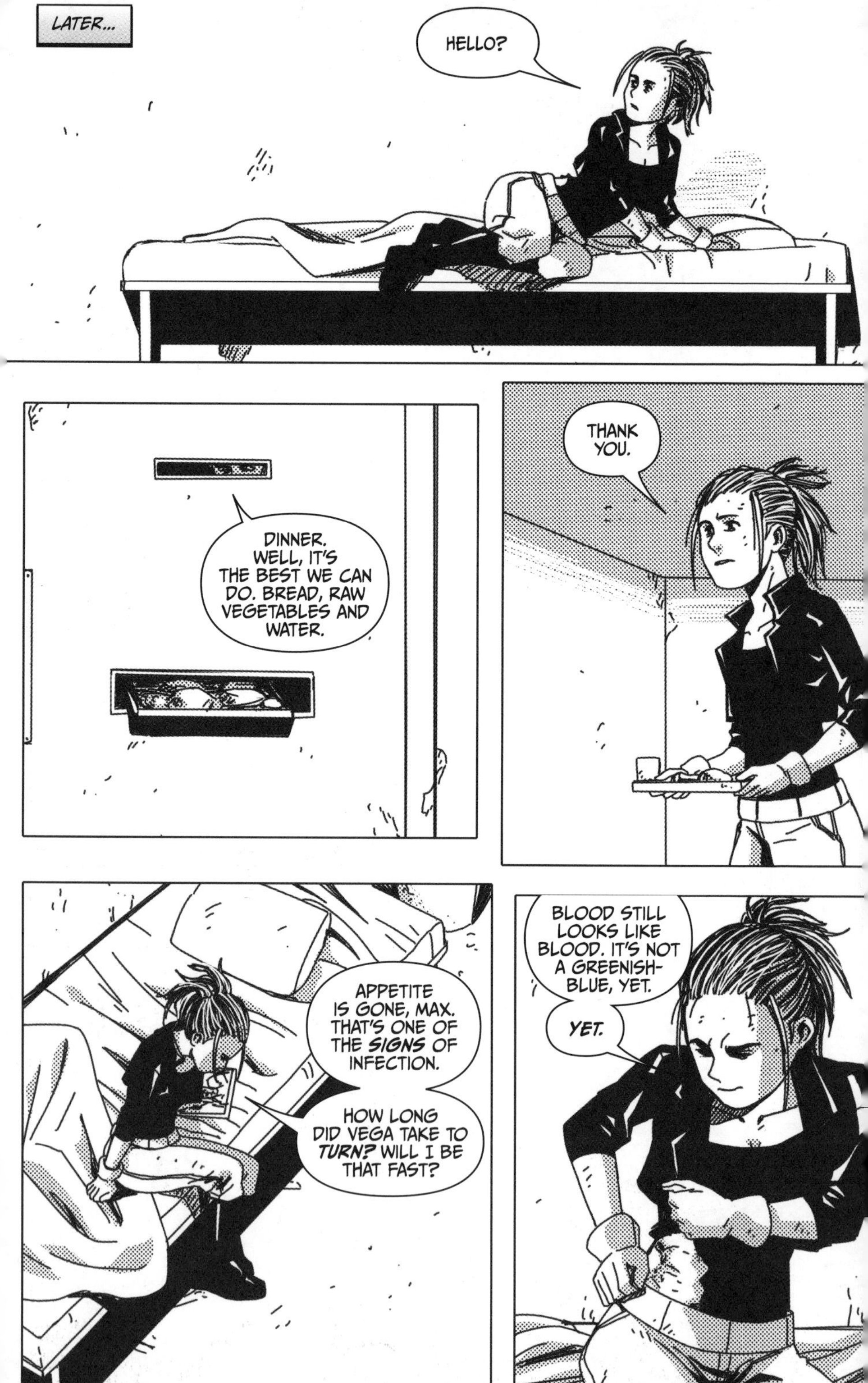
LATER...
HELLO?
DINNER. WELL, IT'S THE BEST WE CAN DO. BREAD, RAW VEGETABLES AND WATER.
THANK YOU.
APPETITE IS GONE, MAX. THAT'S ONE OF THE **SIGNS** OF INFECTION.
HOW LONG DID VEGA TAKE TO **TURN?** WILL I BE THAT FAST?
BLOOD STILL LOOKS LIKE BLOOD. IT'S NOT A GREENISH-BLUE, YET.
YET.

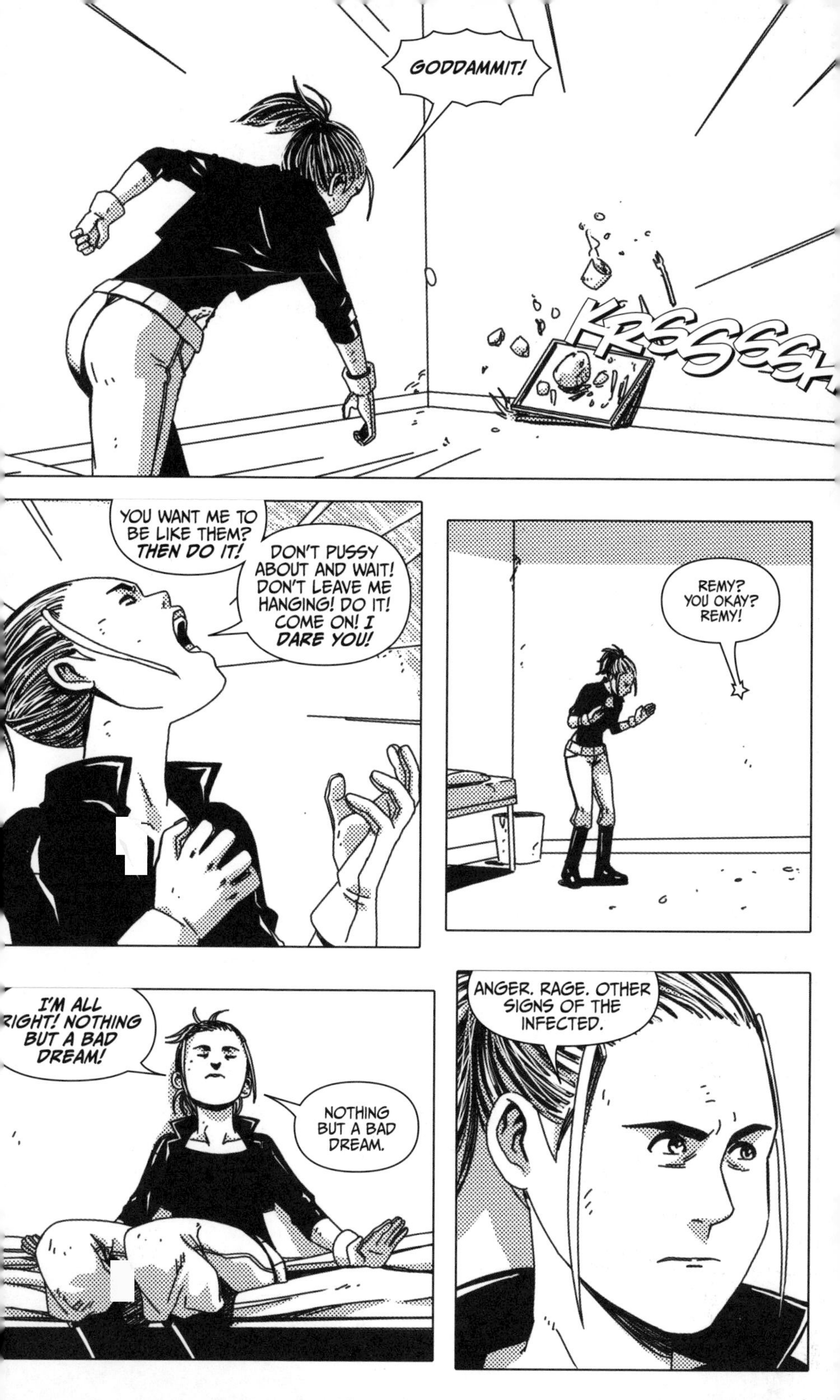
GODDAMMIT!
KRSSSSK
YOU WANT ME TO BE LIKE THEM? THEN DO IT!
DON'T PUSSY ABOUT AND WAIT! DON'T LEAVE ME HANGING! DO IT! COME ON! I DARE YOU!
REMY? YOU OKAY? REMY!
I'M ALL RIGHT! NOTHING BUT A BAD DREAM!
NOTHING BUT A BAD DREAM.
ANGER. RAGE. OTHER SIGNS OF THE INFECTED.

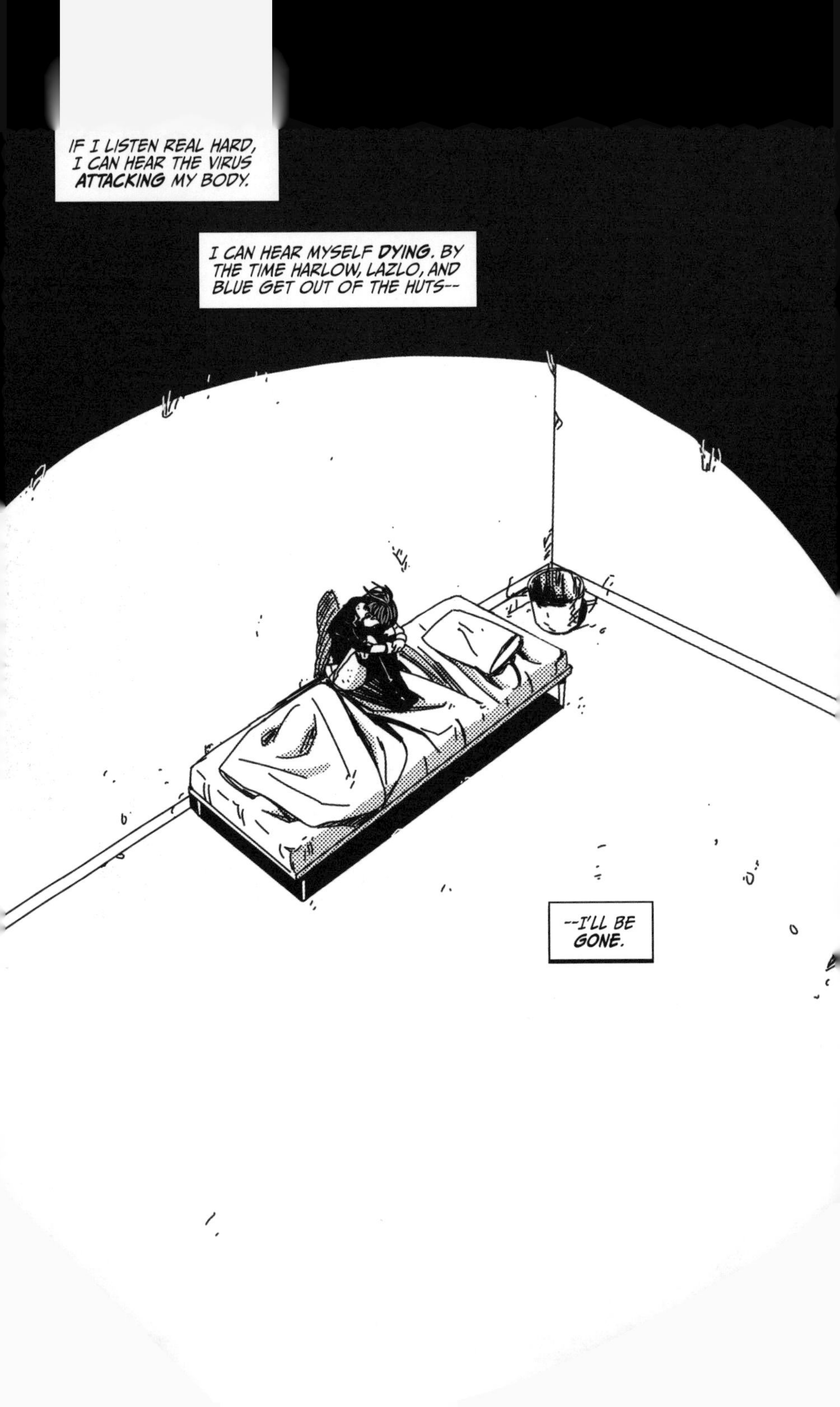
IF I LISTEN REAL HARD, I CAN HEAR THE VIRUS ATTACKING MY BODY.
I CAN HEAR MYSELF DYING. BY THE TIME HARLOW, LAZLO, AND BLUE GET OUT OF THE HUTS--
--I'LL BE GONE.

CHAPTER NINE

THE NEW REGIME

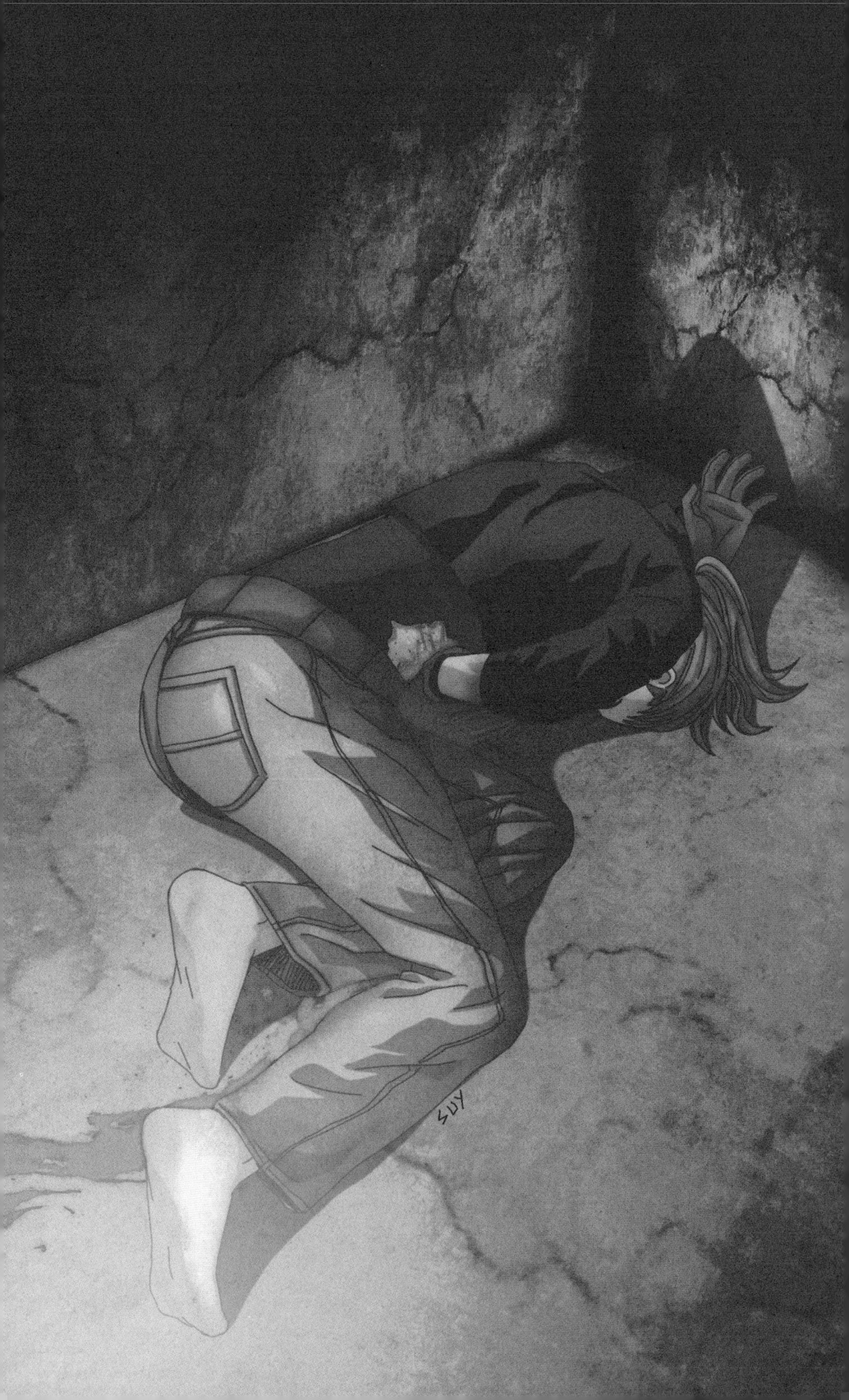
SDY

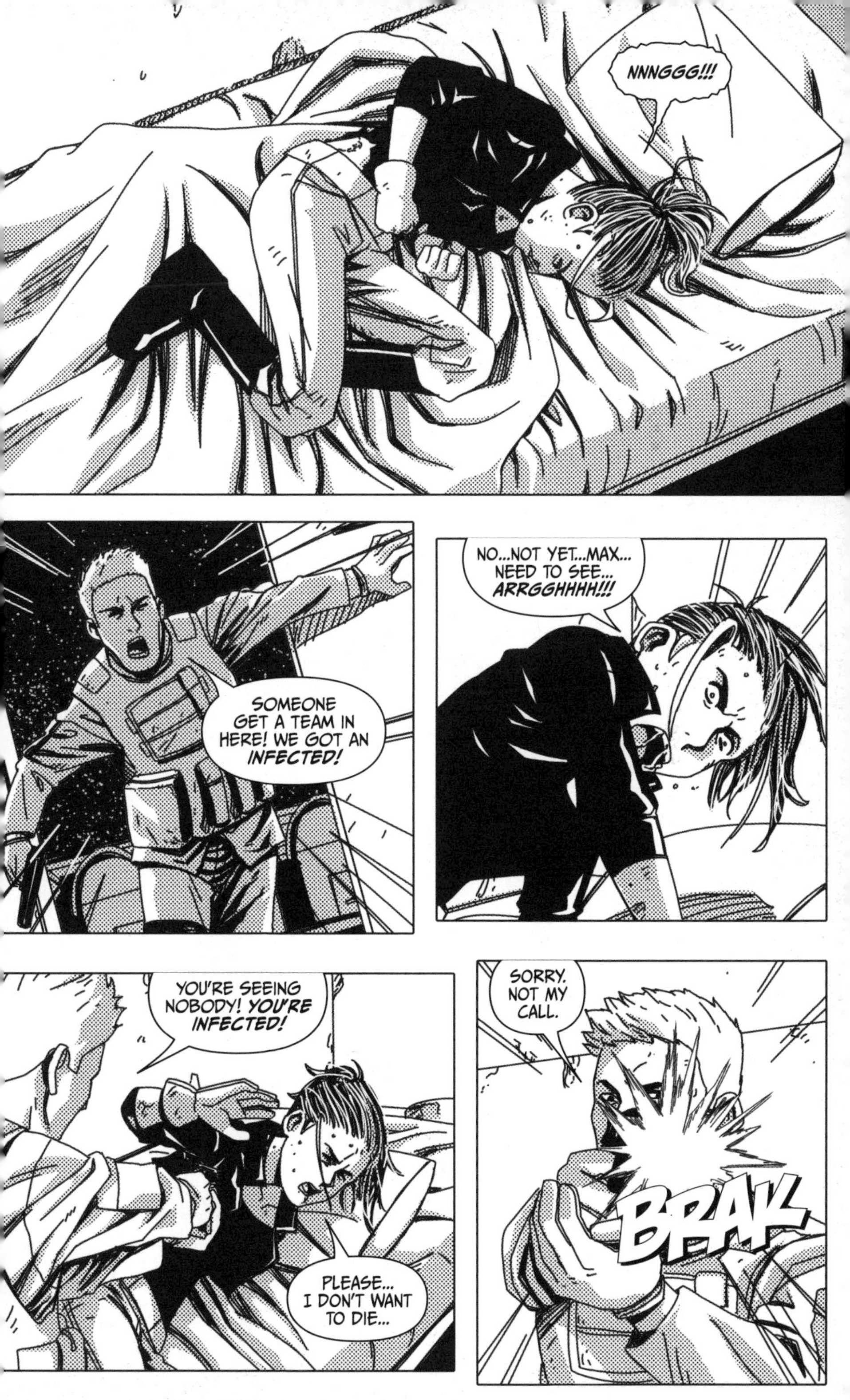
NNNGGG!!!
SOMEONE GET A TEAM IN HERE! WE GOT AN *INFECTED!*
NO...NOT YET...MAX... NEED TO SEE... ***ARRGGHHHH!!!***
YOU'RE SEEING NOBODY! *YOU'RE INFECTED!*
PLEASE... I DON'T WANT TO DIE...
SORRY. NOT MY CALL.
BRAK

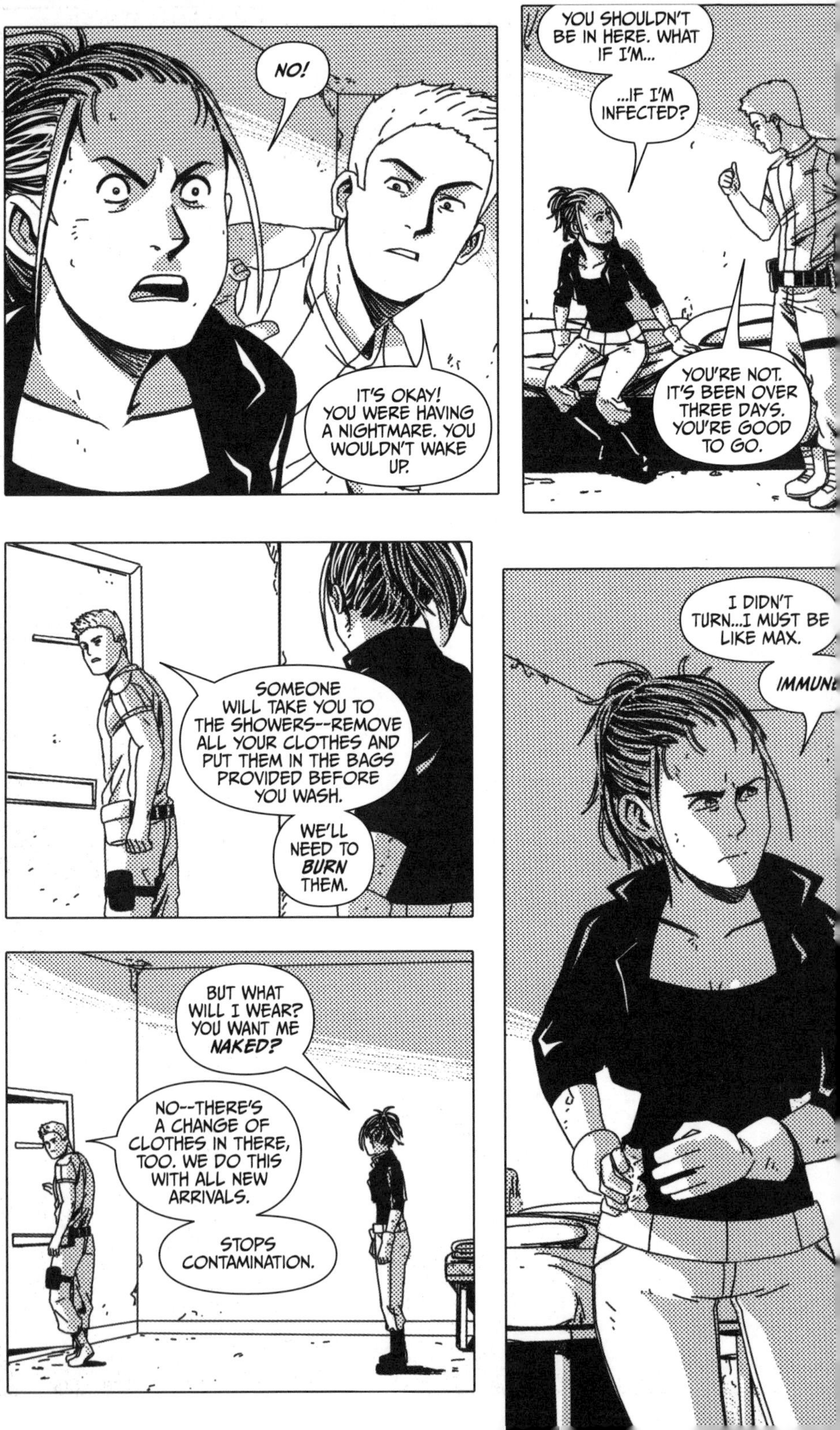
NO!
IT'S OKAY! YOU WERE HAVING A NIGHTMARE. YOU WOULDN'T WAKE UP.
YOU SHOULDN'T BE IN HERE. WHAT IF I'M...
...IF I'M INFECTED?
YOU'RE NOT. IT'S BEEN OVER THREE DAYS. YOU'RE GOOD TO GO.
SOMEONE WILL TAKE YOU TO THE SHOWERS--REMOVE ALL YOUR CLOTHES AND PUT THEM IN THE BAGS PROVIDED BEFORE YOU WASH.
WE'LL NEED TO ***BURN*** THEM.
BUT WHAT WILL I WEAR? YOU WANT ME ***NAKED?***
NO--THERE'S A CHANGE OF CLOTHES IN THERE, TOO. WE DO THIS WITH ALL NEW ARRIVALS.
STOPS CONTAMINATION.
I DIDN'T TURN...I MUST BE LIKE MAX.
IMMUN

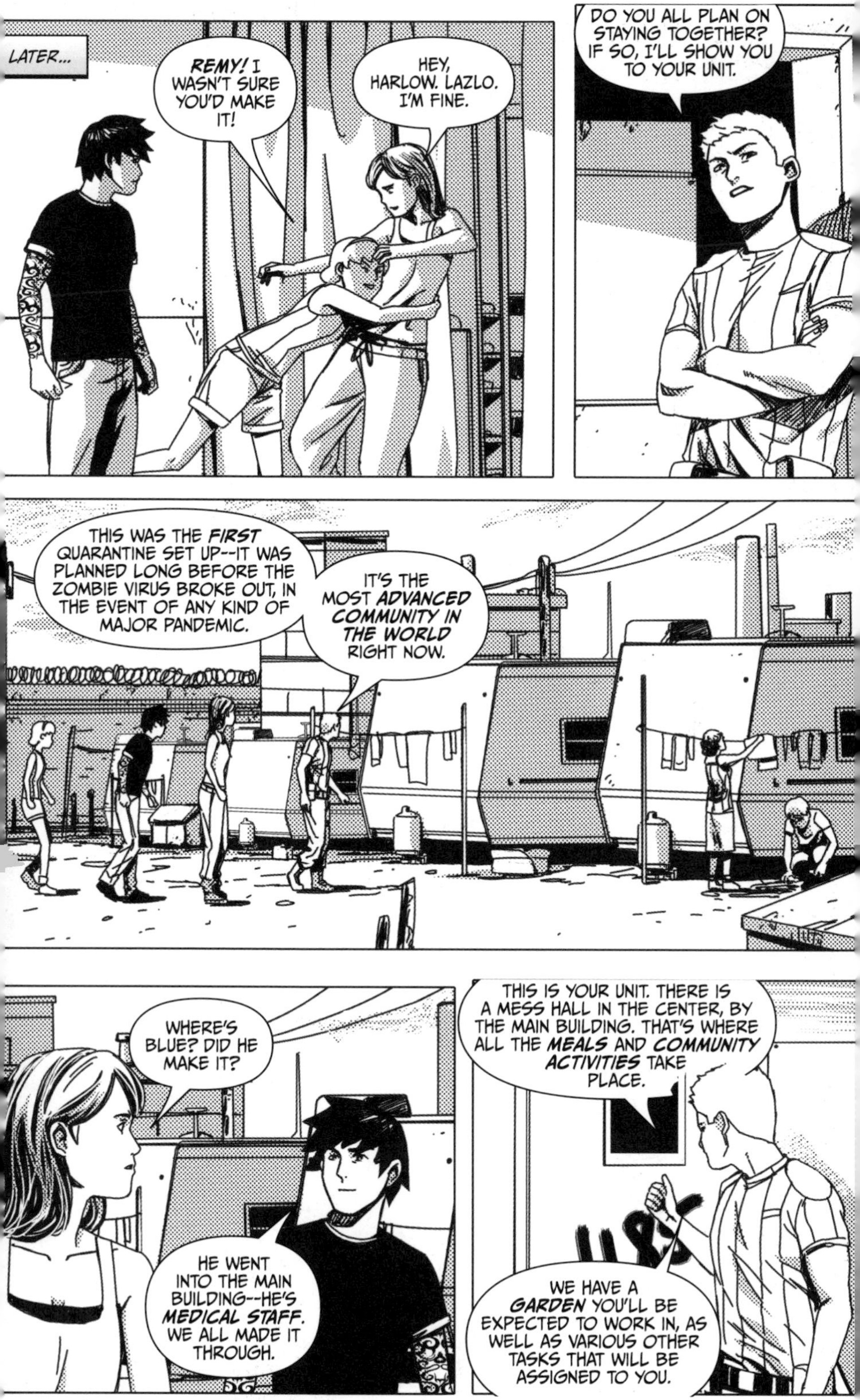
LATER...
REMY! I WASN'T SURE YOU'D MAKE IT!
HEY, HARLOW. LAZLO. I'M FINE.
DO YOU ALL PLAN ON STAYING TOGETHER? IF SO, I'LL SHOW YOU TO YOUR UNIT.
THIS WAS THE FIRST QUARANTINE SET UP--IT WAS PLANNED LONG BEFORE THE ZOMBIE VIRUS BROKE OUT, IN THE EVENT OF ANY KIND OF MAJOR PANDEMIC.
IT'S THE MOST ADVANCED COMMUNITY IN THE WORLD RIGHT NOW.
WHERE'S BLUE? DID HE MAKE IT?
HE WENT INTO THE MAIN BUILDING--HE'S MEDICAL STAFF. WE ALL MADE IT THROUGH.
THIS IS YOUR UNIT. THERE IS A MESS HALL IN THE CENTER, BY THE MAIN BUILDING. THAT'S WHERE ALL THE MEALS AND COMMUNITY ACTIVITIES TAKE PLACE.
WE HAVE A GARDEN YOU'LL BE EXPECTED TO WORK IN, AS WELL AS VARIOUS OTHER TASKS THAT WILL BE ASSIGNED TO YOU.

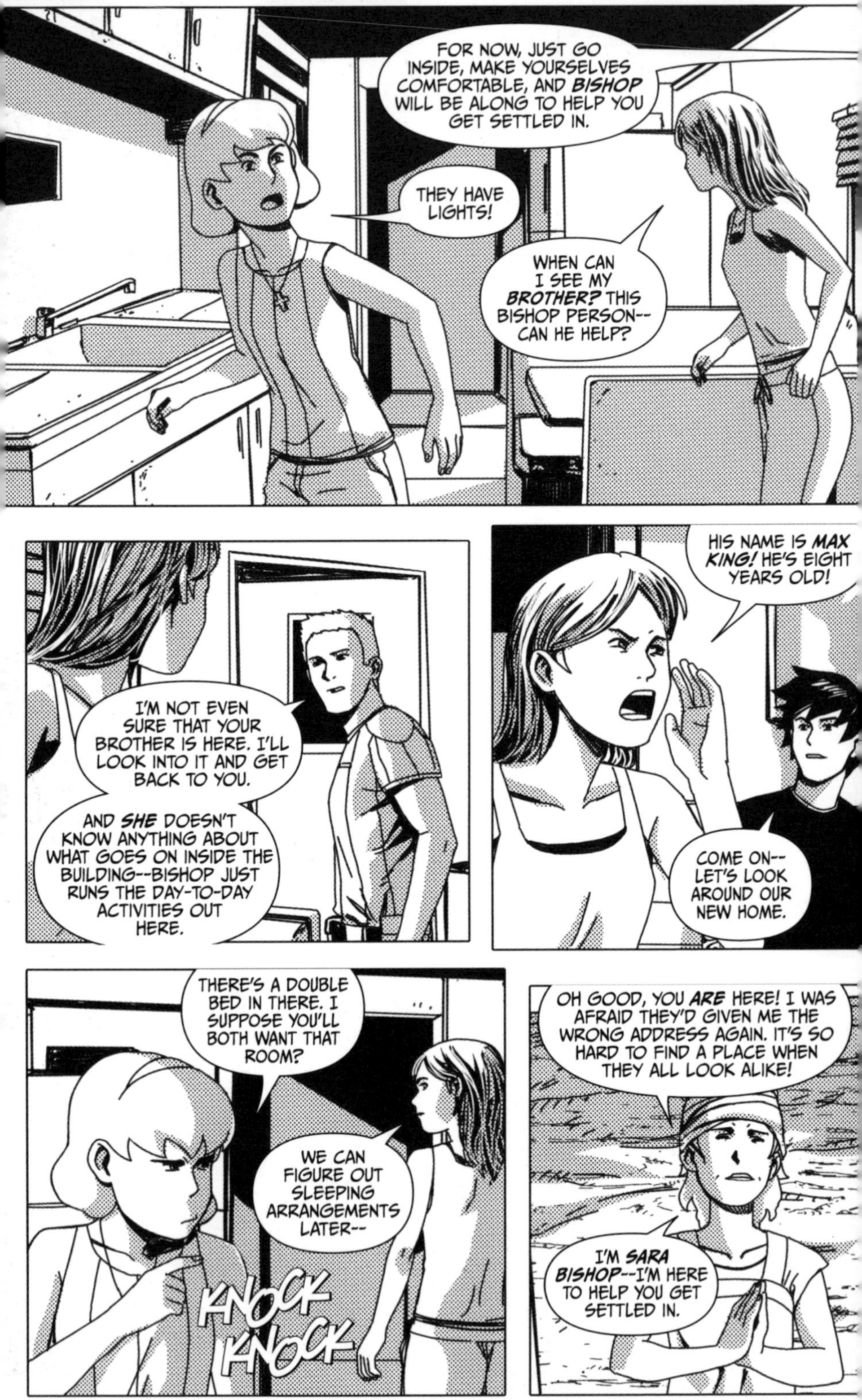
FOR NOW, JUST GO INSIDE, MAKE YOURSELVES COMFORTABLE, AND BISHOP WILL BE ALONG TO HELP YOU GET SETTLED IN.
THEY HAVE LIGHTS!
WHEN CAN I SEE MY BROTHER? THIS BISHOP PERSON-- CAN HE HELP?
I'M NOT EVEN SURE THAT YOUR BROTHER IS HERE. I'LL LOOK INTO IT AND GET BACK TO YOU.
AND SHE DOESN'T KNOW ANYTHING ABOUT WHAT GOES ON INSIDE THE BUILDING--BISHOP JUST RUNS THE DAY-TO-DAY ACTIVITIES OUT HERE.
HIS NAME IS MAX KING! HE'S EIGHT YEARS OLD!
COME ON-- LET'S LOOK AROUND OUR NEW HOME.
THERE'S A DOUBLE BED IN THERE. I SUPPOSE YOU'LL BOTH WANT THAT ROOM?
WE CAN FIGURE OUT SLEEPING ARRANGEMENTS LATER--
KNOCK KNOCK
OH GOOD, YOU ARE HERE! I WAS AFRAID THEY'D GIVEN ME THE WRONG ADDRESS AGAIN. IT'S SO HARD TO FIND A PLACE WHEN THEY ALL LOOK ALIKE!
I'M SARA BISHOP--I'M HERE TO HELP YOU GET SETTLED IN.

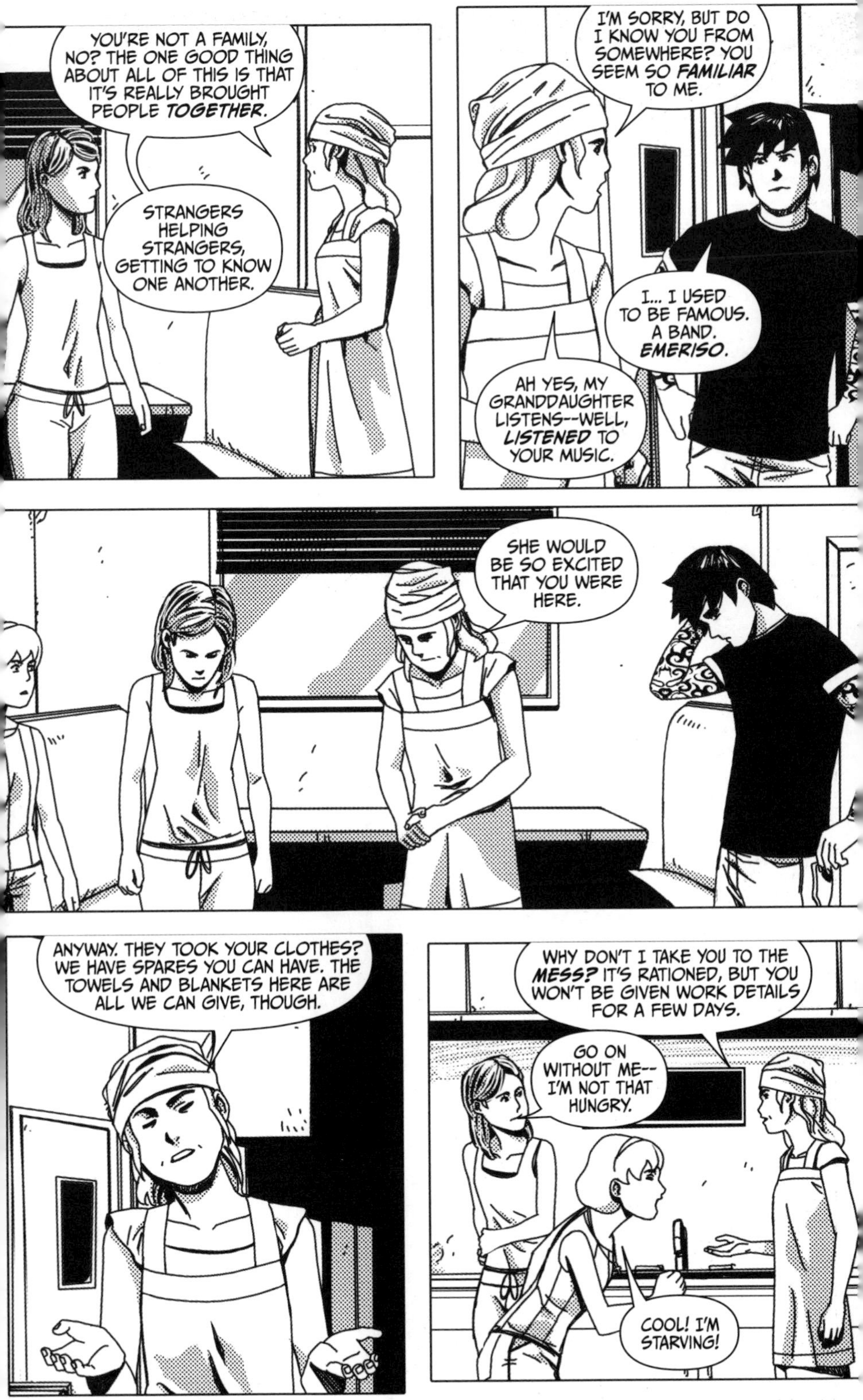
YOU'RE NOT A FAMILY, NO? THE ONE GOOD THING ABOUT ALL OF THIS IS THAT IT'S REALLY BROUGHT PEOPLE *TOGETHER*.
STRANGERS HELPING STRANGERS, GETTING TO KNOW ONE ANOTHER.
I'M SORRY, BUT DO I KNOW YOU FROM SOMEWHERE? YOU SEEM SO *FAMILIAR* TO ME.
I... I USED TO BE FAMOUS. A BAND. *EMERISO*.
AH YES, MY GRANDDAUGHTER LISTENS--WELL, *LISTENED* TO YOUR MUSIC.
SHE WOULD BE SO EXCITED THAT YOU WERE HERE.
ANYWAY. THEY TOOK YOUR CLOTHES? WE HAVE SPARES YOU CAN HAVE. THE TOWELS AND BLANKETS HERE ARE ALL WE CAN GIVE, THOUGH.
WHY DON'T I TAKE YOU TO THE *MESS?* IT'S RATIONED, BUT YOU WON'T BE GIVEN WORK DETAILS FOR A FEW DAYS.
GO ON WITHOUT ME-- I'M NOT THAT HUNGRY.
COOL! I'M STARVING!

NNNG!

WHAT'S GOING ON? ARE YOU OKAY?

I NEED YOU TO GET BLUE. I NEED A DOCTOR, AND HE'S THE ONLY ONE I TRUST.

WHY DO YOU NEED A DOCTOR?

JUST CUTS FROM THE CAR CRASH. GET BLUE.

I'LL BE BACK AS FAST AS I CAN. AND REMY?

YOU LOOK PRETTY WITH YOUR HAIR DOWN.

JUST MY LUCK. TO BE IMMUNE TO THE VIRUS--

--BUT A GOOD OLD FASHIONE INFECTION KILLS ME.

IDIOT. DON'T TELL ME I LOOK PRETTY WHEN I'M IN PAIN.

OW.

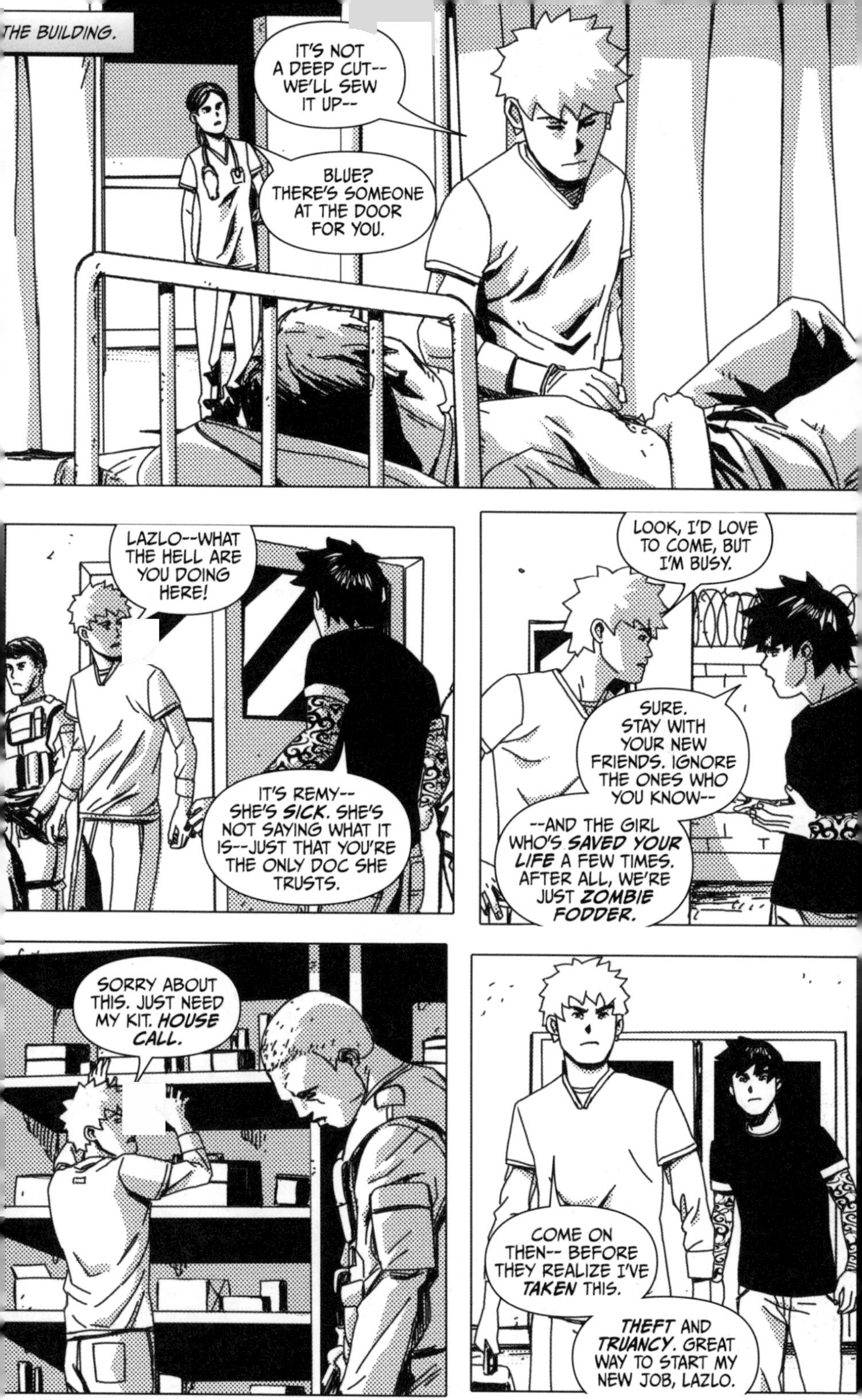

THE BUILDING.
IT'S NOT A DEEP CUT-- WE'LL SEW IT UP--
BLUE? THERE'S SOMEONE AT THE DOOR FOR YOU.
LAZLO--WHAT THE HELL ARE YOU DOING HERE!
IT'S REMY-- SHE'S SICK. SHE'S NOT SAYING WHAT IT IS--JUST THAT YOU'RE THE ONLY DOC SHE TRUSTS.
LOOK, I'D LOVE TO COME, BUT I'M BUSY.
SURE. STAY WITH YOUR NEW FRIENDS. IGNORE THE ONES WHO YOU KNOW--
--AND THE GIRL WHO'S SAVED YOUR LIFE A FEW TIMES. AFTER ALL, WE'RE JUST ZOMBIE FODDER.
SORRY ABOUT THIS. JUST NEED MY KIT. HOUSE CALL.
COME ON THEN-- BEFORE THEY REALIZE I'VE TAKEN THIS.
THEFT AND TRUANCY. GREAT WAY TO START MY NEW JOB, LAZLO.

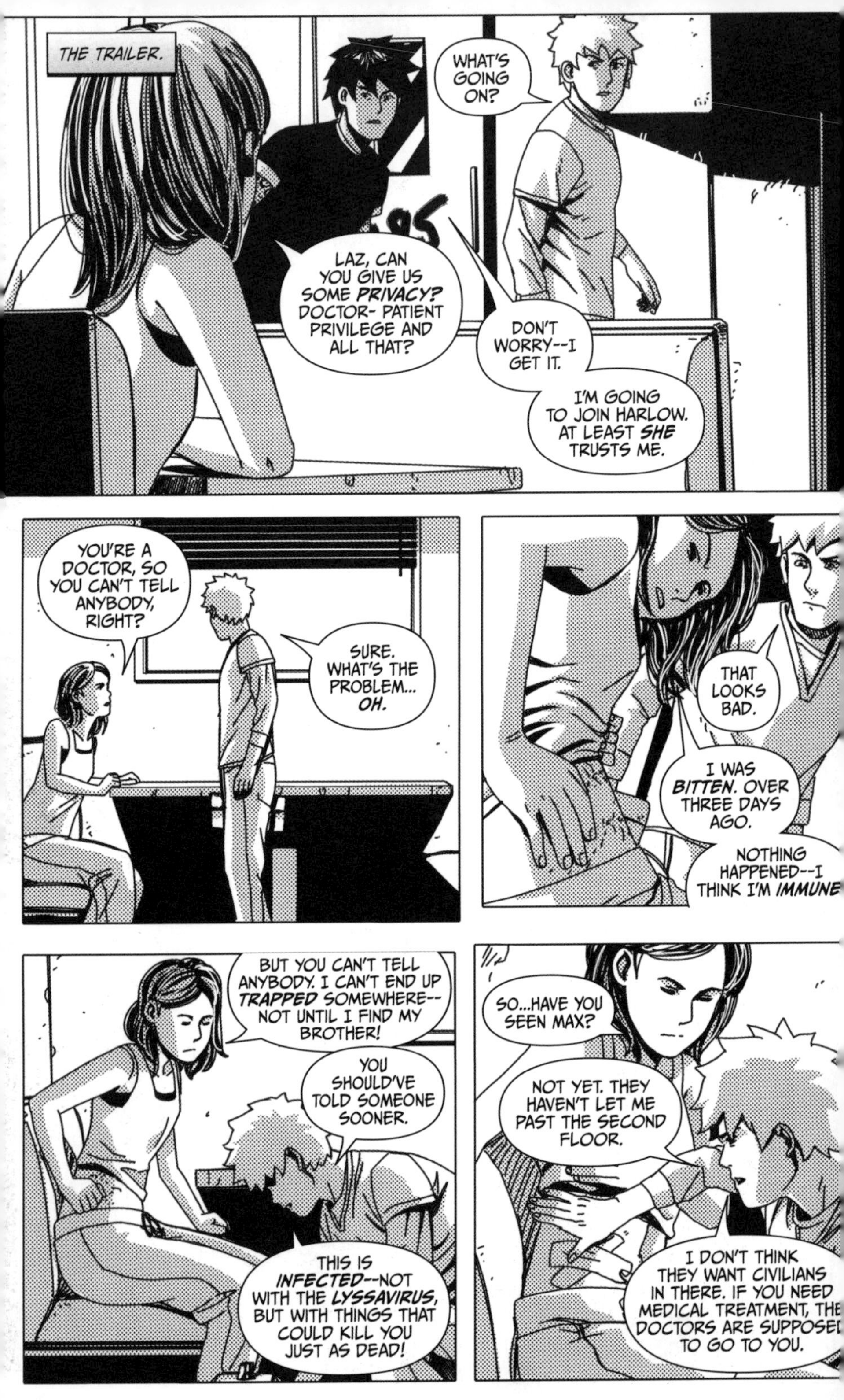
THE TRAILER.
WHAT'S GOING ON?
LAZ, CAN YOU GIVE US SOME PRIVACY? DOCTOR- PATIENT PRIVILEGE AND ALL THAT?
DON'T WORRY--I GET IT.
I'M GOING TO JOIN HARLOW. AT LEAST SHE TRUSTS ME.
YOU'RE A DOCTOR, SO YOU CAN'T TELL ANYBODY, RIGHT?
SURE. WHAT'S THE PROBLEM... OH.
THAT LOOKS BAD.
I WAS BITTEN. OVER THREE DAYS AGO.
NOTHING HAPPENED--I THINK I'M IMMUNE
BUT YOU CAN'T TELL ANYBODY. I CAN'T END UP TRAPPED SOMEWHERE--NOT UNTIL I FIND MY BROTHER!
YOU SHOULD'VE TOLD SOMEONE SOONER.
THIS IS INFECTED--NOT WITH THE LYSSAVIRUS, BUT WITH THINGS THAT COULD KILL YOU JUST AS DEAD!
SO...HAVE YOU SEEN MAX?
NOT YET. THEY HAVEN'T LET ME PAST THE SECOND FLOOR.
I DON'T THINK THEY WANT CIVILIANS IN THERE. IF YOU NEED MEDICAL TREATMENT, THE DOCTORS ARE SUPPOSE TO GO TO YOU.

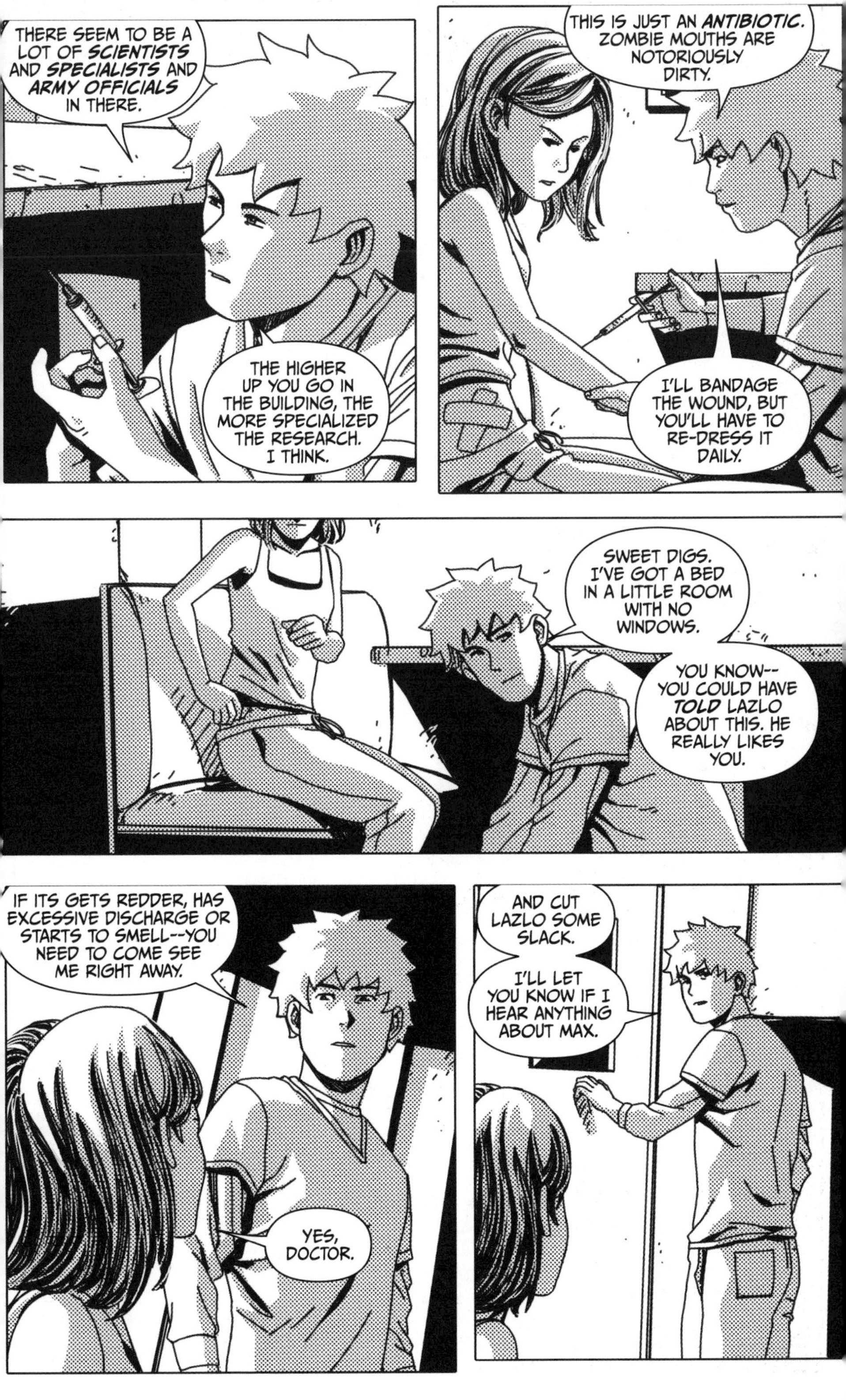
THERE SEEM TO BE A LOT OF *SCIENTISTS* AND *SPECIALISTS* AND *ARMY OFFICIALS* IN THERE.
THE HIGHER UP YOU GO IN THE BUILDING, THE MORE SPECIALIZED THE RESEARCH. I THINK.
THIS IS JUST AN *ANTIBIOTIC.* ZOMBIE MOUTHS ARE NOTORIOUSLY DIRTY.
I'LL BANDAGE THE WOUND, BUT YOU'LL HAVE TO RE-DRESS IT DAILY.
SWEET DIGS. I'VE GOT A BED IN A LITTLE ROOM WITH NO WINDOWS.
YOU KNOW-- YOU COULD HAVE *TOLD* LAZLO ABOUT THIS. HE REALLY LIKES YOU.
IF ITS GETS REDDER, HAS EXCESSIVE DISCHARGE OR STARTS TO SMELL--YOU NEED TO COME SEE ME RIGHT AWAY.
YES, DOCTOR.
AND CUT LAZLO SOME SLACK.
I'LL LET YOU KNOW IF I HEAR ANYTHING ABOUT MAX.

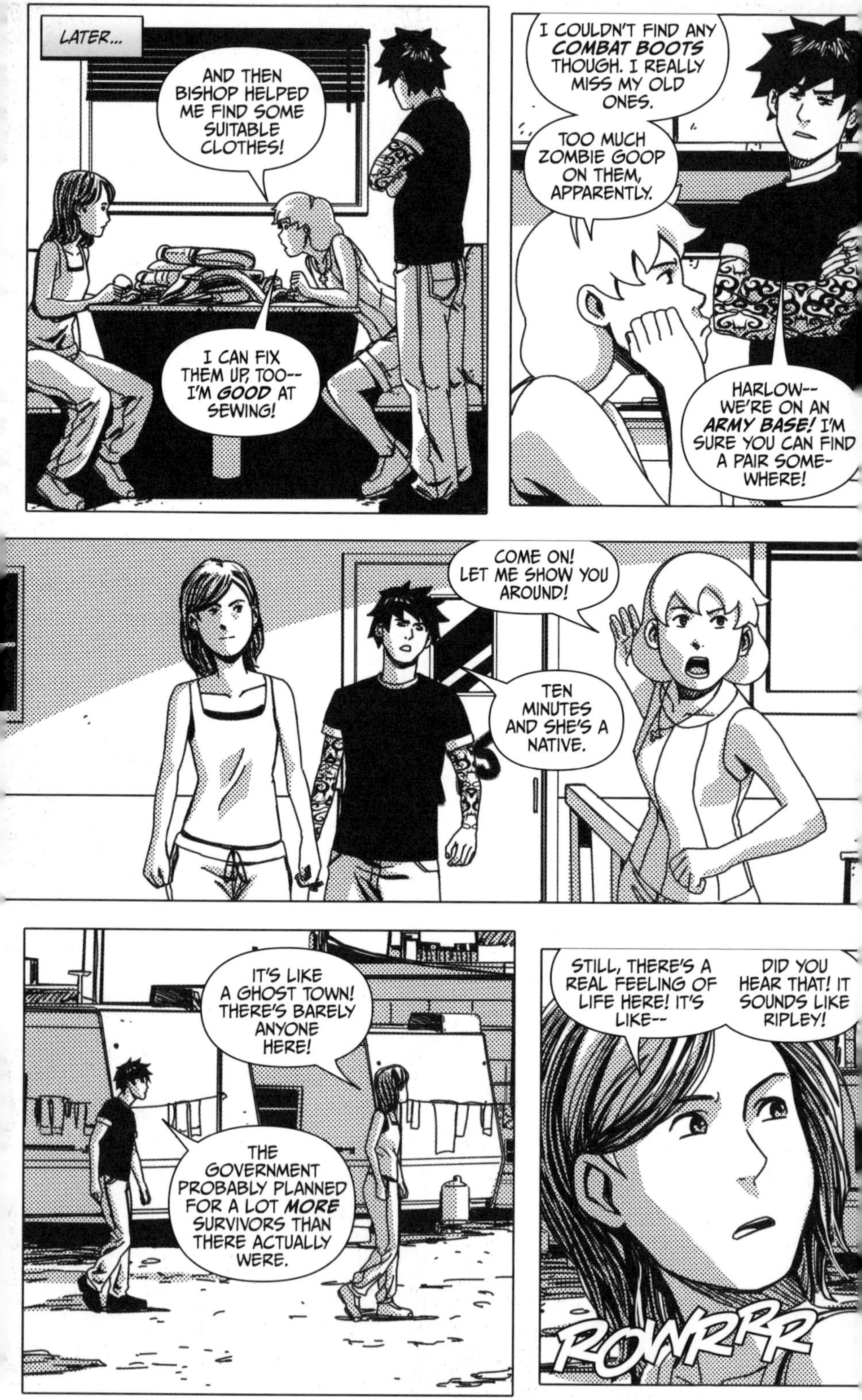
LATER...
AND THEN BISHOP HELPED ME FIND SOME SUITABLE CLOTHES!
I CAN FIX THEM UP, TOO-- I'M *GOOD* AT SEWING!
I COULDN'T FIND ANY *COMBAT BOOTS* THOUGH. I REALLY MISS MY OLD ONES.
TOO MUCH ZOMBIE GOOP ON THEM, APPARENTLY.
HARLOW-- WE'RE ON AN *ARMY BASE!* I'M SURE YOU CAN FIND A PAIR SOME-WHERE!
COME ON! LET ME SHOW YOU AROUND!
TEN MINUTES AND SHE'S A NATIVE.
IT'S LIKE A GHOST TOWN! THERE'S BARELY ANYONE HERE!
THE GOVERNMENT PROBABLY PLANNED FOR A LOT *MORE* SURVIVORS THAN THERE ACTUALLY WERE.
STILL, THERE'S A REAL FEELING OF LIFE HERE! IT'S LIKE--
DID YOU HEAR THAT! IT SOUNDS LIKE RIPLEY!
ROWRRR

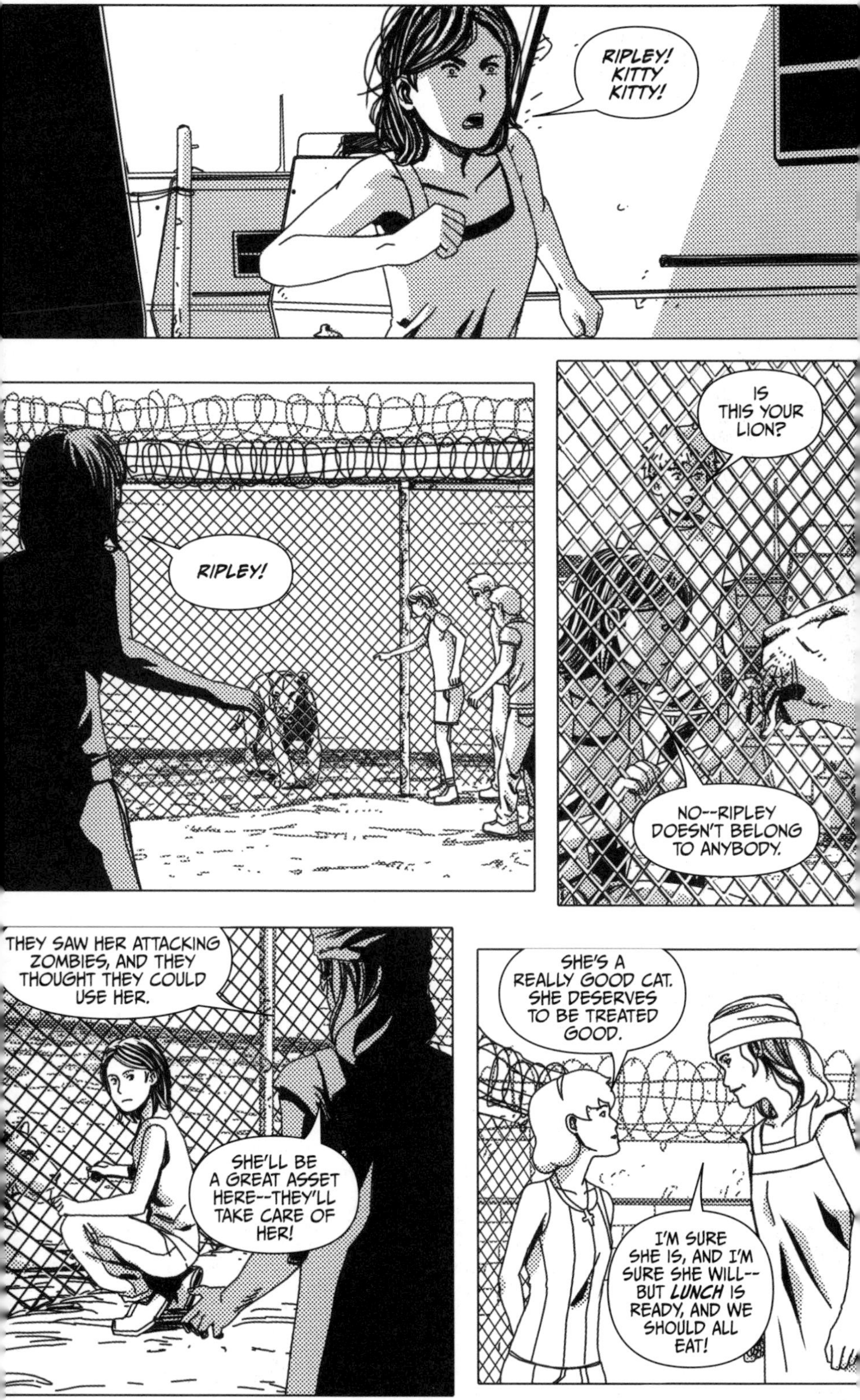
RIPLEY! KITTY KITTY!
RIPLEY!
IS THIS YOUR LION?
NO--RIPLEY DOESN'T BELONG TO ANYBODY.
THEY SAW HER ATTACKING ZOMBIES, AND THEY THOUGHT THEY COULD USE HER.
SHE'LL BE A GREAT ASSET HERE--THEY'LL TAKE CARE OF HER!
SHE'S A REALLY GOOD CAT. SHE DESERVES TO BE TREATED GOOD.
I'M SURE SHE IS, AND I'M SURE SHE WILL--BUT *LUNCH* IS READY, AND WE SHOULD ALL EAT!

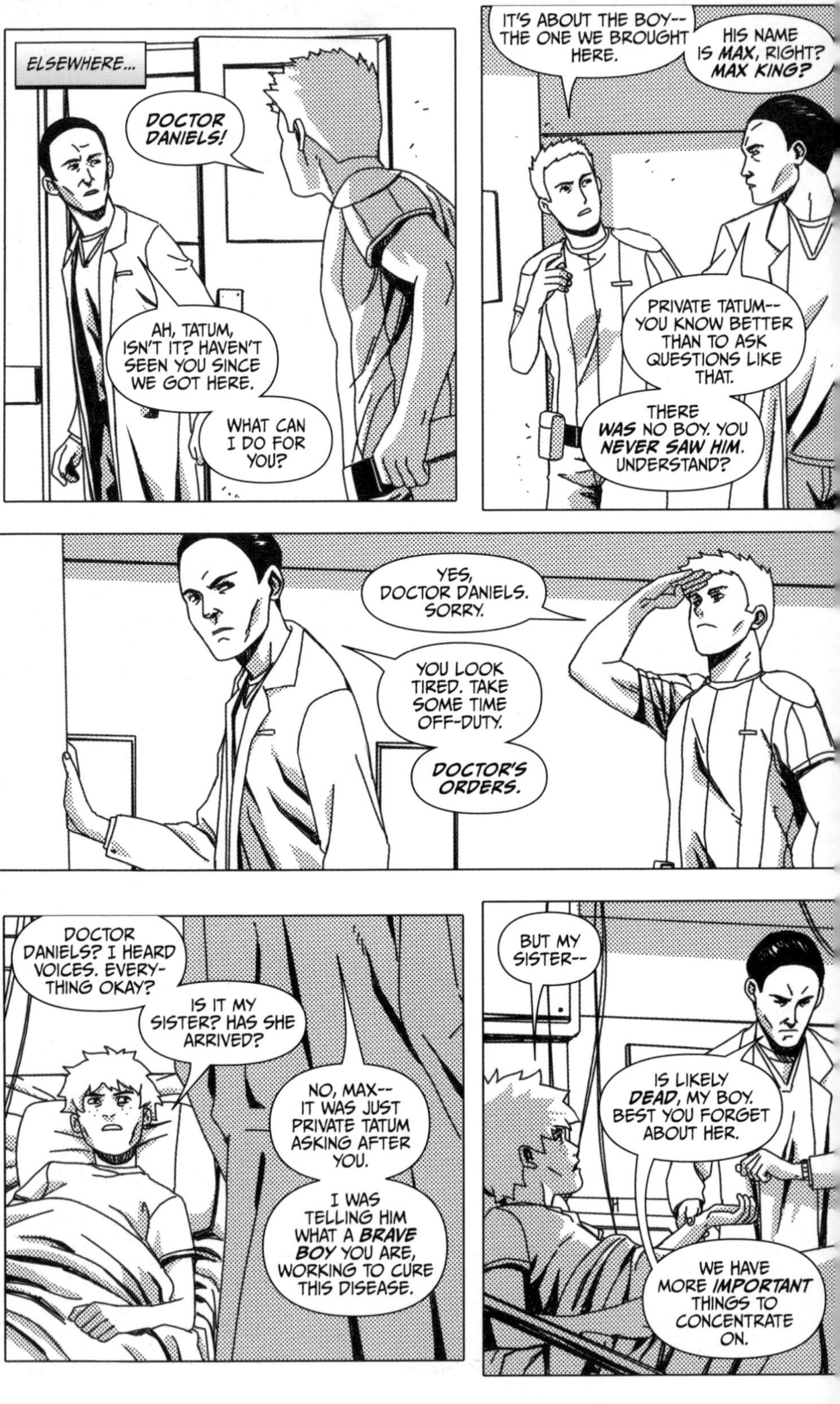
ELSEWHERE...
DOCTOR DANIELS!
AH, TATUM, ISN'T IT? HAVEN'T SEEN YOU SINCE WE GOT HERE.
WHAT CAN I DO FOR YOU?
IT'S ABOUT THE BOY-- THE ONE WE BROUGHT HERE.
HIS NAME IS MAX, RIGHT? MAX KING?
PRIVATE TATUM-- YOU KNOW BETTER THAN TO ASK QUESTIONS LIKE THAT.
THERE WAS NO BOY. YOU NEVER SAW HIM. UNDERSTAND?
YES, DOCTOR DANIELS. SORRY.
YOU LOOK TIRED. TAKE SOME TIME OFF-DUTY.
DOCTOR'S ORDERS.
DOCTOR DANIELS? I HEARD VOICES. EVERY-THING OKAY?
IS IT MY SISTER? HAS SHE ARRIVED?
NO, MAX-- IT WAS JUST PRIVATE TATUM ASKING AFTER YOU.
I WAS TELLING HIM WHAT A BRAVE BOY YOU ARE, WORKING TO CURE THIS DISEASE.
BUT MY SISTER--
IS LIKELY DEAD, MY BOY. BEST YOU FORGET ABOUT HER.
WE HAVE MORE IMPORTANT THINGS TO CONCENTRATE ON.

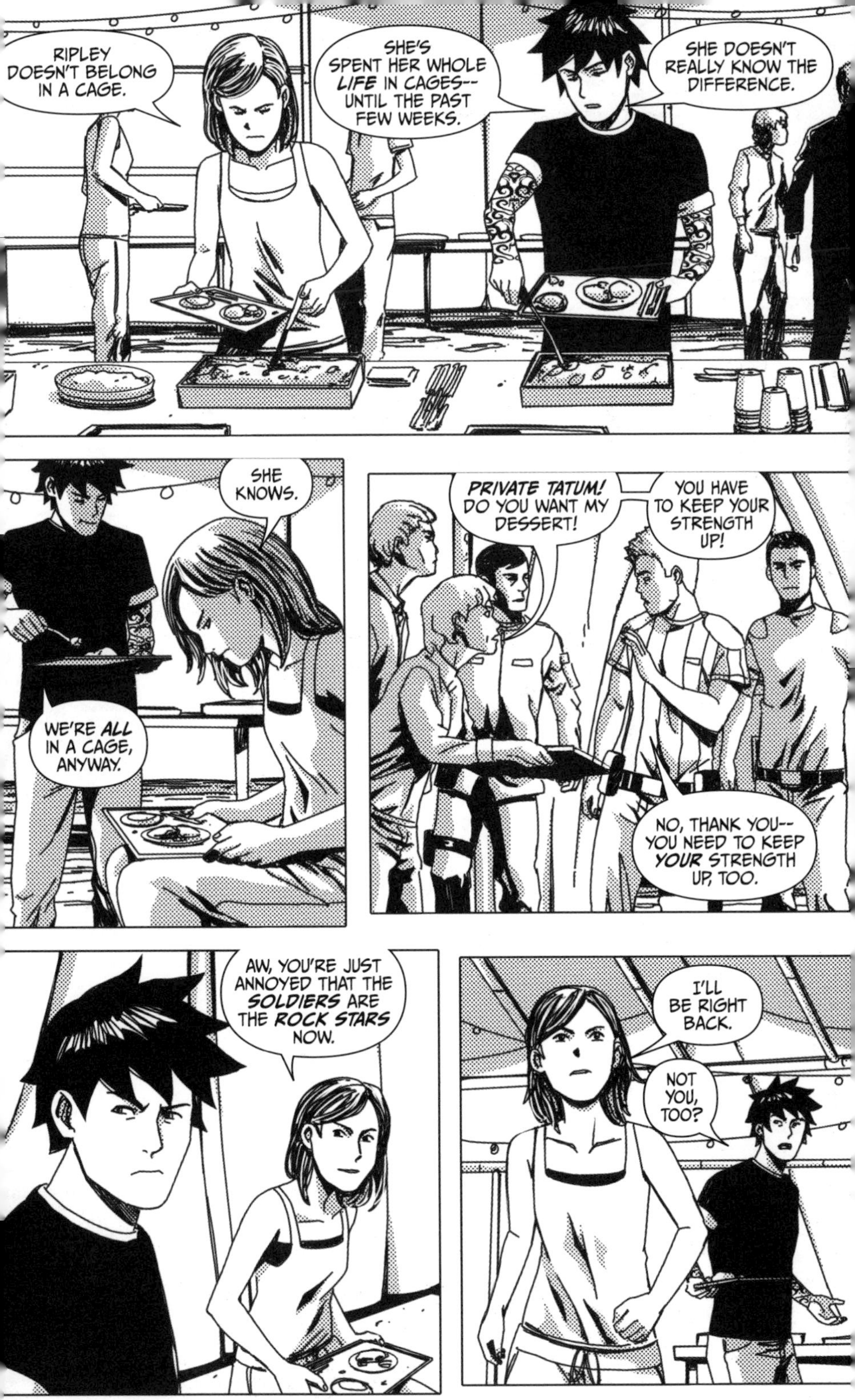
RIPLEY DOESN'T BELONG IN A CAGE.
SHE'S SPENT HER WHOLE *LIFE* IN CAGES-- UNTIL THE PAST FEW WEEKS.
SHE DOESN'T REALLY KNOW THE DIFFERENCE.
SHE KNOWS.
WE'RE *ALL* IN A CAGE, ANYWAY.
PRIVATE TATUM! DO YOU WANT MY DESSERT!
YOU HAVE TO KEEP YOUR STRENGTH UP!
NO, THANK YOU-- YOU NEED TO KEEP *YOUR* STRENGTH UP, TOO.
AW, YOU'RE JUST ANNOYED THAT THE *SOLDIERS* ARE THE *ROCK STARS* NOW.
I'LL BE RIGHT BACK.
NOT YOU, TOO?

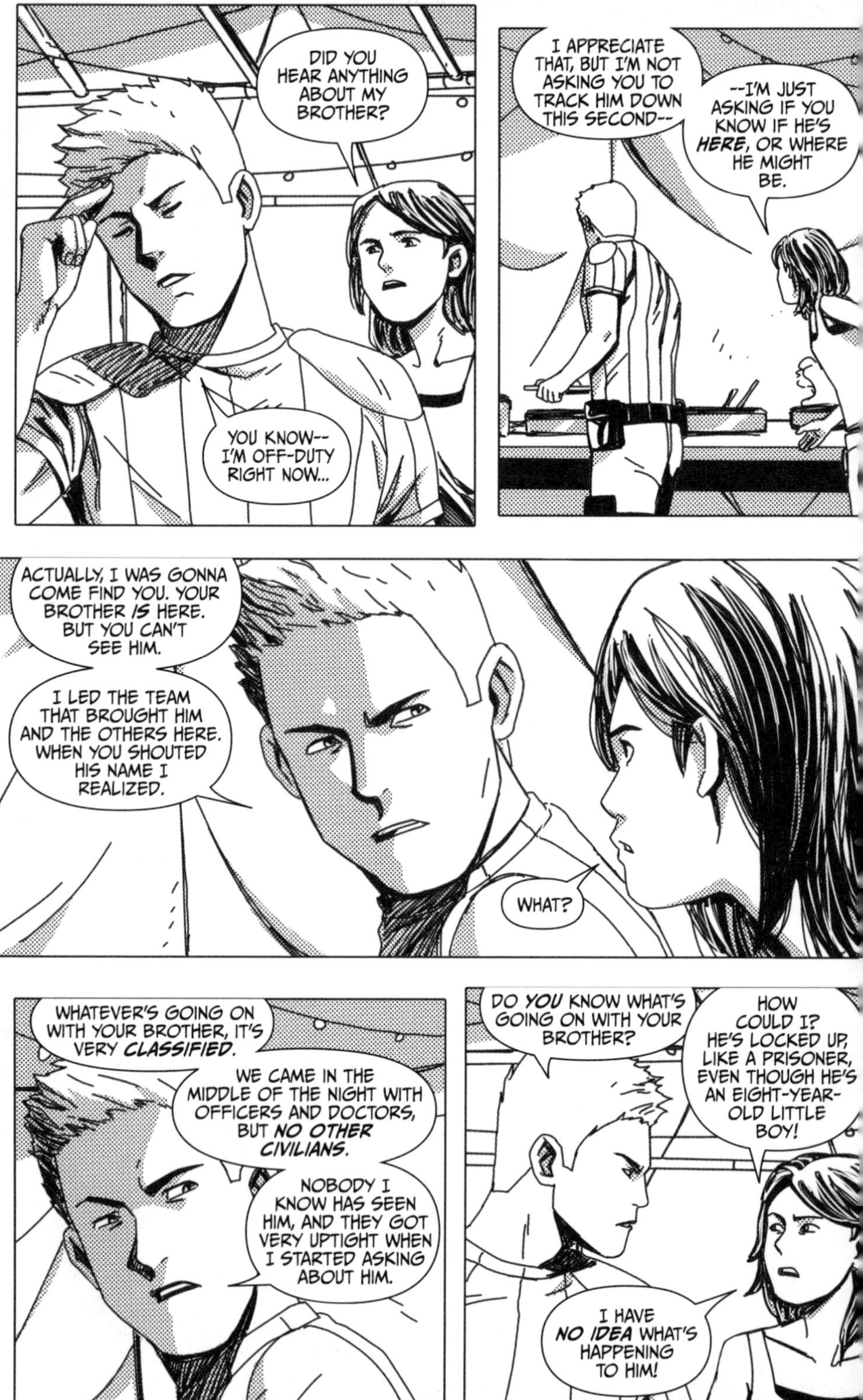
DID YOU HEAR ANYTHING ABOUT MY BROTHER?
YOU KNOW-- I'M OFF-DUTY RIGHT NOW...
I APPRECIATE THAT, BUT I'M NOT ASKING YOU TO TRACK HIM DOWN THIS SECOND--
--I'M JUST ASKING IF YOU KNOW IF HE'S *HERE*, OR WHERE HE MIGHT BE.
ACTUALLY, I WAS GONNA COME FIND YOU. YOUR BROTHER *IS* HERE. BUT YOU CAN'T SEE HIM.
I LED THE TEAM THAT BROUGHT HIM AND THE OTHERS HERE. WHEN YOU SHOUTED HIS NAME I REALIZED.
WHAT?
WHATEVER'S GOING ON WITH YOUR BROTHER, IT'S VERY *CLASSIFIED*.
WE CAME IN THE MIDDLE OF THE NIGHT WITH OFFICERS AND DOCTORS, BUT *NO OTHER CIVILIANS*.
NOBODY I KNOW HAS SEEN HIM, AND THEY GOT VERY UPTIGHT WHEN I STARTED ASKING ABOUT HIM.
DO *YOU* KNOW WHAT'S GOING ON WITH YOUR BROTHER?
HOW COULD I? HE'S LOCKED UP, LIKE A PRISONER, EVEN THOUGH HE'S AN EIGHT-YEAR-OLD LITTLE BOY!
I HAVE *NO IDEA* WHAT'S HAPPENING TO HIM!

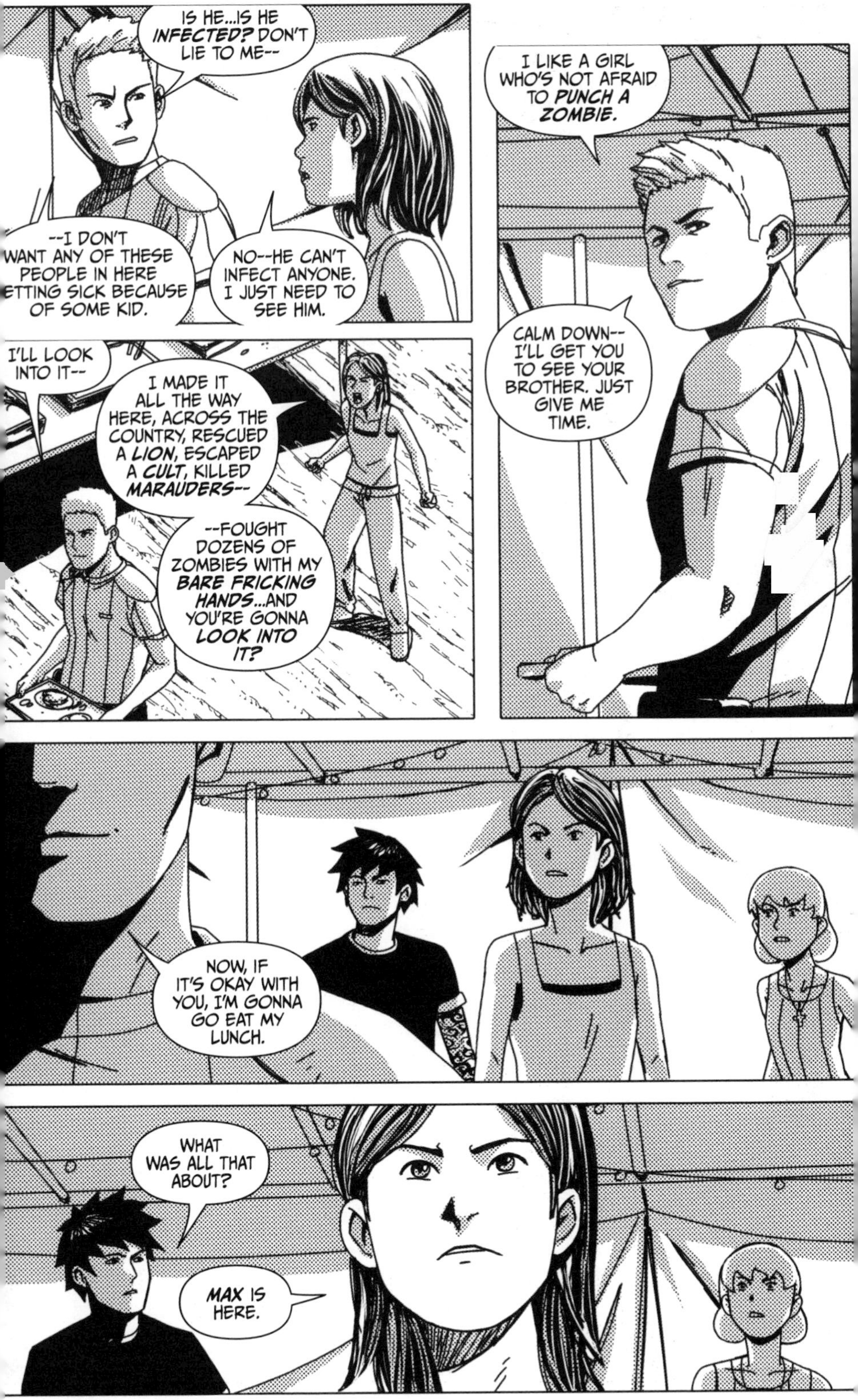
IS HE...IS HE *INFECTED?* DON'T LIE TO ME--
--I DON'T WANT ANY OF THESE PEOPLE IN HERE ETTING SICK BECAUSE OF SOME KID.
NO--HE CAN'T INFECT ANYONE. I JUST NEED TO SEE HIM.
I'LL LOOK INTO IT--
I MADE IT ALL THE WAY HERE, ACROSS THE COUNTRY, RESCUED A *LION*, ESCAPED A *CULT*, KILLED *MARAUDERS*--
--FOUGHT DOZENS OF ZOMBIES WITH MY *BARE FRICKING HANDS*...AND YOU'RE GONNA *LOOK INTO IT?*
I LIKE A GIRL WHO'S NOT AFRAID TO *PUNCH A ZOMBIE.*
CALM DOWN-- I'LL GET YOU TO SEE YOUR BROTHER. JUST GIVE ME TIME.
NOW, IF IT'S OKAY WITH YOU, I'M GONNA GO EAT MY LUNCH.
WHAT WAS ALL THAT ABOUT?
MAX IS HERE.

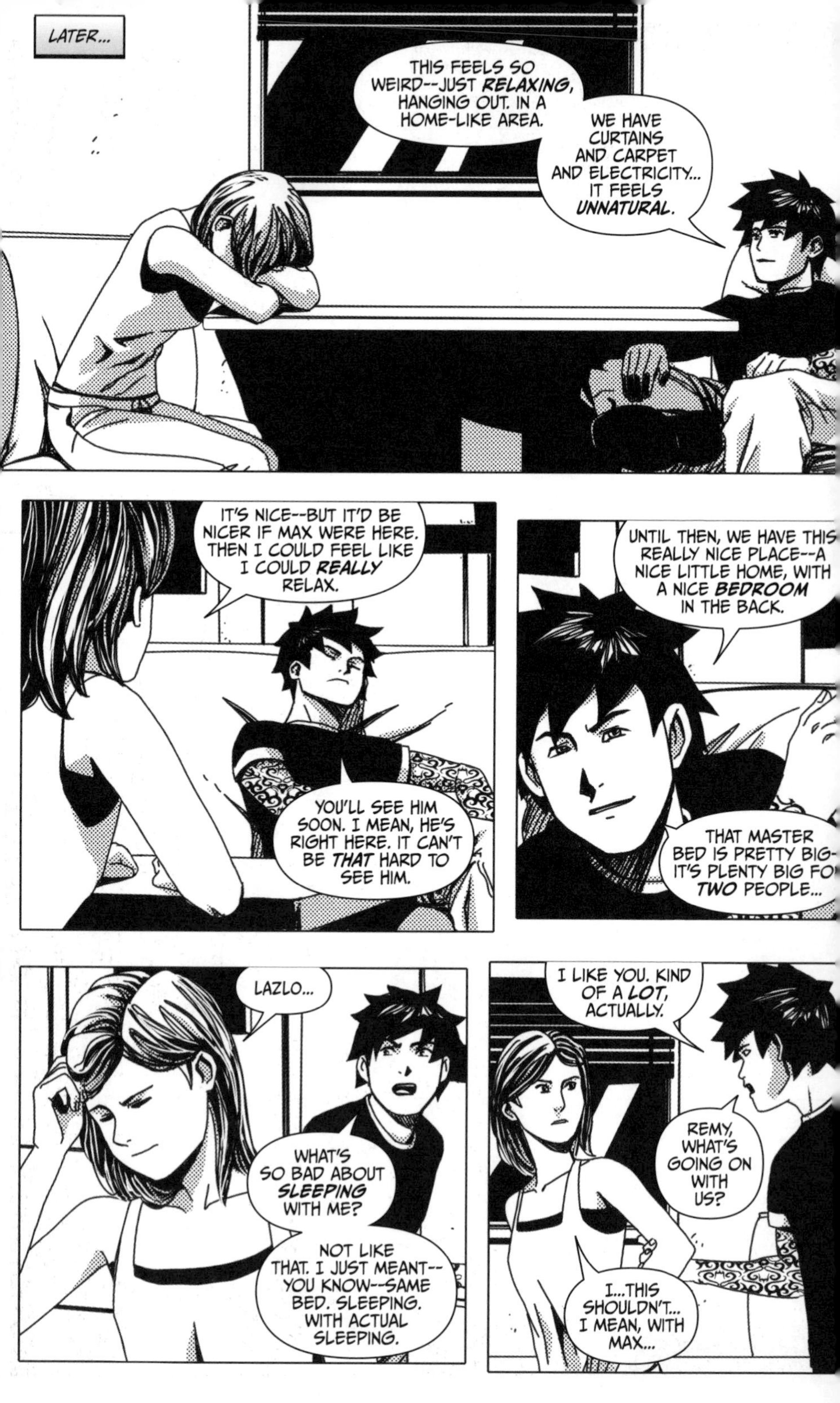
LATER...
THIS FEELS SO WEIRD--JUST RELAXING, HANGING OUT. IN A HOME-LIKE AREA.
WE HAVE CURTAINS AND CARPET AND ELECTRICITY... IT FEELS UNNATURAL.
IT'S NICE--BUT IT'D BE NICER IF MAX WERE HERE. THEN I COULD FEEL LIKE I COULD REALLY RELAX.
YOU'LL SEE HIM SOON. I MEAN, HE'S RIGHT HERE. IT CAN'T BE THAT HARD TO SEE HIM.
UNTIL THEN, WE HAVE THIS REALLY NICE PLACE--A NICE LITTLE HOME, WITH A NICE BEDROOM IN THE BACK.
THAT MASTER BED IS PRETTY BIG- IT'S PLENTY BIG FO TWO PEOPLE...
LAZLO...
WHAT'S SO BAD ABOUT SLEEPING WITH ME?
NOT LIKE THAT. I JUST MEANT--YOU KNOW--SAME BED. SLEEPING. WITH ACTUAL SLEEPING.
I LIKE YOU. KIND OF A LOT, ACTUALLY.
REMY, WHAT'S GOING ON WITH US?
I...THIS SHOULDN'T... I MEAN, WITH MAX...

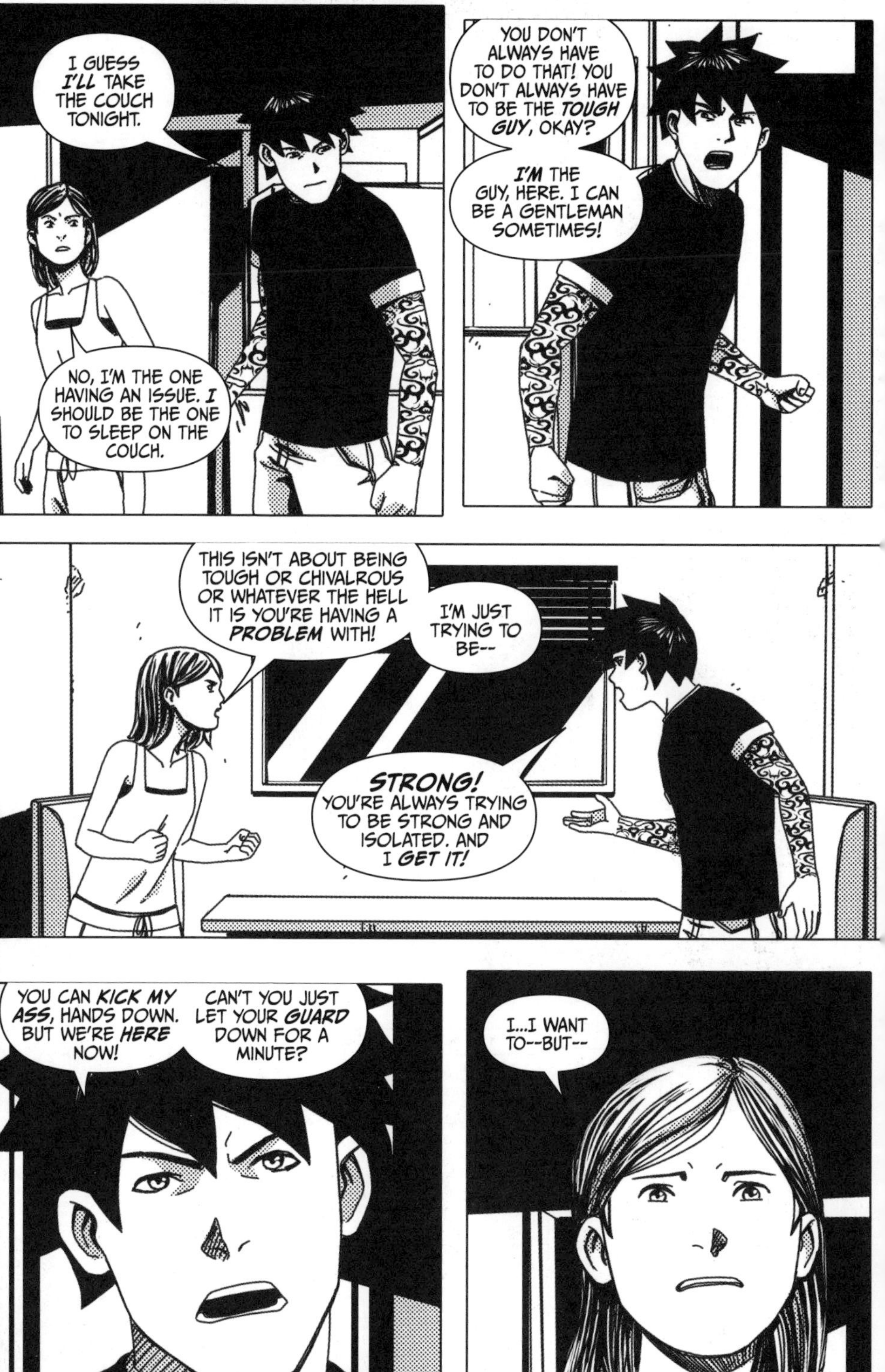
I GUESS I'LL TAKE THE COUCH TONIGHT.
NO, I'M THE ONE HAVING AN ISSUE. I SHOULD BE THE ONE TO SLEEP ON THE COUCH.
YOU DON'T ALWAYS HAVE TO DO THAT! YOU DON'T ALWAYS HAVE TO BE THE TOUGH GUY, OKAY?
I'M THE GUY, HERE. I CAN BE A GENTLEMAN SOMETIMES!
THIS ISN'T ABOUT BEING TOUGH OR CHIVALROUS OR WHATEVER THE HELL IT IS YOU'RE HAVING A PROBLEM WITH!
I'M JUST TRYING TO BE--
STRONG! YOU'RE ALWAYS TRYING TO BE STRONG AND ISOLATED. AND I GET IT!
YOU CAN KICK MY ASS, HANDS DOWN. BUT WE'RE HERE NOW!
CAN'T YOU JUST LET YOUR GUARD DOWN FOR A MINUTE?
I...I WANT TO--BUT--

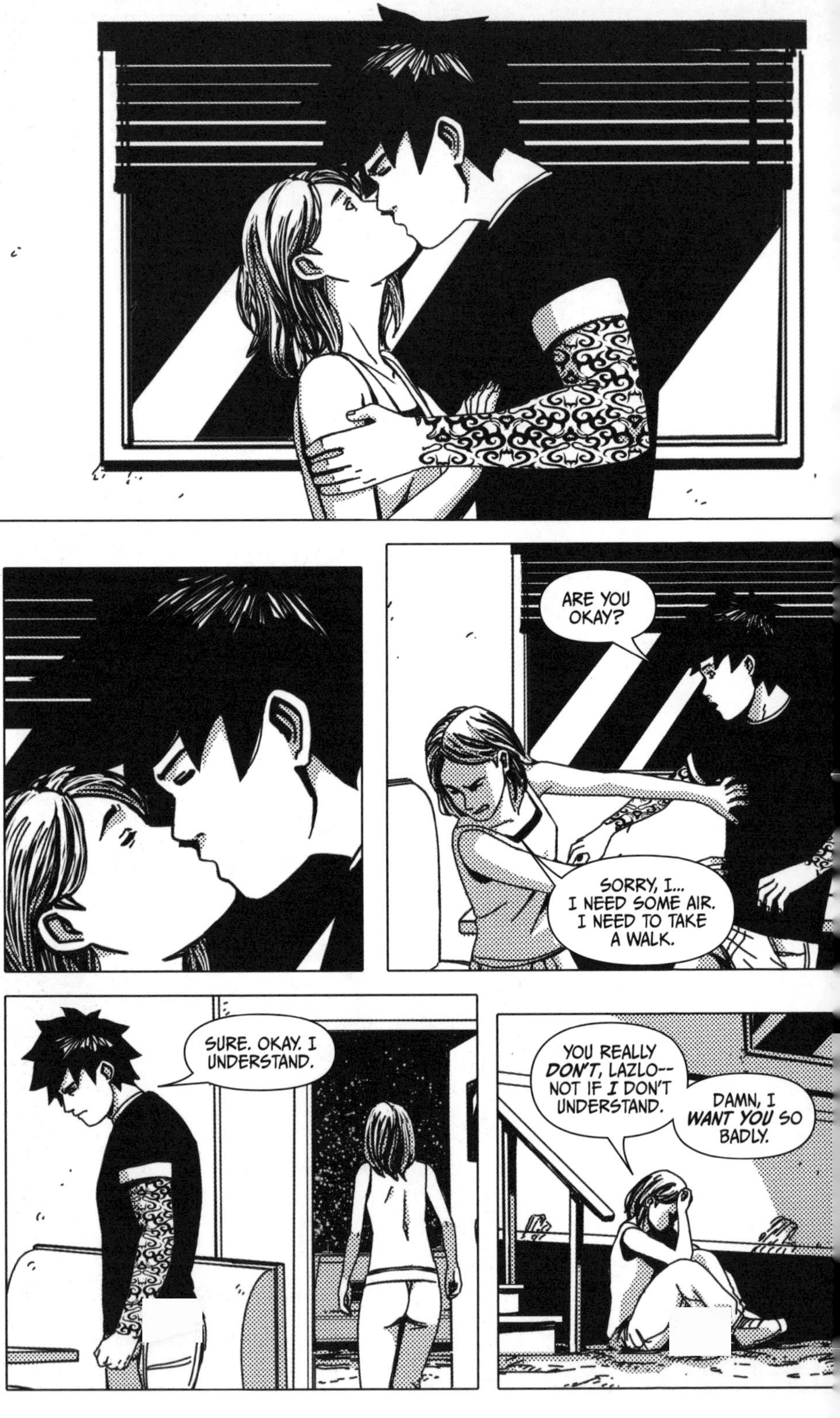
ARE YOU OKAY?
SORRY, I... I NEED SOME AIR. I NEED TO TAKE A WALK.
SURE. OKAY. I UNDERSTAND.
YOU REALLY *DON'T*, LAZLO-- NOT IF *I* DON'T UNDERSTAND.
DAMN, I ***WANT YOU*** SO BADLY.

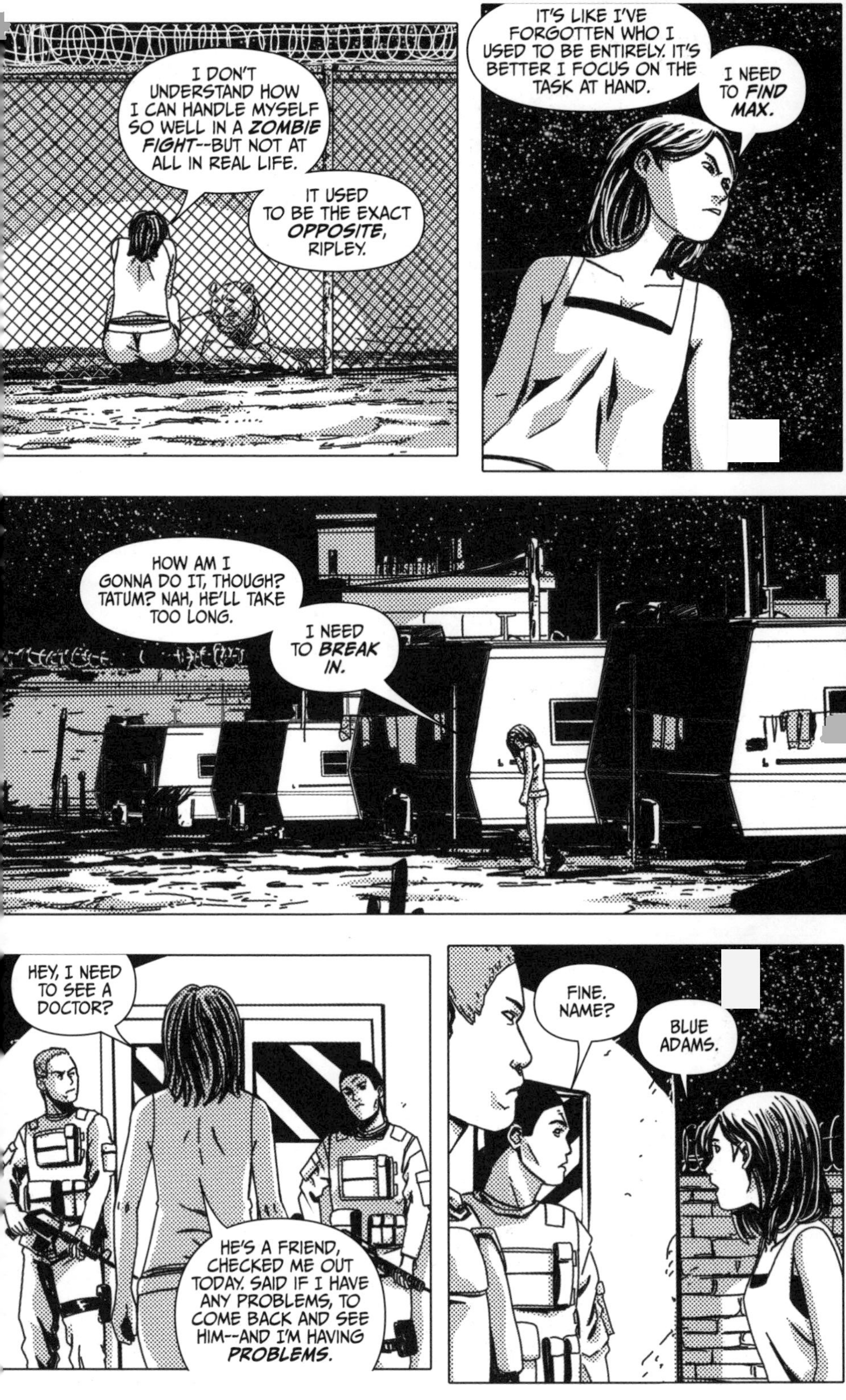
I DON'T UNDERSTAND HOW I CAN HANDLE MYSELF SO WELL IN A *ZOMBIE FIGHT*--BUT NOT AT ALL IN REAL LIFE.
IT USED TO BE THE EXACT *OPPOSITE*, RIPLEY.
IT'S LIKE I'VE FORGOTTEN WHO I USED TO BE ENTIRELY. IT'S BETTER I FOCUS ON THE TASK AT HAND.
I NEED TO *FIND MAX.*
HOW AM I GONNA DO IT, THOUGH? TATUM? NAH, HE'LL TAKE TOO LONG.
I NEED TO *BREAK IN.*
HEY, I NEED TO SEE A DOCTOR?
HE'S A FRIEND, CHECKED ME OUT TODAY. SAID IF I HAVE ANY PROBLEMS, TO COME BACK AND SEE HIM--AND I'M HAVING *PROBLEMS.*
FINE. NAME?
BLUE ADAMS.

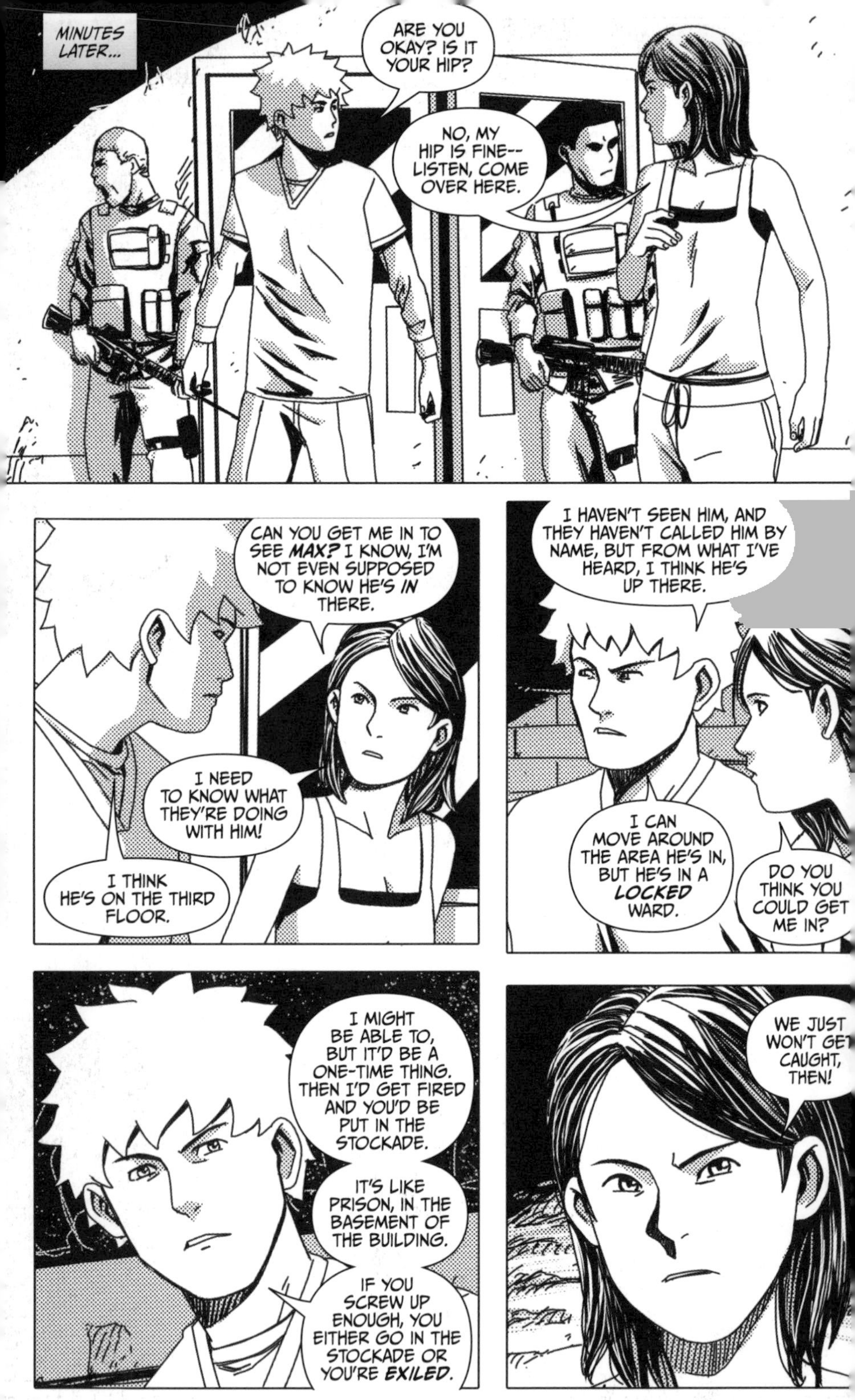

MINUTES LATER...
ARE YOU OKAY? IS IT YOUR HIP?
NO, MY HIP IS FINE-- LISTEN, COME OVER HERE.
CAN YOU GET ME IN TO SEE *MAX?* I KNOW, I'M NOT EVEN SUPPOSED TO KNOW HE'S *IN* THERE.
I NEED TO KNOW WHAT THEY'RE DOING WITH HIM!
I THINK HE'S ON THE THIRD FLOOR.
I HAVEN'T SEEN HIM, AND THEY HAVEN'T CALLED HIM BY NAME, BUT FROM WHAT I'VE HEARD, I THINK HE'S UP THERE.
I CAN MOVE AROUND THE AREA HE'S IN, BUT HE'S IN A *LOCKED* WARD.
DO YOU THINK YOU COULD GET ME IN?
I MIGHT BE ABLE TO, BUT IT'D BE A ONE-TIME THING. THEN I'D GET FIRED AND YOU'D BE PUT IN THE STOCKADE.
IT'S LIKE PRISON, IN THE BASEMENT OF THE BUILDING.
IF YOU SCREW UP ENOUGH, YOU EITHER GO IN THE STOCKADE OR YOU'RE *EXILED*.
WE JUST WON'T GET CAUGHT, THEN!

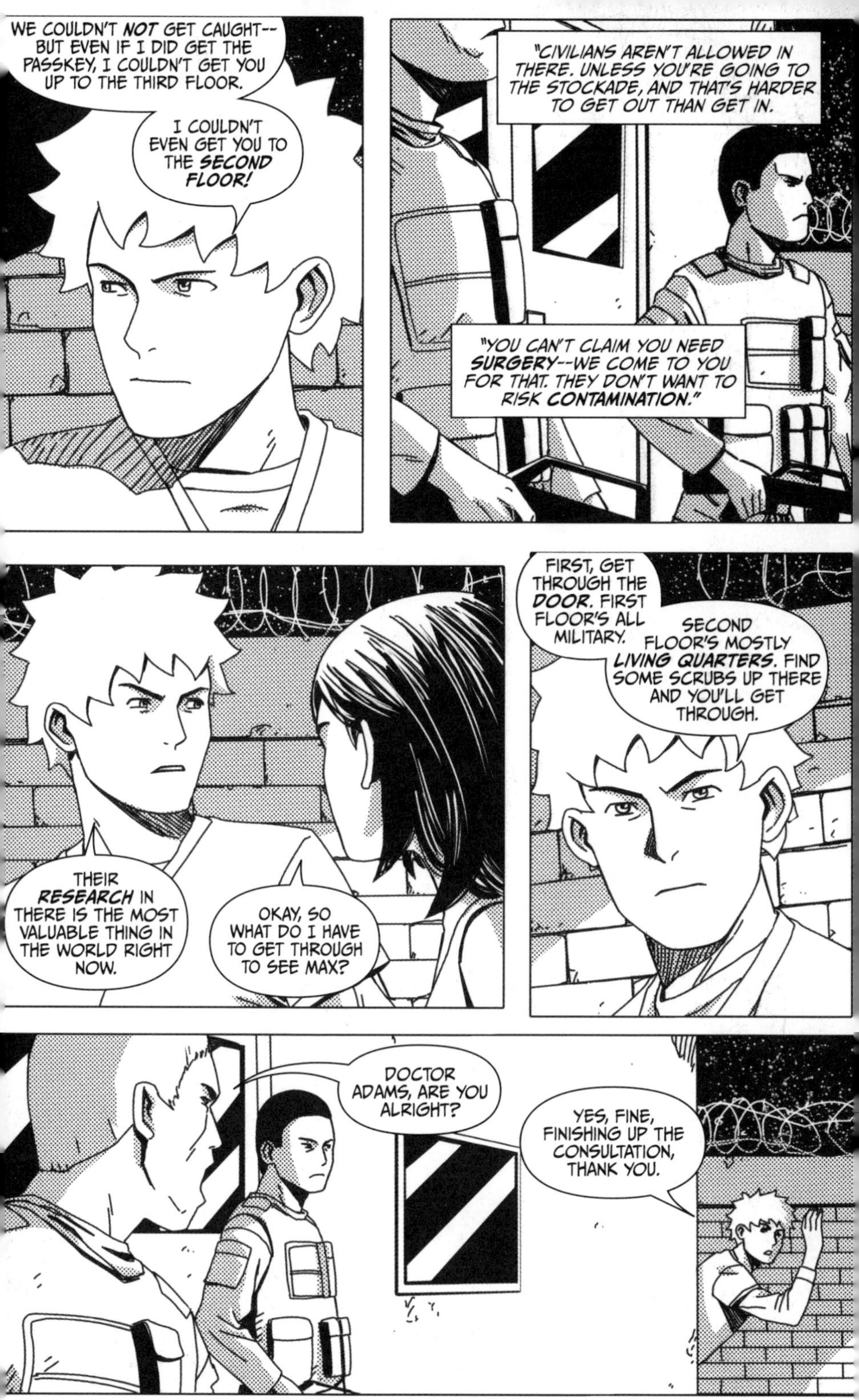
WE COULDN'T **NOT** GET CAUGHT-- BUT EVEN IF I DID GET THE PASSKEY, I COULDN'T GET YOU UP TO THE THIRD FLOOR.
I COULDN'T EVEN GET YOU TO THE **SECOND FLOOR!**
"CIVILIANS AREN'T ALLOWED IN THERE. UNLESS YOU'RE GOING TO THE STOCKADE, AND THAT'S HARDER TO GET OUT THAN GET IN.
"YOU CAN'T CLAIM YOU NEED **SURGERY**--WE COME TO YOU FOR THAT. THEY DON'T WANT TO RISK **CONTAMINATION.**"
THEIR **RESEARCH** IN THERE IS THE MOST VALUABLE THING IN THE WORLD RIGHT NOW.
OKAY, SO WHAT DO I HAVE TO GET THROUGH TO SEE MAX?
FIRST, GET THROUGH THE **DOOR**. FIRST FLOOR'S ALL MILITARY.
SECOND FLOOR'S MOSTLY **LIVING QUARTERS**. FIND SOME SCRUBS UP THERE AND YOU'LL GET THROUGH.
DOCTOR ADAMS, ARE YOU ALRIGHT?
YES, FINE, FINISHING UP THE CONSULTATION, THANK YOU.

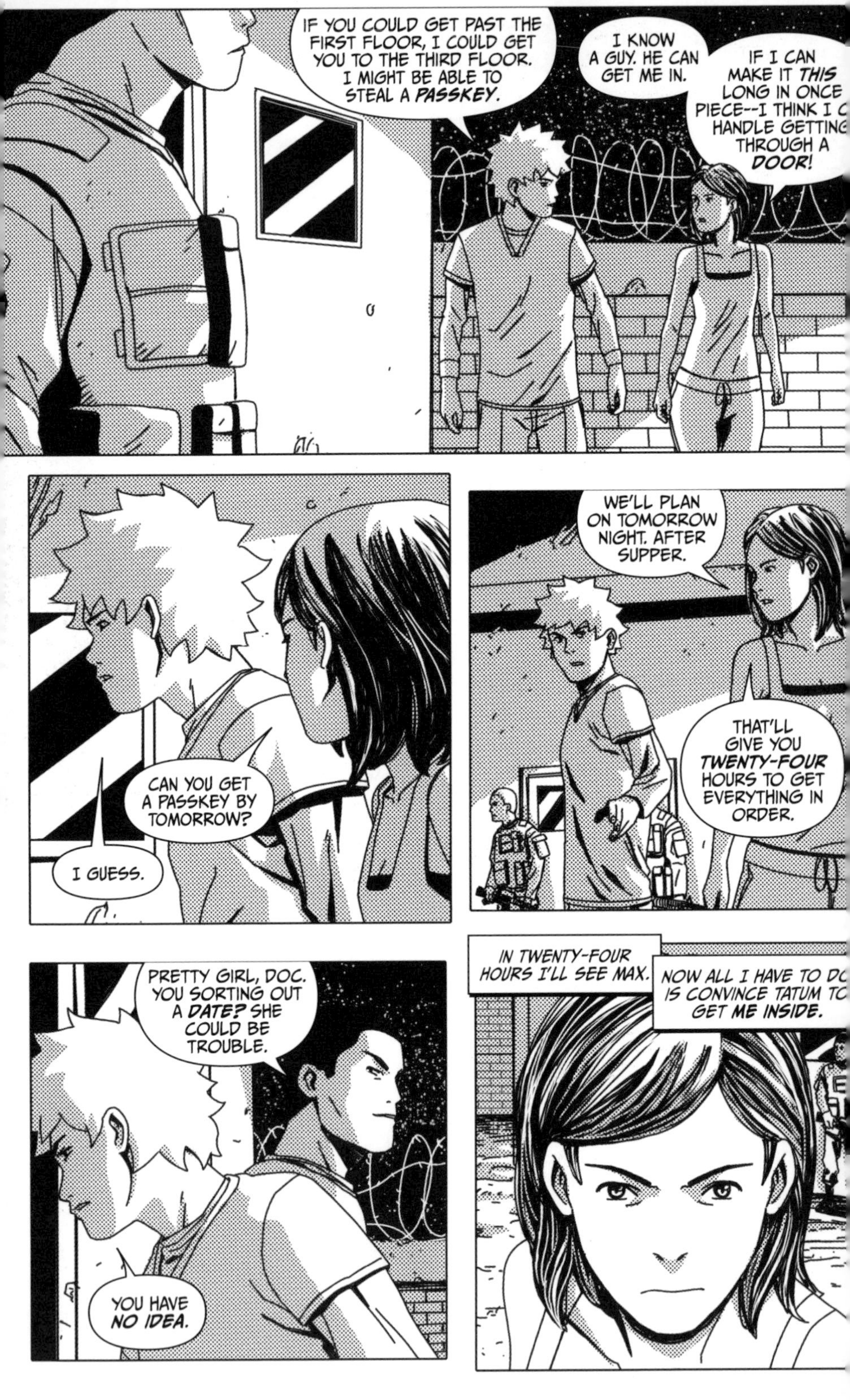
IF YOU COULD GET PAST THE FIRST FLOOR, I COULD GET YOU TO THE THIRD FLOOR. I MIGHT BE ABLE TO STEAL A ***PASSKEY***.
I KNOW A GUY. HE CAN GET ME IN.
IF I CAN MAKE IT ***THIS*** LONG IN ONCE PIECE--I THINK I C
HANDLE GETTING THROUGH A ***DOOR!***
CAN YOU GET A PASSKEY BY TOMORROW?
I GUESS.
WE'LL PLAN ON TOMORROW NIGHT. AFTER SUPPER.
THAT'LL GIVE YOU ***TWENTY-FOUR*** HOURS TO GET EVERYTHING IN ORDER.
PRETTY GIRL, DOC. YOU SORTING OUT A ***DATE?*** SHE COULD BE TROUBLE.
YOU HAVE ***NO IDEA.***
IN TWENTY-FOUR HOURS I'LL SEE MAX.
NOW ALL I HAVE TO D
IS CONVINCE TATUM T
GET ***ME INSIDE.***

CHAPTER TEN

ENDGAME

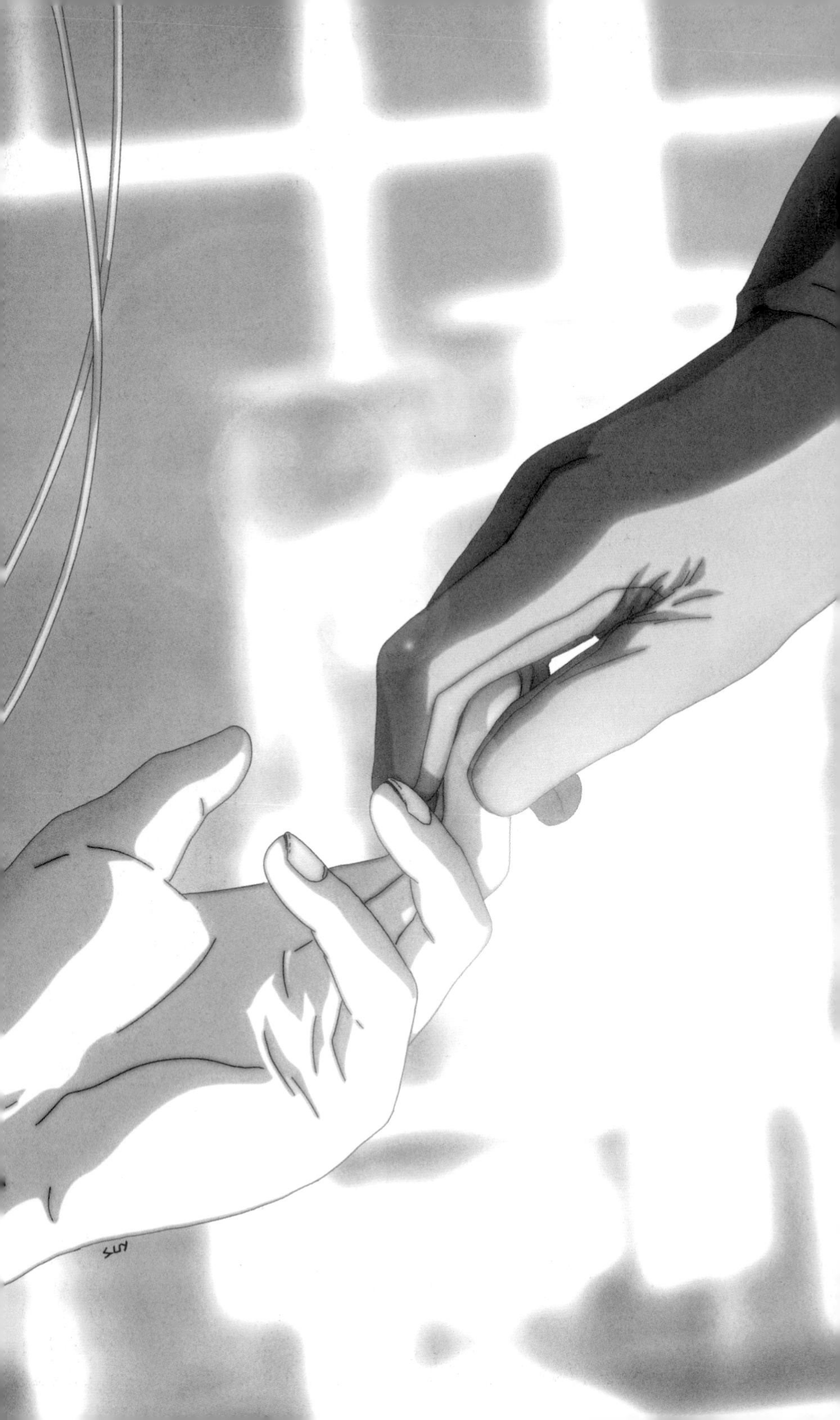

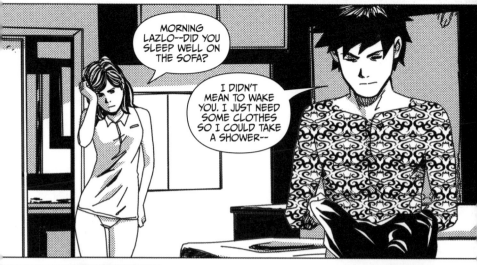

MORNING LAZLO--DID YOU SLEEP WELL ON THE SOFA?

I DIDN'T MEAN TO WAKE YOU. I JUST NEED SOME CLOTHES SO I COULD TAKE A SHOWER--

--I KNEW MY... PANTS...

UM, YOU'RE NOT WEARING ANY...

I KNOW. IT'S FINE.

HAVE YOU SEEN TATUM?

NO. I JUST GOT UP. WHY?

WHAT DO YOU NEED HIM FOR?

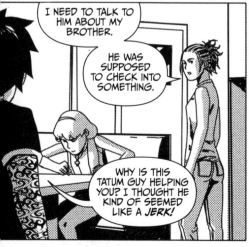

I NEED TO TALK TO HIM ABOUT MY BROTHER.

HE WAS SUPPOSED TO CHECK INTO SOMETHING.

WHY IS THIS TATUM GUY HELPING YOU? I THOUGHT HE KIND OF SEEMED LIKE A JERK!

WHAT ARE YOU DOING? ARE YOU GOING SOME-WHERE?"

YEAH-- I JUST HAVE TO FIND TO TATUM.

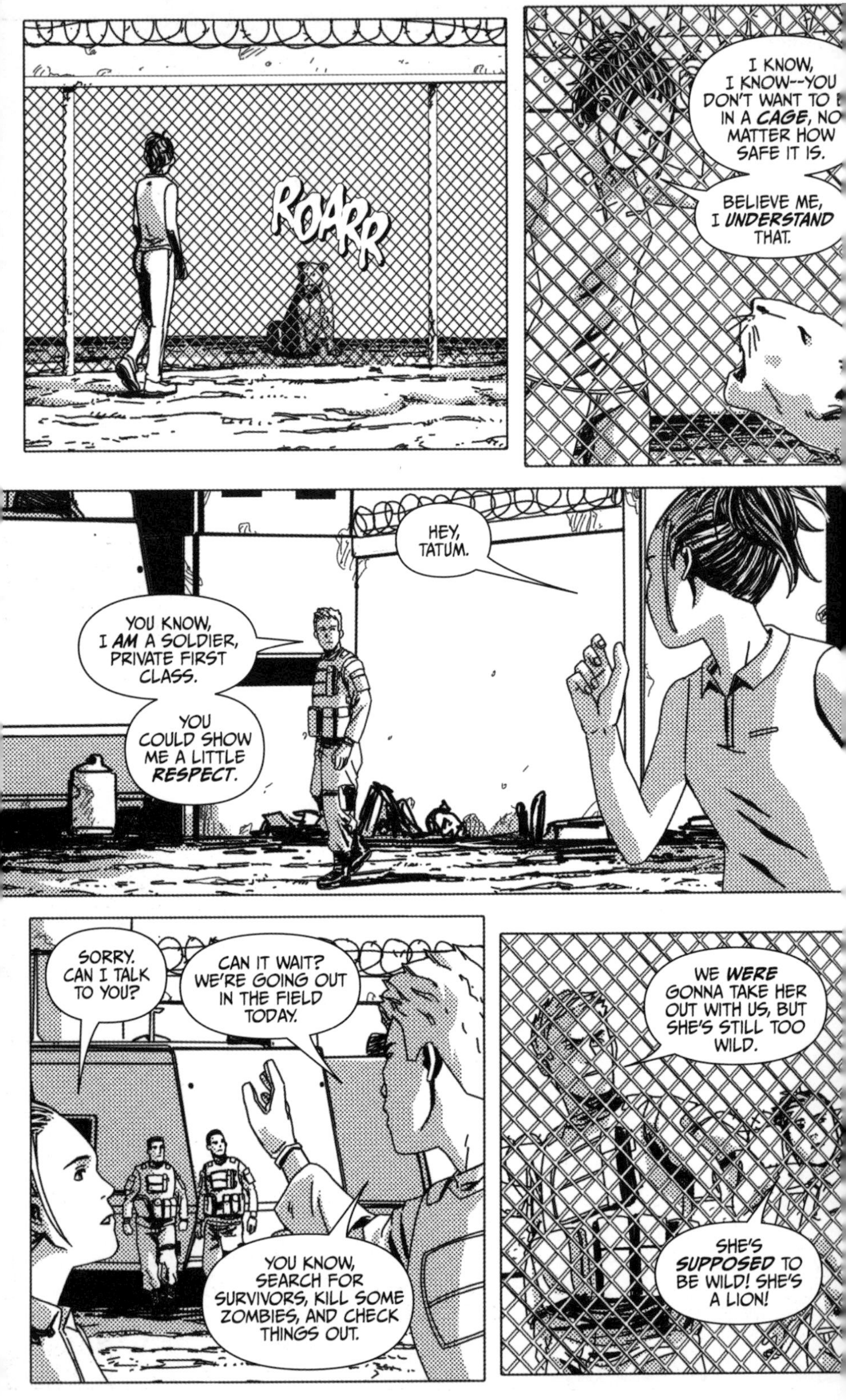
ROARR
I KNOW, I KNOW--YOU DON'T WANT TO IN A *CAGE*, NO MATTER HOW SAFE IT IS.
BELIEVE ME, I *UNDERSTAND* THAT.
HEY, TATUM.
YOU KNOW, I *AM* A SOLDIER, PRIVATE FIRST CLASS.
YOU COULD SHOW ME A LITTLE *RESPECT*.
SORRY. CAN I TALK TO YOU?
CAN IT WAIT? WE'RE GOING OUT IN THE FIELD TODAY.
YOU KNOW, SEARCH FOR SURVIVORS, KILL SOME ZOMBIES, AND CHECK THINGS OUT.
WE *WERE* GONNA TAKE HER OUT WITH US, BUT SHE'S STILL TOO WILD.
SHE'S *SUPPOSED* TO BE WILD! SHE'S A LION!

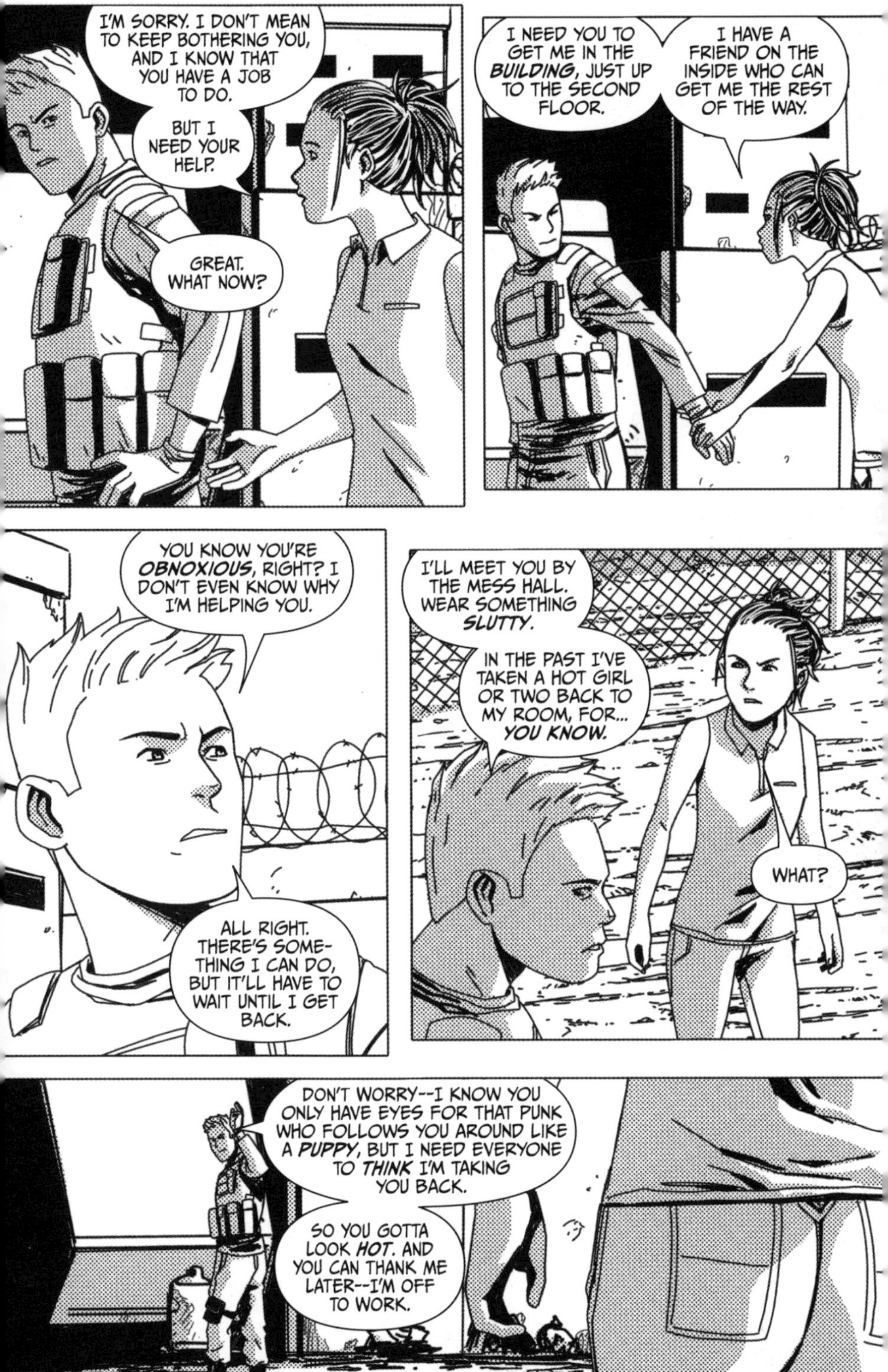
I'M SORRY. I DON'T MEAN TO KEEP BOTHERING YOU, AND I KNOW THAT YOU HAVE A JOB TO DO.
BUT I NEED YOUR HELP.
GREAT. WHAT NOW?
I NEED YOU TO GET ME IN THE *BUILDING*, JUST UP TO THE SECOND FLOOR.
I HAVE A FRIEND ON THE INSIDE WHO CAN GET ME THE REST OF THE WAY.
YOU KNOW YOU'RE *OBNOXIOUS*, RIGHT? I DON'T EVEN KNOW WHY I'M HELPING YOU.
ALL RIGHT. THERE'S SOME-THING I CAN DO, BUT IT'LL HAVE TO WAIT UNTIL I GET BACK.
I'LL MEET YOU BY THE MESS HALL. WEAR SOMETHING *SLUTTY*.
IN THE PAST I'VE TAKEN A HOT GIRL OR TWO BACK TO MY ROOM, FOR... *YOU KNOW.*
WHAT?
DON'T WORRY--I KNOW YOU ONLY HAVE EYES FOR THAT PUNK WHO FOLLOWS YOU AROUND LIKE A *PUPPY*, BUT I NEED EVERYONE TO *THINK* I'M TAKING YOU BACK.
SO YOU GOTTA LOOK *HOT*. AND YOU CAN THANK ME LATER--I'M OFF TO WORK.

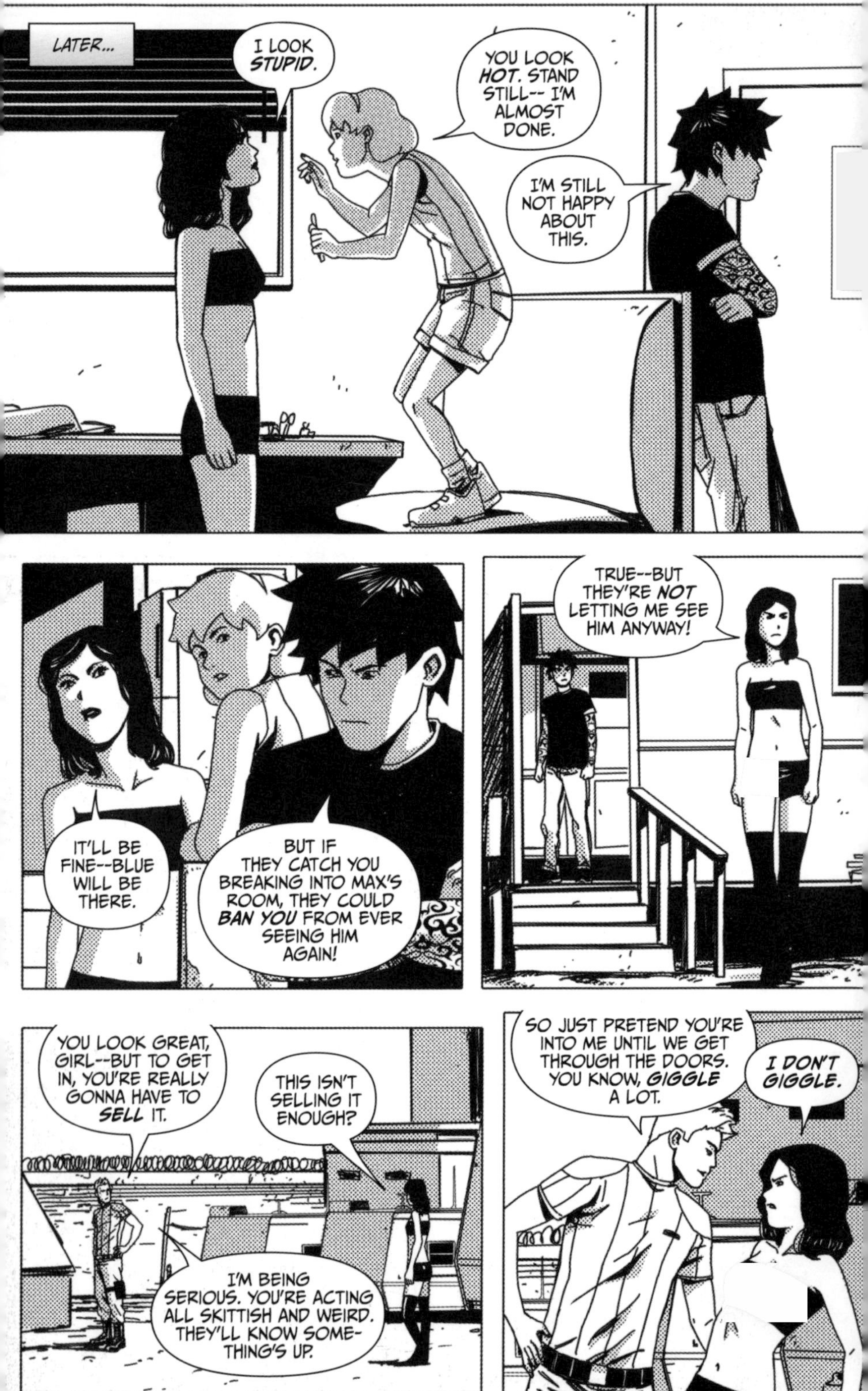
LATER...
I LOOK STUPID.
YOU LOOK HOT. STAND STILL-- I'M ALMOST DONE.
I'M STILL NOT HAPPY ABOUT THIS.
IT'LL BE FINE--BLUE WILL BE THERE.
BUT IF THEY CATCH YOU BREAKING INTO MAX'S ROOM, THEY COULD BAN YOU FROM EVER SEEING HIM AGAIN!
TRUE--BUT THEY'RE NOT LETTING ME SEE HIM ANYWAY!
YOU LOOK GREAT, GIRL--BUT TO GET IN, YOU'RE REALLY GONNA HAVE TO SELL IT.
THIS ISN'T SELLING IT ENOUGH?
I'M BEING SERIOUS. YOU'RE ACTING ALL SKITTISH AND WEIRD. THEY'LL KNOW SOMETHING'S UP.
SO JUST PRETEND YOU'RE INTO ME UNTIL WE GET THROUGH THE DOORS. YOU KNOW, GIGGLE A LOT.
I DON'T GIGGLE.

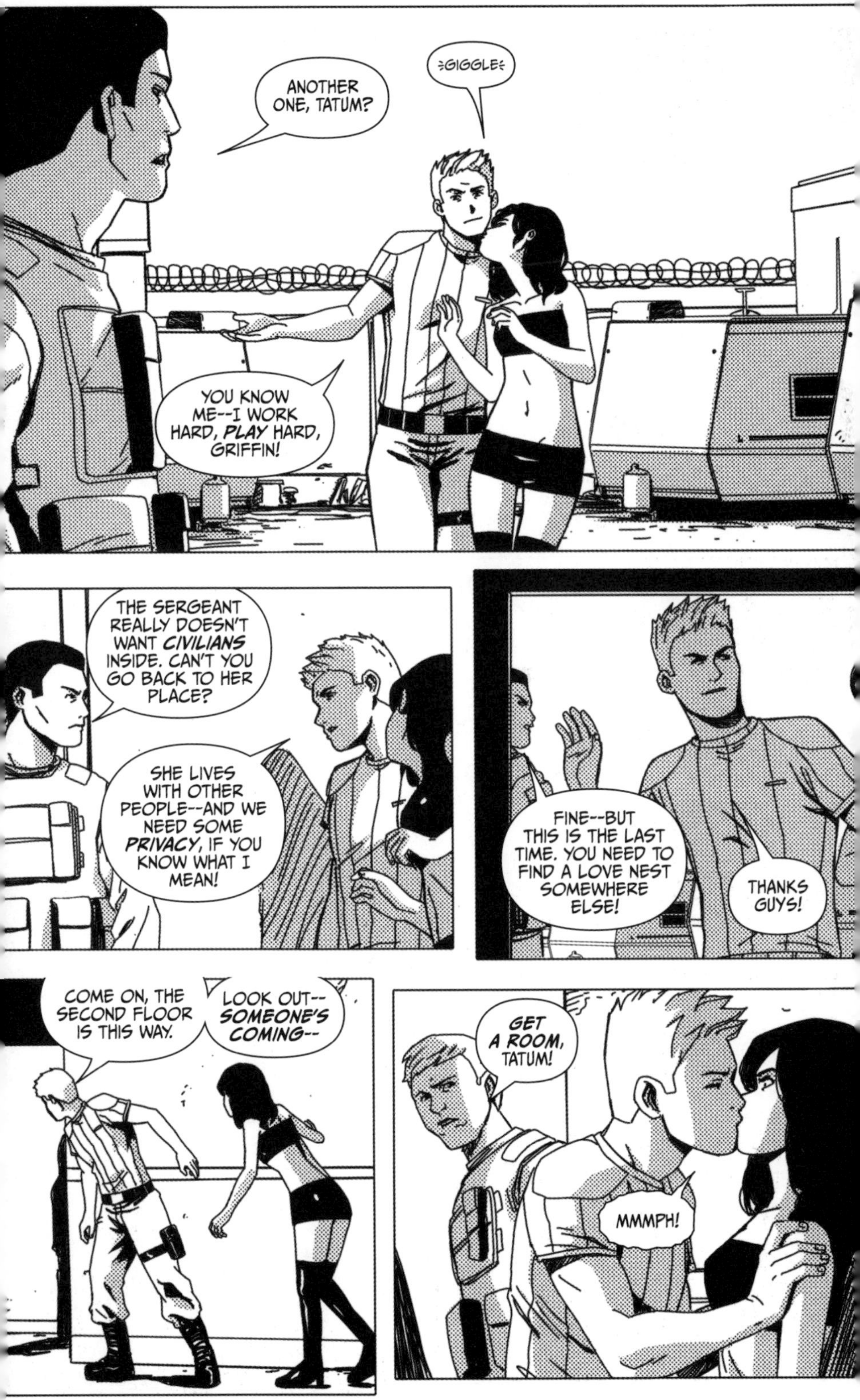
ANOTHER ONE, TATUM?
≈GIGGLE≈
YOU KNOW ME--I WORK HARD, *PLAY* HARD, GRIFFIN!
THE SERGEANT REALLY DOESN'T WANT *CIVILIANS* INSIDE. CAN'T YOU GO BACK TO HER PLACE?
SHE LIVES WITH OTHER PEOPLE--AND WE NEED SOME *PRIVACY*, IF YOU KNOW WHAT I MEAN!
FINE--BUT THIS IS THE LAST TIME. YOU NEED TO FIND A LOVE NEST SOMEWHERE ELSE!
THANKS GUYS!
COME ON, THE SECOND FLOOR IS THIS WAY.
LOOK OUT-- *SOMEONE'S COMING*--
GET A ROOM, TATUM!
MMMPH!

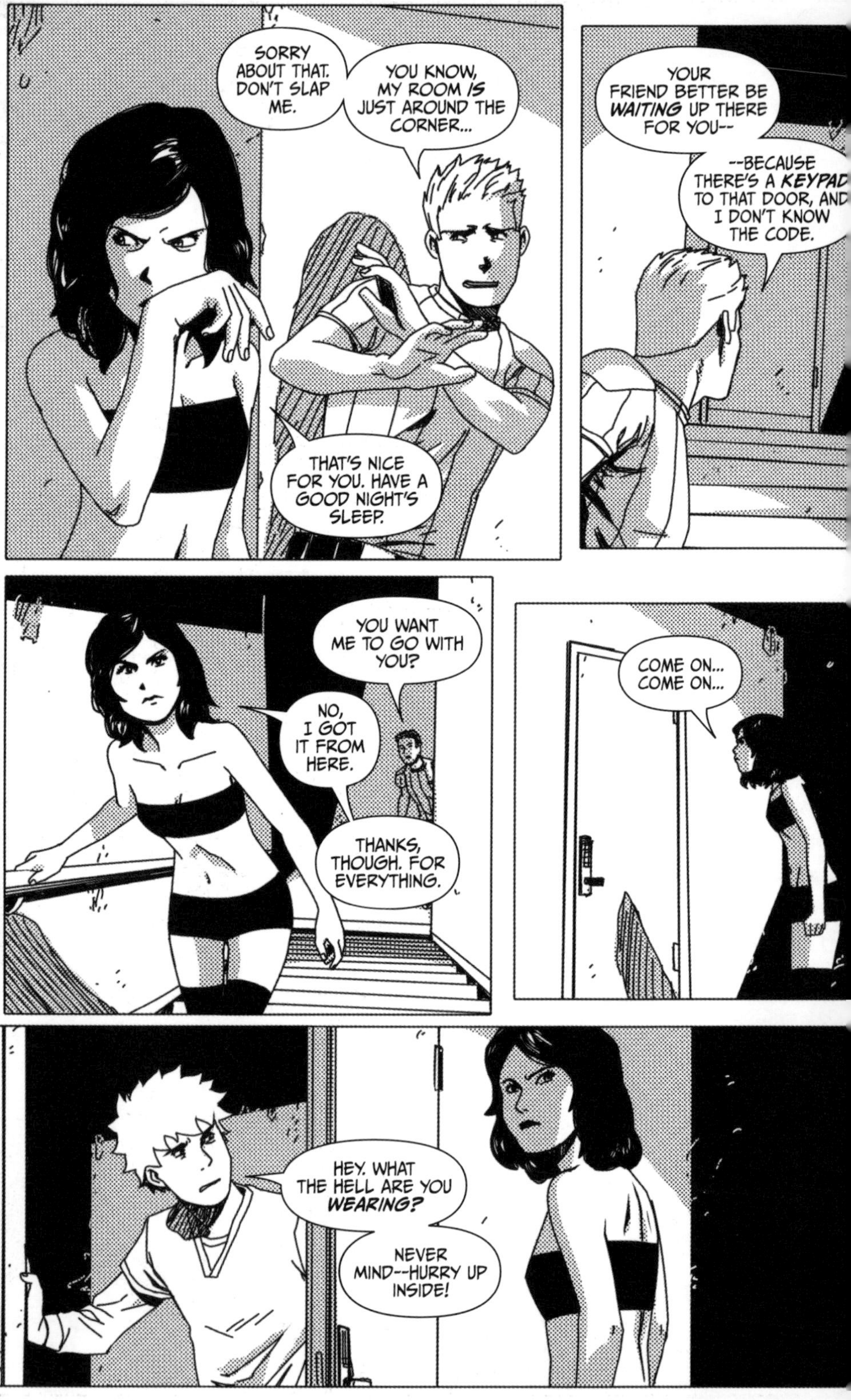
SORRY ABOUT THAT. DON'T SLAP ME.
YOU KNOW, MY ROOM *IS* JUST AROUND THE CORNER...
THAT'S NICE FOR YOU. HAVE A GOOD NIGHT'S SLEEP.
YOUR FRIEND BETTER BE *WAITING* UP THERE FOR YOU--
--BECAUSE THERE'S A *KEYPAD* TO THAT DOOR, AND I DON'T KNOW THE CODE.
YOU WANT ME TO GO WITH YOU?
NO, I GOT IT FROM HERE.
THANKS, THOUGH. FOR EVERYTHING.
COME ON... COME ON...
HEY. WHAT THE HELL ARE YOU *WEARING?*
NEVER MIND--HURRY UP INSIDE!

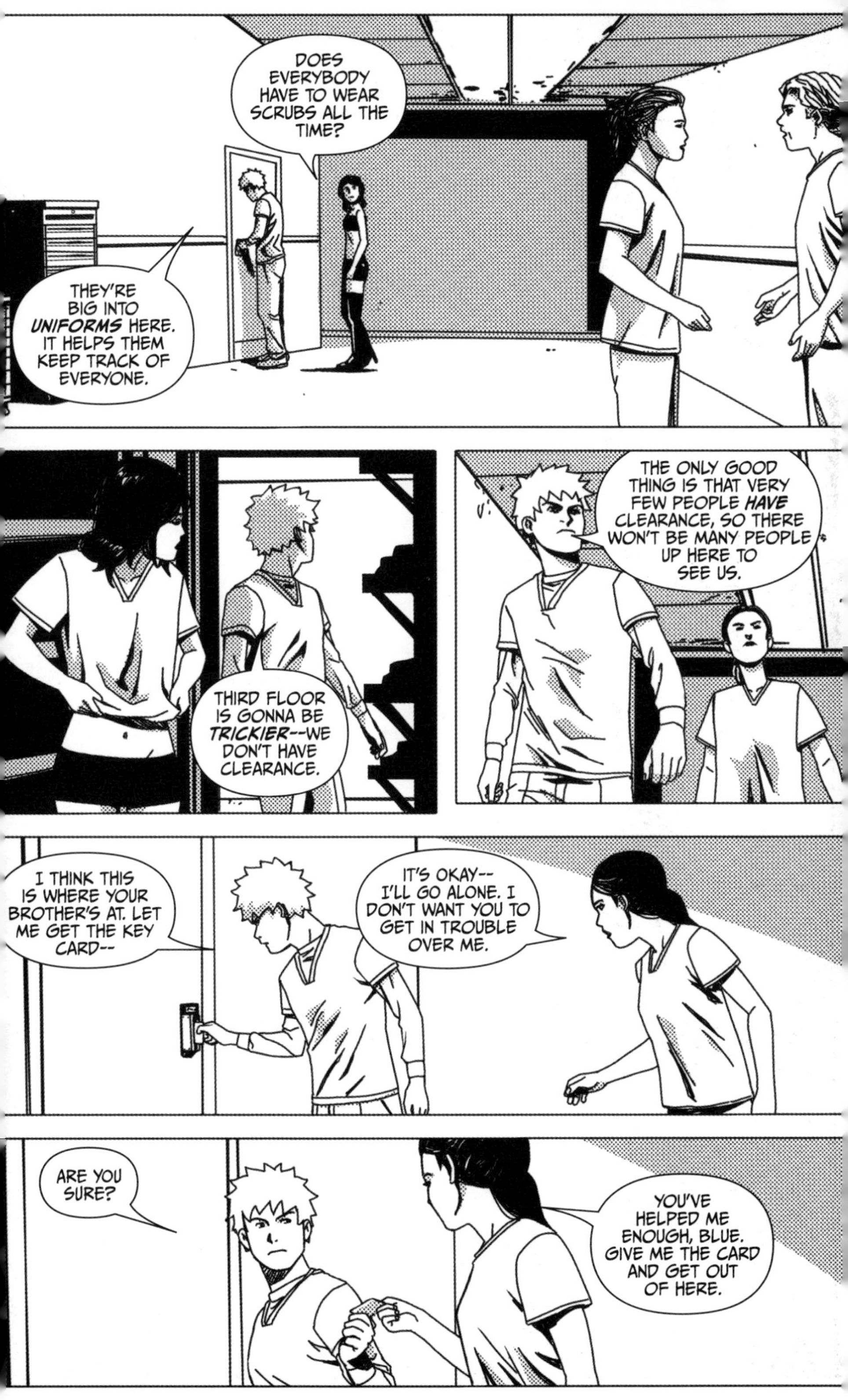
DOES EVERYBODY HAVE TO WEAR SCRUBS ALL THE TIME?
THEY'RE BIG INTO *UNIFORMS* HERE. IT HELPS THEM KEEP TRACK OF EVERYONE.
THIRD FLOOR IS GONNA BE *TRICKIER*--WE DON'T HAVE CLEARANCE.
THE ONLY GOOD THING IS THAT VERY FEW PEOPLE *HAVE* CLEARANCE, SO THERE WON'T BE MANY PEOPLE UP HERE TO SEE US.
I THINK THIS IS WHERE YOUR BROTHER'S AT. LET ME GET THE KEY CARD--
IT'S OKAY-- I'LL GO ALONE. I DON'T WANT YOU TO GET IN TROUBLE OVER ME.
ARE YOU SURE?
YOU'VE HELPED ME ENOUGH, BLUE. GIVE ME THE CARD AND GET OUT OF HERE.

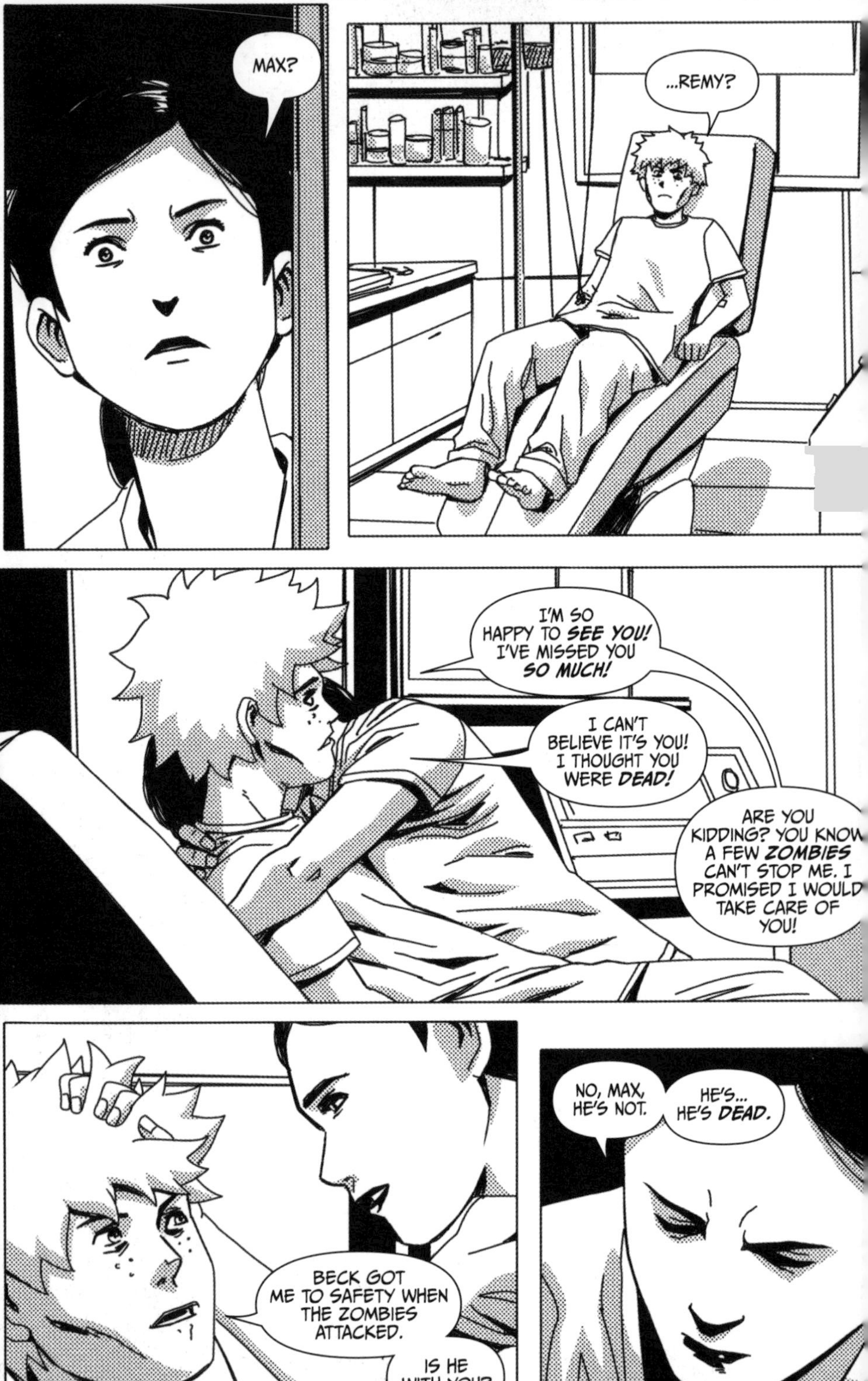
MAX?
...REMY?
I'M SO HAPPY TO SEE YOU! I'VE MISSED YOU SO MUCH!
I CAN'T BELIEVE IT'S YOU! I THOUGHT YOU WERE DEAD!
ARE YOU KIDDING? YOU KNOW A FEW ZOMBIES CAN'T STOP ME. I PROMISED I WOULD TAKE CARE OF YOU!
BECK GOT ME TO SAFETY WHEN THE ZOMBIES ATTACKED.
IS HE WITH YOU?
NO, MAX, HE'S NOT.
HE'S... HE'S DEAD.

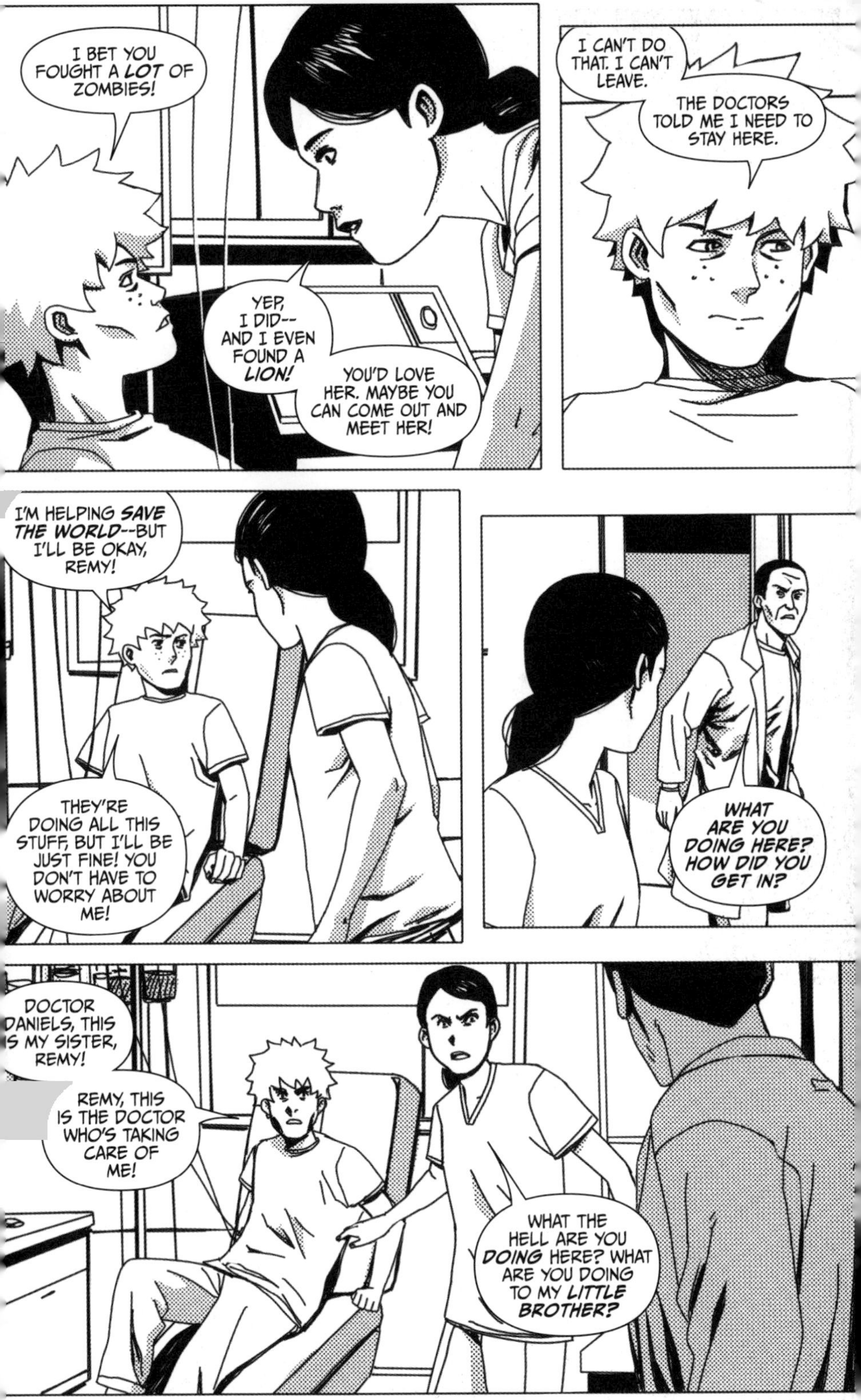
I BET YOU FOUGHT A LOT OF ZOMBIES!
YEP, I DID-- AND I EVEN FOUND A LION!
YOU'D LOVE HER. MAYBE YOU CAN COME OUT AND MEET HER!
I CAN'T DO THAT. I CAN'T LEAVE.
THE DOCTORS TOLD ME I NEED TO STAY HERE.
I'M HELPING SAVE THE WORLD--BUT I'LL BE OKAY, REMY!
THEY'RE DOING ALL THIS STUFF, BUT I'LL BE JUST FINE! YOU DON'T HAVE TO WORRY ABOUT ME!
WHAT ARE YOU DOING HERE? HOW DID YOU GET IN?
DOCTOR DANIELS, THIS IS MY SISTER, REMY!
REMY, THIS IS THE DOCTOR WHO'S TAKING CARE OF ME!
WHAT THE HELL ARE YOU DOING HERE? WHAT ARE YOU DOING TO MY LITTLE BROTHER?

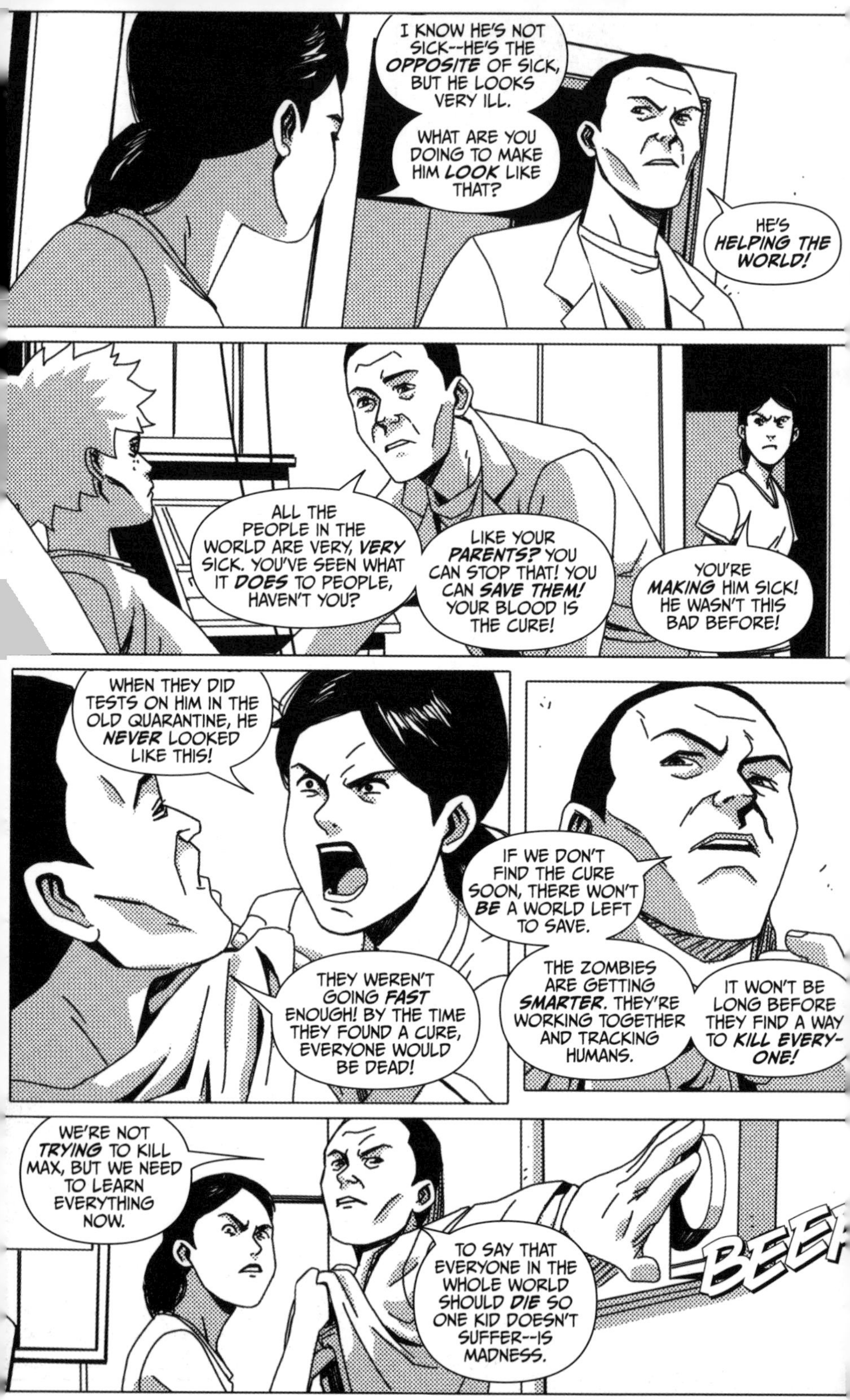
I KNOW HE'S NOT SICK--HE'S THE OPPOSITE OF SICK, BUT HE LOOKS VERY ILL.
WHAT ARE YOU DOING TO MAKE HIM LOOK LIKE THAT?
HE'S HELPING THE WORLD!
ALL THE PEOPLE IN THE WORLD ARE VERY, VERY SICK. YOU'VE SEEN WHAT IT DOES TO PEOPLE, HAVEN'T YOU?
LIKE YOUR PARENTS? YOU CAN STOP THAT! YOU CAN SAVE THEM! YOUR BLOOD IS THE CURE!
YOU'RE MAKING HIM SICK! HE WASN'T THIS BAD BEFORE!
WHEN THEY DID TESTS ON HIM IN THE OLD QUARANTINE, HE NEVER LOOKED LIKE THIS!
THEY WEREN'T GOING FAST ENOUGH! BY THE TIME THEY FOUND A CURE, EVERYONE WOULD BE DEAD!
IF WE DON'T FIND THE CURE SOON, THERE WON'T BE A WORLD LEFT TO SAVE.
THE ZOMBIES ARE GETTING SMARTER. THEY'RE WORKING TOGETHER AND TRACKING HUMANS.
IT WON'T BE LONG BEFORE THEY FIND A WAY TO KILL EVERY-ONE!
WE'RE NOT TRYING TO KILL MAX, BUT WE NEED TO LEARN EVERYTHING NOW.
TO SAY THAT EVERYONE IN THE WHOLE WORLD SHOULD DIE SO ONE KID DOESN'T SUFFER--IS MADNESS.
BEEP

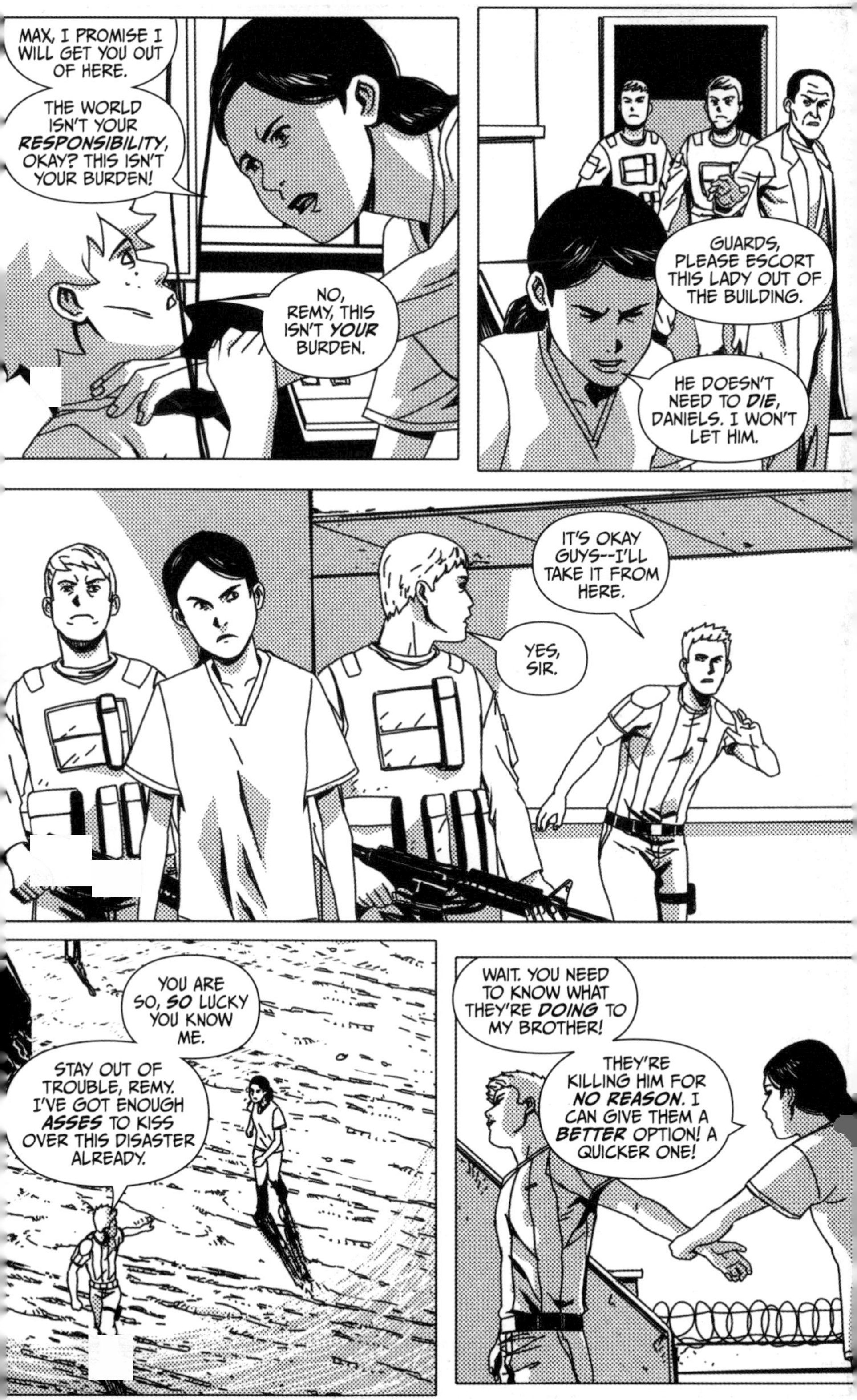
MAX, I PROMISE I WILL GET YOU OUT OF HERE.
THE WORLD ISN'T YOUR **RESPONSIBILITY**, OKAY? THIS ISN'T YOUR BURDEN!
NO, REMY, THIS ISN'T **YOUR** BURDEN.
GUARDS, PLEASE ESCORT THIS LADY OUT OF THE BUILDING.
HE DOESN'T NEED TO **DIE**, DANIELS. I WON'T LET HIM.
IT'S OKAY GUYS--I'LL TAKE IT FROM HERE.
YES, SIR.
YOU ARE SO, **SO** LUCKY YOU KNOW ME.
STAY OUT OF TROUBLE, REMY. I'VE GOT ENOUGH **ASSES** TO KISS OVER THIS DISASTER ALREADY.
WAIT. YOU NEED TO KNOW WHAT THEY'RE **DOING** TO MY BROTHER!
THEY'RE KILLING HIM FOR **NO REASON**. I CAN GIVE THEM A **BETTER** OPTION! A QUICKER ONE!

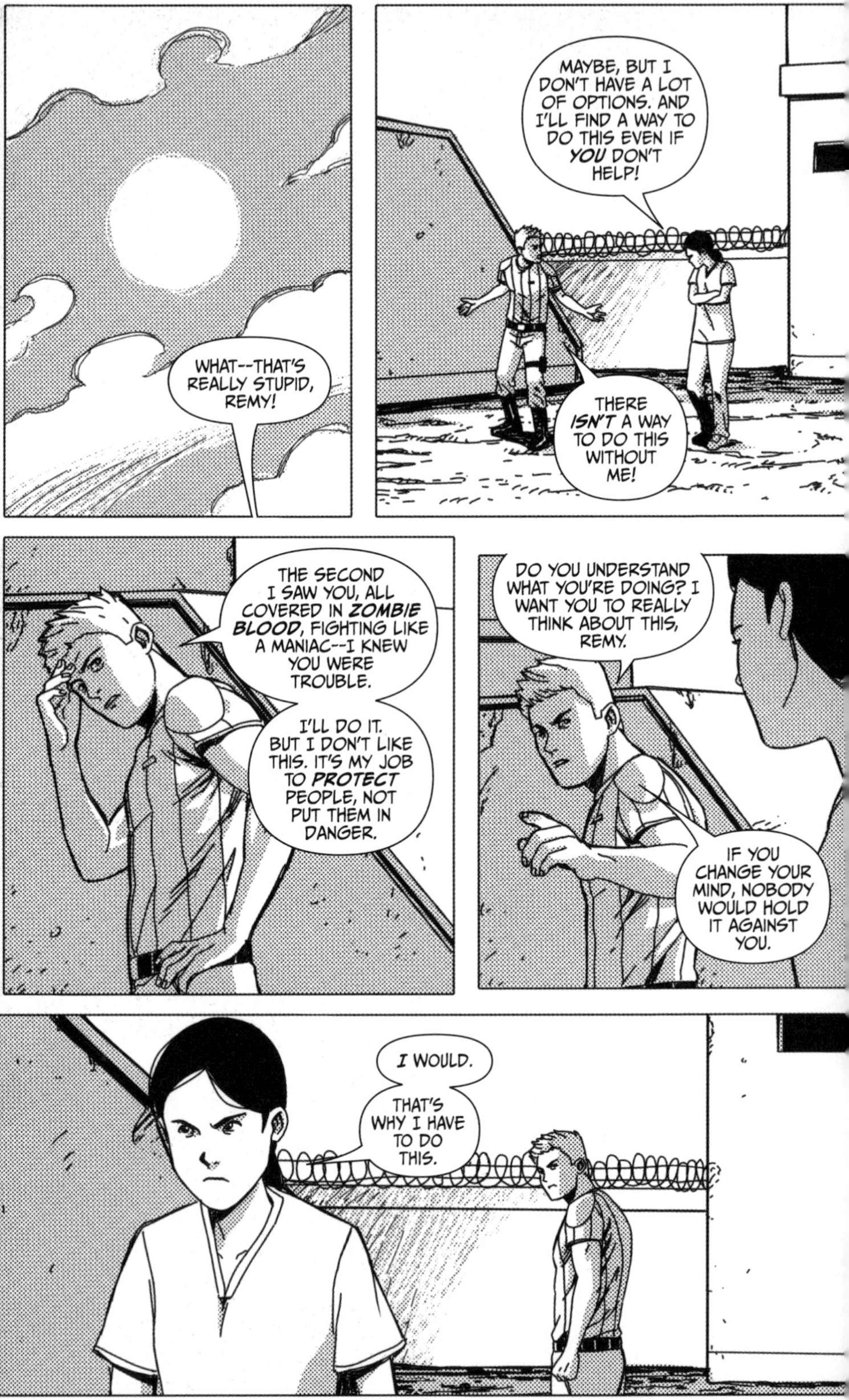
WHAT--THAT'S REALLY STUPID, REMY!
MAYBE, BUT I DON'T HAVE A LOT OF OPTIONS. AND I'LL FIND A WAY TO DO THIS EVEN IF *YOU* DON'T HELP!
THERE *ISN'T* A WAY TO DO THIS WITHOUT ME!
THE SECOND I SAW YOU, ALL COVERED IN *ZOMBIE BLOOD*, FIGHTING LIKE A MANIAC--I KNEW YOU WERE TROUBLE.
I'LL DO IT. BUT I DON'T LIKE THIS. IT'S MY JOB TO *PROTECT* PEOPLE, NOT PUT THEM IN DANGER.
DO YOU UNDERSTAND WHAT YOU'RE DOING? I WANT YOU TO REALLY THINK ABOUT THIS, REMY.
IF YOU CHANGE YOUR MIND, NOBODY WOULD HOLD IT AGAINST YOU.
I WOULD.
THAT'S WHY I HAVE TO DO THIS.

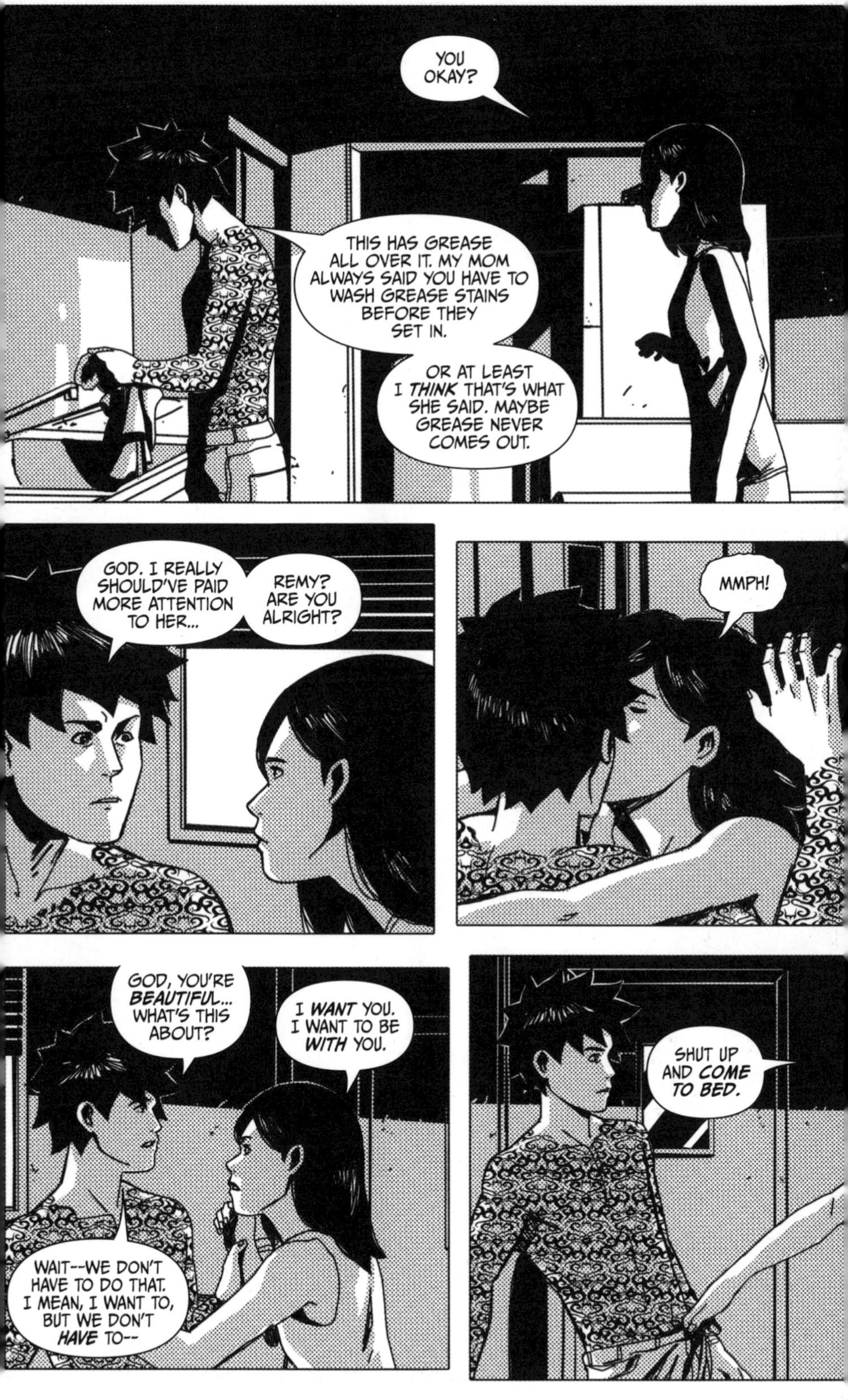
YOU OKAY?
THIS HAS GREASE ALL OVER IT. MY MOM ALWAYS SAID YOU HAVE TO WASH GREASE STAINS BEFORE THEY SET IN.
OR AT LEAST I *THINK* THAT'S WHAT SHE SAID. MAYBE GREASE NEVER COMES OUT.
GOD. I REALLY SHOULD'VE PAID MORE ATTENTION TO HER...
REMY? ARE YOU ALRIGHT?
MMPH!
GOD, YOU'RE *BEAUTIFUL*... WHAT'S THIS ABOUT?
I *WANT* YOU. I WANT TO BE *WITH* YOU.
WAIT--WE DON'T HAVE TO DO THAT. I MEAN, I WANT TO, BUT WE DON'T *HAVE* TO--
SHUT UP AND *COME TO BED.*

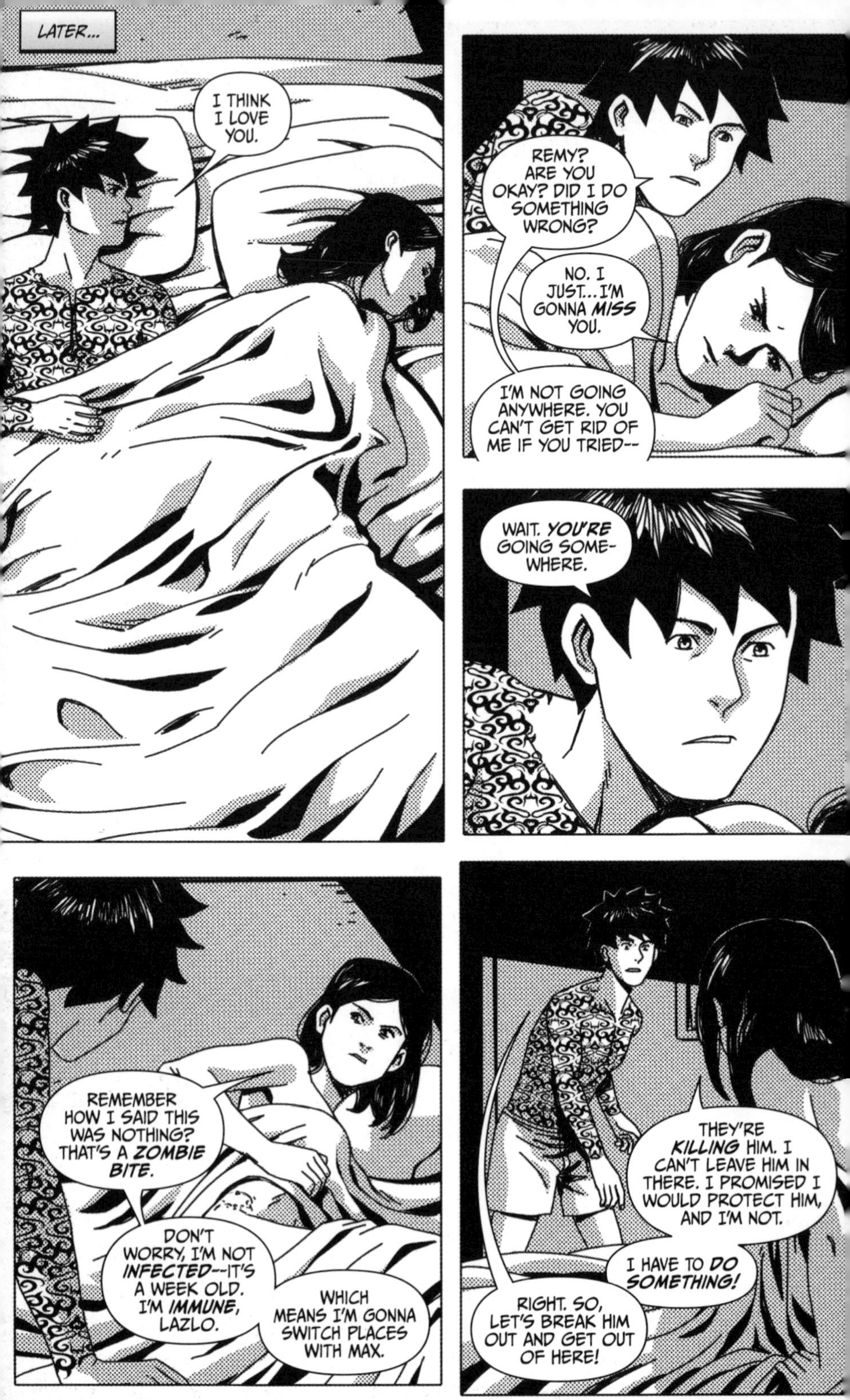
LATER...
I THINK I LOVE YOU.
REMY? ARE YOU OKAY? DID I DO SOMETHING WRONG?
NO. I JUST...I'M GONNA *MISS* YOU.
I'M NOT GOING ANYWHERE. YOU CAN'T GET RID OF ME IF YOU TRIED--
WAIT. *YOU'RE* GOING SOME-WHERE.
REMEMBER HOW I SAID THIS WAS NOTHING? THAT'S A *ZOMBIE BITE*.
DON'T WORRY, I'M NOT *INFECTED*--IT'S A WEEK OLD. I'M *IMMUNE*, LAZLO.
WHICH MEANS I'M GONNA SWITCH PLACES WITH MAX.
THEY'RE *KILLING* HIM. I CAN'T LEAVE HIM IN THERE. I PROMISED I WOULD PROTECT HIM, AND I'M NOT.
I HAVE TO *DO SOMETHING!*
RIGHT. SO, LET'S BREAK HIM OUT AND GET OUT OF HERE!

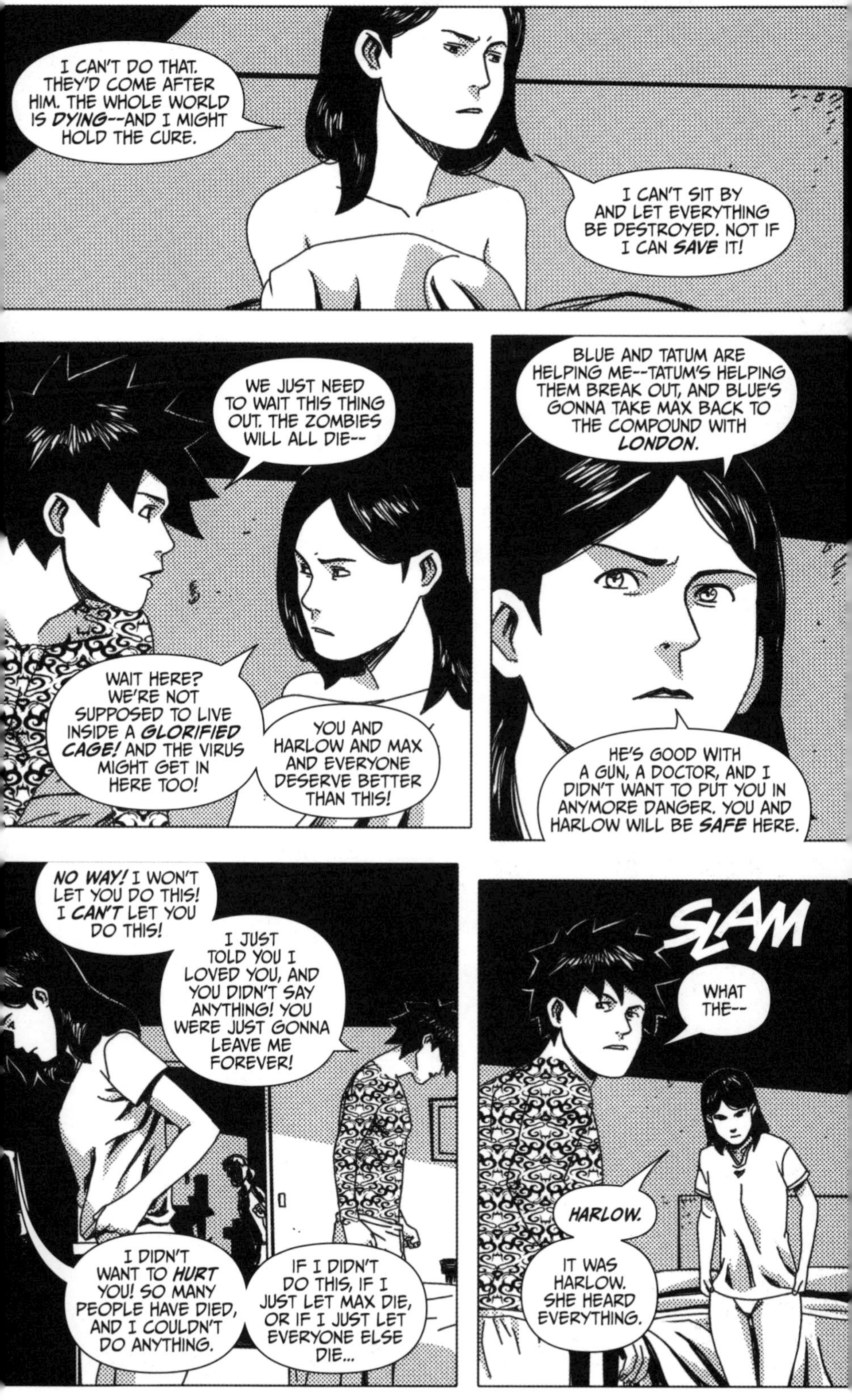
I CAN'T DO THAT. THEY'D COME AFTER HIM. THE WHOLE WORLD IS *DYING*--AND I MIGHT HOLD THE CURE.
I CAN'T SIT BY AND LET EVERYTHING BE DESTROYED. NOT IF I CAN *SAVE* IT!
WE JUST NEED TO WAIT THIS THING OUT. THE ZOMBIES WILL ALL DIE--
WAIT HERE? WE'RE NOT SUPPOSED TO LIVE INSIDE A *GLORIFIED CAGE!* AND THE VIRUS MIGHT GET IN HERE TOO!
YOU AND HARLOW AND MAX AND EVERYONE DESERVE BETTER THAN THIS!
BLUE AND TATUM ARE HELPING ME--TATUM'S HELPING THEM BREAK OUT, AND BLUE'S GONNA TAKE MAX BACK TO THE COMPOUND WITH *LONDON.*
HE'S GOOD WITH A GUN, A DOCTOR, AND I DIDN'T WANT TO PUT YOU IN ANYMORE DANGER. YOU AND HARLOW WILL BE *SAFE* HERE.
NO WAY! I WON'T LET YOU DO THIS! I *CAN'T* LET YOU DO THIS!
I JUST TOLD YOU I LOVED YOU, AND YOU DIDN'T SAY ANYTHING! YOU WERE JUST GONNA LEAVE ME FOREVER!
I DIDN'T WANT TO *HURT* YOU! SO MANY PEOPLE HAVE DIED, AND I COULDN'T DO ANYTHING.
IF I DIDN'T DO THIS, IF I JUST LET MAX DIE, OR IF I JUST LET EVERYONE ELSE DIE...
SLAM
WHAT THE--
HARLOW.
IT WAS HARLOW. SHE HEARD EVERYTHING.

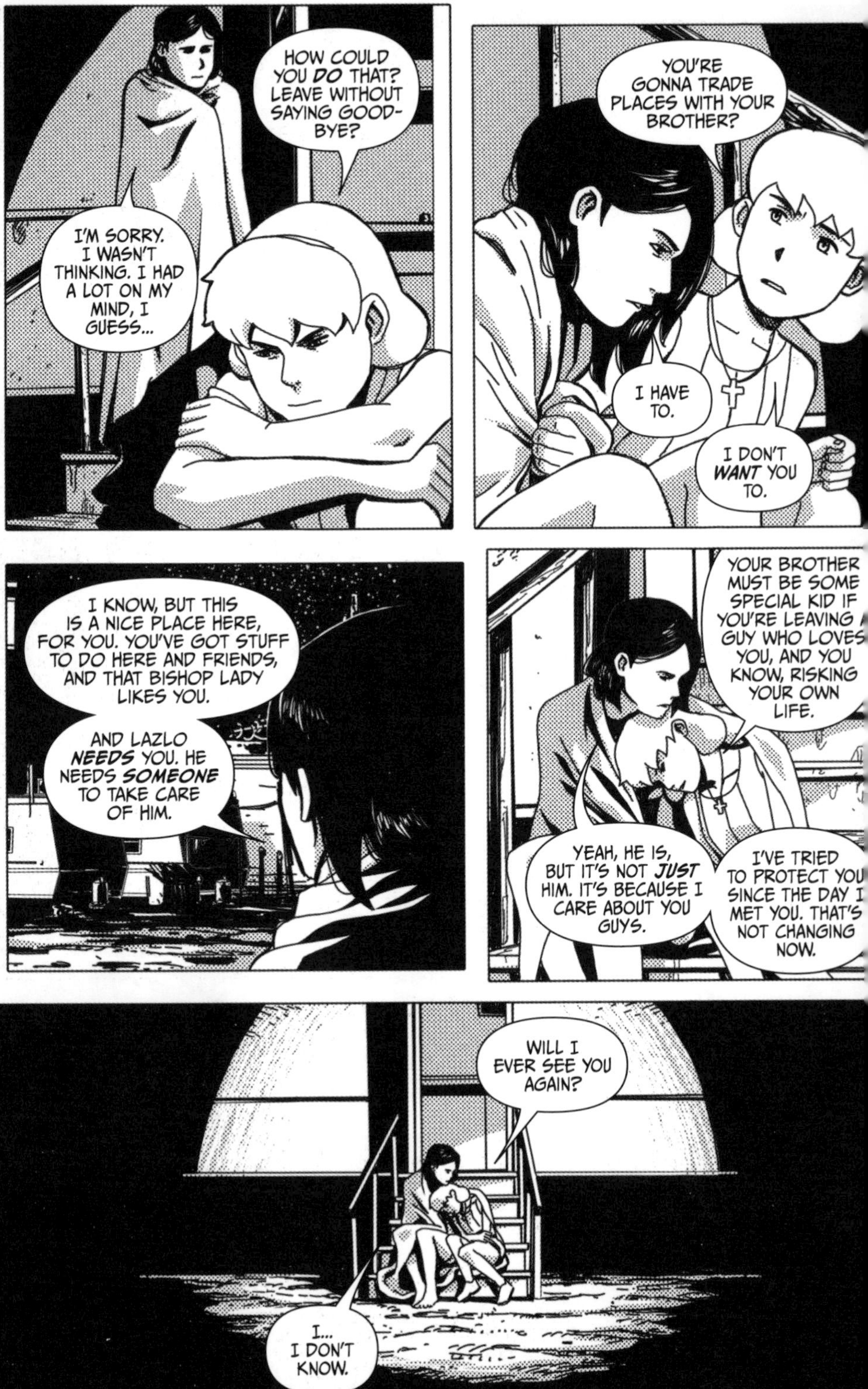
HOW COULD YOU *DO* THAT? LEAVE WITHOUT SAYING GOOD-BYE?
I'M SORRY. I WASN'T THINKING. I HAD A LOT ON MY MIND, I GUESS...
YOU'RE GONNA TRADE PLACES WITH YOUR BROTHER?
I HAVE TO.
I DON'T *WANT* YOU TO.
I KNOW, BUT THIS IS A NICE PLACE HERE, FOR YOU. YOU'VE GOT STUFF TO DO HERE AND FRIENDS, AND THAT BISHOP LADY LIKES YOU.
AND LAZLO *NEEDS* YOU. HE NEEDS *SOMEONE* TO TAKE CARE OF HIM.
YOUR BROTHER MUST BE SOME SPECIAL KID IF YOU'RE LEAVING A GUY WHO LOVES YOU, AND YOU KNOW, RISKING YOUR OWN LIFE.
YEAH, HE IS, BUT IT'S NOT *JUST* HIM. IT'S BECAUSE I CARE ABOUT YOU GUYS.
I'VE TRIED TO PROTECT YOU SINCE THE DAY I MET YOU. THAT'S NOT CHANGING NOW.
WILL I EVER SEE YOU AGAIN?
I... I DON'T KNOW.

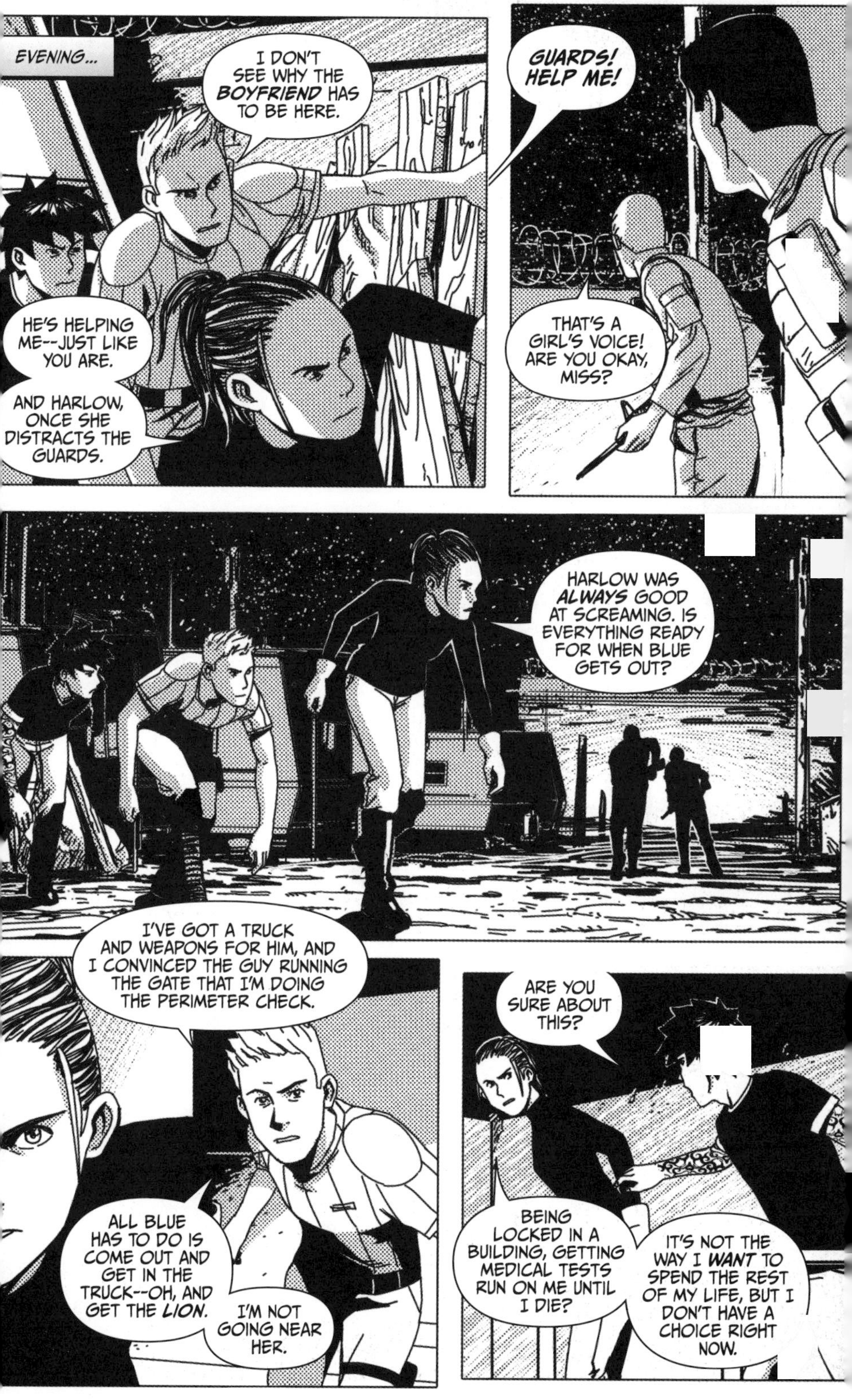
EVENING...
I DON'T SEE WHY THE **BOYFRIEND** HAS TO BE HERE.
HE'S HELPING ME--JUST LIKE YOU ARE.
AND HARLOW, ONCE SHE DISTRACTS THE GUARDS.
GUARDS! HELP ME!
THAT'S A GIRL'S VOICE! ARE YOU OKAY, MISS?
HARLOW WAS **ALWAYS** GOOD AT SCREAMING. IS EVERYTHING READY FOR WHEN BLUE GETS OUT?
I'VE GOT A TRUCK AND WEAPONS FOR HIM, AND I CONVINCED THE GUY RUNNING THE GATE THAT I'M DOING THE PERIMETER CHECK.
ALL BLUE HAS TO DO IS COME OUT AND GET IN THE TRUCK--OH, AND GET THE **LION**.
I'M NOT GOING NEAR HER.
ARE YOU SURE ABOUT THIS?
BEING LOCKED IN A BUILDING, GETTING MEDICAL TESTS RUN ON ME UNTIL I DIE?
IT'S NOT THE WAY I **WANT** TO SPEND THE REST OF MY LIFE, BUT I DON'T HAVE A CHOICE RIGHT NOW.

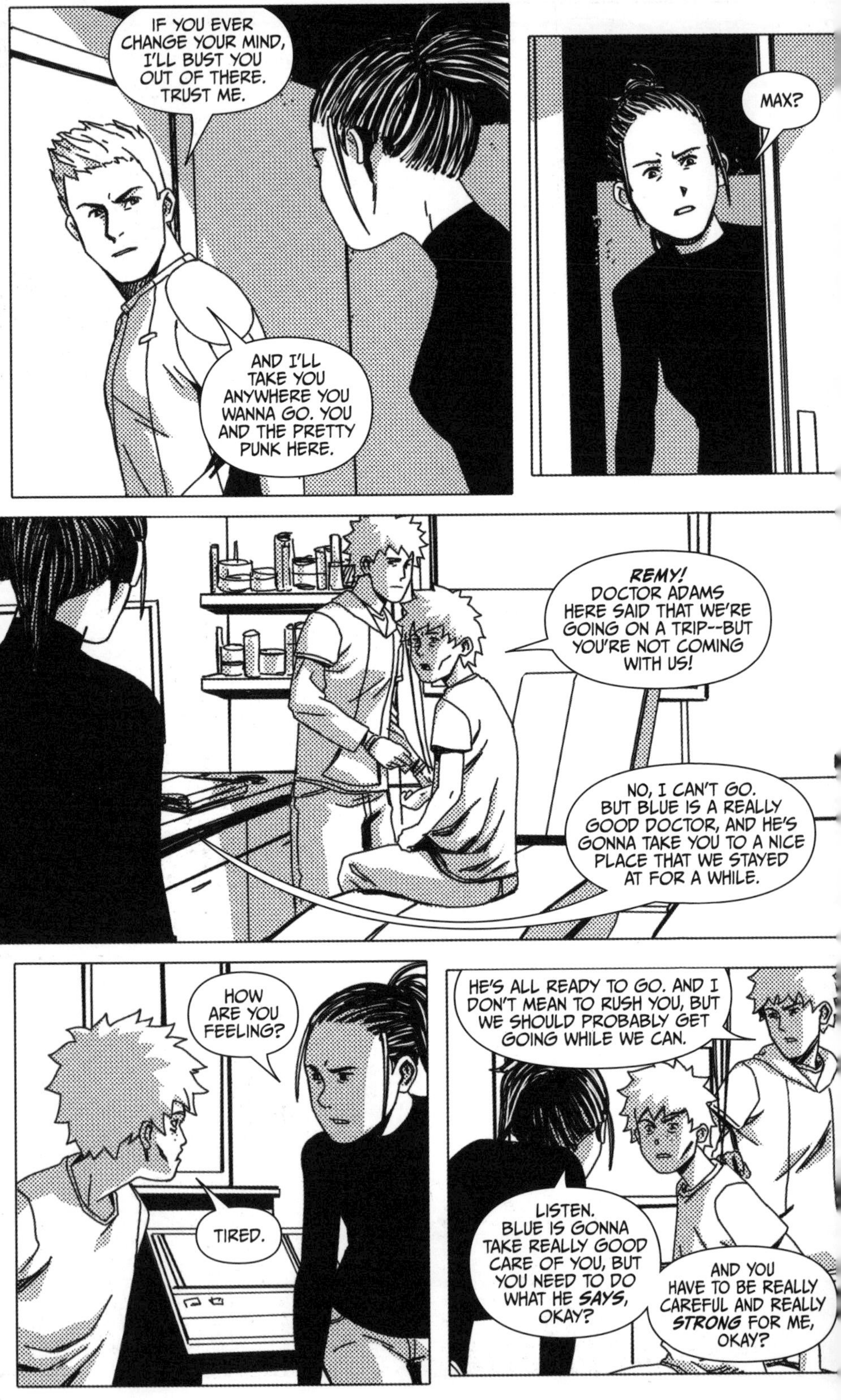
IF YOU EVER CHANGE YOUR MIND, I'LL BUST YOU OUT OF THERE. TRUST ME.
AND I'LL TAKE YOU ANYWHERE YOU WANNA GO. YOU AND THE PRETTY PUNK HERE.
MAX?
REMY! DOCTOR ADAMS HERE SAID THAT WE'RE GOING ON A TRIP--BUT YOU'RE NOT COMING WITH US!
NO, I CAN'T GO. BUT BLUE IS A REALLY GOOD DOCTOR, AND HE'S GONNA TAKE YOU TO A NICE PLACE THAT WE STAYED AT FOR A WHILE.
HOW ARE YOU FEELING?
TIRED.
HE'S ALL READY TO GO. AND I DON'T MEAN TO RUSH YOU, BUT WE SHOULD PROBABLY GET GOING WHILE WE CAN.
LISTEN. BLUE IS GONNA TAKE REALLY GOOD CARE OF YOU, BUT YOU NEED TO DO WHAT HE *SAYS*, OKAY?
AND YOU HAVE TO BE REALLY CAREFUL AND REALLY *STRONG* FOR ME, OKAY?

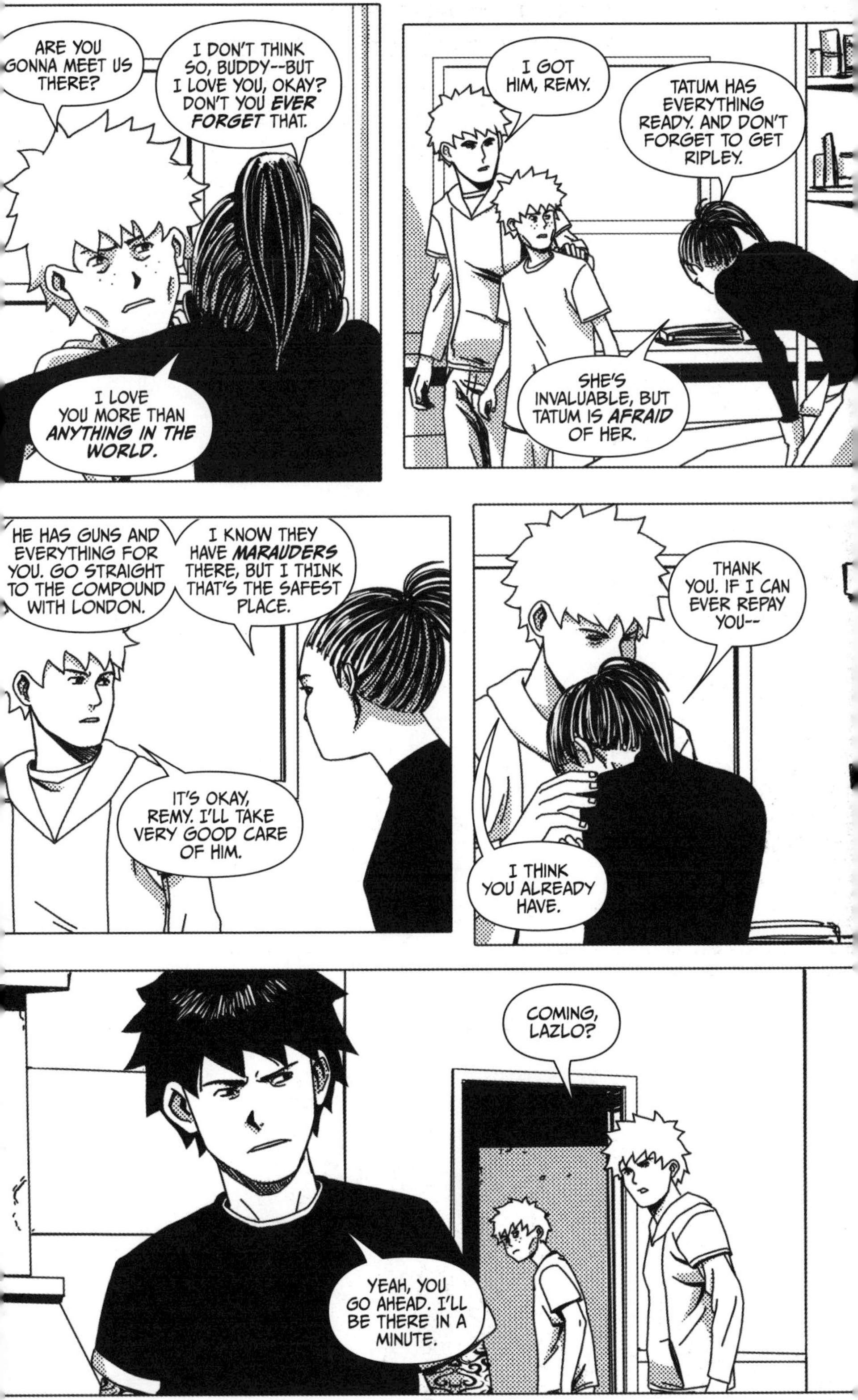
ARE YOU GONNA MEET US THERE?
I DON'T THINK SO, BUDDY--BUT I LOVE YOU, OKAY? DON'T YOU *EVER FORGET* THAT.
I LOVE YOU MORE THAN *ANYTHING IN THE WORLD.*
I GOT HIM, REMY.
TATUM HAS EVERYTHING READY. AND DON'T FORGET TO GET RIPLEY.
SHE'S INVALUABLE, BUT TATUM IS *AFRAID* OF HER.
HE HAS GUNS AND EVERYTHING FOR YOU. GO STRAIGHT TO THE COMPOUND WITH LONDON.
I KNOW THEY HAVE *MARAUDERS* THERE, BUT I THINK THAT'S THE SAFEST PLACE.
IT'S OKAY, REMY. I'LL TAKE VERY GOOD CARE OF HIM.
THANK YOU. IF I CAN EVER REPAY YOU--
I THINK YOU ALREADY HAVE.
COMING, LAZLO?
YEAH, YOU GO AHEAD. I'LL BE THERE IN A MINUTE.

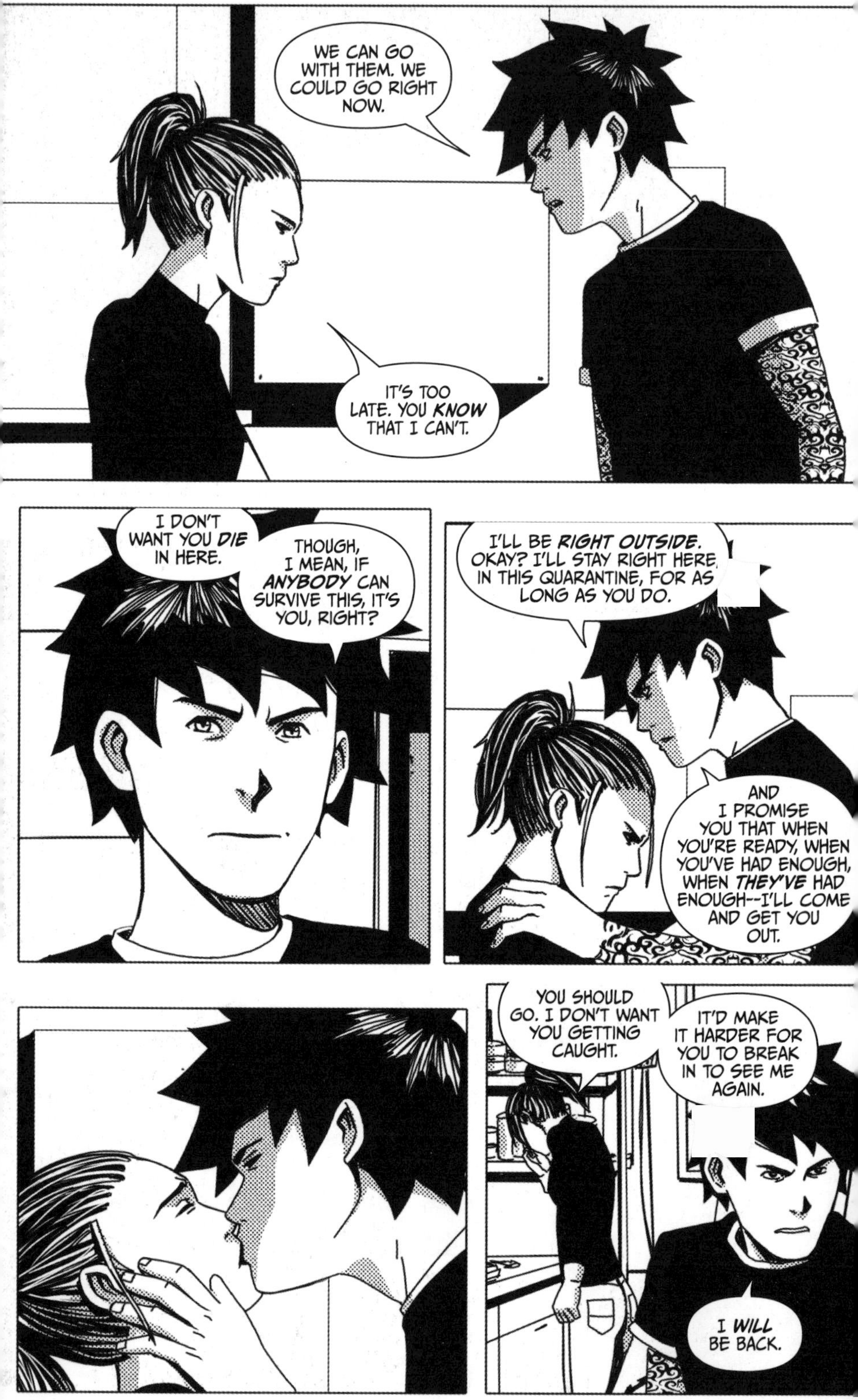
WE CAN GO WITH THEM. WE COULD GO RIGHT NOW.
IT'S TOO LATE. YOU *KNOW* THAT I CAN'T.
I DON'T WANT YOU *DIE* IN HERE.
THOUGH, I MEAN, IF *ANYBODY* CAN SURVIVE THIS, IT'S YOU, RIGHT?
I'LL BE *RIGHT OUTSIDE.* OKAY? I'LL STAY RIGHT HERE, IN THIS QUARANTINE, FOR AS LONG AS YOU DO.
AND I PROMISE YOU THAT WHEN YOU'RE READY, WHEN YOU'VE HAD ENOUGH, WHEN *THEY'VE* HAD ENOUGH--I'LL COME AND GET YOU OUT.
YOU SHOULD GO. I DON'T WANT YOU GETTING CAUGHT.
IT'D MAKE IT HARDER FOR YOU TO BREAK IN TO SEE ME AGAIN.
I *WILL* BE BACK.

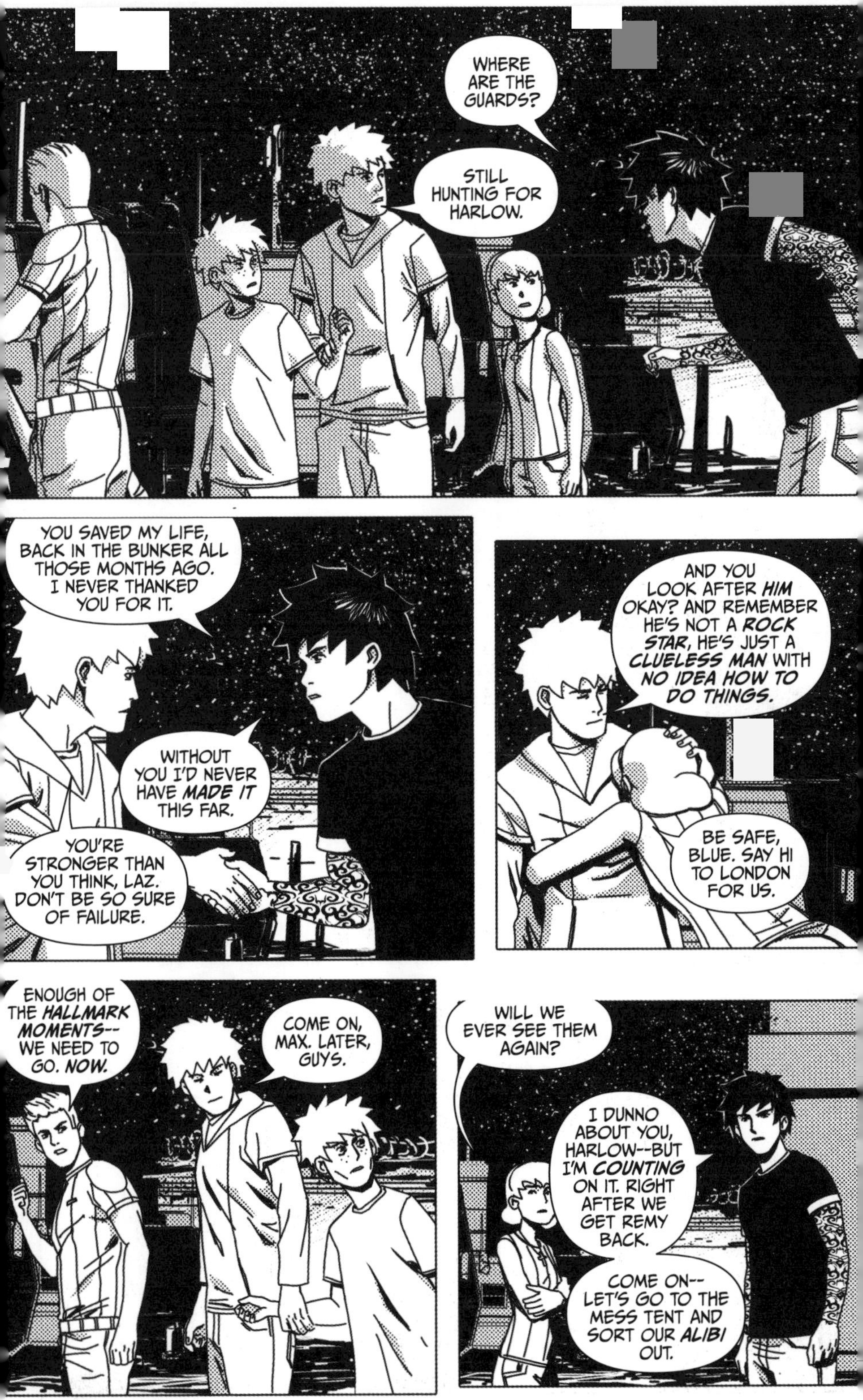
WHERE ARE THE GUARDS?
STILL HUNTING FOR HARLOW.
YOU SAVED MY LIFE, BACK IN THE BUNKER ALL THOSE MONTHS AGO. I NEVER THANKED YOU FOR IT.
WITHOUT YOU I'D NEVER HAVE *MADE IT* THIS FAR.
YOU'RE STRONGER THAN YOU THINK, LAZ. DON'T BE SO SURE OF FAILURE.
AND YOU LOOK AFTER *HIM* OKAY? AND REMEMBER HE'S NOT A *ROCK STAR*, HE'S JUST A *CLUELESS MAN* WITH *NO IDEA HOW TO DO THINGS.*
BE SAFE, BLUE. SAY HI TO LONDON FOR US.
ENOUGH OF THE *HALLMARK MOMENTS*-- WE NEED TO GO. *NOW.*
COME ON, MAX. LATER, GUYS.
WILL WE EVER SEE THEM AGAIN?
I DUNNO ABOUT YOU, HARLOW--BUT I'M *COUNTING* ON IT. RIGHT AFTER WE GET REMY BACK.
COME ON-- LET'S GO TO THE MESS TENT AND SORT OUR *ALIBI* OUT.

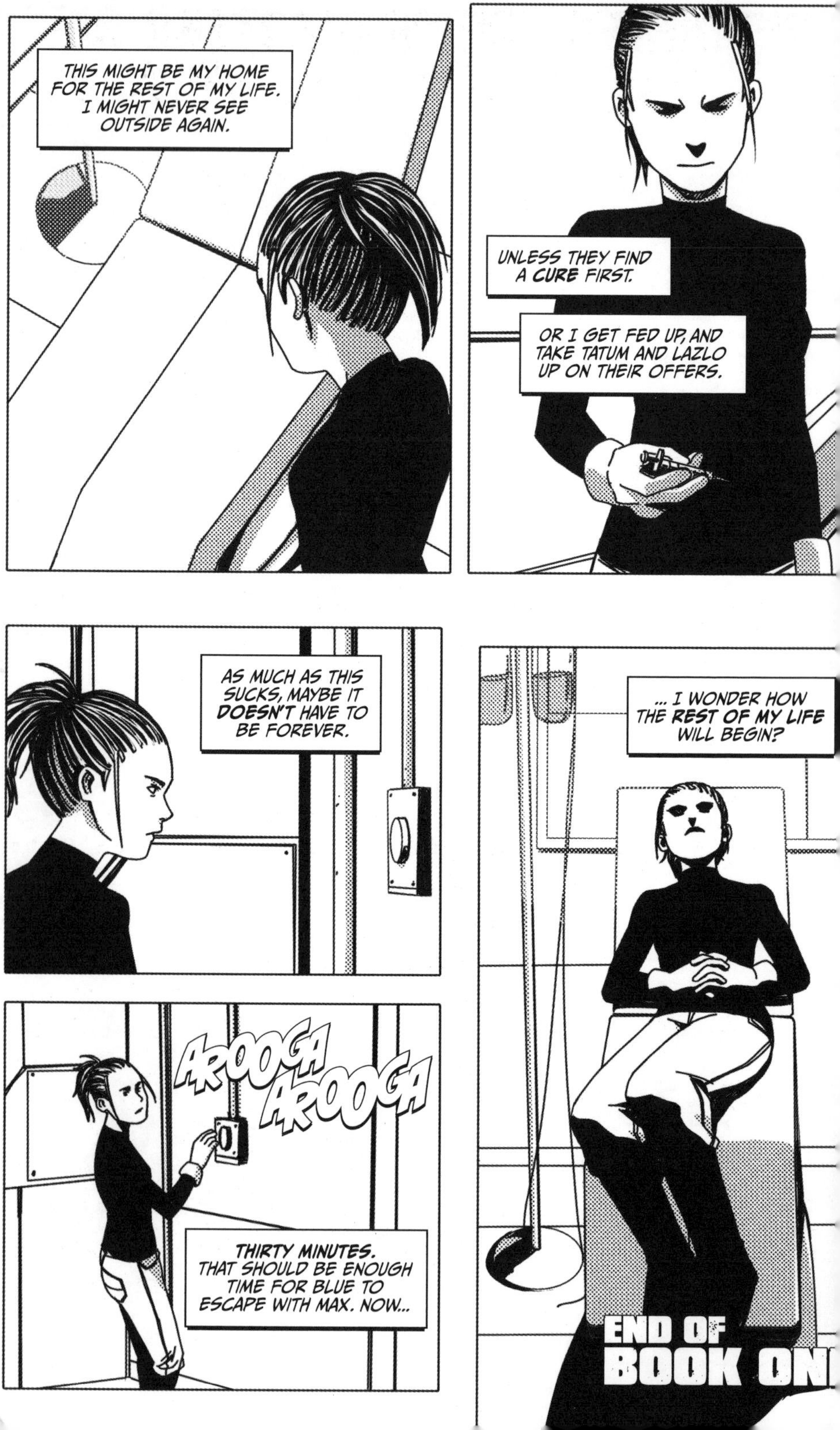
THIS MIGHT BE MY HOME FOR THE REST OF MY LIFE. I MIGHT NEVER SEE OUTSIDE AGAIN.
UNLESS THEY FIND A **CURE** FIRST.
OR I GET FED UP, AND TAKE TATUM AND LAZLO UP ON THEIR OFFERS.
AS MUCH AS THIS SUCKS, MAYBE IT **DOESN'T** HAVE TO BE FOREVER.
AROOGA AROOGA
THIRTY MINUTES. THAT SHOULD BE ENOUGH TIME FOR BLUE TO ESCAPE WITH MAX. NOW...
... I WONDER HOW THE **REST OF MY LIFE** WILL BEGIN?
END OF BOOK ON